CHRIS SCOTT first tried to cross the Sahara on a motorcycle in 1981 describing this and his other early trips in *Desert Travels* (1996). Since then he's travelled in all parts of the desert with cars, 4WDs and bush taxis and has organised and led tours to the Sahara. He's also made short films, including *Desert Driving* – a video/DVD companion to this book – and *Desert Riders* which has appeared on the National Geographic Channel.

His other guidebooks for Trailblazer include the *Adventure Motorcycling Handbook* and he also covers the sandy regions of Australia for *Rough Guides*.

Sahara Overland – a route and planning guide
First edition: 2000; this second edition: October 2004

Publisher
Trailblazer Publications
The Old Manse, Tower Rd, Hindhead, Surrey, GU26 6SU, UK
Fax (+44) 01428-607571
Email: info@trailblazer-guides.com
www.trailblazer-guides.com

British Library Cataloguing in Publication Data
A catalogue record for this book is available from the British Library

ISBN 1-873756-76-3

Editor: John King
Series editor: Patricia Major
Additional editors: Lucy Ridout, Anna Jacomb-Hood and Bryn Thomas
Cartography: Nick Hill
Typesetting and layout: Chris Scott
Index: Patrick D Hummingbird

WARNING: Travelling in the Sahara is unpredictable and can be dangerous.
Every effort has been made by the author, contributors and the publisher to ensure that the
information contained herein is as accurate as possible. However, they are unable to accept
responsibility for any inconvenience, loss or injury sustained by anyone as a result of the
advice and information given in this guide.

NOTE: This book and author's website are not connected with the online
Moroccan/Tucson-based fossil wholesaler using the same name.

Printed on chlorine-free paper by
D²Print (☎ +65-6295 5598), Singapore

SAHARA
OVERLAND
A ROUTE AND PLANNING GUIDE

CHRIS SCOTT

WITH CONTRIBUTIONS BY
GERBERT VAN DER AA, ALISTAIR BESTOW, JOSÉ BRITO, BILL EDWARDS,
CHARLES FOSTER, REINHART MAZUR, CHARLES MEGAW
SIAN PRITCHARD-JONES, FRANK SIMONENT, URSULA STEINER
AND RICHARD WASHINGTON

AND ADDITIONAL MATERIAL BY
GREGG BUTENSKY, EAMONN GEARON, ANDREW GOUDIE, KARIM HUSSAIN,
GRAHAM JACKSON, YVES LARBOULETTE, DAVID MATTINGLY, BERNY SEBE,
IAN THOMPSON, TIM STEAD, RAF VERBEELEN AND KEVIN WHITE

TRAILBLAZER PUBLICATIONS

Acknowledgements

Thanks are due to the many Saharan enthusiasts and contributors who supplied material for free or negligible fees – many far more qualified than me to write this book. A full list appears on p.652. In addition to those credited on the title page with supplying written material, the following have also kindly supplied photos and information: Mick Baines, Gert Duson, Ginge Fullen, Neil Lawson, Bernhard Lorsch, Werner Nother, Michele Soffiantini, Toby Savage Klaus Weltzer and Christer Wilkinson.

A request

Every effort has been made by the author and the publisher to ensure that the information contained in this book is as up to date and accurate as possible. Nevertheless things change, even in the Sahara. If you notice any changes or omissions that should be included in the online updates or next edition of this book, please write to Chris Scott at Trailblazer (address on p.2) or visit **www.sahara-overland.com/updates**.

Regularly-updated information and a whole lot more at:
www.sahara-overland.com

Coming soon: Polish translation of this book

Cover photo: View north from Mt. Tazat, Algeria (Route A7/8) © Richard Washington.

MAP KEY

———— **Track**	———— **Tarmac road**	·············· **Featured route**
🖌 **Rock carving**	🎨 **Rock art**	

CONTENTS

PART 7: ITINERARIES

Sahara Overland

To see the earth in its natural, elemental state, untouched by human endeavour, is a rare and humbling experience. From sun-baked plateaux to sublime sand seas, the Sahara makes a strong and lasting impression. Few experiences can match the thrill of heading out across a trackless wilderness, drinking tea in a nomad's tent, or setting up camp beneath a cliff face fired red by the setting sun.

In a world where mobile phones, signposts, piped water and emergency services are all taken for granted, the thought of visiting a region without these safety nets can and should be daunting. Even with satellite navigation and communication, travel in the Sahara is not without its risks, and some will relish the return to civilisation.

But once you've tasted the exhilaration of travelling for days through the desert, you'll find this satisfaction enhanced by an appreciation of your self-sufficiency and a growing confidence in your route-finding skills.

Along with the ability to navigate competently, suitably prepared and provisioned transportation, be it with two wheels, four wheels or four legs and a hump, is vital to any desert venture. This is something that is often miscalculated by the first-time visitor – it certainly was for me back in 1981 and this is the book I wish I'd had then. Advice on preparation takes up the biggest part of this book because, with the exception of organised tours, it will absorb the bulk of your time and money before you even reach the desert. It's followed by some aspects of the Saharan environment and an outline of travel opportunities. Part 7 comprises detailed itineraries across the entire Sahara to give a vivid impression of what life on the piste is actually like.

DISCOVER THE REAL SAHARA – SOME POPULAR MISCONCEPTIONS

1. Never camp in a oued or a flash flood could wash you away. See p.292.

2. Freezing by night, baking by day? Answer on p.388.

3. Nomads just wander around, free as a bird. See p.406.

4. The Sahara is a sea of constantly shifting dunes. See p.381.

5. Local guides navigate with a sixth sense. See p.299.

6. Sandstorms can bury you alive and dunes can swallow you up. See p.648.

7. You drive on a crust of sand; break through and you've had it! See p.188.

8. Spiders, snakes and scorpions lurk under every stone. Not on p.308.

9. Saharan camels are wild. See p.259.

10. Sandstorms can strip the paint off your car. Actually they can! See p.392.

This book naturally concentrates on the desert regions in the south. Away from tourist towns the people are mellow and the mountain scenery magnificent. Fuel range is moderate and away from **Erg Chebbi** the going is rockier than elsewhere in the Sahara, all of which simplifies vehicle preparation somewhat. Morocco is a common destination as a shakedown for a longer overland trip.

Tunisia

Similar to Morocco in Westernised familiarity but more laid back, Tunisia's drawback, certainly for Brits, is the expensive ferry required to reach it from Marseille or Genoa. But venture south of the camel rides and nomadobilia of the Chott region and you're in the tightly-packed dunes of the **Grand Erg Oriental** (Great Eastern Sand Sea), as definitive a desertscape as anyone could imagine.

Unfortunately for motorised travellers these southern regions are hard to appreciate. A major piste trails a pipeline to the country's southern apex, but unless you're prepared to delve into the unmarked dunes, distances are small and offer little compared to neighbouring countries. The Grand Erg, however, makes Tunisia the easiest place to enjoy a camel tour deep in the dunes.

Prices and touristic infrastructure are similar if not superior to otherwise comparable Morocco, while even in the cities, hassle from traders and kids is low key. Certainly for Brits, Tunisia is more of a transit on the way to Algeria or Libya.

Mauritania

As it is located on what is currently the most used trans-Sahara route, many people shoot through Mauritania (sometimes abbreviated as 'RIM', *Republique Islamique de Mauritanie*). But venture inland and you'll find the Mauritanian Sahara gives you plenty to see without the restrictions that exist, say, in Libya, Egypt or Niger. This is still an essentially untamed country where you can do what you like without stumbling into military patrols or being forced to take guides (though on some routes they're a good idea).

For an Islamic republic, Mauritanian society also comes as a surprise. More than anything else, the conspicuousness and relative freedom of women, from the poorest nomads to the city dwellers, is unexpected. Lighthearted flirtation unheard of in other Arabicised societies makes Mauritania a treat for visitors who normally get a male-dominated view of these countries. On the minus side, Mauritania's recently acquired popularity with trans-Saharan travellers is not lost on the famed entrepreneurial spirit of the Moors.

Assuming you're not just crossing the Sahara (the **Atlantic Route** starts on page 464), a good region to start exploration is the **Adrar plateau** around Atar and Chinguetti; a mixture of dunes and plateaux with evidence of the thousand-year-old Moorish culture as well as far older relics. From the Adrar a route to Tidjikja (see p.481) makes an interesting way of getting south, while roaming in the desolate north and east of the country, you'll have the desert all to yourself.

Mali

A West African favourite, Mali is the home of legendary **Timbuktu**. What's left of this celebrated town, for two centuries an emblem for remoteness and inac-

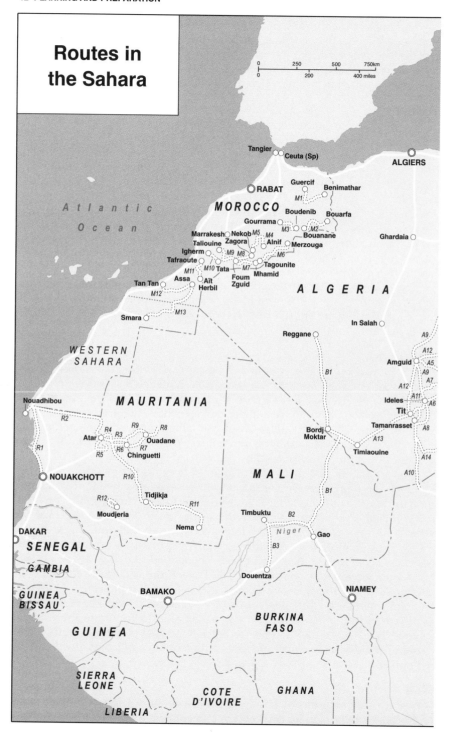

Routes in the Sahara

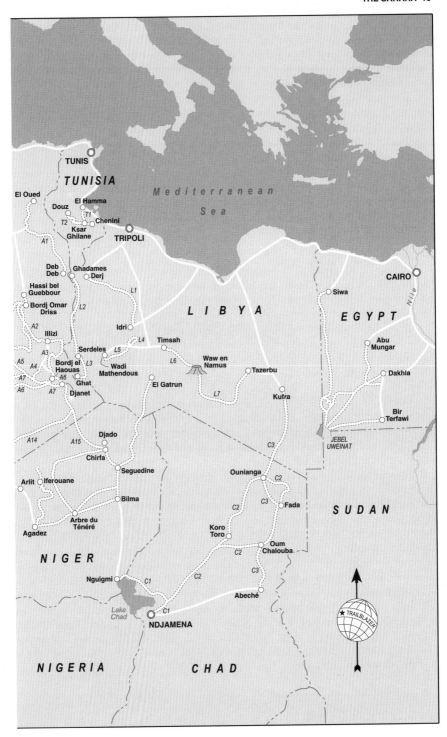

cessibility, sits close to the apex of the Niger River's northward arc into the Sahara. There's not much to see in Timbuktu and the hassle from the kids can leave sour memories, but the boast that you've been there is usually enough for most people, because getting to Timbuktu from any direction is still genuinely tough (see p.580).

There is no developed 'piste culture' in the Malian Sahara, principally because the north of the country occupies one of the Sahara's two hyper-arid empty quarters (the other is the Libyan Desert) with few wells, a negligible population and a relatively bland topography. Furthermore, since the rebellion of the Malian Tuareg in 1992 (see p.413), the once-popular **Tanezrouft piste** from Algeria is barely used by tourists as the region has repelled government control. The activities of smugglers continue unhampered and, although it's possible to visit Kidal and the **Adrar des Ifoghas**, tourist cars that dare take the risk are still preyed on. So, for its size, the Malian sector of the Sahara is the least alluring and the least visited.

Egypt

Presenting a legendarily obstructive bureaucracy for temporary vehicle importation and deep desert exploration, few people visit Egypt just to drive around the desert. Indeed, many bless the day they finally manage to get aboard the Wadi Halfa ferry south into Sudan!

And yet, between the Nile and the Libyan frontier lies one of the Sahara's most historically and prehistorically rich environments: the so-called Western Desert, part of the geographical entity known as the **Libyan Desert** which itself spans eastern Libya and northern Sudan. Logistically and bureaucratically access here is hard-won, especially with your own vehicle. People do do so unofficially which is a risk; a visit is most easily realised using local tour agencies and their vehicles. The focal points are the **Gilf Kebir** plateau in the southwest (location of the real 'Cave of the Swimmers' as featured in the film, *The English Patient*), the **Jebel Uweinat** massif where Egypt, Libya and Sudan meet, and the **Great Sand Sea**.

One reason why this part of Egypt has never seen much traffic is that there are virtually no wells and therefore no inhabitants. Due partly to meteorological vagaries (explained on p.386) the eastern Sahara is much more arid than central or western regions. Consequently nomadism barely gained a foothold here and established pistes southwest of Dakhla are unknown. Nevertheless, this once obscure corner of the Sahara has become a fashionable touristic 'last frontier' in recent years. A string of new **rock art discoveries**, as well as evidence of the activities (before and during WWII) of the likes of Bagnold and Almasy make a visit to the 'Gilf' highly rewarding, even as a mere passenger.

Less demanding excursions that can easily be done in your own vehicle include the ancient oasis of **Siwa** as well as the so-called **Great Desert Road** (sealed), which arches west from Cairo through the Western Desert via Farafra, Dakhla and Kharga to Luxor, though of course this is a faint backdrop to Egypt's world-class antiquities.

Libya

Forget long outdated propaganda about terrorists and anti-imperialist aggression: Libya is nowhere near as dangerous as people would like to imagine. Around the turn of the millennium it replaced Algeria as an authentic true desert destination, until subsequent regulations limited independent travel somewhat. It also boasts the finest Roman ruins along the southern Mediterranean shore. In 2003 the crippling UN economic sanctions (long flouted by oil interests anyway) were officially lifted and almost immediately the procurement of visas speeded up. But, with the advantageous black market rates of the late 1990s having passed, and the relative expense of vehicle importation and the now compulsory guide, the brief promise of independent desert tourism in Libya may have lost its shine.

Libya differs from other true Saharan countries in that its desert is much more developed, and what nomadism existed (mainly in the southwest) has been suppressed by urbanisation. Water, oil and military installations create numerous and sometimes confusing tracks, not all of which are marked on the most recent maps (only the most western parts of Libya received the attentions of the IGN mapmakers). And along the eastern and southern borders, mine fields from WW2 and the little known Chadian war of the 1980s add an unwelcome edge to off-piste exploration.

The scenic and prehistoric wonders of the **Fezzan** region of the south-west are the highlight on the classic tour as detailed on p.560. Routes in the east of the country are longer, more remote and more demanding.

At the time of writing it was not permissible to use Libya's southern borders for Algeria (Djanet) and Niger.

Niger

Once anyone gets bitten by the Saharan bug, a visit to northeastern Niger's **Aïr mountains**, **Ténéré desert** and even the **Djado plateau** soon become desirable. Home of Tuareg and, in the east, Tubu nomads, the early 1990s saw the area cut off as the rebellion of these put-upon nomadic minorities brought trans-Sahara travel through Niger to a halt. These days things are less dangerous and 'the Ténéré' (as the Nigeran Sahara is often abbreviated) is accessible again.

However, it should be noted that since that time not a year has passed without at least one touristic group being robbed, whether travelling independently or with a local agency. The bandits are renegades from the ostensibly resolved rebellion: Tuareg in the Aïr, Tubu along the Djado plateau, and one or the other out in the Ténéré.

Expensive official guides are mandatory to explore this area and, because of this, driving down here from Europe takes some commitment. But until you've seen this part of the Sahara, especially the eastern borders of the Aïr and the Djado plateau, you'll not have seen the best of the desert. The *actual* Ténéré in between the two is just a flat sand plain north of the Grand Erg du Bilma.

Because of the continuing risk of losing your vehicle to bandits, a tour is preferable before committing yourself. Several companies in France, Italy and Germany offer two- or three-week tours of the Ténéré working out at around £100/€145 a day all in. Doing it this way you'll be able to enjoy the experience with a bit more peace of mind.

Algeria

During the 1980s Algeria offered reliable access across the Sahara via two hard, but not too hard, routes: the 1000-mile **Tanezrouft route** from Reggane to the Niger River, and the shorter but more difficult **Hoggar route** to Agadez. Then in the early 1990s political troubles in the north as well as the Sahara-wide Tuareg rebellion shut down tourism and both of these trans-Sahara routes overnight.

Then in 2000, with a reduction of violence in the north (which, incidentally, never affected the south), Algeria came back into vogue for desert travellers as Libya turned the screws on independent travellers. Sadly that promising revival was written off in March 2003 when seven separate groups of travellers were abducted in the Tassili N'Ajjer (full story on p.362). This unprecedented event set back tourism right across the Central Sahara, and the following season saw only a guarded return to the desert.

WHAT CAN I DO IN...

Two weeks
● Leaving Europe on a Saturday morning and back Sunday night (sixteen days), you could spend up to nine days in Morocco including nearly a week on the piste. Although a mad rush, this would be enough time to do most of the Hamada du Draa pistes. Alternatively you could take it easy by hiring a Mitsubishi in Marrakesh or Agadir (about £600/€900 a week) and, as long as you're aware of the limitations of an unequipped and unprepared vehicle, cover the same ground.
● Cross from Central Europe to Tunis for a more leisurely exploration of Tunisia.
● Fly in for a ten-day 4WD- or camel-based tour of just about any corner of the Sahara you choose with a European-based operator.
● Join a 4-day local 4WD tour of Tunisia's Chott region as part of a Tunisian package holiday in Djerba. It's not exactly *Sahara Overland* but they'll probably throw a camel ride in too!
● A fortnight's tour of Egypt's Western Desert, from Dakhla to Jebel Uweinat and the Gilf Kebir, then through the Great Sand Sea to Siwa.

Four weeks
● The classic tour of the Libyan Fezzan plus a visit to the Roman ruins of Leptis Magna and Sabratha, near Tripoli.
● The Western Desert tour of Egypt with a week or two to explore the ancient monuments along the Nile.
● A springtime traverse of the Moroccan Sahara plus visits to the Imperial Cities.

● A fortnight or so in the Mauritanian Sahara (*a lot* of driving). Or ship your vehicle to Dakar or Banjul and fly in – less hectic but more expensive.
● Shipping to and from the above West African ports and exploring Senegal and Mali as far as Timbuktu.
● Some of the longer organised tours of the Aïr-Ténéré or Tibesti-Ennedi with a couple of days to spare either side.

Six weeks
● A relaxed tour of Tunisia and Libya without relentless daily driving.
● As above but continuing into Algeria from Ghat to Djanet, Tam and back to Tunis.
● An easy-paced visit down to Morocco and Mauritania, then shipping and flying back from Senegal or Gambia or selling your car locally (see p.461).
● Rather a rush, but a double crossing of the Sahara: down through Mauritania to Mali, Niger, Algeria and Tunis, or the reverse (logistically preferable).

More than six weeks
● Any of the above as slowly as you like.
● Explore West Africa beyond Mauritania.
● Explore the Tibesti or Ténéré either by driving down through Libya and back through Algeria or shipping to Douala (for Chad) or say, Accra or Port Harcourt for Niger.
● Enjoy a full 10,000km tour of the Sahara from Tunisia, then Algeria or Libya, to Niger, Mali, Mauritania and Morocco, or vice versa. For a trip like this a couple of months would be more like it.

Entry from the north is via Tunisia from Nefta, or from Ghat in Libya which brings you to the Sahara's finest landscapes and most outstanding prehistoric art in the southeast of the country: the **Tassili N'Ajjer** plateau near Djanet and to the west the **Hoggar** mountains around Tamanrasset. The border with Morocco has been closed since 1994 and although there is talk of a thaw in relations, the less scenically impressive Tanezrouft region has seen few visitors, associated as it is with established smuggling activities.

Despite these drawbacks – part of the fluid pattern of African politics – for a single country Algeria offers the best of the Sahara. From sand seas to plateaux, winding gorges and mountain ranges, the full repertoire of Saharan landscapes can be appreciated by simply doing the classic Tunis–Tam–Djanet triangle. Nomadism still flourishes here too, which adds greatly to the ambience of the desert, though guides are now mandatory from border to border. Check the 'Algeria' page on the website for the latest on security issues.

Chad

Unhindered exploration is more than can be said of northern Chad. Here one gets into a realm of Saharan travel that has been unpredictable and dangerous for as long as Europeans have gone there. Never a mainstream tourist destination at the best of times, Chad's **Tibesti** mountains and **Ennedi** highlands are a lure for hard-core Saharans, but can only be *fully* appreciated during lulls in the protracted civil war/rebellion which has plagued the area since independence.

Millions of landmines are the still-lethal residue of a disastrous conflict with Libya culminating in the late 1980s, though it is said that Russia is proposing to de-mine the little-used trans-Saharan route along the west flank of the Tibesti.

With the right vehicle, experience and nerve, Chad's northern massifs and little-known **Tubu culture** will give you an adventure like no other. In your own vehicle, the challenge would be following your own pace rather than being pushed from village to town by expensive and sometimes unnecessary guides, jumpy soldiers and administrative extortion. At the time of writing the Tibesti was out of bounds and the Sudan border in revolt, but in between, tours from Ndjamena can reach as far as the Ounianga lakes and the rock art sites of the Ennedi.

Sudan

Two decades of bitter civil war have cut off tourism from what was once considered one of Africa's friendliest countries – and is still home to one of its most excruciating bureaucracies. Following the railway or even the Nile from Wadi Halfa was many people's introduction to Sudan. Venturing into the unpopulated Nubian Desert or the little-known oases of the northwest beyond the southern sections of the Darb el Arbain (see p.621) or the Wadi Howar is slowly emerging as a new Saharan destination for the committed but is still too marginal to warrant consideration in this book.

People do come up from Ethiopia or Eritrea but in general all you'll see of the Sudanese Sahara is the L-shaped transit from the east to the capital and up to Wadi Halfa. Access from Chad in the west was good for a couple of years, but a rebellion in the Darfur region closed that border in late 2003.

WHEN TO GO

Better to start with when *not* to go. It ought not to come as any great surprise that in summertime the Sahara is a place to avoid. Even on the northern or Atlantic edge of the desert (above 30°N) daily temperatures will top 40°C on most days. In the interior nights will never cool and the daytime temperature will exceed 50°C. These temperatures are not unusual elsewhere in the world of course, but when you add the element of remoteness that's inherent in Saharan travel, summer is just too risky for first timers and not much fun besides.

Consider that the relentless heat puts a permanent strain on your body as well as your vehicle. Unless you're installed in an air-conditioned car, daily water consumption will top ten litres so that a hefty 100-litre payload would not even last two people five days. The effects of these sorts of temperatures are hard to describe until you've experienced them – and then the full force of the pitiless desert is brought home.

And it's no easier for your vehicle. Camel caravans never cross the desert in high summer while a car or bike's tyres and drivetrain will easily overheat just doing simply what it has to to get through. Vehicle failures are common in the hot season; a time when even locals can perish in the desert.

Winter: the Saharan season

If the Sahara can ever be said to get crowded with tourists it's around Christmas/New Year when Swiss, Germans and French make the most of their holidays and grab a bit of winter sunshine.

In December and January Algeria, Libya and Mauritania experience warm days with clear skies. The shortness of the day is the drawback; at 30° latitude (southern Morocco, Ghadames, Cairo) days are only ten hours long. Ten degrees further south (Atar, Arlit, Zouar) you'll get 11 hours of daylight.

Temperatures might exceed 30°C only for a couple of hours in the day but you'll generally only have freezing nights at altitudes of over 1000m. However, although the 'baking days, freezing nights' idea of the Sahara is an exaggeration, winter temperatures do drop considerably after sundown whatever your altitude, so woolly hats, fleece jackets and decent sleeping bags all come in handy.

In the Moroccan Atlas snow will regularly fall above 2500m with occasional blizzards covering a much wider area. Temperatures on the Hamada du Draa will only creep up to 25°C while it's best to expect some rainfall along the Mediterranean coast.

In these sorts of temperatures you can easily get by on less than a litre of drinking water a day which means less to carry and a lighter vehicle, something that's critical on motorbikes and pushbikes. You may grumble about the cold in the early morning but you'll have little chance to complain about the heat.

The transitional seasons

This can be a warmer time to visit the northern Saharan countries of Tunisia and Morocco, though further south the change of the seasons brings temperamental weather in April and October. Many seasoned Saharans consider November to be an ideal month deep in the desert. Days are still long but not desperately hot: 35°C in the low-lying Ténéré, about 30°C in mountain areas.

Nights aren't too cold and from Libya to Mauritania the strong winds bringing a horizon-blurring haze are rare.

The autumn is also the best time to cross the Sahara if you're heading across Africa; at this time you're driving *into* the winter and then into the Central African dry season. Spring can be a gamble. Anything beyond March can bring on *le chaleur* and the onset of summer from Egypt to Mauritania. There's more on the climate of the Sahara on p.384.

The Big Plan

Thorough **preparation** is the first and most critical step when visiting a remote area like the Sahara; if you're travelling independently its importance cannot be overstressed. It will take up more time and consume more money than your actual desert trip, but when done well, good preparation will inspire confidence and ensure a trouble-free trip. In a nutshell this means:
- enough time and money to realise your goal
- information about the area you plan to visit
- a sound means of transport
- the right documentation

A good example of a total beginner having his careful preparation result in a satisfactory outcome is Bill Edwards' camel trek in Mauritania (see p.257). The trio had no experience of what they were taking on and yet ended up travelling from Tichit to Nema unguided, ambitious yet within their abilities by that time.

FIRST STEPS
The early stages of an adventurous travel project are thrilling times as you scan an atlas and trace your finger along likely routes. Perhaps you already have a plan, or maybe this book has given you new ideas. It will also have given you an idea about departure dates. That mid-summer excursion across the Sahara you had outlined may now be revised. Let's hope so. There's more persuasive advice on visiting the Sahara in the cooler months in the Health and Water chapters.

Assuming you're not flying out to join an organised tour (for more see p.31), once you've pinned down a realistic **departure date** (with a bit of leeway for the almost inevitable delays) you can then work back, estimating how much time you'll need to get yourself together. You may be lucky and have a recently-serviced vehicle and some enthusiastic companions, in which case you could be off for a fortnight in Morocco in just a few weeks. On the other hand the Sahara may be the first leg of a big trans-African adventure. In this case you'll need more like one year from the time you pin that new map to the wall until the Big Day.

If you intend to visit the Sahara in winter, start planning in early spring, especially if you've yet to buy and equip a vehicle. This will give you the long

'HELL IS...'

... The desert is a different place without the certainty of the support vehicle. It becomes, then, what it really is....

Sahara Overland Forum

Planning a visit to the Sahara you'll usually know early on whether you want to go alone, with your partner or friends, or as part of a large group. One thing to remember is that although travelling with other vehicles is an important safety factor on certain pistes, it's actually surprisingly easy to meet up with other travellers out there. These sorts of short-term convoys of motorbikes, 4WDs and ordinary cars are often the best travel experiences. Bonded by the security of mutual support you carry few preconceptions about your companions that really matter. Either party can part after a few days or, if things go well, end up travelling for weeks. The spontaneity of this 'ships that pass in the night' scenario can be ideal.

This is not so easy when you set out with your best buddy by your side for an adventure of a lifetime. You don't have to be a black-bereted existentialist to agree with J-P Sartre's pithy observation that 'Hell is other people'. Interpersonal discord is a regular aspect of Saharan travel. People who appear perfectly likeable in a stable home environment can get intensely on each others' nerves once in the wide open desert. Reasons can be many, not least the stress of worrying about 101 things – although packing more than two adults into a Defender is, as we once observed, one way of icing up the inside of the car without air-con!

Alas there is no formula for selecting good desert co-travellers other than whole-hearted, genuine enthusiasm and commitment that's aware that everyday won't be a

picnic. Certainly, flexible, easygoing, even-tempered people who are good cooks, mechanics, sand drivers and linguists and don't mind working hard when necessary are an asset. Unfortunately most Saharans will agree that, while they possess virtually all these qualities themselves, they've very rarely encountered them in other people. I know many a hard-core Saharan who will put up with anything the desert can throw at them as long as it's not Other People.

People want to visit the Sahara for all sorts of reasons: the challenge of driving or riding, saying you've 'crossed the Sahara' or drunk mint tea with a nomad in Timbuktu. Some of course want to get away from people but in the Sahara this can be difficult; if anything the desert forces you up against people's noses which is part of the problem. As desert experience increases so too does a genuine interest in the Sahara, its history and its peoples while sufferance of 'fools' becomes more difficult.

Don't force a friend along just to have someone to talk to or share your experience, just because they 'rode a camel in Rajasthan' once. In my experience, to work well together, all parties must be **committed**, something that's hard to do when you're not quite sure what exactly you're getting into.

The bottom line is go with an optimistic and open mind about your companions. If you're travelling together independently and things turn sour, be prepared to talk it out and go your separate ways if need be. It may compromise your plans but what's left of your trip will hopefully be remembered more fondly. The less flexible situation of organised tour companions is addressed on p.31.

summer days to get the machine ready and tested. Make no mistake, by August you'll be out every weekend banging and drilling and wondering where it's all going to go. Guidelines on outfitting your 4WD, motorbike or bicycle begin on page 105.

Time and money

Optimism is an ingrained human characteristic that enables us to get out of bed each day and carry on. It can also fool us into thinking that everything will go to plan even though we've all learned time and time again, from getting building repairs done to preparing dinner for 8pm sharp, that things always take longer and cost more than anticipated.

Once you've scanned through this book you'll be able to ask yourself honestly if you have the time, the money and the will to see it through. If you've done this sort of travel before you'll be at the great advantage of being able to anticipate the pitfalls. If the idea of driving or biking through the desert starts to look a bit daunting, consider an organised tour. It may not sound as exciting but it will at the very least be a great way of previewing the desert experience or even reconnoitring a certain region without the huge commitment of an overland trip; see Organised Tours on p.31.

One characteristic mistake many people make in their enthusiasm is to overplan, to try and see it all. I still do this every time, formulating plans as if this will be my last chance. It's understandable: with the huge effort required to get to the Sahara you want to make the most of it. Once you're out there or even just on the way down you begin to reel in your ambitious itineraries to something more realistic. *It's extremely rare that a first desert trip unfolds as you envisaged, especially in the more demanding countries.* Expect this. Don't be disheartened when your agenda goes up in smoke. One of the keys to enjoying overland travel in Africa is to **be flexible** in the face of the many challenges that are thrown at you. This factor of the unexpected, impossible to predict and yet almost guaranteed, is part of the thrill.

GETTING INFORMATION

The list below gives the most up-to-date information sources first, as they stand in the UK. Britain is not an especially Sahara-conscious country and the other Anglophone countries are even less so. In Europe you may find you get more help from traditional sources like national tourist offices, motoring clubs and embassies. Certainly France, Germany and Switzerland offer more information (as well as equipment and expertise) for desert travellers than the rest of the world put together.

Internet

For all its inanity and in-your-face commerce, at its heart the Internet deals with information. And for specialist information like travel in the remote Sahara it provides it at a rate that no other media can keep up with.

The Internet can work for you in a couple of ways. You can log onto the main European websites specialising in Saharan travel news. In all cases they will have forums for selling gear, finding travel partners and asking questions (usually the same ones over and over again...) and also publish travelogues, links to personal Sahara homepages, lists of GPS waypoints for remote pistes, book reviews, equipment lists; you name it, it's there. Run by enthusiasts who may also be professionals, their objective runs close to the Internet's pre-commercial origins: an exchange of free information for those who want it.

At the time of writing, my **Sahara Overland website** (www.sahara-over land.com) is the only English-language one. It serves as an online resource for this book with news, a forum, trip reports, country updates, book and map reviews and, until they seal it, a frequently updated page for the Atlantic Route, plus tours and whatever else I've cooked up by the time you read this. But by far the most popular site is the Swiss-run **Sahara Info**, which gets thousands of hits a day and has a comprehensive forum – the key to this type of website. **Sahara el Kebira** is the Italian equivalent and there are a couple of French sites too. As long as they operate, these sites are linked from the www.sahara-overland.com/news page and will no doubt have links of their own going off in all directions.

Another way of keeping up with developments is to latch on to someone's online African travelogue. The trend to post despatches from Internet cafés has created several online diaries in recent years.

What you most commonly get is postings from Internet cafés in African cities, usually a few weeks apart, which are formatted and uploaded by a friend back home. They detail the trials and tribulations and sometimes a little too much of the trivia of trans-African travel but there's a good chance you can communicate with the protagonists via email and get the word about border formalities or other specifics that will go out of date in a book like this and not appear on the official websites.

Sahara tour operators

A sneaky way of finding out the latest information on the accessibility of particular regions is to call up European-based tour operators, make out you urgently want to visit a certain area and ask whether they're running tours there. You may not always get an honest appraisal of the situation, however. They may claim they're booked out till next season when in fact all tours have been suspended owing to political unrest. In fact this information will probably appear on the Sahara information websites very soon, but one way of judging the security of an area is to see if tours are going there.

Other travellers

Although too late to have much bearing on your pre-departure plans, you can't ask for more up-to-date news than from oncoming travellers. They may have just struggled along a piste that you're about to attempt, they may be able to recommend a good local guide or advise on procedures or fuel availability at a remote frontier. With their long delays, borders are a good place to catch up on what's going on over the other side from travellers heading home.

Travel magazines

In Britain the overlanding travel scene is more focused towards long-haul trans-Africa expeditions (when it's possible in its pure sense) or crossing Asia. This predilection is reflected in the travel pages of the newspapers and in travel magazines. Visiting the Sahara rather than crossing it has become a marginal pursuit,

Where and when

The Sahara fills most of seven countries: Morocco with Western Sahara, Mauritania, Mali, Algeria, Niger, Libya and Egypt, and up to half of Sudan, Chad and Tunisia. Choosing where to explore depends on your time, commitment and experience. Not all these countries are safe to visit and they can be broadly divided into those suitable for first-time visitors and tour groups, and those best left to independent travellers who have experience in remote areas and off-road driving.

First-timers

Getting a copy of the **Michelin 741 map** is your first step with a Sahara trip in mind, and looking at it the options for travel appear unlimited. Among first-timers it's common to pick a good-looking route that cuts through the heart of the desert, adding a detour to visit some interesting-looking mountains or a short-cut through some dunes. Only when you start to investigate these possibilities do you realise that exploring this wilderness is full of limitations and restrictions: geographical and logistical as much as political and bureaucratic.

You'll soon realise that most traffic sticks to established routes or pistes. Even these can give you plenty to think about in terms of navigation and driving. Most Saharan travellers have lurid tales to tell of their first desert trip. While they make great stories or even books, being stuck with an ill-equipped vehicle at the wrong time of year with just a 741 for navigation is far from enjoyable at the time. Better to hold back and not bite off more than you can chew. This book attempts to make your first Saharan adventure memorable for the right reasons!

WHERE TO GO

The countries listed below are in order of ease of travel for first-timers in their own vehicles, taking into account: expense, accessibility from mainland Europe and the challenges of bureaucracy, terrain and security. More information on these countries and specific route descriptions starts on p.423. All these countries except Sudan can be visited on organised tours but the conditions and comfort are more of a gamble in the more difficult destinations.

Morocco

Far and away the best place for a neo-Saharan introduction and a good holiday besides. Only the fringes of the Sahara encroach over 'greater' Morocco

A SHORT HISTORY OF PISTES

The French word for 'track' has become the accepted term for off-highway driving in the Sahara, but what are pistes?

Just about all of today's routes in and across the Sahara originated as trade routes over the last few thousand years. Like all roads in the world they link major settlements or economic nodes, which themselves were set up around a reliable water source; the key resource of all settlements.

As the Sahara became more arid following the Neolithic era (see p.384), caravan routes followed a string of wells along the line of least resistance, just as today's highways do. In the Sahara 'least resistance' means avoiding the bigger sand seas (some of which are hundreds of kilometres across) and, where possible, would have meant skirting mountainous, hyper-arid or ambush-prone regions.

Therefore, principal pistes generally follow flat, open ground, linking one oasis to another from the south of the Sahara to the north in as direct a route as possible. The network is completed by minor lateral pistes, a few pushed through in recent years by bulldozers in the course of exploration for minerals. Some major pistes are now sealed roads of course, and during the lifespan of this edition the Sahara will finally become sealed from north to south along the Atlantic Route through Mauritania (see p.464).

In present times, the advent of recreational off-roading has given Saharan pistes a new purpose. Originating in the 1960s with the earliest overland companies, Saharan motor tourism boomed in the 1980s in Algeria, helped in no small way by the glamour associated with the then popular Paris–Dakar Rally. The advent of civil unrest in northern Algeria as well as a rebellion in Tuareg homelands put the brakes on Saharan adventure tourism just as the ownership of four-wheel drives and 'Dakar' replica trail bikes was catching on. Since that time, Mauritania, southern Tunisia, Libya and even parts of Chad have opened up to cater for the European desire to experience the desert, either independently or on a tour.

Route of Tibestian raiding parties to Egei, Kanem & Agadem
Very difficult, no water

A piste well worth avoiding, it seems.

south of the Atlas and north of the Algerian border. The **Western Sahara** territory – Morocco in all but name on the seaward side – is all desert but only the Atlantic route to Mauritania is accessible. Elsewhere it's still a sensitive area until the Polisario question is resolved (full story on p.459, with map).

The dramatic variations in scenery **south of the snow-capped High Atlas** are traversed by several short, clear-cut pistes. Furthermore, the thriving rural Berber culture along with the glories of the Imperial Cities add an extra element which make this an ideal country to dip your toe into the sand. But if it's the grand horizons of the real Sahara that you're after, you're better off heading elsewhere. Northern Morocco can also be hell for the culturally unacclimatised. Though apparently not as bad as it used to be, the hassle here from touts, trinket sellers and kids can drive you to despair. (In the south it's nowhere near as bad.) Not everyone finds the constant pestering unbearable, but the consensus seems to be that if you let it get to you, your experience of this great country will be ruined. If you're curious to explore the wonders of Marrakesh and Fez, consider leaving them for your return north. By this time you may have got the hang of the country and its ways.

especially since the outbreak of the War on Terrorism. In the US the travel media is much the same: a hack reporting on an organised tour or a cliché-ridden 'Bedouin and Starlight' feature are about the gist of it. Just don't give up before you've scanned the **S-Files** on my Sahara website.

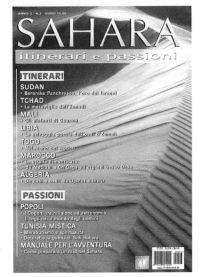

You'll find the best reports – accurate, detailed, radically adventurous and well presented – in the European travel media. The European magazines described below treat Sahara travel with respect and thoroughness and not as some rather eccentric caper introduced by means of a few tiresome camel puns. Even if your French and German are poor, you'll learn more with a dictionary from these stories than from most English features.

Because of their historical connections, the French just can't get enough of the Sahara. French or German editions of *Geo* (the European equivalent of *National Geographic*) are excellent starting points. *Terre Sauvage* also concentrates on wilderness travel and has regular Sahara features; *Globetrotter* is a less glossy alternative. In 2003 *Sahara* (pictured above) came out in Italy and promises to be a quality periodical on the desert.

The 4WD and off-road motorcycling magazine scene is also much more energetic and adventurous than British offerings. With the popularity of Rally Raids (organised BYO car or bike holiday-expeditions) their commitment is impressive: vehicle tests are often done in the Sahara as opposed to in some muddy off-road park in Surrey.

The vigour of German and Swiss publications for hardcore adventure travel is even greater. Along with the German edition of *Geo* you have *Tours Magazin*, where it's not unusual to find a story about a five-star Unimog motorhome pushing through the Rebiana Sand Sea the hard way with *Off Road* specialising in 4WDs. For motorbikers the well known *Motorrad* is supplemented by the more travel-oriented *Tourenfahrer Magazin*.

Travel guidebooks

For detailed and up-to-date information in English there's only one book and I'm afraid this is it! But have a flick through Lascelles' *Sahara Handbook* (still in print) for an idea of what travel was like in the early 1980s, and Jon Stevens' *The Sahara Is Yours: A Handbook for Desert Travellers* for the scene in the 1960s when border guards greeted you with a salute.

As for general travel guides, the **West Africa** editions from Lonely Planet and Rough Guides (updated every 3–4 years) will be essential supplements if travelling in the southern Saharan countries; both companies also publish individual country guides, such as Morocco, Tunisia and Egypt, as do other publishers like Footprint. Written for independent travellers using public transport, all these guides concentrate on the more conventional, easy to reach areas and not the desert. They include copious details on accommodation and where to eat through the entire country as well as 'things to see and do' but feature only the barest details on vehicle itineraries. Wherever you go in the Sahara, you'll find these travel guides essential. This book attempts to complement these guides rather than repeat their listings.

Government Overseas Departments

The UK government's Foreign & Commonwealth Office Travel Advice Unit and its US equivalent, the State Department (both with websites) are civil service departments primarily concerned with preventing their nationals from getting involved in international incidents. Because they have to play it safe they'll often advise against travel to countries that are quite safe, or be very slow to give the all-clear. They are also not always fully aware of arcane regional disputes or the fact that, for example, northern Algeria may be dangerous but the south is relatively safe.

Even with their websites these government agencies cannot be considered impartial, up-to-date monitors of conditions in Saharan countries, especially when things actually improve. Even then, it's the habit of newspaper travel sections to lazily parrot their advice, which is worth noting because your travel insurance may not be valid if your government warned against travel in that country.

Of the two, the US State Department website is more clued up, while the German and French governments' Departments of Foreign Affairs are better still. To keep them up to date, the website addresses for all the above departments are linked from www.sahara-overland.com/news.

Embassies and Tourist Offices   You'll find nothing but 'land of contrasts' pap in the overseas tourist offices for the nine Saharan countries this book covers. Embassy staff, who could not imagine a worse place to go to than the horrible Sahara, will usually supply cluelessness, discouragement or even misinformation.

Visas, documents and money

At the pre-departure stage, gathering the documentation for your Saharan trip is pretty simple, especially when compared to a longer trans-African trip. Things only get complicated when you're in Africa and have to deal with border formalities, which often involve filling out forms in French or Arabic, and getting one stamped before you can get the next one.

A general run-down of documentation needed appears below. For a full description of what to expect on entering Morocco from Spain see page 418, Tunis starts on page 421, Mauritania is on page 464, Ras Ajdir (Tunis–Libya) is on page 545. There are also personal accounts of various trans-Saharan treks in the S-Files on the website.

PASSPORT

If you don't yet own a passport, get on the case straight away; particularly during holiday periods when the issuing process slows right down. It's better not to waste days sitting in a queue watching the ticket counter click by; apply by post to a provincial issuing office instead. If you already own a passport make sure it's valid for at least six months if not a year after your anticipated journey's end as many countries won't issue visas for soon-to-be-expired passports. Your passport needs to have plenty of space in it too: most African visas take up a whole page, let alone the entry and exit stamps, and Niger wastes more space with *vu en passage* stamps at every town checkpoint.

Sometimes it helps to have a second passport, particularly if waiting or applying for onward visas in Africa. Although they don't exactly shout it from the rooftops, in Britain at least, it may still be possible to get a **second passport**

VISA REQUIREMENTS

To cut a long story short, citizens from Austria, Belgium, Canada, France, Germany, Holland, Ireland, Italy, Norway, South Africa, Sweden, Spain, Switzerland, the UK or the USA can get a visa on arrival in Morocco, Tunisia and Egypt, but to visit Algeria, Chad, Libya, Mali, Mauritania or Niger (except French citizens going to Mali, Mauritania or Niger for whom a visa can be issued on arrival) a visa must be arranged in advance.

New Zealanders and Australians require advance visas for all Saharan countries.

EMBASSIES/CONSULATES OF SAHARAN COUNTRIES IN EUROPE

London	Algeria Egypt Libya Mauritania Morocco Tunisia
Brussels	Algeria Chad Egypt Mali Mauritania Morocco Niger Tunisia
Paris	Algeria Chad Egypt Libya Mali Mauritania Morocco Niger Tunisia
Bonn or Berlin	Algeria Chad Egypt Libya Mali Mauritania Morocco Niger Tunisia
Rome or Milan	Algeria Egypt Libya Mauritania Morocco Tunisia
Madrid	Egypt Mali Mauritania Morocco Tunisia
Geneva or Zurich	Algeria Egypt Libya Mauritania Morocco Tunisia

EMBASSIES OR CONSULATES IN OTHER SAHARAN COUNTRIES

Note that, depending on your nationality, a consulate may not necessarily issue a visa. For example, at the time of writing, it was difficult to get a Libyan visa at any of the Libyan consulates in Africa, and currently 'non-Arabs' could only enter Libya via the coastal frontiers with Tunisia and Egypt. Most other countries do not present such difficulties. Relationships with these neighbouring countries ebb and flow and consulates or embassies may close temporarily. Treat the table below only as a rough guide:

Ndjamena	Algeria Libya Niger
Cairo	Algeria Chad Libya Mauritania Morocco
Tripoli	Algeria Chad Egypt Mali Mauritania Niger
Bamako	Algeria Mauritania Niger
Nouakchott	Algeria Morocco (in Nouadhibou) Niger
Casablanca	Algeria Chad Egypt Libya Mauritania
Niamey	Algeria Libya Mali
Tunis	Algeria Egypt Chad Libya
Tamanrasset	Mali Niger

without too much fuss if you can convince them your reasons are sound. Explain that certain visa applications for your African trip will take several weeks but that you need to travel with a passport in the meantime.

Once in Africa avoid surrendering your passport to anybody, including hotels. Offer to pay up in advance instead, although some hotels are just doing you a favour by filling out registration forms for you and then returning your passport. Never hand over your passport to anyone other than a uniformed official and even then be wary in suspicious situations.

VISAS

Because some visas are valid for only three or six months from the date of issue, and because not all Saharan countries have visa-issuing consulates in every European or African nation, you may find that you have to alter your itinerary to accommodate these vagaries, especially if you're planning a multi-country trip. But don't be disheartened – you could get a good look at the Sahara by visiting Tunisia and Algeria. Crossing the Sahara one way and then either exploring West Africa or returning by another route will present a greater challenge which is why few people do it.

This section uses British citizenship as a guide. European nationals will have an easier time, but Canadians and Australians will need visas for just about everywhere. Don't forget to carry plenty of **passport photos** on your travels for visas and other permits.

Getting your visa

Visa agencies can provide the latest information about the ease and expense of visa applications for the Saharan countries. For a price they also provide a speedy postal service and do the queuing for you. This can actually save you money and certainly time if you're busy working or live in a rural area. Indeed, because of the relationships they develop by their regular visits to certain consulates, an agency may have more luck getting your visa than you.

Coming from Europe you do not need to get visas in advance for Tunisia or Morocco, but you do need to arrange one for Algeria or Libya **before you leave home**. Visas for the southern belt of Saharan countries – Mauritania, Mali, Niger and Chad – can in most cases be applied for from consulates in neighbouring North African countries (see box on p.25).

Both Libya and Algeria require an invitation (usually from a tour agency) to accompany your application. This is easily done for Algeria but is a bit more complicated and expensive for Libya. Latest details are on the relevant country pages on the website.

DOCUMENTS FOR YOU AND YOUR VEHICLE

Once you have your visas or their acquisition schedule sorted out, other documents for visiting the Sahara are straightforward to obtain, as long as the dreaded **carnet de passages** (see box on p.28) is not required.

Vehicle ownership document

Your vehicle ownership document is just as essential as your passport. In the UK older people call it a logbook but officially it's a vehicle registration document (VRD or V5). In the Francophone countries of the Sahara it's known as a *carte grise* and at every border you'll need to show it and copy its details onto new forms. It's very important that the details on your vehicle ownership document, **particularly the chassis and engine numbers**, as well as the registration number (*immatriculation* in French) match those on your vehicle. The reason for these elaborate checks is to dissuade you from selling your vehicle, or part of it, whilst in the country. Even slightly damaged engine or chassis numerals (something easily done) may cause complications. If your vehicle has had a replacement engine or even a new chassis, check those numbers now. You have been warned. A British VRD may be unfamiliar to Saharan officials so it helps to mark the registration number as well as the Chassis and Engine number (often the same 'VIN' number) with a highlighter pen. Signing under your name and address also helps give your VRD a personalised look.

If you're driving a vehicle that's not registered in your name an official-looking letter of permission from the individual whose name appears on the ownership papers is essential. An official-looking stamp also helps here.

Driving licence

In Africa you'll hardly ever have to show your driving licence (it's the *carte grise* that counts), but make sure its details are consistent with other documentation and that it's valid long after your trip expires. If, like the old UK licence, it doesn't show the bearer's photograph, it's a good idea to supplement it with an International Driving Permit (IDP). This multi-lingual booklet is an officially-recognised translation of your driving licence and can be picked up over the counter from your national motoring organisation for a small fee; all you need is your licence and a couple of photos. In practice you hardly ever have to show your IDP either, but with its official-looking stamps and your photo it is another impressive ID document to present to a demanding official.

Travel and medical insurance

These days every business associated with overseas travel is keen to sell you some travel insurance as soon as you consider setting foot on a deadly foreign shore. You feel safe and they make money. Ordinary travel insurance (such as that which comes free with some credit cards) probably won't be adequate for Saharan overlanding. Instead, insurance companies who specialise in expeditions or high-risk activities will take on the job at a reasonably competitive price. A recent quote from a UK specialist for an overland trip came to £85/€119 for one month and £95/€133 for two months.

The good thing about going straight to specialists is that they'll understand what 'overlanding' and 'expeditions' really mean. When you say you're off to Mauritania they won't necessarily retort, 'We had our honeymoon in the Seychelles you know, it was luvlay'. Non-specialists may also either underestimate or freak out at the idea of driving in the Sahara, providing either inadequate or exorbitantly-priced cover.

All policies will include the usual cover against theft, ticket cancellation and baggage loss; they will also include vital accident and medical cover, for overlanders the most important aspect. The worst-case scenario would be evacuation by air from a remote location in the Sahara and the need for intensive medical care (see p.356).

PRE-DEPARTURE DOCUMENT CHECKLIST

- Passport
- Vehicle Ownership Papers
- Driving Licence (and IDP)
- Insurance Green Card
- Ferry tickets

Optional/Depending on route
- Travel Insurance
- Carnet (see below)
- Vaccination Certificates (see p.302)

Once you have all your documents it's a good idea to make **photocopies** of everything and keep them somewhere else, including things like passport numbers along with the date and place of issue.

If you're travelling with two vehicles or more, putting a set in another vehicle is a good idea should one vehicle get burgled, stolen or burned out.

CARNET DE PASSAGES EN DOUANE

Many an overlander's planning comes to a sudden panic when they discover the need to finance a carnet (as it is commonly abbreviated). The good news is that, of all the Saharan countries, only Egypt requires a carnet – one reason why so few desert overlanders venture there. But if you're continuing deeper into Africa a carnet will be necessary.

To sum it up, a carnet is an internationally-recognised temporary importation document that allows you to bring your vehicle into participating countries without having to deposit duties or fees with Customs officials (Egypt unfortunately ignores this point).

Carnets are designed to stop you selling your vehicle without paying local taxes. They are issued by FIM-accredited national motoring organisations (in the UK it's the RAC or AA), and are essentially formal proof of your ability to cover the cost of the highest level of duty on your vehicle in the countries you expect to visit. In Africa this is typically around 150% of your vehicle's estimated value. This is not so bad for a ratty Series III or an old Yamaha XT, but with a nice Mitsubishi or a GS1150 BMW it comes to £10,000/€15,500 or more!

You can cover the required sum in one of four ways.
- Leave a bond with a bank in a locked account.
- Get your bank to cover the amount because of your collateral; either money, property or shares.
- Pay an insurance company to underwrite the cost of your carnet. With this option you can pay up to a few hundred pounds; with the above two options, you just pay the cost of the documentation.
- Buy a fake carnet for a few hundred pounds. Usually a last resort and with obvious risks.

Libya issues its own carnet at the border (about £28/€40 for a car), Niger and Mali issue *laissez-passers* for about two pounds a day. Mauritania, Tunisia, Algeria, Morocco have their own temporary importation documents and in Chad they're keen on carnets via the Lake Chad route but less interested if you come and go from the north.

Anything that involves emergency evacuation by air soon becomes astronomically expensive, so the enormous figures mentioned are actually not so impressive at all. Aim for a figure of at least £1 million/€1,500,000 towards medical expenses; twice that would be better.

For Europeans stranded deep in the Sahara, most serious emergencies will involve immediate repatriation but remember: to get a rescue underway you must first make that all-important phone call to the country of issue. Until then you're on your own. As I've found, from some locations this can take days and is perhaps the only situation where a satellite telephone is useful. When you get your policy, look for the **emergency telephone number** and write it clearly somewhere safe like the back of your passport; this way you can direct someone to ring the number if you can't do so yourself. There's more on what to do in emergencies on p.356.

Third party motor insurance

For EU nationals a Green Card extension to your domestic motor insurance makes it valid in Morocco and Tunisia (as well as crossing Europe), but don't count on it. Some UK insurance companies have been known to refuse to issue Green Cards to motorcyclists.

At Tunis no one checks but at Fnideq (Ceuta) they do. For other countries you buy it at the border or soon after. It costs from around £1 a day for a bike and half as much again for a car. In the countries of the CFA zone the insurance you buy on entering the zone will be valid in all the other CFA countries. In Libya, Egypt, Mauritania and Algeria you buy it at the border or the first town, as you can in Morocco and Tunisia if you need to. In Libya cover for a month for a car costs just £13/€18.

While it's nice to think you are insured, treat this as nothing more than a piece of paper. In an African accident, whether your fault or not, it won't be as simple as swapping details. Driving in Africa can be extremely nerve-racking (the full list of potential hazards appears on p.288). If you run down a child or, worse still, a breadwinner you may well be advised by the police to move quickly on, pay someone off and be on your way, or be arrested and locked up. Drive as if you are uninsured. In your instance insurance is only a document the absence of which can drum up a fine at a checkpoint.

Damage, fire and theft insurance

Because of the perceived risks by jittery insurers, this is generally an extravagance for Africa and, in the UK, is only available from insurance specialists for a hefty price.

Nationals of some European countries like Switzerland are luckily able to insure their vehicles for 'Mediterranean countries' which include Morocco, Algeria, Tunisia, Libya and Egypt, something a Swiss friend who lost his Land Cruiser to Tuareg bandits near Tamanrasset once had reason to be thankful for.

MONEY

People get nervous about carrying a wad of money abroad but good old-fashioned **cash** in a readily changeable and local currency is what talks loudest in the Sahara. Unless you expect to be visiting large cities or capitals, **travellers' cheques** are of little use. Despite what you're told, the promise of speedy replacement of stolen cheques requires a phone call – itself a tall order in most of the Sahara. Don't rely on cashing travellers' cheques in the Sahara.

Credit and debit cards are a much more useful way of avoiding pocketfuls of cash. You're unlikely to find the familiar Visa logo in Zoo Baba or Zaouatine but you may well find it in Zinder, Zouerat and maybe one day even in Foum Zguid. A compact credit card or two is definitely an item worth carrying on any trip and makes an ideal and effective emergency stash. Sometime, somewhere you're going to bless that little plastic rectangle for getting you out of a fix, most probably while getting a painless cash advance from a foreign bank, or just paying for a restful night in a plush hotel when you're sick and tired or short on local currency.

Automatic **cashpoints (ATMs)** are becoming more common in desert towns. Credit card companies actually offer the best **rates** of exchange for the

SAHARAN EXCHANGE RATES

These are the official rates at the time of going to press (Sep 2004). Only Tunisian, Moroccan and, at a pinch, CFA currency can be bought in your home country. The others must be bought locally or from touts near the adjacent border. Local fuel prices are on p.421.

	Algeria	CFA(XOF)	Egypt	Libya	RIM	Morocco	Tunisia
1 €	89	656	7.7	1.64	315	11.0	1.55
1 £	130	955	11.3	2.38	459	16.0	2.26
1 SFr	57.5	423	4.99	1.05	203	7.12	1.00
1 US$	71.7	527	6.22	1.31	253	8.87	1.25

Check the latest official rates at **www.sahara-overland.com/exchangerates/**

day of your purchase and in some cases, no service charges. Remember to check card statements on your return in case someone has been taking liberties with your card account. For this reason it is best to use the cashpoints and then pay in cash at hotels, etc.

Best currencies

In the Francophone Saharan countries (i.e; all the ones listed in the table above, except Libya and Egypt) the **Euro** is the most familiar and therefore most useful foreign currency.

In Libya anything is welcome including US dollars, but unless you're coming from America there's no point in changing to US dollars just to change again into Libyan dinars. Egypt's long exposure to mainstream tourism means all popular currencies are familiar.

Some West African countries are part of the **CFA franc zone** (Mali, Niger, Burkina Faso, Ivory Coast, Senegal and Guinea Bissau). French francs used to be directly tied to the CFA at 100:1, but now the Euro does not make such an easy comparison. Also, there are **two types of CFA**, one issued by the BCEAO (currency code 'XOF') which covers all the above countries except Chad. Chad falls in the Central African BEAC CFA zone ('XAF') and had an exchange rate about 5% less than the XOF franc at the time of writing. Make sure you obtain the right sort of CFA franc for your zone (in most cases it will be XOF), or buy the currency in France where they'll know the difference.

Whatever currency you carry and wherever you go, be sure to have plen-

ty of small denomination notes; US$1 bills are widely recognised and a good way to offer a tip or grease a palm, especially as the smallest Euro notes are worth at least US$3. Avoid large denomination notes such as £50 or US$100. They may save space but in West Africa are the choice of Nigerian forgers so are treated with suspicion there.

Organised tours

Joining an organised tour in the Sahara has many advantages over independent desert travel and is a particularly good option for anyone who is unable to take more than three weeks off work. Realistically, of course, we are looking at two quite distinct categories of travellers. These days there are several big tour operators based in mainland Europe who include adventurous desert itineraries in their RTW see-it-all catalogues as well as smaller local agencies in the Sahara.

The two obvious drawbacks with commercial trips are the expense and the lack of independence. However, when you add up all the money you spend on buying, preparing and equipping your vehicle, not to mention getting it down to the Sahara and back home again, the £2000/€3000 price of a tour can start to look like a bargain. As for the lack of independence, this can sometimes be a good thing – the Sahara can be a demanding place to travel through and, as discussed earlier, for some first-time travellers it can provide more adventure than they want. Read any of the gritty anecdotes scattered around this book and ask yourself whether you could or would want to cope with a similar situation. I've been there myself, watching a smoking car by the roadside and wondering if it's all worth it! I've also often paid for tours, both commercial and private, to remote corners of the desert where I would not choose to drive or ride, and have not regretted it at all.

Advantages of a tour

Having booked a tour, you are able to anticipate your departure with excitement rather than the suppressed foreboding that comes with taking your own vehicle. All you have to do is read some books and study a few maps if you like, and buy bits of gear you probably don't need. This lack of pre-departure anxiety is a real treat.

But the biggest advantage of joining a tour is that, with a good operator and local guide, you'll learn a lot about life in the desert. Independent Saharan travellers inevitably discover a great deal about themselves and their vehicle, but if you are serious about learning about the Saharan environment, a tour is superior, being free of the daily distractions facing self-sufficient overlanders. Of course, if you're lucky enough to have the time and resources, the best thing is to try it both ways.

Your tour guide may just be rattling through his script while following his well-worn tram rails, but for you it's all new and informative. He could lead you to many sites of interest: ones as obvious as a panoramic vista from a certain vantage point or as discrete as a secluded rock art site – places that independent overlanders might only chance upon. In between, you might get background information on local life and customs, tea or stopovers with nomads and, let's not forget, the fast track through roadside checkpoints that only a locally-driven car can ensure. All these factors can add up to a rich if

Let someone else do all the chores, you're on holiday!

brief experience of the Sahara, one without the character-building and teeth-gnashing of your own expedition.

Tour itineraries worth their salt will include most nights out under the stars so the passive coach-potato element is minimised. However, these tours are still active undertakings, never more so than when helping push a 4WD out of soft sand. Come the evening camp, you're tired but not exhausted by the day's driving and challenges. The erection of tents and laying out of your bedroll will be just enough work before you go off to watch the sunset while the dinner is prepared. A **good meal** will be crucial, a real highlight to the day, but luckily this is something that is well understood by most operators catering for European clients.

...and the downside

A good local guide, vehicle and in some cases non-African intermediary are the oil on which a smooth tour runs. When these people, or any of the preparations they're supposed to have made, are sub-standard you soon find yourself on a tour from hell, a scene with which many travellers are familiar, even if it wasn't in the Sahara.

When it's bad it's bad, and the loss of independence and not quite knowing what's happening next can become frustrating, but it's the price you pay for convenience. A good tour is one that doesn't drive you to death but recognises that after an hour or two of sitting broiling in the back of a 4WD on a rough piste, tourists need to get out and do something else.

You can make this better for yourself by having a water bottle, snacks and headwear, plus other useful items (like spare film or sun block) close at hand and not strapped to the roof rack. One good tip is to sit on the shady side of the car if you get a choice. If your day's drive is predominantly from west to east for example, sit on the north side of the car behind the driver: suntans may look healthy but half a burnt neck will not impress friends back home as much as you think.

Equipment and food (or lack of it) can also ruin a tour because these amount to some of your few comforts. And, if you've joined the tour as a couple, you may find the lack of privacy gets to you, especially when it comes to sleeping arrangements. Behind it all may be a realisation that what looked good at the promo slide show or in a brochure is just not so enjoyable in reality: the chore of camping, sand, flies, stomach troubles and heat.

Finally, if it's not bad organisation or the relentless pounding without a chance for a break, it can be your fellow passengers that ruin an otherwise good experience. Surprisingly, having a common interest in the Sahara isn't always enough. When people get tired, hot, bored or edgy they soon find things to complain about. The driver or guide are common and sometimes justified targets. One guide I met told me the three couples he'd just led on a ten-day tour had such a mutual antipathy that he had to arrange for them to spend the last night in three different locations! The fact that they'd been cooped up in the back of a Hilux Crew Cab could have had something to do with it.

If it's any consolation, you can be assured that interpersonal antagonism is a regular ingredient of all Saharan travel: packaged, independent or otherwise. The good thing is the desert rarely fails to disappoint so it's rare that other people do much more than taint the memories of a wonderful experience – even if you may not think so at the time.

CHOOSING A TOUR

To avoid outdated recommendations it's best to ask on the website. As you will find, there are no established British operators running true Saharan tours although a few come and go. This means that you need to consider the implications of spending two or three weeks in a group – and with a guide – that speaks primarily French, German or Italian.

With a couple of exceptions (which do not appear to be very successful), only the overland truck companies continue to drive their own vehicles from Europe to Africa, and none of these offers the type of tour discussed here. Just about everyone else now contracts local operators and their vehicles, so ensuring that the country concerned gets a fair slice of the cake.

One guarantee you have is going via a reputable tour operator who's been doing the same thing with the same local agency for many years. The classier their brochure the better will be your own memories; the home-pagey or DTP'd efforts of small-scale local operators should be a warning. In places like Atar, Tamanrasset and Agadez there are scores of seemingly dormant agencies offering the earth, though in reality only a handful of local operators are equipped to do so – and these are the ones who work

regularly with overseas agencies. Don't assume, though, that greater expense is a guarantee of a better time. In the case of two well-known European operators, one of whom charges twenty per cent more than the other, the only tangible difference between them is the thickness of their mattresses; as a guide pointed out, the quality of their guides is indistinguishable. He works for both!

A French charter flight arrives at Atar.

The cost of a tour depends on dozens of factors including, obviously, the local standard of living and accessibility of commodities. However, a few common rules apply. On the whole, camel tours are cheaper than 4WD tours; small groups can expect to pay premium prices; a standard brochure tour costs less than a tailor-made itinerary; and finally, you might be able to strike a better deal if you organise a tour directly with a local agency of guides rather than going through a European operator. Cheap seasonal charters to southern Saharan towns with Le Point Afrique (www.point-afrique.com) for example, make this DIY option feasible, if still a gamble.

Generally for a European departure (usually from Paris) you're looking at around £100/€150 per day. Organised locally it could be half that, plus the cost of your flight. Remember that going direct to the local agency is a radical idea and best suited to personal recommendations: for most people the point of a tour is peace of mind, not cutting costs.

Established European agencies like Nomade, Comptoir du Desert, Suntours and Spezia d'Aventura to name just a few offer two categories of tour: those in a car and those with pack animals. Some include a few days with both. Within these categories there are all sorts of variables, but on the whole you should expect that you will be spending most nights camping out in the desert in small two-person tents or under the stars if you wish.

Mattresses should be provided and will be needed; and you should expect to take your own sleeping bag. All meals should be provided. Most tour operators request that you bring as little luggage as possible but items that you should not leave out include torch, toilet paper, insect repellent, sunblock, hat, sleeping bag, personal first-aid kit, personal water bottle and a jacket for the cold desert nights. Although most tour leaders will do the camp chores themselves (cooking, washing up, packing up) you may be asked to help, especially if you're with a small group. You should also be aware that camping tours do not pretend to be luxurious so you should expect a certain amount of back-to-nature discomfort.

One other important consideration is the length of the tour. Although you will undoubtedly want to give yourself as much time as possible, spending a long period cooped up in a car in the heat, with complete strangers can become galling. For this reason it's recommended that you don't bite off more than you can chew. Two weeks in the back of a car to see the Ténéré may not sound like much, but by the time you get back to Agadez you'll have got your money's worth – as well as your fill of sitting in cars.

On a couple of car tours I've taken, the days off walking in the desert were by far the most memorable. One agency had a great system where, as the drivers packed up in the morning, we would set out on foot to be caught up with later. It suited everybody: the drivers could have a good moan about us or whatever while the guide would show us the birds and the bees and the keen walkers powered on before being bundled back into the cars.

Be aware that after just a couple of days on a 4WD tour, the novelty of being driven about in the sand will wear off and you'll relish every opportunity to get out and stretch your legs. 'Being stuck in the car all day' is the most common complaint on desert tours.

Which vehicle?

There's only so much luxury you can provide in the Sahara but on all 4WD tours the choice of vehicle is central. Remember, because of the distances and type of terrain in the Sahara, most of your time will unfortunately be spent in the car. For this reason, it may be worth establishing what type of vehicle the tour operators use.

In most cases you want to avoid anything in a truck unless it has been properly and comfortably adapted for off-road travel. Trucks are built for carrying sacks of grain not passengers over the piste. The overland truck companies, including the long-established (articulated!) Rotel service, cross the Sahara following the easiest route and, with a couple of exceptions, they don't deal in specialist desert itineraries, just transporting cheap and cheerful groups through Africa.

An ordinary long-wheelbase, air-conditioned, coil-sprung, four-door, 4WD station wagon is the sort of transportation you're looking for. In all the Sahara, with the exception of Morocco, Toyota's 80 or 100-series Land Cruiser is the local tourist transporter of choice, as it has become all over the developed world. If you're interested, its off-road qualities are discussed elsewhere in this book, but suffice to say, the build-quality and comfort of this model

---

ESCORTED AND SELF-DRIVE TOURS

The option of **escorted tours** with your own vehicle has long existed for motorcyclists; a 4WD support vehicle providing a solution to a bike's limited carrying capacity. For bikes this is a big advantage, making riding easier and safer.

Lately, escorted 4WD tours have been cropping up too: combining the support of experienced tour leaders with local know-how and contacts, and the chance to drive your own vehicle.

Back up combined with **autonomy** is what it's all about. It's not surprising to find the idea of going to the Sahara alone a bit daunting, certainly for the first time. On an escorted tour you can enjoy the experience of desert travel without having to cope with the countless ever-pressing worries alone.

As with conventional tours, you'll probably know instinctively whether an escorted tour will be your cup of tea or not. For many Saharan beginners, simply finding one other party with whom to share their desert adventure safely can be hard, and meeting people out there a gamble (although easier than you think). The big appeal is that you are in your own space, effectively doing your own trip but with a group. The time-consuming business of full-on navigation is taken out of your

hands, you can eat your own food and sleep in your own accommodation.

I've led a few tours like this for cars and bikers and have found that for some it was the confidence booster they needed to head off on their own trips the following year. Seen in this way, an escorted tour is a useful recce experience for the real thing.

Unlike in Southern Africa, unescorted desert-ready **4WD rental** is rare if not unknown in the Sahara or certainly very expensive. Unequipped but nearly new Pajeros, Land Cruisers and Defenders are available to rent in Morocco for around £700/€1000 a week, but in most cases a driver is provided.

(along with many other factors) are unrivalled. For a tourist paying up to £100 a day for the experience, any other Toyota model or make of 4WD is inferior. The still common 60- and 75/78-series Land Cruisers (Troop Carriers) found in Algeria and Niger are actually more suited to long-term desert ownership, but don't have the passenger comforts of modern models. Avoid anything with bench seats along the sides of the back like Toyota Troop Carriers (commonly used in Egypt). Expect a forward-facing seat, no more than three abreast in the back and one passenger up front. Land Rover Defenders, common and well suited to stony Moroccan conditions, are on the narrow side but still come with a third, middle 'seat' in the front: don't expect to be comfortable here for more than a few minutes. It's normal on a tour of several days for people to swap seats; naturally the front passenger seat is the most comfortable.

CAMEL TOURS

Joining a camel tour in the Sahara is an authentic way of seeing the desert without the work. You participate in the environment rather than trying to shield yourself from it; you experience every nuance, every minute change in terrain, vegetation, altitude and temperature.

You appreciate the detail of the desert, the random flowers, animal tracks, prehistoric tools and unusual rocks. You can find yourself in parts of the desert that are inaccessible to vehicles, and you begin to appreciate the pattern and pace of life of a desert nomad.

But camel tours can also be difficult experiences. Being constantly exposed to the relentless wind and sun is always tiring and sometimes unpleasant. Water and food supplies may be more limited and less varied than on other tours, and the distances covered will be much smaller; you may even get bored. If pasture is scarce you may have to travel for up to sixteen hours before making camp, and most camel tours require you to walk for a good part of every day – something you may prefer anyway once you've tried a saddle.

If your guides have little experience with tourists they may expect you to be as long-suffering as they are: walking very long distances and making do on a tiny amount of drinking water. And if it all gets too much, you can't just crash out on the back seat of an air-conditioned car and let someone whisk you to back to civilisation. For most people however, the chance to commune so closely with the desert outweighs these hardships,

and Saharan camel tours are popular, particularly with women.

If you're new to camel riding try a short trip before opting for a longer adventure. In Morocco, Tunisia and riverine Egypt you'll find plenty of local tour agencies offering camel outings that last a few hours, or involve just one night out in the dunes.

Although not currently available in the UK, all the well-known European tour operators and even one US outfit organise one- to three-week tours, most commonly in Niger, Libya, Algeria and Mauritania. Groups range in size from six to twenty.

Your tour agency or guide should tell you **what to bring**, but the absolute essentials include a *cheche* or scarf to keep the sun and wind off your head, face and mouth, decent sunglasses (preferably wrap-around ones and a spare pair – or even ski goggles), trousers and long-sleeved shirts, an old pair of comfortable walking shoes, socks to protect your feet from sunburn while riding or if wearing sandals, and a personal water bottle. Baggy trousers (*saroual*) are more comfortable and less abrasive than jeans.

Longer trips or private tours can also be arranged locally if you have the time and make the right contacts; it's also still possible to hook up with the two main commercial salt caravans running in the Sahara: the *Taghamt* between Agadez and Bilma in Niger and the *Alawa* or *Tifiski* caravans from Timbuktu to Taoudenni in northern Mali (see p.269).

Details on the practicalities and experience of organising your own camel travels start on p.256.

One thing you probably can't research is the quality of the vehicle's driver. The taciturn guys behind the wheel are rarely the owners so drive these vehicles like we drive rental cars: hard. I've seen tour vehicles tearing along the brutally corrugated piste up to Assekrem. On another tour I marvelled as owner-drivers nursed their old, overloaded hacks through the dunes.

Organising local and custom-made tours

One way of feeling less of a sap stuck in the back of a car is to create your own itinerary and organise a tour yourself. Several Europe-based tour operators claim to offer this service subject to minimum numbers; others provide contact details for their local agents and let you sort it out – in theory saving you their cut. Bear in mind, however, that if you're proposing an unusual or extreme route, there's likely to be a reason why tours don't go there. The terrain may be too hard on the well-used local vehicles, tribal disputes or mines may make it dangerous, or it may just be that it's an area that no-one knows well enough (though this will rarely be admitted).

Doing a custom tour need not be more expensive than an off-the-shelf tour as long as you remember that tours are priced with certain minimum numbers: usually at least two cars with three clients in each. Two cars also create a safety margin in remote areas. A cosy group of any less may end up paying more per day than a standard tour. That's the price of exclusivity. **Camels** are a bit different, of course (see opposite).

In the Sahara local agencies boast the ability to organise special interest tours for naturalists, archaeologists, geologists and the like, or to undertake an itinerary of your choice. Be sure they're going to come up with the goods and not just lead you along their set route pointing out camel footprints, the odd stone tool or wind-carved rock. Ask them what they expect to show you to ascertain whether the claimed special interest is genuine or, as is most likely the case, just a sales gimmick. If you have a custom-made itinerary in mind make sure they, or your guide, really know the area you want to visit. It is customary for local operators to say 'yes, of course' to anything and then fail to deliver.

Others will just give it a go and let Allah provide. I was once assured that a oued I wanted to follow was 'too stony' and that the driver/guide knew a better piste through the dunes. It turned out he knew no such thing and we wasted the next two and a half days digging and pushing the car out of soft sand and looking for a well – we ran out of water on the first day, which was another indication of his irresponsible attitude. We eventually regained the oued, but by that stage had lost our enthusiasm for the tour and respect for our guide and felt ripped off for wasting two days of our precious tour at £50 a day each. Having you pay for their exploration is a real treat for these guys!

And last but not least, if you turn up in some outback town and want to hire a local car with driver, expect the vehicle to have seen better days. If it's not costing much then you get what you pay for, but stick to a major piste and don't risk anything too adventurous. African drivers (and even expatriate Europeans as in the case above) have a fatalistic attitude towards vehicle maintenance and repair, not helped by the scarcity of spare parts. At the very

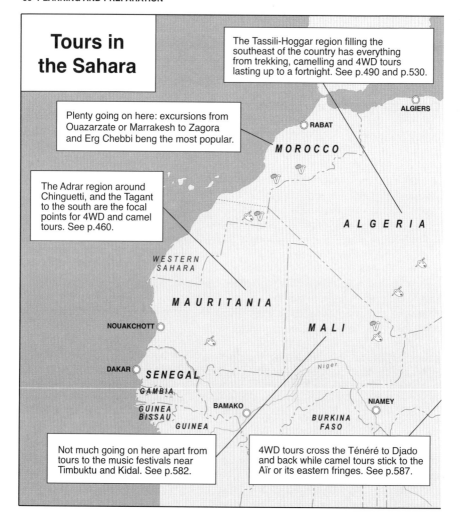

Tours in the Sahara

The Tassili-Hoggar region filling the southeast of the country has everything from trekking, camelling and 4WD tours lasting up to a fortnight. See p.490 and p.530.

Plenty going on here: excursions from Ouazarzate or Marrakesh to Zagora and Erg Chebbi beng the most popular.

The Adrar region around Chinguetti, and the Tagant to the south are the focal points for 4WD and camel tours. See p.460.

Not much going on here apart from tours to the music festivals near Timbuktu and Kidal. See p.582.

4WD tours cross the Ténéré to Djado and back while camel tours stick to the Aïr or its eastern fringes. See p.587.

ALGIERS

RABAT

MOROCCO

ALGERIA

WESTERN SAHARA

MAURITANIA

NOUAKCHOTT

MALI

DAKAR

SENEGAL

Niger

GAMBIA

GUINEA BISSAU

BAMAKO

NIAMEY

GUINEA

BURKINA FASO

least check the vehicle has a jack and wheel brace that works, a thick plank to support the jack on soft sand, a spare tyre with air in it, and enough water and fuel for the planned route. In some places you will find meeting all these demands will actually be quite a tall order.

COUNTRY RUNDOWN FOR TOURS

Just about all the established European operators offer country-specific Saharan itineraries. Below is a general round-up of the Saharan regions they cover. You'll find much more detail in their brochures.

Morocco

There's plenty of everything in Morocco but for the desert you want to keep south of the High Atlas as do just about all the routes

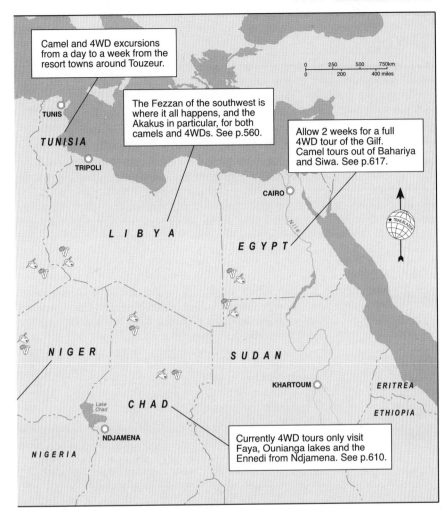

Camel and 4WD excursions from a day to a week from the resort towns around Touzeur.

The Fezzan of the southwest is where it all happens, and the Akakus in particular, for both camels and 4WDs. See p.560.

Allow 2 weeks for a full 4WD tour of the Gilf. Camel tours out of Bahariya and Siwa. See p.617.

Currently 4WD tours only visit Faya, Ounianga lakes and the Ennedi from Ndjamena. See p.610.

described in the back of this book. One exception is the Telouet–Aït Benhaddou track, a popular and stunning deviation on a trip from Marrakesh to Ouazarzate or Zagora. Any piste crossing the arid Anti Atlas will also be outstanding and a visit to Erg Chebbi is also a favourite. Since Morocco is a mainstream destination, you'll find plenty of ideas and options in the relevant Lonely Planet or Rough Guide.

The lack of dunes makes Morocco a poor destination for prolonged camel treks, though there will be plenty of two-hour or overnight options available from the southern oases like Erfoud, and those along the Draa Valley (possibly incorporated into your home-booked tour). Erg Chebbi near Erfoud is the exception (enough to satisfy most people that they've 'seen the Sahara'), with groups shipped down from Marrakesh to do camel overnighters here.

Mauritania

The Adrar region is the focal point of Mauritanian desert tourism with the standard tour coming up the highway from Nouakchott to Atar, turning east to Chinguetti and Ouadane and then down through the desert to Tidjikja and back west via Moudjeria. It packs in the miles but you'll see the best this exceptional country has to offer. Other tours fly straight into Atar and do a smaller loop. Note that the Toyota Hilux Crew Cabs commonly seen in Atar are a cramped substitute for the long-distance comfort of a Land Cruiser, even if it's an older 60-series model.

Along with Sudan, Mauritania has the largest and healthiest camel economy in the Sahara. Large caravans are commonly encountered and camel is the staple meat. So, if you're not tucking into one wrapped in a kebab, there are excellent opportunities for camel tours in the Adrar region, or through the dunes of the Ouadane south of Chinguetti. Longer and more scenically variable treks lead down towards Tidjikja (or vice versa): at least two weeks and as good as it gets (see p.481).

Mali

Timbuktu is the overrated goal here, with 'tea in a Tuareg tent' encounters part of every tour that visits the fabled city. Elsewhere the Tuareg rebellion and continued smuggler/bandit activity see the Malian Sahara of the Adrar des Iforhas rarely visited these days.

There's not much happening in Mali that you can't do a lot better in Mauritania or Niger but see p.269 for an account of a self-organised camel tour to Taoudenni.

Niger

The Aïr mountains and Ténéré desert have for years been among the Sahara's tourist highlights; it's the first place European film crews head for to replicate a Sahara feature done by a previous crew. Because tourism is not flourishing as it was twenty years ago, the cars (Land Cruisers mostly) have all seen better days, though some agencies do run comfier 100-series models. Go for the longer, three-week tours which should include the occasional rest day.

The environs of the Aïr are the best place for cameling – the traversal of the Ténéré with a salt caravan is a forced march more suited to hard-core cameleers. Anything offering a combination of Aïr mountain village life and the dunes to the east around Arakao, Adrar Chiriet or Temet will provide a camel tour to remember. There's more on cameling in Niger on p.278.

Algeria

For a year or two until 2003 things had been looking good in Algeria. Even Brit operators who knew Algeria from the old days were getting in on the act as they knew well that the whole region between the dramatic

Hoggar mountains near Tamanrasset and the Tassili plateau in the southeast offers everything you'd want from the Sahara. Like Niger, vehicles here are mostly Land Cruisers, some past their prime. Indeed the difficulty of buying and registering old overseas machines makes the selection distinctly ratty.

What can be done in a car in the region described above can be done equally well on the back of a camel. The Tassili N'Ajjer plateau is inaccessible to vehicles anyway, so tours always use camels or mules. Elsewhere the Tefedest and Adrar Ahnet regions to the west are rewarding venues.

Tunisia

You'll see plenty of nearly new Land Cruisers bombing over the corrugations between Matmata, Chenini, Ksar Ghilane and Douz; fun excursions but not really the desert. If you get a chance, choose a tour including a visit deep into the Erg Oriental.

Tunisia is a good place for a classic camel trek. The sand sea in the south offers the perfect environment for what most people imagine cameling through the Sahara to be. The dunes may get monotonous after more than a week, but your fantasy will have been fulfilled.

Libya

These days visiting Libya on a tour is easier than doing it yourself. Many entrepreneurs have moved into the business and itineraries have settled between the Roman ruins of the coast and the desert in the southwest Akakus. With direct flights to Tripoli, two weeks is plenty of time to appreciate the above highlights. Vehicles are a selection of old and now newer Land Cruisers.

Camel commerce in Libya has long given way to modern development and, unlike in Algeria, the indigenous camel-based nomadic culture has been subsumed. But the non-driveable reaches of the Akakus or, better still, the Tadrart are the best places for a ten-day camel tour.

Chad

An almost continuous rebellion in the north means there's not much going on in Chad for organised tourism. Vehicles will be old, regular tour dates scarce though, as already mentioned, it is possible to get up to the Ounianga lakes and the Ennedi massif.

Not least because of the above situation, camel touring in the north of Chad is unknown.

Egypt

Visits into the Western (Libyan) Desert can only be undertaken with a guide and local vehicle, so tours are the only option here. Remote desert tours are not high on Egypt's tourist menu so vehicles (Land Cruiser

Troop Carriers with bench seats) tend to be functional rather than pampered, though the better operators use 100-series Toyotas.

 Cameling in Egypt is usually a photo opportunity or a token excursion, the Libyan Desert in Egypt being far too arid to support camel tours.

PART 2: VEHICLES

Most drivers won't need persuading that a 4WD is a good idea in the Sahara. However, it's surprising how far you can get in an ordinary car, while there are dozens of different types of 4WDs, not all of which are up to the job. The first part of this chapter is designed to give you an introduction to the basic elements of a typical desert vehicle to help you decide whether your current or intended vehicle is right for the trip you have in mind. The second part reviews individual models, including campers and trucks, in more detail.

What about conventional cars?

In the next couple of years, about 80 years after the first Citroëns managed to cross the desert, the Sahara is expected to be sealed from north to south along the Atlantic route, theoretically opening it up to regular traffic. But even without sealed roads, travellers have long crossed the desert in conventional cars, and a few have explored the desert in **modified 2WDs**. Choosing to explore the Sahara in this way is a bit like cycling: a deliberate decision to do something the hard way, but not as foolhardy as it sounds. It's common for over eighty per cent of the bangers in the Plymouth–Dakar Rally to finish – a lot more than that other hyper-expensive rally ending in Dakar.

Why a 2WD?

In most cases it is for the same primal motivations as the famous road-crossing chicken: 'to get to the other side'. Along the major transit routes, the Hoggar, Tanezrouft and now the sealed Atlantic, people have hammered their road-going saloons, usually to sell them in West Africa.

It's not the lack of 4WD transmission that makes a 2WD hard work in the desert. Low **ground clearance** along with a build not designed for an off-road beating are the main drawbacks. In all but the softest sand it's primarily decent clearance, not all-wheel drive, that enables a vehicle to keep moving – ninety five per cent of the time a car won't require all-wheel drive in the desert. But it takes just one rock to crack a sump, a series of boggings to fry a clutch – and that remaining five per cent can take hours to get through.

Experimenting with a modified 2WD in Morocco just prior to publication. A longer desert tour was planned. Full story on the website www.sahara-overland.com/merc

I've helped push and pull Peugeot 504s, Kombis and Transit vans across successive oueds and come across 2CVs breaking in half. Most of the wrecks that litter the main trans-Saharan pistes are old road cars. But it's also worth recognising that the Long Range Desert Group manage to cruise all over the Libyan Desert in 2WD Chevrolet and Ford trucks, the authors of the *Sahara Handbook* did much of their exploring in an air-cooled VW camper, and Cyril Ribas has roamed even further in a stripped-out Citroën 2CV. As agony aunts are wont to remind us, it's not what you've got, it's how you use it.

Road cars: what to look for

Looking out ov my window now, an endless stream of cars rolls by and it's hard to know what makes one make or model better than another. What's been used out there before certainly helps narrow things down, but **price** too is a factor because it's hard to imagine anyone spending even half the £3000 or so it takes to buy a decent, desert-worthy 4WD. The whole point is that road cars are easier and **cheaper** to buy, cheaper to prepare and run; in fact cheap enough to abandon. No one's going to go through the whole roof-tent-and-snorkel scenario described over the coming pages on a Datsun Violet, even the SL model. Part of the appeal of a road car is keeping it simple and doing it on a budget. How far you plan to take this depends partly on whether you plan to sell the car out there, expect to have to dump it on the way or have expectations of bringing it back and doing it again.

In most cases people are **buying to sell** which narrows down your choice from what is wanted (see p.461) and what's available at your price. Prices are going to be lowest for high-mileage models. Any fool can buy a banger with ten previous owners for a couple of hundred pounds but what you ideally want is something that's been a second car since new to a well-off family who knew the value of a full service history. With a record like this behind it, a £700 diesel with 200,000 miles on the clock need not be a bad buy.

Recommending marques is trickier but naturally some have better reputations than others. Peugeot is the French brand of choice if for no other reason than the legendary status of the 504 estates (still produced in Nigeria) as the definitive bush taxi until the advent of Japanese minibuses. These 504s may have been petrol engined and have all been bought up in Europe by now, but Peugeot also has a good reputation for producing **diesel engines**; other manufacturers like Ford and Citroën often install Peugeot engines in their cars. The preference for diesel engines over petrol, as detailed in the boxes on page 54 and 56, is as valid for road cars.

There are many old Mercedes saloons still around with prices from €1000. It's worth noting that the prestige cachet of the marque is greater in the UK, although the robust build quality is certainly an attribute. Prices are lower in Europe and if you're thinking of selling out there, **left-hand drive** will be desirable anyway. Fifteen-year-old petrol-engined BMW 3-series are easy to find for less than £500 in the UK, but diesels weren't introduced until later so go for much higher prices. VWs, Audis and Volvos all have a good reputation too but, VW campers apart, are rarely seen in the desert.

Which more or less leaves Ford – cheap and prolific in the UK – and Japanese cars. It's all changed now but in the late 1980s Japanese cars such as

Datsuns/Nissans and Toyotas had all the appeal of a mullet at the Chelsea Flower Show. And yet, rust apart, Japanese build quality from that era, especially Toyota, is second to none, a blessing for moonlighting minicabbers and maybe you too.

As with everything else, the **Internet** is a great place to research a car you might not even have noticed until a few days ago. Somewhere in cyberspace a drooling enthusiast maintains a home-page listing a given model's headlight configurations over the past four centuries. More useful are review websites, both professionally written and merely owners' impressions; just type your model and year into a search engine and you'll soon find them.

Vulnerable sumps, a weak point on 2WDs.

Narrowing it down

To help focus your choice from the plethora of cars available, here are a few more factors to consider. The finer qualities listed for 4WDs are not so relevant as, by taking the 2WD route you're asking for it, so can expect to rough it!

Ground clearance The biggest drawback of all and broadly similar on all cars at around 5" or 130mm. The good thing is that because road cars feature independent suspension the underneath is generally smooth, with no beam axle casings sticking out. They therefore lend themselves well to the fitting of a large **sump guard**. Shorter cars like hatchbacks have a better ramp breakover angle which means they won't get bellied out so easily, but they have much less room too and have front-wheel drive (see p.47).

Body overhangs Also a function of ground clearance and much more varied between models. Saloons and estates all have big back-end overhangs and some have overhanging fronts too. Hatchbacks are generally good at the back and vary at the front – for example Ford's Ka is exceptional at both ends and also has decent ground clearance. Tailpipes, occasionally fuel tanks and, on more modern cars, front spoilers, are all vulnerable to damage. Try to anticipate what will ground out and whether it matters or not. Shortening the end of the **tailpipe** might be convenient to stop it grounding, but the fumes need to clear the body so re-bending it or adding a flexible end is a better idea. Consider the bottom edge of the **radiator** behind that spoiler too. Will it get mashed and pushed into the fan in the event of a nose dive off a small dune?

Wheel and tyre size Larger wheels, like the 16" rims on old 200-series Mercedes, roll over rough ground more smoothly than smaller wheels, while of course increasing clearance on suspension components. They also produce a marginally longer footprint when deflated which helps traction in soft sand. Fifteen-inch rims are found on more modern Mercedes, bigger Peugeots and the like, but hatchback rims go down to 13" or less.

A 'tall' tyre, i.e. one with a **high sidewall** is definitely desirable. You can tell this just by looking at a tyre – its aspect ratio (the second number in the

The humble Citroën 2CV makes a good desert car: light, simple mechanics, good ground clearance and economical. This one's crossing the normally bone-dry Oued Dider on the way to Djanet.
© Gert Duson – www.brussels-capetown.com

tyre size moulded on the side: eg, 185/**75** 15") means how tall it is in relation to its width. A high aspect ratio of 75 or more is desirable for off-roading because it increases ground clearance, provides added cushioning as the tyre flexes over bumps and, most usefully, gives enough scope to deflate the tyre for soft sand without dangerously flattening it against the rim. (If you're making little sense of this, try p.177). But fitting much bigger wheels or taller

2CV DESERT TECH

Taking the ultra-basic, retro approach to the limit brings you to a Citroën 2CV, the French answer to a farmer's utility car originally designed to be able to carry a basket of eggs across a ploughed field without making a mess.

Today it still makes an effective desert machine and was some of the engineering inspiration behind the failed Africar project (see p.49). Engines are air-cooled 450 or 600cc flat twins, front wheel drive with independent suspension.

Assuming you're carrying more than eggs, the main problem in the desert is the **chassis**. An original must be perfect or it will break up on the corrugations. Ideally it should be welded up to 'PO' 'Africa' standard; Citroën's out-of-print booklet (available online) shows where the strengthening is needed. If you're getting serious I recommend a new chassis by SLC (http://members.aol.com/slcchassis/) which is pretty well indestructible.

I've found 125 Michelin **tyres** are too soft in the sidewalls, 145 Uniroyal F560s have a stronger and higher sidewall and ran flat in sand or over the worst of the Moroccan rocks at two bar with no problems. You can also get Dunlop SP50s from French 2CV specialists – said to be even stronger. I ran **tubeless** with no problems; others in the group used tubes

and punctures/failures were a daily event. But take spare tubes anyway. Two spare wheels can fit across the car with 20-litre jerricans behind the seats on their sides; this gives a range of about 800km leaving the rear load area clear.

Keep all heavy weights as far forward as possible because **weight** is going to be your main problem. Think like a bike and get by with minimal gear.

Make sure that your **engine** does not leak any oil – it's vital on a small air-cooled engine. A 4mm alloy **sump guard** plate from the front bumper to behind the exhaust cross box is a good idea, as is a similar plate under the fuel tank. Fit the **stone guard** to the fan housing as well as a very fine 'gravel guard' in the bonnet grill.

Take a spare **fan and pulley assembly** as even the smallest of stones can wreck your fan, causing major overheating. To aid **engine cooling** at slow speeds or in sand remove the panels between the front wings and bonnet. And take at least one **spare coil** as they get damaged in the heat and are difficult to find now.

Finally take some lightweight sand planks as psp is way over the top for a 2CV, and remove the rear bumper as it deflects stones up onto the car.

Sean

INDEPENDENT SUSPENSION

Just about all conventional cars (and some 4WDs) feature independent suspension for superior roadholding. When one wheel goes over a bump only that wheel moves up, the body remains level. This makes for a comfortable ride but has disadvantages on the piste because the ground clearance remains largely the same.

When a beam-axled 4WD drives over a bump the entire beam axle and the body too move up. It does not do much for the ride quality but ground clearance is, if anything, improved.

tyres is not ideal as it **increases overall gearing** so makes crawling up hills and pulling out of sand harder still on clutches and small-engined vehicles.

Front- or rear-wheel drive The jury is still out on which is better for off-roading but it seems rear-wheel drive, as found on larger cars, may have the edge. This could be a misleading impression caused by the fact that larger cars have bigger engines and more momentum, all of which helps in the dirt. Certainly it contradicts the assumption that the **weight of the engine over the driven wheels** of a FWD car (like the 2CV, p.46) is desirable for good traction. All this only gets critical when the going gets rough, of course, but having one set of wheels steering while the others drive may have something to do with better performance in soft sand. And if nothing else the engine layout of a RWD car is easier to comprehend and work on as the engine and transmission are in line with the car. On a conventional front-wheel drive car it's all packed in and, unless you know the car well, it can be hard to tell what's what.

Mechanical simplicity This is desirable for any machine that will be getting hot, dusty and shaken about. It's another reason for choosing older diesels. Be aware that the many electrical functions like windows, sun roofs, central locking and whatnot are all commonly susceptible to dust.

EQUIPMENT CHECKLIST FOR 2WD DESERT DRIVING

If you're planning to sell your car south of the Sahara you're not going to want to spend too much on gear but, especially if you're going alone and into the sands, here are some essential items, besides all the usuals of fuel, water and camping needs.

Remember, when recovering a 2WD from sand-bogging (more on p.180), it's especially important to do a good job first time to avoid stressing the clutch and transmission as you drive out. Get towed out where possible, or get people to push.

- Shovel
- Two tow ropes – or one very long one
- Foot pump or compressor, plus tyre gauge
- Wooden planks or a sand plate cut vertically in two. Even thick strips of carpet will work.
- Cheap airbag jack or a plate to support a regular jack on sand

---

Modifying a road car

The single most important thing that needs to be addressed with a road car in the Sahara is ground clearance and/or underbody protection. The parts that really need protecting are the sump of the engine, along with maybe the gearbox, steering and suspension gear, exhaust pipe, and in some cases fuel and brake lines and an exposed fuel tank.

The simplest way to achieve this is to fix on a sheet of metal: 3mm steel might do or alloy twice as thick. This **bash plate** will earn its keep so it needs to be fixed on well. If you're doing it as you're about to start a piste, wiring on an old oven door with coat hanger wire is better than nothing, but a bash plate bolted solidly onto whatever points are available is best, as they often come adrift. Leave a small gap between the plate and whatever it's protecting; it may help to stuff in some thick, shock-absorbing material like rubber (bits of old tyres would do) so a severe impact is not transmitted directly through the plate to what it's supposed to be protecting.

Raising ground clearance is most easily done on cars with coil suspension all round. The cheapest solution is a **spacer** above or beneath the coil: the car instantly sits higher. Mercedes offer these 'spring pads' in a variety of thicknesses (see the ...com/merc page, they may fit other cars) but anything will do. Extreme levels of this sort of modification will put unaccustomed stresses on standard steering and final drive components, so don't go too far. It's another reason why buying a car with relatively good ground clearance in the first place is a good idea. A rise of the bodywork of around **two inches or 50mm** is the maximum: any more than that and something might snap – don't forget the car will already be heading for a hammering it was not built for. Remember too that the coil sits more or less halfway between the pivoting point of the wishbone and the tyre so a spacer or longer spring of 20mm will raise the car by 40mm, more or less. Getting longer coils custom made is not as expensive as you may think – I paid £150 for an overlength and uprated set for an old Mercedes whose original springs had already been round the planet ten times. A set of standard OE Mercedes springs would have cost £100.

On a rear-wheel drive car it might be possible to lower the differential – usually bolted to the subframe or body – by an inch. This would reduce the exacerbated geometry on final drive linkages to effectively one inch on a suspension rise of two inches, but you'd want to be sure the prop shaft has the play to cope with such a modification.

Torsion bar suspension is also adjustable by repositioning the pivots in the spline; it depends on the model. Don't forget that raising suspension on any road car may negate any normal or even sporty handling characteristics your car may have had. It's worth reiterating then that just as with 4WDs, the easiest way of maintaining your car's ground clearance (and reducing stresses overall) is simply to **not overload it** and keep any heavy weights central and between the axles.

Once you've made the best of your ground clearance and underbody protection, all that really remains is to ensure things like the exhaust pipe and fuel tank fittings are solid (they commonly come loose or fall off on corrugated pistes). For other preparation guidelines, follow the ideas in the 4WD section.

WHATEVER HAPPENED TO THE AFRICAR?

In 1987 Channel 4 TV in the UK ran a series about a revolutionary vehicle called the Africar undertaking a test run from the Arctic to the Equator.

The car was the idea of Tony Howarth who'd become unimpressed with conventional cars' inability to cope with road conditions in Africa, as well as the First World's attitude to exporting unfunctional vehicles to poor nations.

The Africar was an all-terrain, multi-purpose vehicle suitable for *manufacture* and use where the need was greatest – the unpaved roads of developing countries.

Based heavily on Citroën 2CV running gear, its body was made from resin-soaked plywood to enable manufacture from renewable native materials by a low-skill workforce. The engine was to be a supercharged two-stroke opposed twin or four based on marine engines used in the Pacific, with part-time drive to the rear axle(s). Howard firmly believed that a wide track and independent suspension combined with a smooth underbelly free of diffs was the way to maintain all-terrain traction and road manners.

A station wagon, a pick-up and a six-wheeler were built for the Arctic to Equator expedition. The new engine and transmission were not ready so the cars used flat-four Citroën GS engines but encountered regular gearbox problems. Nevertheless, after four months all three vehicles made it to the Equator.

A factory was set up in Lancaster with promises of overseas manufacturing rights. Looking for my first desert car and attracted by the concept, I visited the factory in 1988. But alarm bells rang when the saleswoman stumbled over elementary technical queries.

A month or so later the factory was repossessed and the workers laid off while Tony Howarth hid out in the US for a few years, before coming back to face the music and a short jail spell.

It seems he'd squandered the investors' money on a new engine and gearbox programme and, as the judge observed, 'you were seduced by your inability to face facts'.

The lovely illustrated Africar book can be found on the web for a tenner, but the three Africar prototypes themselves seem to have disappeared.

GROUND CLEARANCE

A 4WD's ground clearance can be measured in four ways:
- approach angle
- departure angle
- ramp breakover angle or belly clearance between the axles
- minimum ground clearance, usually lowest under the axle diffs

On most 4WDs, the **approach angle** is not usually a problem; though on some Range Rovers it's compromised by the front spoiler. Low-slung bull bars or poorly positioned winches can also reduce this angle.

Ideally a **departure angle** should match the approach angle, as it does on the wartime Willys Jeep or a 101 for example. On your average LWB station wagon, however, there's usually a considerable rear overhang made worse by low exhaust pipes, spare wheel placement and tow hitches. It's a compromise needed to give station wagons a usefully long body with a manageable wheelbase.

The **ramp breakover angle**, better understood as belly clearance, is the point when the undercarriage between the wheels grounds as you go over a ramp. Finally **axle clearance**, lowest at the diffs, is important when driving among rocks or along deep ruts, especially on harder surfaces.

On conventional 4WDs axle clearance can only be improved by fitting larger diameter wheels and taller tyres. The portal axle design of HumVees, Unimogs and Pinzgauers is an expensive way of improving axle clearance.

All the underbody angles can be improved by **raising the suspension** and removing running boards and other non-essential paraphernalia along the body's lower edge. Raising suspension along with taller tyres and bigger wheels raises a vehicle's axle clearance but also its **centre of gravity** (as does a heavily loaded roof rack). This all reduces the stability of a 4WD, especially in dunes. The right balance must be struck between adequate ground clearance and a stable loaded vehicle.

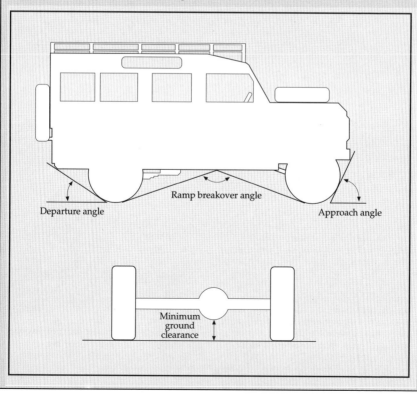

Departure angle

Ramp breakover angle

Approach angle

Minimum ground clearance

SUSPENSION SYSTEMS

In the old days most 4WDs had one-piece beam axles attached to leaf springs and a choice of two- or four-wheel drive. Although this system is still effective and preferred by some drivers, these days the move is towards permanent four-wheel drive with coil springs, a system pioneered on the Range Rover in the late 1960s. Permanent four-wheel drive is the best solution to trouble-free traction and it doesn't take a professor to see that a coiled spring provides better suspension than a bunch of cart springs.

Independent suspension with either coils or torsion bars (found on road cars and the front axle of many Japanese 4WDs) is also an option, improving a 4WD's road manners at some cost to off-road ground clearance and wheel travel (see diagram p.47). For desert driving the strengths and weaknesses of all these options are outlined below.

It's worth knowing that **broken coils or leaves** need not be a show-stopper. With coils you may not notice for months, and with a leaf broken on the articulated side, you can limp home with the axle on the bump stop.

Leaf springs

Pro
● Cheap to replace and easy to uprate.
● Less roll than coils reputedly makes leaves better for load-carrying.
● Secure axle location – few bushes to wear out.
● The inherent damping of closely-packed leaf springs puts less stress on shocks.

Con
● Mounting under the axle makes shock mounts vulnerable to damage.
● Limited wheel travel.
● Short leaves, as on Series IIIs, give a harsh ride; longer leaves (as on Toyota 78s) are much more supple.

Coil springs

Pro
● Cheap to replace and easy to uprate.
● Superior wheel travel to all other systems.

Con
● Can pitch and bounce, especially on SWBs. Body roll can be unnerving.
● Hard coils are as harsh as hard leaves.

Torsion bars

Pro
● A more supple ride than beam axles.
● Used with independent suspension with its related drawbacks to ground clearance.

Con
● Limited wheel travel – not a serious off-road option for a heavy 4WD.

Beam axles

Pro
● Stronger than alternatives.
● The whole axle, including the vulnerable diff, moves up over bumps, maintaining good ground clearance (see p.47).

Con
● The body moves with the axle over bumps which can cause excessive pitching about, a trait which independent suspension minimises.

Independent suspension

Pro
● Less pitching as you go over bumps gives a superior ride in situations where ground clearance is not vital.
● Many Desert rally racers use it so it can't be that bad.

Con
● Ground clearance reduces as suspension compresses.
● Vulnerable to damage and not always designed for an off-road hammering.

Desert Driving in a 2WD

You may have made the most of your ground clearance but in a 2WD you're still missing two 4WD attributes: all-wheel drive and a low-range gearbox. What this means is that when you hit soft sand you must rely on **momentum** to get your through. Maintaining momentum, knowing exactly when to accelerate and when to back off, is crucial to successful 2WD desert driving.

The problem comes when you have to drive a 2WD recklessly fast across sandy creek beds and dunes just to maintain that momentum and avoid getting stuck. Once in Mauritania we came across a trio of Mercedes sedans all with mashed radiators. They'd nose-dived one after another into the same dip, having had to gun their cars over a sandy hump where a 4WD would just drive through at a normal safe speed.

Reducing tyre pressures gives you a bit more leeway before you get stuck, and is essential when you are stuck. As with 4WDs, **one bar** or 15 psi is the optimum pressure, or even less when you're really stuck. When driving through deep ruts, either sandy or stony, which a 4WD can do in 2WD, a low-slung road car has no choice but to drive with one wheel ploughing through the centre ridge and the others off the track to avoid getting dragged to a halt.

Up to a point the smooth underbelly of a car (assisted by a large bashplate on which to slide) plus independent suspension enables the driven wheels to reach down into the ruts and maintain drive. But independent suspension (as opposed to a 4WD's beam axle) is less effective over rocks because when one wheel rolls over a rock or a hump the entire car does not move up with it so compromises ground clearance, something that a 2WD does not have to spare (see diagram on page 47). In this situation a bashplate will be working hard.

In dunes things can get quite hairy. I once met a German couple who'd just come through the tricky Gara Khanfoussa dunes of Route A2 (p.497) in an ancient Beetle. They'd actually driven the route several times over the years – knowing what's in store makes a huge difference which is why some experienced 4WD-ing Saharans can face making what seems like a backward step by turning to a 2WD. It's when you don't know where the danger points are that dune driving in a 2WD can go horribly wrong, as with the multiple radiator mashing described above.

FOUR WHEEL DRIVES

Let's face it, setting off to explore the Sahara is a great excuse to buy a 4WD! The best ones are built for the job and can take on regular tough trips with minimal maintenance or difficulties. Only a few 4WDs score a full hand in the qualities listed below, which are given in order of importance. Lower down the list these features become desirable rather than essential.

Robustness

A true off-roader needs the added strength and stiffness of a separate ladder chassis, a rugged body shell and tough transmission and suspension components that can withstand a pounding. All this added weight does nothing for economy or handling, but such a vehicle will last many years on rough, corrugated tracks that would break a lesser machine.

Mechanical simplicity

In the Sahara you must face the possibility of having to carry out your own repairs. The simpler your car is, the less there is to go wrong and the easier it is for you or a bush mechanic to understand and work on. Manually-operated functions such as gearboxes, free-wheeling hubs, windows, door locks, various adjustments – in fact all the things that are becoming scarce on contemporary 4WDs – are all an asset in the desert.

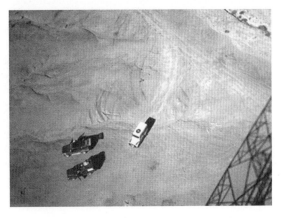

From a distance they may all look the same, but choosing the right sort of vehicle will have a big effect on your trip. Like it or not, you will be in the car most of the time.

Electronically-controlled fuel-metering, traction control and suspension levelling are all wonderful when new and improve a car's performance, but eventually these electronics will start malfunctioning. As the heat, dust and vibration of Saharan travel causes frequent problems with electrics anyway, unfixable 'black box' electronics are an additional liability.

Payload and space

The ideal desert vehicle must have a good carrying capacity, in space and in weight, as both are quickly used up on Saharan trips. This is not simply a question of folded-down rear seats and a roof rack: it means the whole vehicle must be built to carry up to 500kg plus passengers *off-road*, where every component is subjected to much greater stress.

All 4WD manufacturers state a gross vehicle weight (GVW), usually given as the total weight of the car plus maximum payload. Subtracting the weight of the car gives you your payload. On 4WDs this should apply to off-road situations but in practice that's unlikely. Even on Toyotas and Land Rovers the standard suspension wouldn't tolerate an expeditionary payload.

Comfort

While roughing it can be fun for a short while, it wears you out at a time when you need all your energy. A 200km day along an unknown piste will leave you weary, but you'll feel a lot better if the suspension has done what it's supposed to. Comfort also means ensuring that your seating and driving positions are relaxing, that the steering is light, that noise from the engine and your rattling payload is minimal and that your surroundings are kept at the right temperature. Your car will be your home for weeks and needs a well-organised system: accessible and convenient.

Power

Thrashing a small, high-revving engine along sandy riverbeds while clutching the wheel wears you out. Bear in mind that few motoring publications test

4WDs off-road with a full payload, yet in the Sahara this will be your situation, permanently. Responsive acceleration and handling around country lanes will be erased when carrying a four-day, 800km payload of fuel and water. Thus loaded, the typical two-and-a-half-litre turbo diesel engine will be at its limit in the deep sand.

Correct tyres, driving technique and a minimal payload (all rarely achieved without hard-won experience) also help maintain mobility, as does a good power-to-weight ratio, but as Picasso knew well 'there's no substitute for cubes'. If faced with a choice of good suspension or a good powerful engine (what once differentiated Land Rovers from Toyotas), suspension can be easily, cheaply and reliably uprated, an engine cannot (see p.84).

For ordinary desert tracks a power-to-fully-laden-weight ratio of 50bhp (37kW) per 1000kg is a benchmark. In extended soft sand situations such as ergs, aim for 70bhp (52kW) per tonne if you want to keep moving.

Ground clearance

As already mentioned, good ground clearance (see box p.50) is more useful than four-wheel drive in the Sahara. Seated high on a chassis and fitted with large diameter wheels, the body of a 4WD is kept well clear of the ground while typically achieving around 200mm (8") of clearance under the axles.

Fuel economy

Two hundred horse power at 1900 rpm is nice, but economy can be critical and is one reason why diesels are so popular. Economy translates into a longer range, smaller payload and less expense. No desert trip from northern Europe will cover much less than 5000km.

Economy can be maintained by keeping your speed to under 100kph – at an 80kph (50mph) crawl you'll be amazed what distance you can cover on a tankful. Few 4WDs slice through the air like a wing but keeping the frontal area as small as possible makes a great difference at cruising speeds. If you use a roof rack, avoid putting big boxes or other bulky baggage up there for the long, fast drive down to North Africa.

Underbody protection

On the occasions when ground clearance is used to the limit, stout bashplates will reduce damage to vulnerable components like steering linkages, gearboxes and prop shaft joints. Thick steel plates are what is needed here and can be easily attached to frame rails. The best 4WDs have these anyway. Don't rely on the cosmetic plastic guards found on some lightweight 4WDs.

Parts availability and interchangeability

Now that DHL covers the globe, this is not as critical as it used to be, but it's worth keeping in mind. It's one reason for sticking with commonly-used makes and models. Remember spares can come from fellow travellers as well as locals. I once limped back to Europe with a borrowed wheel from one of several Toyota drivers I met at Tunis port. With a more unusual vehicle I'd have been stuck with three wheels.

Setting out with someone in the same type of car reduces the number of spares that need to be carried; running the same fuel also makes sense. The need for creative improvisation or 'bodging' should also be considered when

DIESEL – PROS AND CONS

Pro

● Always cheaper than petrol. In the Sahara between 10p and 30p (€0.2–0.5) a litre.

● At the same capacity, a diesel engine is around 30% more economical than a petrol engine while modern high pressure or 'common rail' engines are at least twice as economical.

● Older diesel engines have few electrical and no electronic components so little can go wrong.

● Being an oil, diesel is less volatile and flammable than petrol – a major safety consideration.

● As long as you can start it, a diesel will chug along happily almost forever.

● Engines are more reliable and last longer than petrol equivalents, especially large capacity, low revving units.

● Diesel engines have superior engine-braking to petrol engines, making steep descents more controllable without having to resort to braking or electronic hill descent control gimmickery.

● Should you run out, diesel's easily available from passing trucks.

● Older style (pre-common rail) diesel engines are more tolerant of bad fuel than petrol engines.

Con

● Pre-common rail diesel engines make about two-thirds of the power of a same-sized petrol engine.

● Diesel fuel is messy and smelly and does not evaporate readily and without odour like petrol.

● When something goes wrong with a diesel it can be hard to fix in the field and expensive to repair.

● Older diesel engines are incredibly noisy. Modern ones are much quieter but still not as quiet as petrol engines.

● You can't hand crank a diesel and even push-starting requires a long run up.

● Some Japanese diesels sold in Europe (e.g. Land Cruisers) have 24-volt electrical systems – good for winter starting but a pain when sourcing electrical components in the Sahara.

● Older turbo-diesels require frequent changes of quality oil.

● The Land Rovers and Cruisers found in the Sahara may well have petrol engines – so diesel spares and know-how may not be as common as you might expect.

● Clean fuel is more critical with diesel fuel injectors (though the same is true of fuel-injected petrol engines).

all else fails. When things go wrong you'll be surprised at the ingenuity of bush mechanics in the Sahara. To you it may be a mechanical disaster but they'll have seen it all before and will have a solution. There's more on improvised repairs on page 196.

Price

For once being hard up is in your favour. Who wants the latest gizmo-riddled 4WD when something a decade older is much more suitable? Not only is older cheaper, it's often simpler, stronger and better proven. It also attracts less attention and if tatty in appearance will be less stealable.

You'll spend much more money preparing and getting to the Sahara than actually being there. In some cases this amounts to more than the cost of the vehicle itself.

Diesel engines

With the advent of electronically metered, high pressure injection systems, the performance gap which once relegated diesel engines to commercial use is disappearing. In the many western European countries where diesel is substantially cheaper, these have been the engines of choice for years. Smaller, quieter and more efficient diesel engines now offer petrol engine performance while achieving double the fuel mileage.

CARAVANS AND TRAILERS

You'll have realised by now that caravans and trailers are a bad idea for Saharan travel. It's hard to think of a piste which would not reduce the average holidaymaker's caravan to firewood, let alone the limitations imposed by the tow hitch and the additional strain on the engine and transmission.

Sturdy off-road trailers do exist. In Australia, towing a purpose-built off-road trailer with an appropriate coupling is common practice in recreational driving, making room for a family in the car. In Europe heavy ex-NATO trailers are cheap, carry 700kg and use sturdy tow jaws rather than the standard ball and socket which would not last ten minutes in the Sahara.

For desert driving the problems come with corrugated pistes which will shake the trailer and pulverise its contents. Larger bumps will get the trailer airborne. Protective packing makes no room for movement and thorough lashing is essential.

The other problem is the frequent need to reverse from near-bogging situations – something that'll occur all the more often with the drag of a trailer. Anything more than a few feet will be tricky and it's at this stage that you'll begin to curse the thing and consider abandoning it. Even on the relatively straightforward Atlantic Route a trailer will be an encumbrance. Leave them at home – and remove the tow hitch while you're at it.

In 4WDs these small capacity engines, typically 2.5 litre, often lose out on the low-down pulling power while trying to achieve brisk, high revving on-road performance: more useful to most day-to-day users. Turbo-charging (discussed below) can help, but modern high pressure or common rail engines (like the Land Rover TD5) now manage to offer both high-speed performance, low rpm pulling power and amazing economy.

Because diesel engines have over twice the compression ratio of petrol engines, the cylinder block and crank cases have to be stronger and well machined which makes them comparatively heavy, as well as more expensive to manufacture than petrol engines. On the plus side a diesel engine will out-last a similar petrol unit and experience fewer problems during that time.

Turbo diesels and intercoolers

Explained simply, a **turbo-charger** uses the 'free' energy of escaping exhaust gases to force more air into the engine. More air improves combustion (like blowing on embers) and more complete combustion creates more power. **Intercoolers** are like radiators which cool the heated charge driven from the turbo to the inlet tracts. Cool air is denser so contains more oxygen; still more power and efficiency is the result. On a diesel you get around 25–30% more power with a turbo; an intercooler is good for another 10%, all with a negligible gain in weight.

Following the demise of simple, naturally-aspirated diesels, just about all 4WDs since the early 1990s now come with turbo diesel engines, offering not only improved power but also a marginal gain in fuel efficiency. They also emit cleaner gases. A notable exception to this trend is Toyota's enduring 1HZ 4.2 litre straight six, still used in the utilitarian HJZ78/79s since it was introduced in 1989. The big 1HZ is one of the best big non-turbo diesels around, at the cost of poor fuel consumption.

Don't be put off by the perceived complexity and racy 'GTi' image of turbos or their claimed sensitivity to dusty conditions. No engine thrives on dust and anyway turbo 4WDs are in a comparatively low state of tune.

Spinning up to 25 times faster than the crankshaft, the turbine can get very hot. Because of these high revolutions turbo diesel engines require special care: top quality 'TD' oil must be used and changed up to every 5000km on older models – even more frequently if you're unsure of the oil's quality. After a fast highway run or a long, steep ascent on a hot day you should give the turbo a chance to 'spin down' before turning off the engine. This way the turbo's not still whizzing round at 80,000 rpm when the oil pump stops with the engine. Usually this practice only means waiting 20-30 seconds and all such cars will have a prominent label reminding you of this precaution. Even if your turbo's not cooking, it's best to leave engines running during short stops in the desert.

Buying used turbo diesels

Because of the need for frequent changes of expensive oil, it's all the more critical to make sure a used turbo diesel vehicle has a full service history before you buy it. Any excessive smoke or rattles that do not clear after a cold start might suggest a vehicle better kept away from the demands of the Sahara.

Don't risk engine problems by fitting an after-market turbo to an older normally aspirated diesel engine. While most manufacturers' turbo diesels started life as ordinary diesels or even petrol engines, they've usually done the development job properly, making modifications throughout the engine if not the whole vehicle to handle the extra compression and cater for the turbine's oil needs. Stick with a standard engine (see also p.84) if you're buying used.

Direct or indirect injection?

You'll notice that some diesel engines have direct and some indirect injection. Toyota's 2H straight six of the eighties was indirect, its current 4.2 turbo is direct. Pre-'92 diesel Range Rovers are indirect, the Td5 is direct. What's the difference and does it matter?

Indirect injection was a solution to tall and noisy engines for small vehicles. All commercial vehicles use direct injection (these days usually with a turbo) but before the advent of common rail induction, most diesel town cars (where space is critical) used less bulky indirect injection engines.

These mix the charge in a small chamber alongside the main combustion chamber. The benefits used to be quicker starting and less noise but at the cost of a relatively subdued throttle response. In recent years noise suppression with direct injection engines has improved to the point where, in big 4WDs at least, direct injection is back in vogue.

Direct injection engines are more susceptible to injector problems so fuel filters must be renewed regularly. One of the benefits of indirect injection engines is that they are more tolerant of bad fuel and imperfect injectors. The old 2.25 Land Rover diesel is a good example.

Off-road, the instant response of a direct injection engine is preferable. Loaded up and trying to get moving in soft sand, you'll need every ounce of low down power. However, on some very rough, boulder-ridden tracks (as in southern Morocco or the long crawl from Zouar to Bardai in the Tibesti), this direct response can be a real pain. As you get thrown around, clinging to the wheel it's hard to stop your accelerator foot involuntarily jabbing the accelerator, jerking the car back and forth (see also p.173).

PETROL – PROS AND CONS

Pro	Con
● Size-for-size, lighter, quieter and more powerful than older diesels.	● Highly inflammable, especially the fumes in empty containers.
● Simple, carburettor-fed engines are easily understood and 'bodgeable' by both amateur and bush mechanics.	● Effervescence creates high container pressures when shaken and/or heated.
● Less battery power is needed to start engines, and hand-cranking or push-starting is easy.	● In hot, slow conditions (or at altitude) evaporation in the fuel pump can cause vapour lock leading to fuel starvation.
● Spilt petrol evaporates quickly and without residual odour.	● Electrics are prone to problems from dust, heat and vibration; all common in the Sahara.
● Old vehicles, especially old uneconomical vehicles with big engines, can be very cheap to buy.	● Unleaded petrol is unknown south of Tunisia and Morocco.
	● There can be many reasons why a petrol engine runs poorly – comparatively few with a diesel.

Petrol engines

These days big petrol engines are deeply unfashionable in Europe where both cost and economy compare unfavourably with diesel. American 4WDs and top-of-the range Land Cruisers and Range Rovers are still available with 4-litre-plus engines, mainly aimed at people immune to this expense, or at the US and Arabian markets where fuel is cheap and powerful vehicles desired.

In Africa the reputation of the early Land Rovers was probably built on their venerable 2.25 litre nails. Crude they may be but you'll still see a few in the Sahara, most of them used only as short-range runabouts. In the Sahara, some tour operators, police and army still use petrol-engined vehicles, usually Land Cruisers though the trend is towards more reliable diesels.

In countries like Egypt, Libya, Algeria, southern Morocco and Mauritania, where petrol is cheap, a Rover V8 or Japanese six-cylinder might be a good idea, being powerful, quiet and in their older incarnations mechanically simple. Furthermore, the chances are that in your home country these older gas guzzlers can be bought inexpensively. A V8 Range Rover, for example, will respond better in the sands than most of the diesel units it was ever fitted with. If you do your sums right, on a visit to countries where both petrol and diesel can be bought for a fraction of European prices, it could all work out less expensive with the right car. Of course whatever you're driving, it pays to fill up every last tank when leaving Libya or Algeria!

One problem with modern petrol engines is that unleaded petrol can be hard to come by in countries south of Tunisia or northern Morocco. If your car runs a catalytic converter on the exhaust system, remove it for the trip or expect to ruin the expensive unit by running leaded fuel. Unless there is a whole lot of critical electronic sensing going on, this won't stop the car running, but the converter will no longer clean the emissions as it's supposed to which could lead to problems with your next roadworthy test.

BODY TYPES

In the desert, a long wheelbase (LWB) vehicle offers the best combination of space and stability. Limitations in some aspects of ground clearance are the compromises you have to make and these are discussed on page 50.

LWB hardtops and station wagons

Overall, a **hardtop** (a three-door van) offers the best body format for up to two people. Because it has no side windows the interior of the vehicle keeps cool, discourages prying eyes and deflects kids' stones. The lack of rear passenger doors leaves the large side area free for mounting sand plates or jerricans. Any rear seating can be easily removed, leaving a large, uncluttered area in which to organise a packing system.

For a long trip a hardtop makes most sense, but most people own more practical **5-door station wagons** for day-to-day driving. With more than two passengers a station wagon is a very good idea of course – don't expect anyone to be comfortable for long with three people in the front, even with a bench seat.

If travelling with just two people, rear seats can be folded flat for a large load area, or left upright making a cargo barrier to hold back a 'surging' payload in the event of a sudden stop. Complete removal of the seats might mean irreversible cutting of the floor carpet behind the back seat but it does free up the area and creates an ideal central position for heavy loads.

Access presents no problems with 5-door models; there's rarely something that's hard to get to. It's a good idea to blank out as many side and back windows as possible to keep out the sun and unwanted inspections.

A LWB three-door hardtop is the most popular body type in the Sahara. This BJ75 Toyota Troop carrier has a non-standard raised roof – often supplied by rental companies in Australia.

For more than two people a five-door station wagon is best, especially with a hinged roof.

Tailgates and other rear doors

Horizontally-split tailgates tend to be found on upmarket or non-commercial models such as Range Rovers, Jeep Cherokees and European-spec Land Cruisers. Vertically-split doors range from one big door (Discovery, Land Rover, G-Wagens and some Pajeros), a 60/40 split (older Troopies and some Patrols) or an equal 'ambulance door' split (African-spec Land Cruisers).

Whichever type of rear door your vehicle has, make sure the rubber seals are in good shape. The boxy rear body of most 4WDs creates a low pressure zone which creates strong suction around the back doors, drawing in the fine dust thrown up by the wheels. With a damaged seal you can actually watch the dust flowing forward like a mist as you drive along. Maintaining a dust-free car in the desert is asking a lot as it will find its way in anyway, but with a bad seal everything will really pour in. One answer is to keep the front door windows or other vents open, assuming you are not driving behind someone's dust already.

Tailgates A tailgate has two advantages for the desert: an **instant table** and a bit of **shade** from the upper tailgate – assuming the rear window's blanked out or draped. The drawback comes from restricting access deep into the interior compared to a back door, although the presence of rear passenger doors minimises this. Because it is a ready-made table, you may find yourself leaning over a lit stove for something or other and catching fire or knocking over a boiling pan. It's worth noting that these are the circumstances in which most injuries happen in overland travel, not from land mines or a hail of bullets during a coup.

Tailgates also make it difficult to mount a roof-access ladder onto the back of the vehicle, unless you can fix something securely onto the upper tailgate, which is often little more than a window frame. The only alternative is bolting ungainly side ladders near the rear corner. Toyota sell this type of ladder for their tailgate models but it's destined for the Africa market so nearly always comes as a package with the Toyota roof rack. Fabricating your own **mini steps** was the answer for my Land Cruiser. I got two steps made in alloy, about 30mm deep and which bolted through the rear wing (fixable with a nut from the inside) but did not protrude beyond the width of the body. With a roof rack to grab on to, stepping from the bumper via the steps onto the roof rack was possible with just one hand.

Vertically split doors Having **one big rear door** gives you a sizeable windbreak, less of a problem fixing ladders and some overhead shade (with a bit of fiddling). Access deep into the back is unhindered. On a **flat door**, such as those on Defenders, attaching a fold-down table hinged inside the door is easy if a bit small. Whatever your car, you're bound to need the extra surface of a camping table as well.

Two doors, equal or otherwise, offer good wind protection and an ideal frame to drape some shade over. The insides of the doors make handy surfaces for mounting water filtration units or storage pockets. Access to the back is good and even if one door carries a heavy wheel, only the other need be opened to quickly sling something in.

Pick-ups

Saharan purists who prize light weight and functionality above all else often favour pick-ups, with either a canvas canopy or no canopy at all. The obvious drawbacks are that they offer less security and weather protection but in the desert these are less significant considerations than elsewhere.

With a pick-up you'll be foregoing the comfort of a permanent and secure shelter, which can be welcome on a windy night, and you'll also miss having ready shade away from the cab. But there are plenty of advantages for this sort of dedicated desert transportation, not least the fact that you'll have a stable and light desert vehicle with a low centre of gravity.

If your packing system is well designed, access is unrivalled and a large lid hinged in any number of ways over the tray reduces the security risk. (Loading the vehicle is covered in greater depth from page 133.) Dust-proofing can be achieved with good sealing but with a pick-up what blows in blows out just as fast.

A Cape-bound Defender pick-up fitted with a demountable cabin. But in strict Germany such vehicles have been getting stick as they exceed manufacturers' GVWs.

Short wheelbase vehicles

Short wheel-based vehicles (usually around 2.3m or 90" between axle centres) have a reputation for off-road agility but lack two important qualities for desert use: stability and payload. What makes a nippy urban runabout or an agile tool in muddy woodland can lose its composure on fast, corrugated pistes. And you'll be lucky to have a metre-and-a-half of load space in the back. This can work if you're travelling alone and are well organised, but the provisions required by two people can make it a very tight squeeze on all but a Moroccan excursion.

A Hilux crewcab taxi in Atar running non-standard 7.50 16" tyres.

You can get round this by using underbody tanks as well as making the most of every nook and cranny, but you're unlikely to escape a load area piled high and probably a roof rack too. As explained on page 133 you may be able to get everything in, but can you get to everything *easily*? Heavily-laden roof racks and high loads inside the vehicle jeopardise stability too.

SWB vehicles tend to pitch forward and back on bumpy terrain more than longer cars, something that's exacerbated by over-hard suspension. They can also slide out unexpectedly on fast corrugated bends if your concentration drops. This can happen to all cars but with a high centre of gravity, once such a car is sliding sideways, overturning is much more likely. These shortcomings can be controlled with thoughtful packing, driving and speed, but the inherent stability of a LWB vehicle, even when it's sliding, makes driving a whole lot more relaxing in the desert.

A SWB car would be in its element on Moroccan pistes, where fuel stages are short and food stops frequent. Indeed there may be times where a mountain road is washed out by a storm (a common event in the High Atlas, but rare in the true Sahara) where a SWB's good angles would help to get through.

Forward controls

This rather ungainly term technically covers all sorts of bonnetless vans or campervans but usually refers to anti-aerodynamic bricks like Land Rover

AUTOMATIC TRANSMISSION: THE ULTIMATE METHOD

Automatic transmission must be the ultimate method of maintaining traction in sand. With torque evenly fed in, no wheel has a chance to spin loose, the thinking and the effort being done by the automatic gearbox. Better still, shock loads are absorbed by the transmission fluid. This makes them popular with fleet operators, such as military forces and car rental agencies, where multiple non-owner drivers might not always treat a manual box lovingly.

A first-time Sahara driver turned up on one of my tours with an 80-series automatic Toyota. Before we knew it we were all embroiled in the small dunes of the northern Grand Erg which the heavy but powerful auto managed no worse than the rest of us. The only time we found the auto box want ing was in tight, small dune formations when the shift from first to second in either high or low box was not ideal: a manual box gave more control and direct response. On all other surfaces, and especially rocks, the auto was easier to drive. As for fuel economy, often thought to be inferior with automatics, in the Erg the auto was a little less economical than my Toyota and about 20% better than a Land Rover Tdi, and on all other fill ups it was up to 30% better than my manual.

This proves that the efficiency and operation of automatic gearboxes has improved greatly in recent years. Alas autos are still not the type of cars that appeal to conservative Saharan or indeed many European drivers who feel secure with the familiar manual gearbox. In the desert the perceived superiority of manual transmission using tangible gears and shafts inspires confidence off the beaten track and in extreme conditions. And importantly manuals are known by bush mechanics whereas most of them would be confounded by an automatic gearbox.

Overheating under desert loads is the main problem; ATF fluid must remain at around 85°C; over 95°C the ATF breaks down and resin forms on the plates, causing slippage. Over 110°C the HCU seals become brittle and drive is lost. The 101 pictured on p.101 used an auto Land Rover box which, after an early failure and an eventual rebuild, ended up with three fan-assisted coolers for reliable operation across Africa.

If you decide to try an auto in the Sahara, make sure that:
- It has the ability to manually lock lower gears (giving direct drive).
- The gearbox has been serviced by auto transmission specialists before you leave.
- It's well protected from rock damage.
- It has a separate and effective fluid cooler, with added fan cooling if necessary.
- You fit a temperature gauge to the auto box.
- You carry some spare ATF fluid.

101s and Pinzgauers and VW buses. In theory, forward controls are ideal desert vehicles. You sit high over the front wheels and without a bonnet have excellent visibility. Body overhangs are minimal and with a moderate wheelbase and 900x16 tyres, belly and ground clearance are good too. They make good load-carriers or campervan conversions.

The engine is actually no further behind the front axle than on a conventional 4WD but because the cab is where the bonnet usually is the load bed is well placed between the axles. The downside is that the engine is right next to the driver which means noise and heat. And, because they are usually dedicated off-road vehicles, the compromises in comfort for long-distance driving are rather too great. There's more on 101s, Pinzgauers and VWs on page 102.

THE MECHANICS OF 4WD

Most town cars are two-wheel drive. One axle is driven by the engine via a gearbox pushing or pulling a car along. In countries and urban areas where reliable, all-weather tarmac roads prevail, 2WD is sufficient. Even when wet, traction with the smooth road surface is reliable.

Elsewhere, all-wheel drive vehicles provide drive to two or more axles in order to improve mobility in situations of poor traction, for example on dirt roads with loose or uneven surfaces, or where there are no roads at all. Obviously, any vehicle that's attempting to travel along Saharan pistes will have to deal with rough surfaces, loose inclines and stretches of soft sand. This means that the improved traction offered by four-wheel drive transmission is desirable.

However, it may surprise you to learn that most mass-produced 4WDs do not have true, continuous drive to all four wheels at all times. Continuous, direct four-wheel drive must address an inherent flaw of the differential mechanism and although the technology for overcoming this flaw has existed for some time, it's far too expensive for mass-produced 4WD cars.

What's the differential?

When a car goes round a corner, the outside wheel travels a little further than the inner wheel, just like the runner in the outside lane of a race track has further to go. As power is fed from the engine at a uniform rate to all wheels, these wheels are expected to turn uniformly, but because of the reality of bends and bumps, wheels cannot do this. This is OK on the wheels of an unpowered axle which roll where they're steered, but wheels on the driven axle must be allowed to follow their varying paths while continuing to be powered by the engine.

This was the quandary facing the designers of horseless carriages in the nineteenth century. They got around it by inventing the axle differential; the bulbous mechanical unit seen halfway along the driven axle(s) of any conventional vehicle.

Without a differential, i.e. with both wheels linked solidly to each other and the gearbox, a car would be very hard to steer. On bends it would want to go straight as the driven wheels locked to each other resist turning through unequal arcs. This tension in the driveline would manifest itself by scrubbing, skidding tyres or, on a heavily-loaded vehicle on a grippy surface, the transmission snapping at its weakest link.

On the driven axle the differential enables power to be transmitted smoothly to both wheels while magically compensating for the slightly varying distances they travel. It's a mechanical wonder that has never been satisfactorily explained to me but it works.

Most drivers of 2WD cars will have experienced the frustrating lack of for-

A car's outer wheels travel further through a bend, so a differential is needed in each driven axle. © Toby Savage

ward motion when just one of the driven wheels loses traction and spins use-lessly – usually when you're parked on mud, sand or ice. This is caused by the unwanted effect of the differential where *all* the power goes to the wheel with least traction – the wheel spinning on a loose surface. No power – and there-fore drive – reaches the opposite wheel and the car stays still. On a conven-tional car it only takes one spinning wheel of the driven axle to immobilise the car. On a 4WD it only takes *two diagonally opposed spinning wheels* to create the same effect. There are various mechanical and electronic solutions to reduce or eliminate this effect (these are discussed below), some of which do provide 'true four-wheel drive' as a temporary measure.

Selectable four-wheel drive

With this 'old fashioned' system the rear axle is permanently driven in the nor-mal way with the front axle brought into play with a gear lever or an electric switch. The car is in rear-wheel drive most of the time, so reducing wear on the front transmission and tyres, marginally saving fuel and lightening steering.

However, when the two axles are engaged to give 'four-wheel drive' there is a problem of differential again. Just as left and right wheels cover slightly varying distances compensated for by the diff', so the front and rear axles can also cover unequal distances. A small variation is enough to cause a build-up of stress in the drive train known as 'transmission wind-up'.

Wind-up

Imagine having each limb twisted in a different direction. That's what's hap-pening to all your transmission components when part-time four-wheel drive is engaged on a hard, grippy surface. On a loose surface such as sand this ten-sion dissipates as undetectable wheel spin, but on a grippy surface such as tar-mac, bare rock or even hard-packed gravel, wind-up soon becomes apparent. Steering stiffens, your transmission clicks and groans, and then a suddenly spinning wheel unloads the wind-up or, if you're unlucky, something in the tortured transmission snaps.

Therefore, you should **avoid driving a 4WD with centre diff locked or in 4WD on dry, hard-surfaced roads** or bare rocks for more than a few seconds. Bouncing over bare rocks will probably unload the stress through an airborne wheel, but on a smooth road you're creating excess wear on the tyres and transmission. Even on a wet road driving in four-wheel drive is not a good idea on selectable 4WDs. A wheel suddenly unloading the wind-up in a fast wet bend could bring on a disastrous skid.

Only engage selectable four-wheel drive on loose surfaces where you need the extra traction. On most Saharan pistes this only includes steep inclines, sandy oued crossings, soft patches and dunes.

There is a school of thought that suggests four-wheel drive should always be engaged on loose surfaces as it spreads the power and returning shock loads over all four wheels. If you're racing this might well be the case, but on the average piste where exceeding 80kph is cause for comment, there's really no need unless the terrain or an extreme payload demand it. I found that in the desert in a selectable 4WD, I'm in 2WD 98% of the time. After a few hours on the piste you'll get the feel for what is needed and within a few days you'll know exactly when to bring the front axle into action.

Freewheeling hubs

The front axle of a selectable 4WD may be disconnected at the gearbox, but all its transmission components, the front prop shaft, diff and axles right up to the hubs will be turned around by the wheels. All these heavy components being turned to no effect create drag and so consume power.

At some stage a bright spark came up with the idea of disconnecting the axles or half shafts from the wheels and so invented the freewheeling hub (FWH). One FWH fits into the hub of each wheel and allows locking or unlocking of the front axle from the wheel. When unlocked, the rotating front wheel will not be connected to the transmission components behind it which will remain still. The benefits of this in the prevalent two-wheel driving mode are reduced fuel consumption, lighter steering and reduced wear on the front tyre and axle. Some people question the real saving in energy, but the lightened steering cannot be denied.

The drawbacks are that when you *do* want four-wheel drive you have to stop, get out, lock each hub by hand, get back in and then engage four-wheel drive. When you return to the highway you hop out and unlock the hubs again. In the Sahara this is not the nuisance it sounds as in practice once you begin a long piste you manually lock the hubs so four-wheel drive can be engaged from the cab without getting out. It might use a fraction more fuel but only the most miserly driver (I've met them!) will go through the rigmarole of stopping, hopping out, fiddling with the hubs and getting in again, crossing a soft patch and then reversing the procedure. Then again, if you're sure there's a long section of smooth, firm piste ahead, unlock the hubs – if you haven't got power steering your arms could probably do with the rest.

Freewheeling hubs have been around for years but they were never fitted as standard to Series Land Rovers which had selectable four-wheel drive. Nevertheless just about every owner will have fitted FWHs by now. This has brought up the possibility of unreliable units failing under heavy use which of course includes driving in the Sahara. In practice this is extremely rare with the best-known brands. On most Japanese four-wheelers FWHs were fitted as standard and were as tough as the rest of the transmission. If you use aftermarket FWHs in the Sahara but are nervous about their ability to take the strain, carry the original hub components as back up.

Automatic freewheeling hubs

With the need for innovation (or novelty) things never remain simple for long. Some 4WDs, notably Shoguns, Nissan Patrols, Troopers plus Ford and Jeep, feature automatic FWHs. Some Mitsubishis even offer a freewheeling front differential. All this is to save you getting out and locking the hubs manually, to be fair not something everyone likes to do in the pouring rain on a muddy track when there's something gripping on the radio.

While these auto features make life easier, in the Sahara the simplest, most reliable manual system is always preferable, and partly for these reasons none of the above 4WDs has caught on in the Sahara. Indeed, one gets the impression that these manufacturers were trying every possible option before giving up and following the full-time four-wheel drive example taken by modern Land Rovers (see p66).

Maintenance and care of freewheeling hubs On a vehicle fitted with FWHs it pays to turn the hubs on for a few miles in every thousand to stir up the stagnating oil and purge any condensation through the breather pipe. You can leave the car in two-wheel drive when you do this. Also, never engage four-wheel drive with the hubs unlocked – you could damage the hubs. It's another good reason for getting into the habit of locking the hubs on the piste in readiness for four-wheel drive, and unlocking them back on the highway.

And make sure *both* FWHs are engaged or disengaged. It's sometimes possible to get distracted between the wheels by a flat-looking tyre or an unhealthy engine noise, for example. Try not to imitate a lazy Mauritanian driver I travelled with once. He left the furthest FWH on his Toyota pick-up locked and only got out at the last possible minute to lock the one by his door. At least the twenty two of us squashed in the back and on the cab roof ensured he had good traction!

Permanent four-wheel drive

Most drivers have little interest in how their car works, they just want it to go. The new breed of 4WD owners fit into this category: they want to enjoy the advantages of 4WD ownership without necessarily understanding what's going on behind the scenes. Because of this, manufacturers have found that a permanent four-wheel drive system is one less thing to be misunderstood or used in the wrong circumstances.

With this system road holding is improved at a slight cost to neutral steering and possibly fuel economy. Better still, there's no need to fiddle with levers or FWHs when moving from conditions of good to poor traction.

The central differential

However, because the permanently driven front and rear axles would soon create inter-axle transmission wind-up as described earlier, an additional differential must be fitted between them. This central diff incorporated in the gearbox enables the permanent transmission of smooth power to all four wheels without wind-up. It's a neat idea until you remember that, diffs being what they are, when just one wheel loses traction, all the power goes via the central and relevant axle diff to that wheel. When one wheel spins on a full-time 4WD you stop.

So, to maintain a full-time 4WD's all-terrain ability, the central diff must be lockable, either manually or, as is the current trend, automatically. Locking this central diff has the same effect as a part-time 4WD with four-wheel drive engaged. Traction is greatly improved but inter-axle wind-up again becomes a problem.

This must be understood clearly. Full-time 4WD with the central diff locked provides near-optimum traction but will also wind up the transmission. Therefore the same limitations to driving on hard surfaces must be observed: **lock the central diff only when you really need to and never engage it with the power on with wheels possibly spinning;** it won't like it.

Viscous couplings – a neat solution

An alternative to the mechanical central differential is found in viscous couplings: a quieter and snatch-free method of transmitting power to the axles using technology similar to automatic gearboxes. A viscous coupling is basically a chamber filled with fluid and a pair of vanes. One vane is propelled by the engine, the other propels the axles. As one vane spins, the drag in the fluid turns the other vane and the car moves forward. The lack of solid linkage eliminates the problem of inter-axle wind-up and the nature of the fluid ensures that the speed of the vanes is virtually identical. If the rotation of the vanes differ, the viscous fluid warms up and, unlike most heated fluids, thickens, restoring even power to both axles. A little power and direct drive might be lost on this system but you're unlikely to notice. It's such a good idea that one wonders if diff-less axles with lockable mini viscous couplings in each hub might not be the answer to true four-wheel drive.

Viscous couplings are found on Land Cruiser VXs, Range Rovers, late Discoverys, Shoguns and Cherokees. If they don't do so automatically, they can and should be locked like a conventional central diff when necessary.

On-demand four-wheel drive

On-demand four-wheel drive is found on road-oriented cars and SUVs such as Honda's CRVs and Freelanders; it works best in wintry or slimy conditions, but not in the desert. With this system the wheels on the primary driven axle (usually the front) must spin a little before the transmission 'wakes up' and turns the secondary axle. This is no problem on ice and snow but in soft sand the spinning primary axle may be burying itself before the secondary axle catches up and starts turning. Once turning, the second axle struggles to push the bogged primary axle and also spins: result – you're stuck. Freelanders have a certain amount of pre-tension built into the system to reduce this lag but these cars make no pretence of being serious all-terrain vehicles. Because this system is so ill-suited to desert conditions all the 4WDs surveyed in the next chapter have either selectable or permanent four-wheel drive.

True four-wheel drive

Because of the need for, and effect of, differentials, 4WDs are not truly four-wheel drive in all situations. Even with centre diffs locked, it only takes two wheels – the diagonally opposite ones on each axle – to lose traction and deprive you of drive.

Getting 'cross-axled' over rough ground, with two wheels insufficiently loaded or in the air, is rare in the Sahara and there are ways of negotiating obstacles to avoid this possibility. More commonly, diagonally-opposed wheels might spin in soft sand or when scrabbling up a rocky incline. For this reason it's a lot easier to get a 4WD stuck than most off-roading novices realise: driving off-road takes skill and judgement. However, these limitations of diagonally spinning wheels can be simply overcome by:
● An evenly-distributed load over all four wheels
● Reducing tyre pressures to optimise traction
● Good axle articulation
● Axle diff locks
Weight distribution is discussed on page 134, the effect of reduced tyre pressures is covered on page 177, and good axle articulation has already been

considered. Locking mechanisms in the axle diff or electronically sensing and controlling wheel spin are other ways of overcoming the cross-axle syndrome.

Diff locks

An axle differential lock eliminates the sometimes unwanted differential effect, locking the two wheels of an axle so they drive together. Standard on both axles on all G-Wagens, Unimogs, Pinzgauers and optional on eighties Toyota J-series and current Amazons as well as on the rear axles of recent Pajeros and Patrols, differential locks can also be fitted as an after-market accessory to all popular 4WDs.

The locking device in the diff housing is operated by either a cable, vacuum or compressed air with a pump activated by a switch.

With diff locks on both axles (and a centre diff locked, if present) you have true four-wheel drive. What you don't have is much control over the steering, even on a loose surface. Your car may grind resolutely forward or back; it may also dig itself deeper into the sand if you haven't properly cleared the wheels.

Diff locks place an extra strain on the transmission, although when a standard fitting, the vehicle concerned ought to have the components to cope. On a Land Rover stronger diffs and half shafts are a good idea with after-market diff locks. Even then, diff locks can still break the transmission if used injudiciously on hard surfaces or a steep, boulder-strewn climb. Only engage manual units when you're certain no wheels are spinning and only use them for recovery and at low speeds. Disengage them as soon as possible.

Having axle diff locks in Saharan deep sand situations won't eliminate the need to get out and clear the wheels and reduce tyre pressures. If you're using the right tyres at optimum pressures and the right gear and gear range (all explained from p.167 onwards), diff locks will make little difference. They can help in cross-axled or 'wet' tractionless situations, like mud and snow where, with the right type of tyres, they'll help get you unstuck, but they're not the answer for soft sand. I had OE axle diff locks on my HJ61 and the two times I really got stuck (in a flash flood and in a dune 'vortex') they made no difference: I was lucky enough to be towed or winched out on both occasions. Instead of spending money on axle diff locks for a desert trip, get a good air compressor.

Automatic diff locks

Automatic locking diffs work mechanically by keeping the diff permanently locked in a straight line and unlocking it on bends, and they can be fitted in an afternoon. Though they sound like a nice idea, my short on-road experience with a LockRite unit brought up all sorts of weird feedback to the steering and

---

FUEL CONSUMPTION FIGURES

A **conversion table** to mpg or l/100km appears on page 650. Where available, fuel consumption figures have been supplied by drivers/owners in desert conditions. Equipment like roof racks increases consumption while taller tyres render speedometer readings inaccurate. They're offered as a guide only; your own readings will vary.

wince-inducing clanks and bangs as the unit failed to unlock quickly enough on some bends. The need for adjustment in driving style – avoiding powering into bends – is frustrating and my subsequent experience with the apparently ultimate in front and rear manual diffs has proved that they're rarely needed in the desert anyway. If you do choose to fit diff locks use automatic units only in the rear axle of a part-time 4WD. On a front axle, or both axles of full-time 4WDs, manual diff locks are best.

Limited-slip differentials
In the late eighties many Japanese 4WDs featured limited-slip differentials (LSD) in the rear axle of their station wagons and they're still an option on some SUVs. LSDs work by limiting the differential effect so that some power goes to the grounded wheel when the opposite one loses traction and spins uselessly. A bit like auto locking diffs, LSDs have their eccentricities on roads and in some situations need to be 'tricked' into action by applying the hand brake. For this reason, as well as the advent of electronic traction control (see below), they're now decreasingly popular.

Cars like first-generation Patrols, Cherokees and Shoguns and high-spec'ed Troopers featured LSDs. In the Sahara you're unlikely to notice the benefit of an LSD, but if you have one it won't do any harm.

Electronic traction control
As suggested, axle diff locks are a crude but effective way of optimising traction and can only be used in certain conditions and with tough transmission components. Electronic traction control (ETC, to give it one of its many names) achieves a similar effect with less expense and without the need for beefed-up, power-draining components.

Usually allied with anti-lock braking, electronic sensors on each hub read when a wheel is spinning and apply braking to that wheel. The differential effect then feeds all power to the opposite wheel which hopefully drives the vehicle forward. Working continuously on each wheel, the technological wonder that is ETC should subtly translate to continuous forward motion.

In the desert it works well on loose rocky ascents and situations where the axle articulation is being used to the limit, especially with an auto box. On the more commonly encountered soft sand slopes and oued banks, however, I've found ETC swaps frantically from wheel to wheel, braking one and then the other and, if you don't back off, individually digging each wheel into the sand. It's not foolproof.

It must be remembered that with ETC one wheel per axle is driving so you don't have the full-on locked-in traction of an axle diff lock (not that that helps much in soft sand). Furthermore, braking one wheel makes the opposite one spin twice as fast, not at ground speed, so increasing the chance of digging that wheel in. However, and this is the crux, ETC is a system that can't cause damage to the transmission by careless driving and can be used, as off-road expert Jack Jackson put it, 'with no driver knowledge or input required or desired'.

As with diff locks, in soft sand ETC won't replace the need to *think* what you're doing and to manually clear wheels or lower tyre pressures. In-cab tyre deflators do exist (on Humvees, for example, but are banned in the Dakar

Rally, interestingly) but the boffins are still working on retractable scoops which spin into action when sensors detect a tyre's deeply buried in sand.

Finally, as mentioned earlier, the reliability of computer controlled electronic components is something that declines with the age of the vehicle – though if your electronic control unit (ECU) starts playing up in the Sahara, inoperative ETC will be the least of your worries.

Survey of 4WDs

Twenty-five years ago the authors of the *Sahara Handbook* wisely noted: '*All too often, choice of vehicle is guided by subjective factors like style, image, and patriotism. The Sahara is not a place for poseurs. Practical considerations like space, fuel economy, power, strength, budget, availability of parts and mechanical expertise, must dictate the final choice.*'

The same is true today, but since that time just about every vehicle manufacturer has jumped on the 4WD bandwagon and produced a vehicle that, if the adverts are to be believed, ought to be able to cross the Sahara without you even noticing. With so many models available, how can you be sure yours, or the one you're thinking of buying, is suitable?

All 4WD cars are not the same. Of the scores of 4WDs now available, both new and second-hand, only a few models crop up regularly in the Sahara, whether driven by tourists or by local commercial operators (who are even more conservative in their choices). Only those models which have a recorded history of use in the Sahara are discussed in detail here.

Some other 4WDs may be quite suitable but for various reasons (and not necessarily their lack of ability) they are unknown or unseen out there. This includes all the popular American 4WDs, lesser Japanese brands as well as more exotic vehicles such as Unimogs and heavy all-terrain trucks. For either political, commercial, technical, practical or even fashionable reasons, these types of vehicles have never earned the reputation for day-to-day practicality that Land Rovers and Toyotas have gained in the Sahara's demanding conditions.

The ideal Saharan vehicle comes from a limited and conservative range. By choosing one of these you may not necessarily be making a statement about your individuality and belief in personal freedom, but you'll be in for fewer surprises.

All the vehicles listed below are assessed expressly for their potential as long-range desert tourers and overlanders. Drawbacks or strengths listed are unlikely to relate to day-to-day driving or domestic off-roading.

The recreational 4WD scene today

Since the early eighties, ownership of 4WDs has boomed throughout the Western world, but proportionally four-wheel driving has not. If anything, increased environmental awareness in developed countries has curbed the scope of domestic off-roading. Not that this bothers most owners. The current popularity of 4WDs is due to a combination of perceived safety, the image of aspiring outdoorsiness and the desire to (literally) stand above the crowd. True off-road utility which can compromise a 4WD's day-to-day driveability has become a secondary feature, yet it is one of their chief selling points. It's a lifestyle phenomenon not unique to 4WDs of course. Hopefully you're different and you're intrigued by the idea of taking your four-wheeler into the true wilderness and seeing how it performs.

They don't build 'em like they used to

As the popularity of day-to-day motoring in 4WDs has matured, successive models have moved away from their functional origins as new owners have rejected effortful transmission selection, boat-like handling and high fuel consumption.

Urban 4WDs like Vitaras, Rav4s and Freelanders are unapologetically designed to appeal to this image-conscious market, offering nippy, car-like handling, comfort, economy and performance but with a rugged look. At the next level, **family estates** such as Discoverys, Mitsubishi Pajeros, Toyota Prados, and Jeep Cherokees all have a Volvo-esque aura of protection and safety, but all make comfortable desert tourers. At the luxury end of the market, **all-terrain limousines** like top-of-the-range Amazons and Range Rovers offer the mind-boggling sophistication of the most expensive Mercedes, Jaguars and BMWs. Comfort-adding features are controlled by electronics which also manage traction, suspension and engine performance. Yet ironically these impressively versatile machines are unlikely ever to be fully appreciated by their affluent owners except perhaps in the Middle East; a huge market for these types of vehicles. In the Sahara they are about as likely to crop up as Kylie Minogue and her pet sausage dog towing a caravan with a Nissan Micra.

Maintaining competitiveness in the buoyant non-four-wheel-driving 4WD market has led to some compromises. The added **complexity** of today's 4WDs discourages owner-meddling but does not yet translate to sealed-for-life reliability (it's more of a service-for-life-or-lose-the-warranty scenario). Because of this, many less-sophisticated older models are more suited to long-range Saharan travel. The latest 4WDs are, in some cases, literally going soft around the edges, which, if nothing else, makes using a high-lift jack awkward.

TOYOTA LAND CRUISERS

Toyota Land Cruisers have long set standards of reliability and durability to which all other 4WDs are compared. They are now predominant in Africa, the choice of aid agencies, NGOs and local tour operators who want nothing more than a competent vehicle that will keep working for years.

'*Plus solide*' is how a Libyan tour operator running two dozen Land Cruisers summed up the much-debated comparison with Land Rovers, but

---

WEB CRUISING

Land Cruiser model codes are initially confusing. The first letter 'L', 'B' or 'H' (usually followed by a 'J') indicates a diesel engine capacity from 2.5 to 3.5 and 4.0 or the current 4.2. 'F' means petrol.

The next designation, from 40 something to the current 100 something, refers to the series, while the numbers 0–2 indicate SWB, 3–4 are MWB, and 5–8 are LWB. The exception is that 60-series wagons were all LWBs and anyway it's not totally foolproof.

In a nutshell, 45s and 75s are functional utilities (but not the 76s, 77s and bush-spec 105s which are in between), while 60s, 80s, 90s and 100s are better-appointed station wagons.

If it's still up, a good page to explore is: www.toyota.co.jp/Showroom/All_toyota_li

neup/LandCruiser/special/ put up by Toyota Japan to celebrate Land Cruiser's 50th anniversary in 1998, but only the Japanese models are shown here – the HJZ 75 and 78s are missing.

For a description of all Land Cruisers, try Brian McCamish's home page: www .brian894x4.com/ with links in all directions, or Rob Mullen's FAQs at www.off-road.com/tlc/faq, or the Japanese-language Landcruiser Expedition Party: http://home page1.nifty.com/landcruiser/, which has some English text and can be 'Babelfished' (www.babelfish-altavista.com).

The 80 and 100 Series are covered in good detail by the Australia-based Land Cruiser Owners Online: www.lcool.org/.

---

spares availability and after-sales service have also helped make the Land Cruiser the world's most popular 4WD by far.

Just as I wrote this, the BBC motoring programme *Top Gear* showed one of its gratuitous car-wrecking features as a relief from sports cars spinning themselves into clouds of burning rubber. They took a rusty £1000 ex-farm Hilux diesel, drove it down steps, into trees and walls, let the Bristol Channel wash it away overnight, dropped it, dropped a caravan onto it and a wrecking ball into it and then set it on fire. And still it ran! Well Land Cruisers are just as tough.

Right from the start in the early Fifties when, like Land Rover, they copied and improved on the American Willys Jeep, Toyota opted for **big capacity engines** allied with comparatively supple suspension. Among other factors, it is the access to the easy, low-down power from a large engine that makes Land Cruisers so suited to overlanding.

An enduring myth suggests that these big engines are thirstier than Land Rover diesels; I used to believe this myself until I started travelling regularly with both vehicles and found that Land Cruiser turbo diesels achieve equal or superior **fuel consumption**. This myth may be based on the fact that for a long time the only Land Cruiser experience open to Brits was using overseas models in Africa and Arabia which are usually petrol-engined guzzlers. Only since the early 1990s has the 80 series become a common sight in the UK. There may also be an assumption that big engines *must* have bigger fuel bills; you can't have more power without using more fuel. Clearly this depends on the state of tune and efficiency: the 3.5 Rover V8 was always a bit more fuel efficient than the old 2.25 petrol fours.

And so, for the few hard-core Saharans bent on exploring the limits where vehicle performance and reliability must be unquestionable, there is no alternative.

This may all be news in the UK where Land Cruisers have been conservatively marketed and, with high prices, have never made a big impression despite Toyota's chart-topping road cars. Although they've been around since the 1950s, Land Cruisers only appeared in Britain in 1980, in the shape of the HJ60. These never caught on in the UK, being seen as fat, heavy gas-guzzlers, doomed to suffer wide tyres, sideboards and a tow hitch. As a result of this, both the range of Land Cruiser models as well as professional know-how in overlanding with them are still virtually unknown in the UK. This has one good result though: in the UK old Land Cruisers can be a bargain.

Over in France, or anywhere else for that matter, it's another story. The range is much greater and many of the models outlined below are readily available in Europe and possibly in Ireland too.

By and large, Land Cruisers have resisted the gimmickry of other Japanese 4WDs and continued to produce solid, hard-working all-terrain transportation. A bad start to the 80 series lost Land Cruiser some of its legendary reputation, but they remain, as they have for years, the world's best selling 4WDs.

In this book only diesel-engined Land Cruisers are considered in detail and because information on the entire range is difficult to find, especially in the UK, they are discussed here in more detail than, for example, the well-documented Land Rovers. Petrol-engined Land Cruisers are widely used in the Sahara (as well as the Middle East and US) but in Europe most drivers choose diesel for all the right reasons.

60 series

In 1980 the **60-series station wagons** (60, 61 and 62) replaced the ageing and preternaturally ugly 55 model which had been the first Land Cruiser to get some export sales for Toyota. For practical reasons no one is likely to take a Land Cruiser older than an HJ60 (or perhaps a late FJ/HJ45) to the Sahara, so earlier models are not discussed here.

Toyota's 4-litre HJ60 on the way to Choum (Route R2). Not as economical as the turbo version and old examples can be rusty, but otherwise as good as they get.
Some early 60s like the one above featured an attractive side band. My own 60 sported a natty pine-effect band – much to the confusion of passing woodpeckers.

Production of the 60 series ended in 1990 with the introduction of the 80 series, something many Saharan drivers regret. They, and many others, consider that the 60 series' uncomplicated toughness and reliability has never been improved upon by Toyota, and 60s especially are still used and sought after by central Saharan tour operators. In Djanet, southeastern Algeria, it feels as if half the cars in the town are old 60s, many with well over half a million on the clock. Newer 105 series are available, but the **body shell** of a 60 is known to be stronger and more capable of

The HJ61: all the qualities of a 60 but with 30% more power, 10% better economy and no woodpeckers – but substantially higher prices and more regular oil changes.

taking the endemic overloading common in Africa. Their popularity means you could sell a 60-series vehicle out there but, more crucially, it also means that parts are widely available. In Niger, ageing HJs still put in the hours transporting tourists through the Aïr and across the Ténéré.

All 60-series Land Cruisers are **five-door station wagons** with horizontal tailgates, a wheelbase of 108 inches (2.74m) and part-time four-wheel drive. At 2000kg they're big and feel it. The four-speed gearboxes were replaced by five-speeds in 1983, and the flabby leaf springs were marginally improved in 1988.

60-series engines

60-Series Land Cruisers are known for their reliable and long-lasting engines, which are either 3980cc, straight six-cylinder petrol (the 3F version is best) or indirect injection diesel (**2H**), which is more commonly found in Europe. The **HJ60's** pushrod engine only makes around 100hp and is not a fast accelerator, but it's big and lazy, giving plenty of low-down power, ideal for off-road driving while being less sensitive than the turbo version to old engine oil (something that only matters for prolonged engine life, not daily performance). For the moment at least, old HJ60s can be cheaply bought in the UK, partly because African car dealers can't shift right-hand drive cars out there.

Things got even better with the arrival in 1987 of the more powerful **HJ61** with its **12H-T** direct injection turbo diesel. Land Cruiser aficionados acknowledge that the ultra reliable 135hp 12H-T was the best engine Toyota ever made. I ran one for 60,000km and the grunty, tractor-like engine never missed a beat. It's a common delusion that whatever one owns is the best of course, but I can't imagine a better engine for the Sahara when you include the real world necessity of maintaining and working on it. Thirty miles per gallon (10.5 kpl) was attainable at a steady 100kph cruise, while in the dunes, as with most diesels, 5 kpl or 15 mpg was as bad as it got.

HJ61s look just like HJ60s but have the word 'turbo' inscribed on the grill. They're easy to find in France but, because of their reputation, hold their value at around £6000/€9000. The UK jumped straight to the HJ62, a five-speed HJ60 but distinguishable by its two pairs of rectangular headlights. The petrol FJ62 was fuel injected.

Broken suspension again – this time testing Paralever prototypes on Route A8 (the back ones were even worse and got flogged off). A bodge was lashed up but didn't last. In the end I drove home on the bump stop which didn't seem to mind.

Steering, brakes, and suspension

On the minus side, **power steering** is light of course but vague on all 60-series station wagons, and with sand tyres fitted you won't feel secure at over 120kph. The rear drums and front discs don't inspire confidence either, although in the desert great **brakes** are not that critical. All European six-cylinder diesels (including UK models) come with **24-volt electrics**, which provide powerful starting and electric ancillaries that last forever, but it can be hard to get parts in the Sahara where Cruisers are all 12 volt (as are all four-cylinder Toyota diesels and sixes sold in warmer markets). Gear change is slow but positive in all 60-series models, evoking Toyota's origins as a light truck manufacturer, and you're stirring a transmission that's as solid as they come and built to cope with the torque.

You'll almost certainly have to replace the original **springs** and **shocks** on your 60-series' suspension (see page 112). I went through a lot of 'experimentation' with my 61's suspension (see below left) and not surprisingly ended up with Old Man Emu on the back and something Italian and similarly heavy duty on the front. Loaded up in the desert with up to 400 litres of fluids and all the rest was not a problem, but unloaded around town it was, of course, a dog. For what it's worth, I removed the front anti-roll bar rather than replace the bushes. It made no difference to the handling.

Spare-wheel location and body mounts
On all 60s (as well as 80s and 100s) the **spare wheel** is mounted truck-style, under the body at the back. It's released by a winch (prone to rust seizure) that's operated by the crank you use for the bottle jack. One often reads complaints about the mounting of the spare, the risk of damaging it and the compromise in the departure angle. In all my experience of desert off-roading in 45s up to 100s, I've never so much as scratched the spare. Even a wide 31/10.5 x 15 tyre doesn't hang below the departure angle. It's hard to think of conditions in the Sahara where the spare would be any more vulnerable than the rest of the undercarriage.

One situation where it does get in the way though is when you're bogged down to the axles and want to reverse out. Then the tyre needs clearing of sand along with the diffs, etc, which makes extra work. With the alternative positions being inside, on the back door (tricky with a tailgate) or on the roof, a Land Cruiser's placement is best for this heavy load: low, out of the way and easy to get to without hernia-inducing lifting.

All Land Cruisers have **rubber-mounted bodies** to allow the chassis beams to flex a little without the body doing likewise and popping all your windows (Land Rover bodies bolt directly to the frame). Rubber mounts should be checked on older vehicles though they easily outlast the body and suspension. Because the chassis moves in relation to the body, **roof racks** must be mounted to either one or the other. It's quite hard to attach a rack to both but I've seen it done, and when off-road something has to crack, usually the brackets holding the rack in the roof gutters or, as on an FJ45 I once owned, the access ladder attached to the rear bumper. A gutter-mounted rack is simpler and lighter and strong enough for Saharan loads.

Rust
This is what you really need to look out for on an ageing HJ60 and is partly why they get so cheap in the UK. Inspect the front edge of the rear wheel arches (close to a body mount), the rear chassis channels behind the rear spring hanger, the ends of the cross tube on which the rear shocks mount, bubbling paintwork on the upper tailgate (not so serious) and the upper corners around the windscreen seal which will leak (as they can do on 80s, funnily enough). Also, check the state of the roof gutters if you're planning to mount heavy loads on a roof rack.

The 70 series

In 1984 the 70 series was introduced to replace the 40 series of long- and short-wheelbase, no frills workhorses, equivalent to Land Rover's 90/110s and subsequent Defenders. Indeed it was the 70s which helped drive export sales of Land Rover's utility models underground, something from which they never recovered.

HJZ70-series pick-ups, the modern camel of the Sahara, on the Beach Piste in Mauritania. There were over twenty of us in the back and another three on the cab roof!

'Cleaning' the Aqaba in the Gilf Kebir with a 75 while the others dig. But the 1HZ engine gets through a fair amount of fuel in this sort of terrain.

A 78 camper conversion (not in the Sahara). Ostensibly identical but with better brakes, much better suspension, longer, wider, roomier and comfier but, in this format at least, still struggles to better 8kpl or 23mpg.

Designations from 70 to 74 were short- or mid-wheel base, 75 was the famous hardtop 'Troop Carrier' (more on which below) and 76 and 77s are 5-door long-wheelbase station wagons, rarely found outside of Japan. Engines can be deciphered as BJ (four cylinder diesels) and HJ, the 4.2 six which is now as legendary for its run-on-anything durability as Land Rover's 2.25 petrol was in the 1960s.

HJZ75 and 78: the last of the great overlanders

For many years the favourite Saharan bus has been the **HJZ75** or later **78** (known in some places as the Troop Carrier), a vehicle that still retains the better qualities of the old 60s and Toyota's legendary durability. Introduced right from the start in 1984, its 2H engine soon got the unburstable 4164cc, 135hp, 4.2 version (**1HZ**) with which it's still supplied to some markets.

If not a pick-up, all HJZ75s bodies are three-door hardtops with two vertical rear doors and bench seats, or less commonly with a second row of seats (known as an 'RV', found in Australia). Saharan travellers prize the 75's robustness and simplicity (leaf springs, part-time four-wheel drive with LSD, no turbo), for they do nothing exceptionally except keep on going. HJZ75s are unknown in the UK, where the vaguely related SWB Land Cruiser II (HJ70) eventually turned up, but they are widely used as utility vehicles in other parts of the world.

Drawbacks include an unnervingly **narrow track** (axle width), which makes a 75 on 7.50x16 tyres appear unstable next to something like a GR Patrol, especially for inexperienced drivers (a problem with all 4WDs). Some owners fit spacers behind the hubs to broaden the track; Grand Erg in Italy sell 30–40mm spacer kits. **Standard leaf springs**, too, are a weak point and commonly uprated.

Along with the weight and lack of a turbo, this means a 75 is not the best pure dune vehicle, but Troopies last and last, taking punishment in their stride. I've driven 75s in the Libyan Desert squashed flat with 600 litres of fuel running off the roof and half as much water and six people and their gear in the back. It's taking this sort of beating in its stride that makes the Troop Carrier peerless, even among other Toyotas. The feeling of solidity gives the impression it could chug through any obstacle on tickover.

The single fly in the ointment is mediocre **fuel consumption** by modern standards. The dinosauresque indirect 1HZ engine derived from the preceding 2H is not tuned for raw power and lean economy, doubtless contributing to its longevity. Compared to a 12H-T which I know well, these Egyptian 75s lacked the turbo's crisp grunt in soft sand while putting in as little as 4 kpl or 12 mpg struggling across the dune ranges of the Great Sand Sea. Horse power is the same apparently but there is 20% less torque with a 1HZ. On normal terrain you can expect 8 kpl (23 mpg), but if you value engine longevity don't be tempted to fit an after market turbo to try and get something for nothing. The cylinder head won't like it.

There are two other types of Troop Carrier. The BJ75 is common in Europe. The engine is a 3.5 four cylinder, not bad but not the same as the 4.2 six which is no street racer itself. By the time you load up a BJ for the Sahara you will have a comparative slug on your hands. If you're buying a 75 in Europe, make sure you know the difference; open the lid and check the engine is long and has six of things, and not four. The other Troopie is the **PJZ75**, also a 3.5 litre but with an indirect, five-cylinder engine making 115hp. Found in Japan, some were built in South Africa, but the word is the PJs are the ones to avoid; a BJ is OK if it's cheap and the 4.2 six is the one you're after for the Sahara. Other South African-built diesel 75s used a direct-injection 3.9 four cylinder Atlantis diesel engine licensed from Perkins and, like a lot of Perkins engines, more suited to pulling a plough than an overlander.

In 1999 the **HJZ78** was released, to all intents and purposes identical to its predecessor. This was a cunning ploy by Toyota who didn't want to spoil a good thing and alienate previous owners. But a closer look showed the new model had many subtle improvements. The chassis was longer and wider, the wheelbase was 200mm longer and the cab was roomier. In addition, the front and rear suspension were revised. Solid axles were retained, but the front now used coil springs, while the rear had longer, more supple leaf springs. The retention of leaves on the rear is significant: leaves create less roll which all-coil vehicles are prone to and which on a narrow vehicle like a Troop Carrier could be a problem. Drive shafts were also stronger and the brakes and calipers were beefed up so that 75 wheels would no longer fit. To make sure no one could try, the 78s adopted five chunkier studs instead of six as on a 75. Apart from the front coils, these five stud wheels are the easiest way to distinguish a 75 from a 78. The extra space and suspension

BUYING AN HJZ75/8 OR HJZ77

How can one get one's hands on one of these desirable Troop Carriers then? In **Europe** the smaller 3.5-litre-engined BJ75s are most commonly found in Germany, and a few six cylinders, including 78s, also got through before stricter emission rules snuffed out the environmentally-unacceptable engine. Like HJ61s, because of their rareness prices are high; at the time of writing €15,000 for a 1996 75 with 140,000km in Holland or €23,000 for a '99 with 50,000km in France. In Germany an African-based, Euro spec'ed 78 can be bought new for £34,000.

The next best place for importing a 4.2 75 or 78 is **Australia** where Troop Carriers are ubiquitous – the definitive 4WD workhorse. You'll get 12 volts, right-hand drive and almost certainly air-con, twin fuel tanks (totalling 180 litres), a raised air-intake, split rims and a bull bar.

In Australia, government vehicles are often sold before they are two years old which puts plenty, some barely used, on the market. Check on the web for government vehicle auctions which happen at least monthly in each state capital – but note that petrol-engined Troopies are as common as the diesels – avoid the petrols unless you're a sheikh; the 1HZ is bad enough!

The pick-up versions (a 75 or 'HJZ79' in the newer form), found all over Africa, are plentiful down under too, but like most pickups, they'll have been worked hard.

If a 77 or a 76 (or indeed any other type of Land Cruiser, except a 75/78) takes your fancy an easy place to import from is **Japan** where a five- or ten-year-old car is about as fashionable as a mullet on a catwalk. Prices at auctions will amaze you, mileages are low and, as suggested opposite, vehicles are often equipped with every possible accessory and option (and autos are prolific too), so you get a lot of car for your money.

The HJZ77 pictured below was ten years old with 54,000km and after a 10-week wait was delivered to the UK for under £7500 with all shipping and taxes paid. The actual auction price of the vehicle in Japan was £2300 – the rest went in shipping and taxes.

For some reason diesel-engined Troop Carriers were never officially imported to **South Africa** so are scarce and not worth considering for export. The pick-ups are another matter and today half the HJZ79s sold there end up being converted into dual cabs or campers. If you're after importing a 70-series pick-up, South Africa would be a good bet.

---

are the biggest noticeable improvements on 78s, not that a well-sprung 75 was that bad, but the front coils improved the steering and handling.

Then in 2002 Toyota offered the substantially more powerful 1HD-FTE 4.2 litre **turbo diesel engine** for the 80s and 100s to some markets, notably Australia. With its computer-controlled fuel injection the 1HD is of course more modern and economical but in some ways does not fit well with a Troop Carrier's perceived use, just as the similarly superior Td5 was seen as incompatible when fitted to Land Rover Defenders. But that is the way modern engines are going: a computer chip as well as very high pressure injection are seen as essential to make modern diesel engines conform with ever-stricter emission requirements.

HJZ77 and 76: The Missing Link?

The hardtop Troop Carrier is well known all around the world (except the UK) but many owners wish they'd made a 5-door, station wagon model, especially for the RV models which had a second

A Japanese-imported HJZ77. © Andy Bell

row of forward-facing seats. In Australia they're so desperate there's even an outfit which customises Troopies with a second side door.

In fact such a vehicle was produced, in appearance a cross between the 60 and 75 with the 1HZ engine. The **HJZ77** was made from 1990 and the '78-erised' **HJZ76** from 1999 to date. These vehicles were sold in Japan (RHD) as well as in China, Thailand and Malaysia.

Whatever, they are rare and not quite five-door Troop Carriers. For some reason the body and wheelbase are slightly shorter which, as with the Discovery, makes them a bit cramped for overlanding if used with back seat passengers. The official payload too is unexceptional at 600kg which suggests the springs may need uprating (not unusual with all Land Cruisers). But in Japan automatics are common and they usually come with all the fruit, often as fresh as the day it was picked: auto boxes, diff locks, winches, air bags, air con as well as heated side steps. Although I've only looked at one, for a LWB I got the impression they have neither the full-on load capacity of a Troop Carrier, nor the coil-sprung comfort and space of the 80s and in a way the 'low-spec' GX version of the 80 series (see below) answers the need for a basic five-door people carrier.

80 and 100 series

In 1990 the HJ61 and 62 wagons gave way to the all-new **80-series** Land Cruisers with their distinctive rounded bodies and much smarter interior fit and finish. In Britain, certainly, it finally put the Land Cruiser on the map, even if it was just used as a posh shopping trolley and school bus. If you're not bothered about driving something different you can forgo all that importing palaver (see box opposite) and do no worse than an old, ex-family 80 with way over 100,000 miles on the clock.

The suspension sets an 80 apart from a 60: all 80s have **coil springs**, a long overdue admission that Range Rovers got it right twenty years earlier. This gives a smoother ride, especially over corrugations, although it's still necessary to add **heavier rear springs** for a desert payload. Brakes and steering were greatly improved too. Among Saharan travellers, especially the French, 80s are as common as Land Rovers and only slightly outnumbered by Troop Carriers.

European 80s used **full-time 4WD**, another big change from the preceding models. The engines in the earliest 80s models proved to be hastily modified (Toyota had retained but fiddled unsatisfactorily with the big six-cylinder petrol engines and the overhead cam turbo diesel engines from the 60s), and for this reason you should steer clear of models built between 1990 and 1992. The 80s that were manufactured from 1993 received attention to the **1HD-T diesel engine**, suspension, brakes (ABS) and gearbox (viscous coupling lockable in High Range and automatically locked in

An auto 80 in the Grand Erg: probably the best all-round Toyota.

Low). With air-con as standard a vastly improved model emerged, but some turbo engines were prone to early main bearing wear (see the LCOOL website on p.72). An injected 215hp 4.5 petrol engine (1FZ-FE) also appeared at this time to keep the smugglers and sheikhs happy.

Timing belts replaced the expensive but maintenance-free timing gears of the 60s, but what Land Rover never really cured, Toyota got right first time. A timing belt warning light comes on as you turn 100,000km to remind you to get it changed. (Not 'timing belt about to shred, abandon ship!' as I thought halfway down a desolate track once).

GX80 and VX80

Eighty-series Cruisers come in more or less two versions: the basic, 'working' GX models, a common sight in Africa and Australia but not in Europe, and the more luxurious VX models, which dominate the European scene. All **GXs** have part-time four-wheel drive, FWHs and vertical rear doors. They usually come with the Troop Carrier's non-turbo 1HZ engine and the twin diff locks that appeared on some HJ61s are an option on GX80s too. **VXs** feature permanent four-wheel drive, tailgates rather than doors, carpets rather than vinyl and other up-spec interior trimmings and features.

Picking an 80 for the Sahara depends on what's available in your market or how far you're prepared to look. In Europe we have little choice, but driving a VX isn't exactly going to give you nightmares. Its 158hp 1HD-T engine feels less grunty (or should that be truck-like?) than the old 12H-T it replaced. It is smoother, quieter and more powerful, though marginally less economical in manual form. It makes maximum torque at 1800rpm – just like the old Series III diesel, but it delivers *two-and-a-half times* as much! At nearly two-and-a-half tonnes, the power-to-weight ratio of a turbo diesel VX is close to that of an HJ61. Because of all this weight, 9.00 x 16 tyres (see p.117) are worth considering for sustained dune driving – there's no shortage of power or robust components to keep them turning. With this set-up you'll have as comfortable a desert Cruiser as you could want.

Alternatively, if you can find the plain, part-time four-wheel drive GX model, you'll spend less to get the non-turbo power train of the legendary HJZ75/8 but get an 80-series suspension and body. These 'working' 80s are used almost to the exclusion of any other car by the many desert tour operators in southern Tunisia. In other Saharan countries they're the choice of the more affluent aid agencies, government officers and NGOs.

Although there is plenty of space in the Sahara, the VX comes across as a big and ostentatious machine – a touch of the Range Rover syndrome which can work against you in some situations. But of all the cars listed here you do get a genuine all-terrain machine that will work unobtrusively as a day-to-day people carrier back home. In the UK, models from the mid-nineties are now cropping up for as little as £6000. Prospective buyers are often scared off by what look like high mileages of 150,000 or more but, as with older Mercedes saloons, this is not a big deal as long as the car had a good start to life with a regular service history. Their appeal as buses to well-heeled families who can afford to run them often includes a full service history anyway – worth paying the extra for if you plan to keep the car a while.

Problems I've heard of directly from owners include broken coils and odd electrical gremlins like lighting relays. Heavier springs, especially at the rear, are well worth considering and not expensive. Unless you are going for a really radical expedition through sustained dunes, I would go for an **automatic**. It's a pleasure to drive, easy and controllable over rocky terrain compared to a manual and, out of the dunes, around 10-20% more economical than a manual HJ61 which itself sets a benchmark. At one point, an 80 I was travelling with achieved an incredible 40mpg (or 14 kpl) along the tarmac out of Tamanrasset, my 61 managed around 33 mpg (11.5 kpl) while a Tdi Defender delivered 25mpg.

100-series
In 1998 the even bigger **100-series** barges replaced the 80s: heavier, wider, longer and more complex than ever with, horror of horrors, independent front suspension to give car-like driving characteristics. The Amazon also has hydraulic vehicle height adjustment to compensate for its lower ride, electronic Active Traction Control and probably Vehicle Stability Control. In the 4.7 V8 format this Cruiser battles it out for the crown of ultimate all-terrain limo with the similar-engined Range Rover, but apart from delivering Saudi playboys for a spot of Ramadan escape and hunting, neither is seen much in the Sahara.

The turbo diesel engine is largely the same as its predecessor, but with an intercooler adding more power. With the advent of the 100 series, many lamented the end of Land Cruiser's off-road utility, but realistically owners of this type of car are not considering overlanding and anyway, the HJZ78s still fill that hardcore off-road niche. Furthermore, Toyota did not burn its 80-series bridges completely: the **105** model is a plain, GX-style workhorse with a solid front beam axle, part-time 4WD, vinyl interior, 1HZ engine and vertical back doors.

Other Toyota 4WDs
Like Land Rover, Toyota have made the most of their legendary 'Land Cruiser' name and have produced several models that are not purely destined to knock around the tracks of developing countries.

Prado: the 90 series
Although manufactured from 1990 and deriving from the 77 models, in 1996 the body shape changed and the 90 series arrived in the UK under the name Colorado (known elsewhere as a Prado or Challenger) but also carrying the Land Cruiser label. In fact in the UK the Colorado/Prado name appears to have been dropped and it's now simply known as the Land Cruiser, possibly to raise its profile against Land Rovers.

It was aimed right between the eyes of the family 4x4 estate brigade who'd

An old-style Toyota Prado, lately renamed a Land Cruiser: a great 3-litre engine and nearly as spacious as an 80. © Jeff Condon

taken to Pajero/Shoguns and Discoverys, and like them has never been taken seriously as an overland vehicle, even though there is no doubt it would be able and, as all the above cars, more comfortable. Perhaps it's the sideboards that give off the wrong signals. Again, you get an economical turbo diesel, full-time four-wheel drive, a coil-sprung beam on the back, but independent coil suspension on the front. The diesel engine has come with ever more powerful and efficient versions of a 3-litre, four cylinder, lately in a common rail form with direct electronic injection and an intercooler (D-4D) to provide excellent torque and economy for its size.

In 2003 a newer, sleeker shape was introduced to take on the new SUVs, having evolved in the last few years from Mercedes, Volkswagen and BMW. But Land Cruisers are sticking to their off-road origins with a separate chassis, limited-slip centre differential with diff lock as well as lockable rear limited-slip differentials and an array of electronic traction, cornering, suspension and hair-drying aids which, for better or worse, all vehicles of this type now feature. Less usefully and showing their road bias, these models now feature 17" wheel rims – not so good for the Sahara although these could be changed.

Toyota 4Runner with Land Cruiser wheels churning through the Imirhou Canyon: a light vehicle with good clearance at the cost of headroom. © M. Soffiantini

A Hilux crewcab adapted for long-range dune exploration with raised suspension, tubeless tyres and 2000km fuel range.
© Werner Nöther

Toyota 4Runner and Hilux

Not pretending to be Land Cruisers, Toyota **4Runners** (aka Surfs) have become popular vehicles, and a few are used in the Sahara by European tourists. Recognisably based on the Hilux pick-up, the later models of the 4Runner feature the desirable three-litre turbo diesel, plus an LSD in the back, part-time four-wheel drive, torsion bars on the front and a dubious free-wheeling front diff.

The 15-inch wheels are easily changed for 16s but the rear tailgate arrangement (the upper window winds into the lower section) shows its pick-up origins and is not ideal for desert touring. Also, the lack of roof gutters makes conventional roof rack mounting tricky. With 16-inch wheels the body will be high but headroom remains limited. Set up like this a 4Runner looks lithe and aerodynamic: good for economy but not necessarily driver comfort.

As mentioned earlier the **Hilux** is the choice of some desert drivers who can live with the limitations of a pick-up. If not pushed hard or overloaded by an experienced owner, the lighter build will last. The relatively small engine will, of course, be flat out in deep sand and may overheat at slow speeds with a tailwind.

LAND ROVERS

The rugged, fifty-year-old silhouette of the traditional LWB Land Rover epitomises the romance of Africa: the plains of the Serengeti, Bedouin encampments, *Daktari*. When many travellers, and not only patriotic Brits, first toy with the notion of overlanding in a 4WD, it's often a Land Rover that springs to mind. In many cases it's even the prospect of *driving* a Land Rover that accounts for much of the appeal. Such is this marque's extraordinary synonymity with tough, dependable, go-anywhere vehicles, aided in the UK at least by inspired advertising campaigns.

Since that reputation was established, Land Rover have diversified with great success and, although the image of a Defender helps sell the brand, this venerable emblem of the brand now accounts for only a fraction of worldwide sales and is nearing the end of production in the UK in its current form. In part this is due to the **variable production quality** (on all Land Rover models) and the interior ergonomics of Defenders. One only hears of the disasters of course, but owning one can be a lottery, something that to their credit even died-in-the-wool Land Rover owners will readily admit.

In fact 110s/Defenders are now so far behind the times in some areas that many people convince themselves that it is a Defender's **'simplicity'** that makes it a good overland vehicle. Cabin noise, water leaks and all sorts of discomfort were acceptable with the Series IIIs, but the development or even just improvement of Defenders has stagnated while better selling Land Rovers flourish in the 4WD boom.

Whole not unique to Land Rovers, early wear of fundamental components as well as prolonged teething problems can all be incredibly frustrating, which is why they suit enthusiasts who enjoy fiddling and fettling with their vehicles. The ability and widespread know-how to swap engines, gearboxes and even bodies between most models gives Defenders their much-lauded **Meccano-like** quality. It also makes improvements and repairs relatively cheap. But, despite the no-nonsense design, mechanical accessibility and on-the-piste bodgeabilty are no better than in cars from a similar technological era like 60-series Toyotas.

Hardtop 110/Defenders – great image but a Discovery is more comfortable.

If you keep on top of it or you get a good one, your Defender could be almost as reliable as a Japanese 4WD; but like any vehicle, once neglected, either by you or a previous owner (a practice which the perceived toughness of all 4WDs encourages), it could cause you endless trouble.

A 130" crewcab with a box body: more payload area than most people need in the Sahara but could be good for a longer trip.

ENGINE-SWAPPING AND INTERCOOLERS

Land Rovers are often fitted with **alternative engines** to improve the economy of a V8 or the power and reliability of a diesel. The choice is most often a larger Perkins, Japanese or European diesel or, less problematically, Tdi engines into older 110s.

Many options exist but overall they're not recommended for the desert unless you have a long personal history of the conversion and trust it implicitly. Standard engines, however seemingly inadequate, are an asset in the Sahara. You get all the original research and development that few home-made engine conversions can achieve. Remember, you can't just call the recovery service as you might do at home.

Problems of all sorts can crop up with conversions. **Overheating** from misaligned radiators or altered air flow is common. So is **mixed-up gearing** when a diesel motor replaces a faster spinning petrol engine as well as bad wiring or difficult access to filters and other ancillaries. Front springs will also need uprating if the new engine is substantially heavier. Oil coolers, electric fans, overdrives and alternative diffs can fix these but other problems may surface in Saharan conditions which can't be replicated at home.

I had a 3-litre Ford six-cylinder fitted into a Land Rover 101 – admittedly a rough conversion using a lousy engine. Even with an overdrive I ended up with a 90kph top speed and worse still, unexceptional economy (the whole point of the conversion). The engine fan was not aligned with the standard V8 radiator, which necessitated running 90W truck oil and a king-sized Kenlowe fan to keep things cool. Even with heavier springs, the front axle was two inches from the bump stops. But the worst was left for the corrugations to divulge. On these tracks the engine shaking on its rubber mounts kept pulling at the radiator hoses, cracking the solder of the hose manifolds so causing loss of water pressure and a still warmer cab.

Another Land Rover 109 I had came with a big Perkins engine. Series Land Rovers are not built for powerful engines; it's one reason why they last so long. The clutch didn't like it and neither did the gearbox. Had it got to the desert something else would have broken.

Remember, better economy is handy, but a lot of extra power will strain a transmission and suspension and cooling system that was not necessarily designed for it and may need

uprating too. If you feel your chosen vehicle does not have the right original engine, get one that has. The Sahara is not a place to experiment with such things.

Bigger intercoolers

However! Lately there has been a trend for fitting bigger-than-standard **intercoolers** to Tdis and even Td5s which, like a turbo, gives 'power for free'.

Tdis have a factory-fitted intercooler – basically a 'radiator' for cooling the hot and compressed air coming out of the even hotter turbo. While density is improved by compression (the idea of a turbo's forced induction), the by-product of a turbo's added heat means the change is not as dense as it could be.

On a typical 200 Tdi the air leaves the turbo at about 130°C – going through the standard intercooler reduces it to about 100°C which improves density a bit and thereby the all-important oxygen content needed for complete combustion.

Fitting a bigger intercooler reduces the air temperature to an amazing 30°C, greatly improving density and so oxygen levels. The fuelling rate needs to be adjusted to compensate but on Tdis this means just making a few adjustments to the injection pump with a screwdriver. On electronic fuel pumps as fitted to Td5s, a new computer chip is easily installed.

Bigger intercoolers significantly **improve torque** as well as power by up to 30% and marginally improve fuel consumption by around 5%. The temperature reduction in the cylinder head is also desirable.

While it is still true that an increase in power may accelerate the stress on the transmission, the broad and smooth nature of an intercooler's power advantage is about as good as it gets. And the composition of an intercooled charge creates added power at lower revs, the opposite of most traditional power hikes and ideal for desert use.

I briefly drove the Land Rover featured in *Desert Driving*, fitted with an AlliSport intercooler and it bore little relation to the Tdis I'd driven before. Throttle response was far superior and stepping out of an HJ61 was not the let-down – engine-wise – it had been with plain Tdis. In the dunes this made progress far more reliable. Overall, though, in the desert the 61 recorded marginally better fuel consumption, by around ten per cent.

Old Series III Land Rovers are still common in many Saharan towns, if not on the piste...

... elsewhere in the Sahara only the chassis survive – here holding up a tea shack in Atar, RIM.

In short, if you just want to get in and drive, or if you demand an utterly dependable vehicle for extreme desert travel, unless you know your Land Rover inside out (as many do), you may be better off with something else.

One of the big advantages of owning a Land Rover in the UK, especially over a Toyota, are **inexpensive parts** and servicing. Partly because they are so well known and people love to tinker with them (and also, it has to be said, because they need more parts back-up than most!), equipping a Land Rover for an overland trip won't cost a fortune. You just have to juggle up the fact that what you end up spending may have been spent on a trouble-free Japanese car. Furthermore, **new vehicle prices** in the UK have been held down in recent years in an attempt to end the absurd but very popular practice of buying a fully UK-spec'ed new vehicle from Europe for much less than it cost in the UK. Now you get a lot of car for your money, and being in a Land Rover adds an expeditionary esprit to your adventure that no other vehicle can approach. The crash in early Discovery and V8 Range Rover prices also makes them worth a look.

Don't believe the commonly-held belief that African villages are full of knackered Land Rovers ready to be cannibalised for parts. Series Land Rovers are seen around the towns but out on the piste the most common sight is a bare chassis half submerged in sand. All the frequently-needed goodies have long since been pinched or sold to your predecessors.

Despite all this, and thanks to its enviable if outdated reputation and that stirring, no-nonsense, 'curves-be-damned' profile, one in every four cars used by Saharan tourists is a Defender. Among trans-African overlanders, they may be even more popular. Part of this is the perception of their ability in **extreme off-road** terrain. This is due to the suppleness of the suspension system in tight situations like jungles, where outright power is less of an issue, as demonstrated in the gruelling Camel Trophies of fifteen years ago. In such terrain it's hard to imagine a Troop Carrier performing better. But in the Sahara, axle-twisting terrain is very rare when compared to the more common power-sapping soft-sand scenario. By far the most axle-twisting piste I've ever done in the Sahara is the ascent to Assekrem from Hirhafok (Route A6) via the pass of Tin Teratimt. At the time we did it (in 2000) it had not been maintained for years and pushed all our cars' suspension to the limit. In front of me an early model Discovery and an 80VX managed the loose and eroded ascent and subsequent wash-outs just fine in Low Range. But next day, having reversed the route, the Discovery broke a radius arm while the 80 mashed a radius arm bush. I thought I'd got away with it but a day later my 61 broke a leaf carrying the Discovery's payload. So, although all vehicles were driven to 'something-breaking' point, none ever got stuck even though they weren't Defenders.

This section concentrates on the **110s** and **Defenders** as these are by far the most popular Land Rovers used in the desert. Range Rovers and Discoverys are reviewed later. Even though they are capable if in good shape, **Series Land Rovers** are no longer a viable option. Old 110s, Discoverys and Range Rovers are now as cheap as a decent, desert-ready Series Land Rover. What few Series III Saharans there are are hardcore enthusiasts who know their vehicles intimately and are well aware of their limitations. For a first-time Landroverer with only moderate under-bonnet curiosity and little interest in expanding it, a later Land Rover would be more suitable.

There are countless enthusiasts' **websites** on Land Rovers, as well as expedition home pages detailing Land Rover vehicle preparation. About the best **forum** going is www.lrenthusiastforum.com.

SHIP OF THE DESERT

People often assume Camel Trophy Land Rovers were purpose-built for desert travel. Perhaps it is the distinctive colour, known as 'sandglow', perhaps the robust appearance, or the rack of jerrycans on the roof. However, the reality is a little different.

I have taken my Camel Defender 110 on several desert trips, but have only come across one other Camel vehicle in the Sahara. They are sturdy expedition vehicles, but the Camel Trophy competitions mostly plugged their way through rainforests and swamps, only rarely venturing into true desert (notably the 1997 Mongolia event), and the vehicle specifications reflect this. Here are a few things to bear in mind if you are thinking of using an ex Camel vehicle in the Sahara.

Firstly, Camel Trophy 110s are **heavy**. After you have slapped on a roll cage, winch, roof-rack, and all the other bolt-on armour which Land Rover Special Vehicles lavished on their sandglow Defenders, you are cutting deep into margins imposed by your gross vehicle weight, leaving less for essential loads like fuel, water etc. You need to balance this against the benefits which accrue from the extra hardware. A roll cage provides peace of mind on steep dune descents, but lack of trees in the Sahara hin-

Veteran of the last Trophy in the Ubari Sand Sea. © Toby Savage

ders self-recovery by winch. This extra weight is also an issue when the going gets soft. Coupled with the Tdi's lack of power (at 2.5 litres, it's a baby compared with the lumps found under the hood of most desert-going Toyotas), you're likely to be looking at a lot more recovery activity than if you were in a lighter vehicle.

Finally, if you get terminally stuck out in the desert, the last colour you would want your vehicle to be is desert-coloured. The opposite is true, of course, if you're looking for a discreet campsite close to a smugglers' piste.

Kevin White

110 and Defender

The 110 first emerged in 1983 with the old 2.25 engines or V8s. A year later the diesel grew to 2494cc (67hp) and a petrol four followed a year later, giving 83hp. In 1986 the first 2.5 diesel turbo indirect injection was introduced, the **2.5 TD**, producing 85hp. It's commonly accepted that this engine is bad news for overlanding (overheating problems and cracking heads) so avoid it, no matter how cheap. Go for the defending and dog-slow 2.5 non-turbo diesel if you must, or better still just get a Tdi.

The all-new **200Tdi** engine was introduced to the renamed **Defender** in 1990 (along with the new Discovery) and in 1994 all Land Rover diesels got the more refined 300Tdi direct injection 2.5 engine. Other differences between a 110 and a Defender are negligible, apart from the transmission. The Defender name was primarily a marketing move to help introduce the new Tdi engine.

Apart from a few early models (like the 'intermediate' Stage 1 V8s), all post-Series Land Rovers use the proven **transmission and suspension** set-up of the early Range Rover: full-time four-wheel drive with a central-locking diff and beam axles on coil springs. It offers class-leading articulation which aids consistent traction without resorting to LSDs or axle diff locks. Shocks sit out of harm's way inside or behind the coils, and ground clearance, approach and departure angles are excellent for the 110-inch (2.79m) wheelbase. A Defender claims to have a payload of 1000kg but not surprisingly it sags out on standard springs with less than half that weight. **Heavy-duty coils** are essential on the back (taken from a 130", for example) with rear springs fitted on the front.

All this adds up to a competent off-road package apart from **engine** choice and ever-troublesome gearboxes. The ancient four-cylinder petrol unit which helped make Land Rover's name in the 1960s never stood a chance against today's performance and emission standards and slipped away unnoticed in 1994. This left the similarly venerable V8 guzzler (discussed below under 'Range Rovers') and the 2.5 Tdis.

Tdi engines

It's an often-raised lament that Land Rover never saw fit to give their workhorse the diesel engine it deserved. Even the electronically-managed Td5 made you wonder what they had against going over 2500cc – although a bigger Ford engine could be waiting in the wings. For years all Land Rovers sold in Australia were immediately fitted with a 3.9 Isuzu unit, and Australian four-wheel driving needs are similar to those of the Sahara.

Top: a loaded 2.5-litre Tdi will be at its absolute limit in the dunes. **Above**: A Land Rover's flat wings make a handy table.
© Yves Larboulette

300 Tdis work hard in the Grand Erg but don't get much more stuck than bigger-engined vehicles.

There's only so much **power** you can squeeze out of a two-and-a-half-litre turbo, even with a bigger intercooler, and the only way, until recent technological advances with high-pressure injection and electronic engine management, was by making the engine spin faster.

In deep sand a loaded Tdi lacks pulling power at low engine speeds. The only way to keep moving is to resort to Low Range. No drama though, they always get through, but with this lack of easily-usable power, gear-changing needs to be brutal and the gearboxes don't like it.

On the road a Tdi Defender (for some reason it gets a Discovery engine detuned by around 12%) will be flat-out at 100kph in the desert. Unloaded and around town, **fuel economy** can reach the high 20s mpg (10kpl), but once kitted out and working hard in an overland situation an average of 15 mpg (5kpl) in Africa was recorded (this, on an admittedly overloaded vehicle). My own experiences touring with Tdis were never quite that bad, though never better than a Toyota HJ61 or the 80 VXs accompanying us – not at all what I'd expected from Tdis.

As for reliability and longevity, the engines themselves are strong and, notably, don't overheat despite the hammering they get in dunes. But **timing belt breakages** were a problem with 300 Tdis up to the introduction of the Td5 engine which reverted to a timing chain. In case you don't know, when a timing- or cam-belt snaps without warning the pistons usually make a mess of the valves. There's little point in carrying a spare belt in this instance – a new cylinder head or even new engine is required. It seems as long as the pulleys are correctly aligned at the time of manufacture (some were, some weren't) and the original belt gets past 30,000 miles, you're in the clear. Officially, you then want to change it every 60,000 miles. If you buy a 300 and the owner doesn't know when the last belt was changed, fit a new one, although by now one would have thought all 300s have been through their belt-breaking and replacement-kit cycles. A good way of checking if it's wearing is to inspect the drain hole in the bottom of the cover with a bit of hooked wire. Have a root around; any black fluffy matter is timing belt shavings indicating wear from misalignment and the need for a replacement kit. Kit 1 includes modified pulleys with lips to hold the belt on; if this doesn't work fit Kit 2 which includes modified pulleys and a new front cover. A yellow mark on the timing cover should mean that either kit has been fitted at some stage by a dealer. But don't overlook the need for **periodic replacement** (as on *any* vehicle with these belts). Other than that, on a long trip it's worth taking a spare water pump and alternator – cheap and easy to fit if the old ones pack up.

So 200 or 300 then? Unless you own a 300 Land Rover lore has it that, despite the chronic gearbox, the 200s have the edge, being simple and more economical. The broadly similar 300 was quieter and more refined but had lots of irritating problems: alternators packing up, the cam belts of course, cylinder heads cracking and short-lived water pumps. It is a bit faster, but not by much. The bottom line with Tdis (200 or 300, there's not much in it) is to get one that's been well looked after, not run on a shoestring.

Gearboxes and rust

The Tdi 200 engine may be the choice but the gearboxes are not, with the transfer lever jumping out under load or refusing to engage Low no matter what you do: a weak point of the **LT77 gearboxes** from the introduction of the 110 through all the Tdi 200s up till 1994. One owner I know was on his third gearbox in 100,000 miles. The day he could not engage Low to get round a dune was the day which led to an accident which destroyed his vehicle and nearly killed him (not *directly* attributable to the gearbox...). Others I've met have literally got through a gearbox in one, albeit hard, Sahara trip!

The much earlier **four-speed boxes** were reputedly stronger than the five-speeds which followed with the 110s, as are **Santana gearboxes** fitted to Spanish 110 and 90 V8s (little help though it is, knowing this!). One well-known problem was premature wear through lack of adequate oil feeding the output shaft bearing leading to the transfer box. In 1994 the better R380 box was introduced with the 300Tdi engine but it is still not without problems usually caused by premature wear. And fitting an R380 box to a 200 engine is not a bolt-on swap.

In Europe at least, automatic Defenders are rare and rarely matched with Tdis, although the **ZF auto box** is said to be more reliable than the LT77 and R380 (not saying much). Most auto boxes get to meet a Tdi when the owner of an auto V8 (usually a Discovery or Range Rover) finally cracks and installs a Tdi. The power and torque characteristics of a V8 and a Tdi are not compatible so technically the gear change is no longer happening at the optimum time. An auto gearbox specialist can alter the valving in the gearbox so it changes gear at whatever torque/speed you want, but most people just live with it changing gear at the wrong torque/time.

It has to be said that such a modification wants to be well tested before the heat and stress of the Sahara – a cooked auto box could be impossible to fix out there. When a manual gearbox on any car starts going, it rarely just packs up but usually refuses to engage certain gears, as Toby Savage recalls: '*The lay shaft bearings became progressively more noisy, leaving only 4th (out of 5). Fourth is direct drive through the gear box and bypasses the layshaft. It sounded like a dustbin full of nails in any other gear so I drove home from Tunisia in 4th low/4th high. It was not too bad actually. Perfected my low to high and high to low changes and managed a creditable 55-60 mph. Avoided all the autoroutes etc and enjoyed rural France. Tried the other gears when a mile from home and they sounded AWFUL!*' Now you know. You will have plenty of warning signs and sounds and will always manage to scrape together some sort of forward progress, even if it is in reverse!

Don't assume that because Defenders have aluminium body panels that they're light and won't **rust**. The good thing is that the structural rust is limited to the steel chassis and the bulkhead so there are no rusted wheel arches, roof gutters or windscreen edges to deal with as there can be on older Toyotas or Discoverys, for example. Furthermore new chassis elements (if not a whole

FINISHING THE JOB – SANTANA PS10

With Land Rover having abandoned its utilitarian origins, even with the Defender, in 2003 Santana, the former Spanish assembler of Land Rovers, introduced the PS10.

While clearly resembling a Defender, the PS10 has kept what worked well with Series Land Rovers while finally nailing the still all-too-current complaints.

Powered by a 125hp, Bosch-managed Iveco 2.8 intercooled turbo diesel (as used in Bremachs and Daily vans – a 106hp non-electronic 'Euro II' is available) you get on-the-move, lever-engaged 4WD via Santana's renowned LT85 gearbox, no FWH, and all running on parabolic leaf springs.

Santana PS10 – a sorted-out Defender.

Chassis and body undergo a comprehensive *all*-surface rustproofing process with the body mounted on 14 polybushes and capped with a one-piece insulated GRP roof. Thick gutters will support a rack securely while most body panels are steel.

Eliminating the seat boxes, centre 'seat' and rear bulkhead means more space front and back, a real advance over the archaic Defender. Tyres are 235 85 x 16s but a wider track means narrower wheel arches, so there's more room in the back and a wider back door. A huge, 100-litre plastic fuel tank has a range of up to 1000km and, like the roof, could be easily repaired and won't rust.

Gear change seemed a bit crude on the models I drove around a muddy track, though the parabolics (two front leaves, four at the rear) felt firm enough to manage a desert payload without alteration. And articulation proved supple enough to maintain traction without resorting to ETC or diff locks, or indeed coil springs.

At low revs the Bosch management helps in this respect, but this is still a small engine compared to a Toyota and not as smooth as a Td5.

With Defender production to be sold off overseas, here is a basic, working 4WD that, on paper at least, would make a great overlander in the no-frills, solidly-built mould of the Toyota Troop Carrier.

chassis), including outriggers for the body mounts and rear cross members, are readily available to weld on once the rotten pieces have been cut off.

Td5 engines

The five-cylinder direct-injection turbo diesel intercooled Td5 has been out long enough to offer an impression of its performance in the desert. In Discovery specification it develops 136 bhp, 122 bhp in a Defender, which relates to a 9% increase in power and 13% more torque from the 300 Tdi.

Despite these figures, on release many testers lamented the lack of low-down grunt in the new engine while recognising a modest power increase at higher rpm. And overall, it seems **fuel consumption** is a little worse than the 300s. Clearly its advances in efficiency are limited to emissions rather than economy. Still, the timing belt has been abandoned in favour of a **cam chain** – a stronger unit being necessary in part to help turn the injector pump on each cylinder which squirt at 1500 bar, two-and-a-half times more than a Tdi. And because of superior filtration, oil changes are now every 12,000 miles with primary filters lasting through three changes. You may not save on fuel bills, but you will on oil and filters.

It was the **electronic engine management system** (ECU), common on all diesels these days, which grated with potential Defender overlanders who understandably liked the idea of being able to diagnose faults themselves. The great appeal of diesels for overlanding is that there have been few electrics and no electronics to go wrong, compared to most petrols. Assuming the engine starts, it reduces the potential causes of bad running to fuel or mechanical agents. Worse still is the engine **immobiliser** which is part of the ECU. A driver from the Land Rover Experience admitted to me these become permanent engine-stoppers in wading situations – rarely an issue in the Sahara of course, but disabling it is worth considering for wet overlanding environments. How to do it is not something you'll find in the owner's handbook.

The early Defender Td5s were said to have an appetite for ECUs; an uprated alternative was introduced in 2002 but some have found it does not work on the older models even though it has replaced their part number. Injector wiring harnesses can also cause a misfire after about 60,000 miles as the insulation breaks down with heat and oil inside the rocker cover. But they only cost £45 and are easy to replace.

These modern high-pressure injection engines demand very **clean diesel**, something that one cannot rely on in Africa. The high-pressure **in-tank fuel pumps** seem to be very sensitive to this so a spare is definitely worth carrying in the desert (they cost around £240). As one Td5 reader reports: *'It happened to me in Sinai when running out of diesel and buying some doubtful stuff from some Bedouins. I know three Td5 owners in Cairo and all have already replaced the pump at least once. Take care on your diesel or have a spare pump with you. I do both...'* On a similar theme, it's worth knowing that the water-in-fuel warning light can come on due to a faulty water sensor on the fuel filter, rather than actual water, but if you're not sure, drain the filter anyway. Mechanically though, the Td5s seem as bombproof as their predecessors.

As for the unreliability of the electronics? I've only met one Td5 owner who'd come up from South Africa and was stranded in Agadez for a couple of months trying to unravel the problem. It's not something you can do with a piece of wire and a bulb anymore. Other overland Td5s I've driven with, or heard about, have managed fine over several trips. In reality, apart from early ECU failures which seem to have been engineered out in later models, problems with electronics only set in after several years when corrosion gets to the contacts. You can help delay this eventuality by using the special grease that Land Rover produces to keep connections clean.

110s/Defenders in the desert

On the plains lack of power is not that noticeable but the **suspension** certainly is. A Rover-scorning friend once replaced his BJ75 with a 110, marvelled at the suspension and never looked back. There's none of the wallowing and bouncing from bump to bump as with all but the stiffest leaf springs. With a coil spring set-up it's more of a boat-like rolling from side to side. As long as heavy-duty units are fitted, it means you can maintain momentum, keep an even speed and so save even more fuel. **Shocks** do work harder on long-travel coil vehicles and I've heard of Defenders frying their dampers to a crisp on corrugated Sahelian pistes. Driving without shocks is a bit more difficult on coilers than on leaf-sprung vehicles whose rubbing leaves create their own damping effect. Carry new spares or the old ones you replaced.

A 110 powers up onto the Gilf Kebir towards Shaw's Cave (see p.626). Actually, it's got a 3.5 Toyota engine.

In dunes or sandy oueds the small engine has to work hard but it always gets through with help from Low Range. The best you can do is **not overload** the vehicle as in this state a Td5 owner recorded a miserable 4.7kpl or 13 mpg around Lake Chad.

The cramped **driving position** has been a source of complaint for decades and will continue to be so, along with water leaks and early rust, until the bolt-together Defender is replaced. Until then the 'middle front seat' is better removed and replaced with a more useful cubby box, even if the driver still ends up jammed against the door. It's something you get used to. **Power-assisted steering** was an option on 110s, though finally became standard on Defenders. On any loaded desert vehicle you'll welcome it. As mentioned before, the LT77 **gearbox** which came with the 200 Tdi can be bad news and needs to be shoved firmly into low range (and sometimes held there) when pushing hard through soft sand.

When it comes to preparing the vehicle, the **shape** of the Land Rover is a definite plus even if the wheel boxes waste a lot of space. Payload is good and can be maximised with crates, jerries and any box-shaped container. Making your own customised containers fit without rattling is easy too, as there are no curves or steps to complicate your design. Outside, the flat surfaces make mounting sand plates and other extra gear easy, and the flat wings make an ideal small table on which to make a sandwich or rest a cuppa. This may sound trivial but it's a real asset at lunchtime where you may not want to get a table out. Furthermore, the steep glass angles (including the windscreen) mean that less sunlight penetrates the vehicle therefore keeping it and you cooler for longer.

The Td5s come with **electronic traction control** (ETC) as described on p.69. It may work well in mud, snow and on rocks but in sand you'll find old fashioned BTC (brain throttle control) makes all the difference (along with tyre-pressure regulation). My own experience with an ETC Discovery on the fringes of Australia's Simpson Desert (as Saharan as it gets down there) proved that in the end there was no substitute for airing down, though the ETC may have helped pull the car through in some marginal situations.

Extra long 130" Land Rovers are also available but with that sort of **wheelbase** you're pushing your luck with the belly clearance over dune crests and oued banks. Even less suitable for long-range desert use are 6x4 or 6x6 exotica, converted by the factory or anyone else, often for emergency services. They may turn heads at Tescos but a standard LWB can comfortably carry all the needs of up to four well-acquainted people.

Compared to Toyotas the prognosis on Defenders may sound grim. Reliability is undoubtably inferior, but then Toyota's reputation in this respect is possibly the best in the world so comparison may be unfair. Land Rovers are no worse than many French or Italian cars and it's worth remembering that they're the second most common car in the Sahara and they always get home.

OTHER POPULAR 4WDS

Nissan Patrol

Nissan's Patrol offers the truck-built toughness of Toyotas without quite matching the build quality, popularity or indeed the high prices. After Land Cruisers, Patrols are the next best Japanese 4WDs for the desert. MQ models from the eighties were basic: much more utilitarian than Land Cruiser 60s but better built than Land Rovers. In the UK if you find a solid, non-rusty example with the truck-like 95hp, 3.25-litre diesel six it will approach Land Rover's simplicity and Toyota's reliability. Suspension is leaf-sprung and four-wheel drive is part-time with automatic FWHs and a manual override from 1986. The gear change is agricultural, but the whole drive train right to the wheels is as strong as any 4WD. As with any vehicle from this era, watch out for rust on the tailgates and the chassis. You can pick them up for under £2000, making them a viable alternative to an HJ60.

Patrol GR

Patrols perked up in 1989 when they got the smoother, free-revving **2.8 diesel engine** which soon became turbo-charged, making 114hp. A year later they built a winner in the GR (aka GQ) range. With its coil springs and square-edged, flared arch body, this is what most people associate with a Patrol. The six-cylinder 2.8 turbo diesel is an excellent engine for its time and over 150kg lighter than the huge TD42 diesel which was also offered, making 124hp without a turbo and a lazy 200lb.ft of torque at just 2000rpm – a bit less than

---

BUS OF THE DESERT

Between 1989 and 2001, Spain produced a series of Nissan Patrols with high roofs (known as a Merco) primarily for commercial use. These models featured part-time 4WD with leaf springs, 12-volt electrics, no diff locks and a basic interior with few electronic devices. The non-turbo 2.8 diesel six is particularly suitable for desert travel compared to the underpowered 2.5 four. The 2.8 has a low torque giving maximum power at low range. The near-100hp makes them slow and lazy on highways, but in the desert they have enough power to easily cross dune fields with more than 800kg of cargo. The tractor-like gearbox is basic but strong and efficient. They have two vertical rear doors, the spare wheel under the back, (like Land Cruisers) and the bumpers are solid and flat, good for hi-lift usage.

The LWBs provide plenty of space but with a roof-rack they're over 2.2m high although the wide track gives stability. The major drawback is the standard 15" rims. These are too small, giving a bad ground clearance and a poor ramp breakover angle.

High-roofed Nissan Merco Patrol in Mauritania. © José Brito

For desert expeditions it is advisable to fit 16" rims, protect the front undercarriage with a bash plate and reinforce the suspension (a couple of extra leaves and a re-bending are enough). The fuel consumption, with four travellers and around 500kg of cargo is: 8.3kpl on highways and hard pistes, 5.8kpl on sandy pistes and 4.8kpl in the dunes.

José Brito

Nissan Patrol fuelling up at Hassi bel Guebbour – a good-value alternative to a Land Cruiser.

Toyota's similar IHZ though it's no longer offered in the Patrol.

And unlike the early Toyota 80 series, they got the GR right first time. It needs a big engine to push 2230kg of 4-litre diesel GR. With its big 16-inch wheels (exchangeable with drum-braked Toyota wheels, incidentally) it's an ideal desert tourer. And even today it still retains the **part-time 4WD** while most manufacturers have turned to fool-proof full-time set ups.

Patrols look big, too big for comfortable town driving but are at ease in the wide-open Sahara. At 117 inches the widely-spaced axles are nearly three metres apart. This makes for good angles, but belly clearance over dunes or creek banks could be a problem (as illustrated on p.50). The GRs are as stable as a pyramid: the wide track and huge wheelbase give a long load area, though the width is not that great as the body tapers significantly upwards. The overlong tailgates of its MQ predecessor were replaced by doors, the larger of which carries the spare. Better-equipped ST models came with rear axle diff-locks and the ability to disengage the anti-roll bar and release the axle's full articulation with a lever in the cab. Other models had LSDs.

The latest models have lost the angular look but now feature a four cylinder direct injection 3-litre turbo with electronic management and around 20% superior economy to the old 2.8 six. All in all, you can't go too far wrong with a Patrol, as long as it's in good condition.

Mercedes/Puch G-Wagen

These days in the UK the G-Wagen or G-Class is rare and yet the marque's solid engineering makes a G a functional, if expensive and eccentric, choice. The original 460-series **240 or 300GD** 4- or 5-cylinder Gs from the 1980s were based on a military design and were heavy, underpowered and slow. Up to

Encounter with a lone Mercedes 300GTD (six cylinders and 170hp) at Berliet Balise 21 near the Niger border (see Routes A14 and A15).

a point, however, these older engines share components with the saloon cars commonly found in some Saharan and West African countries.

Actually built by the same Austrian factory which manufactures Pinzgauers (see p.103), you get **twin diff-locks** and part-time four-wheel drive on the later 461-series models, with the **290GTD** five cylinder direct injection turbo diesel making around 93hp. Better appointed and seriously expensive, the **463-series** uses full-time 4WD – a similar model separation as Toyota's fully-fruited VXs or working GXs.

Much is made of the presence of these twin diff locks (with a third central lock on the 463s) as if it's a really serious off-roader, but they're featured on many Toyotas and are only a mechanical alternative to more sophisticated electronic traction control devices – both make little difference in soft sand (though mud is a different matter).

Suspension on all models is coil and though the articulation doesn't match the best Land Rovers, durability comes close to Mercedes' once-legendary standard. Former desert explorer Tom Sheppard who alone has taken all sorts of Land Rovers off the map for several decades, now drives a G-Wagen.

Range Rover

It's ironic that what's regarded as one of the most accomplished off-road vehicles sees less dirt than any other Land Rover product, if not most 4WDs. The car which got the jump on the contemporary 4WD boom is now Land Rover's hi-tech flagship: a heavy, powerful assortment of platinum-card gizmology that still manages to come out tops, on and off the highway. It's a winning combination of true off-road ability and style, comfort and power.

Now that they've been in production for nearly four decades, older models are well within the budget of a first-time Saharan. Newer models are phenomenally expensive, so only the 'old shape' pre-'95 'Classics' are considered here. Just don't forget that **rust** is as much a problem as on any old vehicle: in addition to the upper tailgate, the rear chassis, bulkhead and doors are the first places to look. A Range Rover may be made of alloy but those panels are thick and the car weighs from 1800kg to well over two tonnes.

V8 engines

The point of taking a Range Rover to the Sahara is that petrol models are **cheap** to buy and despite the fuel cost in getting there this can work out in your favour (see estimate below). The older **carburetted** (i.e. pre-EFI) engines can now be bought for less than a thousand pounds; they're simple to understand, maintain and fix. The later **EFI** 3.5s from the mid-80s on offer mildly improved economy but this engine was not too reliable and was a pain to diagnose. The 3.9 EFIs from 1990 to 1995 when the so-called Classic shape came to an end were said to be better, but go from £2500.

From 1981 to 1985 around 126hp was coaxed from the carburetted 3528cc V8, but the torque was neither outstanding for its size (just 194lb.ft), nor delivered that low (2500rpm peak). It might sound great with a split silencer but was no sand-churner, which explains why the low-stressed V8s can last. The electronic 'black box' (ECU) used to manage the injected V8s (as well as other Land Rover engines) had a bad record for reliability at that time and could be a liability in the Sahara. So carry a spare or stick with the carburetted V8s or, if you must,

Range Rover waits for a storm to break.
© Yves Larboulette.

a Range Rover diesel (though think twice about conversions, see p.84). If payload is not critical, **LPG conversions** (commonly applied to the V8s) are worth considering as they'll save you money getting to Africa: once there LPG is unknown but ordinary petrol is cheap.

To save you working it out I can tell you that your **average fuel bill** for a typical 5000km UK to Central Sahara tour would be around £360 in a Range Rover as opposed to £170 in an HJ60. Only with an HJ, or any diesel for that matter, you can kiss goodbye to the possibility of electrical faults and dodgy high-altitude carburation on the drive up to Assekrem. On the highway expect up to 18mpg or 6.6 kpl, on the piste around 14.3mpg or 5kpl, while in the dunes you'll be doing at least 9mpg (3.3 kpl). Either way it adds up to a **huge fuel payload** for any long piste though I'm told correct tyre pressures and keeping the engine at the right temperature (block off the oil cooler in winter) make a big difference to optimal fuel consumption. With a V8 you want to try every trick in the book.

The Rover V8 has a long heritage which adds up to a wide range of know-how, even if these days that know-how is focused towards snorty off-road racers rather than overlanding. In a standard tune the engine boasts a longevity which few petrol engines can match. With **regular oil changes** the 3.5 can roll past 100,000 miles with only the flurry of fuel bills to show for it. Oil quality and level are important if you're not to prematurely wear the camshafts (although replacement is straightforward and due at around 100,000 miles, about the same as the 5-speed boxes). Electrics and fuel delivery, specifically **vapour-lock** in hot situations, are where the main problems lie in the Sahara.

Diesel engines

Classic Range Rovers came with various diesel engines over the years but none ever hit the mark for Saharan travel: the original 2.4 VM effort of the mid-eighties was an asthmatic sheep in wolf's clothing with a tendency to blow head gaskets. In 1992, 200 Tdis were fitted, hardly a recommendation in this big car, but with more torque at lower rpm. The later BMW 2.5s were also known for their lack of power at low revs.

Desert Ranging

After a diesel Defender, driving a Range Rover is a pleasure: much quieter and more elbow room though barely more powerful. All models have power-assisted steering whose lightness can accentuate the body roll of older models on which interior fittings tend to come away in your hands. Even today the build quality and the reliability are hit and miss – a Land Rover characteristic.

With a 100-inch (2.54m) wheelbase on a short body and the spare inside, there's not that much room unless you remove the back seats. Even then, sleeping with the tailgate closed is an indulgence only shorter people can enjoy unless you fold the front seats forward or figure out some shelf system. As with all Land Rovers, the alloy roof guttering can only carry so much weight before unfurling. Spread the load well and use wide feet on the rack.

A Range Rover does not carry its payload as well as a Defender. Saggy back ends are a common sight in the Sahara, so fit **heavy-duty coils** to carry all that fuel. Removing the anti-roll bar under the axles will free up the **full-**

wheel articulation but of course will result in more body roll. In this state corrugations must be driven with care as the relatively short wheelbase means reduced directional stability. Post-1992, the Vogue LSE had a 108-inch (2.74m) wheelbase, but this upmarket air-suspended model is unlikely to meet most people's budgets for a desert car.

Taller 750 16R **tyres** *can* be fitted but the wheel arches need to be trimmed back unless your suspension is higher and firmer. As a result, many owners struggle with the standard 205 tyres in Saharan situations, and it *is* a struggle. If you take this route choose your tyres carefully: fit the tallest that room allows. The Range pictured on p.95 is running tubeless 245/75R16s.

Land Rover Discovery

The UK's bestselling family estate introduced in 1990 has a lot going for it compared to a Defender but is still a rare sight in the desert. And yet it sold so well there are plenty of early 1990s diesel models to be found for under £3000.

A Discovery does nothing worse than a Defender except not look the part and as Land Cruisers prove, not looking the part does not affect function in the desert. And a Discovery offers Range Rover comfort and ride but without too many bits falling off or the stigma of the 'rich man's toy' which I've seen work against owners at borders. It may not carry loads like a Defender and the rear floor pans and wheel arches rust like spoons, but the modern levels of comfort add up to as good transportation as any.

Tdis are obviously the ones to go for and are far more common, though there is a school of thought which suggests buying a little used **Mpi** (a short-lived 2-litre petrol lemon) and sticking a decent diesel in.

Which Tdi, 200 or 300, adds up to the same factors discussed above though Discovery make a useful extra 10hp in both versions. With **gearboxes** it's the same story though it's worth noting that both Discovery and Range Rovers have a **transfer box ratio** about 15% higher than off-road oriented Defenders. This can work against them in gruelling terrain, but then they have the extra power to deal with it. Many Defender owners fit the higher ratio transfer boxes anyway, once they've upped the power with a bigger intercooler for example.

As on Range Rovers, 7.50 (or 235/85 R16) **tyres** can be a squeeze, though this will raise the gearing still further. Whatever, I've watched standard 205-tyred Discoverys struggle in the sands where those with 7.50s managed fine, partly because ground clearance is not so good.

The abundant **stowage areas** and pockets show that they thought carefully how real people use cars and what their needs are. And the spacious, airy interior is about as far removed from a Series III 'submarine' as you can get; very 'Range'. Spare tyres sit on the back door where hinges and rust can cause problems. This spare-on-the-back-door arrangement on all Land Rovers has been a weak point in

Land Rover Discovery.

the Sahara for as long as they've been there: vibration from corrugations is hard on the tiny hinges. After-market spare-wheel carriers are a wise move on any Sahara-bound Land Rover and Mantec's version enables the door to be opened from the inside, both useful and safe. Officially the roof can take only 75kg and some 'expedition' **roof racks** weigh up to half of that figure so a spare wheel and a couple of empty jerries is all you'll get up there without extra bracing.

With a **wheelbase** of 100 inches (2.54m), overhangs are good, though inside the curves inhibit optimum packing. All that nice **glass** might make an airy interior but it also makes a hot one, exacerbated by the steeply raked windscreen. Blocking out as much glass as possible will keep the inside cool and be less of an invitation to thieves.

The best of the rest

These include the **Mitsubishi Pajero** (Shogun in the UK), winner of several Dakar rallies and the third most popular Japanese 4WD used by Saharan

tourists (after Toyotas and Patrols), though rarely used by locals. Better known as a family 4WD estate which the Discovery was built to compete with, Pajero's appeal is limited by an over-complex transmission system which tries to be the best of all worlds. It's the sort of thing that sounds great in adverts but doesn't add up on the piste where either part-time or full-time four-wheel drive is fine. Things like automatic free-wheeling hubs which unlock in reverse are not much use in the Sahara where

Dakar Rally winners but not popular with overlanders. © Mitsubishi-Motors

reversing from sand in 4WD is a common necessity. A similar system on some Patrols offers a manual over-ride.

If you find a late 1980s or early 1990s Pajero in good condition (Shoguns were bestsellers in the UK at that time) you'll find the 2.5 turbo diesel engines unexceptional in performance and the front torsion bar suspension more suited to the road where most Pajeros stay. Don't overlook possible problems with rust either, especially bad before the mid-1980s, after which it seems that most manufacturers got to grips with anti-corrosion measures.

Overall, be they high spec'ed Pajeros grey-imported from Japan (usually a little more expensive) or the original and older Shoguns, they don't offer much more than a Discovery which now can be easily bought for a similar price with its cheaper spares and better suspension.

Lada Niva

Lada's little **Nivas** were quite popular vehicles in the 1980s and were even used by some Soviet-aligned Saharan countries at the time. The car is quite unusual: it has no chassis, full-time four-wheel drive and coil suspension (independent at the front) and is powered by a 1.6 litre Fiat-derived petrol engine. Conversions to 2.5 Peugeot engines were popular but even with the standard engine, the Lada's light weight of around 1150kg gives it a better power to weight ratio than a turbo diesel Toyota. You get big (but narrow) 16-inch wheels giving excellent angles and clearance.

Although it's reasonably well built and nothing actually breaks, the unrefined interior and small engine give it a limited appeal. Its biggest plus used to be the price but now many of them are disappearing back to Russia where demand has escalated and though still cheap at under £1000, they are very rare. The snazzier Cossack or Hussar versions are a flashy Niva with no special advantages in the desert.

Although it's no Rolls Royce, a Lada Niva is not to be confused with other Ladas. This one's exploring Egypt's White Desert.
© Toby Savage

CAMPERS AND TRUCKS

Initially a truck might seem like the ideal Saharan transporter, especially for a large group or fitted with a proper motorhome body. They're big enough to carry anything, have huge tyres that can roll over any obstacle and are four-wheel drive too! Unfortunately, for the true desert they're not as practical as they appear and, fun though they initially are to drive, for most desert travellers a **LWB station wagon or hardtop fits the bill much better**.

When a heavy truck gets stuck in sand it can take hours to get it moving and in dunes these sorts of vehicles are particularly cumbersome if not completely out of their depth, no matter what you see on Paris-Dakar videos! There isn't a hi-lift jack long or strong enough to raise an 8-ton MAN motorhome out of the sand.

A huge payload and sometimes a low purchase price can be tempting though. Since the end of the Cold War, **surplus NATO** hardware has been pouring onto the civilian market, including robust old 2- and 4WDs of various shapes and sizes. While some, like the multi-axled MAN missile launchers, are tough enough to drive through a house (ring the bell first), the driving experience in anything ex-military will be crude to say the least. At the right price smaller, more purposeful ex-military forward control one-tonners can make a tempting proposition for a Sahara trip. Bereft of all civilian comforts, their no-nonsense functionality has a certain appeal. But again, the reality of day-to-day running and driving a vehicle proves that the middle road – a 4WD car – is preferable.

Ageing **Magirus**, **Mercedes** and **Renault/Saviems** are still used in the Sahara. Their rugged character may appeal to young groups of Saharan adventurers who are as yet immune to discomfort and want to share running costs while enjoying the convenience of walk-in living quarters. Moving towards the other extreme you pass through **Iveco** and **VW Synchro campers**, or slightly more purposeful **Bremach**-based machines and end up with the hyper-expensive purpose-built **Unimog-** or **MAN-based** conversions, usually owned by retirees who've sold up and can now afford to explore the world in style.

Doing it on the cheap. **Left:** A flatbed Magirus with a caravan tied on the back; 2WD but with good clearance. **Right:** From around £1500 you can get this 30-year-old ex-Army Marmon with a 4.2 Ford V8, diff locks and air brakes but still a crude and noisy drive. More Unimog than 101 on paper, but for the same money and fuel consumption you could get a nice Range Rover.

Left: A Bremach camper can be bought for not much more than a new Defender but its 2.8 Iveco engine makes only around 100 or 120hp with turbo. Iveco also make their own Daily-based 4x4 campers with a similar engine (see p.102). © www.Allrad-Christ.com. **Right**: 1970 AL28 Hanomag. Four overloaded AL28s made a nine-month west–east crossing of the Sahara in 1976, but only one actually got all the way to the Nile (see p.338) © AMR.

Any sort of **all-terrain camper** might be desirable on an extended round-the-world trip, especially one where the climate can get miserable and cold (or where you don't want your itinerary governed by the seasons). But for the Sahara and even Africa you may find living in a cabin hot and claustro-phobic.

It's worth recognising that in general one cannot wait to get out of the vehicle after a day on the piste, while cooking and eating outdoors is also a pleasure. And even if it's not set up for it, on the odd inclement night you can make do inside the regular station wagon. Whatever sort of accommo-dation module you may plan to live in (see more about demountable cabins for pick-ups on p.61), it will have to be really something special to beat being outdoors and alongside your vehicle in Africa. Don't forget that as a rule, the modern trend for roof tents (discussed on p.152) replicates a near-instant sleeping accommodation set-up which is always nice when you've had enough and just want to crash out.

Land Rover 101

From 1975 to 1978, Land Rover's 'pallet-on-wheels' **101FC** was manufactured exclusively for the army, but once it appeared on the UK civilian market in the

4WD TRUCKS – PROS AND CONS

Pro	Con
● Old examples can appear cheap to buy.	● Although generally diesel powered, they still use a heap of fuel: don't expect more than 5kpl (15 mpg), even on the road.
● High GVWs and a large payload area on some make them hard to overload.	
● Plenty of room to fabricate a cabin or a caravan body.	● The basic suspension and forward-mounted engine make some hot and noisy.
● Over-engineered toughness makes them hard to break.	● Don't overlook extra running costs such as higher ferry tariffs, hard-to-find spares and very expensive tyres.
● Old trucks have simple diesel engines that are easy to understand and work on.	
● Big wheels and clearance make under-body protection unnecessary.	● No matter how big the engine, the weight of these vehicles makes them very hard work in dunes. They are slow.

mid-1980s it quickly caught on as an unusual enthusiasts' vehicle. With prices having fallen as the last glut of 101s are retired from service it has potential as a good desert load-carrier, particularly as by now many owners have cracked under the pressure of fuel bills and installed a diesel engine.

Proven in prototype form on an expedition across the width of Africa, the 101 uses Range Rover's V8 power and full-time transmission, but on **leaf springs**. However, these springs aren't the rock-solid configuration of the Series III but a suppler version using broader, longer but fewer leaves. They help provide reasonable agility, much boosted by the short wheelbase, excellent angles, the tough 4-speed LT95 gearbox and 9.00x16 tyres. The 101 was originally intended to tow a powered trailer, effectively making an articulated 6WD vehicle. Unfortunately the coupling proved unreliable and worse still on acute turns the trailer tended to push the 101 over!

These days the novelty of 101s has run its course although it's now possible that prices are edging up towards 'collectable' status. You may get a complete and running RHD 12v 'General Service' (GS) example for as little as £3000/€4500. A GS has a full-length canvas cover going over the cab, which can make an airy, **spartan interior**, clearly more suitable for load carrying than living in. Heavier hardtop ambulance or 'radio-bodied' 101s exist, often with 24v systems. The ambulance's broader body really does stick two fingers up at the theory of streamlining. These can be bought from £4000/€6000 and can make a secure if cramped habitat once the interior has been domesticated. A raisable roof will improve life in the back for people over four feet tall.

You'll not want to be running the original bar-grip cross-ply **tyres** but radial 9.00 16s can be expensive and the choice is limited. It's possible to fit 20-inch wheels from a 404 Unimog – they

A radio-bodied 101 in Egypt's White Desert. This one used the original bar grips but had a 300 Tdi with ZF4HP22 auto gearbox plus air-con returning around 21mpg.
© enableafrica.net.

This GS 101 supporting a Sahara bike tour proved to be a good load-carrier but for what it cost me to convert to diesel I would have been better off keeping the V8.

are the same stud pattern but need a spacer on front to clear the steering joints. At 10.5 x 20 this brings in the much greater range of commercial truck tyres without raising the body height too much.

Using a 101 in the desert A 101 is very much of the crude Series III era, but with even greater attention to **operator discomfort**. The driving position is cramped, upright and truck-like with noise from the adjacent V8 or whatever's put on there instead. The brakes are nothing special and with no power steering, even with radials, slow speed manoeuvring is hard work. The flapping tarp of a GS can get irritating but, if new, should be waterproof though is obviously not dustproof or secure.

Faults particular to 101s are few, the best known being the acute angle of the front prop shaft, causing premature wear on the universal joints, but that's hardly drastic. The position of the air filter intake inside the front wheel arch came last in the Golden Jerrican Awards for three years running, but on left-hand drive models a hose can easily be extended up to hang off the 'roll bar' – itself another design flaw – or via the battery box on a right-hand drive version (see previous page).

These gripes apart, **fuel consumption** with the standard V8 is the biggest drawback; 5kpl will be normal with a staggering 3kpl in dunes. Diesel conversions are popular but need to be thoroughly worked out with attention to gearing, engine cooling, engine mounts and access and the almost insurmountable challenge: noise. Ear plugs are the cheapest solution. A diesel 101

Small campers. **Left:** an Iveco Daily 4x4 with a camper body that's high enough to stand in – more than can be done in a standard-bodied 101 for example.
Right: Sand-blasted VW camper shells are common in the Sahara – they were once popular and despite great ground clearance the old air-cooled rear-engined models were a bit of a liability. This subsequent watercooled Synchro T3 model from the late 1980s features permanent 4WD and all the advantages of a VW, namely normal driving characteristics. A few T3s were made with 16" wheels with suspension and gearing to match and even diff locks. The lowest gear is a very low crawler gear – a nifty alternative to the complexity of a Low Range transfer box. Without a pop-top roof a VW is low but it doesn't need a ladder to get into either.

costs around £6000/€9000, the price of a good Land Rover or Toyota, so you have to be a real 101 fan to spend this much.

In the Sahara, not having to worry about scraping bumpers is a relief and sitting over the front wheels you can't ask for a better view. Ground clearance is rarely a problem and the big tyres aid the suspension and spread the load well. However, a 101 is best used for its intended purpose: **load-carrying** rather than touring. Carrying the excess gear for a small group of 4WDs or a bike tour sees a GS in its element. It's worth noting that for ideal weight distribution and traction placing heavy items further back, the opposite of a normal 4WD, works best.

Pinzgauer

Now built in the UK by Automotive Technik, **Pinzgauers** were an early 1970s' development of the agile Haflinger and are better compared to Unimogs. All those 101s pensioned off by NATO have now been replaced by Pinzgauers. Like all short or narrow but high vehicles, Pinzgauers are known for their instability in careless hands but are admired for their mouth-watering **specifications**: portal axles, independent coil-suspension, auto gearbox and diff locks at every turn, all hanging off a tubular chassis which houses the transmission.

Alas, they used to be saddled with an uninspiring 90hp, 2.5 air-cooled petrol **engine** which will only do around 4kpl on the six-wheeler and 4.6kpl on the 4x4. The old factory quoted 5.5kpl and thereafter a 'litres per hour' figure off-road that you probably would not want to calculate.

Like 101s, Pinzgauers come with a full-length tarp or a hardtop body, more streamlined than 101 versions and with back as well as side doors. All the petrol-engined 710 or 712 series had 24v electrics. From 1985 a smoother six-cylinder water-cooled VW 2.4 turbo diesel was introduced, making 108hp, but these Pinzgauers, distinguished by the more prominent nose, remain astronomically expensive and are not that much more fuel-efficient. The latest Pinzgauers use a five-cylinder 2.5 VW turbo diesel making around 135hp in the 714 4x4 model or the longer 718 6x6, and top speed is a reasonable 110kph, making getting to the Sahara tolerable.

New generation Pinzgauers on tour. Better for load carrying than living in.
© automotive-technik.com

On a Pinzgauer full **articulation** is limited unless fully laden, but unlike a 101, axle diff locks ensure that traction is not lost when a wheel lifts. Theoretically the six-wheeler, which is rated to carry nearly 2000kg, may have a worse power-to-weight ratio but will spread that weight over another pair of wheels. It

Pinzgauer 4x4 – a refined 101 but diesels are rare, expensive and noisy.

Old Magirus truck in Djanet, probably an air-cooled multi-fuel V8 as used locally. Note how on all these trucks the cab is separate from the body – an essential feature to allow chassis flex without breaking the body or mounts. You can still have a cab-to-body join portal but it must be articulated, like the rubber concertinas linking train carriages.

A Unimog-based camper conversion – at least £100,000-worth second-hand and giving an impression of invulnerability.
© www.terracross.com

A MAN-based motorhome is around £85,000 new. It may not have the cachet or technical flair of a Unimog but will do the job in the Sahara where a Mog's radical suspension articulation is not so critical.
© www.terracross.com

may sound ideal for sand but on dune crests the length, and high centre of gravity, will be quite a handful. Overall, if you're determined to take a 'Pinny' to the desert, the four-wheeled version in its purchase-affordable old petrol format is the best choice for normal budgets.

Unimogs and larger trucks

Widely considered the ultimate all-terrain utility vehicle, **Unimogs** are used by armed forces, forestry agencies and most commonly by local authorities the world over. Nothing else comes close for people who need a versatile working vehicle for a variety of applications and where cost is not a drawback.

The guys at Mercedes seemed to have thought of everything when they designed the Unimog in the 1940s: diff locks on each axle; a channel chassis designed to flex and body mounts to cope with this; coil-sprung suspension; portal axles offering huge ground clearance and reduced torque loads; oil-bath air filter; 6–8 gears plus Low Range. But the agricultural-style, three-point linkage and front and rear PTOs belie the fact that for most users a Unimog is a nippy tractor rather than a slow 4WD truck.

These days owned by Daimler Chrysler, it is for these more mundane service applications that most machines are sold, rather than leading an expedition into the unknown. The very latest U400s look more like roadsweepers on steroids rather than all-terrain support vehicles.

So, the ultimate off-road vehicle must be the ideal transportation for the Sahara, an environment which documentary voice-overs commonly remind us has 'the harshest terrain on Earth'? Not really. The Sahara is generally flat and when it isn't, no vehicle no matter how capable can get through at a pace much faster than a hobbled camel. The prime difficulty for vehicles in the

Sahara is soft sand and dunes, something that a Unimog manages no better than any other vehicle with appropriate tyres at the right pressures, although it may be able to carry a bigger payload.

In fact the high centre of gravity exacerbated by fitting a camper body on the back and allied with a short wheelbase can make Unimogs unstable in dunes – and when a vehicle like this gets stuck *a lot* of digging is involved. Another aspect commonly overlooked is the **low gearing**. Designed for crawling over rough terrain or towing huge loads means Mogs are flat out at under 90kph while **fuel consumption** will never exceed 5kpl. Add to that the noise of an engine by your side and again you need good reasons for choosing a Unimog.

If you're sure they are for you the square-cabbed **U-series** from the 1970s onward are the ones to go for, and the longer machines in particular with a wheelbase of 3.25m. They are suffixed with either a -50 (eg: 1250) or an 'L'. Designation numbers also correspond broadly to horsepower so if you drop a zero a U1300L (a 5.7 litre, six-cylinder) gives you 130hp and a U1700L (same engine but with a turbo) churns out 170hp. If considering fitting a camper body on the back, 130hp is a minimum figure to be looking at.

Unimogs are in reality too specialised for long-range desert touring and the camper body quickly compromises their famed agility on tricky pistes. A Unimog converted into a motorhome is as close as you can get to a genuine go-anywhere campervan, but at considerable cost.

Less radical and marginally less hyper-expensive as a professional conversion are 2000-series based **MAN trucks** – ordinary commercial lorries but fitted with AWD transmission and tougher suspension; but we're still talking the price of a small house. For a fraction of that cost a similar but older and cruder 4WD truck based on an ex-army DAF or Bedford or a civilian Magirus (as pictured on p.100) could be outfitted from a few thousand pounds.

Vehicle preparation and equipment

For anything more than a two-week hop to Morocco or Tunisia, your vehicle will require modifications and additional equipment that will almost certainly cost as much as, if not more than, the actual desert trip. Broadly speaking this can be divided into **improving** some of your car's current systems (most notably tyres and suspension) and **adding equipment** to make it a more effective and comfortable long-range desert tourer.

The domestic 4WD after-market scene is dominated by flashy accessories many of which are of no use whatsoever in the desert (or indeed anywhere else), while the European overland outfitters sell some amazingly expensive products that you can easily make yourself. It's possible to spend a fortune making your vehicle look like a post-apocalyptic assault vehicle, but this chapter and the next aim to help you spend your money on the **right things** while suggesting home-made alternatives.

The single biggest mistake first-timers make is over-equipping and/or overloading their vehicle.

Overloading – the single biggest mistake nearly everyone makes on their first overland trip. This Toyota carried a ton, much of it high up. The vehicle eventually rolled, and had to be cut down into a convertible for the rest of the trip.

GENERAL VEHICLE CHECK

A common anxiety among adventuresome first timers is the assumption that only expert **mechanics** would dare venture into the Sahara in a car. While it helps to have an aptitude and sympathy for mechanical things (most easily learned the hard way by years of owning old bangers!), you don't have to know how to strip an engine and put it together again. I certainly wouldn't have a clue. Out in the desert a logical approach to fault diagnosis and sometimes a lateral, improvisational approach to solutions works fine. Rather than mechanical skills, **long-time ownership and knowledge** of your vehicle will give you confidence, or at least a familiarity with its ability, especially if it's more than a few years old and has had several owners.

When checking over your vehicle, focus your efforts on what counts: the basics of **engine, transmission** and **suspension**. Make sure these three things are in good order before you start burning through cubic dollars on extra equipment. At the very least the vehicle should be serviced well in advance of your departure with **fresh oil, coolant and air-, oil- and fuel filters**. Doing this yourself is a minimum amount of involvement. Fit new **consumable items** like tyres, fan belts, ignition components for petrol engines, radiator hoses, batteries and even an alternator, exhaust system and radiator, but keep any items that are used but still serviceable to take with you as spares or to use later. Taking new stuff out there is not the same: there's nothing worse than discovering that your spare fan belt is the wrong size when you need it most. I once spiked a stubborn oil filter to remove it during an oil change in the dunes only to find that the identical-looking replacement had a different interior thread. **Fit new stuff now and take used spares**, where appropriate.

Engine

In just about all cases the original engine in standard tune is best. Land Rovers in particular are often fitted with alternative engines to improve or replace worn-out originals. Such experimentation is best left for home use. In the Sahara, problems with overheating, broken engine mounts or over-stressed transmissions are common with such adaptations.

Be under no illusion: your engine will at times be working hard in hot, demanding conditions while carrying a heavy load, something it's probably never done before. Any serious leaks, noises, poor performance or intermittent problems must be fixed before you leave home.

WHAT YOU NEED ...

These items are essential for an extended trip into the Sahara south of Morocco or central Tunisia and are discussed in detail below:
● Suspension and shocks capable of carrying the maximum load over rough terrain.
● Five good tyres, better still six.
● Tyre-repairing equipment.
● Recovery equipment.

● Additional fuel capacity and water containers (see next chapter).
● A user-friendly packing system (see next chapter).
● Tool kit and workshop manual.
Camping gear is essential too, of course, and is covered in its own chapter starting on p.151. Navigation and maps start on p.316.

... AND WHAT YOU DON'T NEED

The following items may appear essential for desert-touring but in practice they're unused by experienced drivers while some have no practical use in the Sahara at all.
● Bull bar and light guards. These are essential in countries where livestock emerging from foliage is a real menace but in the Sahara visibility is good, night-time driving is inadvisable, and the danger from wandering camels is minimal. Light guards are probably more useful for urban driving than in the desert.
● Raised air-intakes and cyclone pre-cleaners. The sound principle behind raised air-intakes (RAI) is that they draw cleaner, cooler air higher up. In practice, if your vehicle's standard air-intake system is correctly designed, an RAI actually makes little difference. A 'snorkel' is the same thing, but designed for deep wading without sucking water into the engine; useful in temperate and equatorial regions, but not in the Sahara.
● Full expedition roof rack. Two or three custom-made roof bars are sufficient to carry bulky or seldom-used items. See page 144.
● Winch. There's nothing to winch off in the desert except maybe a buried tyre (which takes ages) or other vehicles (which can tow you out with a KERR).
● Car compass. Setting a magnetic compass to read accurately inside a vehicle can be impossible or give variable results. Your GPS's compass feature is more accurate and reliable (see p.319).

Cooling systems

In the dunes smaller 2.5-litre engines will be working flat out at slow speeds, a recipe for overheating. In these conditions you'd expect the temperature gauge needle to get close to the red zone, especially crawling through soft sand in a tailwind, but likewise it should drop readily as the airflow increases. Because it's hard to know just how your loaded vehicle will respond in the heat of the desert, play it safe and fit a new or reconditioned **radiator** (especially if it's ever been repaired), along with new hoses and belts.

Old desert lore advises only fresh water should be used in the radiator in case of a survival situation (antifreeze being poisonous). It sounds prudent but overall you're much better off with the slightly higher boiling point and corrosion inhibiting properties of antifreeze. You can always distil the coolant if things get that desperate (see p.359).

Big, four-litre Toyotas are fitted with huge radiators and powerful fans that rarely overheat. Smaller or older engines

The remains of an engine fan stripped by a pebble thrown up while crossing a oued. A back-up electric fan saved the day.

must work harder and may benefit from a 'tropical' fan with extra blades (available for Land Rovers). Alternatively, on any vehicle consider supplementary (as opposed to replacement) **electric fans** such as those made in the UK by Kenlowe or Pacet. Not built for off-road, frames can work loose on corrugations and spin into the radiator so make sure the mounting is solid and that the retaining bolts are secured with locking compounds – and check it regularly.

Running **thicker engine oil** is another way of keeping things cool. In Europe 15W-40 has become the norm but 'old-fashioned' 20W-50 increases your cooling range. If things get desperate straight 40W can be used but let the engine warm up gently on cold mornings.

Airborne dust demands regular air-filter maintenance, especially when driving in convoy.

Air filters

As mentioned earlier, raised air-intakes or snorkels have little cleaning effect on most vehicles but people like them because they look good – I've even heard of people asking for twin snorkels! Certainly clean air is vital for engine longevity and the air filter, airbox and attachment hoses should be kept in top condition, inspected and cleaned, sometimes daily in very windy conditions.

Work out where your particular 4WD draws its air. Series Land Rovers and some Toyotas suck the air through an oil bath, an ideal system for the desert, though the easily-neglected oil should be checked and changed regularly. Sixty-series Toyotas draw it inside the front of the front wing, ahead of any vehicle-borne dust, while early Discoverys draw it further back through the gap between the front panel and the door, not so good as dust from the front wheel gets sucked right in.

Air filters come in the standard **corrugated paper element** which can be cleaned from the inside out by tapping or with compressed air but will eventually need replacing. Because you're probably only visiting the Sahara rather than emigrating there, a new standard paper element will probably be sufficient for a month's trip; use your air compressor to blow it clean after a particularly dusty run and maybe take a spare if you expect to be driving in convoy where the rear vehicles tend to

Washable foam filters outlast conventional paper items but must be cleaned regularly. Carry a spare outer sleeve.

inhale more dust. **Greasing** the inside surfaces of an airbox is a useful dirt-biking practice which catches still more dust and sand before it clogs the filter.

Alternatives to bulky spare filters include similar-looking fabric **water-washable items** for Toyotas and aftermarket **oiled foam filters** similar to dirt-bike filters. These must be **cleaned and re-oiled regularly** if they are to work as well as a new paper filter, but last much longer than a standard paper filter. They feature an outer sleeve which catches

Note how grease has captured the sand and other particles on this half-cleaned airbox. It means the air filter stays cleaner longer.

just about all the dust before it gets to the inner core. By taking a spare, pre-oiled sleeve, you can replace the dirty one with a fresh item to clean when you get a chance. Use the correct extra-sticky **filter oil** (available in aerosols) which doesn't seep down to the base of the filter like engine oil does. Clean the sleeve in petrol (diesel will do), let it dry, oil it, and squeeze out the excess. It's a messy job so it might be worth wearing dishwashing gloves or squeezing the filtering element inside a plastic bag. Foam filters aren't generally available in dust-free Europe but can be bought inexpensively in Australia and the US; try Uni Filter or Finer Filter. Do not use the wire and gauze models of K&N filters that attach directly to the carburettor of some engines so eliminating the airbox. They are far from suitable for dusty overland use and will guarantee premature engine wear before you even get home.

Cyclone pre-cleaners

A cyclone pre-cleaner is an induction chamber that fits onto the end of a raised air-intake pipe or near the standard air-filter intake (if there's room). Angled fins around the induction mouth cause the air to swirl into a spin as it gets sucked in. Heavy grains of sand are thrown out through slits by centrifugal force or drop down and collect in a pre-cleaner's bowl which can be cleaned out. Cyclones are primarily designed for use with slow-moving quarry vehicles or static engines (generators etc) working in very dusty environments. Much of the cyclone effect is lost at higher speeds and, like raised air-intakes, they can take some power from the vehicle at higher revs. All they really do is save your air filter getting dirty too quickly though in a true sand- or dust-storm (when it's safer to stop anyway) they'd be unlikely to cope. Nevertheless, they do look the business!

A cyclone pre-cleaner with a bowl to catch heavier grains and a home-made flexible pipe. A rigid pipe would cause less turbulence.

Fuel filters

African fuel has an exaggerated reputation for dirt to which diesel engines are particularly sensitive, but filling from a garage's fuel pump is usually reliable. If filling from oil drums, as you must at Dirkou or in northern Chad, any water or sludge present will be at the bottom of the drum so consider leaving the last few litres in there.

Diesel engines should have at least two filters between the tank and the injector pump and all should be checked and possibly cleaned or renewed before departure. On good 4WDs a drainable **sedimentor** or **water trap** is usually located inside a chassis rail or at the back of the engine compartment and can get overlooked until completely blocked or rusted up. Unscrewing the drain plug or unclipping the glass bowl allows you to tap off any watery sludge that may have been brought up from the tank.

The **disposable cartridge** fuel filter near the injector pump in the engine bay is less easy to miss and is usually good for 20,000km, depending on your car. Set off with a new cartridge and take a spare. Replacing a filter cartridge is a good way of learning how to bleed air from a diesel system – something you'll need to do should you run out of fuel. **Running out of fuel** is also a good way of clogging up these filters and the sedimentors before them, as the engine sucks in all the crap in the bottom of your fuel tank. This is when you will need that spare cartridge. Try not to run the tank to the limit.

Carburetted **petrol engines** are less sensitive to dirty fuel and carburettors are easily dismantled and cleaned – something that should be part of a pre-departure service. An **inline fuel filter** is worth fitting into the fuel line between the fuel tank and the carb where it can be easily monitored and cleaned if necessary.

On all older vehicles, or those which have done a lot of travel in dusty areas, draining and **flushing the fuel tank** won't do any harm apart from being a thoroughly messy job. As mentioned above it's when you run low on fuel that sludge or rust from the base of the tank can be sucked up into the fuel lines and cause problems.

Transmission

Your transmission will be put to the test in the Sahara, much more than your engine. If there's any undue slack in the drive or if gears jump out or are hard to engage (including low-range selection), you can be sure that desert driving won't make it any better. **Prop shafts** in particular have a hard time on rough tracks. Check there is grease in the telescoping section, fit a gaiter to keep out dust and also check the four **universal joints** (UJs). They frequently wear unnoticed or lose retaining bolts so should be regreased or better still replaced on an older vehicle, taking the old ones as spares.

Land Rovers were once notorious for **half-shaft** (axle) failures on the rear axle and are still known for their short-lived gearboxes. Salisbury axles fitted on Series IIIs were a solution, but half-shafts are still thinner than on other 4WDs. A factory spokesman once explained this as a built-in weak point to protect less-accessible components from damage (rear shaft shafts can be replaced without even removing the wheel). Half-shaft (though not gearbox) failures with 110s and Defenders are rarer. Gentle driving and not overloading will avoid all breakages but on an old Rover it may be worth pulling out the back half-shafts and inspecting the condition of the splines which slip into the diff, the point where they tend to snap. **Reconditioned gearboxes** themselves are not expensive in the UK and may be the easiest way of ensuring peace of mind with a Land Rover.

Naturally the **clutch** will also be working hard, especially in dunes or soft sand where some slippage will occur under extreme loads. One way of testing your clutch is to drive the vehicle right up against a solid wall, put it in top gear, rev to 2000rpm and let out the clutch. If the clutch is worn it will slip; if it's OK the vehicle will stall immediately. Another way is to drop the revs uphill in third, and then accelerate hard to try and induce slippage. Most manufacturers offer heavy-duty clutches, always worth considering even if stiffer clutch pedal actuation is one of the results.

Undercarriage protection

Have a good look under your car and try to visualise where rock damage might occur. It's impractical to completely protect the many underside components but at the very least the gearboxes and fuel tank should have thick steel plates protecting their casings. You never need these items until you accidentally hit a rock at which point they make the difference between minor damage and a ruined transmission. I'd sooner forget the night when I drove over a TV-sized boulder near Ghat in Libya. The front prop, one gearbox bash plate and a rear shock were all destroyed, but when I actually inspected the boulder next morning I was amazed the car was driving at all. The boulder was taken out into the desert and shot.

In standard form some 4WDs are badly designed or deficient in this area and coil-sprung Land Rovers have particularly **exposed steering arms** in front of the axle, a vulnerable point on all 4WDs. Land Rover offer an accessory bar that is better than nothing, and after-market manufacturers provide a range of far superior protection plates from bumper to bumper. Only the steering arms and exposed parts of the engine and transmission need protection; diff guards are not necessary in the Sahara unless you plan to be racing over rocks.

Being almost as low as the diff, **rear shock-absorbers** and their lower mounts are also vulnerable, especially on 60-series Land Cruisers. There's not much you can do here but drive with care through rocks, or avoid them. Coil-sprung Land Rovers wisely have the shock positioned behind the coil. The lower retaining bolt on poorly positioned shocks can also get a bashing and may be worth protecting from damage – fabricating a protection plate is an easy job.

Rear **fuel tanks** are also vulnerable, a good reason to fit heavy-duty rear springs. Toyota got round this problem by putting the spare wheel below the tank, but other tanks right at the back of the car could get damaged. **Sill protection bars** are not necessary unless you're worried about damaging your Land

A full-length bash plate protects the underneath of this Mercedes sedan. © AlliSport

Rover's bendy alloy sills. Choose ones which don't reduce ground clearance while being strong enough to work with a high-lift jack.

The **exhaust system** is difficult to protect because it needs good air flow around it. Ageing exhaust systems regularly fall victim to corrugations, so if yours has seen better days, install a completely new system (ideally not a cheap pattern copy from a quick-fit outlet), along with new rubber mounts.

Suspension

Four-wheel drive manufacturers often give impressive GVW (gross vehicle weight) figures: Land Rover Defenders, for example, are rated at 1000kg. What they don't always tell you is that without **uprated suspension** that weight will leave the vehicle with its front wheels pawing the air. Most vehicles will need uprated suspension to cope with an expeditionary payload, and the best way to determine this is to load your vehicle and see how far it sags. The correct amount of extra suspension is that which makes the car look just over the normal level when fully loaded.

As with tyres, suspension is either a compromise or a dedicated desert modification, and you should be aware that what works well in either leaf or coil format fully loaded in the Sahara will give an unsupple, bouncy ride without the payload – something to consider if you want to enjoy comfortable rides at home after your trip. However, soft suspension in the desert means continuous bottoming out against the axle rubbers (make sure these are still there and in good condition) and having to keep slowing down for mild bumps. It's harder on the tyres too which get compressed when the car bottoms out and of course it reduces your ground clearance which leads to other problems.

One gadget I've seen used is **air helper springs** – a tough air bag that can be hand pumped up to modest pressures (up to 3 bar or 43 psi) depending on your payload. They would seem the answer to the rough ride of an unloaded vehicle on heavy-duty suspension.

I've found that a good brand of after-market suspension for all types of 4WDs, leaf and coil sprung, is Old Man Emu (OME), Australian-made. OME springs come in three strengths: for the Sahara, 'medium' should do the job. Note, however, that their shocks have a less good reputation, depending on who you ask.

For **coil-sprung** Land Rovers, Range Rovers etc, the usual trick is to fit rear springs on the front axle and heavy-duty springs on the rear, or springs from a 130" (a simple task compared to replacing rusty old leaves). This raises the height back to normal levels when fully loaded which is ideal. Resist the urge to go over the top with raising suspension; a vehicle's stability is greatly compromised by just an extra couple of inch-

Rear air helper/assister spring on a 109 using parabolic springs. For various other reasons this vehicle was extremely unstable, one bag got pushed off and the other punctured, but others have reported air bags a good solution to adjustable suspension and varied payloads. They fit better inside coil-sprung vehicles.

es above standard. Use the 'looks normal and level when fully loaded' rule as a guide. Don't forget that fitting high-walled 16-inch tyres will also give some extra height.

Old-fashioned semi-elliptic **leaf springs** can be uprated, but are more expensive to replace than easily-engineered coils. Adding a leaf or two to the pack and re-bending the current set (not such a bodge as it sounds) are some things you can do with leaves. A good leaf-spring manufacturer will be theoretically able to dial in exactly how much lift you want or the desired height when loaded.

Secondary semi-elliptic leaf springs on any 4WD have a habit of cracking in African conditions but this is no drama compared to a main leaf breakage and is easily fixed by a bush mechanic. Some consider that the lateral rigidity of leaf springs makes them superior load-carriers: the HZJ 78 retains leaves on the back and my experience is that, contrary to the impression that they are crude 'cart springs', a good leaf set up is as good as a coil system and, in semi-elliptic forms, should not get through dampers so often.

Parabolic leaf springs are commonly found on commercial vehicles and have come on the 4WD market in recent years. Here, their real success has been in replacing the spine-rattling OE spring configuration of Series III Land Rovers into something that actually works. Unlike semi-elliptic springs, parabolics use just two or three leaves which touch only at the axle and at either end, and whose thickness tapers from the axle outwards at a 'parabolic' rate (ie at a rate which relates to the square function of the length). In the ideal world a single parabolic leaf will work but for overland applications (and perhaps because of people's reluctance to trust a seemingly skinny single leaf spring) two or three leaves are fitted. Because they do not rub against each other they lose the damping effect of the inter-leaf friction of semi-elliptics so **heavier-duty shock absorbers** must be matched with the new springs.

My own experience with *prototype* parabolics on my 61 was not so good – the two-leaved rears bottomed even before I left home and I swapped back to OMEs in the desert. Later on that trip the two-leaved fronts both snapped coming off a small dune ramp at an angle. It does support the impression that less metal, however cleverly designed, cannot absorb an (admittedly unusually angled) impact as well as a pack of five or six semi-elliptics. Then again, I've since heard from the next tester with the same vehicle that his parabolics spring worked fine in the Sahara with a full load.

Bushes and shocks

If you're upgrading your suspension take the opportunity to fit new bushes. Worn rubber bushes give vague steering and clunky suspension and transmission, especially on the radius arms which hold coil-sprung axles in place. **Polybushes** take longer to wear out and come in a variety of densities but aren't necessarily better. They may take ages to wear but they will split and because they are firmer they can pass on the wear to other metallic components like bolts and mounts. We once had a Discovery snap a rear radius arm on red polybushes. It was an early model (later radius arms were thicker) and we'd just been up and down the Tin Teratimt Pass to Assekrem which tested all our suspension over the limit, but the feeling was that the unflexible polybush exacerbated the failure. There's nothing wrong with genuine rubber bushes other than that they need to be replaced more often and they don't come in nice colours. While they last they actually absorb shocks better and a new set is typically half the price of polybushes.

As mentioned above, **shock absorbers**, more correctly described as dampers, are vulnerable to damage on some leaf-sprung vehicles. Heavy-duty items which won't blow apart over pounding corrugations are the way to go, on the rear at the very least. There's no need to buy a trick set of dial-controlled racing dampers whose attributes you're unlikely to appreciate, just a known brand. **Take old shocks** as spares; problems are common and even new ones can break, bend, seize, leak or get inadvertently crushed by rocks. A car is driveable with a missing damper but a spare front and rear unit take little space and can be sold on at the end of the trip.

Oil or gas shocks? The worst sort of terrain shocks have to endure is a washboard or corrugated track when shocks are being pumped up and down several times a second. Naturally this creates high temperatures which can lead to premature wear or seizure. Oil may seem a natural damping medium but it has gone the way of cross-ply tyres. Gas, usually in a sealed bladder to prevent leakage, can damp as well while creating less heat. Gas shocks still use an oil or some kind of fluid, but they run cooler and last longer.

Minimising the 'greenhouse effect'

Despite the many benefits of driving station wagons in the Sahara, their acres of window glass is not one of them, creating an unwanted 'greenhouse effect' inside the car. All-round vision is not vital on the piste and rear-view mirrors are adequate for keeping other vehicles in sight so **blanked-out windows** keep your vehicle and its contents much cooler. At the very least the fixed rear-side windows are worth blocking as are those on the rear doors or tailgate.

Professional stick-on **tinting** looks good but is expensive and doing it yourself can get messy if done badly (trapped air bubbles in the heat). **Painting the windows** with a water-soluble paint like whitewash, or cutting cardboard to fit are the simplest solutions. If colour co-ordination is important, graphic-arts shops sell mounting card in various shades up to A1 size which can be cut to shape and stuck on with duct tape. Keeping a piece of card taped to the upper tailgate window is tricky when it's raised in the horizontal position (but very useful as a sunshade when cooking on the lower tailgate). An all-round alternative requiring a bit more work is **curtains** which can be open or closed and add a homely feel if you're planning on sleeping in the vehicle. Whatever you choose, lighter colours are more reflective so transmit less heat.

Cool cabin

On any type of vehicle the cabin will also get hot, from the engine as well as from the sun, especially when you're driving south in the Sahara. The aerodynamically swept-back windscreens of modern station wagons like Discoverys allow a lot of sunlight to penetrate the vehicle (with their near vertical glass angles and forward controls traditional Land Rovers are superior in this respect).

There's not much you can do here: a stick-on **sun visor** across the top 10cm of the windscreen helps a bit while a fixed exterior visor tends to be a noisy wind trap. Smooth black plastic **dashboards** are especially prone to cooking in the sun, wafting unwanted heat over the occupants. Laying or pinning a towel or piece of carpet across this area greatly helps reduce heat glare though properly moulded carpets are available for many Toyotas (but not in the UK).

You don't have to drive in the Sahara to know that the inside of a car can easily reach 40°C when left standing in the sun on a hot day. Getting into a car like this can be very uncomfortable (powerful fans and air-con are a boon here). **Shading the windscreen**, from inside or out, allows you to park into the sun and so present a totally sun-proof surface. I've used a roll-down awning attached to the roof rack's leading edge, held in place with velcro and tucking under the wipers when in use. Thin bits of dowelling are sewn into the top and bottom edges to stop flapping. Unrolled in a couple of seconds and otherwise

A roll-down sunshade helps keep the cabin cool while parked up.

out of the way, it keeps the cabin much cooler during daytime breaks. If you're going to be out of the car for a while, anticipate the moving sun by hanging a towel from the sunny-side door top and then slam it. If you're running a fridge, remember that all these strategies will help it work much more efficiently (and so reduce the battery load) by keeping the interior cooler.

TYRES

If there is one thing that prospective overlanders fret about more than anything else, it's tyres. The thought of having your trip or all-terrain efficiency ruined by choosing the wrong tyres is galling. The good news is that in the desert, tyre choice is not as critical as it can be in other off-road environments, particularly mud. But because of your payload and the hammering tyres get, you will need good-quality ones. Tyre repairs are discussed on p.201.

Ordinary drivers distinguish tyres by their **tread pattern**, these days as much a factor of marketing as function. What matters much more in the Sahara, is the integrity of the tyre design and the **quality** of the construction – something that is hard to distinguish and is why people choose cheaper brands which look just as 'black and round' as more expensive tyres. Because most piste surfaces are predominantly gravel or firm sand, in the Sahara the finer points of tread design are not that crucial; you'll slide on loose gravel whatever the tyre type. However, in soft sand and dunes some tread patterns and sidewall constructions do make a difference. Soft dry sand is just a pile of grains with negligible traction so gently **compressing** rather than clawing is the most effective way to maintain traction.

Pure sand tyres have no tread whatsoever, creating severe limitations in just about all other driving conditions so are not recommended unless you plan on staying in the ergs. In the real world of Saharan overlanding you may have to drive across rainy Europe as well as through sand seas so a dense, 'closed-block' road-based tyre tread works best. You may be off-roading but an aggressive-tread patterned mud tyre with sharp shoulder blocks is designed to claw at the ground in search of grip. In sand it won't find any and will merely dig itself in while on the road it will whine, wear fast and offer poor grip in the wet.

In general choose AT (all terrain) designated tyres from quality manufacturers over MT (mud terrain) or M&S (mud and snow) designated tyres (205 x 16 M&S tyres are particularly hopeless in sand). Providing they're a good brand in good shape, your current tyres might well be adequate for the Sahara and will certainly do in rocky Morocco where a desert/sand tyre like a Michelin XS is unnecessary.

As with all things, you get what you pay for. An expensive Michelin (who also own BF Goodrich) may last twice as long as other brands and in the desert the better-known brands and not their cheap and cheerful equivalents are recommended. There are no absolute rules; much depends on rim types, driving style, experience and engine power characteristics. Desert drivers will say their tyres are the best if they've not encountered too many problems.

Left: M&S remoulds – unsuitable in sand, especially on smaller engined 4WDs.

One thing is certain though: drive a heavy car fast on any tyre in an under-inflated condition and you risk **overheating** which damages the structure of the tyre and will cause problems down the track.

This is particularly important as new tyres are hard to find in the Sahara and most second-hand tyres you get out there are not fit to hang off a jetty. Suitable tyres also give fewer punctures and cope better with the low pressures needed for **flotation** in sand.

One trans-African overlander I met had endless problems with BF Goodrich ATs fitted to a Troop Carrier, but in all other respects a BFG AT is a good tyre. I don't regret the day I dumped my Yokohama 'XSs' with their continual punctures (rusty split rims did not help) and fitted tubeless BFG ATs. Many travellers on longer trips use the rugged **Michelin XZY**, a plain-treaded truck tyre that won't turn any heads but lasts for years. The only drawback with XZYs is that, being 12-ply rated, they don't spread well for soft sand driving and are very stiff when it comes to changing. They're also said not to grip well on wet roads compared to a tyre with a more sophisticated tread.

Remember that along with suspension, your tyres will carry the brunt of heavy-shock loads over rough terrain for weeks on end, not just weekends away. Don't take chances with tyres just because they'll wear out anyway. Save money elsewhere but replace old or inappropriate tyres with the best you can afford.

MICHELIN XS AND COPIES

Known throughout the Sahara for nearly forty years, Michelin's XS 'sand' tyre used to be as much a feature of day-to-day desert motoring as jerricans and PSP. Copied by just about every other major manufacturer, the 7.50x16 XS and its imitators, chiefly Bridgestone's V-Steel Jamal ('VSJ') and Yokohama's B402, are commonly used by locals as it's all that's available.

Many overlanders think if you're going to the Sahara you must get Michelin XSs, often inaccurately described as 'sand tyres' (they're an all-round desert tyre). But the fact is the era of Michelin XS is over. Tyres and vehicles have come a long way since the late 1960s when every trick in the book was needed to keep a 60hp Land Rover moving.

These days desert-ready 4WDs put out at least twice as much power and have better suspension. Tyre technology has also moved on so that the thin but vulnerable XS sidewalls that were necessary to spread a long footprint at low pressure are no longer essential (although they work better than a

A 7.50 XS and 9.00 Yokohama. A desert icon but other tyres are better all round.

thick, 12-ply truck tyre)

So you can say goodbye to tarmac whine and wandering, rolling in corners and hopeless grip on wet tarmac, mud and snow, and inner tube punctures (a tubeless version was never made). There are only a couple of factories in the world still making them.

Dimensions

Tyres are measured in two or sometimes three dimensions: inner diameter (corresponding to wheel rim size), **tread width**, and sometimes the aspect ratio. These are sometimes given as a mixture of inches and millimetres which can be confusing. The first two dimensions are self explanatory; a 7.50x16 tyre is nominally seven and a half inches wide and fits a 16-inch rim. Note that it's the **diameter** or height of tyres that makes a difference in sand and not, as many imagine, the width. The reason for this is a popular misconception regarding low tyre pressures: when you deflate a tyre its contact area with the ground *lengthens* rather than broadens. A 7.50x16 achieves a longer footprint than a wide 15-inch tyre at the same pressure and is therefore more effective in soft sand. Seven-fifties may not look very butch, but they work because of the long, caterpillar-track-like contact area achieved by a tall tyre. Despite the appearance of bulging sidewalls, width is barely increased. For the average two ton/110 hp station wagon a tyre of seven and a half inches width is ideal for the piste; anything wider is not necessary.

Where shown, the aspect ratio refers to the height of the tyre sidewall as a percentage of its width. A 235/85R16 tyre (equivalent to a 7.50x16) is approximately 235mm wide while the sidewall height is 85% per cent of that figure (200mm). For the desert you want tyres with a **high aspect ratio** of around 80 because this represents a taller sidewall so corresponds to added ground clearance when firm, and a longer contact area when deflated. High aspect ratio or high profile tyres are undesirable for fast road-driving as they squirm and flex under cornering forces. Your 4WD won't feel so stable on the road with tall

TYRE SIZE AND ITS EFFECT ON DISTANCE READINGS

Some of the tyres recommended here will be taller than the manufacturers' standard fitment so, having a greater circumference, will affect the accuracy of the speedometer as well as the trip counter – the latter being an important factor in the desert. There are more details in the 'Navigation and Maps' chapter on p.319.

tyres (high pressures help) but off-road, and especially at ultra low pressures when the effective height of the tyre is reduced, they will still maintain good ground clearance.

The 'R' refers to **radial** construction which just about all tyres are these days and which also happens to perform better at low pressures as well as being easier to change by hand. Apart from commercial use in very rocky areas or muddy off-road motorsports, **cross-ply** tyres are a thing of the past.

Some tyres also have a **speed rating** designated by letter codes; 'M' equals 130kph (81mph) which is the practical top speed of most desert-bound 4WDs – most tyres you'll buy will be rated higher. Each letter represents an extra 10kph so N = 140kph/87mph, P = 150kph/93mph, Q = 160kph/100mph and so on. This letter can also be matched with a three-figure **numerical load index** which translates to the maximum load the tyre is designed to carry at optimum pressure. A load index of 100 is a good benchmark as it equates to 800kg; each additional digit equals another 25kg, so '101' = 825kg, 102 = 850kg, etc. Four tyres each supporting 800kg equal 3200kg, half a ton more than the heaviest 4WDs popular in the Sahara (unladen), but remember that the rear tyres will at times be under much heavier loads depending on the fuel and water payload.

Tyre height

One problem with reading tyre dimensions at face value is that some tyres of equal nominal size are bigger than others. The **actual height** of a tyre is never printed on the carcass but is something that makes the difference between the tyre fouling the bodywork of your car or not. Functional-bodied off-roaders such as Jeep Wranglers and Defenders have plenty of room in the wheel arches but more sophisticated station wagons such as Discoverys and Pajeros have limited space. Fitting a tall tyre on these sorts of vehicles can be a problem unless you're prepared to fiddle with steering-lock stops and the more radical cutting back of body work. It's worth noting then that Michelin's 7.50x16 XS is 828mm high while Yokohama's equivalent B402 is just **808mm high**, possibly enough to make the difference on your car. Some manufacturers post tyre dimensions on their websites (or will have them on hand) which can be a useful guide to knowing if a tyre will fit your car.

A true sand tyre, little or no tread but not much use in other terrain.

When buying **inner tubes**, again insist on quality, not what happens to be on the shelf in your size. Over-the-counter inner tubes tend to be stocked for their price not quality as most people are not buying tubes for the Sahara. Michelin Airstop or any other well-known extra-thick brand will probably have to be ordered in the UK.

Oversize tyres

Expert Saharan drivers are always looking for ways to improve their car's desert-worthiness, especially in deep sand where all the hard work is done. Taller and wider **9.00x16 tyres**, fitted as standard to Pinzgauers and 101s, can offer a solution – with certain limitations. Though commonly done in the UK (European laws on tyre sizes are much more strictly enforced), fitting bigger tyres cannot be done with impunity. The larger, heavier tyre increases the **strain** on the transmission not designed to turn such a tyre, rather like very heavy boots would protect your feet but tire your legs and hamper your agility. Braking performance can suffer too, as will wear on wheel bearings. They will also **raise gearing** by up to 20 per cent which, with a relatively small engine, puts extra strain on the clutch and diminishes the ability of the low-range gears.

Because all these components will already be under stress in the Sahara, 9-inch tyres are best fitted to big-engined vehicles like some Patrols and Land Cruisers whose tough, truck-like transmission components can handle the extra strain. Though even they have their problems. A friend once had to make a 1000-km round trip from the northern Ténéré to Djanet to get new wheel bearings for someone who was running 900 16s on his Toyota. And at that time the northern Ténéré was not a place to be left alone for long. Fitting 9.00x16s on a Land Rover or older Range Rover will be asking for trouble. The 6-cylinder 1-tonne Land Rover of the early 1970s came with 9.00x16 tyres and, when it ran, regularly snapped half-shafts in expedition situations.

Tubeless tyres

Traditionally it has always been assumed that off-roading at low tyre pressures requires tubed tyres. The sealed air chamber inside the tyre can be run at the very low pressures desirable for soft sand without the perceived risk of sudden air loss. Heat generated by friction between the tube rubbing against the inside of the flexing tyre has always been a limiting factor, which is one reason why XSs and the like are limited to 20kph at absolute minimum pressures. Furthermore, it has been thought that the ease of repairing or fitting new tubes is essential on the piste, when compared to tubeless tyres, but short of an utterly destroyed sidewall, this is not the case.

The range of desirable high-profile road-pattern tyres may be slim, but for example a **235 85 R16 tubeless** has exactly the same dimensions as a 750 x 16 and works just fine in the dunes at one bar while feeling much safer on wet roads. There is also a perceived risk of a tubeless tyre **pulling off the rim** with sudden air loss when cornering hard at very low pressures. This has proved unfounded in my experience, although I've heard of momentary losses of air reducing the pressure a little as the bead gets pulled over – something that is easily fixed by pumping up. Only one person has ever admitted to me that they pulled a tubeless tyre off the rim, and that was when they were really try-

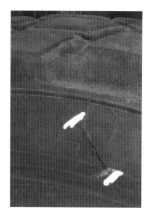

The previous white mark on this tubed tyre shows how this sidewall split is growing day by day. A day or so later the tyre was finished.

ing. More problematical is a dented rim losing the air seal – worse on alloy rims which cannot be bashed back into shape as easily as steel rims. This I have experienced, but in that case the dented rims were the least of the problems – the car was all but destroyed. However, until tubeless tyres really catch on there will be little chance of finding an exact replacement in the Sahara except from another tourist. Therefore, **two complete spare wheels** are better than just an additional spare tyre – a precaution that many desert drivers practice anyway. Note that a part-time 4WD can run different-sized tyres in 2WD if necessary and most locally available 750s exactly match the tubeless size mentioned above.

In recent years experienced desert drivers have been turning to tubeless tyres for the Sahara. The rationale is that at ultra-low pressures when tyres can slip around the rim in high torque/high traction situations, the valve of a tubed tyre would get ripped out (a problem common with motorbikes in the same situation). A tubeless tyre can slip harmlessly around a rim while still maintaining an air seal (some polishing and hardening of the bead may occur, eventually reducing the air seal – roughening and softening the bead is the solution). The risk of the tyre pulling off the rim at low pressures has proved to be minimal with normal driving through sharp bends – and **cooler operating temperatures** without tube friction are an added benefit.

The biggest problem was thought to be with **punctures** or if the tyre does come off the rim. Tubeless rims have a lip to help locate the tyre's bead on the outer edge of the rim. Breaking the bead to change a tyre can be done with the techniques described on p.202, and remounting – getting the bead back over the lip – can be done with the aid of a 16" bicycle tube.

Puncture repairs in the tread of a tubeless tyre are easy – you just find the hole, remove the foreign object and ram a gluey **plug** into the hole with the special tool. Pull the plug half out and snip off the excess; the puncture is fixed. This handy practice is said to be illegal in Europe where tyre removal and **vulcanisation** from the inside is the preferred method that keeps tyre shops in business. Because of this you may have trouble buying the plug and tool kit from a tyre shop (BMW bike shops sell them for their bikes, which also run tubeless tyres). We've repaired heavy Amazon tyres with this method in the desert and got home fine. It's certainly more effective than removing a tyre but it would be worth getting the plug properly repaired once back in Europe. Repairable **sidewall damage** would certainly require vulcanisation where a tubed tyre might be successfully patched on the inside.

Among tourists, using tubeless tyres in the Sahara is becoming the norm even though it's still unknown to conservative locals. Indeed tubeless tyres hold significant advantages and if you are unsure or have a dented rim, fitting a tube will always get you home.

Pumps and compressors

For tyre repairs as well as for altering tyre pressures over varying terrain, some kind of pump is essential and a powerful air compressor is highly recommended in the desert. Besides saving time and effort, it means you're never reluctant to drop pressures (which means fewer boggings) or to re-inflate again – crucial to avoid premature tyre wear and damage.

Manual pumps come in the familiar foot pump cheaply bought from motor accessory shops or tall slim hand pumps. Both take about 300 pumps to gain 1 bar (15 psi). Multiply that by four wheels with two people at 35°C and that's a lot of pumping. Manual pumps are a useful back-up but used alone are barely adequate for Saharan motoring. If you are buying a footpump, get the better brass model not the cheap steel one which will soon pack up in the sand. Use it on a board or sand plate to keep sand out of the mechanism.

Compressors

Your engine generates electricity so it's sensible to use that energy to power an electric compressor. The best compressors for the desert use electric motors to power a small piston engine to pump air. The power drawn by the electric motor and the pumping capacity of the piston (along with the ability to keep cool) determine the efficiency of the compressor. Prices range from £20/€30 to over £400/€600, the more expensive examples quickly pumping large volumes of air irrespective of pressure and without overheating. Note that besides the options described below, it is possible to modify a car's **air-conditioning compressor** to pump air for the tyres. Obviously your air-con will no longer work so it's the sort of modification which suits an older car where the fitted air-con system has packed up and is no longer

Three hundred pumps per tyre at 34°C can undermine morale.

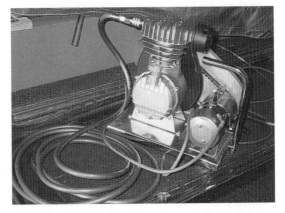

A powerful air compressor, like this one from Grand Erg, is a much under-valued accessory in the desert.

A 2.6 cfm Viair compressor from Matt Savage available in a kit and a 12-metre air line.
© mattsavage.com

worth repairing, or a unit salvaged from a wrecked car with air-con fitted.

Forget all **cheap compressors** from car accessory shops that plug into your cigarette lighter PTO. These cheap units claim to reach an impressive-sounding 200psi (in a bicycle tyre perhaps) but what really counts is how many **cubic feet per minute** (cfm) they can push, especially as pressure builds up. In the real world these units will take at least ten minutes to pump up a 7.50x16 tyre from dune to road pressures and before all four wheels are done will probably have overheated and cut out. These gadgets are not designed for the heavy demands of big tyres and desert driving.

At the next level you have 'recreational 4WD' compressors which wire directly to the battery, not a dashboard PTO. Designed for the off-road market in the US and Australia, expect to pay at least £100/€150 for something that pumps out **at least 1.5–2 cfm**. ARB is well known for use with their diff-locks but along with QuickAir and Viair, ARB also produce bigger, portable units which pump at about 2.1 cfm at low pressures though the rate decreases rapidly as the pressure in the tyre builds up. To avoid flattening the battery **keep the engine running** if re-inflating several tyres.

At the top of the range are what might be called 'expedition' air compressors specially made for, or by, European Saharan vehicle outfitters like Grand Erg or Därrs. Costing up to £400/€600 they're a good idea if you're running large tyres, expect to visit the Sahara regularly, or are supporting a multi-vehicle expedition.

Weighing in around 10kg, they are designed to be portable though they're more convenient permanently mounted out of the way and wired to the battery with a switch. The difference between these very expensive compressors, with oil-cooled barrels the size of moped engines is that, unlike other units, they'll continue to pump around 80–90 per cent of their maximum flow rate at high pressures where an ARB or Viair slows down to 50–60 per cent. A Grand Erg 400VA compressor can comfortably re-inflate a dozen 7.50x16s from 1 to 2 bar before it starts getting hot, taking about two minutes per tyre. The 700VA model pumps 50 per cent more air (91 lpm max) and inflates tyres correspondingly quicker than the 400.

If you're working a compressor hard like this, keep it **out of the sun and in a breeze**, and on all compressors, especially those mounted inside the engine bay, check their air filters (where fitted and accessible) once in a while.

Although I see people using them, an **air reservoir/tank** does not really save much time while taking up more space as well as being a dangerous chamber of compressed air and another thing to leak. Only the more powerful compressors will be quickly capable of filling a useful-sized tank to full pressure, but these are the units that are so efficient you won't need a tank in the first place.

RECOVERY EQUIPMENT

Standard recovery items for desert driving include a **jack, shovel, sand plates** or ladders and a **tow strap** or **rope**. High-lift jacks are well known to all off-roaders and though heavy and awkward things to stow, and dangerous if used carelessly, their ability to lift a two-ton car quickly makes them, or something like them, indispensable in the Sahara. Your car's standard jack, ideally a **hydraulic bottle-jack,** should be retained as a useful back-up and has its uses when you want to fully jack-up the vehicle to make repairs. If your bottle-jack is missing or you have inferior pillar- or scissor-jacks, replace them with at least a 2-ton bottle-jack and make sure that its fully extended length suits your 4WD's higher axles. Unlike high-lifts, bottle-jacks are best placed directly **under the axle**, not on a chassis rail. This way the jack lifts the wheel directly and not the compressed weight on the suspension and then the wheel. It's this placement which makes them awkward to use in the desert and is why high-lift jacks or air bags are more useful. Details on recovery techniques appear on p.181.

High-lift jacks

Designed in 1905 for logging operations and since adapted to 4WD use, two brands are well known in Europe: the original Hi-Lift made in Illinois and the virtually identical Canadian Jackall version. Available in four- and five-foot lengths, the shorter jack is adequate for ordinary 4WDs. Hi-Lifts come in forged and more expensive and stronger cast versions. Again, the forged version will do for an average two-ton 4WD.

The jack works by 'walking' up the jack's stem as you crank the handle. Flick the lever **with the handle in the upright position** and it walks back down the stem again as you crank the handle until the weight is released. It's essential to **read and understand** the instructions which come with these devices – being US-made, the Hi-Lift's handle and booklet are plastered with warning labels.

The **jacking point** must be capable of taking the car's weight; ideally this is the chassis or a flat-bottomed bumper attached directly to the chassis as found on Land Rovers and 'working' Toyotas. Adapters that fit into bumper holes or plates are available to use the jack with Defenders. Before first using the jack look carefully under your bumpers for the best place to take the weight, ideally where the bumper bolts directly onto a heavy chassis rail. Well-placed bolts will prevent the jack sliding sideways; if not it's wise to bolt or weld on some kind of slot so that the jack's foot locates securely, especially on the rear which needs more effort to lift. Sticking marking points on the bumper helps swinging the heavy jack into the right position without scrabbling around making sure it's in place. It's these little details that make using the jack simpler and more secure; when you're worn out from digging out yet

An Australian jack adaptor which enables you to hi-lift directly off a wheel hub on certain vehicles with chunky protruding hubs, instead of having to lift the whole car and *then* the axles when you jack up the body.

High-lift jacks are inexpensive but need strong jacking points and care in use.

again you don't want to have to hope for the best or concentrate on making a secure placement.

In soft sand the jack will sink down before lifting the car so a **jack pad** is needed to spread the weight. Sand plates, a shovel's blade or a spare wheel will do but a 20cm by 30cm block of wood around 4cm thick is better and won't get damaged. Again you'll need to locate the jack's base securely onto the block, to prevent slippage.

Lifting the rear of a fully-loaded car can be difficult; try it at home before finding this out too late. Lifting the front (effectively a shorter pivot), even both wheels, is quite easy. When fitted with a top clamp, a high-lift jack can also be used for crimping or bending (useful for fitting springs), or as a short-distance winch or hoist. For this application chains or cable must be used, not rope. A high-lift jack can also enable swift recovery from sand (see p.182).

Air bag jacks

Air bag jacks are tough vinyl balloons the size of a dustbin which are inflated by the car's exhaust and can easily lift one side of a 4WD. For something like a Discovery an air jack rated at two tons will do the trick; for a heavy Toyota 80-series four tons is a better bet.

Air jacks are a rare sight in the Sahara where conservative drivers stick to traditional techniques and equipment. However, for effortless sand recovery or even righting overturned vehicles, an air jack is ideal, spreading the weight over a large area and requiring no strenuous or dangerous jacking. I've never been a fan of heavy, cumbersome and dodgy high lifts and was happy to replace mine with an air bag which is lighter and requires less effort. The number of occasions when you actually need to jack the car right up are fewer than you think, especially as your desert driving techniques improve. The bag needs less than 1 bar (10psi) to lift a car so no engine damage can occur, although the **exhaust system** must be sound if it's to survive as well as fill the bag efficiently. On my 61 it started blowing through a braided section between the engine downpipe and the exhaust.

One thing you must give consideration to is where to **position the jack**:

HIGH-LIFT JACK SAFETY

Never work under a vehicle that's being lifted or is resting on a jack, high-lift or otherwise. Use a jerrican, rock or spare wheel to take the vehicle's weight and chock the wheels unless they're well embedded in the sand during a recovery. On soft ground jacks can begin to lean and then suddenly slip sideways without warning. This is why secure location points on the car and the jack pad are necessary.

When you operate the jack, **extend the handle fully** to make sure the peg springs securely into the next notch on the stem with a click. Smooth operation can be a problem if your jack gets gunged up with sand (keep it in a dust-proof container or splash some water – not oil – onto the mechanism). Grip the handle securely, wear gloves and avoid putting your head between the handle and stem – difficult to avoid as you lean hard on the jack for the final lift. Should your hand slip before the peg clicks in, the handle will flick back with a speed and force that will knock your head over the horizon.

Light-weight people may have difficulty jacking up the rear of a fully-loaded car at all, so practise at home before it's too late – an air jack (see below) is the answer).

the ideal smooth, flat surface is not present under a 4WD with a separate chassis. Choose the position carefully or make a load spreading adapter remembering you're lifting half the car's weight onto this point. At the very least a thick piece of carpet should be used between the undercarriage and the bag – and something similar on the ground if thorns or rocks are present.

Airbag jacks are ideal for the desert where their wide footprint works well on soft sand. And they're much lighter than a high-lift jack.

Sand plates

Sand plates (or 'ladders') work by creating a temporary road surface onto which cleared wheels can drive, gaining some grip, momentum and hopefully sustained forward motion. The principle has spurred many variations or improvisations: rubber floor mats, grass or towels when desperate, rolls of chicken wire or canvas, wooden planks, or purpose-made items such as easily stored rolled-up sections of chopped-up car tyres (bakkie matts) joined with wire, metal ladders and, easily sourced so most commonly seen in the Sahara, perforated plates of steel (PSP) or aluminium.

In its original form, **steel PSP** is a WWII artefact; the interlocking sections of three-metre long plate were once used to make temporary roadways and even landing strips (this must have taken a lot of PSP!). Like high-lift jacks, PSP has been adapted to desert use and is cheap to buy from military surplus outlets (usually in full three-metre lengths). But although very **cheap**, steel PSP is very heavy and all versions are wider than they need to be for all but a truck. Furthermore, the jagged interlocking teeth can be nasty to handle.

The PSP look is much copied and adapted, and these days is available in smoother, lighter **aluminium** from 3 to 5mm. Go for the thicker version as 3mm alloy plate will bend easily. Plates are also available in, or can be made from, **fibreglass** (GRP) or Kevlar which is lighter still. They have the added advantage of flexing a bit and so contouring with the ground whereas alloy plates can get bent and may need bending back to be fitted back onto a car. This contouring also improves grip. Avoid so-called 'waffles' which are repackaged oil rig decking and weigh a ton, though they have their uses as 'bridging ladders' to get over a ditch (unknown in the Sahara, but a possibility in the Moroccan Atlas). Some recommend a section for each wheel, but for an ordinary 4WD **two sections** about 1.5 metre long are sufficient. Only heavy trucks will need two pairs of steel plates to get through.

Heavy steel PSP doesn't get any lighter if you paint it with alloy paint! Spanner mounts are also cumbersome. Ideally you want a quickly detachable system using no tools so you don't have to think: 'can I be bothered to undo the ladders' when stuck.
Below: Home-made GRP sand plates with simple brackets and bungy lashings.

Conscientious clearing of all wheels and the undercarriage, plus low tyre pressures, are more effective than sand plates as the box on p.183 proves, and all types of sand 'plates' become less necessary as your skill in reading and driving through sand grows. For years I carried a pair of GRP sand plates and never used them until one occasion when I was so stuck in a dune bowl the only way out was winching. On every other occasion, reversing, being pushed out, lifting the wheels and filling in the holes, and/or deflating tyres did the job.

The standard length will do the job on a LBW 4WD but it's good to know that sections at least 50cm shorter than your wheelbase are best because as one wheel rolls off the plate lifts up and then ideally drops back to the ground before the next wheel rolls onto it. Too long a section will stay up and may get jammed into the wheel arch. Thrown up plates is also something pushers should watch out for. This unwanted effect is partly why **articulated** versions have caught on. The only type I've tried are '**bakkie matts**' from South Africa, made from old tyres wired together which can be rolled up. They are less than half the cost of alloy or GRP sand plates but are heavier than they look. One problem with non-rigid matting is that it can bunch up as a vehicle pulls away so that there is less of a mat for the following axle to roll over. A more gentle technique ought to be adopted with these mats, but even then I've heard of one person who shredded his bakkie matts after repeated use.

As for actual **sand ladders**, these are now rarely used. For an equal surface area steel items are even heavier than PSP and clearly lack the surface area and 'flotation' of a plate or mat, tending to sink without effect and get buried. The fact that the wheel might have to lurch from one rung to the next creates uneven traction and makes things worse. Marking the spot with an upright shovel helps locate buried ladders; another technique is to tie on clip-on ribbons.

In the end, anything will do the job, but having used all the above versions and more besides, I've found that (solo trips excepted) none is essential to experienced drivers, while the lightness of flexible and well-finished **GRP plates** is the least cumbersome and is as effective as the metal equivalents. They bend with the ground's contours so improve traction, but spring straight again.

Bakkie matts (**top**) roll up out of the way but are heavier than they look. Notice below how they bunch up; not good for high-power recoveries. By comparison the sand ladder (**below**) with widely-spaced rungs (found by chance probably years after it got buried and lost) is less effective.

Mounting sand plates

Whatever type you choose, sand plates need to be **securely mounted but easily accessible**. Having to climb onto the roof rack to unstrap them every time you get stuck is very tiresome: on a bad day you may be using the plates every half-hour. The ideal mounts are quick-release clips which bolt on the car's side or roof rack, or a clamp which screws on by hand.

Any other method should imitate this concept: a hook to take the weight and a quick-release strap or clip to locate the plate and pull it down. Avoid having to use any tools to unmount the plates or ladders. Fixed against the side windows of a hardtop, the plates can double up as a security and shade device. Assuming you have the clearance and the plates are short enough, another option is slipping them into 'C' channels between the roof rack and the roof. A simple strap or elastic is all that's needed to keep them from slipping out. This idea would work well under the front edge of a rack on any vehicle where the roof line drops.

Shovels

A shovel has many uses in the Sahara: burying waste as well as digging the car out. The best type to choose is one with not too large a blade – so anyone can use it without straining – and a full 'D' handle that you can grip and angle firmly rather than the cheaper 'T' handles as found on the ex-Army shovels available in the UK for a fiver. As with sand plates, mount your shovel firmly but accessibly. The long-handled shovels recommended by some to use under the car are in fact very awkward. To clear sand it's simplest to get right in there

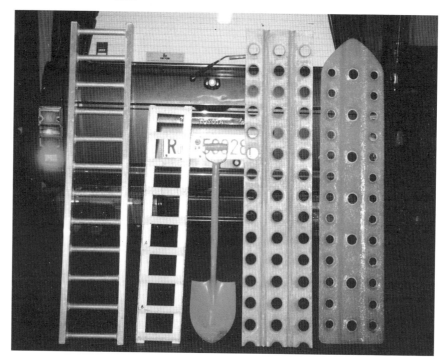

Take your pick (or shovel) from the left: alloy sand ladder is incredibly light and strong but expensive to make and hard to find; shorter home-made steel version is very heavy but cheap; ideal sand shovel has a 'D' handle as pictured but perhaps a slightly smaller blade; alloy 'PSP' but without those nasty edges – a popular choice but tends to bend; GRP sand plate from Grand Erg – light and bendy and the pointed end tucks in well under a wheel, but also expensive.

and use your hands. So-called 'pioneer tools' like pickaxes and sledge hammers are not necessary in the Sahara unless you're planning to trailblaze a new piste through the hills. If so, don't forget some gelignite.

A simple way of mounting sandplates. Stick a bolt out of the body, add a rubber sleeve and then weld the right nut onto a strip of metal and bend it into a handle to mount the plate. Another handle idea is the black plastic knobs which hold down spare tyres in Fiats.

Tow ropes

A tow rope or strap (the latter more easily rolled up and stored) is an essential part of any overlander's equipment. Synthetic materials are best; 3-core **nylon rope** being the strongest and with a bit of give. It should be kept in a bag out of direct sunlight and away from sharp edges which can cut or wear individual strands. **Nine metres** is a standard length and the minimum necessary for towing or righting an overturned vehicle in the desert. To recover a vehicle from deep sand, dune crests, a wet chott or feche-feche a stretchy **'kinetic' rope** (discussed in Recoveries p.184) is much more effective than an ordinary tow rope. In sand, conventional self-recovery with a couple of people pushing is usually quicker than setting up a tow.

Two straps can be easily joined with nothing more than a tightly rolled-up magazine or a stick.

Both are less dangerous than shackles which are lethal if something breaks, particularly during high energy kinetic recoveries, although a couple of shackles rated at four tons or more are useful accessories if one car has towing rings rather than hooks.

Tow hooks are best though, avoiding the need for shackles altogether. JATE rings (high-specification towing rings) should be fit for the task and bolted securely to a longitudinal chassis member, not just to the bumper or a chassis cross member.

BATTERIES AND SOLAR PANELS

Using electrical ancillaries from the car's normal 'SLI' (starting, lighting, ignition) battery when your engine isn't running risks flattening the battery, especially when you then try and start an ill-tuned engine on a cold morning. Jump-starting from another car is the simple answer (or tow-starting if no jump leads are available) but this assumes another vehicle is around.

Because the primary battery is such

An ex-army shovel on a slightly longer 'D'-handled shaft. It's fitted to the roof rack with quick-release Verschluslager mit Gummispannband clips from www.daerr.de, part # 209241400400.

An easy and safe way of joining tow ropes.

Tow hooks solidly mounted on chassis rails are more convenient than rings.

a vital component, especially with a diesel, a **second battery** is a good idea and essential if you're running a fridge or other item which consumes electricity around the clock. A second battery also enables you to use electrical appliances in the evening without having to worry about the main battery. In addition it provides a back-up should the main battery fail.

There has been a trend to use **deep-cycle** or 'leisure' batteries as second batteries. These differ from SLI batteries in that they're designed for long, slow discharging and regular flattening so are suited to running accessories on conventional touring campervans. But they are not designed to provide the short powerful burst of 'cranking' amps needed to start a cold engine and then

Poor starting on a cold morning is no problem if there's someone to help – but a second battery is always a good idea.

quickly recover. In the desert starting the engine is more important than keeping the milk from going off so, especially for solo vehicles in remote areas, having two SLI batteries is advisable.

However, **sealed batteries** like Odysseys or Exide Maxximas, to name just two, are designed with both high cranking amps *and* the ability to withstand repeated discharging. These dry cell or **gel** batteries can be discharged up to 400 times while still providing lashings of cold cranking amps. They are also built to resist vibration damage (which in the Sahara can be a battery killer as the insides break up on corrugated pistes) and won't even leak if they crack. And of course the benefits of not having battery acid evaporate or spill, or emitting explosive, corrosive gases does not need underlining. For the Sahara, quality sealed batteries are one less thing to worry about.

Be aware that sealed batteries are more lead-dense so can be **heavier** than regular lead-acid batteries for which your car may have been originally designed. Because battery trays can corrode from the fumes of old lead-acid batteries, it's worth checking that your **battery tray** is up to the extra weight and expected hammering. Defenders keep their battery/ies under the left seat, strong enough and 'sealed-for-life' which means virtually no dangerous fumes, but if they're smaller than standard you'll want to be sure they're securely mounted, especially as you tend to forget about them under the seat. A solid location eliminates movement which can lead to chaffed or broken cables, shorts and possible electrical fires.

Recharging batteries with a split-charge system

Obviously the second battery will need recharging somehow and, short of constantly rotating the two batteries or using a solar panel as a separate charging source (see p.132), a common method is a **split-charge system** which enables a second battery to get charged from the car's alternator, something any 4WD alternator ought to be able to manage. A split-charge system also **isolates** the two batteries when the engine (and therefore the alternator) is off, allowing only the auxiliary battery to be used for electrical accessories.

A couple of methods of battery isolation management exist: a solenoid switch or an electronic diode. The **solenoid switch** method is simplest, a mechanical unit that can be repaired manually should it fail or jam. It requires running the second battery in parallel with the main one (i.e. positive terminals connected to positive and negative to negative), thus doubling the amperage (power) although reputedly shortening battery life in the long run. With this system it's best to start with two new and identical batteries.

When you turn on the ignition the solenoid is switched on giving plenty of starting power, though at the same time reducing the individual recharging times of the batteries. With ignition on but the solenoid off, the batteries are isolated and ancillaries run from the second battery will only drain that unit. The problem comes when needing to start a car with one good and one weak battery. As soon as two batteries are connected (i.e. when you turn on the ignition), they will equalise. If your second battery has drained to half its power overnight, connecting it to the fully-charged battery will only result in three-quarters of the potential power, possibly not enough to start your engine.

Over the years I've heard of all sorts of problems with split-charge systems, usually finding one has two flat batteries. With the system wired up in this way a **manual isolating switch** is essential for occasions when you think the second battery may be dangerously drained – a marine-type four-option rotary switch works well. Fitting it in the cab of the car is ideal so you don't forget it's there or whether it's on or off. Once the car has started or, better still, once it's been running for a while and the main battery has recovered from the effort of starting, you can manually reconnect the solenoid and allow the batteries to be recharged together. The equalising of power will have no negative effect once the engine is running and creating electricity from the alternator.

Better still is wiring the solenoid switch to the **alternator output**. This avoids the two batteries being connected during the critical engine-starting phase, the second battery only being linked once there is output from the alternator (usually a few hundred rpm above tickover and certainly not during starting). One V8 Land Rover I know that was wired up in this way had no problems, even with a totally flat spare battery. Oil pressure and temperature sensors can also be used to activate the battery isolating the solenoid independently of the ignition switch.

Some solenoid battery isolators are not suitable for vehicles with electronic engine management (i.e. just about all modern turbo diesels) as they can cause sharp voltage surges or spiking that can upset electronic management units. (You may have noticed 'EFI-safe' jump-starting cables which incorporate anti-voltage surge protection). For these vehicles (i.e. those with internally-sensed voltage regulators) certain **diode battery isolators** can be used, but you need to be certain it's the correct type with additional diodes that moderate any voltage surges.

Otherwise, a diode battery isolator can be used on any vehicle with an externally-sensed voltage regulator (usually pre-EFI) and is an automatic system requiring no switches. The diode acts like an electronic one-way valve, sensing voltage drops from each battery and directing the alternator's charge towards it. The undesirable equalisation of unevenly charged batteries is avoided, keeping them permanently isolated and independently charged. You miss out on the advantages of paralleled batteries and a diode takes up nearly a volt drop in the charging circuit, but you can always join them up with jump leads if necessary plus the second battery can be run totally flat and it will be recharged once the car is running. By avoiding 'automatic' paralleling it does not reduce battery life but does have the disadvantage of being an unfixable 'black box'.

24-volt engines

Like trucks, diesel-engined Land Cruisers and some Patrols sold in Europe use two 12-volt batteries in series to power a 24-volt electrical system, ensuring reliable cold weather starting of the big diesel engine. Sixty series Cruisers are 24-volt throughout (including ancillaries right down to bulbs) while 80-series and later feature 24-volt starting but 12-volt ancillaries. Running a second pair of batteries is excessive; a single 12-volt back-up will do.

Nevertheless, wiring in solenoids and diodes can get complicated if like me, you don't know your amps from your watts and consider experimentation in the Sahara with the vehicle's batteries risky. I met an 80 in Agadez once which was having all sorts of split-charged battery problems. These vehicles are more suited to the solar system of charging an auxiliary battery.

Maintaining batteries with solar power

Even with all the split chargers in all the bars in all the world, what better place to exploit the sun's free energy than the Sahara, an environment famous for sunshine! A solar panel of around half a square metre can put out 40 watts, plenty enough to keep a spare battery in shape with just a couple of hours charging a day. In fact, with a panel and a single, good quality gel battery, you can eliminate the need for a back-up/auxiliary (assuming you're not running fridges and the like). That's less weight and less expense while still having a guaranteed method of recharging a flat battery as long as the sun shines in the Sahara (it may take a few hours).

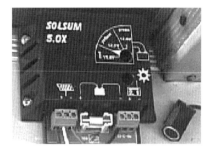

Unless you have a switch, an inexpensive regulator is necessary to stop a solar panel cooking your battery.

The great advantage of this system is that it's totally independent of the car's charging and electrical system – no split-charging systems needed. A solar panel is connected to the secondary battery (larger panels should use a **regulator**) and that battery can, for example, be wired to its own cigarette lighter PTO mounted around the car or an inverter (see opposite).

In cloudy Europe **solar panels**, from BP/Siemens or Unisolar, are expensive compared to the US or Australia where this technology is much more widely used, just as it is in parts of the Sahara. It was once used to help light up the desolate Tanezrouft piste but soon got vandalised. If your caravanning or overland equipment supplier can't help you may find yachting chandlers a good place to look, or buy from the US off the Internet.

Unisolar offers rigid panels or flexible vinyl mats that can be rolled up when not in use (about 20% more expensive). Their 'US32' rigid panel is a good size and can be found for as little as $160 in the US (UK suppliers manage to convert that to nearly £300!). About as wide as a car, a foot deep and an inch or less thin, it puts out 32 watts, nearly 2 amps and has an operating voltage of around 16.5 volts. You may find some ex-army places selling alluringly cheap solar panels, but being for military applications, they're usually 24-volt which might give your regulator something to think about.

A solar panel has the added advantage of being able to **charge a flat car**

battery (albeit very slowly) should the alternator fail; a handy, get-you-home measure which I heard worked for a stricken Mitsubishi in the Tibesti once. If you have two batteries you can solar charge one during the day while the other runs the car until it goes flat. Driving in this manner, the battery will last even longer if you don't use any of the car's electrics – even taking the brake-light bulbs out will help.

Above: Having a removable panel on a lead is not a bad idea should you park up for a few days with your vehicle in the shade. **Below**: This 3-way PTO can be quickly swapped to run off the car battery or the solar-powered battery.

Inverters and 12-volt adaptors

Inverters are inexpensive electrical gadgets which convert a car's 12 volts DC into 240 volts AC (household voltage). It sounds a great idea and people assume a black box enables you to make toast on the dashboard while hoovering the boot. Inverters can be useful for running power tools, your favourite bedside lamp or even microwave ovens (if powerful enough), but inverting **consumes a lot of battery power** which is why most units need a cooling fan. Choose one rated at 300 watts or more and avoid

using any appliance with a heating element which draws huge amounts of power.

If available, buy a simple **12-volt adapter** which plugs into the cigarette PTO for items like laptops, two-way radios or digital cameras (which are around 8–12-volts anyway). This is a more efficient (and quieter) way of charging these sorts of devices. Try and set up an auxiliary electrical system where the inverter gets used only occasionally or for short periods rather than every day.

Loading and packing

Packing up to half a ton into your car while keeping nearly all your equipment accessible is an organisational challenge. The best way to start is to sort out how much **extra fuel and water** you need to carry with you (this will depend on your destination), and where to put it. Together these two vital fluids can add up to over fifty percent of your payload but once stored out of the way can be forgotten about apart from replenishment.

Once you've done that, work out where you're going to **sleep**: on the ground, in the car or on the roof? The pros and cons of the different sleeping options are outlined in the 'Camping' chapter on p.151. Having done that you can then work out a plan for adapting the interior of your vehicle. All the advice in this chapter relates to the most commonly-used station wagons and hardtops, though the general principles also apply to pick-ups and trucks.

Principles of packing

It's difficult to imagine day-to-day life in the desert, which is why a **test trip** is such a good idea, even if it's just a weekend's camping. Even then you can expect to refine your packing system as you go along, though essentially it boils down to **sleeping**, **cooking**, **eating** and **washing** plus occasionally, **recovery** and **repairs**. Try and visualise your daily chores in the order that they happen: getting up, cooking and eating breakfast, having a wash, topping up fuel tanks if necessary, packing up and moving on with a stop for lunch and then making camp for the night.

The diagram below shows an ideal layout for distributing your gear, using density and frequency of use as guides. In a nutshell, **heavy items should be packed low and between the axles**, while **regularly-used items should be accessible** without having to move anything out of the way. The principle is that nothing become too buried. Five-door station wagons have better accessibility so are more versatile. As with all the ideas in this book, don't pull your hair out trying to duplicate them exactly. The diagram is just a guide to what works best but may not always be easy or cost effective to put into practice on your chosen vehicle.

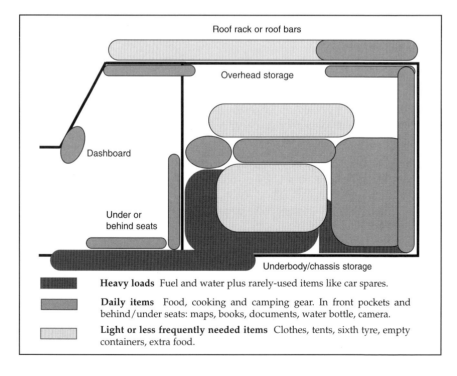

Roof rack or roof bars

Overhead storage

Dashboard

Under or behind seats

Underbody/chassis storage

Heavy loads Fuel and water plus rarely-used items like car spares.

Daily items Food, cooking and camping gear. In front pockets and behind/under seats: maps, books, documents, water bottle, camera.

Light or less frequently needed items Clothes, tents, sixth tyre, empty containers, extra food.

LONG-RANGE FUEL AND WATER SUPPLIES

In Morocco, short stages and lack of fuel-devouring soft sand means a standard 4WD fuel tank is adequate, and if travelling in the cooler season a 20-40 litre water container is sufficient for two people. Elsewhere in the Sahara, where your fuel and water requirements will be much greater, you'll have to carefully consider how and where to carry these primary and very heavy commodities. **Jerricans** or **tanks** are the two choices for both fuel and water; the former inexpensive, the latter more convenient.

Jerricans

For travellers who don't expect to be making a lifetime of Sahara travel and haven't got limitless funds, jerricans provide the simple answer to increasing your vehicle's range. Available sometimes still unused from military surplus outlets for around £5/€8, they make reliable and robust fuel containers.

An LRDG jerrican at Ain Murr well, Sudan.

The standard steel jerrican is a German design (hence the name) from the late 1930s, developed to support their blisteringly effective *blitzkrieg* invasions. The fact that the design remains unchanged shows how well they succeeded with the ergonomics of carrying, pouring, sealing and storing. During the war in North Africa, the LRDG prized the discovery of any jerricans, while the Germans were ordered to destroy them on retreat.

A jerrican holds 20 litres (4.45 gallons) when filled in the upright position. This leaves an **air gap** just below the handles which shouldn't be filled with fuel (by tipping the can backwards) unless you're really desperate. The air pocket, as well as the X-shaped indentations on the sides, enable the can's sides to bulge as fuel expands; especially the case with petrol which is more volatile than diesel. Once warmed and shaken on your roof, take care to open the cap very slowly (the cap's clamp design makes this easy) to avoid a spurt of fuel, which, besides being dangerous, is messy and wasteful.

Nifty vinyl funnels; available from www.zoelzer.de

A **clamp-on spout** (some with an integral gauze and breather tube) should make topping-up while holding a heavy can easier. But I find these clamp-on spouts often don't seal well, fuel runs down your leg and their internal gauze slows down the flow rate, prolonging the effort. A wide-bore **funnel** takes half the time. Rigid funnels get messy with

Cheap siphon-pump – tastier than a mouthful of diesel.

diesel and are awkward to stow, so I prefer the 'collapsible' vinyl items with the end snipped off to make the hole bigger. Store them in a plastic bag or flat lunch box. Cut-down mineral water bottles will also do the job and you can chuck them after use.

Better still, leave the can where it's stashed on the car and siphon the fuel into the tank either with a simple tube or a **manual siphon-pump**. Until mastered, the mouth-sucking method to get a siphon going is understandably unpopular with motor fuel. If you have no siphon pump bury the whole hose into a full jerrican (a flexible, clear, thin-walled hose is best). With the other end fully submerged, put your thumb over the end and draw out the tube which should stay full of fuel. Poke the tube into the tank filler and the weight of the dropping fuel will create a siphon.

Jerricans themselves can be knocked about for years: I've never seen a welded seam leak, though **cap seals** do leak. You can buy spare seals or, failing that, a chopped-up inner tube clamped across the mouth will work. Once rust or flaking paint begin to come out of a jerry, either make sure you use a fine pre-filter or get another jerrican. Neat ten-litre versions are available and even mini five-litre mod-

Top: A roof full of empty jerries and drums on the way to a fuel dump; in this quantity not an ideal place for long-term storage.
Middle: a simple wooden crate made to take ten steel and plastic jerries for fuel and water – a solution for this 80VX driver who did not want to modify his vehicle radically for a single desert trip.
Bottom: jerrican-mounting frames are a neat and unobtrusive way of mounting jerries while keeping the roof free for tents and suchlike.

els, all using the same clamping cap. They can also be robust containers for spare motor oils and other fluids and make good jack stands when working under a car.

There is said to be a small risk from **static electricity** in the dry desert atmosphere when refuelling vehicles, especially petrol. Earth the car by touching it before opening the cap and pouring in the fuel.

'Jerricans' copied in **plastic** should never be used for long-term fuel storage. The soft slab sides and screw-on caps are unsuited to the expansion and will swell like a balloon before splitting, leaking or bursting. I once drove a car carrying nearly three dozen cheap plastic jerries on the roof. Within a couple of days fuel was running down the sides of the car as the liquid expanded and caps leaked; I even had to use the wipers as it ran down the windscreen. It was very messy and bad for the rubber components.

Mounting jerricans

If your car has a nearly adequate tank fuel range and you're only using a couple of jerries, lashing them down securely inside the car simplifies things so long as you don't mind the small risk of fuel odour (no matter how careful you are, there's always some spillage). Make sure they don't chafe and rattle by wrapping them in carpet or sitting them in a wooden crate. If the seal is good a jerrican can safely be stored in any position. More than a couple of jerricans are better stored outside the vehicle; keeping them on a roof rack is a temptation but not good practice when full; fitted on the side they're easier to get to but require the sort of drilling into the body that only die-hard desert drivers have no qualms about.

Very handy are **jerrican-mounting frames** (see bottom picture opposite), which don't protrude when not in use so cause no problems with use in mainland Europe where, as with oversized tyres, regulations for such things are strict. In the UK, AlliSport makes them from alloy or they are easily fabricated yourself from 1-inch angle. In Britain you'll also find the cruder and heavier metal ex-army '**baskets**' into which a jerrican can be locked. These work well on back doors, can be used on their sides, under the load bed of a truck or even bolted inside a vehicle for a secure placement, although you could do all those things with the frame and save space. If used on the side of a vehicle they stick out too much and look dangerous.

When fitting jerricans into these baskets or right across the width of a roof rack bear in mind that petrol expands when heated and shaken (diesel less so), so may get jammed in until the pressure is released or the contents cool.

If you do end up stacking them across the roof as some long-range Sahara tour operators have to do to pack more tourists in their cars, make sure there are extra mounting points **on the roof rack** and that you mount them all at one end where the rack is stronger, not in the middle. Eight full jerries on a roof rack are the weight of two adults: across corrugations on dunes having that weight in such a position could not be worse for vehicle stability.

Long-range fuel tanks

If you're planning on doing regular desert trips, or a long overland one, extra fuel tanks either second-hand, home-made or specially designed for your vehicle, are much more convenient than jerricans, but add up to an extra expense.

Interior tanks

The ideal location for mounting either a lorry tank or a custom-designed tank is on the floor immediately behind the front seats. On a hardtop this makes access to the filler difficult but unless fitted right by a door interior fuel tanks should never be filled at a garage by reaching inside the car – there will always be some spillage. African pump attendants are very diligent and fill up tanks to just over brimming and with diesel this will be especially messy. Instead, fit a proper **filler cap and hose** from the body of the vehicle into the tank. This will mean cutting into the body or replacing a window with perspex and mounting a filler into that, but it is the only way to guarantee fuel not being spilled inside the vehicle.

To top up the vehicle's main tank a **fuel line with a tap** can be plumbed to the neck of the vehicle's main tank or unrolled and hung into the main tank filler, filling it with a simple gravity feed. Using this loose fuel pipe method it's easier to **record fuel consumption** by filling the main tank via a jerrican, thereby measuring your fuel off 20 litres at a time. Initially this eliminates some convenience but once you get the measure of your vehicle's fuel consumption characteristics in all types of terrain, regular fuel consumption measurements will no longer be essential, merely interesting.

Alternatives to measuring fuel used with jerries include a 'dip tube' ideally read from the centre of the tank (a mere dipstick may be hard to read). Insert the tube, put your finger over the end and withdraw: the suction will have retained the fuel level in the tank which could be measured against a marker.

Above: a new 160-litre lorry tank picked up from an army disposal site for just £25.
© Andy Bell
Below: 200-litre oil drum of fuel keeps this V8 Range Rover on the move. Both would require some serious back springs.

Or, fit an exterior fuel level tube on the side of the tank, though this needs to be well protected from knocks and read on level ground.

You can, of course, siphon or electrically pump the fuel from the auxiliary tank into the car filler, so avoiding the need for any leak-prone fittings except the cap and a breather pipe, but this is a bit basic. An old car fuel pump may do the job cheaply if slowly during an evening stop. It is always desirable to decant the fuel to the lowest level at every reasonable opportunity.

Lorry tanks and oil drums

A 100-litre-plus rectilinear **lorry tank** picked up from a commercial breakers, cleaned up and mounted behind the front seats (the ideal location short of underbody mounting) will probably cost less than five jerries. At twice that volume, lorry tanks become a real bargain, albeit an incredibly heavy one when full. With one of these you could increase your range to nearly 2000km and considering that the UK has the most expensive fuel in Europe, real savings can be made with huge tanks when returning from the Sahara. Another advantage of buying a used lorry tank is that it's made for the job and comes with fuel line fittings, including breathers (see below) and even a fuel sender and gauge.

If you can't find a lorry tank, used 200-litre (45 gallon) **oil drums** can easily be found on the Internet. The shape isn't ideal to save space or mount securely, but it's a ready-made fuel container as strong as a jerrican.

Home-made long-range tanks

An alternative to a get-what-you're-given lorry tank or oil drum is having something made-to-measure. It's more costly but every inch of space can be used to the full and mounting brackets can be positioned to use any existing fixtures in the car. **Mild steel** of 1.5mm is the ideal material; stainless steel or aluminium look nicer but cost more. Whatever you use, interior **baffles** must be incorporated to add strength and reduce surging, which is why a lorry tank is ideal. Go for the biggest volume you think you'll need. With any box tank height x width x breadth measured in 10cm units will give the volume in litres (more or less). Therefore a tank that is 30cm high, 50cm broad

Simple home-made steel box tank built to fit with a capacity of 135 litres, but heavy and seven times the cost of seven jerricans.

and 120cm wide adds up to 180 litres or nearly 40 gallons).

As with any tank, a **breather** is essential. A breather is simply a pipe leading from the top of the tank to the outside air, enabling air pressure inside a tank to remain equal to its surroundings, so eliminating leaks caused by unequal pressure. Using a sealed 210-litre auxiliary tank in Morocco once, the extreme altitude changes caused my tank to regularly flex its walls with a loud clank as it expanded in the rarefied air, especially evident when nearly empty (air expands more than fuel). Unscrewing the filler cap equalised the air, but had to be done again at low altitudes to avoid implosion.

A steel tank itself is very unlikely to burst, but welds, taps, hose joints or seals will easily leak if not perfect, and this can be smelly or dangerous. A breather pipe should rise up high above the tank and feature a U-bend or a loop to stop sloshed fuel spurting out. A splash plate inside the tank where the breather outlet is located also helps in this respect. I also plugged an inline fuel filter on the end of my breather for good measure and on my Land Cruiser jammed the end of the pipe somewhere in the rear air-vents near the tailgate pillars.

A tubular sill tank on a Land Cruiser 60 makes the most of the wasted space between the body's sill and the chassis rail. The filler is on the wheel arch.

Underbody tanks

These purpose-built tanks are made to fit in the wasted voids underneath various 4WDs and, though they cost a packet, can double or triple your range without you even knowing they're there. Outside the UK, Land Cruisers are all available with factory-fitted auxiliary 90-litre chassis-mounted tanks plumbed to the main tank with a gauge and taps. With Land Rovers it's well known that SWB under-seat tanks can fit a LWB, increasing the capacity by 45 litres each side, though one overlander reported that the reduced air-flow caused overheating in his diesel 109.

Wide Land Cruiser 60s and 80s have masses of room between the longitudinal chassis rails and still more between the rails and sills, as do many 4WDs. With their full-length wheel arches, hardtop LWB Land Rovers waste a lot of space between the rear wheels and the front doors although the chassis rails are relatively close together. A 60-series Cruiser can easily take a 70-litre tank between the rails without any modification. With Land Rovers a better position for long-range tanks is behind the sills.

In Australia you can find a range of underbody tanks from 40 to 200 litres mostly for Toyotas and Nissans. They are also available in Germany for G-Wagens and Land Rovers but are very expensive.

On all these versions fitting can be complicated, requiring new or split filler caps, and piping that may be best left to the manufacturer, in some cases adding further to the cost. As you can see, this is serious money for effectively half a dozen jerricans but when fitted they enable you to save valuable space, keep the enormous weight of fuel positioned low down and enjoy vastly increased range.

Fabricating and fitting your own underbody tanks is not a simple gravity feed top-up operation. If plumbed permanently into the main tank it requires an understanding of the function of fuel return pipes as well as careful routing to protect fuel lines from damage in this vulnerable position. A better idea might be to keep them independent of the main tank, topping them up with an electric fuel pump or siphoning via a jerrican. This is perhaps the ultimate solution to carrying fuel: not too expensive if the tank shapes are simple but keeping the vast bulk of extra fuel out of the vehicle and as low as possible. Should one tank rupture all the fuel need not be lost.

Water containers and tanks

As with fuel, water can be carried in jerricans or tanks. Unlike fuel you will need access to your water several times a day so its positioning and accessibility should be considered accordingly. Having to pour water out of heavy 20-litre containers can work for a few days' camping but on a longer trip you'll want a system that avoids lifting heavy weights and wasting sloshed water –

in-built taps, siphons or electric pumps are all good solutions.

One advantage of using a multi-jerrican or container system is that it's easy to estimate your remaining reserves accurately: with water tanks you have to make more of an educated guess. Another good thing about multiple containers is that should you fill up with water that proves to be polluted it's easier to isolate that water without contaminating all your reserves. Plus jerries can be

A 20-litre Swiss army water bag (right) is robust, easy to use and takes up no space when empty. The Orlieb bag (left) is less usable but both are good alternatives to fixed water tanks.

carried to an inconveniently-located tap or well one by one for filling; a quick method even if it does involve heavy lifting. This **compartmentalisation** of water has real benefits and is one reason why, even if you're using a single tank, it's worth bringing at least one 20-litre water container along as well: at the very worst you may need it to 'walk-out' in an emergency.

Jerricans and plastic containers

Metal jerricans are robust but have the disadvantage of not showing how much they contain at a glance and, being four times the weight of a 20-litre plastic container, they're unnecessary for water. There's also a chance they'll get mixed up with fuel-containing jerries. If you do end up using jerricans for fuel and water, differentiate them clearly: white or blue is the customary colour for water; red, or the standard green, for fuel.

Not all the thin **translucent plastic containers** bought from camping shops are tough enough to knock about in the back of a 4WD, especially if they're being moved and used every day. Choose a thick, well-moulded example and check that the cap seals well by pressing the walls together (kneel onto them if no one's looking); if air leaks out so will water – not a great problem if the container is kept upright, but messy. Much tougher are the **black plastic**

HOW MUCH WATER?

Advice on how much water to carry, where to fill up, and how to ensure it's drinkable is given from page 135, but as a guideline, for two people doing the standard Central Saharan pistes in mid-winter, plan a capacity of **10 litres per person per day** between watering points for all uses including washing. Increase this to 15 litres per day in late autumn and early spring or on extreme pistes and *at least* 20 litres per day in summer.

These estimates include emergency reserves; they are not what you should expect to consume each day. It's not a bad idea to have at least one jerrican always full of water and never used except in an emergency, as well as getting into the habit of being frugal with water, no matter how much you're carrying.

On the floor behind the front seats is the ideal location for water or fuel.

20-litre water containers available from military surplus outlets, but these will definitely need to be tested as leaking caps are common. Get the newest and cleanest you can find and have a quick sniff inside to make sure nothing's died in there. The reason these containers are black is to eliminate the growth of **algae** brought about by exposure to direct sunlight: something that happens quicker than you think but won't kill you. More important is keeping water out of the sun to keep it cool.

Built-in **taps** are convenient but a source of yet more leaks. Taps incorporated into the cap are better than protruding taps at the base of the can which are sure to get knocked about and eventually leak. With a tap-in-the-cap make sure there is a second small cap to enable the water to pour out smoothly. In general, if using several plastic containers, have only one with a tap, the rest plain. This way you only end up with one leaking tap instead of half a dozen. Once a day or so the tapped container can be filled up from the plain ones or the tap-cap transferred to a full container.

As with fuel, the ideal storage area is behind the front seats. With a station wagon it's easy to fit fuel cans on one side and water on the other but on hardtops plan to have water containers accessible, which may require an electric pump to get the water from their ideal location to the back door.

Other containers

Alternatives to rigid plastic containers include **collapsible PVC tubes**, a modern version of tractor-tyre inner tubes once adapted for the same purpose, or indeed a nomad's goatskin *guerba*. Available ready-made from Opposite Lock 4WD or motorcare.com.au in Australia, or easily fabricated to your specifications by a PVC mouldings manufacturer, they're designed to lie on the floor behind the front seats of a station wagon and deflate as the water is drawn out via a built-in tap. A good space-saving idea if protected from punctures, a water tube can make a useful auxiliary container, taking up very little room

Exterior-mounted water jerries need to be light proof to inhibit the growth of algae.

until needed for a single very long stage without wells. Another good thing is that you can take them out easily when not in expedition mode.

Still another way of transporting water I've heard used by a couple of Saharan travellers is bringing your own **bottled water from home**! Like the PVC tube, space increases as the water is used up: square-shaped 5-litre containers will be most space efficient and the empty containers will undoubtedly be welcomed by locals. In practice this system is preferred by travellers visiting remote areas like the Western Desert where there are no wells whatsoever, or those wanting to maintain autonomy while saving time by avoiding all settlements and possibly unreliable wells when travelling way off-piste.

Water tanks

As with fuel, built-in water tanks provide a neat, single water storage unit which works best in conjunction with an **electric pump** or, if positioned appropriately, a gravity-fed tap (see left). Robust plastic tanks in various formats, capacities and with threaded ports are easily available from plastic moulding manufacturers as well as some caravan or overland outfitters. Don't bother trying to wash out and use a tank that once held fuel, it will always carry the taint of diesel or petrol.

With hardtops the back of the vehicle is not an ideal **position** for this heavy weight, yet it's the most accessible for drawing and replenishing water. On any vehicle heavy water and fuel should be positioned low and between the axles, ideally on the floor behind the front seats. A pressure-sensitive electric pump (which starts working when a tap is opened) is eas-

ily plumbed in but, as with fuel, think about breathers and ease of replenishment as well as a secure, vibration-proof fixing to the vehicle's body. Use copious amounts of carpet as lagging, especially if the tank is made of metal or a brittle plastic. If nothing else, ratchet tie-downs work well if you do not want a permanent fitting.

With a tank centrally mounted in a hardtop, it's best to fit an exterior filler cap into the body of the car, clearly marked 'Water'. With a five-door station wagon, refilling the tank is less awkward. Generally it's best to keep water inside the vehicle rather than in a chassis-mounted tank where it will get hot from the engine and exhaust.

A moulded plastic 100-litre water tank. The tap avoids the need for pumps.

Refilling can often be done by hose from a garage, even in the Sahara, though be prepared to deal with a fixed tap (carry some hose) or a well. Try and anticipate how you can most easily fill the tank without accidentally sloshing water everywhere or transferring laboriously from bucket to tank. Make the tank filler at least as big as a car's fuel filler so a large volume can be easily and quickly poured in via a funnel or whatever. Whichever way you do it, make it simple and foolproof. As with all systems and operations, try to visualise yourself working in adverse conditions: a sandstorm, a rush or while you're sick. The easier a repetitive task, the less chance there will be of making errors because 'we couldn't be bothered to top up the water, it's such a hassle'.

PACKING SYSTEMS

Going to the Sahara is not like taking off for a fortnight's holiday: you can't just throw your suitcases in the back, put your shades on and hit the road. You must organise and carry a temporary home in your vehicle for the next few weeks so your goal is to store everything as efficiently as possible, trying to ensure that everyday items are easily accessible, that everything is securely protected against damage from bumps and corrugations, and that the weight is kept low and evenly spaced.

Once you've sorted out how and where to carry your water and extra fuel, and whether or not you're going to sleep in, on or outside the car, you're left with food, cooking equipment, camping gear, clothes, personal items, car spares, toolkit and recovery gear. When deciding where to put all that, try and visualise your **daily chores** as mentioned at the beginning of this chapter. The diagram on p.134 should give you some idea as to the most appropriate zones in a car for storing all your gear. There's more detailed advice on how to store food and camping equipment starting on page 151.

There are as many packing systems as there are Saharan travellers; some are illustrated on the following pages. There's huge variation in **cost** too: some people spend thousands of pounds on specially-designed fitted modules, complete with built-in tanks, storage boxes and a kitchenette, while others make do with half-a-dozen cardboard boxes and a set of tie-downs. Desert travel already requires enough expenditure on vital items such as tyres, heavy-duty suspension and ferry tickets. In my experience, with the opportunity and imagination it's satisfying to design yourself an effective storage and camping system that suits your needs and doesn't cost a fortune.

Unless you've bought a pre-equipped car you'll be starting from scratch. The **important factors** to consider when organising a good desert-ready packing system are:

- Secure, vibration-proof fitting
- Convenience and access
- Low centre of gravity
- Cost
- Demountability (to a certain extent) if you don't want your car to be permanently modified.

Roof racks

A roof rack frees up space inside the vehicle from bulky clutter so greatly improving accessibility. Roof racks are disapproved of because they encourage overloading, and overloading in the worst possible place where it can cause instability. Try and use a rack only to store light, bulky and low-value items, not fuel and water or regularly-used items. Remember too that the bare rack, let alone the baggage, will increase fuel consumption by *at least* ten per cent. Whatever's loaded on the roof, keep the

The fitted plywood interior of a 30-year-old Land Rover Carawagon. Nice looking but very rattly.

frontal profile low to minimise drag, and streamline containers where possible. Racks made of round tubing further reduce turbulence and wind noise, but are more expensive.

Though heavier, roof racks have the advantage over roof bars in that they have a peripheral frame which makes getting up as well as lashing down items much easier. Fitting a **plywood baseboard** to the rack is a good idea; this keeps the sun from heating the roof of the car and also helps spread the load (including your own) across the structure. If you fit this yourself, take the chance to measure up and cut a few **10cm circular holes** where the longitudinal and lateral cross members meet, so making effective lashing points by simply knotting a loop of rope or hooking a tie-down to the rack. Another way is screwing a bar with **slidable lashing points** that can be moved around as necessary. Usually used in the backs of pick ups they can work well on a roof rack or even inside a hardtop. Lock-n-Slide bars are manufactured by the people that make Hi-Lifts.

The alloy gutters of Land Rovers are well known for not being strong enough to carry a substantial load on the roof so any rack must have extensions reaching down to steel body mounts. Other vehicles' steel guttering will be up to the job, provided there's no rust in there and the rack uses several wide feet. Note that cracked pillars and windscreens are common symptoms of overloaded or inadequately supported roof racks. I was in a heavily-loaded 109 recently and could see the whole body flexing from side to side in the front windscreen frames while on some bends the doors would fly open.

If you do end up carrying heavy loads on the rack, expect to have to drive much more carefully. The owners of the Toyota pictured on page 65 boasted that they carried a ton, much of it on the roof. Halfway through their trans-African trip the top-heavy BJ45 rolled unexpectedly on a smooth dirt road. They ended up sawing off the top half of the car, giving away their excess gear in an impromptu roadside market and carrying on south. They also commit-

ted another mistake in the mounting of their rack: they attached it both to the roof gutters and to the chassis. Land Cruisers and many other 4WDs have rubber-mounted bodies to permit some chassis flex and reduce interior noise and vibration. Because the body moves independently of the twisting chassis the tension repeatedly broke their gutter mounts without them understanding why. With a rubber-mounted body, attach the rack either to the body or to the chassis (the latter

Alloy Land Rover gutters can't hold a heavy rack alone and after a sudden drop or extended corrugations the guttering begins to 'unroll' blocking the doors from opening. You'll notice one clamp has been removed to allow the door to open. G-Wagens have a similar design but are made of steel.

really is overkill unless you're carrying a herd of buffalo on the rack).

Land Rover bodies are made of alloy panels which are less strong. They get round this by bolting the 'fragile' body shell directly to the very rigid chassis: one reason why Series Rovers give such an uncomfortable ride and why current Rovers feature long travel coil suspension. In this case a chassis-mounted rack is more desirable if rarely implemented because of the complication or expense. As mentioned earlier, struts dropping down from the rack to solid chassis mounts front and rear easily overcome the limitations of soft gutters.

Roof access

Some kind of **roof-access ladder or steps** is a good idea, and obviously essential if you're planning to sleep on the roof. If you're dithering about spending the extra for a rack with an access ladder, do it, you won't regret it. Even though you can easily haul yourself up by standing on a bumper, wheel top, spare wheel and window sill, one day you'll slip and injure yourself. The back corners of Land Rovers are ideal for access ladders but cars with tailgates are more awkward. Ladders hanging from the upper tailgate or on full-width doors put a strain on the hinges and can only work with the door closed or tailgate lowered; ladders on the side aren't ideal either. The light and effective solution is to bolt a couple of rungs or steps onto the back corner. You'll see many African Land Cruisers have neat Toyota access rungs bolted to their corners – you can probably buy these out there.

Roof bars

A full-length platform is not always necessary. A couple of gutter-mounted roof bars can carry rarely-used gear such as a spare tyre, PSP and a shovel. Roof bars or ladder-racks can be bought from car accessory shops but are usually designed for commercial vans, not overlanders. Make sure you get something that has the necessary rigidity and robust mounting clamps or get something made to fit. As with all racks the important things to remember are wide feet to spread the load in the gutter and a secure mounting bracket. Square-section 50mm aluminium tubing makes a strong and light roof bar while the gutter brackets may be easier bought from a rack manufacturer than made yourself.

Interior storage systems

Obviously some sort of containerisation is needed to help organise and locate your payload. Some ideas are given below but whatever you choose, go for **several medium-sized boxes** rather than a couple of large ones. A medium-sized box of, say, 40 litres' capacity is easier to pick up and move while not being so big that the things at the bottom require protracted unpacking. If you do choose a deep box, put another box in it so it can be pulled out and the lower half easily accessed. You can pile rucksack-sized bags of clothes, mattresses and bedding on top of all your boxes, as they're light, help muffle the rattles and are easy to lift out of the way. A rucksack is a good idea anyway in case you end up walking out or flying home.

Keep things simple. It's easy to get carried away using every last nook and cranny to stash away small items which are awkward to retrieve or forgotten about. Then again, certain non-fragile items which you'll use rarely if at all –

like vehicle spares – can be stashed out of the way between the rear body panels of the rear wings. Larger items like spare shocks can be attached securely under the body to chassis rails or behind bumpers. Zip ties or wire backed up with duct tape does the trick.

Line the back of your car with carpet to dull the ever-present **rattling**. It's something you won't be able to gauge until you hit your first corrugated piste, but a rattling payload soon

Two, inch-deep steps are bolted to the rear pillar of this Land Cruiser. With practice you can step from the bumper onto the roof using just one arm

becomes extremely irritating. Tying everything down with **straps** also helps minimise rattling and stops things from sliding about and breaking.

You may find it useful to draw yourself a small map identifying the location of various items as it's possible to forget your ingenious packing layout weeks later. It's certainly wise to label similar-looking containers with their contents or use differing colours. I'm not the only person to have turned their car inside-out looking for obvious items I was sure I saw just a few minutes ago!

Lastly, a **cargo barrier** is a very good safety precaution. It can be an interior tank or just a wire dog guard bolted to the body behind the back seats of a station wagon. Stories of all sorts of drivers being killed by things hitting them from behind are not rare. Think about how your luggage will react in a frontal impact or in the event of rolling over.

Containers

Plastic crates and lidded metal boxes are most popular and best used in combination.

Choose **vertical-sided plastic crates**, not the tapered ones which stack within each other when empty. Vertical-sided crates don't waste space and pack more securely side-by-side. Buy quality items made of thick soft plastic rather than brittle thin ones. Make sure the handles are up to the job: you don't want to come away with just a couple of handles when yanking a loaded crate out of the back. Measure the dimensions of your payload area. There are enough varieties of plastic crates available at home-accessory and DIY stores to find a set that will almost perfectly fill out your rear compartment with little room to move about. Use blocks of wood to fine-tune the location and eliminate shifting.

Well-made Zarges **alloy boxes** can be bought from military surplus outlets or new. It's worth having one such box, strong and dustproof, either locked to the roof rack (if packed with lightweight items) or inside for secure storage.

Home-made frame supporting plastic crates on an HJ75. That's an Engel fridge on the left. © Geoff Kingsmill

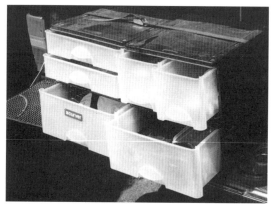

Plastic stackable drawers from a DIY superstore; an inexpensive solution to compartmentalised storage...

... but banana boxes are an ideal size, strong and rattle even less. What's more, they're free.

Storing all your stuff in Zarges boxes is over the top. **Steel trunks** are cheaper but tend to rattle more and are best lined with carpet. Därrs has a broad range of all these types of metal box.

Drawers or cupboards really are the ideal solution to accessibility without having to lift out box after box. Slide-out boxes, either crates on a frame (see photo) or boxes on shelves, is the easiest method.

I once tried the latter by fitting two or three shelves into the back carrying **banana boxes** with the bases inverted into the lids and the handle slots strengthened with duct tape. Banana boxes may sound like a joke but I copied the idea from a German veteran whose boxes were on their sixth African outing! Banana boxes are free, strong, the ideal size and rattle-proof.

While time-consuming to conceive and make, the heavy 15mm boards could hold five or six boxes each. Locating strips screwed to the shelves stopped the boxes sliding out and if you measure it just right everything will fit neatly. It's a crude but cheap way of achieving easy access, though plastic crates on a metal frame slide out more easily.

On a later vehicle I modified this system by simply using a set of

Curver 'Workshop' stackable drawers. Four of these 20-litre units were enough to hold various items for daily use, weighed next to nothing and stood up to several month-long Sahara trips. One problem with plastic is that it begins to look so grubby after a while.

Lashing down

All these boxes are useless if not lashed down. Jamming them in is not enough and piling bags on top is still not good enough for the piste. A vehicle rollover would create the worst circumstances for unsecured baggage but much more often it's the rebound of the springs out of a dip that lifts loose baggage into the air momentarily whereupon it drops back down with a wince-inducing thud. This is when things get damaged. With the containers securely lashed to the floor and their contents snugly packed, it's possible to endure hours of corruga-

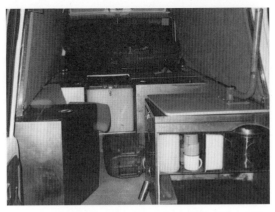

Stainless steel interior from Grand Erg in Milan. Note fold-down beds on the side walls.

Another Defender with a similar conversion. Simple latch cupboards on the right and stove and sink on the left. Sleeping compartment is in an alloy roof wedge accessible from the inside.

tions with nothing more than a loosened jar lid, while still being able to get to things.

Station wagons, especially those with rear seating removed, actually offer more potential fittings for lashing points than some commercial vehicles. Land Rover hardtops are a case in point as they still don't have common sense **lashing points** as standard and will probably never get them.

Straps, tie-downs and other fixtures

Fittings and straps don't have to be enormously strong, just sufficient to stop the containers launching themselves over bumps; quick-release straps make access and, more importantly, relocation effortless – often overlooked when you're packing up in the morning or in a rush. Stronger 1-inch ratchet straps or **tie-downs** have strong hooks and can hold anything from a tyre to a motorbike on a trailer. Elastic bungees may not be strong but have a

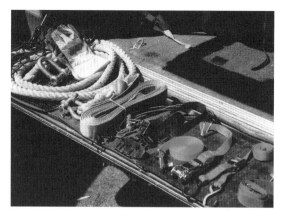

A selection of straps for towing and lashing down. Carry plenty of spare tie-downs and elastic bungees.

multitude of uses. Carry an excess of straps and tie-downs: long, short, thin, wide, ratchet, quick release. They're always useful but tend to go missing or get worn through. Lengths of **chain** (in old bicycle inner tubes to prevent rattling) and a few padlocks are also useful for securing high lifts, sand ladders etc in populated areas while strips of **inner tubes** themselves, knotted into loops make excellent, renewable bungees to secure anything from shovels to firewood. And there'll come a time when a length of **string or rope** will prove useful, for a clothes drying line if nothing else.

Fitted options

Specially-designed fitted storage systems (some examples are illustrated on the previous pages) are intended to replicate a motorhome's cupboards and fittings in the back of a standard 4WD car, something that's only partially effective in such a small space. They generally comprise a set of boxes of various sizes and shapes, often designed to fit the contours of your vehicle exactly. In a typical system you would get a kitchen box with built-in two-ring gas stove and bottle, detachable wind-break, and space for pans, oil and washing-up liquid and other tall items, plus five other boxes, some deep enough to store bedding, others only large enough for packets of food. As with the best motorhomes the boxes are designed to be versatile so you can arrange them to double as tables or seats or a large flat surface area on which to sleep.

However, they are better suited to cooler areas of the world or longer overland trips, where inclement weather may make you want to huddle inside the car. As you spend all day driving in the car and maybe even the nights sleeping in it too, eating at cramped tables really is for agoraphobics only.

Other stowage ideas and places

Elastic nets, as found on the back of coach seats and in Discoverys, are easily fitted to any vertical or overhead surface and very useful for stuffing light objects out of the way but not out of sight. Larger elastic **cargo nets** up to half a metre square with hooks in each corner are available from motorcycle shops.

A compartmentalised **shelf** fitted across the width of the car above the windscreen makes a handy stowage area, especially on vehicles with inadequate door pockets and other stowage areas. In Australia they make fitted ones for Land Cruisers and the like.

Camping equipment and food

Part of the pleasure of motoring in any wilderness is being able to park up anywhere and establish a temporary home in potentially spectacular surroundings. To do this you need to carry well-thought-out equipment for sleeping, cooking, eating, drinking and washing, all of which should be packed, stored and organised so as to make camping as hassle-free as possible. Some days on the piste will be hard and tiring and this is when a smoothly operating camp will be appreciated. You don't want to fuss about for an hour or more erecting a flapping tent or setting up a kitchen when all you really want is a cup of tea and a lie down. As with most aspects of overland travel, the aim here is for convenience, accessibility and securely packed and reliable equipment that's simple to operate and easy to store away.

SLEEPING ARRANGEMENTS

Travelling through the desert in a car it's both possible and desirable to sleep as comfortably as you would at home. Overlanding is tiring at the best of times, and you're a lot more likely to make serious errors of judgement and to fall out with travelling companions if you haven't slept properly for days. Although some people enjoy the simplicity of doing as the nomads do and **sleeping on the ground**, this seems to be an acquired taste for back-to-basics Saharan purists and there's nothing to be gained from giving yourself this extra endurance test unless you know you'll enjoy it.

Where to sleep

Unlike bikers and cyclists, car drivers have the luxury of several different options when it comes to sleeping arrangements, none of which need take up unreasonable amounts of space or weight.

If you do sleep in the sand, one tip I've found that works really well is to scrape out a flat **trench** with your foot just a few inches deep and as long and wide as you are, then throw your sleeping or mat on top. The curved up sides replicate the 'sinking in' impression of a good mattress and make an instantly raised level for a pillow. Try it if you sleep out, you'll be surprised how snug and cozy it feels.

A cosy spot in the Grand Erg after a couple of days dune bashing.

Ground tents

Tents are cheap, light and simple to erect; they create a sense of security and privacy, can protect you from insects and other creatures and should keep out the wind, sand and even rain. The best tents to go for are the **self-supporting** geodesic ones; avoid anything that relies on guy ropes as tent pegs can be a pain in sand and hard work in stony ground. Go for a tent capacity of much more than the typical allocation the catalogues give – they are a tight squeeze. Two people will appreciate the space of at least a three-person tent and in a car the extra kilo or so of a bigger tent is not a problem. Self-supporting tents can be easily picked up and moved around should the shade move, the wind change direction or you find yourself too close to something's burrow for comfort. On hot nights the fly sheet can be left off, the inner tent acting as an insect net while allowing any breeze to pass through.

The chief drawback of sleeping on the ground is the fact that you can't just park up anywhere and set up camp. You'll need to find a smooth, flat area – not easy in the middle of a huge *hamada*. Of course, if your tent is narrow enough you can put it on your roof rack if the ground looks uninviting, assuming the rack is clear of gear.

Inside the vehicle

Sleeping inside the vehicle is the idea behind motorhomes and truck conversions, but can be cramped and claustrophobic in an ordinary-sized 4WD. With this option you never have to worry about where you stop, plus you've got the security of the body around you, which can be comforting in certain places and gives you protection from whatever the weather throws at you.

Unless your vehicle is loaded to the roof (in which case it is almost certainly overloaded!), you should be able to squeeze in the back for the odd night – a useful option if you want to keep a low profile near a town, if there's a storm blowing or if you just can't be bothered to erect the tent. But if sleeping in your vehicle is your permanent plan you must obviously arrange your gear to form a strong, flat surface or, more easily, have a board that is either permanently fitted or that slides or swings into position. A **bed-board** permanently fixed across the car halfway between the floor and the roof is ideal in that it enables you to stop and just crawl in the back for a rest or even lie there while being driven – handy if you're feeling poorly. Boards that slide in must usually be in several parts, but on a hardtop can be stacked on top of each other behind the front seats to unfold or slide onto otherwise unobtrusive side supports. On a relatively long and narrow Land Rover this works well, but wider cars will need heavy, strong boards if they're not to collapse under your weight. The idea behind the **built-in systems** is that the strong storage containers are designed to take the weight of sleeping adults, in the latter case with just the fitting of a couple of boards.

Roof tents

Like sleeping inside the car, having a roof tent gives you the freedom to stop and camp on any kind of terrain. A roof tent puts you up in the breeze and gives your car a 'second room', welcome on a long trip or if there are a few of you. They are particularly suitable for Africa but less effective in stormier, colder environments. Whatever type of roof accommodation you opt for you'll need a strong roof rack that's capable of supporting the weight of two adults, and some kind of roof-access ladder or rungs as discussed earlier. Of course, all this won't do your aerodynamics or fuel consumption any good.

A pair of Eezi-Awn rooftents. A rear overhang (see below) can be better in that it gives you shade over the rear door area, if that's where you cook.
© Toby Savage

You can put any two-person self-supporting tent on the roof, but if you can afford it, a purpose-built roof tent from Howling Moon, Hannibal or Eezi Awn (to name just a few of the South African manufacturers from where most such tents originate) will make your nights comfier and more fun. Made of durable canvas, most of them fold in half on a frame on your roof rack. Unfolding with minimum effort, some of these tents will be up in less time than it takes to get an ordinary tent out of the bag and laid on the ground.

These canvas roof tents cost a rather hefty £600/€1000 (about 50% more than in South Africa). The best ones to go for hang off the roof on a board supported by the ladder. Generally a **back or side overhang** is most useful as it creates some handy shade in a useful area. Many of these tents have integral mattresses which add to their bulk and your fuel consumption, and some have good venting systems which work well in sub-Saharan or tropical areas but not so well in a strong desert wind.

You may sometimes have trouble finding good level patches of ground and it's surprising how desirable it is: for a good tip see p.292. An alternative to canvas fold-out tents is the Italian Magiolina which uses a waterproof GRP case which winds up to erect the tent, but these take up the whole roof and cost even more than all-canvas tents.

Mattresses, camp beds or hammocks

Wherever you decide to sleep – on the ground, inside the car or on the roof rack – you will have no regrets if you do so on a high density, **deep foam mattress**. At about 80mm thick and made of open-cell foam, they are bulky to store and, in the UK at least, quite expensive, but can be almost as comfortable as a proper bed.

Avoid the foam mattresses supplied in vinyl sleeves with some roof tents as they're sweaty. Instead, make a close-fitting **case** for the mattress from washable, comfortable but snag-proof material such as heavy-duty cotton or upholstery fabric. Before you sew the sleeve, think about how you're going to store the mattresses in the car. Unless they fit in a roof tent finding a good place to keep them is a problem. A full-length mattress of two metres can be cut into two unequal sections (the longer section to match the width of the car) and a fold sewn into the sleeve. This enables two mattresses to stack relatively compactly.

Even with a natural fabric sleeve, foam mattresses get clammy by the morning so, like all the bedding, are worth airing; hang them over the tent or roof rack while you're making breakfast.

Air beds or lilos take up much less room than foam mattresses but are much less comfortable and have the perennial problem of punctures, and to a lesser extent, inflation (a compressor helps). Even then they're sweaty and with double air beds the lighter person will roll into the dip of the heavier – not always desirable even with loving couples! Individual airbeds are better but overall they are to be avoided.

Camp beds are another thing of the past, being even bulkier than mattresses and not that comfortable anyway. On the dry ground of the Sahara they offer no particular advantage and allow cool air to pass underneath; this is desirable only in the heat of summer when the hard ground retains its heat and actually warms you up – very unpleasant. If getting away from crawling insects is your priority, sleeping in a zipped-up tent, in the car or on the roof offers all the answers.

Hammocks sound like an even cooler way of getting above the ground but in the desert there is rarely anything to hang them from except a pair of vehicles. Also, try spending a night in a hammock before you go... you'll find yourself very stiff and distinctly banana-shaped (and banana-coloured) by the morning. If you insist on hammocking, go for the wider transverse Mexican-style nets where you sleep across the width of the hammock so gain a flat, more stable sleeping area, though these are only suitable for one person. Save your hammocking for the jungle.

In a bid to outdo Japanese gimmickry Land Rover experimented with this gearbox-oven below the middle seat. On older models Low Range third is equivalent to Gas Mark 6.

Make the most of sleeping comfort and go the whole hog with **bedding**: a duvet with pillows is much nicer than a sleeping bag which may be warmer and more compact but can limit leg movement which, depending on how you sleep, makes you feel cramped in the mornings. Some better brands of sleeping bags can zip together to make one large bag. A duvet, sheet and pillows can be easily rolled up into a bundle, strapped up and thrown anywhere in the back or in a dustproof container on the roof.

COOKING EQUIPMENT

If you're cooking for no more than four people, you can manage quite well with a twin-burner camping stove plus a supplementary means for boiling water at lunchtime without having to set up the stove. The choice is mainly between **bottled gas** (available locally though not always in handy-sized bottles), powerful but fussy **petrol stoves** and an open fire.

Locals cook on open fires or gas, usually making a frame for the gas burners. Below: an old twin-burner gas stove folds out of the back door of a Carawagon.

Gas stoves

Butane gas is the standard fuel for powering camping stoves and is common in African and European countries with no mains gas. It has many advantages. The flame lights instantly and burns cleanly, the stoves are simple, light and cheap to buy, bottles can be bought or refilled even in the desert and certainly in big towns right across the Sahara (albeit usually the

big 20kg bottles). **Fittings and threads** may not match what you bring from home but you can buy it all out there cheaply (stoves included) and a standard 5kg bottle of gas about the size of a football will easily last two people a month, especially if another source is used for boiling water. The main drawback is that they don't put out as much heat as petrol stoves and can be prone to poor vapourisation in sub-zero temperatures (keep the bottle warm on freezing nights). Another problem is that a gas flame is quite weak compared to a petrol stove, so unless you cook inside you'll need to set up a windproof position.

Petrol stoves

Coleman's well-known petrol stoves are an alternative but have the drawback of running poorly on ordinary petrol (more on p.233) so even if you're running a petrol vehicle you'll need to carry unleaded or better still 'Coleman fuel' (refined petrol, 'white gas'). For a larger group, Coleman do a three-burner model but these are probably available with gas stoves too. I've found Colemans powerful but poorly designed and fiddly to use compared to gas.

Open fires and pressure cookers

Cooking solely on wood is possible in parts of the Sahara, but you're further depleting an already scarce natural resource that should be left for any remaining nomads. In some parts of the desert, like the Hoggar (a particularly barren place), cooking on open fires is said to have been outlawed altogether for tourist groups. If you do use wood, be economical or bring plentiful waste wood from home, you'll find it everywhere. Campfires are convivial, but avoid huge blazing bonfires using scarce desert wood.

Cooking on an open fire is agreeable, but use wood sparingly, or better still bring your own.

Whatever you cook on, a **pressure cooker** speeds up cooking and makes it easier to cook on a single ring. Bring the cooker up to pressure then take it off the heat and wrap it up or put it by an open fire. You can then cook whatever's going with it and by the time that's done whatever's inside the pressure cooker will be ready to eat. They may appear a bulky item to carry around in the desert, but if you're cooking for more than four people who want to eat more than a variety of tinned foods, they can expand your culinary repertoire.

Boiling water

There will probably be plenty of times when you just want to boil some water – for lunchtime soup, mid-afternoon tea or a warm wash – without having to set up your stove or use up one of the valuable two rings while something else is cooking. A small single-burner camping stove is a handy alternative heat source, but the small cartridges are hard to find in the Sahara. Better to take two 5kg bottles and use one for quick boiling and the other to supply the stove. To keep things simple you can attach a burner head directly to the bottle so there's no need for fiddly hoses. Set by a wheel out of the wind it's a quick way of boiling water in a kettle or pan.

Volcano kettles and thermos flasks

Volcano kettles (to give one of their many names) are a nifty solution to fast boiled water. A volcano is a cylindrical container with an outer chamber con-

A volcano kettle and a flask – a handy way of making hot water and keeping it hot, all helping to save stove fuel.

taining water and a perforated base to allow air to get in. Any combustible material (twigs, paper, grass, sand soaked with petrol) is stuffed into the central 'chimney' and set alight. Acting on a similar principle to Trangia stoves, this actually works better in the wind.

The large surface area inside the chimney quickly heats up the surrounding water jacket, making full use of the heat energy. Once you get the hang of lighting it (a squirt of lighter fuel will speed things up greatly) and know how much fuel to use the volcano will boil a litre in three to four minutes. To me the corked, aluminium **Kelly kettle** version available in the UK appears unnecessarily complicated, with a separate stand, grill and pot-type handle. Although the performance is the same, I've found an Australian one-piece, galvanised mug-handle version (see photo, p.156) much more in tune with the simple ethos of the volcano.

Washing with sand – but not on your mum's best Teflon pot.

Finding **fuel** is surprisingly easy in most parts of the Sahara – except in dunes and on barren hamadas, for which occasions it's worth keeping a sack of twigs as a back-up. These kettles give you the satisfaction of efficiently using combustible waste and whatever you come across while offering the performance of a gas stove. In fact, a volcano can double as a conventional kettle on a gas stove by simply putting a cap over the top of the chimney to retain the heat (the lid of a tin can does the job).

A thermos flask is worth taking on any camping trip and nowhere more so than in the Sahara. Filled in the morning when the stove or volcano is up and running, a quality thermos will easily keep water or beverages hot enough till the evening, providing you remember to pre-warm the chamber with some boiling water first. The robust all-metal flasks are best. The plastic pump-pouring 'coffee-morning' flasks popular in France seem a bit flimsy for desert conditions and appear more suited to keeping water cool.

Fridge-freezers and cool boxes

Depending on your attitude, a **fridge** is either an unnecessary luxury or an essential accessory for your cooking needs. Ask yourself what you'll be putting in it once you get to the desert and your perishable supplies from home have run out. Refrigerated products are a rarity in the Sahara and cooling canned drinks (or drinking water) is an extravagance. It's surprising how cool a car can remain, even without air-con, if you keep the sun out where possible. While unpacking a car during a 30°C lunch break, you'll be surprised just how cool some buried and sealed items can remain from the previous night.

Unless you're dead set on enjoying fresh dairy products (while they last) it's better to adapt your food needs to **non-refrigerable items**, especially once you see the cost of a desert-ready fridge. For example, many sauces need refrigeration once they're opened, so buy small bottles and use them in one go. The same applies to long-life (UHT) milk. Hard cheese actually lasts very well without a fridge, indeed at the end of one six-week trip through Algeria we wondered what the red ball of Edam really contained, having only mildly rubberised over that time in the back of a hot-running soft top. Butter or margarine will remain fairly solid if kept out of the sun and well-buried vegetables can be stored in pieces of cloth to prolong their lives. On a recent trip (admittedly in mid-winter) we had fresh salads right up until the day we returned to civilisation – two weeks later. With a bit of thought, it can be done.

Engel fridge. Nice for luxuries
but how long will they last?
© expeditionexchange.com

Engel fridges

If you're sure you want a fridge in the Sahara, Engel is the Japanese brand that's renowned for being up to the task of cooling and even freezing food while shaken about in the back of a 4WD. Engel fridges start at around £350/€570 with a 16-litre capacity, with prices rising to over £800/€1200 for 39-litre fridge-freezers. The 29-litre fridge-freezer model is a popular choice, being a useful capacity but not too big (though still the size of a pair of jerricans). Most Engel units are steel bodied (smaller ones are plastic) and open from the top so no cool heavy air drains away.

What makes these fridges/freezers so expensive is their compact and efficient motors, capable of running off 12- or 24-volt car batteries as well as domestic AC while drawing minimum power. Other cheaper fridges use different cooling technology but they're not quite up to the demands of Saharan travel. Engle's 29-litre model can draw as little as 1.6 watts at an ambient temperature of 30°C to keep the contents at 5°C – a little higher than a domestic fridge. Trying to freeze things will work the motor much harder and draw more watts. Remember that ensuring efficient cooling by the fridge minimises the drain on your battery too.

Cool boxes

If you like the fridge idea but can't afford an Engel, a plain insulated plastic coolbox or Esky might be for you. With thickly insulated walls and a top lid, they're designed to keep food cool usually with the aid of a bag of ice or one of those slow-thawing blue ice blocks (neither of which is available in the Sahara). Nevertheless you can still use the insulation properties by opening the box to the cold overnight and opening it as little as possible in the day. Even though they are cheap, for the space they take you may find even cool boxes are not worth it unless you are buying local meat.

Fridge and cool box tips
● Reduce air space – solids and fluids retain their temperature longer.
● At night put some water bottles out in the open; around dawn put them back in the fridge.
● Keep the vehicle shady and ensure the fridge is out of direct sun.
● Try and maintain airflow through the car when stationary.
● Open the fridge as little and briefly as possible during the heat of the day.

Cooking utensils

There's no need to buy gimmicky camping equipment like nesting pots if what you have at home will do the job. Some breakable items like plates are better in plastic (though paper plates save water and can be burned), but a china mug can be easily protected and is nicer to drink from. Also, a car has room enough to carry a few morale-boosting luxuries – for example, fresh coffee from a cafetière or an espresso coffee pot can make an early start less daunting.

When **packing** utensils, envisage a typical cooking scenario and group things together for easy access. Keep small, loose items like cutlery and tin-openers together in a small box and wrap clanking items in tea towels to stop them rattling against each other.

A kitchen box

- Large saucepan
- Small saucepan – not essential but can be useful
- Frying pan
- Volcano kettle
- Personal water bottle
- Hanging 10-litre 'day bag' for water – avoids lugging out a heavy jerrican if you don't have an electric pump or tank with a tap
- Thermos flask
- Kitchen knife
- Chopping board – doubles as a useful windbreak for cooking stove
- Sieve/colander (draining pasta water from a saucepan is manageable but is a common cause of scalds, as well as 'spaghetti sablonese')
- Tin-opener
- Deep plastic plates/large bowls – take a spare for covering things or for visitors
- Large plastic or china mugs – useful for cereal, too
- Spoons and forks
- Washing-up bowl – makes a general purpose container, and can also be used for washing clothes
- Paper towels – better than tea towels which soon get grubby
- Washing-up liquid and pan scourers – you can save water by washing plates and pans in sand; sand removes leftovers and leaves a clean plate but works better on hard surfaces like china or stainless steel
- Cutlery box – avoids losing things
- Tupperware boxes or deep-screw plastic jars
- Condiment box (or drawer) for all herbs, spices, nuts and condiments
- Transparent plastic bags – useful for wrapping but identifying leakables
- Cloth bags (make your own) for storing vegetables
- Large plastic bag or bin liner for keeping bread fresh

FOOD

Don't assume you to have to eat badly just because you're travelling in the wilderness. The expectation to suffer by eating corned beef round the clock is a particularly English affectation. While it can be fun to get back to basics don't forget this is your holiday and a good meal may be the day's only highlight. With some careful planning before you leave home and a small but well-stocked stash of home-bought food supplies, you can supplement locally-bought provisions and make desert meals something to look forward to, not just a means of counteracting malnutrition.

Spices on offer at Zagora's weekly market.

MAKING BREAD

Even in the Sahara it's rare to be more than four days between settlements and a chance to buy fresh bread.

But, even if you don't choose to park up for a while or are undertaking a long slow route, fresh bread every day can be a treat, as demonstrated by the popularity of domestic bread-making machines.

Nomads have traditionally baked bread in sand heated by the embers of a fire; it's a common treat on a Saharan tour. Embers are pushed away, a dip in the sand is scooped out, with sand and embers put back over to bake the dough. But this unleavened *taghella* (to give it the Tuareg name) is rather dense and hard work once it's no longer fresh.

Tortilla-like **flat bread** is quicker to make on a frying pan: a mixture of flour, water and a bit of salt. Add an egg or two and use milk instead of water and you have **pancakes** which can be a treat either savoury or sweet.

But to give bread a bit of body without the heaviness of *taghella*, you need yeast, time and a bit of practice. On one tour we did in the Gilf we were over two weeks in the desert with no provisions. Our cook laboriously made up some dough with the all-important yeast and let it rise for a couple of hours. He then rolled out lumps into flat round discs, fried them on a hot plate and soon we had fresh, hot **nan**-like bread which was chewy and a whole lot more satisfying than *taghella* or stale baguettes.

The price for this is the time it takes to make it – it's not something you'd want to do every night, but you won't regret it if you do.

Making leavened bread using a jack handle and an oil drum lid.

Local food

Overstocking with food supplies from home is a common mistake; after all you're going to the Sahara, and organising provisions for each day is one less thing to worry about. Plus you would get to eat what you like, not what's available. But even if you intend to spend most of your trip piste-bashing in remote corners of the desert, you'll find yourself passing through villages and small towns every so often, and where there are people there is food.

Much of the fun in being in the Sahara is in mingling with local people at the markets and experimenting with exotic foods. It can take some getting used to but will give you a chance to socialise in an authentic way before you disappear back into the dunes.

Of course, local food may be in short supply – deep in the desert produce from the oases is minimal, quality and variety are limited and prices high, but chances are that, if you're not too fussy, you'll be able to at least partially restock every time you pass through inhabited areas. The first step then is to try and anticipate how frequent and how reliable your market stops will be.

Bread (*khobsa* in Arabic) is one thing you'll find in any desert town, available for next to nothing either from the **bakery** (*kusha*) or redistributed to a corner shop, though hardly ever at the market. In the Francophone Saharan countries you'll get baguettes, though they are a bit denser than what you'd get in France. Further east traditional flat breads are the norm.

From mid- to late winter you'll find **oranges** for sale at roadside stalls, markets and oases throughout the Sahara. Cafés and coffee houses in even the smallest towns often offer freshly-squeezed orange juice at this time of year.

Dates are a staple desert food and are sold everywhere year-round. They sometimes contain unappetising maggots which might disagree with your stomach; bite into the date sideways to reveal the pit and open up the date to see if anything has got there before you.

Most Europeans are squeamish about buying local **meat** – usually mutton or goat or, in Mauritania, camel – hanging as it does covered in flies. However, so long as you cook the meat

Date with a wriggly surprise.

thoroughly (grilling is best), you shouldn't have to worry about whatever the flies have done to it. But in reality, storing, cutting, preparing and cooking fresh meat is such a hassle that most desert travellers can't be bothered with it and stick to tinned stuff or vegetables. One way a cook managed to make fresh meat last in the desert with only a cool box was to part-cook it in large amounts of *ghee* (refined butter), though any fat would probably do, and add some salt. Two weeks later we were still eating fresh meat. Another way to keep meat fresh is to keep it alive. One time in the Ténéré we came across some nomads and bought a sheep. It was slung on the roof and was killed that evening in the camp.

Most **restaurant dishes** throughout the Sahara are meat-based; to avoid getting sick, try to choose a dish that's freshly cooked for you rather than something that's been stewing away tepidly for several hours. If you're invited to eat at a nomad's tent or someone's home, you may be honoured by having a goat freshly slaughtered for the occasion.

Regional provisions

In **Morocco** and **Tunisia** you're sure to find fruit and vegetable stalls or shops in every small town, as well as a grocery store selling tinned food, pasta and rice. For variety, freshness and spectacle, the best places to shop are the weekly markets (*souks*) held in all small towns in Morocco and Tunisia; guide books should tell you on which days these take place. You can also get fresh French-style bread in every small town in Morocco and Tunisia, and in Morocco flat brown bread the size of a hubcap makes a change from baguettes.

Fresh bread is also available in every small town in **Libya** and **Algeria** from the bakery and sometimes from small grocery stores. In Libya you can often only spot the bakery by the queue of kids with empty bags and baskets lined up outside waiting for the bread to come out of the oven. For a quarter of a dinar (the smallest note) you get five loaves and when you buy less some bakers may give it away.

At the markets or roadside stalls we found potatoes, cucumbers, tomatoes, zucchini, aubergines, onions, okra, parsley, pomegranates, lemons (all around 2LD/kg) and apples. In some small shops (eg in Nalut and Sebha) you can also get a reasonable selection of dried foods, including pasta, biscuits and jam, as well as tinned tuna, processed cheese and chocolate spread. Prices seem expensive but are about the same as in Europe. The new road which

Spreading out across a *raïma* is a relaxing way to dine. Below: a lovely Salade Aïroise.

finally reached Djanet, Algeria, in 2001 vastly improved the range of goods there, with the corner shops next to Djanet market amazingly well stocked with tinned and dairy goods plus local produce. Illizi and Tamanrasset are better still in their selection.

In **Mauritania**, Atar has plentiful supplies of vegetables and some fruit for sale in its main market; you can buy bread and brochettes here too, but usually only in the late afternoon. There are plenty of corner stores in Atar, selling a few canned foods, soft drinks, biscuits and sweets. Remember, if it grows locally or in the same country or the Far East, it may well be cheap, but if it's been imported from Europe it will be the same price as back home. The Sahara of **Niger** being much more remote it will only be Agadez where you can stock up well, though at a higher price. Throughout the Aïr local boutiques will have some goods to supplement locally-grown produce while on the far side of the Ténéré, Dirkou is a remarkable frontier town of unexpected vitality and intrigue. On the trade route to Libya, you can get everything from a haircut to a new magazine for your AK. The regional capital, Bilma, to the south, is a ghost town, by comparison.

Basic food supplies

Even assuming you'll be able to buy sufficient fruit and vegetables every three or four days, you should always carry some **back-up food** to cover the days when you run out of fresh food or don't make it to market in time. Aim for a mixture of quick and easy tins, weight- and space-saving dried food with short cooking times to save fuel, and some simple sauces that only need water but are palatable. A few packets of pasta and/or rice are always a good standby, as are tinned kidney beans, chick peas, tuna and mackerel, or anything else nutritious and palatable that's in a can; don't take too many cans as they weigh a lot and don't take anything you haven't tasted before you leave. Tofu-like halloumi or paneer hard cheeses last for ages and fry up well with a bit of pasta sauce. The same goes for those freeze-dried 'just-add-boiling-water' meals in a bag you get from camping shops. They may be light to carry but on tasting one we threw the rest away. Packets of dried tomatoes, dried mushrooms and dried onions are good back-up vegetables. Take oil, salt, pepper, tomato purée (in a tube which can be reused over a long period, not in a can which cannot) and a few herbs and spices to jazz up your meals and make them taste different from the night before.

Take plenty of *enjoyable* snacks – crisps, chocolate, cakes – and think twice about overly wholesome and overpriced energy foods that you think are suitable for an expedition but would never normally eat at home. Dried fruit and nuts are full of the right stuff but soon lose their lustre (buy dates in the desert instead). Wholegrain bars make handy snacks but are similarly boring after a while.

Lunches and evening meals

Long-life **spreads** and fillings are a good idea as bread is so ubiquitous right across the desert. With cheese spread, long-life paté, jam, Nutella or peanut butter, you can make fast and filling sandwiches for breakfasts and lunches. Sometimes you need a lot of spread on old bread to make it palatable. If you have a fridge, fresh cheese is a nice treat; if you don't, try taking hard cheeses with you and keeping them in the coolest part of the car, wrapped in cloth rather than plastic once opened. Butter or margarine will last fine out of a fridge, though is best kept in a sealed box. Olive oil makes a good substitute.

A good lunch and snack option are instant **cup soups** – instant Japanese miso is more refreshing than the traditional instant soups and a good source of salt. As a change from bread we made up **salads** for lunch, usually concocted from tinned fish with a few pine nuts, herbs and dressing. You can also use up any rice or pasta left over from the previous night's meal, which is why it's worth taking a couple of empty tupperware boxes with you.

Evening meals can be the most convivial time of the day, especially when you're travelling in a group, and sometimes camp cooking can be a real pleasure. But it can also be a chore at the end of a long and tiring day, especially if there's a strong wind, or if it's cold. Food that works particularly well for speedy, **hassle-free** evening meals includes pastas that don't take long to cook (eg gnocci), served with a packet cheese or pesto sauce, instant noodles, and pre-flavoured risottos (which can be enlivened with sun-dried tomatoes and dried mushrooms). You'll also appreciate fast-cooking meals if you're running low on cooking fuel.

A sample list of basic food supplies

- Pasta, especially the fast-cooking varieties such as tortelloni and gnocci
- Packets of pre-flavoured risotto – fast, easy and tasty
- Rice – varieties with dried vegetables or spices mixed in are handy, but keep some plain; that savoury taste gets nauseating
- Instant noodles – very useful when you're too tired to do anything more than boil water
- Tinned beans, eg kidney beans, chick peas, black-eye – can be added to anything and are full of protein we're told
- Tinned vegetables like sweetcorn or new potatoes, or a ratatouille mix
- Dried onions – light and add flavour to anything
- Sun-dried tomatoes – add interest and flavour to anything
- Dried mushrooms (porcini are tastiest but need pre-soaking)
- Packet soups
- Packets of mix-with-water sauces, eg cheese (some types need milk or butter), mushroom and pesto
- Tubes of long-life vegetable paté from health-food shops – tasty, long-lasting, compact
- Nutella – for that chocolate hit!

- Tinned fruit – a quick sweet hit
- Muesli bars – don't melt, and make palatable snacks for a while
- An isotonic 'sports' drink for when you're dehydrated or think you might be soon; the South African 'Game' brand is tasty and inexpensive
- Oil – make sure you buy one with a screw top, not a flip lid
- Salad dressing
- Salt and pepper
- Dried herbs and spices
- Tomato purée in a tube
- Biscuits – sweet and savoury
- Coffee and tea
- Sugar cubes – simpler than powdered sugar, saves on spoons and spillage
- UHT long-life milk

Packing and storing food

The cardinal rules of packing apply here too. Firstly, don't take too much. As described above, when you're in the desert you should always be able to find some provisions every few days. When shopping for your basic supplies, think carefully about **weight and space**, which essentially means go easy on the tins and cartons. Dried stuff is of course very light, but anything that requires reconstituting needs water.

However carefully you **pack your food**, extensive travelling on rough pistes can play havoc with pretty much anything. Lids of all types (jars, bottles, tupperware boxes) undo themselves, paper packets and plastic sacks rub against each other and split, vegetables get bruised, and it's even been known for milk to turn into yoghurt from all that shaking! Encase breakable and leakable items in transparent plastic bags (for easy identification) or tea towels.

Whatever packing and storage system you decide on, you'll need to have several different **compartments** for your food supplies. These should be labelled so that you know more-or-less instantly where to locate something. The idea of pre-planning your meals, with everything in ready-sealed bags seems sound but would only really be necessary for an overworked cook catering for a large group; be flexible and enable choice from your supplies. We found it useful to keep one small 'day box' (containing tea, coffee, milk, energy drink powder, a couple of spreads and soups, a few snacks) for breakfast, lunch and snack items behind the front seats. With a drawer system it's very easy to compartmentalise dried veg, pasta, rice, condiments etc, which makes locating things very easy. As with anything heavy, if you have a box of tins you should try to store it low down in the car.

Remember, all this advice, especially on what to eat, is merely based on a preference and is here to give some ideas; it's not a specially-designed Saharan diet. The simplest advice is: try to eat as you would at home.

CAMP LIFE

Tables and chairs

Don't plan on eating in the front of the vehicle even if the seats are comfy. On most days you'll cherish the opportunity to get out for a change of scenery and if something gets spilt it's a mess. Even if you have a tailgate or a table hingeing down from the back door, a folding **table** with a couple of folding **chairs** makes eating much more comfortable. As ever, there's plenty of designer camp furniture out there but for eating a chair with an upright back is best, if not as comfortable as the various cleverly designed geodesic chairs which have become available. Those are very relaxing but not so good at a table with a plate under your chin. Both tables and chairs with legs joined in a continuous bar along the ground are better than straight legs which sink into the sand. Also useful, though not necessarily for meal times, is a simple **folding stool** – handy for sitting on while doing wheel repairs, for example, and for keeping things off the ground when you've run out of flat surfaces.

Having said all that, it's not impossible to feel rather foolish, sat at your camp table in the middle of the desert with a napkin tucked under your chin. Taking the indigenous approach to eating and relaxing – on a large carpet or **tarpaulin and cushions** – can be most agreeable, and soft furnishings don't break or rattle about. Any old rug or piece of carpet will do and it's easily rolled up and slung on a roof, but bring along some big firm cushions to give support. It may sound pampered but I've found that some sort of **back support** or some way to get your backside just a few inches off the ground (a jerrican with a cushion for example) really is much more comfortable, especially for eating. Lying on the ground you're forever having to move around as one limb goes dead or joints get stiff.

Awnings

You'll always find you gravitate towards shade, usually a lone tree for a lunch break. But for the occasions when nothing turns up (this is the Sahara, after all!), an awning that unrolls from the side of the car or over the back can make lunch breaks or longer camps much more enjoyable than huddling under the shadow of the tailgate or squashed along the shady side of the car. To be fully useful a **three-metre-square** surface area is best, giving enough shade for up to four people without having to shuffle around as the sun moves round.

I made the mistake of choosing an old plastic tarpaulin I'd had lying around for years for our awning; a heavier **natural fibre** would have been much less rusty and may have flapped less, as I found when spending a couple of days under an Eezi-Awn awning. Don't underestimate the effect of the daytime breeze: it will make your awning flap and crack irritatingly and come adrift if not secured thoroughly. The simplest method is a pair of two-metre poles in each corner held in place by a three-

Welcome lunchtime shade at Hassi Mislane (L2), but avoid light plastic tarps which flap irritatingly in the wind.

metre guy pegged or weighed down. Choose long, wide pegs for sand and bang them right in – in rocky terrain anything will do, including a rock. Proper camping awnings which roll out of a tube like a shop front don't need guy lines as they have their own rigidity built in. They are very convenient and would be very welcome on a longer overland trip across Africa.

Lighting

One thing regularly underestimated is the need for good and reliable lighting when camping, as you'll soon realise when you try to hold a torch in your teeth while rummaging in the back of your vehicle. Around Christmas, the most popular time to visit the Sahara, daylight lasts from 8am to 6pm so there'll be a good four hours of wakeful darkness in need of illumination. A full moon and stars can help a lot, but not when it comes to chopping onions rather than the ends of your fingers. **Good lighting** is an important safety consideration. Just as the home is the most dangerous environment, so too, despite the desert's many more obvious dangers, is your nightly camp.

The **courtesy lights** in the car are of some use and most station wagons feature a second light over the back doors as well as in the usual position. They obviously won't be bright enough for camping, so something more effective needs to be set up to undertake the evening's chores. Unless you're a die-hard retro, avoid **lanterns** powered by paraffin, gas or petrol. Paraffin storm-lanterns are relatively feeble and smelly, while anything with a fibre or silk mantle, even the bright Coleman petrol-powered models, doesn't stand a chance of surviving intact on Saharan corrugations unless you are very careful. Other rechargable electric 'lantern-looking' lights by Coleman are ridiculously bulky for what they are.

Adjustable, roof-rack-mounted spotlights powered from the car battery are bright but consume a lot of power, and raised tailgates will get in the way. I've found the best combination of versatility and minimal power drain is a **fluorescent tube** powered from the battery. These consume next to nothing, have no bulb filaments to fracture and provide an adequate spread of light – if not, a second tube certainly will. On my 61 the light jammed neatly into the upper tailgate handle, shedding light directly onto the tailgate.

With a side-opening door it's not so easy. A rod sliding out of the roof rack makes a good hanging point unless you choose permanent mounts

available from caravanning shops, less fiddly in setting up but not quite as versatile in where they shine. Kept on a wire, tube lights can reach to a tent on the ground or the roof, though in this case it's worth adding a switch where the wiring goes into the bulb so you don't have to tear yourself out of your cosy repose to turn it off.

A pair of fluorescent light sticks on long wires make enough light without using much power.

Head torches are very handy of course, especially for night-time toilet outings. And keep a powerful hand torch ready for emergencies.

All lighting will attract **moths** and other insects and small animals, even in the depths of the desert – frustrating when they take a dive for your food. Some night places are worse than others (vegetation and recent rainfall may have something to do with it) but there's not much you can do about this other than occasionally turning everything off or setting up a brighter decoy light to lure them away. That will fool them.

Desert driving

Technically, driving Saharan pistes is less difficult than many imagine. Nevertheless it's vital to have an understanding of what your vehicle can and cannot do. The agility and indestructibility of 4WDs is often overestimated by beginners – not helped by adverts depicting 4WDs driving up dam walls or perched on mountain peaks.

In reality, your fully-loaded four-wheeler is as much a lifeline to you as a camel is to a nomad; the provisions and equipment that it carries are crucial to your survival, so you must **learn how to use it** in off-road conditions. Tourists in 4WDs have died in the half-hour drive between the desert resorts of Erfoud and Merzouga in Morocco because they did the wrong thing when the car got stuck. Actions as basic as engaging freewheeling hubs, reducing tyre pressures or even just putting the car in four-wheel drive (all exacerbated by summer-time temperatures, it must be added) have led to such disasters because people fail to appreciate the limitations of these go-anywhere 4WDs. You can't just turn off the highway, pull a lever or two and drive wherever you like: effective four-wheel driving requires skill and judgement and a familiarity with the attributes of your car's ground clearance and transmission.

In the Sahara, tracks never stay the same for long so concentration on navigation is also vital. The need to maintain smooth progress and not get stuck, while at the same time keeping an eye on the big picture, is what gives desert driving its edge. You may have come here to get away from it all but you won't get away from the need for constant **decision-making,** from trivial issues such as where to make a lunch stop, to fundamental life-or-death calculations about routes and fuel consumption. Like any new skill it has a steep learning curve and satisfaction in its mastery. The fact that your well-being depends on safe driving will never be far from your mind once you are out there.

Sympathetic, defensive driving means protecting the vehicle's components as well as its occupants from damage.

When the text advises to 'engage four-wheel drive' this corresponds to 'engage central diff lock' on full-time 4WDs with a manually operated control (such as most modern Land Cruisers and Rovers).

Situations and techniques in this chapter are specific to desert driving, not general off-roading.

OFF-ROAD DRIVING: SOME BASIC TECHNIQUES

The standard Saharan driving scenario goes something like this. You're driving along a flat **piste** (track) that stretches off into the distance, clearly, vaguely or with many braided deviations. You're averaging around 40kph in third or occasionally fourth gear, slowing down every so often to cross some bumps without flattening your head on the roof. If you're near hills or in a valley, there'll be sandy- or stony-bottomed **oueds** (dry creek beds, wadis) to cross, measuring anything from a metre to a kilometre wide, and you'll probably have to engage the lower gears and possibly four-wheel drive to negotiate them. Things never stay the same for long. You may come to a rough patch of basalt **hamada** that needs to be driven over slowly to preserve both the tyres and the well-being of passengers, after which you might find yourself speeding up across a perfectly smooth claypan. Occasionally you may venture into **dunes** which can be a white-knuckle ride, even if they're easy, as the whole attitude of the car and the required driving style changes.

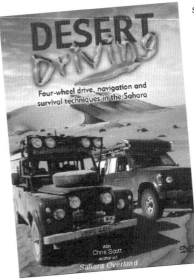

Many of the driving and recovery techniques described in this section are vividly demonstrated in the 82-minute dvd, *Desert Driving*. Filmed entirely in the Sahara, you can buy it off the website.

This **variable terrain** demands your full-time **concentration** as you try to maintain a smooth optimum speed; stretches of truly smooth, obstacle-free piste are so short and so rare that they'll be gone before you have a chance to appreciate them. In fact, it's actually impossible to take your eyes off the track for more than a few seconds without wandering over some suspension-jarring bump. Meanwhile, you or your companion will be watching the compass or GPS as well as occasionally referring to a guidebook or map and keeping your group or guide vehicle in sight and looking out for landmarks.

All of which makes desert driving a demanding exercise. Traffic and conditions permitting, on a highway you can pretty much sit with one finger on the wheel close to the speed limit while eating a sandwich and fiddling with the tape player. In the

TAKE IT EASY

Always drive within the limitations of:	... and be aware of the consequences of:
● your experience	● damaging or rolling the vehicle
● your car's abilities	● getting lost
● the terrain	● running out of fuel
● visibility	If in doubt, slow down, assess or turn back.

desert both hands will be clamped to the steering wheel and both eyes fixed on the ground ahead as you trundle along at 50kph. In good off-road conditions you can cover up to 400km in a day. That doesn't sound like much, but come the evening it will feel great to turn off the engine and enjoy some stillness and silence.

Traction: how to keep your 4WD moving

Traction from your powered wheels, better understood as 'grip', is what keeps your car moving forward. On a good surface two-wheel drive is sufficient but off-road, four-wheel drive spreads power over all four wheels, doubling the traction and making wheelspin – loss of traction – less likely. It's the difference between running up a slippery hill (eventually your feet will slip) or crawling steadily up on all fours.

Traction, and therefore forward motion, is reduced or lost when one or more powered wheels begin to **spin**. Besides using too much power, wheels most commonly spin for four reasons:

● The ground surface is too loose or fluid.
● The tyre pressure is too high for the type of terrain.
● The car's weight is resting on its undercarriage, not the wheels.
● One wheel is in the air (over very rough ground).

Any of the above situations will result in loss of forward motion and, if you don't dip the clutch soon enough in the first example, bogging. Getting stuck in soft sand is discussed later in the chapter, but first it's best to get to grips with a 4WD's angles and ground clearance.

Crossing a steep-sided trench or a low ridge

The third situation listed above, with part of the car's weight resting on its undercarriage, can be fairly described as having exceeded the limit of **ground clearance**. This can happen when driving over rocks but in the Sahara is more commonly used up when negotiating a creek bank or gully, straddling a dune crest or simply sinking right down to the floor pan in soft sand (more on which below).

When crossing a **narrow**, **steep-sided trench** or negotiating a low rocky hump, a good way of not getting bellied-out is to traverse the obstacle at an optimum angle of 45 degrees. (Note that this only applies for low ridges or narrow trenches on flat ground, and not slopes, dunes or creek banks which should always be negotiated straight on; see below.) Drive off in low range (see below) for maximum power and control and let each wheel drop individually down the lip or crawl over the ridge, effectively shortening the wheelbase so improving the ramp breakover angle. It can help if a passenger stands in front of the vehicle and guides the driver over the obstacle. Again, it's hard

Crawling down oued banks like this is rare on the piste.

to visualise a situation where such acrobatics may be necessary (I've never had to do the 45° thing) but it's something that coil-sprung Land Rovers manage better than most standard vehicles.

When crawling in or out of a steeply-banked oued or across a channel that's been cut by a flash flood, you may become aware of an inadequate **departure angle**. In most cases you'll choose a place where you know you won't ground the back bumper to the point of lifting the back axle. But there are various ways of minimising inadequate clearance, all of which involve altering or eliminating the step to suit your car. These include:

- Piling rocks or spare wheels against the step.
- Shovelling or pick-axing away the lip of the step.
- Using supported sand ladders or bridging ladders (ultra rigid sand plates) to make a ramp.

All the above may sound very 'Camel Trophy', but the fact is the only time you would ever have to do this on a normal Saharan piste is if storm flooding had cut some steep-sided channels. This does happen, but passing traffic wears away the edges of such gullies in a day or two. You're more likely to encounter this situation if you find yourself **off-piste**, usually after trying to take a short cut. If you've chosen to drive off-piste you're probably an experienced desert driver in a suitably-equipped vehicle. But if your short cut has turned sour or, more seriously, you've got onto the wrong track and have stumbled into rough terrain, the answer is simply to turn back before you get stuck. If something goes wrong, no one will look for you, much less find you, off the piste.

Low range – when and how to use it

The presence of low range is what separates true 4WDs from fashionable around-town runabouts like RAV4s and Freelanders. A low-range gearbox, usually selected by a lever close to the main gearbox lever, gives you as many gears as high range, but at a much lower ratio and also more closely spaced. Using it gives the impression of more power as the car accelerates easily if briefly in each gear. Typically in a five-speed car, low-range third is close to high-range first and low fifth the same as high second or third.

On a part-time 4WD (Toyota 60 and 70 series, or the Santana PS10) engaging low range automatically selects four-wheel drive, but of course manual freewheeling hubs must also be turned on. Low range gives much greater **throttle control** on inclines (as described above) as well as the ability to pull away in power-sapping conditions like soft sand (see below). For the vehicles recommended in this book low first is too low for most situations apart from crawling over rocky steps or down very steep banks.

Pulling away in low second or third means less chance of wheelspin on a loose surface while still providing enough power. Because low-range gears have **extra close ratios**, the step up to the next gear is smaller than in high range. In practice this means upward gear changes are less likely to bog the engine so you keep moving – essential in dunes. Low range is not an alterna-

---

LOW RANGE CHECKLIST

- For power and control.
- Engage at a standstill or walking pace.
- Don't forget FWHs or central diff locks.
- Avoid too much power, especially on grippy surfaces.
- Only use low-range first for extreme rocky steps or steep descents.
- During sand recovery, pull away in low second or third.
- Avoid long runs in low-range top.
- Avoid changing gear on difficult sections. If in doubt, choose the lower gear.
- Making smooth changes into high range on the move can take practice.

---

tive to high range, it's more of an extension. Change back to high range at the first opportunity, although small-engined vehicles will need to use low range more than others.

It's best to **select low range at a standstill**. Try not to yank or force the lever – easier said than done on some Land Rover gearboxes which have a tendency to jump out of low range into neutral when under load, which can be alarming on a steep incline. Make sure the transfer lever is fully engaged and if necessary fix (or get the passenger to hold) the lever in position, keeping both hands on the wheel. Usually the fact that you're bogged or about to try something tricky means you've come to a stop anyway. Once moving, you can change up to high range – useful in dunes – although achieving this without undue clunks takes some practice.

Be aware of the additional torque or leverage that low range imposes on the transmission components: be extra smooth with the clutch, throttle and gear changes, especially on hard surfaces or with powerful engines. Also, avoid driving for long periods in low-range top. The higher engine revs combined with the low ground speed can overheat the engine. See below for more on the correct use of low range in sand.

Corrugations

Perhaps the worse type of surface regularly encountered on dry, dusty tracks are corrugations. In French they're called *tôle ondulé* ('corrugated iron'), in other parts of the world 'washboard surface'. These maddening formations of parallel ridges across the track are made either by the braking and acceleration of passing vehicles (they get worse either side of a bend) or by the unyielding suspension of heavy trucks (corrugations appear on the most-used tracks). Wherever a track allows vehicles to speed up and the ground conditions are right, corrugations form. They're not unique to the Sahara, but in wealthier parts of the world dirt roads get graded smooth every so often.

Whatever their origins, the experience of driving over four-inch high corrugations is like driving without suspension. At their worst the entire car, its contents and occupants experience a jack-hammer **pulverisation** that feels sure to break something. On lesser cars it eventually does: fractured exhaust mounts are common as is damage to brackets that hold any movable component, even the engine and gearbox itself. Once, after a particularly vicious couple of hours in the Adrar, all the nuts holding the engine of an old Land Cruiser to its clutch housing were loose. And in Algeria I once came across a limping 2CV that was slowly breaking in half. **Punctures** are also common on corrugated pistes as the tyres take the brunt of the hammering and overheat, followed by the suspension. A Series Land Rover is agony – anything with coil springs makes the experience more tolerable.

About the only good thing to say about corrugations is that when you come across them you can be sure you are on a **major track**. I've had occasion to be delighted to re-experience that familiar underwheel juddering while searching for the right track. If you're lost and you find a corrugated track, you can be pretty sure it leads somewhere significant.

Driving on corrugations

Corrugations are at their worst when the rocky or vegetated nature of the surrounding terrain makes deviations impossible. On the Ksar Ghilane and Fadnoun examples given in the box below, the tracks can sometimes braid

A corrugated track waiting for you somewhere in the Sahara.

out, which at least gives you the impression that you've found the least bad stretch.

One way of dealing with the hammering is to **accelerate** up to around 80kph. At this speed the vehicle is literally skimming over the surface. It's best not to think what the suspension and tyres are going through but at least the cab and contents can feel isolated from the worst. However, because you're skimming from the crest of one bump to the next your vehicle is not really in touch with the surface, which is dangerous. Short-wheelbase vehicles, especially those with high loads, can spin out on bends or as you weave across the track trying to find the least bad section. It's a matter of getting the feel for the car and seeking out the 'optimum harmonic velocity' with secure traction and directional stability, something that's different from vehicle to vehicle or may not even exist. At times it just becomes unbearable and you resign yourself to juddering along in second while trying to think of something else.

The good thing is that corrugations rarely go on for long, and really agonising stretches last only a few hundred metres. Nevertheless, after such a hammering any weak link in the car is apt to break. Following a hard day of corrugations it's worth thoroughly **checking** battery, exhaust pipe, tank and roof rack mounts, wheel nuts and food containers; in fact pretty much anything that's attached to anything else. If nothing's fractured after the first really bad session, the chances are it will survive.

CORRUGATION BLACKLIST

- Chinguetti–Ouadane (via plateau), RIM
- Tam–Assekrem (east approach), Algeria
- Tahifet to Tam, Algeria
- Ksar Ghilane to Chenini, Tunisia
- Timsah to Waw Kebir turn-off, Libya
- Derj–Bir Gazell, Libya
- Aïr mountain tracks out of Agadez, Niger
- Agadez–Tazolé, Niger
- Siwa–Bahariya, Egypt

ROCKY MOUNTAIN TRACKS

Unlike on the plains or plateaux, the course of mountain tracks is usually obvious which makes minute-by-minute navigation unnecessary. Mountain tracks can also include very scenic stretches as you wind through canyons or get a chance to look back from a pass onto the sandy plain you've just crossed. However, **visibility** in the hills will not be very good and in certain desert areas like Morocco's Anti Atlas where traffic is relatively regular, oncoming traffic should be anticipated, although this is usually more relevant to speedier motorbikes.

The increasingly rocky and steep eastern ascent to Assekrem Pass in the Hoggar.
The western ascent is almost undrivably loose.

Rocky ascents

When gradients get more severe, as little as 1:3, the track surface can become gouged out by spinning wheels and this gets exacerbated by rain runoff. At times a track can also pass over bare steps of rock whose sharp edges can damage tyres and dent rims. In these situations, and all conditions where you cannot see the end of the obstacle, **walk the section first and plan your route**, moving rocks and filling holes as necessary.

Although it does not feel right, once you get moving it's better to let a tyre slowly pass over a sharp rock rather than try and avoid it and risk damaging the vulnerable sidewall. A tyre's tread is much thicker than its sidewalls. Leaning out of the window may not be enough. If the tyres need to be positioned accurately or there is a risk of grounding the undercarriage, get someone to guide you from ahead. This is a time to engage four-wheel drive and low range, crawling forward slowly but surely. Assuming the traction is very good on dry rock, keep the central diff **unlocked** on a permanent 4WD to avoid inter-axle wind-up. Part time 4WDs in four-wheel drive will just have to deal with possible wind-up.

Hand-throttle ascents

Sometimes a very rough surface will rock your car from side to side and, together with the need to steer away from a precipice, this makes smooth progress hard to control. As you're thrown around your foot can inadvertently jab the accelerator causing the car to lurch forward and back (bracing your foot against the footwell helps), possibly spinning a wheel and losing traction. On a very steep incline (again, only a couple of the pistes in this book include these ascents) this loss of traction can see your car slide backwards.

One way of ensuring smooth forward motion is to pull the **hand throttle** out a couple of notches and take your foot off the accelerator. Hand throttles are standard on most diesel Land Rovers and Cruisers; on other vehicles you

Covered from all angles. The steep, loose and washed-out ascent from the Afara plain onto the Tassili plateau (A4) is easier to control using a hand throttle. Without it the inadvertent jabbing of the accelerator as the car rocks about can break traction.

can make a hand throttle using a **choke cable**. Driving like this you'll still roll around but the engine will rev evenly whatever you set it at. Control is much improved, enabling you to concentrate on picking the smoothest path around the boulders, loose stones and ditches and away from the edge. This technique also works well on stony oued crossings (common in southern Morocco). It makes progress smoother and spares the transmission. An extra dab with your foot to the pre-loaded accelerator can be given when a bit more power is needed. (Hand throttles also make useful 'cruise controls' on long empty highway stages, giving your aching right leg a rest). This is not an approved highway driving technique of course so keep under 100kph and be ready to instantly release the hand throttle if necessary.)

Should you **stall the engine** during a steep ascent the technique outlined below is the one to follow (and is worth practising beforehand on any gradient, unless you always drive up rough slopes with this page open by your side).

- Leave the stalled vehicle in gear, then:
- Engage the footbrake and the handbrake and turn off the ignition.
- With the brakes still on, depress the clutch, engage low-range reverse and release the clutch.
- Make sure that the front wheels are still pointing straight ahead.
- Release the brakes slowly. The vehicle will creep back onto the transmission.
- Without touching the accelerator or clutch, start the engine in gear – the vehicle will lurch into reverse and slowly descend the slope, with you looking back and steering a straight line. Dab the brakes if you feel the need but in low reverse you should be going extremely slowly, much less than walking pace. If possible, have someone guide you down.

With this controlled descent completed, try and work out where you went wrong and why you stalled. It's best to take on steep hills without changing gear, and if in doubt, always choose a **lower gear** or low range; that's what they're for and they will help guarantee an ascent.

Steep descents

From the top, slopes have a habit of looking worse than they are. On a steep but loose or stepped descent, the following procedures work best and are similar to a controlled hand-throttle ascent. This sequence applies to anything from clambering down a steep oued bank to descending a long stony hillside.

● Ascertain if there's an easier way down.

● If the descent is severe – this is only likely in an off-piste situation – **walk down first** to plan your route, marking points to place wheels and clearing rocks or filling holes as you go.

● Consider lowering tyre pressures for better traction, rocks permitting.

● Get someone to guide you from ahead around the worst obstacles.

● Engage four-wheel drive and low-range second or first gear.

Descent from the Atakor massif in the Hoggar: low range first and keep off the brakes and accelerator.

● Move off, keeping both feet on the floor and away from the brake and accelerator pedals. Resist the urge to brake unless absolutely necessary – you will probably cause a skid. If you are in low first you should be doing about 1kph. Concentrate on the path or your guide's instructions until level ground is reached.

● If the vehicle slides, do not brake; it will make things worse. Instead, keep your nerve and accelerate gently to allow the wheels to catch up with the ground speed. Then back off the throttle and allow the vehicle to slow with regained traction. If it slides again, point straight down the hill, track permitting and ride it out. In this crisis situation you may feel safer not wearing a seatbelt – it makes jumping out of an out-of-control vehicle easier, but in all dangerous recovery situations where speed is involved seatbelts make crashing or rolling a vehicle much safer.

Clearing rocks before descending a long-disused piste on the Hamada el Hamra in Libya.

SAND

Not surprisingly, soft sand is the most common reason for getting stuck and dunes the most common place to wreck a vehicle. Sand is not like any other surface, including mud or snow, and there are certain well-known techniques and practices which you should adopt in order to keep moving or recover your vehicle when it's up to the axles in sand.

One often reads of keen desert expeditions cranking up the publicity by practising on coastal sands in temperate latitudes. It may look the same and will

Marshalling the driver down in low first; it's steeper than it looks!

get you as stuck if you try, but it's much more humid than true desert sand so more forgiving. For most overlanders, the first experience they have with sand is when they get stuck in the Sahara. Dune driving is considered later but first, flat sand.

Driving on soft sand

If the sand is in the form of a firm sheet, such as the Selima Sand Sheet along the Sudan–Egypt border, or the northern Ténéré in Niger, you have little to worry about and can enjoy some serene driving. But on most pistes and even sand sheets you'll always come across patches of **soft sand**, usually along river courses where fine grains collect, or along the edge of sand seas, but as often in any other place for no discernible reason.

Negotiating big dunes in the Great Sand Sea – extreme sand driving. © M. Soffiantini

When the sand softens you feel the engine drone and the car slow as power is sucked away. If it's just a soft patch the car will pick up speed again. If not, **change down quickly** and accelerate smoothly. In this situation your vehicle's momentum, greatly aided by the **flotation** of the tyres, is what keeps you moving. If you anticipate lots of soft sand on the immediate route ahead, consider lowering your tyre pressures (see below). Power on smoothly, engaging four-wheel drive if you feel you need the extra traction and you'll get through. If you lose momentum and sink in, **traction** will be necessary to get moving again and to keep ploughing on until the ground firms up.

In most cases, such as in small oueds, the **momentum** of a two-ton car, even at low speeds, is enough get you through. Elsewhere you must do all you can to maintain speed. Avoid any sharp turns or sudden ascents which create extra drag and lose you momentum. Watch out for rocks and grassy hummocks. Keep in high range (if you have the power) using lower revs: wheel-spin is less likely so traction is maintained.

If you know you're going to get stuck, admit defeat early and depress the clutch *before* you come to a standstill: otherwise the wheels simply spin themselves down into the sand. Learning to give in early will save you a lot of exhausting digging (see below).

One technique I've heard of but keep forgetting to try is moving the steering wheel from side to side as you push through sand. Although it appears contrary to the advice about minimising wheel drag, the theory is that sand building up ahead of the front wheels flows away to either side as the steering wheel is turned, rather like a snow plough. Without the build-up front wheels have less sand to push through or over and are less likely to sink. It's may be worth trying with less powerful cars that need every trick in the book, but I get the impression it makes little difference.

Reading sand

Depending on the type of sand, driving in existing tyre tracks can be better, but this is not always the case. In **dense sand** where a deep, steep-sided trench is formed by a passing wheel, the ruts can drag on your wheels and slow you down, so you're better off pushing your own way through. At other times the **pre-compressed** sand of an earlier vehicle can be easier. There is no firm rule. You have to experiment and learn from experience.

Generally **the lighter the colour of** the sand the softer it is. One interesting theory suggests light sand is old sand, its grains leached of all its mineral colour into pure crystals, worn smaller and rounder by time. **Darker sand** is younger and has larger, more angular grains which interlock better and give better support to a passing wheel.

Grey-surfaced sand can be so-called *feche-feche* (see p.179). Hit that and clouds of the dusty yellow powder below the grey surface explode around the car. If you stray onto feche-feche, trying to maintain momentum while steering back to firmer ground is your only option. Recovery from feche-feche is hard work.

Some **dark volcanic sands** like those around Waw en Namus in Libya can be as soft as light sand, while any sand supporting vegetation may be firmer, giving a bumpy ride over the tussocks.

Indistinguishable soft patches can clearly be seen once a vehicle has passed.

Tyres in sand

Flotation, or the reduction of ground pressure, is achieved by spreading a car's weight over a larger surface area, either by fitting larger tyres or drastically deflating standard ones. This increases the contact area with the ground – the snowshoe principle – which prevents sinking in. Note that it is the *diameter* or height of tyres that makes a difference in sand and not, as many imagine, the width.

The reason for this is another popular misconception regarding low tyre pressures: when you deflate a tyre its contact area with the ground *lengthens* rather than broadens. A tall tyre, such as the **7.50x16** ubiquitous in the Sahara, achieves a longer footprint than a wide 15" tyre at the same pressure.

Knowing when to turn back is the key. You'll get a feel from the car and the terrain for when it's not worth continuing.

The rings – exaggerated for clarity – show how a tyre's contact patch lengthens rather than broadens at low pressures, so greatly improving traction.

A tyre spread out at one bar shows why high sidewalls are desirable to maintain good ground clearance at low pressures.

Seven-fifties work because in sand the tread is less important in aiding flotation than the long, caterpillar-track-like contact area achieved by a tall tyre. Despite the appearance of bulging side walls, width is barely increased – if it were, the sidewalls would soon puncture. The tall sidewalls of a 7.50 tyre also help maintain ground clearance when in a deflated state. This doesn't mean you have to get out and let your tyres down at every soft patch. As long as you maintain momentum, you're much better off using four-wheel drive to get through.

Tyre pressures

The first-time desert driver quickly learns the huge difference **very low tyre pressures** make to driving in soft sand. As Ralph Bagnold discovered nearly eighty years ago while driving a truck into the Great Sand Sea: '*Prendergast let more air out of his lorry wheels so that the pressure was only 15 psi instead of 90. The result was marvellous. The lorry sailed along...*'

Because as road drivers we are all reminded by safety experts to keep tyre pressures at correct levels, letting them down seems contrary to good sense. Equally off-putting is the thought of having to laboriously pump them up again in just a few hundred metres with a hand or foot pump or a slow compressor. The solution here, already emphasised on p.121, is to get a powerful compressor.

Below are **guidelines for tyre pressures**. Ideally tyres should be **measured when cold** but in the desert this is not practical except at the start of the day. The pressures will vary according to your vehicle's weight and tyre size: these recommendations suit a GVW of around 2400kg. A lighter vehicle requires lower pressures.

- Full load, fast highway: 3.2 bar   (47 psi)
- Piste or rocks: 2 bar   (32 psi)
- Soft sand: 1.7 bar   (25 psi)
- Dunes   1.2 bar   (17 psi)
- Emergency recovery, soft sand: 0.7 bar (10 psi)

In all situations err towards higher pressures but recognise that if the conditions demand 1 bar, 1 bar it's got to be. 'As high as possible, as low as necessary' is a good maxim. It's all this up and downing with tyre pressures that makes it important to **check** them every morning.

Check also for sidewall damage on both sides and re-establish the optimum pressure for that day. Running tyres at low pressures can cause particu-

FECHE-FECHE AND CHOTTS

Feche-feche is a much overused term to describe any ultra-fine powdery sand or **bull dust** which claws away your momentum while rising up in spectacular dust clouds behind you (see the picture on p.82). The yellow dust often re-settles with a fluffy texture which you'll learn to recognise and avoid... or turn round and blast through again with someone behind a lens. When you hit it the tyre makes a distinctive hum as clouds of dust billow around the vehicle and you press the accelerator to the floor. The answer here is to keep moving while trying to avoid the worst-rutted sections.

These tracks are through mild feche-feche; a dark pebbly surface with pale yellow powder underneath.

True **feche-feche** is another thing altogether and if you're unlucky enough to drive into it, you'll know it. It's a crust of baked grey mud which I've only found close to erg edges in a dried-lake formation not unlike a chott (see below). Driving onto the crust you break through straight away and sink into the deep bed of the flour-like yellow powder described above. It will take every ounce of your engine's power to get back onto firm ground. On a bike I've had to paddle desperately back to the 'bank', screaming the engine in first gear with a ten-metre roost spurting vertically from the back wheel. My companions urged me to repeat it for a great photo, but I was in no mood to go near it again! In a heavy car it's more likely you'll sink in almost straight away and can do nothing but reverse or hopefully be towed out. Expect to move little more than a sand plate's length at each attempt.

Chotts, also known as *sebkha*, are salt lakes found on the desert side of northern Atlas ranges (more on p.382). Like their counterparts, the claypans and mud flats found along water courses, chotts can be wonderfully smooth to drive over. At other times the drying creates a rough crumbled surface seemingly created by a herd of cows. The danger with chotts as opposed to claypans is that the surface may look firm, but recent rain (not necessarily nearby either) may have raised the water table so that you're looking at a crust 'floating' over saturated salty sand. Sinking through this is one of the messiest and most difficult recovery situations and it will take several hours of shovelling, pushing and towing to extract yourself.

You may come across evidence of these **boggings**, either old and hard baked or fresh and messy, the latter serving as an urgent warning about the conditions around you. On the causeway across the Chott el Djerid in Tunisia you'll spot places where tourists have gone down for a burn up and got their fingers burned instead.

If you can't avoid them, keep to the edge of chotts or follow good tracks across them. Darker patches may indicate a soft surface but as in dunes, you can never be sure.

A water-logged chott near Lac Maider, M6.

lar problems, including overheating, which is discussed below. Something else to watch out for is that **loose-fitting tyres** (usually old ones that have been on and off several times) can slip around the wheel rim, owing to the combination of extreme torque and enhanced traction (a condition more common on bikes with knobbly tyres). You'll notice the tyre valve leaning over which means it's getting dragged round the rim. Eventually the valve may be ripped out. Before this happens deflate it and reposition the tyre and valve against the wheel rim.

The softer your tyre the more it flexes. On every revolution the tyre side-wall is squashed as it meets the ground and springs back as the weight is released. This is happening continuously, ten times a second at 60kph. As with any flexible material this movement creates internal friction in the rubber which manifests itself as heat. **Overheated tyres** can lead to all sorts of problems, not least punctures. An easy way of checking if your tyres are getting hot is to touch them. If the sidewalls are very hot to the touch you must slow down or increase the pressure. At extreme low pressure of 1 bar or less you should never exceed 30kph for long periods.

As explained above, tyre pressures increase as they warm up through the day. Furthermore, the tyres on the sunny side of the car get hotter still. Take this into account when you're doing the hand test and also when you're measuring or lowering tyre pressures. Expect one side to be at least 10% higher if it's been in the sun. Assuming the tyres were all equal to start with, reduce pressures with your watch or by counting (one minute each wheel, for example) rather than with a tyre gauge. Because tyres pressures increase as they get hot, consider bleeding some extra air out in the course of a long day through dunes.

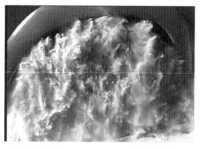

Don't do this – every second of spinning equals a minute of digging.

STUCK IN THE SAND

Despite all the above advice you'll probably get stuck in the first soft sand you encounter. If you stopped early, you should be able to reverse out without digging or pushing. Once back on firm ground, have another go, accelerating through the soft patch or taking another route.

The biggest mistake made by novice or stubborn sand drivers is **not stopping soon enough**. You plough on ever more slowly until you're revving the engine but not moving forward and finally release the clutch with a judder from the wound-up transmission. You try and reverse, but that's no good and deeper in you go. You try going forward, this time in low first and the torque spins you down into the sand a little more. Finally you admit that your 4WD is not so all-terrain after all and that you're embedded in the surroundings. Depending on how dogged you were, or how soft the sand suddenly became, all the tyres will be buried up to the wheel rim.

Getting unstuck

When you've realised that your wheels are well and truly bogged, you first need to decide whether it's best to go forward or back: if you're on a slope, always aim to descend the gradient. Checking that there's still air between the undercarriage and the ground (if not, see below) **scoop or shovel the sand** away from the sides of the wheels. A pair of hands works as well as a shovel and sand is clean so there's no excuse for everyone not to get down to it. Dig away a smooth **ramp** in whichever direction you're going. Clear the sand away right down to the bottom of the tyre. There must be no lip to roll over if the tyre's to have a chance of recovery first time. Depending on tyre pressures and the terrain ahead consider letting some air out. If it looks like the beginning of a sandy section, let down to 1.4–1.7 bar (20–25 psi).

Take the time to clear a wheel well.

Once this is done to all four wheels, drive out in low second or third or high or low reverse and keep going until you're on firm ground. If there are a couple of people around to **push**, so much the better as this can make the difference between getting stuck or getting through. There should be no need for sand plates and the whole business should take no more then five or ten minutes.

With a long section of soft sand, the pushers should run with the car and push again if the car hits another soft patch or until they can't keep up. If driving forward it's possible to hop onto the back bumper as the car picks up traction and jump off to push again as necessary. Don't try this on bumpy or hummocky ground though: if the driver is going flat out to get through, it's impossible to hold on at the back.

Down to the axles

This situation becomes less frequent as you learn to read the sand and to stop early. It need never happen at all but at some time, especially in dunes, even the most experienced driver can plough into an indistinguishable soft patch and sink before they know it. Usually the dragging axles stop the car going too deep, but that's deep enough.

Recovery from this situation is going to take two people at least half an hour. There are three main methods of getting out: using a **high-lift jack or air bag**, digging with a **shovel and sand ladders**, or **towing** out. Whichever it is, letting the tyre pressure down if you have not already done so will make a big difference. If you're heading into dunes, it's time to reduce to one bar anyway.

Be aware of the risk of **sunburn** and **dehydration**. Wear a shirt and a hat or cheche while you're working and take a good swig of water when it's done. If it

Usually a quick scoop-about to clear the wheels is enough. Having done that, all hands to the bumper makes all the difference. Most of the time you don't need sand plates and all the rest.

goes on like this in stops and starts for hours, prepare a rehydration drink (see p.164). For ideas on dealing with overturned vehicles and side-slope recoveries, see page 193.

Recovery with a high-lift jack and air bags

This method requires no grovelling under the car with a shovel and is the quickest and most effective. Jack up the front of the car until the wheels are above the sand. In this situation there should be no need to chock the rear wheels which are well entrenched. With the wheels in the air, push the sand into the holes and lay down a sand plate if you think it's needed. When you lower the car the axles should be well clear of the ground and just on the plate.

Repeat the same for the rear, noting that you, your jack or your jacking point probably won't be able to lift both wheels clean in the air on a LWB wagon. One wheel at a time then, repeat what you did with the front wheels. Reduce tyre pressures and drive out in low second or whichever gear is best to avoid a labouring engine and clutch or spinning wheels.

With **air bags** it's the same procedure but you do one **side** of the car at a time as an air bag cannot securely lift the front or rear of a vehicle without it rolling off the bag to one side. It's great to watch the wheels rising from the sand as the bag creaks and you hold the nozzle against the exhaust. It's also a lot less physical effort than a high-lift. With the wheels in the air, push sand into the holes, lay a plate if you need it and drive off.

Recovery with sand plates

This is the traditional but rather more effortful method, getting down and frantically scooping or digging the sand from under the car and around the wheels quicker than it flows back. A shovel is useful for the axles but even short ones are hard to use under a car where hands are easier.

Whichever direction you decide to drive out, clear the axles, fuel tank, and whatever might drag. Shovel away sand from the

High-lift (**top**) and air-bag (**bottom**) recoveries.
Simply raise the wheels, push in the sand and lower the wheels. No digging or even sand plates needed.

tyre sides and level out a ramp in the recovery direction. Clear the sand right down to the base of the tyre, even if it means moving vast quantities of sand that slide back into the hole.

Once this is all done push your sand plates (or whatever's available) just under the tyre so that it can drive onto the plate easily without a step; pointy-ended plates, like those by Grand Erg, work well for this. People sometimes carry four sections of sand plate but really a pair is adequate. Shove them right against the tyre in whichever direction you're heading: if

Try to get the plate under the tyre. To guarantee this, some kind of jacking is needed.
Inset: Recovering the plates.

you're reversing put them under the back wheels so once they've passed over them, the front wheels can use them too, to get some momentum going. Reduce tyre pressures if you haven't already done so and have a look at the best way out if it's not obvious. If you can't go back, walk forward and **stamp on the ground** with your foot: a firm print means driveable sand, an oval blur means it's probably too soft to support a car and you'll want to try and find another way. This is a typical dune scenario, of which more below. The inconvenience with sand-plate recovery is that they have to be retrieved; also rigid metal plates can damage the underbody of the car as they get spat out by spinning wheels.

A SAND RECOVERY COURSE

I once hired a guy to do a tour in Mauritania which at one stage might have been better described as a Sand Recovery Course. One day, contrary to my proposed itinerary (the usual problems with guides) we were persuaded to take a 'half-day shortcut' through the dunes which went on for days.

At one point we took two hours to cover just 100m, a multiple recovery that dragged on because, having only a handpump, our driver didn't want to let the tyres down. Within 200m it happened again, and then again 10 metres later, by which point it was mid-afternoon and, exhausted, we insisted on having a rest. This went on all the following day and half of the one after that, by which time we'd covered 40km – pretty much walking pace, even in dunes.

On the last day, heading back to the planned route now just a couple of kilometres (but a morning's pushing) away, we all ended up walking from stage to stage, reconnoitring a firm passage for the car by stamping our feet on the sand to the amusement of a nomad girl who had ambled up to sell us

trinkets. As our tour leader had no sand plates ('too heavy'), no high-lift jack ('can't buy them here') or shovel ('they'll just nick it'), and was reluctant to let down the tyres ('there are lots of stones ahead') or listen to the nomad girl's advice ('what does she know?'), we struggled back to the piste with murmured curses and jocular bantering.

After that we all considered ourselves experts in basic sand recovery and survival using only grass, our hands and the sweat off our backs.

Without proper equipment or reduced tyre pressures this recovery took two hours.

Recovery with tow straps and snatch ropes

Shovelling, laying sand plates and even inflating an air bag are all hard work, especially if repeated several times a day. With a single car there is no choice of course, but with another vehicle, towing makes sense: you can be free in a couple of minutes.

Non-elastic tow straps are not always very effective in dune recoveries; the towing car just kicks up sand. However, they are needed for highway towing, righting overturned vehicles (see p.193) and other 'non-kinetic' applications, so carry both.

The strains in towing a vehicle stuck in the sand mean that towing points on both machines must be strong, ideally attached directly to non-rusty chassis rails. **Tough hooks**, be they part of a tow strap or attached to the chassis, are more reliable than shackles. **Ropes** made from synthetic as opposed to natural materials are best (3-core nylon being strongest and with a bit of give) but should be kept in a bag out of direct sunlight. Straps are less bulky and easier to store than ropes.

But as is demonstrated in the photo on the left, the direct pull of a tow strap or normal towing rope can lead to wheelspin in very soft sand. In this sort of situation snatch ropes (see below) work much better, but non-elastic tow straps or ropes are useful. Highway towing is easier with such a rope and in the rare event of an overturned vehicle, **a non-elastic strap is essential** to right the vehicle with control and not yank it over onto the other side (see p.193).

Learning from the master. A KERR is carefully laid in position. Note the slack left in the rope, a deliberate move so that the car driving away has a bit of speed before beginning to take up the rope's elasticity.

Having the towing vehicle face the bogged vehicle works best as the driver can monitor the progress of the recovery. At a hoot or other agreed signal, and assuming some digging has been done to clear the stranded vehicle's wheels, both vehicles should drive, even if there is some wheelspin involved. But if sand is getting sprayed about with no movement, clearly the bogged machine is heavily stuck – use the recoveries described earlier.

Snatch towing using kinetic energy recovery ropes (KERRs), to give them one of their names, is commonly done by the mud-driving off-road community but I've found works very well in the desert.

Getting stuck in mud can be much worse than sand; the liquid mire tends to suck cars down and worst off all, it's messy. A KERR is nothing more than a strong but elastic rope. It will stretch by about thirty per cent to reach a maximum length and then act like a normal tow rope. But at the point when it starts pulling the bogged car there is a mass of energy stored in the rope, waiting to be released, greatly multiplying the pulling force.

SAND DRIVING SUMMARY

- Use momentum and acceleration as well as 4WD to get through.
- Admit defeat early and stop before the car is dragged to a halt on spinning wheels.
- If appropriate, reverse out and take another run or find another route.
- If lightly bogged, a quick scoop around the wheels is often sufficient. Shovels, jacks and sand plates are not necessary.
- If deeply bogged, clear the wheels and undercarriage properly and reduce tyre pressures to ensure a first-time recovery.
- If not reversing, check ahead first.

- A couple of people pushing makes a big difference.
- One bar in the tyres and correct use of gears makes all the difference.
- Avoid revving the engine and slipping the clutch. Use low second or high reverse.
- Keep moving until back on firm ground or a downslope, however far it is and however far the others have to walk with the sand plates.
- Remember, pumping up tyres afterwards is easier than more digging and pushing.

KERRs work particularly well on dune crests which can be an awkward recovery at the best of times, requiring the digging away of large amounts of sand. With a KERR just hook up, leaving some slack as in the picture opposite, and tow away. The strain on the vehicles, though immense, is linear and smooth and the lunge is not hard to control. As mentioned before, towing points must be especially strong due to the forces involved; they are much greater though more progressive than regular towing. There are many tales of broken shackles

As the energy in the KERR peaks and is released, this Land Rover is yanked off the dune crest; a fast and effortless recovery, but one that requires solid towing points.

hurtling through windscreens and out the back, or cars being systematically stripped of their bumpers.

Occasionally you may find yourself pulling out **bogged-down 2WDs**. For your own safety take care where you attach the strap on their car. Road cars have few tough mounting points and in deep sand a bumper will rip off and fly right at you – avoid shackles, if possible.

Keep towing ropes and straps in a bag to protect them from damage and, if damaged, do not use them for heavy recoveries.

DUNE DRIVING

Dunes, and especially ergs (sand seas), present the most challenging and dangerous driving conditions in the Sahara. They come in many shapes and sizes, from the grassy hummocks found in larger oueds, to thousands grouped together in country-sized ergs which take days to cross. You'll see dunes along nearly every piste, even if you don't have to drive into them.

For many enthusiastic off-road drivers the chance to drive across the rippled banks of a Saharan dune is a major fantasy. Their benign appearance is inviting and driving can be exhilarating, urging you to power up slopes and, with a flurry of churning sand, tip over the crest and blast back down.

The reality is that dune driving, be it in a recreational domestic setting by

Dune casualties.
From the **top**: A 25-metre leap off a dune could have been fatal. For the car, it was – everything was bent. © B. Lorsch.
Middle: Head over heels down a dune; the wreckage at La Goulette. © Pir Corbettone.
Bottom: A gradual tip over – the consequence of not making a direct dune descent.

the sea or deep in the Sahara, is probably responsible for more broken necks, crushed roofs and abandoned vehicles than any other terrain. When they want to thin the field to a more manageable size in the Dakar Rally, a stage through an erg is set up. By the other end half the contestants are usually out. Some are carried out.

Several not necessarily obvious factors make dunes hard work and potentially dangerous:

● The condition of the sand is unpredictable and hard to read reliably.

● Because of this, it's crucial to maintain momentum but forward visibility is limited and, in certain light conditions, even treacherous.

● Without a local guide or reconnaissance on foot the concentration required to keep moving is very fatiguing for the lead driver, especially first-time dune-drivers.

● No matter how big or deflated your tyres, soft sand saps power and works engines, cooling systems and transmissions hard. Any weakness will be quickly exposed.

● Many descents are not possible to reverse.

● Dunes are generally uninhabited and without wells.

● Recovery of an irreparable vehicle may be impossible.

If that's warned you off then good, although these words probably won't sink in until you've experienced dune driving for yourself. Curiosity will lure you in anyway, but at least you'll know what to expect. Safe dune-driving is something even locals get wrong occasionally. For a tourist it takes several trips to get the right feel for it.

Minor dune formations

As mentioned at the start of the book all pistes avoid soft sand and dunes where possible. The two classic trans-Sahara routes through Algeria follow firm terrain with just a few well-known sandy sections. The old Atlantic Route could be done in an ordinary car, albeit with quite a beating. Other pistes, like the southern route from Djanet to Tamanrasset (p.509), can snick through the Erg Admer at a narrow point while a little further north, the

Ghadames–Serdeles piste along Libya's western border (p.553) actually passes over the Algerian border to avoid the worst of the Erg Ubari. It still includes a 30km section through real dunes that will give you pause for thought.

One small dune formation – most often encountered off-piste – is a parallel series of **small dune waves**, sometimes found alongside ergs or more often downwind of a natural wind funnel (KM400 of Route A14 for example).

On the brink. Resist the urge to dick about in dunes – in the desert or by the sea, this is where most accidents happen.
© Toby Savage

Less than half a metre high and not always visible in the glare, these nasty 'speed humps' can wreck a car's suspension if hit at high speed.

Into the ergs

Crossing an erg means taking the line of least resistance. Most of the massive Saharan ergs are composed of vaguely linear rows of dunes separated by corridors, known as *gassis* in some countries. Because of the prevailing north-easterly wind in the Sahara, just about all these ergs have their gassis oriented along the wind direction: north–south in the Great Sand Sea of the Libyan Desert in Egypt; north-east/south-west in the central and western Sahara. Travelling in these directions through an erg is possible; attempting to cut *across* the corridors is extremely hard work and involves much zig-zagging up and down to find a passage over to the next corridor.

In Libya the traversal of the Erg Ubari's eastern arm between Idri and the Sebha–Ghat road is a popular challenge. Even with zig-zagging the distance between the roads is around 160km. You can be sure that if you just keep going south you'll make it to the road.

I've met bikers who have done this crossing in a day and other groups of 4WDs who took eight days, with a guide! There are no continuous tracks or markers. GPS waypoints are of little use as Route L4 (see p.564) will probably show. You just drive along the line of

On the dunes above Lake Gabroun, Libya.

MORNING CRUST AND OTHER MYTHS

One is forever reading in off-road driving manuals and ill-informed mainstream media about sand having a **magical crust** over which one must drive lightly so as not to break through to the softer sand below.

In my experience, this crust is a rare phenomenon found on serirs across which no piste passes, though the crust on true feche-feche or chotts (see p.179) is well known.

Sand is simply either firm enough to drive across, so soft you get stuck, or somewhere in between; there's no such thing as sand crust, it's one of those 'deserts are freezing at night, would you believe it!' myths that appear to have become irritatingly lodged in the popular imagination.

One also reads that soft sand is **firmer at dawn**, having cooled overnight with condensation binding together to form a crust.

The dawn crust theory sounds plausible and may occur in more humid northern areas of the Sahara like the Grand Erg in Tunisia, but one hot afternoon in the Erg Ubari we gave up, exhausted, and left it till the next morning – when to me at least the sand seemed just as bad!

This impression of improved early morning traction was explained to me by a dune-driving expert. According to him, as tyres heat up during the day the pressure inside increases up to 20%, making the tyre harder and so less effective in sand. Overnight the tyres cool down and sag and hey presto, traction may be much improved.

least resistance until it gets blocked and you're forced to find a way over to an adjacent corridor. At times it's just impossible to go against the grain. In the anecdote on page 183 we could see the Btâh Chinguetti just a few kilometres to the north but were continuously forced south-west by the low dunes' orientation.

For many reasons small dunes are the most demanding to drive through. Closely packed crests demand very quick thinking (above) with the risk of getting trapped in a vortex – a very awkward recovery without a winch or kinetic rope.

Small dunes

Just as hard as driving against the grain in big dunes is driving, in any direction, through small dunes: good examples being Route A1 in the northern Grand Erg Oriental on p.493, Erg Chebbi in Morocco or even the very short drive to Ksar Ghillane from the palmerie (p.539). Small dunes seem to be a feature of the northern Saharan fringes, as they move into the desert they get higher and develop in lines with the characteristic gassis or corridors. Whatever aeolian attribute it is that makes small dunes, the result is a lack of linear formations and instead, a maze of slip faces and crests.

Driving a vehicle on these sand waves is hampered by **poor visibility**, making it hard to locate easier routes until you're nearly on them. And short run-ups over crests mean that getting bellied-out is a regular occurrence, as also is simply running out of thinking time as you try to maintain momentum by driving in any direction that will go. This can all end up with you getting trapped in a small vortex or car-sized bowl where, in my experience at least, the only way out was on the end of a winch cable.

Dune-driving techniques

If you can **go with someone who knows** a way through, be it a local guide or experienced tourist, grab the chance. You could save hours wondering where to go and how to get there, or days getting out of the dunes, as has happened to a few travellers I've met. If you're going without a guide go with another car or two. To drive alone into unknown dunes really is pushing your luck. If you can get a motorbiker along, so much the better. Offer to carry their baggage as a lightly-laden bike makes a useful reconnaissance vehicle and can save you driving into a situation you can't get out of. Better still, if you're planning on doing some long dune routes, invite a competent off-road motorbiker or quad rider along. They really will be an asset, but only if they're good riders on unladen machines.

The following advice assumes you're doing it without a guide. Before setting off undertake a full **vehicle check**, especially the cooling system which will be working hard. Also check the security of the luggage should you take off or roll over. Try and pack all weight low to lower the centre of gravity, for example by taking a spare wheel off the roof rack and storing it securely inside the car. And don't haul ridiculously huge quantities of **fuel and water** for a short crossing (another reason why the eastern Erg Ubari is a popular excursion) though expect doubled fuel consumption – on most diesels bank on 4–5kpl (14 mpg) and about twice that with a petrol engine – and carry enough water to be safe should the crossing take much longer than expected. Once underway keep your general orientation in mind but do not expect to drive in that direction for more than a few hundred metres. If there are tracks follow them but do not assume they lead the way you want to go.

Always aim to reduce upward gradients and so the chance of getting stuck. Traverse *gentle* dune banks in a gradual diagonal **ascent** – steeper slopes must be tackled head on to avoid the risk of rolling. Corridors and long dips offer a natural line but often the sand at the bottom can be very soft. The windward side of dunes (the shallow slope) is usually firmer, as will be some rippled dune banks.

Try to **maintain height** by riding these dune banks. By keeping high you always have the advantage of steering down a slope if you feel the car sinking. There are times when you

A deadly vortex in Erg Chebbi, a good example of the small dune sand seas prevalent in the northern Sahara.

Taking a small dune ridge at a very shallow angle. It might have worked but the car hit a soft patch and was on the brink of turning over.

have to drive all over the place, even back where you came from, just to maintain momentum and try to regain some height from where you can try again. On other occasions, especially in the **small dunes** mentioned earlier, you have to tear around a bowl formation like a 'wall of death', using the momentum gathered to get you up a bank and over a crest that could not be taken with a simple right-angle turn (see diagram, below). You can also use this 'contouring' of a dune bowl to give yourself a few more seconds to work out a route.

Away from small dunes the general pattern is to find the gentle but usually firm windward slopes of the dune or a corridor and then gain height to a saddle or a crestable dune and drop down the loose slip face. The reverse is not possible which is why a return through an erg should take a different route. It is the infinite configuration of dunes within the general pattern of firmer and less steep windward slopes and unascendable slip faces that makes driving so unpredictable and dangerous.

If you have the power, keep in **high range** as the gear characteristics are more conducive to sand traction. Land Rovers and other small-engined cars may need to stay in Low Range most of the time and Low Range will be necessary in any vehicle to get moving after getting stuck – aim to change up to

Coming over a crest from Point A with the only safe way out being a low crest at Point B, there's not much chance that you will be able to turn right and get over the slope; the turning forces will slow the car down and bury the tyres.
Better then to ride around the sand banks to gain speed and approach Point B straight on with more control.

high range soon. Changing up into high on the move has got to be done quickly to work smoothly. Stay in low top until you're moving fast on the flat, or better still descending an incline, clutch in, shift back to high, and then move the main gear lever from top gear to third. The change to high can be made smoother by double-declutching, a gear-changing technique from the days before modern synchromesh gearboxes, but this takes time to master and twice as long to implement. If your car is especially clunky when changing from low to high on the move, do it at a standstill, i.e. on a downslope.

Speed versus visibility

One of the paradoxes of dune-driving is that you must go fast to avoid getting stuck but **speed** is dangerous when you can't see what's over the next crest. A motorbike, a more stable quad or just a co-operative passenger can all be extremely helpful. To drive up a big dune without knowing exactly how steep the other side is or what its orientation is can be extremely nerve-racking. This is where all the accidents happen and I have seen people burst into tears following the shock of coming over a dune a little too briskly. Hit a crest with a steep drop too fast and the vehicle

You can crest a dune at a safe speed, but turn away from a direct descent and this can be the result.

takes off, noses into the soft slip face and overturns or rolls. Worse still, you crest the dune straight on as your instinct suggests and at the right speed, but find the slip face dropping at an angle to the left or right and your vehicle rolls sideways. Never assume that the descent matches the approach slope and **never descend a slip face at an angle** as the car could easily roll over with its wheels facing uphill, a very time-consuming recovery. If you do find the rear

wheels sliding round as you descend a slip face, do not brake. Steer downhill and accelerate, changing up a gear if necessary, to regain a straight-down descent of the slope.

Without doing a **recce** on every crest, dune driving is a lottery. Trudging up dune after dune is tiring, but it's the only way to avoid surprises, which is why it's better to be in a group. It only takes one person to find a way through for all the others. Reconnoitring is a vital job that can often be made easier if the individual rides on the back bumper of the car (assuming good hand-holds) to save frequent getting in and out. Recces may not be necessary for every single

Descending a sand slope at an angle to avoid some rocks, the back wheels begin to slide round. In the end I steered into the slide and drove slowly over the rocks. Interestingly a following car on XSs managed to hold the angle – maybe they're not so bad after all!

crest, but if you get lazy it could end badly. It doesn't have to be anything as dramatic as rolling the car: a one-foot lip taken at running pace made a Defender land with such a thump that the rack bent down the alloy guttering so the driver couldn't even open the door!

Hand signals and two-way radios

The above case happened because the driver misunderstood our guide's **hand signals**. The 'patting' gesture which looked clearly to them (and me following) like 'floor it' actually meant 'slow down'. Don't make this mistake. The whole group should understand common signals: left; right; faster; slower; steep drop; slope angles this way; and of course STOP. Follow guidelines precisely. When someone indicates to be sure your wheels cross right *here*, they're saying that for a reason. **Radios** (see p.347), when they work, can be a clearer

Too much gas. But the following car, going just a little slower, got bellied out. The knack is to back off with just enough speed to plough through the crest and end up pointing downwards, then accelerate again.

method of communication but a pointed arm is pretty unequivocal too.

Cresting dunes

Cresting dunes safely requires accelerating up to the edge in high second and backing off just as the front wheels roll over the edge, letting the momentum ease the vehicle over the edge so it comes to a rest pointing downwards with its rear wheels more or less along the flattened-off crest.

It's natural to be timid as you watch your windscreen fill with sky at the very edge, but **stopping too early** means straddling the crest on the belly of the car. This situation is not as bad as it looks because, unlike getting stuck on flat ground, shovelled sand falls away down the slopes so clearing the undercarriage is easily if not quickly done. You don't have to get the vehicle on its wheels (probably impossible anyway), just get some weight back on them. If the car is horizontal or leaning a little **forwards** and you want to continue the descent, scoop away more from the front edge and then get two or three people to push up the back bumper as the car drives forward. There'll be plenty of sand thrown about but if you've cleared away enough the car will churn its way onto the down slope. If you've stopped at the top of a descent you don't want to make you'll have a lot of digging to back the car up: if possible tow the car back.

Not quite enough speed over this crest, but a quick push up the back saw it scrabble over.

If the car's tilting backwards it will have to back out. Same procedure, but push up under the front bumper as the car drives back. In this instance the driver should be very careful to **reverse slowly in a straight line**, perpendicular to the slope. It's much easier to get into a weave or fall into a dip and roll a car when reversing. That's exactly what happened to a Belgian guy I met in Nefta once. He'd been touring through the Grand Erg Oriental for a few days and on the southern edge, near Hassi bel Guebbour, lost control as he reversed off a failed ascent and rolled several times. The car had no windows, a pointy roof and was being beaten back into shape by Nefta's metalbashers.

As you reverse from a failed climb, back up a slope if there is one so you can get a good run up for the second attempt. This time, knowing the nature of the far slope, you can run up to the crest with the right amount of speed and tip over the edge to snick into first and drive down the far side.

Side slope recoveries and fallen vehicles

Short of falling over, the most difficult dune recovery is when a vehicle has become stuck on a slope and is perilously close to tipping over. The slightest alteration in balance, even just getting out of the car, could see it go over, though usually the embedding in sand makes them more stable than they look.

More than ever it's important with a leaning vehicle to **take your time** and think it through properly. You're not going to get any more stuck. Obviously keep people away from the underside of the vehicle if it looks perilous and get a rope on the high side with people pulling on it until another vehicle can get into place to take the strain. Without another vehicle around it just takes major excavation under the high wheels to get the vehicle more level. You won't get a jack under the low side, though an airbag jack may work to push it up, but this is dangerous. Just resign yourself to digging and be thankful it is till on its wheels.

With another car (and room for it to manoeuvre) attach the rope to a high point like the roof rack; two points if the rack is less strong alloy because no rack is designed to take a lateral force like this. (With no rack put a strap through the car and round the roof, in one side and out the other.) You can't expect to pull a car upright before the rack bends, but as the towing car eases back sand will fall in under the unloading lower wheels. A couple of goes will right the car. Then with more clearing of wheels and laying of sand plates, slowly tow the car directly backwards (again, assuming there is room) until it's on level ground.

Fallen or overturned vehicles are rare but, crash injuries notwithstanding, you should again take your time to make a recovery without further damaging yourselves or the vehicle.

Most vehicles will fall on their side. If it's on a dune slope (as in the photo on the right) the only way is to drag it down to level ground, something that can only be done with another car. If you're alone you're in deep trouble and have a couple

A strap pulls the vehicle over (**top**) to get some sand under the wheels on the low side. Now less precariously balanced, it's towed down the slope (**bottom**) and back onto the plain.

Top: It may look drastic, but the only way is to drag this car down to more level ground where it can be pulled back onto its wheels (**bottom**). Within an hour it was running just as before. © Toby Savage

Inset: An indistinguishable low rise saw this Land Rover tip over harmlessly. **Main picture**: A hasty recovery can do more damage than the fall, so take your time. Dig holes beneath the wheels to reduce the leverage and keep clear of straining tow straps. With another vehicle, airbag jacks are useful aids in this situation. © Jean-Paul Larboulette

of days' digging to look forward to. Once the vehicle is on level ground, a strap around a chassis rail will give enough leverage to lift the car, though digging pits for the wheels to fall into reduces the towing force required.

There is a temptation for people to help with the lifting but it's safest to let the towing car do all the work; it can easily manage. If something breaks, the helpers could be crushed as the vehicle falls back.

Following such a recovery, besides all the expected problems of tumbled up baggage, broken windows and leaking fluids, once a car has been on its side for a while, **oil can run into the combustion chamber** if any valves happen to have been open when the engine stopped. Trying to start a car in this state may not work if all cylinders are flooded as the oil creates a hydraulic lock and the crank jams. But if only one cylinder is flooded with oil, a big engine may be able to fire up just long enough to bend or break the con rod of that flooded cylinder. This applies to both petrol and diesel engines. Left unattended, eventually this oil might drain back down past the rings, but it could take hours and you'll never know for sure. So, before you try and run the engine, it's necessary to **loosen all fuel injectors** or spark plugs and turn the engine over, expelling any oil from the combustion chambers. A few turns will do. After that, check the oil level and the car should fire up, but expect a bit more smoke than usual from the pipe.

Shadows and lack of perspective

If you think all this sounds hairy, there's worse to come. During the middle of the day when the sun is overhead there are no **shadows** to give you an idea of the lie of the slopes. It's even worse on a cloudy day. This doesn't occur on every occasion in the desert but when it does you have the impression of driving on clouds. All around appears to be the same featureless hue: you can't distinguish level ground from a steep slope and it's extremely disconcerting.

I've ridden a bike in these conditions and completely out of the blue I rode into the side of a dune and fell over. I couldn't tell that the slope was there. All the **perspective** of shade and colour which we use to judge distance and surface were absent in the surrounding monotone. Only the horizon divided the sand from the sky, giving a guide to balance. Riding into a dune bank in these conditions was lucky. Driving off a dune crest is usually disastrous. As explained, not every dune crossing at noon will be like this, but when you encounter this phenomenon the only answer is to stop and wait for the sun to

The position of the sun can affect accurate reading of the relief, especially in dunes. With the sun behind you, shadows defining the ground ahead can be hidden from view.
An overhead sun casting no shadows at all can also lead to disorientation when driving in dunes.

False impression of a continuous smooth ascent

Hidden shadow zone

drop a bit and give some definition to the land. Some recommend using DIBS mirrors which reflect a spot onto the ground ahead, but these have to be constantly adjusted unless you happen to be travelling in a straight line – and they won't reflect anything in the Sahara if your bearing is between 90° and 270° as the sun's behind you.

Low sun angles are also dangerous and not only in dunes. The difficulty of driving into the rising or setting sun, especially with a bug-splattered windscreen, is familiar to most road drivers. But in the desert the sun at your back presents a similar difficulty in defining relief – something you'll find evident when driving a Saharan piste from **south to north**. You'll notice a glare that wasn't there before because all the shadows that help define the relief of the ground are facing north and obscured by the relief. It's odd but not alarming, and occasionally you might crash over a ridge or into a pothole that you couldn't distinguish. We were once going north along the eastern banks of the Erg Tifernine in Algeria (A12), heading for Gara Khanfoussa, and the eye strain, made no better with or without sunglasses, was enough to cause a headache.

In dunes this lack of facing shadows is similar to the overhead sun situation, and again could mean falling down a slope that simply was not seen. Be aware of this when dune-driving west in the early morning or east at dusk.

DUNE-DRIVING SUMMARY

- Never go alone unless you accept the consequences.
- Go with someone who knows the way.
- Anticipate doubled fuel consumption and exhausting recoveries.
- In a group establish hand signals or use radios.
- In a group take obstacles one at a time to avoid collisions.
- Try to maintain height.
- If unsure, stop and reconnoitre on foot.

- If the engine gets hot, park into the wind with the engine running and bonnet up.
- Descend slip faces vertically. If you start sliding sideways down a slip face, steer downhill and accelerate. Do not brake.
- In extreme boggings reduce tyres to 0.7 bar but keep speed down.
- Re-inflate tyres as soon as you return to firm ground.
- GPS waypoints are less useful than you think and can distract from the big picture.

Vehicle maintenance and repairs

Ideally you want to leave home with a serviced vehicle that's going to require little or no maintenance and only the occasional repair. In reality you have to be ready for anything, based on your confidence in your vehicle. In a modern Japanese car you could expect nothing to go wrong at all. This is just as well with cars produced over the last decade as they're not designed to be repaired by their owners.

Make sure you have a **service manual** for your vehicle, preferably one that's designed for home users and includes advice on elementary troubleshooting and fault diagnosis. Even if you don't understand every page of this manual, someone else might. Official factory manuals are necessarily much better as they tend to be written for trained mechanics with specialised knowledge and equipment.

Regular vehicle checks

Get into the habit of doing regular vehicle checks. Certain things should be checked daily, such as tyre pressures, oil and coolant level. In practice you'll give up the all-over daily checks once things have settled down and a few consecutive inspections have come up with nothing, but definitely do a full check before setting off on a long piste or after a very rough day's driving. **Home-made fittings** are especially prone to failure on the first corrugated piste.

So that you don't overlook anything, I find it's useful to print out a **list of daily vehicle checks**, get it laminated and keep it in a door pocket. By keeping it handy you can easily refer to the list and tick off various items with just a quick prod, pull or glance.

Outside and underneath
- Tyres: pressures and sidewalls.
- Underbody: leaks and damage.
- Free play in prop shafts, UJs and pinions.
- Exhaust mounts.
- Spare wheel.
- Suspension and shocks.

Engine bay and front
- Engine oil level.
- Radiator water and hoses.
- All belt tensions.
- Battery/ies: connections and mounts.
- Air filter connections.
- Water pump free play.
- Other loose fittings.
- Lights and grill.

Top
- Roof gutter clamp fittings.
- Other roof rack attachments.

Inside
- Fuel tank and tap.
- Water tank.
- Lashing points and loads.

TOOLS AND SPARES

You'll need tools to work on every fitting in your car short of removing the engine and taking it apart (though some might feel safer with the means to do that too). It sounds like a mobile garage but in fact adds up to a good-quality socket set, spanners, screwdrivers and some pliers.

As mentioned already, it's common for untested home-made modifications to give problems so, aside from these standard tools, you'll need some miscellaneous materials for improvised repairs. Try and visualise what might break under the strain and how you'd fix it. The following list covers items that I've found useful and others that seem so but were rarely used:

- Spare nuts, bolts and hose clamps in various sizes.
- Various jubilee clips and cable ties, very handy.
- Duct tape, very handy.
- Hand drill and drill bits (rarely used).
- Pieces of thin alloy plate (or save some tin cans).
- Length of chain and links.
- Hacksaw, hammer and file.
- Big screwdriver/lever.
- G-clamp big enough to use on a car bumper.
- WD40 spray.
- Electrical wire of various lengths and gauges, plus solder.
- Plastic-coated gardening wire and wire coat hangers. Useful.
- Epoxy glue, radiator sealant, silicone gasket sealant, fuel tank/crankcase repairing paste, thread sealant. All useful.
- Safety goggles for working under the car or in wind-blown sand.
- Short block of wood for supports, spacing or hammering without damage.

The philosophy of spares

The quantity of spares you take is also related to your confidence in your vehicle, plus the length and difficulty of the trip. You need to strike a balance with essential items and trying to outdo Sod's Law that states if you don't take it you'll need it.

I know one guy who travels in an ancient IIA with *everything*, but he also knows how to fix everything in his vehicle and on occasion has had to. Meanwhile, I travelled for years in my 61 with nothing but some old shocks and radiator hoses cunningly stashed away so long ago I've forgotten where. Part of the reason I'd bought a Toyota was that I wanted to avoid the potential gnawing anxiety which can bear over a trip. In the end my 'take nothing and you'll need nothing' gamble paid off and when I needed to I always managed to limp home on broken springs or three and-a-half tyres. One could say that

I'd adopted an African fatalism, tempered with the pragmatism of knowing what could stop me in my tracks and what I can actually fix (a short list).

With a vehicle doing its first trip it's understandable to be nervous of every noise and rattle and dwell on the galling possibility of a meltdown after months of preparation. Having come through that experience and out the other side I believe some trips were not meant to work out but that strangely, there also appears to be a certain amount of 'paying your dues' which rubs off subconsciously on making better decisions next time. Once a machine has proved itself and you get to trust it a major hurdle has been overcome and you can begin pushing your exploration to greater levels. It is certainly a great relief to be able to get nagging vehicle worries behind you and focus on the trip and the environment.

Anyway, **mark all spares** clearly if you wrap them up to save messing about when looking for the right item. Useful for any vehicle are a **head gasket**, best placed between stiff pieces of cardboard and taped against any flat surface to avoid bending. A spare **alternator** picked up from a breaker's can give peace of mind (check it's working before you stash it), as can a spare **water pump**, inexpensive when new and, like an alternator, easily replaced if it fails. Certainly check the state of the carbon brushes in the alternator and the **starter motor**, another handy item to pick up from a breaker's.

A full set of **electrical ignition components** for petrol engines will be necessary – condenser, distributor cap and HT leads and spark plugs and caps – as they often give problems in dusty conditions. Carburettor spares like diaphragms, floats and jets are also useful as is a **fuel pump**. All cars should have plenty of spare electrical fuses. A French glossary of these and many other parts as well as vehicle problems appears on page 649.

It might be an idea to have diesel injectors serviced before departure, though I've never heard of problems with these in the Sahara. A spare **glow plug** or two is a good idea as are **fuel filters** should you run the tank dry and suck up some crap. If you think you need to go as far as valves, piston rings and big ends you're either a keen home-mechanic or taking the wrong vehicle. Plan to carry a complete change of engine- and gearbox/diff **oils** and half a litre of **hydraulic fluid** to top up leaks. A spare **clutch plate**? Well, you certainly can't get far with a burned-out unit so consider fitting a new heavy-duty unit at home and taking a spare one along as back up. It all depends on your car's age, payload, route and your confidence in undertaking such repairs. Carry a spare **radiator cap** as it's possible to get distracted and lose it. The same goes for **fuel filler caps**.

IMPROVISED REPAIRS

Use a logical approach to fault diagnosis and, if necessary, a lateral approach to problem solving. This was demonstrated by James Stewart and his chums in the classic desert survival drama *Flight of the Phoenix* where a mixed group of oil workers and engineers led by James Stewart managed to build a single-engined aircraft from the wreckage of their crashed machine. Miraculous engineering like this is only possible in the celluloid imagination, but on a less epic scale such improvisation is at the heart of many bush-mechanic remedies and helps keep many desert vehicles running.

It's beyond the scope of this book to offer detailed mechanical information so this advice is generalised and, to some, rather obvious. With just about all the bodges listed below it pays to drive slowly once a repair has been made and to check it frequently. Very often they're not initially effective, especially if sensitive to vibration, and you may have to try something else. These ideas cover only vital items that must be addressed to maintain mobility. Usually, if you can get the engine running, however badly, you can keep moving.

All this messing around will no doubt get your **hands** dirty. If you're not using surgical latex gloves (available in bulk from car shops and chemists), use heavy-duty washing-up gloves. Alternatively, wash your hands in a mixture of liquid soap or washing-up liquid

Front leaves all broken. Luckily it was the half with the shackle, so the rear of the spring still located the axle in position. Any attempt to keep the axle off the bump stop with wood and straps soon crumbled, so in the end the axle sat on the rubber all the way home. On another occasion with a broken radius arm and a loose rear axle, a chain was wrapped around the axle from the rear bumper while a winch cable ran under the car and took up the tension from the front. There is always a solution.

and sand or sugar and then rinse in a little water – a very effective way of removing grime.

Common fixes

An engine that won't start can almost always be put down to a problem with the **electrics** (common with petrol engines), **fuel** (possible with diesels) or **electronics** (in modern cars, and usually terminal). Work at possible causes systematically and try to avoid turning the battery over and over in the hope that it will catch. Check electrical connections: is there a spark at the plugs, or fuel coming out of loosened injectors?

If an **alternator** has packed up, start the car off another battery and keep it running, removing things like brake-light bulbs and anything else that would discharge the battery. Keep the engine running; a diesel engine can be kept running all day and all night, while petrol engines are more sensitive to prolonged low-speed running. Either way, if the **starter motor** has failed, constant running will be essential unless the terrain and another vehicle permit tow starts. Check that the starter isn't jammed or slipping first by giving it a sharp tap with a rock or hammer – a trick that's worked for me before. If the starter jams it can be down to corroded contacts which can be cleaned up once the starter is off. **Tow starts** are best

What, no Radweld? Resoldering a leaking radiator with a tyre lever heated in a fire.

achieved in a high gear. Start off in neutral and, once moving at a good speed, depress the clutch and engage third gear in high ratio.

Split **radiator hoses** can be bound tightly with wire and then duct tape, although replacement is better. Leaks from fragile old radiators are to be expected, either from cracks or stones. Egg yolk is said to work but proper radiator sealant is best, assuming the hole is not too large. A radiator does not have one core winding up and down in series, but has parallel elements, so it's possible to bend the exposed ends of a fractured element closed with pliers if you can't glue it up or otherwise block it.

Split tyre sidewalls and even inner tubes can be sewn in an emergency but you'll have to keep the pressure high on a repaired tyre to avoid undue flexing, and a tube will need a big patch. Put another patch on the inside of a sidewall repair so the tube doesn't rub, but don't expect this to last long. You could fill a damaged tyre or one without a tube with sand to give it some shape, but it would need to be filled right up, something that's tricky to do and even then may not work. Grass and other foliage certainly don't work, but clothing might do the trick.

A holed or sheared **exhaust pipe** can be fixed with a splint-like alloy sleeve wrapped around the break and fixed with a pair of hose clamps, unless a small crack or hole can be repaired with a bandage. Breaks at the silencer join are less easy to fix: fit a sleeve loosely on the pipe end and push it into the can and then the clamp down the sleeve. A car can run fine without a silencer, especially a turbo diesel.

A bar of soap rubbed into a **cracked petrol tank** is an old bodge though the epoxy pastes made for the job are better and can be strong enough to hold a thread and bolt in other situations. Replacement gaskets of any type can be made from cardboard, providing the single piece is big enough.

This broken chassis was repaired with a plate welded on using a pair of car batteries. The fact that the pick-up was carrying one of those demountable cabins probably contributed to the failure.

It's possible to **arc weld** off two (or better still three) 12-volt batteries attached in series making 24/36 volts and plenty enough amps (home arc-welding machines produce about 30-40 volts). A jump lead attached to a pair of Mole grips can hold a welding rod and bits of thick cable or wire can join the batteries if necessary. Take the batteries right out of the car and if unsealed protect them from sparks (batteries produce explosive gas) and prepare the welding area well. It's not going to do your batteries much good in the long term so is best for emergencies only, but I've seen a broken chassis repaired with battery welding.

Arc welders are easily found in desert towns and always busy, but although **welding rods** can be in short supply – bring your own as well as a welding glass; they're tradable commodities. However, alloy welding is unknown so repairs with gluing, rivets or drilling and bolts are your options. Alloy is rarely a structural element in cars, though auxiliary fuel or water tanks made of aluminium can cause problems if they come adrift and crack.

Vapour lock occurs in hot conditions when petrol vapour blocks the passage of liquid fuel through the fuel pump. Letting the car cool down is one answer: draping the fuel pump with a wet rag is the instant solution to cooling it and condensing the vapour. Vapour lock is not a problem with diesels.

Under the car, bent **track rods** can be removed and bent back by heating in a fire if necessary. They don't have to be perfectly straight. A severed metal **brake pipe** can be crimped and folded over, saving loss of brake fluid and keeping effective braking on the other wheels. With a rubber pipe, fold it over and crimp it with a small hose clamp or a zip tie.

If any **transmission** component from the back prop shaft to the axles fails, you can continue in front-wheel drive only with the car effectively in four-wheel drive or, on cars with permanent four-wheel drive, by locking the central diff and continuing at a moderate pace.

It's worth remembering that, despite the much-repeated stresses of desert travel, it's very rare for a vehicle to be completely stranded and unrepairable and it is worth recognising that, even though you may not think so now, the more irresolvable the problem, the greater will be the ingenuity of you or the people around you in fixing it.

TYRE REPAIRS

Motorcyclists are used to the sometimes laborious job of changing tyres by hand, but most car owners are blissfully unfamiliar of this task. You hand the flat over to the guy at the tyre centre and with the aid of his press the job is done in ten minutes. In the Sahara, the need for self-sufficiency includes performing your own tyre repairs, the most common cause of immobility. In most cases this means merely changing a wheel and getting the tyre fixed at the next town, a repair you can afford to put off or pass on if you have a **second spare**. If not or you're feeling energetic, the tools you will need for this task are:

● Jack. High-lift or air bag jacks are easiest to use (see below), but you'll need the vehicle's standard bottle-jack or a wheel stand as a back-up.
● Wheel brace (include a back-up socket in your tool set).
● Tyre levers. Use good-quality tyre levers made of hard metal that won't bend; your tyre dealer can order them. Two at about 60cm long and no more than 25m wide are ideal. A pair is usually enough though sometimes a third short lever can hold the bead up as you lever the next portion.

Thorns are a common cause of punctures, especially in the sub-Saharan Sahel. Be wary of parking in the shade of acacia trees.

- Puncture repair kit plus alcohol (cologne or petrol will do, but diesel is too oily) and talcum powder or chalk.
- Spare inner tubes. Tubes often get ruined in a puncture; bring at least four.
- Tyre-pressure gauge. The sliding rod types are said to be reliably accurate but digital ones, just as widely available, are easier to read. Avoid the cheap circular dial types which are notoriously inaccurate.
- Pump or compressor (see below).
- A bead-breaking tool such as Tyrepliers – a crafty Australian device designed to lever the bead off bit by bit.

   If you've never changed a car tyre before, let alone a chunky 4WD tyre, here are a few tips. First of all, **practice at home**, not the Sahara. Learning tyre changing out in the desert when you may need the tyre to keep moving will be stressful and may lead to mistakes. If you're buying new tyres for your trip, have a go at mounting the spare, or even all five yourself (by then you really will be an expert!). Observe the **careful jacking precautions** outlined from page 122. If the car needs to be jacked up on soft ground for any longer than it takes to swap wheels, lower it back down onto a rock or a couple of jerricans (ideally, full). In the desert, work on a **sheet** laid out on the shady side of the car and wear stout footwear and gloves where possible.

Wheel changing – step by step

1. Try to park on firm, flat ground in 4WD, in gear and with hand brake on.
2. Chock front and rear wheels.
3. Remove spare tyre and jack.
4. Loosen wheel nuts.
5. Jack up the car.
6. Check wheel chocks.
7. Finish undoing the bolts and remove wheel.
8. Fit spare and refit nuts loosely.
9. Lower vehicle from jack.
10. Tighten wheel nuts fully.
11. Try and ascertain the cause of the puncture.
12. If not repairing immediately, restow tyre and jack.
13. Check all tools are replaced and that the pressure in the newly-fitted tyre matches the others.
14. Remove chocks and drive on.

Breaking the bead

Removing tyres presents two challenges, breaking the bead or edge of the tyre and levering it off a one-piece rim (split rims, unknown in Europe but fitted to Toyota 70-series, avoid tyre levering but can still be stubborn). With a good technique and the right tools there should be no huge effort involved but it's still hard work when you're stressed and hot.

   Take your time and follow the steps

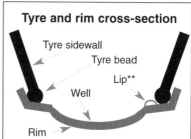

Tyre and rim cross-section

Tyre sidewall
Tyre bead
Lip**
Well
Rim

Identifying tyre and rims parts. The lip** only appears on tubeless rims and exists to hold the bead against the rim.

Left:
Using a TyrePlier bead-breaking tool.
Right:
You can also use a high-lift jack to break the bead. With tubeless tyres, you'll find you need it.

outlined below. Some wheel and tyre combinations are harder to separate than others: new tyres can fit too snugly onto rims and old tyres can rust to steel rims. A **hot tyre** is more malleable than a cold one; a recently punctured tyre will be hot, but if you've left it a while, warm it in the sun.

● Stand on the tyre sidewall to try and push the tyre off the rim into the well; this rarely works unless the tyre is a loose fit.

Alternatively you can drag the tyre under a bumper and **jack** the car down onto it. This can be tough on the sidewalls but the rounded corners of a high-lift base shouldn't do any damage. As a last resort you can try the African method of **driving** over the rim to break the bead. With either method, squirting some **soapy water** into the rim can help, as it can when remounting the tyre.

● With the bead off one side you are ready to lever the tyre off. The important thing is to make sure the side of the tyre opposite to where you're levering is pushed into the **well** of the tyre. In this position it gives the tyre bead the necessary **slack** to be levered over the rim. Kick the tyre repeatedly into the well as you lever round. Excessively hard levering can damage the tyre's bead. Breaking both beads can make levering off the tyre easier but means more remounting work later. Once you get about 20cm of the bead over the rim the rest is easy.

Tyre changing on tubed rims – step by step

1. Remove valve cap and unscrew valve core with valve tool, taking care that the valve core doesn't shoot off as the air escapes.

2. Break the tyre bead off the rim. On off-set wheels with unequal rim widths, the narrower rim is easier to break.

3. Lever off the tyre.

4. It may now be possible to drag out the tube, but it's sometimes easier to completely remove the tyre from the wheel.

5. Carefully inspect the tyre tread and sidewalls for damage. Pass a hand across the inside of the carcass to find any possible protuberances. In thorny acacia country you may find several thorns

Pressing the rim out of the tyre.

pushing through. Subsequent rocks tend to push the thorns in deeper so they must all be removed to avoid continuous punctures for days on end.

6. Either replace the tube or repair it (see below).

7. If not already powdered, some talc sprinkled inside the tyre helps a fresh tube align itself without creases.

8. Refit the valve core and fit the partially-inflated tube back into the tyre, trying to avoid any twisting and with the valve perpendicular to the rim.

9. With the tyre upright, fit the narrower rim into the tyre, seat the tube in the tyre and push the valve through the rim. If the valve stem is short you may want to screw on the valve tool to stop it slipping into the wheel during fitment.

10. With the tyre back on the ground begin levering the narrower rim (if offset) out of the tyre. As you work round make sure the bead opposite the levers is fully in the well giving the much needed slack for the final push when the tyre pops over the rim. Soapy lubricant and an acceptance of your mortality helps reduce the effort.

11. Check that the valve is straight and inflate the tyre.

12. Complete wheel-changing steps described in points 8 to 14, above.

Repairing tubes – step by step

In practice it is best to **replace a tube** rather than repair it, but a time will come when you have to repair a tube, so it's best to know how.

Make sure you press the patch securely onto the tube, eliminating all air bubbles. Using a roller ensures a good seal.

Locals in old bangers will often try to scrounge patches and even tubes. You may have spare patches but think twice about giving away tubes. Patches are available in every town.

1. Inflate the inner tube to help locate the puncture. Passing it over your eyes or wet lips can help sense the air jet from a pinprick hole. You're unlikely to have the luxury of a bath to dip the tube in and look for bubbles, but if you do, use it. Otherwise spit on possible puncture holes and watch for bubbles. Don't assume there is only one hole, especially in thorny country or if the wheel travelled for some distance while flat.

2. Once the hole (or holes) is located, release the air and roughen the area around the hole with some sandpaper.

3. Clean off the sandpaper and rubber grit with a solvent like alcohol, perfume or petrol.

4. Choose your patch, apply a thin film of glue to the area and wait till it's dry to the touch.

5. Unpeel the patch (usually it's the **foil or clear side which should be stuck to the tyre)**. Using a roller or a screwdriver handle on a solid surface, press the patch firmly to the tube, making sure the entire edge is stuck down. Sprinkle some talc over the gluey excess and complete the appropriate tyre repair as outlined above.

6. Once you've refitted the wheel, **check the wheel nuts** after a few kilometres. Six-stud Land Cruisers, in particular, are known to loosen their wheel nuts which can sometimes end in sheared wheel studs, but any wheel change should be followed by a wheel-nut check at the first stop.

Remounting tubeless tyres

Having established that tubeless tyres work fine in the desert, even at the very low pressures needed in sand, the other problem is removing and mounting tyres in the field.

Unlike with tubed tyres, the need for this is pretty rare of course. The ease of fixing tubeless tread punctures **from the outside** is their most obvious advantage (see p.120). Presumably for safety reasons, this practice is illegal in much of Europe where tubeless tyres must be repaired or vulcanised from the inside.

Nevertheless, a situation may occur when you need to remove or just remount a tubeless tyre back onto the rim. The problem is getting the bead of the tyre over the small lip which you get on tubeless wheel rims (see diagram, p.202), without an inner tube to push it on. Normally you need a blast of high-pressure air to get the tyre mounted, otherwise air simply escapes before pressure builds up as the tyre never makes a seal.

This sort of high-pressure air is something you usually only find in a tyre shop or get by using the **Icelandic Technique**: squirting lighter fuel through the valve housing and igniting a small explosion which usually mounts the

tyre and possibly dismounts your eyebrows. I've never tried this as the bicycle tube technique below worked out fine but I'm told: *'The fuel I always use is Butane cigarette lighter gas, first jack up the problem wheel, then arrange the tyre with the biggest gap between tyre and rim at the top, spray in the Butane (a stock 205 x 16 RR tyre usually requires about a 4 second burst of butane gas). Then stand back and throw a lighted match at the gap. With a loud pop the tyre is back in place ready to be reinflated to working pressure.'* Now you know.

The **bicycle tube technique** seals one side of an unmounted tubeless tyre and, trapping the air, enables the build-up of pressure to mount the tyre onto the wheel rim. With the loose tyre fitted inside the rim, put it on another bare rim or something similar like an oil drum or jerry. This ensures that the full weight of the tyre is resting – and so sealing – the lower tyre edge against the rim. If you do it on the flat ground,

Using the 16" bicycle tube method to help get a seal while remouting a tubeless tyre. It helps to lift the rim off the ground so the bottom on the tyre is resting on the rim, while the bicycle tube seals the top edge.

the weight may be on the tyre not the rim which will cause air to escape.

Now cover the bicycle tube with soapy water and tuck it into the upturned rim and pump it up to get a snug fit. Try not to overinflate the tube (as shown with the over-width rims on the preceding page) because a bike tube tends to stretch unevenly around the valve which will lose the seal.

With the bike tube tucked in, remove the valve core from the tubeless rim (this greatly speeds up inflation) and inflate the tyre. You'll need more than a foot pump and may need to jiggle the tyre around and push or pull the bike tube to ensure a good seal but as soon as you get it right the tyre suddenly seals and inflates quickly. The soapy bike tube should come away even with the tyre nearly in place. To finish, refit the valve core and pump the tyre up to the desired pressure.

Riding the Sahara

Exploring rather than simply crossing the Sahara represents an extreme of adventure motorcycling that either appeals to you or fills you with dread. Unsupported motorbikes are not the ideal vehicles for this sort of travel and, more than ever, thorough planning and preparation are crucial.

The biggest problem will be **carrying enough fuel and water**. Riding a fully-loaded bike on remote, rocky pistes is very demanding and something that's best left to experienced riders. Plan well within your range and limit your tour to the cool **winter** months. Never consider riding in the Sahara during the summer months (May–September). With temperatures up to 45°C, you'll need to drink every half hour and daily water consumption will exceed ten litres.

These bike chapters assume that you're riding in the desert unsupported and independently. Riding with 4WD support is logistically straightforward but it also takes away the raw edge of doing it off your own back. Then again, an unladen bike accompanying a 4WD or two makes an ideal reconnaissance vehicle in the desert, skimming over soft sand where the heavy cars can get bogged for hours.

Which bike?
Motorcycling in the Sahara takes a lot out of a bike, in some cases more than the manufacturer intended which is why, as with 4WDs, a limited range of models is regularly used. These days most trail bikes will do the job and there are a few models that are genuinely suited to the rigours of the Sahara.

What sort of bike you choose depends on what sort of riding you plan to do in the Sahara: simply crossing the desert and heading on south across the continent, following some of the main pistes in this book, or hardcore off-piste exploration. Whatever you choose, a solid stock machine with sensible modifications is best for the long ride. For the first two categories listed above

For the Sahara a 600cc single is best: two KTMs, a 650GS, XT600Z, XR400 and a Dominator.

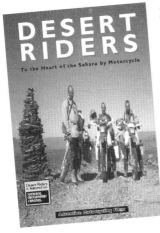

Much of the new material for this section appears on the *Desert Riders* dvd and www.adventure-motorcy-cling.com/desertriders

you can probably get away with a twin cylinder or even a modified multi. They will get you through the desert and, out of the soft sand or rocks, will make a comfortable ride.

For anything radical it has to be a **single**, because they are light but still adequately powerful. Singles will make any real desert biking much less fraught, though maybe at the price of comfort in getting down there. These days all singles of around 600cc have enough power to carry a load over anything you can throw at them without straining and they are less intimidating to ride in difficult terrain.

I don't discuss every single marque here, just the most used. Suzuki DRs and Kawasaki KLRs are great machines but I've never seen a KLR650 in the Sahara and DRs are only a bit less rare. These models are described in my *Adventure Motorcycling Handbook*.

If you're buying a bike specially for the Sahara, get it well in advance of your departure so that any problems and modifications can be sorted out. Whichever machine you choose, consider the following important qualities:

● Lightness
A typical load of up to 50kg (plus fuel) will annihilate any agility and reduce braking performance as well as accelerate wear on tyres and chains. A trail bike will become as nimble as a road bike, while a heavier twin could really be a handful except with an experienced rider.

● Economy
This is what rules out most two-strokes. An average economy of around 17kpl (51 mpg) is a good target. Aim for an extra 20% cruising on the highway and 20% below average in dunes or against strong winds. It's worth noting that, despite their drawbacks, **fuel-injected bikes** are around 15% more economical than equivalent carbs, and a lot smoother besides (surging notwithstanding), plus injected bikes don't get sick at altitude.

● Comfort
Trail bikes, with upright seating positions and sometimes buzzy single-cylinder engines, are tiring to drive over long distances, especially along European autoroutes with dirt-biased tyres. A **small windscreen** or fairing is a good idea, even on the piste.

● Mechanical simplicity and accessibility
Compared to cars, bikes are more mechanically reliable in the desert, but if things do go wrong you'll be on your own. Toyotas and Land Rovers may be used by locals and tourists alike, but anything bigger than a moped, let alone a dealer, is rare between the Mediterranean and southern Africa.

● Agility

A proper trail bike's 21" front wheel, steering geometry and wide handlebars all aid off-road control, as do knobbly tyres, long-travel suspension and ground clearance.

● Reliability and robustness

Over the years certain marques and models have earned a reputation for dependable reliability and robustness. These are the ones most commonly seen on the piste and listed here.

KTM Adventure

For once a marque's success across the board in the Dakar Rally reflects also on independent desert riding: **640 Adventures** are built from the ground up for the job and are not just trail bikes with big tanks and decals. 'Off the shelf overlanders' is how one owner describes them. KTM have come a very long way from the spitting, recalcitrant thumpers of the 1980s.

The whole integrated purposefulness is reflected in the build-quality and design. The tank holds a very useful 28 litres while the frame (if not early side-stands) is known to stand up to heavy crashes.

Avoid the early slide carb models – the later CV carbs from around 2001 give much better fuel economy and smoother running. Power is crisp and responsive and matches the quality suspension. And with it comes the availability of overlanding

KTM Adventure: light, powerful and strongly built, the best pure desert machine going.

gear from the usual suppliers. There is plenty around: extra tanks, pipes, racks and all sorts of goodies all the way up to rally spec.

The main problems (apart from engine failures due to the crankshaft bearing or con-rod) add up to **vibration** from the relatively high-compression engine and the notoriously **uncomfortable seat** which can make long road rides tiring – though the windscreen makes this less bad than it could be, and alternative seats are available. All the better then to get on the dirt as soon as possible, where this bike shines and you'll forget all about your numb backside. Alloy sprockets used to have a habit of wearing fast, and the vibration means you need to keep a check on fit-

You don't have to buy an Adventure – an LC4 with a big tank makes a light Adventure without the screen but both engines require frequent oil changes.

tings. You can alter the CDI unit to allow the bike to run on low-octane fuel – something that only BMW have also got to grips with.

Even secondhand Adventures are expensive – less fancy **LC4s** are more common and once fitted with an Adventure tank and other mods will give you a functional Adventure.

Yamaha XT

Once the most popular range of bikes used in Africa, Yamaha's XT series, specifically the 600cc (now 660cc) Ténéré version, was a groundbreaking machine and is often still the first bike people think of when considering taking on the Sahara. These days XTs have stagnated and lost their original deserty focus and are now in the shadow of BMWs and KTMs.

XT500 on the way to In Guezzam. The 19" front wheel and road tyres were a bad idea.

Well over 20 years old but the original Ténéré is still a great machine once the suspension and seat are firmed up. All following models were heavier and had inferior components.

If you find one, an ex-rally XT600Z with all the big tanks and mods makes a good overlander if the engine's in good shape.

Arriving in 1983 the original kick-start **600Z Ténéré** (34L) was the first off-the-shelf overlander following the many home-cobbled XT500s which ploughed through the Sahara. Standard features included a 30-litre fuel tank which managed not to be huge, o-ring chain (radical for the time), powerful brakes and lights, an oil cooler and YZ suspension, all wrapped around a simple air-cooled, four-stroke, single cylinder engine based on the exceptionally economical XT550. With only minimal alterations, early model Ténérés still make reliable overland machines even if they are now pretty scarce.

Subsequent models like the electric start 1VJ moved away from this ideal, despite some detail improvements (notably in the positioning of the oil tank and cooler, and bigger air boxes). Electric starts, rear disc brakes and fairings paid for retrograde cost-cutting features elsewhere, and the tank was down to 23 litres. Although the original kick-start Ténéré's soft suspension was greatly improved, later models were heavier and appeared to be less mechanically durable and less economical.

The cheap, small tanked **XT600E** (3TB, 3UW) kept going throughout the 1990s, wringing out the XT reputation and was only finally dumped in 2003 long after its sell-by date. Nevertheless it managed to be seen as superior to the **five-valve 660cc Ténéré** introduced in 1990 which never really caught on in the Sahara, being 30kg heavier than the first XT600Z and with only a 20-litre tank, barely worthy of the name.

In the UK, David Lambeth (see advert in the back) is the XT Man and always has a good stock of fresh-engined **twin-lamp 3AJs**. These came out just before the 660 in the late 1980s and are the best Ténéré that are readily available these days. They're not too old, carry a decent 23 litres and like the original can be made ready for the desert without great expense once the common **fifth gear** problem has been checked. This gear pitting is not a problem unique to 3AJs but because these models get chosen and used on hard overland trips, it crops up sooner. (On all big thumpers you can preserve the gearbox and final drive chain by not lugging the engine at

The twin-lamp Ténéré is the best of the bunch, from an era when bash plates were actually made of metal not plastic.
© Geoff van de Merwe

low speeds, no matter how good it sounds.) A 'twin-lamp' is your basic, early 'KTM Adventure', not quite the quality build but for half the price.

Among the enduro exotica, **TT600** Belgardas are tuned XT600 engines in either a racy S version with quality suspension or a lower specified E model equipped with an electric start. Although the S model is less radical and more stable than an equivalent XR, the TT600E model would still be a good choice and may be available in the UK, through grey or parallel importers bringing bikes in from Italy. Problems are the leaky upside-down forks and, some say, the Italian build quality which does not quite match the Jap-built examples.

Yamaha finally cranked out a new XT in 2004, the **XT660R** – really a replacement for the XT-E which was now doing regular shows at Dinosaur World. The 660R is no desert bike, just another cool single which is popular in Europe. The weight is around 170kg and the new water-cooled engine features **fuel injection** and low slung pipes with a catalyser, all to help it pass European emission controls. The pipes mean there is no bash plate, just less ground clearance so it would have to be modified round the side to enable effective underbody protection. The gearbox is said to be much stronger though. The tank is only 15 litres but it won't be long before someone offers something bigger, and the rims are alloy which is a step up from the XT-E.

People are put off by electronic fuel injection, but besides helping to save the dolphins, it offers a smoother response

The XT660R is really a new XT-E, not a Ténéré: fuel injection will smooth out the engine, but those pipes will get a bashing.
© Yamaha Motor Co.

as well as better economy. The problem with electronics, as we all know, is that they can pack up out of the blue.

For the moment then, like old Land Rovers, there is enough of an industry and know-how keeping old, air-cooled XTs on the road and ready for the piste. For the full Ténéré story and comprehensive tech-chat and advice, check out www.xt600.de – it's in German but well worth babelfishing.

Honda

Honda's broadly similar **XL** range never really got to grips with the success of the Ténérés, although the early twin-lamp XLM of the mid-eighties was a pretty good attempt: big tank, tubeless rims and a low seat height, but you'll struggle to find one now.

The XL series took a big step forward with the NX650 **Dominator**, which is still around, featuring a great motor and handling to match. Second-hand machines are nothing special but you can get a useful 23-litre Acerbis tank.

The best Honda single still available must be the **XR650L**, an ideal blend of the electric-start Dominator motor in an XR-derived frame with decent suspension from CR motocrossers. It's been available in North America since the early 1990s and has only lately come to Australia and almost the UK.

XRL1; a bit of a shed out of the crate, but with a few mods a decent alternative to a KTM. Full story at www.adventure-motorcycling.com/desert-riders.

As you can probably tell, we chose XRLs for my Desert Riders Project in 2003, importing three from Western Australia (some places now import them into the UK). It was a toss up between an Adventure which, once we'd fettled with our XRLs, we could have probably got for the same price. Once the chronic carburation was sorted out the biggest problem was the **seat height**, not made any better on our machines which were fitted with 40-litre tanks perched up high. But in the desert they never missed a beat; our main reason for choosing Hondas over KTMs. Fuel consumption was in the

XRL2: great handling with a good electric start engine.

mid-50s mpg (19kpl) on mine, one bike was oddly 20% worse and the lightest rider was always 10% better. At one stage in the dunes oil temperatures got up to a worrying 150°, but we ran synthetic oil from new and the motor sounded as good when we got back. Overland Solutions made our racks and strengthened the rear subframe – essential for the loads we were carrying.

Compared to my old XTs the best thing about the XRL was the great stock **suspension**. We messed them up a bit by fitting harder fork springs to cope with the tank, though did nothing but jack up the preload on the back. To be honest, even with the weight we carried at times, we could have got away with the stock suspension and enjoyed a lower bike and less 'sinking boat' cornering. Interestingly, I was the only one to change my original spokes for galvanised steel, and only mine broke, though all the wheels needed tightening after the rocky sections. You can still read the lowdown on my XRL, from selecting which bike to preparation as well as recorded sat chats from the desert at www.adventure-motorcycling.com/desert-riders.

The only other popular Saharan Honda is the super-reliable **XR750V Africa Twin**. A smooth, heavy dirt road cruiser, it is well out of its depth in deep sand.

Two things owners complain about with XRVs are the **weight** and the unreliable electric **fuel pumps**. Positioned alongside the back shock, it's the contacts that usually corrode; your best bet is to fit a Mikuni vacuum pump, similar to those on KTMs (see africaqueens.de). That said, it's the only problem you ever hear about with ATs, along with perhaps the need for a better **back shock** for big loads and two-up riding. It's a testament to the high mileage

Is that the fuel pump he's checking? Some riders like a hefty machine and this XRV with a 40-litre tank managed all the pistes the Adventure behind it did, though with maybe a couple more tumbles: www.atic.org is a good website.

these smooth V-twins can put in. Reliability and comments like *'it keeps on going after a severe hammering'* are what just about all owners comment on.

The only other Hondas out there are old **XR600s**, not as common as you might think in the desert and a bit too frail in the engine and flimsy in the subframe for hard off-road touring. As with all these **enduro bikes**, what you gain in lightness and agility you can lose in fuel economy, relatively short-lived if high-tuned engines (compared to trail bikes), and comfort.

I've also travelled with **XR400s** on my tours – again, a bit slinky to be carrying much baggage but with a bigger tank and alongside a support vehicle this would be a great machine, easy to ride, not as revvy or thirsty as you might think and not, by coincidence, the choice of many dirt tour operators as a basic but solid machine that can take an off-road beating.

XR650R with a full alloy jacket. Fast and well sprung, but a bit juicy.

Surprisingly, considering their racy profile, I've seen a couple of alloy-framed, water-cooled **XR650Rs** being used in the Sahara. Once adapted for the desert they're seen as a powerful but Honda-reliable equivalent to a KTM.

The price is higher fuel consumption than something like an XRL and higher maintenance, all important factors in the Sahara. And despite that alloy frame XR-Rs are not that light and lack an electric starter, which you'll come to appreciate.

BMW

BMW's reputation for overland machines is nearly as old as the brand. Many people have taken the Boxer twins on long world trips and now that the fuel-injected 650s have sorted out their early surging woes, there's a lighter alternative to the big twins.

Even though a variant won the Dakar in 1999, for a single the original **F650 Funduro** is a heavy desert tourer. At 17.5 litres the standard tank is neither

Rotax-engined BMW F650; fast, but not well suited for soft sand traction.

here nor there (although Acerbis do a 27-litre replacement), and the 19" front wheel makes tyre choice limited (an MT21 will squeeze on using, for example, a Honda VT500 mudguard). These days a Funduro would have to be pretty cheap to lure you away from its fuel-injected cousins.

Fuel economy is good (though not in sand), and a tough fairing plus neatly tucked-in water-cooling gear make the Funduro worth a look. In Libya once I found its only drawback was the rela-tively revvy Rotax engine, fast on the road but lacking in low-down pulling power in the sand – something that XTs do better. I actually got stuck in the sands of the Erg Ubari several times on a F650 where an XT600 would have chugged through.

F650GS resting. The 'Dakar' version is a better choice.

Released around 2000, the F650GS comes in three versions; the **F650GS 'Dakar'** with longer sus-pension, a 21" front wheel and a taller screen is the one you want. All models use electronic fuel injec-tion with an 18-litre underseat fuel tank. That may be small, but you can count on at least 10% better fuel consumption over the most economical Dommies or XTs. With a full tank a Dakar weighs over 190 kilos, but that seat (2" higher than a GS) is wide and can be lowered a bit.

Compared to the old Funduro, the injected 650s

are a huge improvement. The EFI smoothed out the low-rpm running: you can pull away from 1500 rpm without shaking the drive chain apart. It's still a revvy machine but a whole lot more enjoyable to ride, feeling agile, light and stable.

Electronics are a concern but at least the Dakar does not have the rectifier mounted behind the bashplate as on early GSs (the lower, roadgoing model with a 19" front). Speaking of which, **bashplates** are little more than pressed tin but with some attention to protection

Replacement carbon-fibre bash plate on this admittedly lower GS was cracking up. Even if you have to make it yourself, an alloy bash plate is best.

(better hand guards), water hoses and a still higher screen, the Dakar makes a great desert bike.

The 650s use a **catalyser** to clean up emissions. Normally these must run on unleaded fuel which is unavailable in most of the Sahara. However, I'm told that you can run the cats on these bikes for 'a few months' on leaded before the cat clogs up or stops working. When this happens it won't affect your bike, but it will affect the emissions when it comes to your next road-worthiness test.

On all bikes fitted with cats (usually with EFI) you can replace the stock cats and silencers with a no-cat aftermarket pipe and the bike's electronic emission sensor will adjust the fuel injection accordingly, meaning the machine should run fine.

The website with all the answers is US-based www.f650.com.

Paralever Twins

BMW's shaft-driven dual-purpose 800-1000 Paralevers and the subsequent injected 800, 1100, 1150 and now 1200cc **GS flat twins** are a heavy proposition for the true Sahara, but that hasn't stopped people taking them there since the year dot. The old pre-injection twins boasted good accessibility, great engines (if not electrics) and reasonable suspension. Although heavy, the weight is low which makes the bulk easier to handle until you get out of shape.

For the Sahara it is these **Paralever** models of the early 1990s which are preferred as they lack the electronics and greater weight of the fuel-injected machines which are covered in the *Adventure Motorcycling Handbook*.

Paralevers came out around 1986 featuring a great improvement over the original 800G/Ss limited suspension. The single-sided 'Paralever' swingarm counteracted the shaft's torque effect under acceleration but, more usefully, was firmer.

The R100GS has a small wind-screen, a better idea than you think on

BMW R100GS set up for ultra-light desert touring.

An HPN R100GS heading across Africa. They can hack the Sahara crossing OK, but off-road exploration is easier on a single.

any desert bike. A few riders I know have learned to handle their GS in the sand – besides skill and nerve the way they do it is by taking minimal luggage. And the reputation for reliability is not that great. One rider I met who'd done a quarter of a million kilometres on his Paralever said he'd changed everything single on the bike at least once.

The weight and feel of a flat-twin BM gives a completely different ride to singles. Less agile, but much more comfortable once loaded and on the move, the whole machine is reassuringly stable in a way unmatched by big singles. It's when you get in ruts, on rocks or need to cross dunes that this mass can get intimidating. You have to be master of your machine or else it will eat you up. If you're heading for the sands, **knobbly tyres** will be vital to help point your GS where you want to go.

Broken stators and diode boards are a problem, but this can be due to overloading the system with extra lights, electric vests and other gadgets that road tourers like to do. You're unlikely to need any of these accessories in Africa, but an uprated or spare rewound stator and diode board will give you less to worry about.

For the Sahara avoid the R100GS 'Dakar' variant with a heavy half fairing wrapped in daft crash bars. You can make a much better 'Dakar' yourself with a 43/45-litre tank from Acerbis or HPN along with the masses of equipment, from frames up, available to make GSs better dirt tourers.

There are several **websites** for the twins: www.ukgser.com covers all GSs, including the injected twins and singles; in the US www.airheads.org sticks to the twin valvers as does www.hpn.de who make some very tasty specials.

Bike preparation

Don't be in any doubt about the hammering your bike is going to get in the Sahara. It must be ready to handle the corrugations and likely falls while still being controllable on the piste when carrying your provisions for several days at a time. This is a task that the most commonly-used machines handle amazing well with little more than a stiffer back shock, a big tank, rack and better tyres.

Realistically, a **range of 600km and three days** is the best an unsupported bike can easily handle without reprovisioning – a fuel payload of around 35 litres. It may not sound much but it is fuel-carrying capacity which defines the limit. If this chapter's advice could be reduced to two words, they would be '**travel light**'. Besides offering agility in the dirt, a lightly-loaded bike puts less stress on already hard-working wheels, suspension and transmission.

Plan to fit in a **test run** to see how the bike handles and if everything works. The fewer surprises you encounter in the nerve-racking early days of the actual trip the more you'll gain in confidence. If you doubt whether any component will last the entire length of your planned trip, renew it. This applies especially to things like tyres, chains and sprockets which wear faster in the desert.

PREPARING YOUR BIKE

Before you leave you must have confidence in your bike's ability to handle the Sahara. The basics points of bike preparation are:

- An engine in good condition and suspension that can handle the load.
- A securely mounted luggage system.
- Adequate fuel and water range, including a reserve.
- Good tyres and strong wheels.

Engines and fuel

Most modern, single-cylinder engines have a relatively high compression ratio and run badly on the low-octane fuel (usually below 90 ROD) you'll some-times find in the Sahara. Signs of an engine straining on poor fuel are a light tapping (known as 'detonation' or 'pinking') from the cylinder head even under gentle throttle loads, as well as power loss and overheating. Air-cooled engines run best on the highest octane fuel available, so **octane booster**, a fuel additive, can be worth taking on a long trip. Available at off-road competition shops, a litre lasts up to 1600km on low-grade fuel, assuming 10cc per litre and 17kpl (50 mpg). Of course the likes of KTM and BMW offer alternative or reprogrammable electronic ignition for this very need, and fuel-injected bikes cope better with low octane: the 650GS and Dakar can run on 91 octane.

Fuel filters and vapour lock

In desert areas, dust is always present in the air and even in fuel, plus old jer-ricans may have paint flaking off the insides, so an **in-line fuel filter** in your fuel line(s) is a good idea. (Injected bikes will have their own, super-fine fil-ters.) The cheap translucent, crinkled-paper element type works better than fine gauze items, which most bikes already have inside the tank as part of the fuel tap assembly. Note the arrow for direction of flow. Paper in-line filters can be easily cleaned by simply flushing in a reverse direction with petrol from the tank.

In hot conditions fuel filters can create **vapour lock** (evaporation of hot fuel in the filter body before it gets to the carburettor), which leads to fuel star-vation. When the bike cuts out and cools the fuel will eventually condense and run into the carb again... until it all gets hot again. Vapour lock is worse when your tank fuel level is low and the filter body itself gets hot. We're talking temperatures of over 35°C here – a maximum in the Saharan travelling season. I've only had this happen once, on a Funduro in Libya in April. A piece of cardboard keeping the heat of the barrel off the fuel line filter did the trick.

To get round it top up your tank and pour water over the fuel filter – you'll see it fill up with fresh fuel instantly. Then wrap it in a damp cloth and think about some more permanent insulation from the heat (like the cardboard men-tioned above or moving it away from the engine's hot air-stream).

Clean foam filters in petrol, soak in engine oil, squeeze, dry and reinstall.

A better way is to soak with proper air filter oil which, unlike engine oil, doesn't soak to the bottom and stays nice and tacky.
Use a cut-down water bottle to soak it and squeeze dry over the bottle so none of the filter oil is wasted.

Air filter

Air filters will require possibly daily cleaning during high winds or sand storms. Because of this the best ones are reusable multi-layered **oiled-foam** types such as those made by Twin-Air or Uni Filter. Carrying a pre-oiled spare in a plastic bag is not a bad idea either.

Make sure that your airbox lid seals correctly and that the rubber hoses on either side of the carburettor are in good condition and done up tightly. It's worth working out where your air filter breathes and how that location will cope when the rear wheel is kicking up a roost. Many riders remove the induction snorkel on top of the airbox to improve response but that of course can let more sand in. If they're in a bad position, a baffle to keep thrown up sand from piling in is a good idea.

Greasing all surfaces inside an airbox is messy but catches more grit so keeps the filter cleaner for longer. You can rinse a re-usable foam with petrol and then soak it with engine oil, but proper **air filter oil** does the job much better, and if you're careful not to waste it, you don't need to carry that much for the typically weekly clean. Should you run out, engine oil is better than nothing.

Cooling

On an air-cooled bike an **oil cooler** is not an essential addition as long as you avoid the hotter Saharan months. If you do decide to fit one, dry sump engines (those with separate oil tanks) lend themselves more easily to this modification, as any of the external oil lines can be cut and a cooler spliced in with extra hosing.

Mount a cooler up high and in front of the engine; under the headlamp or cut into your fairing. Accessory manufacturers may make kits to fit your bike, but a good-sized oil cooler from a crashed street bike or car will do. On the way down to the desert you'll need to block off the cooler with tape or bypass it altogether – something easier done on home-made jobs – as an over-cooled engine wears quickly and runs inefficiently.

Some bike accessory outlets produce **oil temperature gauges** which screw in to replace the cap/dipstick in the frame of oil-in-the-frame XTs, XRs and the like. These can be as useful if not *better* than an oil cooler in that they actually show you when it might be a good idea to cool off (usually in dunes) before something blows up. Touratech do a replacement sump plug sender for many models which will attach to the wire of a car-type oil cooler gauge. I fitted one to my XRL but never got the gauge to work. Better still is an **IMO Rally computer** – a nifty electronic gadget that can give readings on all sorts of things (mostly to do with speed, time and distance), including oil temperature, at the push of a button (if not calculating an average oil temperature reading for the last month, along with maximums and minimums).

An IMO Rally computer is not just handy for rallies – it's a clock, speedo, odo and even an oil temperature gauge.

Water-cooled engines should not need an oil cooler. If the needle heads for the red, things are getting too hot (this is the Sahara, after all) and you must let them cool down. Water temperature gauges tend to be pessimistic and imprecise, but continued hard riding in deep sand at 40°C will eventually cook the engine. Before a head gasket blows point the bike into the wind with the engine running and allow the radiator to cool the engine. On any bike in the desert consider using thicker engine oil: **20-50 motor oil** is recommended at hotter times of year. With any thick oil, remember to warm up your engine gradually on cold mornings to allow the oil to thin out and do its job. In desert areas it's normal to experience a 30°C temperature variation between dawn and mid-afternoon.

When making a stop on a very hot day, **keep your engine running** for a while or do not turn it off at all, especially with air-cooled machines. When the bike stops moving, the sudden lack of airflow over the motor or through the radiator causes the temperature to rise dramatically. Turning the engine off at this point causes the temperature to rise even further and it's not uncommon to notice a loss of power due to a slight seizure of the motor when moving off again. By keeping the engine running during brief stops on hot days, the oil is kept pumping around, cooling the engine.

Tanks

For very long pistes all bikes will require either a double-sized fuel tank or a bulky **jerrican** of 10 or 20 litres, and in some cases even this will barely be enough. Jerricans are a cheap way of augmenting fuel range and can be dumped or sold when you've finished with them. A good way to get rid of one is to exchange it for fuel at a filling station. These guys can always get rid of jerries so ask for at least what it cost you in fuel.

Luckily for the sort of bikes most people are considering,

With GPS as back-up, an advance fuel dump can extend your range to 1000 km and beyond.

A 24-litre Acerbis tank on an XR650R. The pannier tanklettes, also from Acerbis, are too small and space-wasting to be useful.

A pair of Acerbis pannier tanks of eight litres each on an LC4; works well with soft luggage or on a rally.

Taking the time to mark your big tank with an estimated capacity level is a good idea.

Ten-litre under-jerries on a big GS.

plastic tanks are readily available. Although a major expense, a tank holding up to 40 litres is preferable to using up valuable space with jerricans. A big tank places the heavy weight of fuel in front of and below the rider, close to the machine's centre of gravity. In this position it has a less pronounced effect on the balance of the bike, though you'll certainly feel the difference when you first try and ride off with 40 litres of fuel sloshing about. If the tank goes below the carb and needs a fuel pump, so much the better, the weight is low: on *Desert Riders* we found 40 litres of fuel sloshing around above carb level was hard work. Choose **vacuum fuel pumps** like the Mikuni on KTM Adventures which work off the carb.

Among others, Acerbis makes a range of large plastic tanks to fit many dirt bikes, from 20 litres up to a 45-litre tank for a GS. Although they're expensive, plastic tanks do combine the best in strength and lightness as well as providing resistance to vibration damage. They can be easily repaired with glue and are far superior to home-made **alloy tanks** which few people use these days.

Make sure you mount a big tank well. Some Acerbis tanks come with feeble fitting kits that won't be up to the hammering a full tank gets on corrugated tracks – some of the frame support 'mushrooms' supplied will struggle to cope. Lagging along the top tube helps take the weight, or simply starting from scratch with your own fitting system. Check out the *Desert Riders* web pages to see how I tackled it.

A 40-litre tank is all very well, but as mentioned, on our XRLs they were very high which did no favours for handling or stability (they were originally for XR600s). Some of the guys managed to get a depression professionally pressed in on the underside so the tanks could clear a redundant seat fitting nut and sit

Left: a Tesch in-pannier 11-litre tank; pricey and a bit clanky. Plastic fuel or ex-chemical containers are cheaper, lighter and just as robust. **Right**: A 40-litre tank plus a disposable 20-litre drum gives a 1000km range, still as little as three or four days riding.

an inch or two lower. Every inch helps here, but too low without resorting to a fuel pump means you can't get the full range from the tank's volume as the final couple of litres are below carb level. Next time I would consider a more modest-sized main tank of around 20–25 litres and keep the rest of the fuel low and either alongside the engine or at the back a bit like the BMW opposite but not using heavy steel jerries.

Chains and gearing

Shaft-drive systems are virtually maintenance-free and in this respect they're ideal for desert bikes, but they're usually fitted to heavier machines which as we know bring about their own problems. Chains and sprockets are more vulnerable to wear and lubrication immediately attracts sand which rapidly makes things worse.

Sealed **o-ring chains** have a quantity of grease between the rollers and pins, sealed in with tiny rubber rings between the rollers and side plates. Only when those rubber seals begin to wear out after many thousands of miles will the chain begin to wear out like an ordinary chain. Manufacturers have since come out with somewhat gimmicky 'X-' and 'W-' ring chains (effectively, multiple seals), some of which are guaranteed for 12,000 miles. With these sorts of chains, chain aerosol sprays are not needed nor should they be used in the sands. For *Desert Riders* we were testing various systems: the other two fitted DID 'gold' x-rings while I tried out a similarly-priced RK 'XW' ring, also made in Japan. Result: the DIDs barely needed adjusting while my OK RK needed about three or four adjustments in 5000km.

Good-quality **steel sprockets** are essential to get the best from an o-ring chain: avoid lighter alloy versions. And beware of buying cheaper, pattern 'chain and sprocket kits' from some mail order suppliers who sell obscure brands of chains and inferior steel sprockets. Original equipment (OE) sprockets matched up with a good chain will give you 10,000 miles of trouble-free use.

A cheap o-ring chain ruined this sprocket in just 4000 Saharan kms. You can't go wrong with DID x-rings.

One tooth larger 'road' sprocket gets zip-tied to the frame for the run home.

The good thing with chains as opposed to shafts is that you can easily **alter gearing**; most bikes come too highly geared out of the crate anyway.

For the highway run down to the Sahara you'll want road gearing, but when the going gets gnarly, it's easy to swap the front sprocket with a one-toothed smaller item and so raise the gearing. You'll get better control in stony oueds as well as better response from the lower gears when you most need it.

Chain tension

Your chain should be adjusted to provide **40mm of slack**, measured midway along the chain *with your weight on the bike*. On most trail bikes with long travel suspension, this will give an impression of an overly slack chain when the machine is unloaded and at rest, but this slack will be taken up once the suspension is compressed to the correct level when the bike is on the move. Expect a certain amount of tightening and polishing of the chain towards the end of a hot day; this will slacken off to the correct tension as the chain cools during the course of the night.

WHEELS AND TYRES

Modern trail bikes are built with lightly-spoked alloy wheels to reduce unsprung weight and improve road performance. Some rims are not up to the heavy beating they'll encounter over the potholed tarmac and rocky pistes of the Sahara. Back wheels will at times be carrying greater than maximum permitted loads and are particularly prone to damage.

You can save yourself a lot of bother by fitting **heavy-duty spokes** or, better still, upgrading your wheels with **quality rims** by Akront, Excel or DID. The advantage can be the difference between having to check and possibly

Check your spokes regularly, in the early days and especially after very rocky terrain or potholed roads. Twang each spoke for a good, even tone. Dud ones will sound flat. Using a good-quality spoke key, turn each nipple in small increments until it sounds right.

tension your standard wheels every few days, and being able to confidently ignore the strengthened items for the entire trip. As with sealed chains, and knobbly tyres, this is one modification worth making if you have some tough desert riding lined up.

On *Desert Riders* all our spokes got loose, and a few of my HD spokes broke – easy enough to replace without taking the tyre off. They definitely needed more maintenance than previous wheels I've run on my XTs.

It is possible that the combination of our heavy racks on the, at times, tough terrain took their toll on the wheels as never before.

Tyres

Tyre choice is always a problem: how to achieve grip in all conditions with long tyre life. In the desert you can save yourself the angst by simply going for good-quality knobbly tyres. They work fine on dry tarmac and grip brilliantly in the dirt, transforming your overloaded barge into something that can inspire confidence.

Run down to the start of the piste on old road tyres which you can choose to bury for the ride back. But when the tarmac ends, you won't regret knobblies.

On the road they do wear fast and are dangerous on wet tarmac. If you're heading down the Atlantic Route to West Africa now, though it will probably be all tarmac by the time you read this, you could get away with a trail, or even a long-wearing road, tyre. If you have any off-roading planned a better compromise is to ride down to the tarmac's end on any old tyres, dump them and then fit hard-wearing knobblies for the piste. Whichever tyre you choose, make sure it has at least four plies; anything less is designed for light unsprung weight and will not be resistant to punctures.

Michelin Deserts and Pirelli's MT21s

Among Saharan riders two tyre types have earned a reputation for reliability, grip and long wear; Michelin Deserts and Pirelli's MT21s. Designed for the Dakar Rally, Deserts are the real thing, not some trendy marketing gimmick. Riding on **Michelin Deserts** with heavy-duty inner tubes (Desert tubes are available) and strong wheels is one of the best modifications you can make to your bike if you intend covering a high mileage off-road while heavily loaded.

Their notorious stiffness is a bit of a myth; it depends a lot on your bike's rim. They can be fitted easily provided you use good tyre levers, lubricant and the right technique. This will probably be the last time you will have to use your levers until the tyres wear out thousands of kilometres later; punctures with Michelin Desert tyres are rare. To allow the flattening necessary for optimum traction Deserts can (and sometimes have to) be run virtually empty of air. For the tyre's sake, speeds should be kept down, but Deserts are built for this sort of abuse. We used Michelin T63s on the rear for Desert

Pirelli MT21 rear tyre fitted to the front of an F650: great on the piste but hairy in the wet.

Michelin Desert tyres can be a tight squeeze but they're worth it, especially on bigger machines.

Riders and had a few punctures. On the front we used Deserts. In retrospect, our XRLs were probably heavier than we were used to and a Desert on the back may have worked better.

Pirelli's MT21s are road-legal tyres which manage to achieve an excellent compromise between off-road grip and acceptable road manners, the accent being on the dirt. A combination of a rounded profile, low knobs and hard rubber make it an ideal alternative to a Desert for front or rear wheel. MT21s are emulated by Michelin's T63 (which has the Desert pattern), Metzeler's Karoo, Bridgestone's ED660/1 and probably a few more by the time you read this.

Depending on the type of tyre and weight carried, **1 bar or 14 psi** is the optimum all-round **pressure** off-road, 0.7 bar for soft sand, and 1.5 or more on rocks or fast, hard piste.

Tyre creep

Besides causing a tyre to overheat, riding at the very low pressures necessary for traction in deep sand can, especially with very torquey engines, also cause the tyre to slip around the rim. As a result of braking and acceleration forces

The leaning valve indicates tyre creep; eventually the valve may get torn out.

One way of eliminating tyre slippage is by fitting self-tapping screws into the rim just deep enough to bite on the tyre.

the inner tube can be pulled around with the tyre, eventually ripping the valve from the tube. Therefore, for low-pressure use it's essential to have **security bolts** (also known as rim locks) fitted to both rims to limit excessive tyre creep. These devices clamp the bead of the tyre to the rim and, if not already fitted, require a hole to be drilled in the rim for the clamp. KTM make an especially good light rim lock which will fit any bike.

Keep an eye on your valves. If they begin to tilt over it means that your security bolt may need tightening. Always keep the nut (usually 12mm) at the base of your valve loose, or do not use it at all. These nuts (some tubes have knurled rings which can only be finger tightened) are only useful as an aid to refitting tyres.

Self-tapping screws are an alternative to security bolts, which can unbalance a wheel and get in the way when changing tyres. They can be screwed through the rim so that they just bite onto the tyre bead. Two set at 180° intervals each side of the rim should keep the tyre in place.

Punctures

Punctures are the most common breakdown you'll experience on your trip. Before you leave you must know how to fix them yourself; unlike in a car you can't carry a spare. Practise at home so that when the inevitable occurs you can be sure the operation will be done smoothly.

Among your **spares** you should include some washing-up liquid (or liquid soap), talcum powder to sprinkle over a still-gluey repair, plenty of patches and rubber solution and, depending on your tyres' sturdiness, at least one spare inner tube per wheel.

Many touring riders rate puncture-sealing fluids like UltraSeal which do an amazing job of plugging thorn pricks, but the best way to repair a puncture is to fit a new tube without pinching it, though with some tyre and rim combina-

Three ways of changing tyres. From the **left**: letting the bike sit on the swingarm or boxes – not so stable and sandy on the chain; **middle**: sitting on an alloy box – turn the box upside down so you don't damage the lid; **right**: laying the bike on its side, stable but can be hard on the rack. Another way is leaning the bike over on its sidestand until a wheel is in the air and jacking a box or stick under the bash-plate or opposite footrest; not so stable.

tions this is easier said than done. Puncture-sealing fluids are fine but avoid labour-saving aerosols which are messy, unreliable and usually explode in your panniers before you use them. Also include a good pair of tyre levers, a **pump**, a couple of spare connectors for the pump and an air-pressure gauge. Compressed CO_2 cartridges save pumping but eventually you're going to run out; save them for an emergency. Inexpensive electric **mini-compressors** available from car accessory shops can save a lot of sweat, but you must carry a hand pump as a back-up. We were given mini compressors and, sure enough, they proved to be

as cheap as they looked and packed up in the heat and dust. No one's really made a reliable mini-compressor for bikes yet and even hand pumps can fail. Having two forms of tyre inflation (or certainly a pump for each rider) is not a bad idea as without it you are stuffed.

Changing tyres is not everyone's favourite job. The best thing that can be said is do it slowly and carefully, although keeping your cool in 30°C halfway along a remote piste when you're not sure what's

Take your time, be systematic and work on a tent to keep sand out of the wheel bearings. Strip off some riding gear but wear headwear and finish off with a drink. An alloy box makes a handy bike stand.

ahead can be asking a lot. Don't be too proud to let someone else in your party who is better at tyre levering do the job. There is nothing as galling as realising you've pinched your last tube, but last time I managed a new one: somehow leaving a short tyre lever in the tyre! The instructions on the car pages about ensuring there is enough slack in the well to mount the tyre (p.202) apply here too. You should not have to strain too much so make sure the tyre is in the well by kicking it in there. There is a full, step-by-step photo sequence on puncture repairs in the *Adventure Motorcycling Handbook*.

CARRYING THE LOAD

How to carry the gear necessary for basic survival in the Sahara is your biggest challenge. You can't escape the need for fuel and water because as you'll read in the survival section, *fuel is distance and water is time*. Nor can you get away without a robust luggage system that will take the hammering – but the enemy is always **weight**. To do it right takes a high level of commitment or the experience of a few trips. Everyone returns to the Sahara with less stuff.

It boils down to a choice between soft fabric panniers or hard metal containers mounted on some kind of rack. Overloading is a common mistake: remember your nimble trail bike will handle like a lilo full of porridge once it's fully loaded and in the sands.

Whatever you decide, it's important to distribute heavy weights **as low and as centrally as possible**. Doing this will greatly enhance the balance and control of your machine in the sand – it will feel lighter even if it isn't. Light things like clothes, sleeping bags or empty containers can go on the back of the seat or in front of the headlamp. If you're carrying extra fuel in jerricans, unless they are mounted really low (as in the photo on the left), top up the tank regularly to keep the weight in an ideal position midway between the axles.

Newsflash: this bike is ridiculously over-loaded...

... the result is a very slow and unstable machine, even on an easy piste.

Hard or soft luggage

Whatever space you have will always be filled to brimming. Keep it small and you'll take little, use big containers and you'll fill them with less-than-necessary stuff and overload your bike. For a short trip (less than three weeks) soft luggage will be adequate. On a longer transcontinental trip, hard luggage might be better but it adds weight and is time-consuming and expensive to fit. Overall for the Sahara, where security is not an issue, **soft luggage is best**.

Soft luggage

Soft luggage usually means **throwover panniers** slung over the seat with a rucksack or kit bag across the back. This system has drawbacks but is light, cheap and versatile. Throwovers can stretch, burn, melt, fall off, tear, disintegrate or simply get stolen. Some of these drawbacks can be overcome with careful thought and design in how they're mounted. One problem particular to trail bikes is their high silencers. Even with heat shields it's still possible for panniers to get pressed on to the pipe at high speed or when bouncing over rough ground: nylon tends to melt, canvas burns. The best solution is to hook the front edge of your panniers on to the frame to stop them sliding back and to fabricate a **proper guard** around the silencer to prevent contact.

A **light frame** as opposed to a full-on rack is not a bad idea with soft luggage if it helps the stuff to stay on and not burn up.

As light as it gets: two Ortleib throwovers and a backpack, yet the bike still carried over 40 litres of fuel.

Hard luggage

At first thought hard luggage might sound like a good idea, being secure, and strong, but a good system is heavy. Forget any non-metallic panniers designed for smooth road-riding, they won't last.

After years of popularity with continental riders, **aluminium boxes** have finally caught on among the Brits who'll be able to stop making their own out of of Land Rover panels. But for true off-road riding, alloy boxes have many drawbacks. They need a heavy rack to secure them and they stick out which gets in the way of your shins when paddling. This in turn can lead to paranoia when crossing sandy oueds where you get nervous of needing a dab for fear of a bite from the pannier's edge. While on rocky or tight mountain tracks such as the western descent from Assekrem (A6) wide boxes limit where you can ride as they bash into the sides. On our XRLs with the silencer on one side and the battery on the other, the boxes sat especially wide. (We all agreed that for the sort of riding we were doing, next time we'd take slimmer boxes or soft baggage.)

One good thing about Touratech's, and probably some other makes, is their ability to come off quickly. A quickly detachable box has many uses as a bike stand, seat and table, laundry bucket, or

This hefty Tesch pannier caught a rock on the side of the track and sent the rider flying. The table feet built into the lid didn't really work. Lighter Touratech panniers have mounts designed to break off, though this doesn't always happen.

... but one good thing about wide hard luggage is it makes a bike easier to pick up.

A home-made rack from footrest to indicator supporting the bike's sub-frame. If carrying metal boxes, a ledge along the bottom (as on the rack below) takes the strain off the mounts.

Overland Solutions rack for an Africa Twin to carry Touratech Zega cases. The way the boxes sit in the trays means actual mounts can be quick-release but don't need to be heavy duty – having both is tricky.

It doesn't all have to go inside. Strapped to the lids is a tent and an empty fuel can (makes a handy stool too). Kit bag goes across the back. Note the many grab handles; helps pick the bike up.

just something that can be whipped off to make maintenance easier. The crux is that the q/d fitting must be genuinely q/d while being strong enough to keep the box on in all conditions.

As for accessibility, Touratech offer neat, box-shaped **holdalls** which slip straight inside their 35- and 41-litre Zega boxes. It's an idea worth imitating with your own alloy cases. A kit bag of light stuff works well behind the seat as it doesn't need heavy rack support and won't hurt when the bike rebounds and whacks you.

Racks

If you're restrained enough to travel light, you can get away with using soft luggage without a rack like the LC4 on the previous page. But even with, say, a ten-litre jerrican on the back seat, the rear subframe on some bikes can flex, possibly inducing a weave on loose surfaces, especially if you're running road or trail tyres. And on rough ground subframes can sag or crack.

In the end the relative flimsiness of modern-day single-shock subframes (especially some XRs and other bikes not designed for passengers or payload) convinces most desert bikers that even a basic baggage frame or rack is a good idea and is easy enough to make yourself. Bernd Tesch makes off-the-shelf overlanding racks, but they're heavily built. Advice on building your own racks is covered in the *Adventure Motorcycling Handbook* but in the UK Overland Solutions have acquired a great reputation for making strong custom racks for any bike, as well as a whole lot more besides.

Tank bags and day packs

Valuable or frequently-used personal items that don't fit in your jacket are best kept in a **tank bag** or on your body. Avoid those multi-storey road touring tank bags, they'll be continuously sliding off on the piste. Keep a tank bag small and handy like the BM on p.215, or do without.

If you need more baggage space, a waist bag or day pack is ideal and very convenient. **Day packs** aren't quite as handy to use, but whatever's in there, you can be sure you won't lose it. One tip: use a day pack which is a bag with a drawstring opening and be careful with the more common ones which open full out with a two-way zip; unless the zip heads are joined together or zipped down one side they can work themselves open on rough pistes and everything drops out, something that's less likely to happen with a drawstring on a bag.

Don't put vital things like **money and documents** in external packs and bags: they're easily snatched by opportunist robbers or pilfered by pickpockets. Instead, keep items that you can't afford to lose zipped inside your jacket pocket.

Water containers

The best way to carry water while riding is in a **hydrator** in your backpack; basically a water bag with a hose that clips to your shoulder straps. This way the water is secure and it's easy to drink while riding – small regular sips are better than big glugs when you stop. Camelbak set the ball rolling years ago but seems expensive for a bag with a hose. Platypus are another brand but I've found their less soft bladders can acquire pinprick leaks. With either you don't have to buy the full pack, but can just buy a bladder and hose which fits on your own pack, cutting or melting a hose hole on the top of the bag to avoid having the zips together up top (see above).

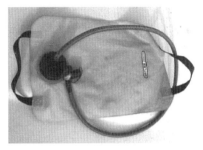

An Ortlieb converted into a hydrator with a bit of pipe and a clip. But you'll need the clever 'bite spout' to avoid dribbling. You can buy it from an outdoor shop.

Your main water container should ideally be around 10 litres, double that for remote desert sections. Ortlieb make nylon water bags in various sizes which can also make bulk water holders that will cram in and can be adapted as a hydrator. The good thing about **water bags** is that they get smaller as they empty. Rigid containers are nearly as light but they take up space and can be awkward to lash down.

A couple of 10-litre Ortlieb bags make handy containers, save space and double up as a pillow. But I find the caps rather stiff and awkward to use and some leak.

Testing your system

Once you've finally set on a baggage system, even if it's just two paper bags and an elastic band, it's essential to take the fully-loaded bike – including full tanks and cans – for a test ride. See how it rides and if custom-made components make contact with the swingarm or tyre on full suspension travel.

Riding your bike in this state for the first time will be quite alarming and as you wobble along the street you'll wonder how on earth you're going to make it across the Mauritanian Empty Quarter. This may be your last chance

It may be the Sahara, but it will be colder than you think, especially on the highway approaches to the piste. Dress accordingly.

to seriously re-assess your personal requirements and consider cutting down on weight. While the bike's loaded up, lay it on its side; if you can't pick it up again it's just too heavy and unless you're certain there'll always be someone around to help you, you must reduce or re-arrange the load.

Protection and comfort

Motorcycling in the Sahara involves covering long distances off-road. Either can be tiring and together they can be exhausting. Bikers are used to roughing it and making do, but don't spare your own comfort.

However small, a **windshield** or small fairing is a good idea and need not hamper off-road riding; once you're standing up you can see over it. Handlebar fairings (see p.212) are adequate and don't weigh too much. At the right height and adjustment they'll help reduce neck strain and make boring highway cruising more tolerable. You can make your own version to extend from a plastic headlight cowling. A frame-mounted fairing as on late Ténérés, Transalps and F650s will obviously provide better protection but be prone to damage. It's really the screen that is most useful on the way to, and in, the desert.

Trail-bike **seats** are notoriously slim and sometimes too soft. The KTM

A neat bashplate and water tank on an LC4. Every desert bike must have a metal bashplate of 3-5mm alloy – and extending it as above to hold water or tools makes sense. It protects the whole engine, foot controls as well as your feet. You'll be surprised by the dents they'll collect.

Adventure's plank is a legendary butt killer. Slim saddles are only useful when you have to stand on the footrests over rough terrain. Consider replacing the foam with something firmer or replacing the saddle altogether with a broader home-made item. Then again, I fitted a wider front saddle from a GSX750 on my XRL, hoping for greater comfort. Swapping with one of the other bikes which merely had shortened its original Honda saddle showed there was no noticeable difference – they were as bad as each other! It's hard to know what works; wider must be better and well-known Corbin saddles, though wide, feel oddly firm but many riders swear by them. Again, a fully-loaded test ride will show up any discomforts that may not have been evident during the planning stage. It's usual to be utterly exhausted after a hard day on the piste, especially if there's been lots of rocks. It's at this time, late in the day, that many biking accidents happen. A lightly-loaded and comfortable bike gives you the ability to endure the extra distance that could make the difference. A large comfortable seat, elementary wind protection, an effective silencer and a little room to move around will all help.

Two-wheel camping

Camping in the Sahara can be pretty basic on a bike, not least because you never really have any substantial shelter and there's only enough room to carry bare essentials. But it's surprising how satisfying this can be, partly because on some days anything is preferable to riding another metre and also because it demonstrates how little you need to get by, even in a desert. At the end of the day you can ride off behind that dune or up a valley and pretty much feel like you have the whole desert to yourself.

As mentioned in the car chapter, **sleeping**, **cooking**, **eating** and **drinking** are the basic elements of camping (washing is something you do on a bike when you have water to spare). The greater the comfort and efficiency of these elements, the better will be the quality of your Saharan experience: on a bike it needs to be. As with all biking gear, it depends how committed you are to saving space and weight. A tasty meal followed by a good night's sleep is important to allow your body to recover after an exhausting day's riding. There are no easy solutions with desert biking which is why it generally suits the young and hardy.

Tents, sleeping mats and sleeping bags
For most of my early biking trips I never carried a tent or even a mat, choosing to simply lie in a sleeping bag on my clothes. Doing it this way I can't say I ever had a great night's sleep, especially if I ended up in a rocky area. In the Sahara the wind generally stops at sunset and the popular myth about the desert being 'scorching in the day and freezing at night' just isn't true in my experience, though the typical daily temperature range of 25 degrees centigrade may give this impression.

Disturbances by creepy crawlies are also much exaggerated in the cooler months. The worst you'll get is gerbils

An inner tent can provide adequate shelter without too much weight.

burrowing around for your food scraps. However, lately I've gone soft and have taken to bringing an inner tent whose chief benefit is a psychologically comforting shelter. Crawling in and flopping out after a hard day's riding can be a real tonic. You don't have to use it every night. On a calm windless night, simply lying it on can be just as good.

There's no need to get an expensive ultralight design capable of withstanding a Himalayan blizzard. For the Sahara a simple two-pole crossover design will stand up without pegs and cost from £30/€50. With these sorts of tents around I'm amazed to see people still fiddling with tent pegs and guy ropes. Don't bother with the fly sheet either, the unproofed inner tent will be good enough to keep the cold off and allow condensation to pass through which is more comfortable. It's also an effective mosquito net, handy if you're heading for the Sahel and beyond, and makes a good ground sheet for tyre changes (see p.225) or impromptu picnics.

Lash out on a quality three-season bag – you won't regret it.

Sleeping mats and bags

Foam sleeping mats are bulky for the comfort they offer. Though expensive for a piece of open-cell foam in a bag with a plug, the **self-inflating Therma-Rest** type sleeping mats work amazingly well. I've managed for a few years with a three-quarter-length Ultralight. It has not got a puncture yet, nor have I had a problem with sand getting in the valve, though using it in or on a tent may help. It rolls up to the size of a pair of toilet rolls; that much space I don't mind using up for the comfort it gives. See also my tip on digging a sleeping trench on page 151.

As for **sleeping bags**, compactness and warmth within your budget is what it's about. Get the best you can afford which means spending over £100/€150. Seasonal ratings are notoriously optimistic and vary from one brand to another so always choose a three-season or higher. If you can afford it, science still hasn't found a way to improve on the lofting qualities of **down**, at its best plucked from virgin white geese (not to be confused with inferior *feathers* which are sometimes mixed with down at a clearly specified ratio). Not only does down fluff out to fill a large volume (the key to insulation), it compresses better than any man-made fabric and will do so for many years. Warmth for warmth, a down bag will be more compact than a synthetic one and feels much nicer too. Down can get ruined in water, or at least takes a long time to dry, but as you're going to the desert the quick-drying qualities of synthetic sleeping bags are hopefully not needed.

One drawback that I've always found with sleeping bags is that, sleeping in a tube, you are unable to move your knees up which means you may end up with a stiff back in the morning. A few years ago I invested in an egg-shaped Yeti bag which gave more leg movement while still maintaining the insulation and compactness of the cocoon.

Air your bag out every morning by turning it inside out and letting it hang in the breeze on your tent or bike. Especially with down you want to minimise the number of washing cycles as much as possible as it reduces loft in the long run. Synthetics don't have this problem.

Lighting
On long winter nights you'll need some lighting in the evening, and a good spread of light around your camp makes life much easier. The bike's parking light is too weak and the main beam risks flattening the battery. A **head torch** is the most compact – on *Desert Riders* we used incredibly compact Petzl Zipkas which may not have burned holes in the night but used an energy-saving LED filament. A good head torch and the night sky is all you need.

Cooking, eating and drinking

Relying on wood for cooking is too much of a gamble in the Sahara. With a car you can pick up firewood where you find it, but on a bike this is not possible. A small **petrol (gasoline) stove** is the answer; you have a tank full of the stuff so if you run out, not being able to cook up a brew is the least of your problems. If anything it will be the other way round. Running out 14km short of Timimoun one night, I poured the 50cc from my Optimus stove into the tank to get me another few hundred metres down the road.

Fuel is handy but food will become a real highlight to your day, so pick your favourites. All the stuff above had been buried three months earlier and was a real treat to dig up!

The problem with petrol stoves is that modern ones are designed to run on '**white fuel**', a cleaner petrol than that which comes out of Saharan fuel pumps. Lead-free is better but is only found in the northern cities, not in the desert. Prolonged use of local two-star (*normale*) may eventually clog the generator (feed pipe) or jets with soot. I would guess this process takes a couple of months of daily use, so either take a **spare generator** (if applicable to the model you use) or take a gamble and hope the stove won't block before you head back. Taking a litre of white fuel defeats the object of saving space and weight. Better to fill your bike's tank with unleaded when you can and top your stove up at the same time before you get deep into the desert where ordinary leaded fuel is all you'll find.

Using local leaded fuel your stove may spurt and smoke a bit before it fully heats up but once hot, petrol stoves put out much more heat than gas and are more resistant to wind. The wind shields which come with most stoves are pretty ineffective, so work out a proper wind break with your baggage to increase efficiency and save fuel.

Anything that claims to run on **multi-** or **dual-fuel** is either a play on words (ie: it runs on leaded *and* unleaded – big deal), a compromise in the jet size, or requires a fiddly changing of jets. In the desert you need a simple petrol (gasoline) stove, not something that claims to run on diesel, kerosene, white fuel and Orangina.

The Coleman 533 I've used for years (renamed a 'Sportster' in some markets) claims to run on white fuel and unleaded, but I've always run it on African fuel with an occasional burn-through on unleaded when I get home.

EQUIPMENT CHECK LIST

This is an essentials-only version of the list that appears in the *Adventure Motorcycling Handbook*. In the Sahara your attitude to weight and space is critical. Every rider who returns to the Sahara takes less baggage.

Travel documents
Passport
Vehicle ownership document
Cash, credit cards and travellers' cheques
Travel tickets
Green Card and/or Third Party Insurance
Passport photos

Camping
Sleeping mat
Sleeping bag with stuff sack
Inner tent

Cooking
Petrol stove
A few lighters
Pan scrubber and tea towel
Spoon and fork
Cooking pot
Swiss Army penknife with tin opener
Washing-up liquid
Mug
Water bag(s)

Toiletries and First Aid
Liquid soap and flannel
Washing detergent
Small towel or sarong
Toothbrush and paste
Toilet paper
Universal sink plug
Anti-diarrhoea medication
Rehydration powder or drink (see p.164)
Aspirin and plasters

Clothing
Riding boots
Socks
Underwear
T-shirts or shirt

Fleece jacket
Riding jacket
Gloves
Leather trousers or MX pants
Hat
Crash helmet and goggles
Spare dark lenses or sunglasses

Navigation and emergencies
Maps
Compass
GPS receiver
Mini binoculars

Bike spares and tools
Spare keys
Front and rear inner tubes
Puncture-repair kit
Bike pump and back-up compressor
Tyre levers
Tyre pressure gauge
Control levers
Spare air filter
Wire and duct tape
Spare nuts and bolts for rack fittings
Instant gasket, epoxy glue, radiator sealant
Jubilee clips, electrical wire and connectors
Spark plug(s)
Petrol pipe
Spare bungees and straps
Sockets, Allen keys and spanners
Mole grips
Cross- and flat-bladed screwdrivers
Pliers with wire cutters
Spoke key
Mini hacksaw with spare blades
Top-up oil and rag

Miscellaneous
Headtorch plus spare batteries
Camera and film
Pens and notebook
Books (guide/phrase/reading)
Calculator
String or rope

I'm still on the original generator and I've heard that if it blocks up you can take out the wire inside, try and clean it or eliminate it to get a rougher flame. To start it you simply pump it up, turn on the fuel and light it. This sort of uncomplicated design is the key for all sorts of overlanding equipment. Which brings us to what I call 'red bottle' stoves made by various manufacturers, with the fuel bottle attached by a hose or pipe to a compact burner. The idea I presume is that it's more compact to pack but takes a bit of assembly. I've tried an Optimus Nova which squirted fuel from the jammed clip-on connection, and have watched new MSRs spluttering and permanently blocking after a couple of hours' use, despite cleaning and replacing parts. Others have reported reliable results from red-bottle jobs but they cost twice as much as a 533. They require fiddly assembly which can lead to leaks or let in sand, as well as regular cleaning maintenance, the last thing you want to do when you're hungry. Other drawbacks many mention are the noise of some 'red bottle' stoves and the poor heat control; either all or nothing.

Also worth considering is **stability**, both on the ground and for holding pots; there's nothing more frustrating than watching your half-cooked dinner tip into the sand. In my experience Coleman models are ideal in this respect: the squat, compact shape of the one-piece unit sits securely on the ground, and the wide burner gives off plenty of heat and support for a pot. 'Red bottles' have very cleverly designed fold-up burners but lack a large base for anything but a small pot.

Getting into camping takes some adjustment and clumsy accidents are common when you're tired or still getting used to the whole business. A reliable, uncomplicated and stable stove goes a long way to minimising this.

This Coleman 533 'Dual Fuel' stove has worked fine for years on Saharan fuel and puts out plenty of heat. Note the 300cc flask. Filled up along with the morning brew, it enables a hot drink at lunchtime without the need to get the stove out.

One-pan cooking

It may sound extreme but a half-litre **mug** and a one-litre **pan** with a lid will do. A plate is unnecessary and a spoon and a penknife are all the cutlery you'll ever use. You can cook your rice/pasta, put it in the mug with a lid on top to keep it warm, and then, if you're not simply throwing something in with the pasta cook whatever else you have and chuck the pasta back in – just leaving one pan and one cup to wash. Avoid pouring hot water away, use it for soup or washing up. Don't get drawn in by trick titanium cookware from camping shops. A sturdier stainless steel saucepan (from Woolies) with a spot-welded, rather than riveted, handle will take rough use and sand cleaning without getting grubby or bent.

Take the chance to eat in **roadhouses** and cafés when you can to stave off the inevitable boredom with your own food supplies as well as making them last. For more ideas on food see p.159.

One pan, a mug, a stove and a spoon is all you need.

Stopping for water from the Tanarine village well in the Oued Samene.

Clean water

People tend to be very squeamish about drinking water from desert wells and rock pools but in my experience a **water filter** or tablets are not necessary in the sterile and barely populated Saharan environment. Only once you get to warmer tropical countries is there a risk from polluted well water or food due to the higher temperatures and denser populations with poor sanitation. In this case **sterilising tablets** like Katadyn's Micropur are best, leaving no unpleasant taste as chlorine- and iodine-based tablets do.

Remember tablets sterilise but they don't remove impurities. This may be just harmless silt but to get rid of it you need a filter. Even without a filter a packet of tablets will be useful. You never know when you might need them and if ever in doubt, use them.

Riding in the desert

The moment you first set wheels on the piste is usually a shocking one. Suddenly everything is brought sharply into focus. You're heading out into the desert on a machine that steers like it has two flat tyres. At the first patch of soft sand you slither about and maybe even fall off. With a dry mouth you stop and ask yourself, is this wise?

Old colonial sign at the south end of the Fadnoun plateau in Algeria. This once-great piste between Illizi and Djanet is now sealed but is still a fantastic ride.

The good thing is that, just as you got the hang of riding your heavy rig on the highway, so you'll get used to riding in the sands. In the desert it's not so much the actual riding as the relentless **concentration** demanded by riding *and* navigating that will wear you out. Although you'll often be riding through spectacular scenery, the only chance you'll get to appreciate this splendour is by stopping, either by choice or accident. On some tracks you can find yourself staring so intently at the ground ahead that when you stop you experience the mild hallucination of the ground moving away from you.

Accidents happen in the early days when you're still getting the feel for your machine. They also happen later when you become over-confident. After that, you'll have acquired the right balance of caution and confidence. Fifty miles an hour or 80kph is the safe maximum speed on any dirt surface. Faster than that it's not possible to react quickly enough to the ever-changing terrain.

Riding in the Sahara is never predictable. Never take risks, resist the impulse to show off and always ride within the limitations of:

- your vision.
- the terrain.
- your experience.
- your bike's handling abilities.

At the same time you must be fully aware of the consequences of:

- having an accident.
- getting lost.
- running out of fuel or water.

It's not uncommon for bikers to lose their head a bit in the desert and belt off across the sands at full speed. On my desert tours (where the bikes are not loaded of course) I'm amazed there are not more broken necks: this is one reason why I rarely organise them now. Riding this way is very exhilarating until you come across a rock, a soft patch or a shallow depression, indistinguishable in the midday glare. At this point the front wheel gets deflected or digs in and you fly over the bars, closely followed by your cartwheeling machine. In this type of accident it's the bike that usually causes the injury to the rider: on most desert trips I've seen, come across, or heard about, riders who have come to grief in this way.

On the pistes

Most pistes in the Sahara are easy to navigate but sometimes challenging to ride. Many tracks will be rutted, occasionally obscured by sand, dotted with rocks and, as likely as not, corrugated.

Corrugations are a miserable fact of dirt-roading and are best ridden with knobbly tyres at slightly reduced pressures, a well-supported sub-frame, a comfy seat and a firmly-wrapped kidney

The 400-km Graveyard Piste (A2) south of Hadjadj well; one of the best biking routes in the Sahara.

belt. A bike's narrow track means that it's possible to find a tyre's-width section of piste which gives a smoother ride, or even to cut-off along the side of the track.

Even on a smooth track you must always be vigilant for loose rubble that could take out your front wheel. Always have the brakes and clutch covered, ready to slow down or change gear at the sight of an obstacle. No matter how good your suspension, always aim to avoid bumps and therefore the chance of losing control.

Soft dunes near Tichit in Mauritania – if you don't ride light you'll sink and could get swallowed up. © Karim Hussain

Ride light
First-timers on the dirt tend to tense up, gripping the bars with stiff arms as the bike does its own thing and they absorb all the bumps like a plank. Try to relax your body which, when rigid, actually has a detrimental effect on handling. On rough terrain resist clenching the bars; instead hold them loosely, guiding the front end while allowing the bars to bounce around loosely in your palms.

By being relaxed and responding fluidly to the knocks you'll preserve yourself and your bike from sudden and ultimately tiring shocks. Riding light includes **weighting the footrests** (see below) over any cross ridges or V-shaped dips and using your body rather than the handlebars to steer. During the course of a long day on the dirt you'll find this kind of responsive riding saves both physical and mental energy. Alert, smooth riding is the key and is satisfying to master. It will certainly take a few days of piste riding.

Standing on the footrests
Standing up on the footrests over rough ground is the most important technique off-road beginners should adopt because when you're standing up:
● suspension shocks are absorbed through your slightly-bent legs and not directly through your back
● your bike is much easier to control
● being higher up, your forward vision is improved

Contrary to the impression that standing up raises your centre of gravity and makes you less stable, it actually has the opposite effect. Standing up transfers your weight low, through the footrests,

Standing on the footrests greatly improves machine control as well as visibility.

rather than through the saddle. This is why trials riders and motocrossers always tackle tricky sections standing up on the footrests.

When standing up, grip the tank lightly between your knees to give your body added support and to prevent the bike from bouncing around between your legs. Padding on the inside of your knees or on the tank helps here.

It's not always necessary to stand right up; sometimes just leaning forward, pulling on the bars and taking the weight from your backside onto the footrests for a moment will be enough to lessen a jolt. As you get the hang of riding on the dirt, standing, just like sticking your leg out on a slithery bend, will soon become instinctive., as will briefly unloading the saddle to lessen an impact. In a nutshell: **stand when you must – sit when you can**. The key is to preserve energy with smooth, efficient riding.

Riding in sand

Even when flat and firm, Saharan sand requires a high degree of concentration and riding is at its most demanding when you're forced along a track that's been rutted by car wheels. Riding *along* rather than just *across* a sandy oued presents the most difficult condition that a desert biker regularly encounters. Here you can find yourself having to stand up for kilometres at a time when confined to long stretches of one- or two-foot-wide ruts.

Sand-riding can be hair-raising and you'll often come close to falling off, but the techniques described below are the only way to get through short of paddling along at 2kph. The keys to riding in soft sand are:

Knobbly tyres The control gained by using proper off-road tyres has already been underlined and in the sand you'll appreciate it more than ever. Quite simply the extra grip and directional stability they give makes sand-riding less dangerous and more fun. Unlike on a 4WD where tread is immaterial to cornering, a motorbike needs knobs to lean over securely on the dirt. Trail tyres are a compromise for the road and just aren't the same. Knobbly tyres will transform a bike in the desert.

Low tyre pressures Dropping air pressure to as little as 0.3 bar (5 psi) lengthens the contact patch with the sand, dramatically increasing traction and reducing wheelspin; it works even with a trail or road tyre. It can mean the dif-

ference between riding confidently across a sandy section or slithering around barely in control, footing constantly, loosing momentum and finally getting stuck or falling over.

The trouble is, in this under-inflated state, a tyre gets much hotter, due to the internal friction created by the flexing carcass. Being soft and hot the tyre gets more puncture prone. Keep your speed down on very soft tyres and be sure your security bolts are done up tight as it's in just these low-pressure/high-traction situations that tyre creep occurs.

Ultra-stiff Michelin Deserts originally designed for heavy Dakar racers have to be run at extremely low pressures to spread well in soft sand.

Momentum and acceleration These are often the only things that will get you through a particularly soft stretch of sand, so don't be afraid to stand up and accelerate hard at the right time. A quick snap of the throttle in a middle gear gives you the drive and stability to blast assuredly across a short, sandy oued. No matter how much your bike weaves and bucks around, keep the power on and your backside off the seat for as long as it takes. So long as the front wheel remains on course (or even if it doesn't) you're moving and also most in control. Keep off the brakes, especially the front. If you need to slow down use the engine to decelerate and be ready for the bike to become unstable at this time. Riding like this is very tiring, but in most cases even trying to slow down and stop will mean falling over or getting stuck.

Sometimes it can be better to just push it through.

Confidence This is not something you can learn but it is something you can try and nurture. We talked about it a lot on *Desert Riders* as we recognised that if you came to a horrible twin sandy rut oued crossing and showed the slightest bit of doubt, you'd blow it. This often happens when you're tired and think, 'oh no, not another one'. The prospect of yet another semi-out-of-control launch into a oued can be galling. You need to gas it, but going fast feels dangerous, especially when you're worried that a quick dab will have the metal case snapping at your shins.

I remember along the Graveyard Piste there is a very fine-sand oued crossing near the Illizi end that always kicks up heaps of dust. I'd filmed there in the car a couple of months earlier, knew it was ahead but secretly hoped we'd somehow bypassed it. When we came to it the other two guys took it like any other oued and scraped through while I flapped about and fell down two or three times. You need to be firm with these oueds and remind yourself you've done it before and can do it again.

Another time a couple of us cocked up the Oued Imirhou crossing on Route A4 – I shot off at a tangent up the oued trying to keep moving but got buried. It took a quarter of an hour with two of us pushing to get the bike to the other bank. Sometimes it can be better to just push it through.

Braking and turning

Brake and turn gently in soft sand. When very soft it's best to avoid braking altogether and simply roll to a halt, otherwise the trench dug by your brakes might keep you there when you try to pull away. If this happens, hop off and run alongside in first gear until the bike's moving freely without wheelspin and jump back on – easier said than done with some luggage systems, and an invitation to perform a face-plant.

As anyone who's ridden on a beach knows, **turning** hard on smooth sand creates its own berm, or lip of raised sand, enabling radical foot-out cornering. On a desert plain, wide gradual turns under firm acceleration are best made using your body weight rather than turning the handlebars and leaning. No matter how far the tread goes round your tyres, the best traction and therefore the greatest stability is achieved with your bike upright. Even though it's fun, avoid sliding around; there'll be plenty of occasions when you get crossed-up involuntarily.

Sandy ruts

If you can avoid having to ride through a sandy rut, do so. If they are unavoidable because of vegetation or rocks either side, about 40kph in third gear is the best combination to maintain stability when riding along sandy ruts; the low gear and high revs give quick throttle response to further difficulties you may encounter. Slow down through the gears not the brakes, and don't be reluctant to rev your engine hard if necessary.

Even just pulling away on this sort of churned-up soft sand can get you stuck. There is the redline technique, the paddling technique or running alongside, pushing and hopping on technique. It varies with riders and bikes.

If you find yourself riding in a deep rut, stay in it and don't try to cross ruts or ride out unless absolutely necessary. If you must change ruts, hurl your bike and weight in the chosen direction while standing up and gassing it. The right combination of body positioning, throttle control and steering (all greatly aided by knobbly tyres) should see you make it.

Getting stuck in sand

Getting a bike stuck in the sand is nowhere near as big a problem as getting a car stuck, and a solo rider is usually able to get moving again without assistance. You may have hit an unexpected soft patch in the wrong gear or at too slow a speed, and gradually your bike gets dragged to a halt as you drop frantically through the gears.

Left: Well and truly buried, the result of turning and trying to ride up a bank – the loss of momentum meant I had no chance (see also the diagram on page 190). **Right**: The easiest solution is to lean the bike over, fill in the hole, pick the bike up and, with the bashplate now off the sand, push it out in first gear with the engine running.

In this situation do all you can to **keep moving**. As you slow down to walking pace, pull in the clutch to avoid futile wheelspin and, with the engine still running, hop off the bike. Push the lightened bike with the help of the engine, jumping back on once you're moving on firmer ground. This sort of activity is tiring and not something you want to do more than a few times a day but keeping moving is the only answer to even more laborious digging, pushing and shoving.

Nevertheless, sometimes you get caught. When the **wheels are buried** up to the hub and the bottom of the engine is resting on the sand, turn off the engine. The bike will be standing up by itself at this point so lay it on its side. Kick the sand back into the hole dug out by the rear wheel and pick the bike up. Think about lowering tyre pressures if you haven't already done so. Start the engine, let the clutch out and push the bike forward. If the rear wheel begins spinning again, as may happen on an upward incline, stop immediately. Try and flatten the ground in front of the wheels so that they have no lip to roll over and consider letting still more air out of the rear tyre, even if it means you have to re-inflate it again once you're free. Also consider dragging your bike around so that it faces down the incline, from where it will get moving much more easily. This may require removing your luggage.

Getting bogged down in sand is usually the result of limited experience, of not reading the terrain correctly, of having too high tyre pressures or of spinning your wheel when you should have got off and pushed. As you become more experienced on the dirt these events should occur less and less, if at all.

Dune-riding

When passing an alluring range of dunes the temptation to dump your baggage and have a quick blast can be hard to resist. On my solo biking trips this was never the case as the idea of thrashing about in the dunes was far too risky. Motorcycle accidents are most common in dunes where riding anything heavier than a 250cc dirt bike is just too dangerous. For your own safety avoid riding in dunes for fun. If it's part of a piste, commit yourself to the task single-mindedly and if there is a way round it, take it. The sand may appear cushion-soft but a cartwheeling bike landing across your back is not.

In the dunes – as dangerous for bikes as for cars; see pp.185-95.

Dunes can be a maze of varying, similarly-coloured slopes, sometimes hard to distinguish. Most accidents happen when the speed you're compelled to maintain on soft sand sends you over a drop (see diagram, p.195). If you're lucky it'll just be a harmless tumble; if not it's the end of your trip and the beginning of a stressful evacuation.

Limit your dune-bashing to mornings or evenings when the low sun makes better shadows. Let your tyres right down, wear protective gear and don't lose your head.

Some of the general principles in the 4WD sand driving section (pp.185-95) will also be helpful and a baggage-free dirt bike can be a real aid to navigating cars through dunes.

Riding straight down some steep sand slopes is not possible while boxes get in the way if you try to descend at an angle. The only answer is laborious manhandling.

In the dunes, never let your concentration drop while riding, attack soft sections standing up on the footrests and with the power on. Maintain momentum at all costs, even if it means slithering around and riding in the totally wrong direction, or jumping off and running alongside. You can expect your engine to get very got in the dunes as you will be revving it to the limit in every gear. Keep an eye on the temperature and stop to let it cool down if necessary.

Approaching crests on a bike is very tricky compared to a 4WD as you don't have the stability or the four-wheel traction. It can often be easier to plan to fall over on a crest rather than go over the edge and fall down with your bike behind you. Having fallen on a crest, it is easy to pick the bike up and walk it down if necessary. One problem we found with our wide metal boxes is that they dig into the slope even when you try to just walk a bike down. Riding straight down some steep slip faces is not possible so the only answer is to manhandle the bike down, which is easier with two people.

Rocky mountain tracks

In rocky regions like the Tassili Hoggar in Algeria, tracks provide the type of terrain where a well set-up bike is at its best, being faster, easier and more enjoyable to ride than any other form of transport.

However, the danger here lies not only in damaging your wheels and getting punctures, but also in colliding with an oncoming vehicle or riding off the edge.

Some rocky mountain sections demand reduced speed for no other reason than uncertainty about what is around the next

The Tarat piste (Route A3); one of the best mountain tracks in Algeria.

Even this big GS is managing to cope with the gnarly ascent to Assekrem. Good balance helps; if you go too fast you could damage the rims. Check spokes after a heavy day on the rocks. © Jeff Condon

corner or over the brow of the hill. Keep your hands over the handlebar levers and be ready for anything: grazing camels, tracks cut by floods or covered in fallen boulders, or deep sand.

Again, in the mountains as much as anywhere, you must ride within the limits of your visibility and the terrain. Read the ground constantly. A steep descent may end at a sandy creek or wash-out, while a steep ascent rarely continues down the other side in the same direction. After just a few hours of this you'll find your judgement and reflexes improving noticeably. As much as anywhere, try and ride light to reduce impacts.

Some very stony tracks don't even give you the chance to worry about

---

RIDING OFF-PISTE

Choosing to ride off-piste, directly across country with no tracks or markers to guide you, is perhaps the most authentic and exhilarating form of travel in the Sahara.

Most people dabble with the off-piste experience by taking short cuts between recognised routes and landmarks, or just riding a few kilometres off the piste overnight to get a feel for the truly wild Sahara.

But extended off-piste riding is not for beginners: in addition to having the riding skill and dependable machines, it requires a realistic appreciation of what your are letting yourself in for.

You should already know the region well and be familiar with its range of mapping and how to interpret the maps. Satellite images may be of some use, but again experience is needed in interpreting them. The terrain you'll ride on will greatly affect your progress and fuel consumption; study maps at around 1:200,000 scale to try and visualise the terrain. Canyons can offer an easy-to-follow route but can be full of boulders, vegetation and alluvial sand and offer no escape.

It goes without saying that you'll be on your own so a satellite phone (see p.352) is an essential safety back-up. Ride in a group of three and monitor fuel and water closely.

Note that some countries don't allow travel off tracks and in some places you would not want to do so anyway for your own security.

Into the unknown: some days in the Tassili on *Desert Riders* we covered just four kilometres. Yet out in the Ténéré we managed over a hundred times that figure.

oncoming traffic. The western descent from Assekrem is sometimes so washed out that you're riding on scree and will be struggling to keep your panniers from bashing into the rocks. By the Libyan border the aforementioned Tarat piste becomes incredibly rocky south of Imirhou. In a car it's not a problem, you just chug over the rocks in Low Range, but on a bike some ascents are very challenging, requiring clearing rocks or even walking the bike up. Keep tyre pressures high on this sort of terrain and check your spokes the first chance you get.

Road-riding

Before you get to the piste you have to ride on African roads. While it may be easier on your back, the roads of North Africa can be stressful in the extreme, especially during the first few days and in big cities. You must be ready for anything: sudden stops without brake lights, cutting in, aggressive drivers, excitable children, things thrown out of windows, dead animals, live animals, holes in the road, a barbed-wire road block. The list goes on and on.

Every year of motorcycling will stand you in good stead as you try and anticipate the hare-brained driving of most commercial drivers. In Africa ancient jalopies, lorries overloaded to breaking point, and speeding limos make a lethal mixture. Big bikes are unknown here and rarely considered by other road users.

Once you get to the desert regions, **potholes** and the encroaching sand present an added danger. With potholes you'll have to concentrate hard as the sharp edges can easily dent a wheel rim; be prepared to manoeuvre or brake hard – or just keep your speed down. Generally you'll have an easier time of it than cars but if the road gets really bad you may have to choose the option of riding on the dirt alongside. It may not be quicker but will prove more consistent than a badly-damaged road.

Another hazard on a tarmac highway in a desert area is **encroaching dunes** with tongues of sand across the road. Oddly enough in both Algeria and Libya you find sand over the road around 31°N. If the dune is right across the road two ruts are usually formed by passing traffic and to ride through successfully you must balance speed with caution. Although it's momentum that gets you through, riding into these sandy ruts at highway speeds will almost certainly knock you off. The sudden build-up of sand in front of the front wheel will dramatically alter the castor effect of the steering and flip the wheel sideways, sending you over the bars.

Suddenly having to ride on soft sand after hours of vacant cruising along the highway takes more adjustment than most can manage in the few seconds they have to think about it. Again, accidents are common here. If you don't want to paddle over the dune – not a bad idea if you're riding on trail tyres at road pressures – slow right down to about 40-50kph, drop a couple of gears and accelerate hard, allowing the back wheel to weave around while you concentrate on keeping the front wheel in the middle of that rut.

Remember the **3 'A's of African riding**: Alertness, Assertiveness (*not* aggression) and most of all, Anticipation. Ride to survive.

Cycling in the Sahara
(Based on material by Yves Larboulette)

A few years ago, I had the urge to visit Mauritania, but with only four weeks' holiday it was impossible to manage it by motorbike or 4WD, so I decided to fly there and explore the desert by bicycle. I was not interested in life or death struggles or 'crossing the Sahara' – cycling was just the most obvious option.

The idea of cycling in the Sahara sounds crazy but with careful preparation it can be a rewarding way of experiencing the desert. By travelling slowly you see things more closely, and you'll inevitably have much closer contact with the locals than you would on a motorbike or in a car. Our sense of space is defined by the time it takes to travel to limits such as settlements, borders or dwindling provisions, and the faster we travel, the more space we need to feel free. On a bicycle, as on foot, you don't need to travel enormous distances to feel free so there's no need to imitate 4WD drivers who try to achieve an autonomy of 2000km or more.

Having said all that, travelling through the Sahara by motorbike or car is difficult enough, but with a bicycle it is extreme. Desert cyclists require excellent mental preparation, top physical fitness and proven equipment. The cyclist's biggest problem is very **limited autonomy**. You might need ten litres of water a day, but carrying more than 20–25 litres on a bicycle is impossible when trying to pedal over sandy or corrugated tracks. The key to success is painstaking preparation, and to respect the desert and the limitations of both you and your bicycle to a far higher degree than motorised travellers need. It is essential to be extremely careful when choosing the region you plan to visit, your route, and the season in which you travel. And you must travel with a flexible attitude that accepts the use of passing transportation when the riding is too hard or boring.

WHERE TO GO

Cycling in the Sahara does not automatically have to mean *across* the Sahara, though this is often the motivation for most first-timers. To get a real feel for the desert it's not necessary to suffer endless kilometres of pedalling and pushing through desolation. A visit to the peripheral regions of the Sahara in **Morocco or Tunisia** poses fewer logistical problems while offering much more variety *and* a taste of the Sahara. They are the easiest and most rewarding countries to cycle through as well as being easy to reach. In addition, eco-minded travellers will appreciate the fact that it's possible to get you and your bike there by train and ferry, without having to rely on planes.

However, the most crucial factor here is **temperature** – the countries of North Africa are significantly cooler

Shade at last, but beware of punctures.
© R Verbeelen

than those of West Africa, which means you have a much more realistic range in Tunisia and Morocco than you do in Mauritania, Niger or Mali, where 'winters' are effectively dry seasons with average daytime temperatures of 30°C. In fact, aside from Mauritania, described below, the Sahara regions of **West Africa** are not suitable for bicycle touring. Even the Sahel is very difficult to explore by bicycle unless you stick to the tarmac, and you'll largely depend on other vehicles in these areas.

Don't expect to ride every single trail.
© R Verbeelen

Morocco and Western Sahara – The Atlantic Route

After Algeria, Morocco is probably the most interesting of the Maghreb countries for cyclists. Marrakesh would be an ideal starting point. From here you only have to cross the Tizzi-n-Tichka Pass (no mean feat at 2260m!) and the Sahara lies before you, where you'll encounter much less hassle than in the north.

The **High Atlas** has beautiful scenery and friendly people and the fit cyclist will find many rewarding loops there, though expect snow in the higher passes from November to March.

The **Sahara** starts south of the imaginary line linking Agadir, Ouazazate and Er-Rachidia, with many tracks leading to settlements over manageable distances. An energetic fortnight's **road riding** would run from Marrakesh over the Atlas to Ouazazate, Boumalne-Dades, Tamtatouche, Assoul, Goulmima, Er-Rachidia, Rissani, Tazzarine, Zagora, Foum-Zguid, Tata, Akka, Tiznit, Agadir and back to Marrakesh, totalling nearly 2000km but about as fine a cycle tour as Morocco offers.

Of the Moroccan **pistes** described in this book, Routes M3, M4, M9 and M10 would all be interesting and possible on a tough mountain bike, assuming the season is right. Early spring or late autumn would be best on the longer pistes, avoiding the need to carry excessive quantities of water and making use of any wells along the route.

For those planning to travel down to Mauritania, the **Atlantic Route** (see p.464) will have been sealed by the time you read this so you can theoretically cycle on tarmac from anywhere in Europe across the Sahara all the way to Dakar. Winds and water range for the 1500-kilometre stretch from Layounne to Nouakchott will be your main problem.

Tunisia

Tunisia offers a variety of attractions to the cyclist without the hassles of Morocco, but as many of the most tempting routes are in the north of the country they do not really qualify as Saharan cycling. The actual desert is confined to southern Tunisia and is largely covered by the dunes of the Grand Erg Oriental, which rules out cycle touring off-road; in addition, much of this is a military zone where cycling would not be encouraged. However, the region immediately to the south of the **Chott El Djerid** holds some possibilities. The northern stretch of Route T1 passing the oasis of **Ksar Ghilane** on the edge of the Grand Erg Oriental would be feasible on a bike, as long as you don't mind the occasional bit of pushing. On all tracks in Tunisia you should expect tourist cars and motorbikes to be driving at excessive speeds, a more pronounced problem here than in Morocco, as few appreciate the vulnerability of the touring cyclist.

Getting **provisions** doesn't pose much of a problem in Tunisia as settlements and wells are very close together. Like Morocco, Tunisia has its fair share of obstinate guides, persistent vendors and stone-throwing children, all of which can make camping wild in the central agricultural region difficult, but there are inexpensive hotels and restaurants in almost every small town. If you take the regular ferry from Marseille or Genoa to Tunis, you can then get you and your bike transported quickly south by taxi or train.

Mauritania

Mauritania's prospects for bicycle touring have improved with a new road along the Atlantic route and another reach up to Atar. Some interesting excursions are possible. The Mauritanian Sahara is mostly flat but settlements are far apart. Expect very high temperatures in the interior, even in winter: 35°C in January is not unusual.

A major drawback is that there simply is not much **traffic** in Mauritania and much of it is full to the brim. Hitchhiking for free is unknown and you may be charged a lot for a lift. I was asked 10,000 ouguiya from Akjoujt to Atar on the roof of a truck – but that's Mauritanians for you! As everywhere in Africa, taxis leave only when full. You should expect to pay for your bike as if it was an extra passenger. A worthwhile alternative to taxis is **internal flights**: Nouakchott to Tidjikja costs around 6000 oogs by taxi, but only 7000 oogs by plane.

Atar is a good spot to head for. From here, an ideal week's tour would take you out to Chinguetti via the New Pass and back via Amogjar (Routes R3 and R4). The ride on to Ouadane along the plateau (R9) will be very hard on your wheels but is the only way of cycling there; very soon you'll wish you hadn't bothered. In **Chinguetti** consider doing a camel ride in the sand dunes surrounding the town. If you find yourself back in Atar and heading south to Nouakchott, don't miss the 40km excursion from the main road to the wonderful oasis of **Terjit** (p.472).

Algeria

The tenth biggest country in the world, Algeria's network of tarmac highways offers a keen cyclist the chance to make a Grand Saharan Tour. It is also the most scenically impressive of the Saharan countries and will fulfil many of your Saharan expectations.

With an entry from Tunisia at Nefta you can ride west to Timimoun and Reggane or south to Djanet and Tamanrasset. However, officials may not let bicycles pass and with the restrictions on independent travel at the time of writing they may urge cyclists to use public transport. Trains, planes, buses and taxis will transport bikes, although officially trucks are not allowed to carry hitchhikers. See the 'Algeria' page on the website for the latest.

If you don't want to ride deep into the desert you can make a satisfyingly ambitious tour of the **north Algerian Sahara** by starting in El Oued near the Tunisian border and heading west via El Golea to Timimoun beneath the Grand Erg Occidental, altogether around 1000km. In Timimoun turn north to Bechar (around 460km) from where you can take the train back to Algiers or turn south for Reggane and the road east to In Salah. Although this route is all on roads it includes some long stages in the desert.

The road heading south to Tamanrasset might suggest the possibility of cycling all the way to Niger, but that would be a mistake. **South of El Meniaa** things become tough: the 400km route to In Salah crosses the monotonous and windy Tademait plateau. You may have to rely on passing vehicles for water which is an undesirable way of travelling in the Sahara, although currently it's mandatory to join a convoy to travel south.

South of In Salah, the distances get much longer between watering points and the road surface is at times either ruined, diverted or covered with sand drifts. You would need about seven days to travel the 660km from In Salah to Tam. From Tamanrasset you could transport your bike to Djanet somehow (flights are cheap and a fun way of enjoying the desert is from the air), from where a fabulous sealed road leads north over the **Tassili N'Ajjer plateau** to the oil fields of the Grand Erg Oriental and back to El Oued.

Libya
Libya is not well suited for cycling. The roads are mainly flat but the distances between places worth seeing are enormous and, compared to Morocco or even Algeria, most of the landscape is boring at pedalling speeds. Clothing might prove an awkward issue in traditional Libya and a woman riding a bicycle might be considered disgraceful. Adults don't use bicycles in Libya so spare parts will be scarce. A traverse along the coastal route from Egypt to Tunisia is possible of course, but it's not the Sahara and the traffic along this road is at times crazy.

Egypt
Some hate it, others love it. The best opportunity for the advanced desert cyclist would be the **Oasis Circuit** via Baharija, Farafra, Daklah to El Khargha and Asyut on the Nile. Besides that, very good possibilities exist for riding and hitching: Egypt has a good public bus network and trucks are allowed to offer lifts. The Nile also has a railway running along it if the wind's against you.

WHICH BICYCLE?
Mountain bike or touring bike? The answer is: both are suitable as long as they have been appropriately adapted. **Touring bikes** have geometry trimmed for riding stability. Their rear triangle is long enough to prevent your heels hitting the panniers and the seating position is comfortable. Drop handlebars give better streamlining which, as anyone who's ridden a recumbent bike knows, makes a very big difference. If you choose a touring bike, the toughness of the wheels must be considered, as well as rims which can take big (700 x 47C) tyres. Touring bikes are also more comfortable, lighter and faster on the highway, but are difficult to control off-road. For any of the road tours outlined above, a touring bike would be best.

Mountain bikes have a higher centre of gravity with a slightly higher rolling resistance as well as heavier frames. If you choose a mountain bike make sure the rear triangle is long enough and has mounting points for racks. Don't choose a model with a racing position unsuited to touring, and go for a handlebar combination with multiple positions.

Frames and other components

These days it doesn't really matter whether your **frame** is aluminium or steel as aluminium frames have advanced enough to be reliable. Steel frames are more elastic and often you'll hear that steel frames are easier to repair in the bush. But be aware that modern steel frames are made with very thin tubes and in case of a fracture, traditional welding may not work, though, if available, braising may do the trick. The bike should have a **long wheelbase** with a long rear triangle, a stiff frame, comfortable handlebars and well sealed bearings. Select simple, solid, well-proven components, which are easy to repair (such as Shimano SIS which are not sensitive to sand and are simple to repair and adjust). If prolonged sections on tarmac are expected it's advisable to fit a **Triathlon handlebar** for both types of bike. Use medium-grade Loctite on all threads of screws that hold accessories as well as on the spokes.

Avoid sophisticated equipment like hydraulic- or XT V-**brakes** which also put an enormous strain on the rims. Medium-priced components, e.g. from the Shimano LX range, will do the job perfectly. Choose a freewheel with seven **gears** over one with eight or nine. The more gears you have, the narrower the chain has to be; high wear and breakages may be a result. Keep dust and sand off the chain and chain wheels. When greasing the chain, clean it and use only a little oil, wiping off the excess.

A GPS is probably not necessary but your bike should be equipped with a reliable **trip meter**, an essential device for keeping track of how far you've travelled and so estimating your position.

Wheels and tyres

Nowadays good alloy **rims** are at least as tough as steel rims. If you have a choice, select a large rim, e.g. 25 or 26mm, as they are stronger. Spokes should be double butted and made out of stainless steel. Wheels with 36 spokes are stronger than wheels with 32 or fewer.

Whether you prefer a touring bike or mountain bike, use large **tyres** with

reinforced sidewalls. They will give you better going and comfort on the tracks and are less prone to damage caused by sharp stones. Nevertheless, avoid knobbly all-terrain mountain-bike tyres as they have a high rolling resistance, wear rapidly and attract thorns. Use robust tyres especially made for touring: one of the best is the Schwalbe Marathon XR which is available in 700 x 47C and 26 x 1.9. Other companies offer similar ones like the Top Touring 2000 from

Tyres and wheels get a hammering on this sort of terrain. © R Verbeelen

Continental. These tyres will have a slight rolling resistance penalty over street tyres, but have little negative profile in the centre and can be pumped up hard. Punctures will be few and wear will be low.

Punctures

The best way to avoid punctures is to avoid **thorns** at all costs. Stay at least 100m away from every acacia tree and regularly check the tyres for thorns. The smaller ones need some time to work through and if you're lucky you could remove them with pliers or tweezers before they get too far.

Like many riders, I haven't found sealants and liners very effective. A **sealant** does not plug the leak at low pressures and makes a mess of the tyre,

New tubes are better than patches in the heat. © R Verbeelen

making patching impossible. The same applies to self-healing tubes (e.g. Specialized Airlock). The sharp edges of **liners** also cause flats if not perfectly seated. Latex tubes work well at low pressures and do not puncture as easily, but they're expensive and heavier.

Suspension

There will come a day on the piste when you curse your rigid fork! Prolonged riding over corrugations is extremely tiring and some suspension will relieve strain from the bicycle and improve driving security. Luckily, suspension forks nowadays are reliable but still require maintenance at least every 100 hours or so. Spare parts will be impossible to find in Saharan countries. The Swiss **Parallel.rs** fork is available for 26″ and 28″ wheels, has an extremely simple, virtually maintenance-free construction and is serviceable with basic tools. Another advantage is the rack could be fixed to the suspended part of the fork.

Full suspension bikes have drawbacks: they're too maintenance-intensive and contradict the 'keep-it-simple' idea of bicycle touring.

EQUIPMENT

You've probably been told enough by many people but it's worth repeating one more time: save weight under all circumstances! But how much is the limit? Consider this rule of thumb: if you are able to carry the bike with baggage (not including water) over more than about 100m the weight is acceptable – or you are a body builder.

If the number of things to stuff into the panniers is growing and you find it difficult to decide which items should be left at home, try a systematic approach. Make a list of all the items and their weights, including panniers, clothes, etc. Add up the total weight. Now eliminate the most obviously unnecessary items and take a closer look at the list. Compare the weight and usefulness of all the items and you will know what to leave at home. You might not notice unnecessarily heavy items for the function they perform: a plastic bottle containing sugar weighs 120g, a nylon bag only 20g and takes less space when not full.

Racks and panniers·

There is a good choice of tough **racks** on the market. The rattle of bad roads and tracks stresses a rack and its fastenings, often resulting in cracks, especially in aluminium alloy racks. For this reason, Cro-Mo steel is preferable for desert touring racks. The Bruce Gordon, Blackburn and Tubus brands are well known for their solid but light build.

Some people recommend only using **panniers on the rear** and adding a small rucksack on the rack. That makes sense if you're not carrying much baggage, but overloading the rear of a bike can make you lose steering control, and the front might even lift on steep inclines. For piste riding I would set the limit at about 20-25 kg on the rear. If your load exceeds this you'll need a **front pannier rack**, but be aware that this will affect your agility and create more wind resistance and, in off-road conditions, front panniers will ruin your steering control. Use the front pannier rack to distribute weight on your bike, not to overload it! Waterproof panniers (e.g. Ortlieb or Karrimor) could be used as a washing tub or bucket to raise water from wells. Although it sounds a good idea, avoid carrying a **rucksack** on your back – over longer periods, it's torture as it puts extra weight on your already stressed backside. **Handlebar bags** are very convenient for storing light, fragile and precious things for everyday use such as camera, tools, diary, maps, compass and so on. They should have a quickly detachable fastener that allows you to take them off the bike.

Tools

A compact universal tool saves weight but is not always as versatile as individual tools – and if you lose it, you've got no tools at all. Take all the tools you'll need to execute the usual repairs like **changing spokes**. Doing this on the chain side will require a freewheel removing tool. A **chain riveter**, spare sections of chain and spoke wrench are essential, and if your bike does not use an Ahead Set you'll need the spanners to adjust the steering head bearings. Your **hand pump** should be solid; you'll use it frequently. Don't forget to lubricate it (I used sun lotion when I had nothing else left). You should learn how to **true your wheels**. Bad roads and rough tracks plus slinging the bike onto trucks will give them a hard time.

In big cities you might find some spares for modern bikes but not in rural areas so take essential items with you. Patches for inner tubes will be easy to find; most wheels in Africa are 26″.

Using wells can greatly reduce your payload. © R Verbeelen

Water

On a bicycle, your route is determined by the number and frequency of water supplies along it, and by how much water you can carry. One litre of water weighs one kilo. It's essential to plan your route wisely as your margin for error is virtually non-existent. Depending on the weather and effort, a person will require 5 to 10 litres of drinking water a day. Pedalling in the midday sun may raise consumption to 15 litres. With a temperature of around 30°C you'll require about **5–10 litres of water per day** as well as isotonic drinks to replace minerals lost in sweat.

At 30°C you'll require about 5–10 litres of water per day. © R Verbeelen

You must be vigilant about your water consumption because the wind dries the sweat so quickly that you will barely notice that you're losing lots of liquid. With the sustained physical effort of cycling, **clean drinking water** is much more crucial than for the low-energy needs of motorised travellers – you don't want to get too sick to cycle on to your next water supply. Therefore you need to be extra careful about local water and other locally-made drinks: *zrig*, an unpasteurised and unrefrigerated milk drink in Mauritania, is very refreshing and nutritious when fresh, but also the cause of serious illness as I found to my cost. See page 312 for details on how to purify your water.

I used **Ortlieb water bags** to carry my supplies; these proved to be very strong, but I wouldn't recommend them in areas with an uncertain water supply as they can easily puncture. Plastic containers of about 5-6 litres or bottles of 1–1.5 litres are more robust, if bulky.

If your water supplies rely on **wells**, take a thin rope of about 50m and a suitable container such as a collapsible bucket as not all wells are equipped with these. Never rely on unconfirmed supplies for water as some wells marked on a map can be very difficult to locate (as Karim found east of Tichit, see p.352). I once searched an area for two hours and did not find a well. Later, some shepherds showed me the right place, covered by a metal sheet and lots of sand. The perfect camouflage.

On some sections, your water supply will probably depend on **passing vehicles**, a common but very risky way to overcome the limited autonomy of a bicycle that has led to many close shaves for desert cyclists. Tracks are seldom clearly defined, except in rocky terrain. Especially on the plains, they braid out. Everybody is searching for the easiest passage and you may see the dust from a car 3km away but they won't see you waving an empty water bottle.

Food

With your body under the constant strain of cycling it pays to be very careful about what you eat and drink. Basic foods like bread, rice, spaghetti, potatoes, onions, different vegetables and fruits are available at the local markets but quality and availability will vary. It might be a good idea to bring a few light and compact supplies with you, but try any boil-in-a-bag speciality camping meals before you leave home as they can be quite disgusting. Dates are an excellent snack but avoid low-quality camel fodder; open each date to check for maggots wriggling around the pith (see p.161). In the Sahel countries, nutritious peanuts are widely available. Carry plenty of green tea and sugar; both are good for you and handy as presents to others.

ESSENTIAL BIKE TOOLS, EQUIPMENT AND SPARES

- Lock
- Oil
- Puncture repair kit (50 patches minimum)
- Grease, if the bike has regreaseable bearings
- Nuts and bolts for racks and accessories
- Wire and Epoxy glue to repair cracked racks and other gear
- One tyre
- Two inner tubes
- Cables for brake and derailleur

- Set of brake pads
- Spokes, ten of each type with nipple (generally this means three different lengths – check that they fit)

For an extended tour
- Use two or three chains alternately
- Axle for the rear hub
- Freewheel
- Replacement trip meter

Camping gear

A **tent** is heavy and bulky but I'd recommend using one. A good night's sleep is essential to recover from the day's exertion. Rain is not so uncommon, especially in the Atlas. Depending on the region and season, protection from animals such as snakes, scorpions, ants and spiders will be useful too. When evaluating a tent look for a light and robust design that's easy to pitch and resists strong winds. A **sleeping mat** is a trade-off: the self-inflating ones are the most comfortable but are susceptible to punctures. On a short trip of around a month I'd recommend a self-inflating one but for prolonged trips or those in the thornier Sahel I'd go for a closed-cell mat.

In most regions of the Sahara, wood could be easily found so it's not always necessary to carry a **stove**. A wilderness stove such as the Sierra model will outperform many fuel stoves but its fan needs batteries. On the other hand, relying on wood to cook means that you have to collect it, and at the end of a very tiring day this may be the last thing you feel like doing. A combination of wood cooking and a very small, simple petrol stove (e.g. Borde or Optimus 123) may prove effective. In Morocco and Tunisia where Camping Gaz cartridges are easily available, one of the light, easy-to-handle Camping Gaz stoves is a good choice when you can't find a café.

Clothing

Clothes have to be functional and comfortable, keeping you protected from the elements and, where necessary, warm. Clothes also tell a lot about the person wearing them. If you want to experience the traditional hospitality of the desert people – something that is much easier to do on a bicycle than with motorised transportation – you should adapt your clothes to Islamic customs. Your behaviour and appearance can make the difference between rejection and sincere hospitality.

Avoid wearing **shorts** in public; in some countries they are considered underwear! Tight clothes, outlining your body and showing exposed skin is as bad, especially for women. Despite the huge tolerance towards crass tourists you may experience hostility from rural people. Loose, airy clothing of natural fibres is the best solution, thanks to the dry climate. In the colder seasons micro-fibre underwear may be necessary. For me light **bike-touring trousers** that could be transformed into long shorts worked best. They respected local clothing customs and allowed better ventilation when needed. Some people also like the traditional baggy *saroual* trousers, though you'd need a pair of cycle clips to keep them out of the chain.

Your face, hands, neck and eyes are permanently exposed to the sun so should be covered whenever possible. For the head a large hat or even better the traditional *cheche* works well. The cheche protects you from sun, wind, dust and dehydration but can be awkward to combine with a helmet.

The back of your hands will get sunburnt very quickly – use **gloves** which will also protect your palms from chafing. Any other exposed skin should be protected by sun lotion. Quality **sunglasses** are a must.

RIDING IN THE DESERT

Depending on the region, October to March is the most pleasant time. The Michelin 741 map has a useful **climate** table but temperature information should be taken only as a guide: in Tidjikja the average maximum for December is given as 27°C, but was well over 30°C during my visit. Meanwhile the High Atlas in winter will be snowy above 2000m. The weather in the Sahara is not as predictable as some think.

Pedalling in sand – as hard as it looks.
© R Verbeelen

In hot areas or seasons, travel during the early hours of the day when the air is still cool and the wind is light, as it is at the end of the day. Have a long relaxing siesta (bring a book) and only set off again when the temperature starts to drop in the late afternoon. At this **pace** you could expect to cover about 60 to 120km a day on bad roads and good tracks, depending on your fitness and the wind. On very bad tracks with lots of pushing, 30–50km a day may be all you can manage, sometimes much much less. In the Sahara the prevailing **wind** blows from the north-east. Plan your route with an awareness of this fact. The wind not only slows you down, it also dehydrates you if you don't protect yourself properly, so increase your water consumption. Remember, you're unlikely to be carrying more than two days' supply of **water** so plan the route within your capabilities and dependable watering points. Even with the best material and preparation, the desert is always stronger than you are.

The difficulty in riding a loaded bike over tracks and sand is **greatly underestimated**. Sure, fat tyres will help but the only way to cross long soft sections is to push at 3 to 5kph with increased effort – and therefore increased water consumption. When you have to push the bike over long sections, carry some of the baggage in a rucksack to reduce the pushing effort. Never assume that pistes are easy to travel over. Sometimes the **sand** on the piste is much softer than that beside it so experiment. When a sandy patch is less than 100m you could try to pedal through, maintaining a gentle steady cadence to prevent wheelspin. It'll be impossible to keep a straight line so just steer the bike vaguely in your direction using light steering and shifting body weight to change direction.

PART 4: TRAVELLING BY CAMEL

Not everyone is drawn to the idea of seeing the Sahara from a motorised vehicle or even a bicycle. The authentic desert experience must surely be on the back of a camel, though the initial romance of the idea may soon be rubbed down to something more raw once you have sat on a camel for a few days.

One thing nascent cameleers should appreciate is that most of the time one **walks** with camels; they are employed more as mules than horses, to carry the essential provisions needed by a pedestrian in the Sahara. Riding is less comfortable.

Where to go

Two countries stand out as having genuine camel economies which are not solely dependent on tourism: Mauritania and Sudan. Camels are exported

from these places to other Saharan countries for meat, load carrying and even as status symbols for *arriviste* nomads.

Elsewhere genuine trading **caravans** do still exist, from Timbuktu to the salt mines of Taoudenni in northern **Mali** and across the Ténéré in **Niger** from the nomadic settlements around Agadez to the salines of Bilma in the east. Joining one of these caravans is still possible but is arduous in the extreme, walking from before dawn for over twelve hours a day on a bowl of gruel. The Aïr region of Niger is a much better place to enjoy a camel tour and experience the authentic Tuareg nomadism that goes along with it.

In southern **Algeria** the camel economy dwindled with the decline of the tourism which supported it before the 1990s; if not the Tassili the Tefedest north of Tamanrasset makes a good destination. Camels in **Libya** are as little known as genuine nomadism (a political and environmental factor), though there are sure to be camel trips in the popular Akakus region. Hyper-arid environmental considerations also eliminate the possibility of camel travel in the Western or Libyan Desert of **Egypt** beyond token oasis excursions out of Bahariya or Siwa. To camel in this country you're best off making your way to the Bedu camps of the Sinai – an area beyond the range of this book.

Which leaves **Morocco** and **Tunisia**, the latter being by far the better choice for camel excursions of up to a week or more in the sands of the northern Grand Erg.

On the following pages three cameleers, Bill Edwards, Alistair Bestow and Charles Foster, offer more detailed advice and impressions on the dromedary experience from Mauritania, Mali, the Aïr and Sudan. These impressions may seem to contradict one another but that is to be expected as the customs of camel travel vary across the Sahara.

Mauritania
Bill Edwards

In January 2002, two friends and I flew out to Atar in Mauritania. Upon arrival we purchased three camels, engaged the services of a local guide, and set out for Nema, where we intended to sell the camels. We had no prior experience of camels or desert travel, although we had done a lot of preparation and research. Even after three months and 800 miles on the road with the camels, the last 250 done without a guide, I'm no expert on camels; this account is not definitive – it is a record of what we learned from our experiences.

Logistics and planning
Before anything else you should work out **how many** camels you will need. You need enough camels to carry all the food and water required by the party, and your equipment. This depends on the route you're taking. Both you and the camels require food and water:

● Water is obtained from wells. You will need to fill water containers for your own requirements (you won't have to carry water for the camels – they can go **three or four days** without water). The greater the distance between wells the more you will need and thus the more water you will have to carry. Your daily requirement will depend on the **time of year** – we needed about **five litres** per person (for drinking and cooking) in January, rising to seven in late March.

● You'll have to resupply with food in towns along the route. The further apart the towns, the greater the load.

● Camels can satisfy the bulk of their food needs by grazing on bushes and shrubs at night, and during stops. This can be supplemented by grain bought in towns. If your proposed route is not well vegetated, you will need to carry more grain, so will need more camels to carry your food and water.

Camel stats
● In general camels can carry around **80kg** on a regular basis.

● They can cover roughly **30km** in a day over flat terrain – this will be reduced if you're making steep ascents or crossing dunes.

A caravan ascends the Amogjar Pass in Mauritania.

Our route required three camels for three of us. It was relatively well-vegetated and wells were at the most four days apart.

Basic camel handling

Pretty much all working camels in Mauritania will be fitted with a nose ring. This is a metal ring passing through the camel's nostril and is the key to controlling the animal. You need to tie a cord or 'nose rope' through the nose ring. When you are not using the camel – i.e. during rest stops or overnight – you

need to **hobble** it. This means tying its front ankles together with thick rope, to stop it from straying too far. When the camel is hobbled the nose rope should be removed as otherwise it tends to snag on vegetation as the camel browses. So, at all times, your camel should be either **nose-roped or hobbled** – otherwise you won't be sure of controlling it.

Hobbling camels limits their wanderings while enabling them to graze.
© Bill Edwards

To fit a nose rope to a hobbled camel you need to approach it calmly and quietly. The height at which a camel normally holds its head will put the nose rope out of reach. A well-trained camel that you have got to know will often lower its head for you and allow you to thread the nosering. If you are unfamiliar with the camel, or it's feeling uncooperative that day, it may stretch its head out of reach, bite and gnash at you, and wheel around to get its head away from you. On these occasions, if the nosering is on the camel's right side, you need to get up close to the camel's right shoulder. You then need to loop the nose rope over the top of his head – this is best done by flicking a length of rope under his head, up and over the left side and catching the end as it comes over the head. This takes practice. You can now pull the head down using the rope, and put one hand on top of the head. This tends to subdue a troublesome camel. With your other hand you can thread the nose rope through the nose ring and tie it off. This also takes practice to do one-handed, and a nose rope with a toggle on the end is invaluable at these times.

Once the nose rope is in, a trained camel will become much more docile. You can now let the rope hang, and crouch down at the front feet to undo the hobble rope, taking great care not to startle the camel. Whenever you are in this position next to the feet you need to be very vigilant to avoid being kicked.

Using the nose rope you can lead your camel around. If you want it to sit, e.g. for loading, you pull down on the rope whilst making a rapid 'tsh,tsh,tsh' noise. The exact noise used will vary across the Sahara. To get him up again tug forwards on the rope and make a rapid tutting noise.

Before hobbling a camel do not undo the nose rope, but leave it trailing on the ground. Kneel down next to the camel's front feet, as ever exercising great caution. Pass the hobble around the far ankle twice so it is encircled once. Leave roughly equal lengths of rope on either side. Twist the ends of rope around each other several times before tying them off around the near foot. If the feet are too far apart you can literally pull or push them closer together with your hands – a trained camel won't seriously object to this. Once he's hobbled, you can remove the nose rope.

Tracking

Each night, you need to hobble your camels and turn them loose to graze. Unless they are allowed to roam overnight they will not get enough to eat, so tying them up is not an option. Since they are hobbled they will hopefully not go far. Ideally you should organise your morning routine so that somebody is able to set out after the camels at first light.

Often they will not have gone far and will be clearly visible. Otherwise you will have to follow their tracks. One simplifying factor is that they will almost invariably move together – if you find one you find them all. We had three camels initially and we always found them together in the morning. Later we sold two and replaced them. For two or three days these two new camels moved separately overnight from our remaining original camel, but after that they all moved together.

Following the tracks is generally straightforward if the camels have moved across sandy ground. There is a thin layer of sand in most desert environments, enough for the camels to leave tracks at any rate. Problems arise if they have crossed bare rock or if strong winds have blown away the tracks. On regions of bare rock there will be depressions and gullies filled with sand where they may still have left tracks. It's helpful to observe the camels for a while each evening to see which general direction they are headed in. If there are no tracks at all you will have to set out in your best guess of the direction they went in, and keep your eyes peeled. A pair of **binoculars** helps and indeed these are prized by herders right across the Sahara.

Our biggest worry throughout the trip was being unable to find our camels in the morning! The consequences are obvious. This is one good argument for taking along a **guide** who knows camels.

On the march

Exactly how you load your camels will depend on the design of saddle you have and what you are carrying. Make sure the loads are high on the camels' backs and **well-balanced**. It is a real pain to have to continually adjust badly balanced loads once you are underway.

Rather than each leading a camel it is easier to organise them into a **chain**. You tuck the nose rope of one camel underneath one of the saddle ropes on the camel in front, but do not tie it off. If one of the camels bolts they should not be tied together – a

On the march. © Bill Edwards

strong tug on a nose rope could rip the nose ring out of the camel's nostril. While one person leads the whole chain it makes sense for someone else to walk at the rear, so you will notice if any kit drops off or, as often happens, the rear camel becomes detached from the chain. You feel pretty foolish when you glance back only to see that you've left a camel a quarter of a mile behind you!

The camels will cope fine with most types of terrain. When traversing dunes you must take care not to lead them down the steep side of a dune. Especially with heavy loads, they can stumble and break a leg.

Even during winter you will probably want to sit out the hottest part of the day. When choosing a lunch stop look for somewhere with shade for you and grazing for the camels. You should unload and hobble them and remove their nose ropes.

Stopping for the night

Towards the end of the day you need to start looking for a good camp. A particular consideration when moving with camels is that there should be some grazing for them nearby. This ensures that they will be well-fed, and also means they will probably not stray very far overnight.

After unloading the camels you can leave the nose ropes in and let them wander unhobbled for half an hour or so, but keep an eye on them. This is the only time they have when they are neither loaded nor hobbled!

Camels need to eat something every day even if they don't drink. If there is no grazing, grain is a good alternative to straw. © Bill Edwards

Grain

Once you've set up camp bring the camels in to give them some grain, about 1 or 2kg each is a good amount. More is required if there is no grazing near your camp. We used to lay out their ration on an old blanket, and then lead them all over to it. As they get towards the end of their meal they will start to squabble over the dregs, often snapping and biting at each other. If a camel is behaving particularly badly a couple of whacks with a stick will generally keep it in line. Our first guide, Ahmed, used a well-timed punch in the face to chastise a greedy camel. It may be that some of your camels are weaker than others – these will need more feeding so you should lead away your stronger camels before all the grain is eaten.

Knee hobbling

Occasionally you will not want to let the camels roam overnight. This could be because you need to be sure of making an early start, or because you know there is no good grazing anywhere nearby and you don't want the camels to go straying for miles. On these occasions you can knee-hobble the camels. Hobble the camel around his ankles as usual, then sit him down. Remove the nose rope. The camel's front legs will be bent at the knee – the knee sticks out in front, with the lower leg tucked back underneath the upper leg. Loop the nose rope three or four times around the lower and upper leg together, just back from the knee, then tie it off. This needs to be done tight enough to stop it from coming undone, but not so tight that it cuts off circulation in the leg. With one leg hobbled the camel will find it practically impossible to stand up. If he is absolutely determined to get up you could hobble both knees, which will make it impossible to stand.

You should only knee-hobble camels in exceptional circumstances. Going without food for a night will have a serious impact on their strength. If you have to, you should pick a comfortable sandy spot for the camel to sit for the night, and if possible gather some food and place it within reach, so that he has something to eat overnight.

Wells

Your camels will not need to drink very often. During winter months ours could easily go for a week without water, but by March they were drinking at every well we came to, that is, every two to three days. Nearly all wells will have troughs next to them for watering animals. The camels will drink if they need to. However, if it is hot and you know that there won't be any wells for a long time, you should actively encourage them to drink.

Camels can drink up to 100 litres at a time. The fluid is actually stored in the bodily tissue, not in the hump as many imagine. The hump is actually a reserve of fat indicating a well-fed animal.

Stopping in towns

Bear in mind that when stopping overnight to resupply, you cannot keep the camels in town – you will have to camp one or two miles outside the settlement. Someone should stay with the camels during the day while the rest of the party goes into the town. Around most towns there might be scattered smallholdings – be careful that your camels don't eat any crops.

Health

All our camels lost weight on the trip. Of the original three, two were so seriously emaciated by the halfway stage that we had to replace them. I think this was because one was too old, and the other too young. The remaining original and two replacements finished the trip without major difficulty, but all were a lot skinnier and weaker than when we had started. Several locals, including our first guide, told us we were pushing them too hard, but on the other hand we were setting a much slower pace than many of the Western experts (Michael Asher, Wilfred Thesiger) had suggested was possible. I have come to the conclusion that any camels carrying loads all day for an extended period will lose weight. Between caravan journeys they are rested and graze all day for several months. Some deterioration therefore is inevitable, but you should do your best to minimise it. It was a cause of major concern to our guides if we were unable to find a camping spot with grazing for the camels, and on several occasions we pushed on after dark to ensure that they would have something to eat that night.

One of our camels developed a sore just under its tail, where a saddle rope ran. Once the sore had formed there wasn't much we could do. A way of preventing this is to thread a short length of plastic hose onto the rope where it runs under the tail. The hose should be of sufficiently large diameter that the rope can slide freely through it.

Buying and selling

The inexperienced face two hurdles in the camel marketplace – lack of camel knowledge and ignorance of local market rates.

Good camels

The key point here is that they should be well-nourished – all camels will lose weight over the course of a long trip so they need to have enough to start with. You will be able to make out the dim outlines of ribs on all but the very fattest of camels, but you don't want a camel which has a clearly visible skeleton. In my experience (limited admittedly) a **decent-sized hump** is a good indicator of a well-nourished camel, and you should avoid those camels which have little or no hump. Clearly you should avoid a camel with any obvious injury or problem – a limp for example.

Secondly, if you have little experience with camels, you will want well-trained and reasonably docile animals. Ask the potential seller to thread the camel's nose rope, get it to sit down, saddle it, get it up, and let you lead it around. Ask him to hobble it. If the camel is ill-behaved during any of these procedures you should avoid it.

Finally you want to be sure that the camel you are buying is a working animal and not being kept for milk or meat. You can judge this to a large extent by how well-trained the animal is – camels kept for meat will not be accustomed to saddles and nose ropes. In Mauritania only castrated male camels are used as working animals. You should avoid females, kept only for milk, and uncastrated males (bulls) which can be aggressive. The Hassaniya word for castrated male camel is 'zuzal'.

Good price

Without impartial local advice it will be difficult to ascertain the price that a local would pay. Before you buy talk to as many people as possible to get an idea of the market rate.

We started our trip in Atar, where we bought three camels for 190,000 ougiyas each (about £540/€800). Camels seemed to be rather scarce in the Atar region, probably because there had been a major drought a few years earlier.

This might account for the high price, though I think we also paid over the odds, especially since two of them were rather weak. We sold these two in Tidjikja and bought two much stronger camels for 130,000 ougiyas each (~£370/€550), obviously a much better deal. I think the market price in Tidjikja was probably lower (there seemed to be more camels grazing in the surrounding area), but we were also aided by having a trusted local friend in the form of our guide.

Buying

In Atar we found camels to be rather scarce. There was no regular camel market, which meant that we had to ask around. This was a less than ideal situation because most of the people with working camels for sale were nomads camped some distance out of town. Getting a lift out there will cost you in time and money – this makes shopping around costly and it perhaps makes sense to buy the first reasonable-looking reasonably-priced beasts you come across. Try and arrange for the sellers to bring the camels into town for the sale, or you may be faced with a long journey back from the camp.

Bear in mind that as soon as you take delivery of the camels they are your responsibility. You can't keep them with you in town. You will either have to set up camp outside town, or employ someone else to look after them while you make your final preparations.

Hired help

Our landlord was a tour guide. We paid him to help us for several days, buying equipment, sorting out transport to see camels, helping us look after the camels after we had bought them etc. While not strictly necessary someone like this can make life a lot easier in the beginning when you have a lot to think about.

Even if you are very confident of your own navigation you will need to get a guide, at least until you are confident in handling the camels. The most important thing is to find someone who can proficiently handle camels, and can literally show you the ropes.

Mauritanian camel saddle.
© Bill Edwards

Equipment

A lot of camel-specific equipment is best bought locally. You will need nose ropes, hobble ropes and saddles for each camel, sacks for all your food and kit, and a lot of rope for loading. Mauritanian saddles come in two forms: the throne-like riding saddles similar to a Tuareg saddle, and pack saddles which are little more than a wood and metal framework onto which you attach equipment.

If you are unfamiliar with camels you are unlikely to be riding much; it knackers your camels out for one thing. Nevertheless it's worth getting at least one riding saddle in case a member of the party is injured and unable to walk. You also need to buy blankets, which are placed under the saddle for padding.

To carry kit I recommend empty food sacks of woven plastic strands – these are very tough and available from any local food shop. When buying nose ropes and hobbles look for specialised ones with toggles to facilitate tying. We also bought **jerricans** (definitely preferable to traditional goatskins), an axe for chopping firewood, and a collapsible bucket for drawing water from wells.

Selling

This was even more of an adventure for us. Before you try and sell your camels you need to work out accurately what you think they are worth, and strive to get this price for them. We decided we would aim for a price of 250,000 ougiyas (about £715/€1000) for all three. This is quite a depreciation given that we had paid £1280/€1800 for them in total. But you have to consider firstly that there were many more camels in Nema than there had been in either Atar or Tidjikja, and secondly that the condition of ours had inevitably deteriorated over the course of the trip.

We camped a little way out of town and at least one person always remained at camp. Initially we went into town without the camels. We got into conversation with lots of shopowners, tour guides and other random inhabitants of the town and generally let it be known that we had three camels for sale that we'd be bringing to town the next day. The next day we took them to show to various people who had expressed interest and gathered a large crowd along the way. An impromptu auction developed with bids eventually surpassing our target price. We agreed a price with the top bidder and the crowd dispersed. We headed off to the police station where we would sign a contract and the money would be handed over. On the way our potential buyer informed us that his bid had not been serious and he only made it to get rid of all the other bidders at the auction! In fact he was now offering us half his final bid! This turned out to be a common ploy. From that point on we decided only to negotiate with individuals. We eventually managed to get 215,000 ougiyas (about £610) for all three. We might have got more if we had been more patient, but our visas were about to expire.

CAMEL JOURNEY – ATAR TO NEMA

Wanting to experience the Sahara four of us flew to Atar in Mauritania, bought three camels and took them on an 800-mile journey to Nema, where we sold them before flying home. We were 23 years old, just graduated from university. None of us had any experience of desert travel, and no one knew anything

© Bill Edwards

about camels, or working animals in general. We were keen to do the trip independently, and buying and selling the camels ourselves was an important part of the experience for us. We were also keen to do a substantial chunk of the trip without a guide.

Nine months before departure we went to Jordan for a week, where we organised five days in the desert with a local guide and a camel. This didn't teach us an awful lot but it did at least mean that we had seen a camel and a desert, albeit fleetingly, before we arrived in the Sahara.

Upon arrival in Atar we purchased three camels and engaged the services of a local guide. Our aim was to travel south to Nema, via Tidjikja and Tichit, and sell the camels. To break ourselves in we had done a two-week circuit from Atar to Oudane and Chinguetti, ending up at the oasis at Terjit. Now, on the eve of the main trip, we were resupplying in Atar. Our camels, The Beast, White Lightning, and Young'un, were resting and grazing under the care of our crippled, illiterate guide, Ahmed, who spoke only Hassaniya, an Arabic dialect of Mauritania. The night before departure we returned to camp to find a load of nomads sat with Ahmed, united in the view that Young'un would not make it to Tidjikja alive. This was a bit worrying – we had thought our camels were just a bit tired after the practice trip. All we could get out of Ahmed were a few worried glances at Young'un, and 'Insha'allah', basically 'whatever God wills'. Still, buoyed by the purchase of much tinned pineapple, our spirits remained high.

We set off for Tidjikja, travelling across huge rock-strewn plains. Young'un wasn't coping that well, at times having to be lifted to his feet after being loaded. On the third evening we camped in a valley after crossing a wide field of dunes, and were surprised by a nomad family arriving out of the darkness. They were carrying drums – ready for a party. They turned out to be real movers. It seemed that we were required to dance and sing as well, and Len sang a song that they all really got into. It was perhaps fortunate that they couldn't understand the explicit nature of the lyrics.

Ahmed was keen to make it to Ain as Sefra, a nearby settlement, ASAP, to rest and graze the camels, otherwise, pointing to Young'un, he rolled his eyes back, stuck his tongue out of the corner of his mouth and made some gurgling noises. We set off as fast as Young'un could walk. The death of a camel would be a financial blow, and could also have serious consequences if we were caught several days between wells. I guess it would also be quite a blow for the camel concerned.

Camels must eat daily so grain or straw is need in unvegetated areas. © Bill Edwards

After several days crossing an immense basin piled high with rolling dunes, we arrived at Ain as Sefra, the most out-of-the-way place we'd ever seen. We spent three days resting and grazing the camels, during which time Young'un, and now Beast also, degenerated to an almost skeletal state. Ahmed was doing the death face at both of them now. They hadn't been one of the all-time great purchases.

We were approaching Tidjikja six days later, struggling through strong winds. About 15km out Young'un sat down and refused to get up. Apparently that's a sign of imminent death in a camel. After much application of the stick to Young'un's ass he shakily rose to his feet again. Not long afterwards he uttered a half-roar, half-moan, and fell over again. It took a lot of pulling and a lot of stick to get him up this time. Somehow we managed to struggle on until eventually we could see the edges of Tidjikja through the haze, where we made camp. Young'un collapsed again, but it was the last time he'd have to carry anything. '*Al Hamdu li'lah*!' rejoiced Ahmed 'Thanks be to God'.

Tidjikja was going to be busy: Ahmed was going to help us sell Young'un and Beast, and buy better replacements. Also we needed a new guide since Ahmed didn't know the way on and we didn't fancy going alone with new camels. He suggested we take a withered old bloke who spoke French and upon questioning gave a detailed description of the route from memory, which agreed with our maps. We took him on, despite him not having quite the honour of Ahmed (he wore sunglasses and trainers, and wasn't crippled).

Tidjikja was a biggish place, split right down the middle by a wide sandy oued. It was always windy. The townsfolk seemed perturbed by how dirty we were after fifteen days in the desert. We were accosted several times and told to wash more often!

A couple of blokes rolled up who had some camels for sale, over at their camp just out of town. Len and I took a jeep out there to see them, along with Ahmed. After much lying around in the tent drinking horrid tea, the camels turned up. They were pretty big and muscular, very big in fact, and a bit twitchy. In fact their owner seemed to have some difficulty in controlling them. Nevertheless, Ahmed was enthusiastic and said they'd get to Nema. We agreed on a price of 130,000 ougiyas each. The nomads would bring them into town tomorrow and we'd pay there.

The next day was busy: we signed a contract for the new camels and paid, and then conducted an impromptu auction of Beast and Young'un in the middle of town. Predictably we didn't exactly make a fortune on them.

Heading out of town the next morning, Gav

Making a windbreak with the bags. © Bill Edwards

popped into the post office, and found a letter waiting for him. It was the only letter that the Tidjikja post office had received that year. It was a copy of *Playboy*. We weren't sure what the local legal position was on this, but at any rate we set off swiftly out of town on the road to Tichit.

Ahmed had been the perfect guide – he looked after himself, was always up long before us, and was excellent with the camels. Also, most importantly, we didn't speak the same language so it was impossible to have arguments. By contrast there was something of a personality clash between us and the new bloke. It all came to a head in an unfortunate incident when, arguing over which was the best route, we got a bit lost, ran out of water, and couldn't find the next well. It was probably our fault as much as his. Fortunately all ended 'well'. The remaining six days were marked by much bad feeling and argument but also by spectacular scenery. We were walking along the edge of a 100m cliff looking out over sand dunes that stretched to the horizon. I had the impression I was looking over a sea where the waves had been frozen in place (and turned yellowy white). The unearthly effect was completed by the total silence, when you somehow expected to hear the crashing of waves on the rocks.

The final well before Tichit, called Zig, was 65m deep, and we had to attach a camel to the rope and haul water up with a pulley. Approaching Tichit we passed through vast herds of camels, hundreds strong, being taken out to graze.

After the events of the last few days we were certain that we wanted to continue to Oualata without a guide. We were a bit worried that the local police might force us to take a guide, so we decided to stop and resupply in Tichit for one day only. The Tichit–Oualata leg was the longest and most remote but we were confident in our abilities with the camels and our navigation, especially with GPS. Would-be guides in Tichit tried to put us off saying that the route ahead was preyed upon by bandits. We reckoned this was unlikely, but even so, if we were attacked, what was a skeletal old man going to do about it?

So we told the police we'd be hanging around a few days to choose a new guide, then headed off the next day at dawn. Our path lay across a desolate plain flanked by mountains on one side and silver dunes on the other. The palms and buildings of Tichit dwindled behind us, clustered around the tower of the mosque on the hill.

Unencumbered by a guide we were in high spirits and felt like the holiday had really begun. We were traversing flat plains, following the bottom of a huge cliff. On the morning of the second day we

The camels pull up the water at Lekcheb. © Bill Edwards

© Bill Edwards

stopped at the last settlement for twelve days. In Tichit we had been unable to get any foodstuffs beyond rice and pasta, so it was looking like being a bland couple of weeks. In this village we hoped to pick up some onions, instead we just collected three men begging for presents. One old boy followed us for over 5km before our onslaught of expletives finally discouraged him. We were managing precious little interaction with the local populace other than being begged at or ripped off.

We climbed onto the cliff in high winds on the third day, and pushed on to Aratane well. The next two days were spent traversing a difficult field of dunes which was very tiring for us and the camels. There was also no shade from the midday sun so we had to rig up a low shelter out of blankets. We spent three horribly hot hours lying beneath them. The next day was my birthday: the lads let me lie in till 6:30am and produced a chocolate bar they had been hiding since Tichit, and a fresh pair of boxers bought in the UK. This meant I now had three pairs of pants, the most out of anyone on the trip.

The next morning we had to find Tinigart well. We were a little apprehensive after reading the account of a trans-African motorcyclist who nearly died of thirst here because he couldn't find the well. Using our map and GPS we pinpointed the exact location of the well and arrived to find... nothing.

In fact, the map wasn't far wrong. We were on a plateau but about fifty yards away was a canyon, a more likely spot for a well, and we followed camel tracks straight to it.

The next six days passed straightforwardly but with some strong moments. On day ten out of Tichit we were headed for Tagouraret well. It was a really windy day and there was a thick haze of dust in the air. From some distance we thought we saw the well, seemingly surrounded by trees – in fact it was a huge herd of camels being watered. We arrived with our three camels, and began to draw water from the well. Through the haze two huge stacks of rock towered up out of an utterly desolate gravel plain, with isolated dunes scattered here and there. The surroundings were bleak, but the well itself was a mass of activity, with several caravans watering their beasts. We finished up with the minimum of attention and disappeared into the haze again.

Gav has a pretty poor memory for faces and this nearly got us into trouble a couple of days later. We had eaten lunch in the welcome shade of a large boulder and Gav had gone off to round up the camels. Len and I were surprised to see him return leading an unfamiliar camel and with a very agitated nomad in tow. 'This bloke keeps telling me this is his camel!' says Gav, 'but I'm sure it's one of ours'. It wasn't. The nomad found it inconceivable that anyone could mistake one camel for another and was only placated when we intimated to him that Gav was mentally deficient.

A few days from Oualata, a cut on Len's foot became badly infected. We were all exhausted by Oualata and the last three days to Nema seemed like a real chore. In fact they were possibly the nadir of the trip for all of us. Len was in a lot of pain and the camel he was riding had developed a sore under its tail where the saddle rope ran. We had real fun and games trying to saddle him each morning. The whole area was full of grasses whose seeds were tiny balls covered in spines. These spikeballs stuck to clothes, blankets, ropes etc, in the thousands, and the spines would break off in our skin, reducing our quality of life to near zero.

We were broken men by the time we reached the edge of the cliff overlooking Nema. We made camp in a ravine at the bottom of the cliff about 1km out from the town. The ravine turned out to be infested with ticks, which did nothing to improve the camels' mood. I had just finished hobbling White Lightning when my attention was distracted, long enough to receive a solid two-footed kick to the head. Fortunately no concussion, but it left a lump.

It took us several days of negotiation, auctions, visits to the police, arguments, and nearly coming to blows with one would-be buyer, before we sold the camels for a vaguely acceptable price. Auctions in Nema were unorthodox. If someone wants the camels he outbids all the others to remove the competition, then when you come to sign the contract he drops his offer again, all your other potential buyers having disappeared.

We flew out of Nema on Friday. Departures consisted of one building with a single door out onto the runway. Upon the arrival of the aircraft, everyone ignored this door, and leapt out of the windows. Guessing that the seat numbers on our tickets would bear only a casual resemblance to the actual seating arrangements on the plane, we too leapt out of the windows and sprinted across the tarmac.

I don't want to see another camel for a long time.

Salt caravan from Timbuktu

Alistair Bestow

There are but a handful, perhaps even fewer, routes over which goods are transported in the same manner today as they have been for hundreds of years. The route from Timbuktu in Mali, to Taoudenni in the far north of the country, deep in the Sahara, is one of them. Each year between September and April, caravans of camels still ply their way across the Sahel semi-desert region, sometimes via the village of Arouane and on into the true Sahara. At Taoudenni they are loaded with slabs of salt to return with their cargo across the 750km of sand to Timbuktu.

I have been privileged – and I mean privileged – to travel with the Arabic traders in both directions on this route not once, but twice. The first journey was in late 1999, and having found it so rewarding, I returned to Mali in late 2001 to traverse the route once again.

The road from Timbuktu. © Alistair Bestow

Having 'test-driven' camels in Morocco for three days in August 1999 with a guide, I felt ready for a more challenging excursion. I had hoped to travel from Timbuktu north to Arouane, about one-third of the way to Taoudenni. That return journey takes nearly two weeks. I discussed the possibilities and practicalities with several tour operators in Timbuktu (and one in Bamako), and decided that Dramane Alpha seemed the most experienced and practical of them (see box opposite). Amongst the discussions about the possibilities of such a journey, Dramane mentioned that if I wanted to go to Taoudenni, he could arrange it. It was rather a daunting prospect. As I sensed the excitement of such an adventure, my mind also filled with the things that could go wrong. Could I trust and rely upon a person whom I had never met before? Was I both physically and mentally fit for such a journey? What would happen if my guide or I were injured? What if we ran out of water? It was a very sleepless night!

There were three factors in my favour. I had the time to do the journey and I was there at the best time of the year (late October or early November). The cost of the journey was also reasonable too: Dramane's first price, CFA600,000 (approx £600/€900), included the use of the camels, the services of a guide, food and water, regardless of the number of days for the journey. With these factors in my favour, I took a deep breath, and decided to go.

While Dramane was appointing a guide and camels, and drawing together supplies, I had to psyche myself up for the undertaking and obtain some supplies of my own. I already had a sleeping bag, ground sheet, self-inflating mattress, a small one-man tent, sun-block, contact lens solution, ordinary running shoes (I don't suggest heavy leather boots), a water satchel and a head torch. I also had a good thick jumper that, besides keeping me warm during the cool mornings, served as a cushion while riding and a pillow at night. I procured a few multi-vitamins from the local pharmacy, having envisaged correctly that the diet would be poor; several rolls of lavatory paper and matches. (The matches are used to burn the used paper – important in the dry environment where paper has little opportunity to degrade.) I bought a plastic plate and cup, and ensured that a few kilos of dried beans were included in the food rations. The beans were to add both protein and balance to my diet. I also purchased a *bou-bou* (the traditional blue robe) and a *houli* or *cheche* (the length of cloth for a turban), which is de rigueur for travelling with the camels. I was assured that it was more comfortable, and that the camels preferred me to be dressed this way!

When provisioning for the journey it is tempting to buy some extra tinned or preserved food, some biscuits, jam or any number of other foods to relieve

---

TAOUDENNI PRACTICALITIES

My journey was organised by Dramane Alpha in Timbuktu (his name was in the Lonely Planet *West Africa* book, and he organised the National Geographic expedition to Taoudenni in the late '80's).

I had originally planned on going as far as Arouanne and back but he assured me that if I wanted to go to Taoudenni he could organise that too. I was asked to 'budget' for forty days, and his first price was reasonable (CFA600,000 or £600, with no haggling at all).

I left all my documentation and cash with Dramane and we signed a copy of a statement of what I had left with him.

Dramane provided me with a guide, ensured that supplies were procured, and that the guide understood what was expected of him.

---

you from the boring menu which is to come. However, I suggest that these extras be kept to an absolute minimum. Perhaps a chair or folding table would also be useful, to enable relief from the tedium of always eating while seated on the ground. All these are available in Timbuktu. However, the more of these 'special' items you take, the more you separate yourself from the people and culture that you have come to see and the more difficult it is to take and pack and manage these 'extras'. The cameleers sit on the ground to eat and in my opinion therefore so should the tourist. I do not believe that the cameleers would warm to a tourist in the same way if lots of these extras were taken on the journey. I felt weighed down as it was by the trappings of Western culture. Sleeping bags and self-inflating mat, groundsheet, water filter, mint toothpaste and a camera are all foreign to the cameleers. I did take a small packet of dried apricots with me (from Australia) in 2001, and rationed them to one or two a day for Ahmed (my guide) and me. Even then I was concerned that I did not really have enough to share with the other cameleers. Sharing is an important part of the culture. There is a practical reason for not taking too many extras. The distances travelled each day are far and everyone gets tired. It is enough to expect the guide to prepare the usual basic rice and goat stew at the end of the day. There isn't the time or energy to be able to prepare special food for the tourist. I went as a guest of the cameleers to travel with the caravans, to do my best to accept them on their terms, and not to make myself separate from them.

I understood from Dramane that women are able to go on the journey if they wish, although I had not heard of any doing so. His experience is that the least successful journeys are those when a man and a woman (perhaps boyfriend and girlfriend) travel together, unless perhaps they really know that they are both up to the challenge. If people want to travel with the caravans, it is important that they are fit enough to walk a quarter to a third of the fifty or so kilometres travelled each day, and to ride the camels for the remainder of each day. You may like to carry some water, but the camels are loaded with the rest of your gear. (The cameleers, however, never carry water.) It is also important that you are mentally ready for the challenge, ready for the isolation, ready for the size of the desert and ready for the cultural experience.

At this stage, my visa would only last another three weeks, but I was assured by the local tourism authority that it would not be a problem to get it renewed in Mopti after I had returned. It was not possible to get it prolonged in Timbuktu, and it was a fair distance to Mopti. This advice was not quite correct and resulted in some unpleasantness with an official in Mopti after returning from Taoudenni in 1999. The visa was renewed after some haggling, but it would have been much better had I had my visa prolonged earlier in Bamako or Mopti. (I did get a 'prolongation' for my visa in Bamako before my second journey in 2001.)

There are some security issues in the north of Mali, and banditry occurs sporadically at any time. The week before I left Timbuktu for Taoudenni in 2001, a group of four 4-wheel drive vehicles were set upon near Taoudenni. The tourists were relieved of all their cash and valuables and had to limp back, physically unhurt, to Timbuktu squashed into just two of their vehicles. Although concerned about security, I felt comfortable enough knowing that I was to be on a camel rather than a 4WD. I was also to be in the close company of a guide.

Dramane was paid half the cost of the travel before I left, on the understanding that the balance would be paid upon my return. To reduce the risk of losing or being relieved of my valuables, I chose to leave my passport, cash, travellers' cheques and credit cards with Dramane, as well as my exposed film and a couple of souvenirs. We each had a signed copy of the list of items I had left with him. There is nothing to buy en route, even in Arouane, and a passport is a liability. I took a photocopy of the passport on the off chance that an official would need it. None did. After each of my journeys, Dramane returned all my belongings and documents.

In early November 1999, we loaded up three protesting camels at the edge of Timbuktu, were farewelled by Dramane and, with a couple of assistants, and Mohammed, my guide, we pushed off north into the Sahel and, for me, into the unknown. The Sahel region north of Timbuktu is undulating, patchy grassland dotted with hardy trees with fierce thorns. We sometimes came across nomads grazing their sheep and goats. Unsurprisingly, the further north we travelled the patchier the grass, and the fewer the trees. When evening drew in, we simply stopped for the day. Dinner was cooked, and the stars appeared along with the occasional scorpion. I prepared my groundsheet and sleeping bag and slept under the stars.

On both the journeys my guides (and I) called in at their respective families' tents, and stayed for at least one night. Mohammed and Ahmed each came from nomadic families, who move with the seasons to graze their sheep, goats and camels. They located their families by knowing roughly where they could be expected to be found in the expanse of the Sahel, and by asking any other families or travellers they came across.

Colour section (following pages)
- **C1** Rock and dunescapes of the Jebel Akakus, Libya (p.560).
- **C2 Top**: Riding past the volcanic plugs towards Assekrem, Algeria (p.508).
  Bottom: Rekkam plateau, eastern Morocco (p.426).
- **C3 Top**: Approaching the Arbre Perdu, Niger (p.526, p.598).
  Bottom: Rendezvous at Berliet 21, Algeria (p527).
- **C4** Riding in the Grand Erg Oriental, Tunisia.
- **C5** The guelta at the end of Essendilene Canyon, Algeria (p.538).
- **C6** Camel races at Essouk Music Festival, Mali (p.582) © Gregg Butensky.
  Bottom: Fresh salad in the Great Sand Sea, Egypt.
- **C7 Top**: Old fort and market at Faya, Chad © Reinhart Mazur.
  Bottom: Zouar Valley, Tibesti, Chad © Reinhart Mazur.

C1

MISSION
BERLIET
NOVEMBRE 1960

Their family's tents were often situated in the midst of a vast plain of undulating sand, peppered with a very fine patina of grass, so little grass in fact that it made no difference to the colour of the sand from a distance. The families were always very hospitable, sharing their food and water with me, as well as providing fresh camel milk.

Goatskin waterbags or *guerbas* may look the part but are an acquired taste and always leak a little. Water bags from man-made materials may be better.
© Klaus Weltzer

The days were long. Over the course of the journey, we often got up at between 2am and 3am, sometimes earlier, and occasionally later. On one occasion I was even roused at 10.30pm to start the day! Mohammed would dash off into the dark looking for the hobbled camels, as I stirred, packed my sleeping bag, installed my contact lenses and got ready for the day's travel. Breakfast was the traditional three small glasses of sweet tea, a handful of peanuts and a handful of dates (really hard crispy dates with their flavour enhanced by the remains of a weevil or two). The dates are important to keep one regular – an essential health consideration when the rest of the rather poor diet is taken into account.

We walked with the camels for the first few hours until dawn, when Mohammed would stop for prayer, and then we'd ride over the undulating, sparsely grassed Sahel, stopping occasionally for calls of nature. Sometimes we'd cross the track that makes its way between Timbuktu and Arouane, and occasionally see a vehicle. I did not have a saddle for the journey and I eventually did get used to riding the camel without such a luxury. I sat on a blanket, perched on top of the camel amongst the sacks of rice, guerbas of water, cooking hardware and other such necessities tied on with well-used ropes. My camel had a rope from its lower jaw, tied to the tail of Mohammed's camel in front, so steering or controlling the camel was not a skill I needed to master.

Mohammed and I usually stopped for a couple of hours during the hottest part of the day, sometimes finding a tree for shade in the earlier stages of the journey. The temperature reached 35°C. We'd set up a small fire using a few twigs and grass to cook some lunch and make tea. Lunch was exactly the same as dinner – dull rice or spaghetti and gristly goat. After lunch we'd again walk for a couple of hours, before remounting, and travelling on ever northwards.

One of the hardest aspects of the journeys was, in addition to getting very tired (and, I admit it, grumpy from time to time), communication with my respective guides. Mohammed in 1999 knew no English or French, and I no Arabic, so for the month I had no-one to talk to – all communication was by sign language. Despite these difficulties, I believe that the whole experience would have been very different and not as rewarding had I travelled with an English-speaking guide, partner or friend. It would certainly have been easier, but at the same time perhaps I would not have interacted with and observed the cameleers, camels and landscape to the same extent. The character of the journey became different when Mohammed, the three camels and I joined a caravan of sixty or so male camels heading north. The rhythm of life became apparent as the days passed with the caravan. Although I could not speak to them, not knowing any Arabic or Tamachek, they overcame their shyness, I overcame mine, and the character of the six or so cameleers came through over the ensuing weeks. Mohammed was also pleased to be able to talk to someone else, for his earlier verbal isolation from his people was just the same as mine, as long as we travelled alone. My verbal isolation, however, continued.

The head cameleers led the way, while sitting on usually the largest of the camels, with their apprentices at the end of the string of camels, tied lower jaw to tail by rope. The apprentices were usually young men or teenagers, whose job en route was to ensure that the camels remained strung together and behaved themselves, and to pick up any part of the load that fell off. They also made tea in the portable braziers, distributing it to the company. The ratio between camels and cameleers is about fifteen-to-one, so it is hard work for all concerned.

Travelling with the caravan, we no longer stopped for lunch and instead had it on the move. It was called *crème* and comprised millet that had been crushed the night before, then mixed with salt, sugar, a little water and perhaps some spice. The ball of dough was then squirrelled away in a sack for the next day. At lunch time-ish, the raw dough was put into a bowl and dispersed in a large quantity of water and consumed. It looked rather like a bowl of tired dishwater with gravel swishing about at the bottom. It was difficult to consume while on a walking camel, so mostly it was had while walking. Sometimes it tasted good.

Near Arouane the cameleers stopped with the camels for a day or two to draw grass from the clumps that grow in the area. It is made into rope to be used later for carrying the salt, and to make the padded cushions of grass that support the weight of the salt on the camel's back. It was indicated to me at this time that my hands were too soft for making rope – and indeed they were. Rene Caille was the first European of the modern era to pass this way and live to tell the tale. This is how he recorded the process in the early 19th century:

'The cakes of salt are tied together with cords, made of a sort of grass which grows in the neighbourhood of Tandaye. This grass is dry when gathered, but afterwards moistened, and then buried in the ground to keep it from the sun and east wind, which would dry it too rapidly. When sufficiently impregnated with moisture, it is taken out of the earth and plaited into cords, which the Moors used for various purposes.'

© Alistair Bestow

And that is exactly the way I saw the biodegradable rope being made on my journey. Even today, there is no dashing off to the local hardware shop for a few coils of nylon rope.

Beyond the halfway point there is nothing for the camels to browse on – but browse they must, if one wants camels to maintain their condition and be strong enough to carry the slabs of salt. The problem is solved by loading the camels with bales of grass, also drawn or mattocked from the grass tussocks in the area at the edge of the desert. About one-third of the camels in a caravan each carry two large bales of grass to be issued as rations as they progress through the bald desert. Each camel looks comically like a walking haystack. They would like nothing better than to chomp their way into the grass from the camel in front as they walk along. But the cameleers have this problem licked: they muzzle each camel with a short length of rope, to ensure they cannot open their mouths. Some bales are left along the route as the caravan progresses north, to be used on the return journey. Every caravan knows whose bales are whose, and none ever goes 'missing'.

Arouane is a village of a hundred or so souls and even older than Timbuktu itself. Today the rough collection of mud buildings lies on the very edge of the true Sahara, and is surrounded by oceans of sand. There is also a nod to more verdant times, thanks to a handful of struggling trees that were optimistically planted some years ago. Despite its rather desperate outlook, it does have a school and some basic medical services. Mohammed and I had lunch there, and watered the camels at one of the five wells, before moving on into the desert.

Water for the camels is not required often. Every few days we would pass one of a series of wells from which ancient water is drawn from deep below the desert. The process of drawing water requires a rope, a leather bucket and a pulley, and rather than rely on these tools to be at each well, each caravan carries their own. One end of the rope is tied to the bucket, and the other to a camel. The bucket gets dropped into the well, and is hauled up over the pulley by the camel. The bucket is manhandled to the nearby concrete troughs from which the thirsty camels drink. We also fill the *guerbas* with water for our use. I took a water filter with me in 1999, but besides being slow, and being an awkward arrangement to keep 'my' water separate from the others', it clogged up early on and proved useless. I had to get used to the well water, which was fine to drink as long as it was drawn from a well that was not near human habitation and was not contaminated by a camel. I was not ill on either of my journeys. While there was certainly enough water to drink it was insufficient for washing clothes or oneself, or for shaving. I became very adept at washing and rinsing my hands in about 25ml of water and a tiny quantity of liquid soap. The other reason for not washing was a practical one – there was little time or energy for such activities.

The landscape varies during each day of travel. Sometimes it is a continuous stretch of muscles of sand. Sometimes it is rocky hamada – desert strewn with tennis-ball-sized rocks. Sometimes it is so flat and featureless that you cannot discern how far it is to the horizon. Sometimes there was a dried *wadi*, with a flush of surprisingly green vegetation. Sometimes we traversed strings of east–west running dunes of white or apricot or purple-grey. Sometimes there were rocky outcrops and hills. It was never boring. It was also very clean – a feature noted by T.E. Lawrence in his desert travels.

There are regular sites along the route where the caravans stop for the night. A few are near the wells, but most are in areas with some protection from the possible wind. My task at the end of the day was to collect dried camel-dung nodules left by previous caravans, in the apron of my *bou-bou*. It was the only source of fuel once we were in areas where there was no vegetation. Camel dung does not smell, burns well, and is essential for cooking.

We spent an average of 10 to 11 hours a day travelling, either walking or riding, the longest, toughest day being when we rose at 2.15am and finished at 8.30pm. Towards the end of that particular day, my thoughts regarding the question of 'what on earth was I doing here?' were particularly strong. More often though, although we started very early, we would finish travelling in the late afternoon, allowing sufficient light for the camels to browse or have their rations. There was also light for us to collect fuel, prepare dinner and crush millet for the crème the next day and to do some maintenance (e.g. repair broken slabs of salt on the return journey). I learnt fairly early on that neither Mohammed or Ahmed liked beans, and it was obvious that it was very awkward to try and cook them separately, when there was just one fire. I soon fell into a routine of putting a handful of beans in a plastic bottle with some water in the morning, and by the late afternoon, they were sufficiently soft to eat raw, mixed in with the spaghetti/rice goat stew. They were not particularly delicious, but they were nutritious.

We travelled a great deal at night, although sometimes I was in rather a sleep-deprived stupor. It was all part of the dramatic experience of the desert, to see the constellations swing across the sky and to see a full cycle of the moon, without the washout caused by man-made lighting. It was never truly dark. The spectacular stars sprayed across the heavens provided just enough light to see our way, even when the moon had not yet risen. One night I witnessed a spectacular meteorite shower, with blazing trails being painted on the sky every fifteen seconds or so. How could I not be moved by the spectacle?

Taoudenni is set on a plain where once a lake existed, one that dried out a long time ago leaving not only layers of silt, but also layers of salt. It is surrounded by cone hills and rough rocky outcrops. There is no town, village or even a shop here. Taoudenni is merely a moving mine site that creeps across the former lake as the salt is successively exhausted at each location. The buildings are ragged shacks made of mine waste and rare corrugated iron. The only water available near Taoudenni is suitable only for camels – water for the miners and the odd tourist is a three-day camel ride away.

Taoudenni salt mines. © Alistair Bestow

On my first visit I stayed just two nights in Taoudenni, while in 2001 I spent five nights there, giving me not only plenty of time to catch up with some sleep, but also to see how the mines operated. About two hundred people slave away in the mines to scrape together an income. My understanding is that these days none of the miners are actual slaves or prisoners, as was the case until recently. Each mine is operated by two to four people, is the size of a large room and ends up being three to four metres deep. Only picks, shovels, baskets and bare hands are used to remove the rubble to reach the layers of salt, the first of which occurs about a metre below the surface. A slab of salt is 10-15cm thick, one metre long and a metre wide. Using a pick, the salt is trimmed of the exterior dry clay and dirt, leaving a 4cm thick slab weighing 35kg or more, which is ready for the caravan. There are two grades of salt, one for human consumption and the other, a lower grade, for animals. The blocks are worth about £2 a slab in Taoudenni, but their value increases to about £7 per slab once in Timbuktu.

Taoudenni salt miner trimming a slab.
© Alistair Bestow

The miners have first dibs at the camel dung supply in Taoudenni, as there is no other fuel supply for them. Mohammed brought extra dung from the earlier campsites for our needs while in Taoudenni, while three urchins too young to swing a pick regularly scoured around the various caravans camps for camel dung. They carried a large sack and as they cheerfully went about their work, they sang like angels.

Photography is an interest of mine, and due care and respect is needed when taking photographs here, as much as anywhere else. Permission should be requested beforehand, and a 'cadeau' should be offered in return. From experience I learnt that an appropriate gift is a small pack of paracetamol, readily available in Timbuktu, easily carried, and most welcome.

For the cameleers, the return journey is even harder than the journey to Taoudenni. Not only do they have all the tasks they did before, but now they have to load the heavy salt. We would rise at about 12.30am, and for the next two hours it was a very chaotic, noisy affair. The hobbled camels had to be located, loaded with four slabs each and put in the correct order. All this is done in starlight. The camels protest long and loud while being loaded, but are composed and quiet once the task is done. My task was to ensure that the lead camel stayed put and did not wander off trailing a string of camels in its wake. When we were finally ready, we'd push off into the dark at about 2.30am, the only sound being the shoosh of camels' feet on the sand and possibly of a cameleer singing. When the sun rose, it became clear that not only were the camels in the same order as yesterday, but they each carried the same slabs of salt. Evidently, the camel-loading process was not quite as chaotic as it sounded.

On the last night of the journey in 2001, we could see the blinking red light on the transmission mast in Timbuktu in the distance. Ahmed and I rose after the rest of the caravan had departed at the usual 2.30am. We loaded the salt onto his five camels for the last time, and the two of us moved off toward the red light. I practised the few words of Arabic I had learnt along the way, and Ahmed practised the same number of English words, as we made our way along the sandy tracks. At dawn we pulled into the edge of town where the salt was unloaded, and suddenly the rhythm of life with the caravan came to an abrupt end. The town soon came to life, the streets were busy, the markets and shops opened, and the camels were gone. I went to a hotel, had the first shower and shave for several weeks, bought a few bananas from the market, visited a café and had coffee, bread and an omelette. Is it any wonder that travellers considered Timbuktu a rich and wealthy city? For that is exactly what it seems after having spent weeks in the desert.

It was arranged for me to return to Dramane's home to pay the balance of the fee, collect my belongings, and very importantly to provide a 'cadeau' for my guide. After the first trip I was almost embarrassed by not having such a gift ready, but gave Mohammed the blanket I had bought for the journey. Two years later I was better prepared, and was able to give Ahmed a pocket-sized pair of binoculars. In return Ahmed gave me two small blocks of salt, strung together with leather. These *petit sel* had been used to help support and distribute the weight of the large slabs of salt carried by each camel on the journey. I was touched. Although they were heavy, they sat at the bottom of my pack for the next couple of months while I continued my travels in West Africa, and are the best possible souvenir I could have had of this fabulous journey. My guides on each of the journeys had treated me very well. They earned my enormous respect for their knowledge and understanding of the desert, and the way they looked after me. Each of the journeys was different, but both afforded the opportunity to learn a great deal about the Sahara desert, camels, the salt trade, the people and, perhaps most of all, about me.

Tour of the Aïr

Alistair Bestow

Having had a hugely satisfying journey from Timbuktu to the salt mines in Taoudenni in Mali by camel, I was keen for more. I set my sights on Agadez in Niger, and on travel from there into the Aïr Massif. In the month or so that I had, I could have seen much of this terrain from a four-wheel drive (at a cost). However, I chose to travel less distance more slowly, in order to absorb more of the sights and sounds of the Aïr, and to do this the camel is ideal. Being inside a vehicle separates you from the people and landscape, and can diminish the experience, whereas a camel allows you to immerse yourself in the environment which you have come to see, and to get to places where vehicles cannot go.

Having arrived in Agadez in mid-November on the bus from Niamey, I made my way to the Hotel Agreboun in the middle of town. Other hotel guests were few and far between, Agadez International Airport, the main access point for many travellers, having been recently closed for extensive works. The next day I explored the town, in search of travel agencies regarding the options about my travel plans. For an independent traveller it became apparent that it was not going to be cheap. I was quoted prices for camel trekking of about CFA35,000 per day (about £35) and up. The guide I eventually selected cost about CFA25,000 per day, and I received that for which I paid. We agreed on a journey of twenty seven days, being broadly a loop that headed initially north and north-west via the hot springs at Tafadek. We'd then travel north-east to Timia in the central south of the Aïr, south to Mt. Bagzane, east to Tabelot, and then south-west to Agadez. I did purchase the very useful 1:1,000,000 IGN map of the Agadez region, and estimated the distance to be in the order of 500km. The distance per day was then roughly 20km, which I though a generous amount of time for the distance, having been used to travelling about 50km a day in Mali. However, travel is obviously much slower in mountainous country, and perhaps the time to cover the distance was warranted.

We agreed, over a rough written contract, on a total price of CFA675,000, the route, the number of days' travel and that water and food was included, and each kept a copy. I paid about 50% of the agreed cost before we travelled, and would pay the balance on my return. We would depart the next day, and my guide would arrange the required permission from the police for the journey, as well as food and provisions. Before the journey I left some of my belongings at the Hotel Agreboun, rather than carry them into the Aïr.

On the morning of departure a certain amount of food, several goatskins for carrying water and a quantity of cooking hardware had been gathered together at my guide's home. This was loaded into a four-wheel drive for the short trip to a nearby village where we transferred to our three camels. It was only now that I realised the reason the guide had been a little tardy about the price. Not only was I to have a Tuareg guide, but also a cuisinier (a 12-year old boy to do the cooking) and a chamelier (a guy to look after the camels) – and all four of us had to be fed and watered. I though that perhaps we were a little over-staffed, but by now the decision had been made. And in case you are wondering, one of the camels carried two people. We did have a saddle for each camel – a rather narrow Tuareg item which could comfortably accommodate a single buttock. Getting comfortable was possible with a blanket and jumper.

The four of us pushed off north, first walking then riding, across the undulating rocky landscape, criss-crossed with dry riverbeds sometimes lined with thorny acacias and grasses. We called in at villages from time to time, my guide catching up with friends and relatives. Small flocks of goats and sheep wandered about, usually under the supervision of a shepherd.

The day's events were fairly regular: we'd rise at dawn, have bread and tea, load our steeds, and ride or walk until lunchtime. Lunch was usually cooked spaghetti or rice and goat, before moving on again until the late afternoon. We always moved well away from the roads when selecting a campsite for reasons of security, and

© Klaus Weltzer

Stony ascent of Mt Bagzane in the Aïr.
© Alistair Bestow

often camped in a sandy riverbed.

The food for the journey started off well – there being sweetcorn, tomatoes and capsicum to compliment the rice and goat, and sometimes we tried the local flat hard cheese. The food, however, deteriorated when we did not come across any more friends or relatives. We subsisted on very stale bread, rice and goat, flavoured with half a teaspoon of tomato paste. We did not even seem to have any dates, of which I'd seen a plentiful supply in Agadez. Water was drawn from village wells and carried in goatskins, or was taken from a soak in the riverbed, the latter tending to be a cloudy brown colour. I did my best to ensure that the water I drank was treated or boiled to keep the tummy bugs away.

We stopped at the hot springs of Tafadek. I had imagined that they would be located in a corner of a riverbed surrounded by a tiny patch of luxuriant vegetation. Wrong. They were located in the middle of a dry river bed, but were now housed inside two small concrete buildings, with precious little vegetation nearby. They were used as local bathhouses – one for women and one for men. The hot water was supplied via a pipe at the bottom of the communal bath, for which there was a plug in order to conserve the water supply.

Unlike in Mali, where my camel was tied to the one in front, here I had to ride my own camel, and this is when I came to appreciate the different personalities of the camels. Some are obedient. Mine was not. Some are fast enough to keep up with the other camels. Mine was not. Some had a comfortable gait. Mine did not – particularly when moving faster than walking pace. To control the camel after it had risen, I was instructed to cross my legs at my ankles across the camel's neck, and place my bare right foot under a loop of soft wool that hung on the neck of the camel. The theory was that by gently tapping with my foot, the camel would go. Hopefully it would go a little faster if tapped again and was accompanied by a 'tsa-tsa-tsa' command. My camel sometimes responded and sometimes it did not. A single rein was used in order to control the direction of the camel and to bring it to a halt, and a series of 'psh-psh-psh' noises was used to make the camel crouch after stopping. I did get used to it and became fairly competent in riding and controlling my camel. In all I learnt a lot about riding camels, but I suspect that my camel also learnt a lot about me.

The Aïr Massif, as harsh and rocky as it is, is dotted with villages, particularly near the dry river beds. The villagers scratch a living by growing fruit and vegetables. Dates, sweetcorn, onions, lettuces, tomatoes, peppers, oranges, grapefruit and pomegranate are all grown. The water for the gardens is drawn from shallow wells near the riverbeds. Over each well is a wooden derrick of tree trunks and branches carefully tied in place with ropes and string. A pulley, two ropes, a soft bucket, a local boy and usually a camel (occasionally a bullock) work together for hours each day drawing water from the wells. The water pours into channels that make their way into the surrounding small plots. While water pours periodically out of the bucket into the earthen channels, someone in the garden opens and closes the channels to distribute the water amongst the crops. Other people attend to the endless task of weeding. It was very peaceful, quiet and soothing to an observer's eye. It was also hard work.

As we moved further north, the rocky hills became more frequent and the mountains themselves drew closer. After making our way slowly up the dry river beds and rough tracks into the barren volcanic mountains, we arrived in Timia, one of the larger villages, where there was sufficient water to grow fresh fruit and vegetables for Agadez, as well as supplying their own needs. (The pink grapefruit are to die for.) The vegetable gardens and orchards are distributed along the riverbed, sandwiched between the sandy riverbed and the steep barren rocky slopes, not far from the village itself. Also memorable was the fort on a steep hill near the centre of the village, being an echo of the not-so-pleasant past. The fort was damaged during the mid-1990s' rebellion, but is now undergoing some restoration. I spent a very pleasant hour or so at the local water pump, turning the handle of the pump while the women and girls filled their buckets. Seeing a man doing such work amused them, when it was clear that it was a woman's role.

Our food supplies began to run low, and I'd expected my guide to purchase more along the way, but he seemed reluctant to do so. The repetitive goat and spaghetti was getting very dull. I procured some dates, haricot beans and crushed dried tomato powder in Timia, but insisted that my guide buy the macaroni, tea and sugar. While my guide did speak French and I recalled a little from my school days, he chose not to speak slowly or choose simple words, and the discussion deteriorated into a shouting match over who was going to pay for the basic foods. At other times we also had a heated discussion about trying to ration the oranges to one each a day, rather than eating them all in a day or two. We had discussions about the rate of travel, because it seemed to me that we were hurrying along a great deal of the time, forcing a trotting pace out of the camels that proved very uncomfortable. The walking pace was much more comfortable. We were also well ahead of schedule according to my calculations from the map, but discussion on this subject also broke down. My guide and I were clearly not getting along.

We occasionally had salad for lunch, being lettuce, tomato and onion, with some oil and a chicken-stock cube. And as much as I knew that such food in these circumstances is not recommended for health reasons, there are only so many times that you can say 'non merci' without appearing to be rude in declining people's hospitality. It was my undoing. I picked up a case of diarrhoea that was quite persistent. Eventually Norfloxacin became my friend… As much as I had tried to keep my water either treated or boiled, I suspect that the salad was the cause of my ills.

From Timia we travelled south, at times along paths or along riverbeds, and made our way up onto the plateau of Mt. Bagzane, the highest point in the Aïr at 2022 metres. The route was very steep and covered in volcanic boulders, making travel very slow. Frequently we all dismounted to help guide the camels up the tricky course, and I was very surprised that the guide took the

© Klaus Weltzer

camels this way at all. On our ascent, one camel did fall, and there was the painful sound of cooking pots, food sacks and other hardware being crushed, followed by groans from the fallen camel. The stricken animal was 'righted', reloaded, and off we moved, even more gingerly than before. We found a camping spot at the top, amongst the enormous boulders to protect us from the wind. It became quite cold as soon as the sun set, and although I had a good sleeping bag and mat, my guide, the *chamelier* and *cuisinier* slept near the cooking fire that was kept stoked all night. The *chamelier*, like many Tuareg of the Aïr, always wore a fearsomely-long Tuareg sword at his side, and I hoped that I would not see it used. My guide insisted that I sleep close by, because although no trouble was expected, the Aïr does still harbour bandits. I, however, was also concerned about having to sleep in the smoke of the fire (which the others did not appear to mind) and the possibility of embers burning holes in my sleeping bag. More tension between the guide and myself.

Mt. Bagzane is quite spectacular, being part of volcanic remains and covered in boulders, numerous villages and beautifully symmetrical volcanic cones. We descended off the plateau to the east through a deep valley that slashes its side. Water made its way down the valley, providing for more crops and a range of other surprisingly verdant plants. Again the camels had to pick their way slowly down the rocky slope to the plain below. Off on the horizon to the east, one could see the distant dunes of Ténéré. They, however, would have to wait until next time. We travelled a little further east to Tabelot, from where many of the Bilma-bound caravans set off, before heading in a southwest direction for Agadez.

As I suspected from my map, we were still well ahead of schedule, and I was not really surprised when on the eighteenth day we arrived back in Agadez. I would have preferred to have travelled more slowly over the route, rather than spending a number of long days hurrying along on my uncomfortable camel. My guide was not impressed when I paid him the balance of the travel for the eighteen days, rather then for the twenty-seven days he expected. When I was quite happy to go to the police to discuss the matter, as my guide suggested, he then suddenly changed his mind. I think that he had hired the camels for a certain fee, and if I'd only paid for the eighteen days, then he may have made a loss on the cost of the expedition. I did not want him to make such a loss, but neither was I going to pay for services I'd not received. I reluctantly agreed to go on another nine-day journey with the same guide, to

Tazerzait well, eastern Aïr. © Klaus Weltzer

make up the time and see another aspect of the region, and to then pay for the full twenty-seven days. This time we'd go to see some rock paintings to the south-east, and the Falaise de Tiguidit, south of Agadez. The rock paintings, high on a bluff, were very interesting being of giraffe, ostrich and antelope and being several thousand years old. Now, however, the rate of travel slowed to a crawl on some days while we travelled through somewhat dull country, and we did not actually get to the cliff line at all. The last of the nine days were the longest – all I wanted to do was to get back to Agadez.

While the guide and I did not get along particularly well, he did take me to some fascinating places, and returned me safely to Agadez in good shape. We did see some spectacular country, oases, amazingly tough and friendly people, great fruit and vegetable gardens and beautiful villages, all the more interesting having been visited by camel.

Sudan and Sinai

Charles Foster

Travelling with camels can be difficult, frustrating and unpredictable. It can also be immensely exciting. It is the classic form of desert travel, and camels can take you to places that no four-wheel drive vehicle can go.

Camels are good at sand. If they are properly loaded and used to rocky areas, they are surprisingly good in mountains too. Be careful about rocky areas, though. If your camels are not used to rocky areas their feet will get badly cut, and then you have serious problems. Dromedaries (the one-humped camels you will meet in the Sahara) become miserable in the mud and the wet.

To hire or to buy?
You should consider buying only for long expeditions and if you have a great deal of experience. And if you are in those brackets you need no advice from me. But if you are a novice keen to buy, delegate the buying and the subsequent selling to someone local and trustworthy who knows the trade. If you do buy, make sure you build time into the expedition schedule to try your camels out. If you head straight out into the desert with the price tags still dangling from their ears you are unlikely to come back.

For short expeditions of less than a couple of weeks you would be stupid to buy. Hiring a camel at a sensible price probably means that you will get something capable of staggering round the course. Taking the hirer or one of his relatives with you as a guide improves those chances still further.

There are many types of dromedary, and a vast and fascinating literature which compares and contrasts them. In the Sahara the ones you are most likely to come across are the Mehara (pretty ubiquitous, but particularly in the north and central Sahara), the Hageen (mainly in Egypt), and the Beja and Anafi (common in Sudan and East Africa, but also often found in the southern Sahara). In practice there is a huge amount of interbreeding and pure strains are becoming the exception rather than the rule. You shouldn't worry about the reputations of the various strains: you should worry about the reputation of the man hiring you your camels, and the relative decrepitude of the generally unimpressive animals which you will probably have to choose from.

Pre-departure service

The front feet should be straightish, and the front legs straight and close together. The hind feet should be turned out slightly. The front 'elbows' should stand well clear of the chest pad. If you are taking your camels into mountainous areas or over lots of rock, smaller feet are an advantage. Big, dinnerplate feet are what you want if you have miles to go over soft sand. Uneven wear of feet indicates poor conformation, which itself can cause problems after a while, particularly in heavily-loaded animals.

Camels feet generally look cracked and dreadful. Don't worry too much unless the camel is actually lame. Anyone used to looking at horses will be horrified at the look of most camels' hind legs: they generally look wasted and uncoordinated. Cow hocks are pretty much the norm. Again, don't worry: most of the weight is taken on the front legs.

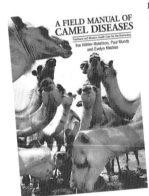

Strong shoulders are much more important than a powerful rump. The hump should be firm, not flabby. An overall picture of robustness is more important than fine points of conformation. A tremendous book on veterinary issues is the *Field Manual of Camel Diseases: Traditional and Modern Veterinary Care for the Dromedary*, by Rollefson, Mundy and Mathias (2001), published by Intermediate Technology.

You should forget most of what you have heard about camels' ability to go without water, and aim to water them at least every three days or so. You can, in fact, condition them to waterlessness over about a month, by progressively increasing the period of absence from water. If you do this properly you will eventually have a camel which can manage without water for about ten days. If you know that you are going into a wellless area for a while, it is important to make your camel drink properly. You can lead your camel to water and you can make it drink only if you give it no water for the previous four days or so. There is nothing cruel about this: it is physiologically sensible.

You cannot, realistically, carry enough water for your camels. Much of the weight they carry will be your own water. Your route and survival will be dictated by wells. Simply because a well is marked on a map doesn't mean that it will have water in it when you get there. Local information is crucial.

Camels can cope without water but need something to eat every day. If there is nothing to browse on, you will need to carry hay, alfalfa or, if (and only if) the camels are used to it, grain. Grain is best ground into a mash.

On the move

You will generally just use your camels as porters to carry your kit, but not you, and the lead camel will be led with a single bridle. It will take you a little while to learn the personalities of your camels and their relations with each other. Camel X will bite camel Y, but not camel Z. Acquiring this sort of knowledge will determine the order they adopt in your caravan.

Of course you can ride your camel, but, at least to begin with, it is a very **uncomfortable** business. If you want or need to try, use the bedouin style – with one leg held more or less straight, the foot of that leg resting on or near the camel's neck, and the other leg crooked round the pommel of the saddle and

Camel feet are made to spread the load on sand, like eskimo snow shoes. Weight for weight, on a human they would proportionally be the size of dustbin lids.

curled down near the other leg. If you try to ride the camel like a horse your crotch will be raw within the hour. You steer with your legs, the bridle and (very sparingly) with a stick.

Although top racing camels can clock 65kph (for very short distances) you should forget about all paces other than the walk. In practice, your expedition will move at your own walking pace.

Correct loading is all-important. Although a well-watered, well-fed camel in good condition should be able to carry 250kg, try not to average more than 150kg per load. An unbalanced camel is an unhappy one and symmetrical loading is crucial. Supervise this yourself, don't leave it to the camel boys. Remember that the front legs are much more powerful than the hind legs.

The day's routine is up to you, not to the guides you have chosen. Don't be bullied into a regime you don't like. What tends to happen is that you get up early, have breakfast, walk until late morning, and then stop in the heat of the day, hobbling or tying up the camels. You would then start up again at about 3pm, walking until the evening. Personally I hate the endless lunch times. Also unloading, hobbling, catching and re-loading the camels is a real hassle. I would rather spend all that time and energy making miles, and so I much prefer a longer, unbroken march. I also think that if it is really too hot to travel in the middle of the day, you might as well cut your losses and do all the travelling by night. In fact it is rarely, despite your guides' moaning, too hot to travel in the middle of the day.

Your guides will try to stop in the places where they and all the other camel drivers always stop. If you can avoid this, do so. Those places tend to be heaving with voracious camel ticks. There is nothing which spoils your enjoyment of the day quite as much as the discovery of a happy family of huge bloated ticks hanging onto your gonads.

Your food is, again, a matter for you. My staple is bread. I take sacks of flour and make bread by mixing the flour with water and pouring it onto the bottom of a wok-like pot heated on the fire. Or you can make rather thicker dough, wrap it round a stone, and bake it in the embers. Bread gets boring after a while, and you will want to supplement it with other things. Dates and other dried fruit are excellent: so is the dried cheese which is pretty ubiquitous throughout North Africa. Tins are nice, and convenient, but too heavy to be

practicable for more than very short expeditions. The dehydrated food you can get in any European outdoor shops is excellent.

A final word about guides: you need them, but do not rely on them. They will tell you that lots of things are impossible. That generally means that they cannot be bothered to do them. They tend to be highly conservative people, who resent being diverted from their usual routes and routines. Do not trust their navigation. If you leave your compass and GPS at home because you are in the hands of a local, you are being very foolish. Try to use guides who have been recommended to you by previous expeditions. And (of course) on no account pay them everything up front.

PART 5: IN THE DESERT

ON THE ROAD IN AFRICA

After hours of semi-comprehensible form filling you finally spring out of the port like a piece of wet soap. Now what? The temptation is to get moving. At both La Goulette (Tunis port) and Ceuta or Melilla (the recommended entry points into Morocco), you can avoid urban congestion and head south without delay. Once you get stuck in with the rest of them, North African driving is not so bad, but in either case try and avoid having your first African driving experience at **night**. The unfamiliarity with local road use and driving techniques added to the lack of visibility are too great a risk for a newly-arrived visitor.

BORDERS AND CHECKPOINTS

The vagaries of border crossings are perennial worries to travellers in Africa. Here are some guidelines; you'll soon develop your own strategies:

- Remain calm and polite.
- Be patient and smile a lot.
- Never grumble or show unnecessary irritation.
- Obey all the instructions for searches and papers.
- Accept delays, queues and sudden 'lunch breaks'.
- Never argue: bite your lip in the face of provocation.
- But do not put up with outright theft or strong hints for gifts; asking for a receipt often helps.

Inland borders, particularly south of the Sahara, rather than the busy Mediterranean ports, are where you may be given a hard time (Soloum, into Egypt, is an exception). Stoicism and good humour will defuse a tense situation. Try to remember that the glamorous benefits of a uniform and an old machine gun soon pale when you're living in a tin shed far from your family and haven't been paid for six months. Recognise that if there is something wrong with your paperwork they have a legitimate right to be awkward. Read the situation. If there's a need to make some payment, stick up for yourself, but in the end, pay up if you want to get moving.

It is important to realise that **bribes** aren't daylight robbery but a way of life in Africa. You may resent this custom but that's just what it is, a custom that oils the wheels. A couple of thousand CFA or a few euros can save hours, and these payments *are* usually tiny in the overall scheme of things. You'll know when you're expected to pay – accept it as part of travelling, but don't think you have to pay your way through every border.

Border procedures

Papers of different sizes featuring impressive stamps are much admired at African frontiers, and you'll amass a fair bit of locally-issued documentation once you start crossing borders. One traveller described the paperwork amassed at Soloum as a 'folder that resembles a post-grad dissertation'.

To give you an idea of what to expect, the most common documents and permits required for each of the Saharan countries are listed below, but these should be viewed as a rough guide only. Apart from visas, unless otherwise stated all these permits and documents should be obtained on site, at the relevant border or office. Some border officials may want to see vaccination certificates – Niger was once known to be serious about Yellow Fever inoculations, but few other countries bother.

Typical border procedure
- Fill out immigration card and get passport stamped.
- Fill out a similar form for your vehicle (your registration document will be needed): an *Autorisation de Circuler* or *Permit de Conduire* (Chad and Tunisia, where a PDC lasts 90 days).
- Fill out currency and maybe 'valuables' declaration form.
- Get carnet stamped (Egypt and Sudan only) or buy local carnet (Libya only).
- Change money.
- Get a temporary importation permit – *Declaration d'Importation Temporaire* – (for most countries which do not require a carnet). In Mali and Niger it is called a *laissez-passer*.
- Rent Arabic number plates (Libya and Egypt).
- Buy motor insurance (Green Cards are valid in Morocco and Tunisia).
- Get passport stamped by police within a week of arrival (Libya only).

Hazards

As you head inland towards the desert you'll soon encounter the broad range of African road users and road conditions. Semi-crippled trucks carrying impossible loads, jalopies lurching along at 20kph, pushy taxi and bus drivers, speed-crazed gangsters in tinted Mercs, donkeys and carts, old men on mopeds, pedestrians carrying tree trunks, deathwish touts blocking the road to sell you pots or pottery. Everyone fights for their bit of tarmac. It may not be as bad as somewhere like India but, along with the heat, culture shock and your aspirations in the desert, it's still nervously exhausting.

Unexpected diversions may give you a premature sample of African off-roading and as you get closer to the desert, dunes may blow across the highway: a much under-rated hazard that should not be driven over at full speed, no matter how smooth they look. Camels, too, may be grazing by the road and

RESPECT THE SAHARAN ENVIRONMENT:
A CODE OF PRACTICE FOR OVERLAND TRAVELLERS

In 2003, section 5.3.1 of a 78-page UNESCO report titled: *The Sahara of cultures and people. Towards a strategy for the sustainable development of tourism in the Sahara in the context of combating poverty* categorised Saharan tourists as 'excursionists', 'discoverers', or 'initiates'.

A final category, 'independents' was described as follows: *'These are essentially travellers who move around in complete autonomy, with their own 'super-equipped' vehicles, and make very little use of local personnel (sometimes a guide, on the understanding that the use of GPS provides access to all places, particularly neolithic sites). They consume lots of water and wood without necessarily realising what the consequences could be and make only minimal purchases in the countries they visit (food, fuel and craft products). As they are unsupervised, they often cause, through ignorance, irreparable damage to the environment and to neolithic sites. It would seem that their presence causes more damage than it might bring additional resources to those regions and their population. They are to be found in Tunisia, Morocco, Algeria and Niger, and less so in the Libya and Mauritania.'*

Some of the errors and exaggerations in the above are obvious; all that is missing are allegations of Satanic rituals and dolphin mutilation. Regrettably this is how overland travellers in the Sahara are being presented.

The ability to travel freely but hopefully responsibly is now being restricted in many Saharan countries. As so often happens, the actions of a few are ruining it for the majority. There is little doubt that poorly-trained local guides (see below) and other locals are as much to blame for the perceived environmental degradation, but it is now necessary to spell out a code of practice for responsible tourism in the Sahara.

• Respect local laws and religious customs (see p.294).

• Always ask people first if you may take their photograph or film them: this is a typical area of tourist insensitivity. Consider the rudeness of being photographed or filmed while walking down your own high street.

• Most local wood resources are not regenerating and are needed by nomads. In areas where there is no nomadism, dead wood may also be part of the local ecology. Cook on gas, and for camp fires bring easily found waste timber from home. Campfires are nice but there is no need for huge bonfires. If you're cold put on a hat!

• It should go without saying, but get into the habit of using water conservatively, both in town and on the piste.

• Most travellers bring way too much food from home. Plan to buy food and other provisions locally; there's more there than you might expect.

• Leave no garbage in the desert, even buried and including biodegradable matter. Burn what waste you can in a campfire or better still dispose of it all in town dumps.

• Avoid the use of detergents in the desert, especially near water sources. Their scent can repel animals which rely on waterholes or well troughs.

• If you need to drain motor oil in the middle of the desert, try your best to collect the waste and dispose of it responsibly; better still do it in a town.

• Think twice about making radical excursions off-piste that will leave clear and permanent traces of your passing.

• Bury all toilet waste at least a foot deep and make an effort to burn toilet paper after use and bury it in the same hole.

• Travel in small groups of fewer than a dozen people to lessen the impact on local resources.

In the end it all boils down to respect for the environment and the people who live there, as well as a desire to preserve the wilderness as you would wish to find it. As mentioned elsewhere, this may mean tidying up after your guides, but it is the responsibility of all desert users to preserve the wilderness for others to enjoy.

There are further guidelines on specific conduct in Muslim countries on p.294 and on appreciating the Sahara's cultural heritage in the box on p.399.

like any animal, should be approached with caution. Eventually, after a couple of days you arrive at the final threshold: your first piste.

Sharing the driving

On a good day's driving without long breaks, 200km is a reasonable distance to cover off-road. One experienced driver can manage this, but by the end of the day it sure is nice to stop. With other equally competent and willing drivers aboard, a couple of hours at a time at the wheel is ideal. This way no one gets either bored or worn out.

Being *allowed* to drive is another matter. It's common for male driver-owners not to want to relinquish the controls of their pride and joy to anyone, or for others to be intimidated by the responsibility of piloting a lumbering two-ton bus through the wilderness.

Conservative as this may sound, if it works best with Him at the wheel and Her over the stove, let it be so. The first few days on the piste will be tiring for everybody, both driver and passenger(s), as all accustom themselves to the new environment. Soon, everyone and everything settles into a routine and you can begin to relax and appreciate your surroundings.

Giving help on the piste

Because traffic is so light on desert pistes, in the Sahara it's customary to wave or flash lights at every passing vehicle, especially those parked by the side of the piste. On the highway, a stranded vehicle won't be stranded for long and it's up to you if you want to get involved in assistance. But on the piste, 'Hi/I'm OK/You're OK' waves are more important and if someone is clearly in trouble or makes a signal to slow down ('patting' the air as if bouncing a basketball), you should offer to help.

The problem can be sifting local chancers wanting a lift from those in genuine need – something you'll work out for yourself. Though more common along highways, some wily nomads will wave an empty water container, a plea some would find hard to turn down, and then once you've stopped ask for sugar, tea, cigarettes and whatever else they can think of.

Fellow travellers with a shared cultural background (i.e., other tourists) will only ask for help if desperate. Be aware that this could involve you in hours or even days of assistance. It sounds callous, but tourists generally help other tourists while locals might help each other as well as tourists – some will see it as a chance to make some cash, others will do it out of a sense of duty.

On my first trip to Algeria I had endless encounters on the trans-Saharan highway before I learned to park a hassle-free distance from the road. These offers of help soon got down to business: changing money or buying whisky. But later, when I was stranded on the piste and in need of help, passing drivers took their deadlines more seriously and no one stopped.

Another time, a little further south of Tamanrasset, a passing truck refused to give a lift to an injured rider I was carrying with some difficulty on the back of my own bike. And only a year ago I was lying crippled by the track when a tourist car drove up, looked down at me and drove on. Charming! Desert dwellers can be surprisingly hard and even mercenary, with little pity for stranded tourists. At times waving a wad of money rather than an empty jerrican or a bandaged arm may be necessary!

Offering lifts

In Africa the sign for a lift is an outstretched arm with a down facing hand, not an upright thumb. Again, giving a lift is up to you and it depends on the situation. In general, streetwise young men will try it on just for a ride in a cool car, while nomads or older men could do with a lift to the next village if local transportation is scarce. If there's no room, they can stand on the back bumper and hold onto the rack, although this is a bit mean for older travellers! Encounters with lone women are unknown and you're unlikely to have room for a whole family. Don't be too paranoid though. Giving a lift or other assistance can lead to interesting discussions, an insight into local life and even offers of hospitality which will enrich your travels.

Not so much fun is when you're forced to give a lift to a soldier or policeman, usually stranded at a remote checkpoint. Depending on your mood and the individual it can be an uncomfortable or interesting experience, but saying no is not usually negotiable if there's a roadblock involved.

Parking up

For lunch stops and overnight camps do yourself a favour by parking **out of sight** of the road or piste. Besides the safety factor of not getting run over or choked by dust from a passing lorry, this avoids giving an open invitation to hustlers and hassles – particularly relevant when you're close to a settlement. But even if you do think you're miles from anyone, it's amazing how often in certain countries you'll gather an audience emerging seemingly from thin air to inspect their evening's entertainment.

It's up to you how you react, but always bear in mind that your looks, clothes, equipment and behaviour are just as interesting to them as theirs are to you. Just as it's fascinating for us to watch a Mauritanian nomad woman weaving a mat, so it is a great source of fascination for them to watch tourists packing up their tents or fiddling about with a GPS. As often as not, you'll be invited to share tea with the onlookers, or even a meal.

Choosing a camping spot

Accept that not every desert camp will be a cosy locale with a backdrop of dunes and fluttering palms. **Shelter** of any kind is what you are looking for and it's common to keep going 'just over that rise' to find somewhere that feels right. It's hard to resist the impulse to gravitate towards any kind of 'shelter' even if it's just a mound of dirt or a car wreck on an otherwise desolate reg. This object

A quiet corner of the Libyan Desert.

anchors you in the sea of flatness and, however insignificant, is actually psychologically desirable for a comfortable night's rest, especially if you're alone or on a bike.

An old adage advises that you should **never camp in a oued** because flash floods from distant rains could rip through your camp causing havoc. Some sources have even claimed that 'more people have drowned in the Sahara than died of thirst' – about as likely as more people dying of thirst than drowning at sea, or freezing to death in the Antarctic. In Morocco, where the run-off from the Atlas can be frequent, steep and fast, this warning is valid in certain seasons but in the deep Sahara, oueds often offer some welcome tree shade or vegetated wind breaks, as well as soft sand rather than gravel. Obviously if there are dark clouds in the sky keep to the high ground wherever you are, but dangerous flash floods are only a real danger in mountain areas, and by the time they get to the plain they're all but spent.

Getting out of the **wind** is a more sensible concern, though as mentioned elsewhere, the wind often subsides with the Saharan dusk. A car-high dune or mound can make your evening camp much more pleasant as well as warmer. Before you set up camp, have a walk around to find the optimum position for your vehicle. A quick way to discern the strength and direction of the wind is to kick up some loose sand. With cars it's usually best to park the nose into the wind leaving the back sheltered, though this depends on your exact sleeping and cooking arrangements. With a bike, if you have no tent a line of baggage against the wheels forms an adequate windbreak for cooking and sleeping. If sleeping on the ground see the tip on p.151 about digging a sleeping trench.

This camping spot is already occupied.
© Yves Larboulette

Open water or damp oueds (or places where there are dead beasts) can be **fly-ridden** – another annoyance though generally only at hotter times of the year or maybe after rain. Mosquitoes, too, can be a nuisance further south. There seems to be no pattern to the location of moths nor a way of getting rid of them short of moving or turning off your lights. **Spiders** also seem to be attracted to bright lights but, as with **snakes** and **scorpions**, sightings are very rare in the cooler months when most tourists visit. Scorpions tend to live in rocky areas so avoid lifting stones with your hands or bare feet. If you're superstitious you might like to imitate the practice of the Nemadi nomads of Mauritania who draw the trace of a snake by their side before going to sleep in the hope that real snakes will keep away.

Almost perfectly **level ground** is more important than you think. Most nights this is not too hard to find in the wide, flat expanses of the Sahara, but sometimes the right spot that's out of the wind and feels right may not be quite flat. An easy way to level off a car on soft sand is to dig sand away from the side of the tyres on the high side. The wheels will sink bit by bit but won't bury themselves like a spinning wheel, so driving away next morning will be easy.

It's also worth noting that areas of loose sand will lose the day's heat quicker than rocky places. A night in the **dunes will be colder** than a camp among flat slabs of rock that retain their heat for hours.

Altitude, too, has a noticeable effect on overnight temperatures. Freezing nights are possible in mid-winter in far northern latitudes or at above 1000 metres.

If you end up near an encampment or village, decide whether you want

After a few days packing up quickly becomes a habit. Burn what waste you can and take the rest with you.

to join in with all the associated hullabaloo and opportunities for social interaction (if invited). If not, it would be best to move away a good few kilometres to ensure privacy and security (they may expect and appreciate it too). It can be quite unnerving when someone looms up out of the dark to 'say hello' when you're in your slippers and have your camp spread out all over the ground. Depending on their behaviour you never know if they are just being friendly, are on the scrounge or have other ideas. In this situation you may prefer to pack up your camp overnight to avoid the nagging fear of theft. This is the main reason why camping **out of sight** of the piste is such a good idea.

CULTURE SHOCK

One aspect of travel health that is rarely talked about is **stress**, usually what you come on holiday to get away from. It will come as no surprise that you'll find travelling in the Sahara just about the most stressful thing you've done in a long time, especially in the early days of your trip. Fears of getting robbed, lost or becoming ill are all the more acute when you're on your own with everything you possess for the next few weeks or months around you. The need for constant vigilance can lead to symptoms of stress: headaches, irritability and absent-mindedness. This kind of tension isn't made any easier by driving along remote tracks with only a little water and fuel for days at a time.

A common way to deal with these perceived threats is to move fast and get your dangerous escapade over with as soon as possible. I've experienced this nervous restlessness in myself and in others, and have recognised it for what it is: an inability to relax or trust anybody for fear that something bad is going to happen. This unfocused anxiety must be separated from the 'running for your life' panic, when your long-cherished adventure is falling to pieces about you. Getting back to a point of safety makes sense at this time.

Fortunately, this understandable paranoia slowly abates, especially when you've had a chance to get used to your surroundings and meet bona fide locals (as opposed to officials and hustlers), who'll offer you a generosity and hospitality that you rarely encounter elsewhere.

Try not to waste the trip for which you've planned so long in useless paranoia. Aspire to get as much out of the people you meet as out of the pistes you drive. It can help if you make things easy on yourself early on. Plan visits to intimidating cities on the way back when you'll have the experience to enjoy a souk and the space to carry home souvenirs.

Personal conduct in Muslim countries

The following advice all boils down to respecting local laws, customs and sensibilities. Many of them derive from the mores of **Islam** which, like other oriental religions, is much more a way of life than modern Christianity is. Travellers can feel excessively nervous about causing offence (especially for women), so that visiting the home of a traditional high-caste Arab, for example, can be a nerve-racking experience.

The best approach is simply to observe and mimic the behaviour of your host and those around you. It's worth noting that it is usually urban Muslims who are the strictest adherents to Islamic doctrine (aside from anything else, a 'more devout than thou' one-upmanship is often adopted to 'keep up with the Joneses'). Desert nomads, for whom life is hard enough without having to worry about impressing their neighbours, tend towards a more pragmatic interpretation of Islamic law.

Islam has great respect for Christianity with which it shares many early myths; Jesus Christ himself is mentioned as a prophet in The Koran and many Old Testament figures appear in both The Koran and The Bible: Abraham/Ibrahim for example. But when the conversation turns to religion, as it often does, Muslims will be contemptuous of anyone who denies the existence of a God so it's best to **suppress any atheistic principles** you may hold dear and call yourself a Christian or whatever.

The **left-hand rule** (a favourite of sniggering book reviewers) is commonly known. Muslims find our use of toilet paper as disgusting as we find their use of the left hand for the same purpose. However, hands are always washed and people do not struggle to perform daily tasks one-handed; like many taboos, this one has its roots in common, hygienic sense. Many of the guidelines listed below are also a matter of common sense:

● For even the most perfunctory exchange, always introduce yourself to strangers with a **greeting** and a handshake: *Salaam aleikum* is the opening greeting, to which *Aleikum salaam* is the correct reply (in shortened form). *Bonjour* will often do instead. Many Muslim men will not shake hands with Western women, though some may view them simply as 'Westerners' while others will get a cheap thrill out of touching a woman for any reason.

● During **Ramadan**, a month of daytime abstinence, Muslims do not eat, drink or smoke during daylight hours and as a tourist it's polite not to be seen doing the same. However, you won't get stoned for publicly breaking the fast and anyway travellers, Muslim or otherwise, are officially exempt from the rules of fasting. People can get a bit cranky towards the end of Ramadan, especially in hotter places but, compared to Arabia, travelling during this period in the comparatively moderate Saharan countries is no problem.

During Ramadan in some countries, Morocco included, sunset is marked by a siren and evenings can be very festive as the starving masses catch up on their drinking and eating. Not so handy when you're in a city is the same siren at 4am when they all get up again to get fed before dawn! Ramadan begins with the first sighting (from Mecca) of the new moon and in 2005 is set to start on 4 October and end around 3 November (the Eid al-Fitr festival is 4-6 November). Note: Muslim festivals are timed according to local sightings of various phases of the moon so it is tricky to date them for future years, but over recent years the dates have been ten or eleven days earlier each year.

● Especially in traditional or nomadic environs, avoid touching other people, passing things or eating with your **left hand**.

● Although hashish may be widely used in some Muslim countries, being caught in possession of hash or other **drugs** will carry stiff penalties. In Morocco, where smoking is widespread, use your wits: in the northern cities set-ups of all sorts are common.

● **Friday** is the Muslim day of prayer, so the weekend begins at midday on Thursday, when many shops and other services close until Saturday morning.

● Unlike some Christian churches, very few **mosques** are tourist attractions. Never enter a mosque unless invited to do so and, when you do, remove your shoes and, if not doing so already, wear full-length clothing.

● While in the desert, or in campsites, you may dress as you wish but, whatever the weather, **dress** conservatively in towns and don't imitate some crass tourists in singlets and shorts. To devout Muslims the sight of bare flesh is offensive and unequivocally provocative.

Hassle

Everywhere in Africa, the eternal difficulty is to distinguish people who are hassling you from those who are being friendly. Though much better than it used to be, parts of Morocco are the worst places for tourist hassle with Egypt along the Nile also hard work. Parts of Morocco (around Merzouga for example) can be hard to handle and even frightening – I've heard of people fleeing

Being a respectful tourist clutching a code of conduct can be challenging when surrounded by jeering kids. Keep your cool and remember the Arabic saying: 'Everything passes.'

back to Spain after just a few days and even being stoned while trying to help stranded tourists. It can be tempting to want to get your own back by making fools of your tormentors or losing your temper. Appreciate that, just like back home, anyone who approaches a tourist has something on their mind and it's not always to welcome you warmly to their country even if these may be their exact words! Anywhere in the world it will be the uninhibited, cunning and opportunistic who approach tourists out of the blue.

How you deal with it depends on your temperament, but overall the somewhat wishy-washy advice of attempting to maintain good humour is the only way. These people are experts in getting you to connect with them: asking in four European languages your name or which country you're from. Remember, once a conversation is initiated you can feel very rude wanting abruptly to truncate it. Your tormentor knows this well. If you don't want to get involved just respond to the initial greeting, smile and then shake your head indicating 'no'. Keep doing this and smiling and doing whatever you're doing and eventually they'll give up and zoom in on someone else.

Bargaining

Whether bargaining for souvenirs or negotiating for services, the first step is to appraise the object or service of your desires and ask yourself what you are really prepared to pay for it. Even if it's over the odds, once you've established this in your mind you should have no reason to feel cheated once you pay it.

When it comes to **souvenirs**, all the time-worn tricks will be tried on you: free shipping, two for the price of one plus a free tin pendant, but stick to your price unless you want the object at any cost. You may well be asked to 'give me your best price', but remember that if you do name a price you'll be obliged to pay it, so don't let any figure pass your lips that you're not prepared to pay.

Bide your time, for this is your greatest asset (along with the wad in your pocket). If you have the chance, look around for a few days and get to know the vendors and what they have (often it's all from the same source). If you find it hard to simply leave, say you might come back tomorrow. Try not to allow yourself to be intimidated, however charming the vendor. In Morocco be wary of being drawn in by a carpet seller to have tea unless you're confident you can handle the extreme pressure that may be put on you.

Agreeing a price for **other services** like mechanical repairs, guides or food is less customary. There's usually a set price for such commodities, certainly for guides and food (although one time at Essendilene Canyon in the Tassili the guardian was much more pleased to receive a sleeping bag as a tip than a few hundred dinars). Locals don't go to the souk every day and engage in protracted negotiations for the same kilo of nuts they bought last week. But if you

---

DEALS ON WHEELS

Establishing the true cost of vehicle repairs can be a bit tricky, especially if they can see you're stuck. One time in Morocco I needed a new wishbone for my Mercedes; it wasn't broken but would be soon if I carried on on the piste.

I stopped at the usual hole-in-the-wall garage and soon we were chasing a guy on a moped around town, from one place to another, before ending at a lock-up full of Mercedes wishbones. Not knowing what one was worth, I called a friend on the sat phone to get a UK price so I'd have a rough idea.

Having established that the used wishbone would fit my car, I was not surprised to hear an initial price greater than for a new one in the UK.

I scoffed at the price in the approved manner, telling him I could get one new for that and eventually, after playing on a few more swings and roundabouts, a price was agreed at less than a new wishbone but with labour included. This suited me fine as to make a mess of the job myself would have taken me days.

Two hours later the car was ready. Did I pay more than a local? Almost certainly, but I wasn't complaining. Right by the garage were the weathered ruins of Sijilmassa which I'd always wanted to visit.

feel you're being overcharged because of your nationality, give it a go or ask the price in advance. In some cases, not to barter is seen as weak and not playing the game. It's all part of the travel experience, with market encounters one of the few occasions you get to interact with locals as normal people. Enjoy it.

Begging and charity

Travelling through the world's poorest Muslim countries will expose you to the widespread practice of begging, from the plainly destitute but also more often from cheeky children. It's common to feel guilt at the thought of your indulgent adventure in the face of the extreme poverty you'll encounter. The gross imbalance of global economies hits you square in the face as you're confronted with millions of needy people and only one of you.

Over the years sponsored overlanders and rally teams got into the habit of throwing out branded commodities as they tore past, be they pens or lighters or stickers (some guidebooks even provide lists of recommended but compact handouts!). Their interaction with the communities is limited to a trail of dust and a glow of goodwill as they watch scores of kids scrabbling in the dirt for their presents.

Ask yourself why you're giving someone money – is it to make yourself feel less bad or to genuinely improve their lives? Begging is endemic in poor Muslim countries like Mali; the giving of alms is one of the tenets of Islam. But in nearby Guinea Bissau, for example, a Christian and truly impoverished country, begging does not exist yet the need is clearly much greater.

While your trip will at least open your eyes to the onerous lives of three-quarters of the planet, accept that you can't help them all. A simple policy to adopt is to give tips or gifts in return for actual help, be it directing you to the right road or hotel, looking after your vehicle or taking you to a mechanic. You may even be put up as a guest. If this happens one of the ironies you'll soon discover is that the generosity and hospitality or Africans is inversely proportional to their wealth. Poor people will ask for nothing but to have the honour of helping you. A small gift of cash or food may not be asked for, but will be greatly appreciated.

Out in the desert between the towns, the nomads living *en brousse* are at the end of the chain when it comes to material goods. Here donations of actual commodities are more useful than money. Food may seem like a good idea and you'll probably be carrying too much, but think about what you're offering. Chances are if they're living where they are they have food, even if the quantities and range are much more modest than yours. You may be tempted to proffer 'luxury treats' which you know they'd never have access to. In my experience this does not go down so well. As with other things, the tastes of nomads are conservative and a jar of pesto with sun-dried tomatoes and pickled anchovy fins may be sniffed at politely but quietly fed to the dogs later. Better to give less exotic products which you know will go down well.

Clothing can be much more useful. Few people realise that the clothes we give to charity shops do not end up being given away free to the world's poor people. They are sold through a chain of clothes traders and end up on sale in the markets of Africa or Asia. Here, for all but the desperate, there is much more dignity in choosing and buying the item you genuinely want rather than

SAINTLY GESTURES

One time a tour of mine was visiting the remote Tassilian village of Iherir. We were invited by the school teacher for tea that evening and arranged for a guide to take us up the valley the following morning.

At the same time I handed over a sack full of clothes, thinking they would be welcome in the narrow, sun-starved valley.

Next morning I noticed the same bag on the way to Djanet with one of the villagers. Oh well, direct action is a nice idea but whatever they could sell them for would still benefit the village.

Another time we were on tour in Mauritania with a Dutch guy who travelled frequently for business. Over the months he'd managed to amass a large stash of cosmetics from the flights and hotels he'd used. His entrepreneurial plan was to set up a little pitch in Chinguetti marketplace and sell Novotel-branded moisturiser and shower caps to the locals. When the day came his scam was a flop. Many thought he was giving the stuff away and when he demanded money they laughed at him.

Things weren't so funny when passing through Amguid village in Algeria one time. We were on our way back north but one of the group had just retired and still had some unwanted work clothing to give out. The fact that he'd wanted to record his largesse on videotape had always seemed a bit odd, but things turned ugly when the rabble stormed his car as soon as the windows went down. This was not the usual cheerful commotion of cadeau-chanting kids, but a truly desperate mob of all ages the like of which we'd never encountered before.

Suddenly faces became rather panic-stricken as his car was inundated with clawing arms and we all had to run for it.

But once out of range the guy got his shot. He pulled up and laid the bags of clothes on the ground and filmed the approaching mob from a safe distance. It was an ugly scene in more ways than one.

the mad rush of the doors opening on an upmarket jumble sale. Desert nomads will probably never get to these markets so a bin bag of your unwanted clothing and old sleeping bags can be most welcome. In mountain areas warm clothing is especially welcome, as is practical footwear and children's clothing. Obviously some consideration to local cultural values is required in choosing what clothes you give.

But just when you think your place in heaven is guaranteed, consider that one Saharan guidebook I read suggested that giving practical items like clothes to children is not always a good idea. The gift, while almost certainly passed on to a parent, can create an imbalance in the family dynamics as the parent is shown as not being the provider. Although this can be interpreted as another trip-wire along the convoluted path of politically-correct etiquette, it does sound plausible, so if you can hand over your gift to a person of responsibility, so much the better.

One thing is for certain: do **stop** and get out of your vehicle to hand over any items. Try to interact with the people respectfully even if, as is likely with desert nomads, you'll have no language in common. And don't necessarily expect effusive thanks; a request for a cig, tea or the shoes off your feet is much more likely!

LOCAL GUIDES

In some countries or parts of the Sahara, guides are obligatory: in the Aïr and Ténéré; in northern Chad; in southwest Egypt; and lately on crossing the border into Libya and Algeria (though these regulations may be relaxed one day). Sometimes this is done to ensure that the local economy benefits from tourism; to keep tabs on traffic; or because of sensitive border areas, mines; or for security reasons (as in Egypt and Chad). Elsewhere the regulations have been introduced to protect the heritage of the desert or as a response to the looting of archaeological artefacts and 'environmental damage' for which independent tourists are blamed. In other areas, hiring a guide can simply be the sensible thing to do; certainly in Chad this is the case at the moment.

In the Libyan Desert of Egypt it is also necessary to pick up a soldier from the border area as a **guard**. The actual usefulness of this guard is somewhat dubious as the guy usually sees it as a chance to slip into a civvy shell suit and be driven around and fed for a couple of weeks. He has no radio or firearm and is another body to feed and water. Libya also requires a policeman as well as a guide to travel with the group.

Guides can introduce you to exotic local customs.

Travelling with a guide can be a relief from endless route-finding and, if you share a language, a wonderful way of learning about the desert. A guide can also help speed you through checkpoints and show you things you might never see if blasting along alone. Modern maps and satellite navigation technology are no substitute for personal knowledge of a route. In fact the guides you hire may not know one end of a map from another. Instead they rely on memory and abstruse natural features to locate themselves. There is nothing mystical in this skill. At best they know their area intimately and even off track can make connections with landmarks, surface features, wind direction and the sun's position to see the big picture, even if they cannot necessarily pinpoint themselves on a map.

But being led by a guide can also detract from the satisfaction of fulfilling your own adventure. Learning the art of successful navigation is very satisfying and gives you a focus and a connection with the desert. But when added to all the other elements of independent travel in a wilderness (not least, the driving or riding), this can dominate a trip and make it less fun.

Having a stranger in your group or even in your car, and often an aloof or unapproachable one, can create unplanned tensions. It's not uncommon to be overly suspicious of a guide and wonder if you are getting your money's worth. Their personality and professionalism can be the key to giving you a miserable or a memorable experience.

Guides and escorts
In places where guides are obligatory or commonly used, you can be sure that there'll be plenty available for hire. In certain towns they'll seek you out, elsewhere you have to ask around or approach a travel agency; personal recommendations by past travellers are the best leads but, as with plumbers or solic-

This guide never said a word but would pop into the frame at every photo opportunity.

itors, these too can prove unreliable. Once a guide becomes popular he may become lazy. One good place to ask is on the forum of the website.

The big question is: what do you expect of a guide? Though it may change, at the time of writing, in Libya and Algeria you won't get past the border post without one. Recently I heard of a tour group whose guide turned up at the border in a normal car and dressed in a suit. Full marks for presentation but *nul points* for a functional vehicle.

Chances are this guy will be nothing more than an **escort**, taking you on an approved route along the highway, something you could do as well in a bus. He may know nothing of the desert and not even be from there.

This demonstrates a problem in the Sahara: very few guides are trained to work in tourism. In oil-rich Algeria and Libya, management of tourism has long been neglected as a secondary, seasonal and unpredictable industry. It's not helped by the fact that the governments of these countries are indifferent to the opportunities that tourism offers their southern populations. A barrel of oil does not demand an en suite hotel room with panoramic views across the erg.

This lack of **industry professionalism** is not at all unique to the Sahara of course. Anywhere in the world, where there's a chance of meeting foreigners and making money from them, there are bogus guides. Today's guides may have worked in mineral exploration, the army or as smugglers and bandits, and can now earn a living running tourists around. Letters of recommendation from former tourists can be easily forged and the prospect of easy money and a ride across country can inspire all sorts of tall stories. Be wary of school-aged hustlers and those guides who see your trip as an excuse for visiting all their relatives en route. Remember, your life may be in their hands, and just because they are born in the desert, it doesn't mean they're infallible – far from it.

In my experience Saharan guides seem to have very little **environmental awareness**, in particular to the disposal of rubbish (a concern more affluent Westerners can afford to indulge). And though they may know the locations of sites, they may have little appreciation or understanding of neolithic rock art, its origins or meaning. For them it's just a job to point places out. I've been shocked to turn up at campsites still littered from the rubbish left by the previous group and have regularly picked around the campsite in the morning, collecting combustible litter to throw into the fire.

Recently much was made of the litter collected on the Tassili N'Ajjer plateau above Djanet, only accessible to pedestrians and pack animals. It was used as an example of how unregulated 'mass tourism' was degrading the region. And yet as long as I have been visiting the Sahara, access onto the plateau and its world-class rock art required a permit from the Tassili N'Ajjer National Park and all groups had to be accompanied by a guide. The fact that they led, cooked and were responsible for these groups and the rubbish they left in the park seems to have been overlooked.

Another problem with guides arises when you want to take them away from their prescribed routes. Nervousness about the condition of their own vehicles can play a part, but guides also feel secure following their time-worn 'tram lines'. They can get distinctly edgy when asked to go into areas they don't know or which will push their vehicles hard. The fact that you have a guidebook full of proven GPS points may not necessarily make them feel any better. I've seen one driver (admittedly not the guide) literally freak out at the thought of heading into the dunes, grabbing a wheel brace and all the cars' keys, yelling 'we're all going to die!'.

On the bright side, when things go wrong a guide's familiarity with the local culture and of course the language can really help. Once when I wrecked a front propshaft in Ghat, our guide took my boomerang-shaped prop round the back somewhere and returned with it an hour later, as good as new. In fact the best guides are the ones you build up a relationship with over several trips; ones who become your friends and take an interest in your exploration. This mutual respect must be earned over time, which is as it should be, but is not always convenient to most Saharan travellers.

Guides' fees

Guides' **fees** vary according to the area, number of days, and sometimes the direction of the route. In the Ténéré, where guides are mandatory, plan on paying around €50 a day no matter how many vehicles, double that if they have their own car. It is a pretty average figure all around the Sahara, even in countries where fuel is much cheaper. For a one-way trip it is not unusual to have to pay for the guide's return fare by land or air.

If you're on a **motorbike**, you'll need to hire a guide with his own car, which will be more expensive. Otherwise, a guide can ride in your vehicle. Proper guides usually take care of their own provisions, except maybe water, but compared to tourists, true desert guides hardly drink or eat anything, often making do with a bag of dates, a bag of flour with which they make sand-baked bread, and with some mint tea.

Sociable guides will share their tea and bread with you, and it's polite to ask them to share your evening meal, but that's up to you – usually they will pick at your Western foodstuffs or politely decline.

Health

Deserts are sterile, barely-populated environments which makes them very healthy, at least in a bacteriological sense. Many of the lurid diseases one reads about in sub-Saharan Africa do not apply to the Sahara itself. Commonly-voiced anxieties about scorpions, spiders and snakes are also unfounded. In the cooler months these creatures are rarely seen and have little to gain attacking a human. There's also an unfounded squeamishness about drawing water from wells, more on which later.

In truth, the real threats to health are more mundane: **sunburn** or mild heat exhaustion are to be expected by new travellers, but **accidents**, usually associated with cooking or working on vehicles, are also common. Motorcyclists are a special case, with injuries from crashing heavy bikes in deep sand being a regular desert tale. Inadvertent **dehydration** can occur from persistent **diarrhoea** or working hard in the sun, while terminal dehydration can be avoided with adequate water capacity and sensible route-planning. Other than that, dry skin and lips are regular complaints but hardly life-threatening.

If you don't feel well after you come back, consult your doctor and tell them where you've been.

BEFORE YOU GO

The health advice given in this chapter is purposely brief. For expert advice you should consult your doctor or one of the specialist travel-health clinics listed below. You might also consider taking one of the many travellers' health books with you: *Bugs, Bites and Bowels* by Dr Jane Wilson Howarth (Cadogan) and *Travellers' Health: How to Stay Healthy Abroad* by Richard Dawood (OUP) are two well-established titles. Most travellers feel safer if they've taken out medical insurance for their trip.

Immunisations

To find out which immunisations are recommended for your trip, ask your doctor. A personal consultation with a travel-health specialist can often save you money as these people generally don't recommend jabs unless they're absolutely essential. This is particularly useful if you're only going to be travelling in the Sahara and don't plan to venture further south. Some diseases – such as malaria and meningitis – only present a significant risk in the warmer, southern parts of a country where there's lots of standing water and a higher population. Some diseases are also seasonal and the clinic staff will be aware of this.

Getting your jabs

These are the most common diseases for which you *may* require immunisation (in the UK, most of these may be given free of charge by your doctor):

● **Polio** This jab clashes with the Yellow Fever jab, so they need to be taken three weeks apart.

- **Tetanus**
- **Typhoid**
- **Yellow Fever** Of the Saharan countries, Chad and Niger are in the 'old' Yellow Fever endemic zone so a Yellow Fever jab and certificate are officially required for entry into these countries. They were regularly required at Assamaka frontier north of Agadez in the old days. Tunisia and Libya may also require proof of Yellow Fever vaccination if you have been in a country in the old Yellow Fever endemic zone (e.g. Chad or Niger) in the preceding six days. And all countries require the certificate if you have just left an infected area (most of sub-Saharan Africa comes into this category). In truth they are rarely asked for these days.
- **Hepatitis A** Try to get the ten-year Hep A vaccine rather than the Gammaglobulin vaccine which is only effective for three months.
- **Meningococcal Meningitis**
- **Rabies** The risk of being bitten by an infected dog is very small, particularly if you don't pet dogs. A vaccine is available but even if you've had it, in the unlikely event of being bitten by a rabid animal you'd then need a follow-up course of two further injections. Consult your doctor.
- **Hepatitis B** The disease is passed through contaminated blood products and unsafe sex. A vaccine is available.

Malaria: prevention and treatment

Most health professionals consider the desert to be a malaria-free zone. In addition, the non-desert regions of Tunisia, Libya, Morocco and Algeria are also classed as malaria-free zones although I once heard from a traveller who was convinced they had caught malaria in Tamanrasset (the population has boomed in recent years and there certainly are mosquitoes there).

In the Sahel region south of the Sahara malaria is still a risk. As malaria (or the dehydration caused by its fever) is the most common cause of death in the world, it's worth taking specialist advice on the risk it poses on your proposed route.

If you're advised to take **malarial prophylactics**, you'll need to start the course of tablets at least one week before you go and continue taking the drug for four weeks after you've left the malarial area. There is a range of different prophylactics designed to cope with the different strains of malaria; some mosquitoes are resistant to particular anti-malarial drugs. In all cases the prophylactics provide significant protection against getting malaria *but they cannot guarantee immunity*. One of the most commonly prescribed anti-malarials for Africa is Mefloquine, sold under its trade name Lariam, which can have serious side effects in some people, including severe depression, anxiety, nightmares and dizziness. If you are prescribed Lariam, consult your own doctor first and try to start the course two or three weeks before your departure so you have a chance to change to an alternative anti-malarial if necessary.

If you decide not to take malarial prophylactics but still think you may be at some risk of getting malaria you could pack an **emergency treatment for malaria** in your first-aid kit, which consists of a prescription-only course of quinine sulphate tablets and Fansidar tablets.

The best way to avoid malaria is not to get bitten by malaria-carrying mosquitoes. They are active between dusk and dawn and tend to hunt at ankle level so cover this area and all exposed skin with **mosquito repellent** or put your feet up. Indoors or out, use an inner tent if there are mozzies about. Avoid campsites near stagnant water and be aware that hotel bathrooms with leaking plumbing are also breeding zones.

Malaria symptoms and self-treatment

The **symptoms** of malaria are fever, headache and shivering, similar to a severe dose of flu and often coming in cycles; there can be additional symptoms too. As malaria can be fatal, you should watch for these symptoms at any time up to a year after entering a malarial area – this includes after you've returned home when you may be fooled into thinking you've only got flu. Therefore, if you develop a fever of 38°C or higher seven days or more after entering a malarial area you should try to get immediate medical help; a simple blood test will show whether or not you have got malaria.

If you cannot get immediate medical help, you should assume that you have malaria and give yourself the following **treatment** straight away. Take 600mg of quinine sulphate every eight hours for three days. After the last dose of quinine, take three tablets of Fansidar in a single dose.

ASSEMBLING A MEDICAL KIT

Organising an effective and compact medical kit is an important step in your pre-departure preparation. It's quite possible to make up your own kit based on the list below. Alternatively you could buy a pre-packed travellers' first-aid kit from a chemist or travel clinic.

A fully-equipped first-aid kit for two adults could cost you up to £150/€225, but the decision on how much medical stuff to take is, of course, a personal one. As with vehicle spares, it's natural to want to try and cover every eventuality when you expect to be several days' drive from help but, realistically, you need to be certain that you will be able to use your medicines and first-aid equipment when it comes to the crunch. For example, unless you really can envisage sewing up a serious wound, it's better to forego the needle and thread and opt instead for adhesive steristrips, which also close large wounds. This also applies to antibiotics and other prescription medicines which rely on you correctly diagnosing the illness before using the medication. If you or your companion start to feel seriously ill, the chances are that you'll head straight for the nearest health centre which – unless you're driving off-piste – probably won't be more than three days' drive away. Of course, you may be lost or unable to drive anywhere, in which case medical

---

MICRO FIRST-AID KIT

Over 25 years of desert travel I have found people's health fears are much exaggerated, as is the need for comprehensive medical kits and most inoculations.

I have had my own accidents and dealt with others' accidents but all I've needed are the following which I carry in my wash bag:
- Aspirin-type pain killers.
- Imodium-type 'blockers'.

- Wet wipes.
- Diarolyte rehydration sachets or isotonic drink powder.
- Ear sticks and ear plugs.
- For plasters I can use toilet paper and duct tape.

Splints and bigger dressings can be improvised from other materials.

self-sufficiency could be a life-saver. Or you may get to the clinic only to find that there are no medicines available to help you so you'll be pleased to have brought your own.

Once you've bought all the components for your first-aid kit it's essential to go through what you've got, reading the instructions for any unfamiliar medications and trying to visualise in what situations they'll be useful. To make treatment fast and efficient, it makes sense to assemble the kit in **easy-to-find sections** that are clearly labelled; you might therefore have separate bags for 'burns', 'wound-dressing' and 'intestinal problems'. Store your kit in a plastic lunch box or a canvas bag. Before you set off, make sure that everybody on the trip knows where the first-aid box is kept, what it contains and how to use it.

Once you're in the desert you'll almost certainly be asked for medicines by local people. Obviously it's up to you to respond as you see fit, but be aware that, if you're not medically trained, it can be dangerous to diagnose other people's illnesses and prescribe treatments, particularly as your patients may have a completely different approach to medicines. Two things that go down well with nomads and are much asked for are aspirin and eye drops.

Medical kit list
The following list includes basic **essentials** plus recommended additions.

General
● **Painkillers** In addition to curing headaches and period pains, aspirin and paracetamol reduce fever and bring down swelling and inflammation. Aspirin is the most effective, but some people are allergic to it, and it should not be used for snake bites.
● **Plasters** For blisters and cuts.
● **Sun block** Despite all your best efforts there will be times when your skin is exposed to the Saharan sun.
● **Insect repellent** Sometimes useful in southern regions.
● **Tweezers** or **sterile needle** Handy for extracting thorns and splinters.
● **Thermometer** Standard body temperature is 37°C.
● **Pre-moistened tissues** ('wet wipes').
● **Eye wash** Soothes eyes when irritated by sand and dust.
● **Moisturising cream** Hands and face can get sore and heels of sandalled feet can crack.
● **Lip-salve** or **Vaseline** for dry and cracked lips, a common ailment especially on bikes.
● **Multi-vitamins**.
● **Lacto-calamine cream** for soothing bites, sunburn and rashes.
● **Oil of clove** for toothaches.
● **General antibiotics** Prescription-only antibiotics such as amoxycillin or penicillin are good for a broad range of infections but should only be used as a last resort when medical advice is not available.
● **Sterile syringe set** to be used as an insurance against getting Hepatitis B, Aids and other diseases from infected needles in sub-Saharan hospitals where hygiene standards may be poor.
● **Scissors** – or use your penknife.

Gut problems and rehydration

- **Imodium** or **Lomotil** Anti-diarrhoea tablets.
- **Electrolyte sachets** Commercial powders for making rehydration solution; isotonic drink powder; rehydration solutions in bulk such as Gatorade. A self-concocted solution of sugar and salt will work as well (see opposite).
- **Metronidazole tablets** Prescription-only antibiotic for amoebic dysentery and giardia.
- **Laxative** for constipation.

Wounds

- **Antiseptic solution** and gauze swabs (cleaner than cotton wool), or swabs that are already impregnated with antiseptic.
- **Melolin dressings** Non-stick dressing for wounds.
- **Micropore tape** for binding melolin dressings.
- **Steristrips** for closing serious/deep wounds when stitching is appropriate but not possible.
- **Bandage and safety pins** for muscular injuries and immobilising limbs (e.g. with snake bite).

Burns

- **Jelonet dressing** Acts like running water to stop further burning and cools the burn down.
- **Flamazine cream** Prescription-only antibiotic cream for burns; also works for severe sunburn.

Limb fractures

- **Inflatable splints** (like tubular 'water wing' buoyancy aids) that slip around the injured limb to immobilise the fracture, though any rigid beam bandaged to the limb will do.

Malaria prevention and treatment

- **Malaria prophylactics** Check with your doctor or a travel clinic to see if they're necessary for you. An emergency course of quinine sulphate and Fansidar (both prescription-only). More on p304.

Coping with the heat

The most common cause of sickness and discomfort in the Sahara is, not surprisingly, **the sun** and **the heat**, wearing you down and drying you out. Prolonged sun on an uncovered head will lead to a headache by the end of the day, a common malady. **Wear a hat** and, to minimise the debilitating effects of the heat, **drink frequently**. After an effortful vehicle recovery or in hotter Sahelian countries you should also guard against the loss of mineral salts in your sweat by rehydrating yourself whenever necessary.

Sweating is the body's main thermoregulatory device and in hot climates sweating is always present even if, due to the aridity, it evaporates instantly and goes unnoticed. On your way south, as you learn to **seek out shade** whenever resting, your skin's sweat glands adapt to the increasing heat by secreting more sweat in order to keep the core of your body at the correct temperature of 37°C. Therefore as you acclimatise you will be drinking more water rather than less. **Thirst** is quite normal and should not be suppressed. Bizarre as it may seem, wearing trousers, hats and shirts with sleeves all help to keep the body cool. The less flesh you expose to the moisture-sapping air, the slower your sweat evaporates – hence the traditional nomad outfit of long-sleeved robe and turban. In fact, Tuareg men and Berber women actively try and make themselves sweat as much as possible by wearing indigo-coloured turbans and veils (dark colours absorb rather than reflect heat). These work as natural air-conditioning units, by trapping the sweat as it cools.

Less dramatically but more commonly, the hot, dry atmosphere can dry out your skin. The most vulnerable bits are lips, hands and, if you wear sandals, heels. You'll need plenty of heavy-duty moisturiser. If your heels get so cracked that they become painful, slather them with moisturising cream before you go to bed and wear socks overnight. Alternatively, wear shoes in the daytime for a few days, which will make your feet sweat more and help soften the skin.

Common health problems in the desert

Diarrhoea

Travellers' diarrhoea is common on any overseas trip and should be no reason for concern unless it lasts for more than a few days. It is caused by consuming mildly contaminated food or water and, having given you discomfort for a while, should flush itself out within 48 hours. If it doesn't it is faintly possible you might have got dysentery (see below) or something worse, so you should get medical advice as soon as possible.

The best way to avoid getting diarrhoea – or a more serious disease like dysentery, typhoid or Hepatitis A – is to be careful about your **food and water**. Disease-carrying bugs are most likely to be present in meals that have been re-warmed or left out in warm temperatures, in raw vegetables (salads) and unpeeled fruit (which may well have been fertilised with human or animal dung) and in raw and undercooked (rare) fish and meat. Be aware too that the camel and goat milk you may be offered by nomads is unpasteurised and could therefore create stomach problems. When cooking for yourself, always wash fruit and vegetables or, better still, use produce that you can peel.

If you get diarrhoea, stop and rest. Drink plenty of uncontaminated water, but don't eat much: plain boiled rice and soup are good; fried foods, coffee and alcohol are not. The main danger with prolonged diarrhoea is dehydration, as you lose water with every bowel movement. To guard against this, take rehydration solution or make some up yourself: **eight level teaspoons of sugar plus half a level teaspoon of salt per litre of water**. Try to avoid taking 'stoppers' like Lomotil unless you absolutely have to: your body is trying to flush out the bug, but stoppers delay this action and so your recovery. In practice, of course, taking these drugs makes travelling more tolerable.

Much less common is **dysentery**, a serious illness which feels like a severe form of diarrhoea but lasts longer. If you have amoebic dysentery, there'll be blood in your stools, but you need to have proper medical tests to diagnose any type of dysentery. Until you get medical attention you should treat dysentery in the same way as diarrhoea. Doctors and travel pharmacies can prescribe antibiotics for amoebic dysentery and you may want to add these to your medical kit just in case.

Thorns and footwear

The best way to avoid getting thorns in your feet is to **wear shoes**. Sandals are cooler and usually more comfortable but don't offer the protection of boots. Thorns can cause infections if they break off deep under your skin. Disinfect the area first, then try and dig under the thorn with a sterile needle before pulling it out with a pair of tweezers. If thorn wounds do get infected, they'll become painful and inflamed and you might need to resort to antibiotics.

Scorpion stings and snake bites

For tourists in the Sahara these are very rare and rarely fatal in adults. Neither snakes nor scorpions are aggressive and will only react violently when threatened. Therefore, avoid surprising them by lifting rocks under which they may have settled and carry a torch when walking around the camp at night.

Scorpions are said to prefer rocky places and are nocturnal, so avoid rocky campsites where possible. Shaking out footwear in the morning is a desert ritual. A scorpion sting is extremely painful and will swell up. The pain should only last for a few hours and the best way to treat it is to take aspirin.

Snakes are very shy but migrate towards sources of warmth at night, which includes you in your sleeping bag. The horned viper is the most dangerous of the Saharan snakes and likes to bury itself in the sand, waiting for its prey, but be reassured that even the most venomous snakes often bite without injecting enough venom to be harmful to an adult and that it can be a matter of days (rather than hours or minutes) before a person dies from a lethal bite, so it's always worth driving to the nearest medical centre. If you come up against a threatening snake, stand absolutely still until it moves away; snakes only strike at moving objects.

The first symptoms of a **snake bite** appear between fifteen minutes and two hours after having been bitten: expect double vision, sweating, increased salivation, faintness, diarrhoea, headache and/or pain in the chest or abdomen. The approved way of dealing with a snake bite is as follows:
● Keep the casualty calm. Panic increases the rush of blood round the body which also speeds up the spread of the venom.
● Wash the bite with clean water and soap to remove any venom from the skin surface. Remove tight-fitting clothes or jewellry that might constrict the bitten area when it starts to swell up.
● Keep the bitten area below the level of the heart and as still as possible to hinder the spread of the venom around the body. This can be done by winding a wide bandage around the whole limb, beginning with the bitten area, and using something as a splint as well. Do not apply a tourniquet.
● It may look good in Westerns but cutting the bite and sucking out the poison will most likely lead to infection.
● Treat the pain with paracetamol tablets, not aspirin, which can worsen bleeding problems in this situation.
● Get medical help as soon as possible.

Scalds and burns

Scalds and burns are common camping accidents, so be careful with stoves, boiling water and open fires. Never cook in the dark, make sure the stove and pots are stable, and drain pots using a sieve rather than a saucepan lid.

To **treat a burn**, you must first stop the burning by flooding it with cool water for at least 10 minutes. If water is scarce, either re-use the same water, use some other mild liquid like milk or canned drinks, or apply a water gel dressing (see first-aid kit). Don't remove any clothing that's sticking to the burn as that might cause infection, but cut away anything that might constrict the injured area when it starts to swell up. Cover the injured area with a sterile dressing or very clean non-fluffy material or plastic bag to stop infection getting in, but do not put ointment or adhesive tape on the burn and do not burst any blisters. If the burn is extensive or deep there is a real danger of serious dehydration so you should drink lots and take rehydration salts. Extensive and serious burns need medical attention as soon as possible.

Protecting your eyes
Sunglasses are essential in the desert, not just for cutting down the glare and so avoiding headaches, but also for keeping the sand out of your eyes, particularly on windy days and when digging your car out. The curved sunglasses that protect the sides of your eyes are best; if you're travelling by bike, goggles are essential and they may be useful on a camel too on windy days. The best way to soothe and bathe gritty eyes is with an Optrex-like eye bath; basically a saline solution.

In practice, **contact lenses** are less trouble than you might expect but take spare glasses as it's easy to get sand embedded in the lens. Alternatively, take a big supply of daily disposable lenses.

Rabies Avoid petting dogs or any other mammals, even if they are not foaming at the mouth. Excitable dogs are a common sight around villages and seem to go for bikers and cyclists. At all costs avoid being bitten by any beast.

Vehicle accidents
Drivers, and especially riders, should bear in mind that in the case of a serious accident in the desert, medical help will be a long time in coming. If you do need intensive care or a blood transfusion you should be aware that not all African blood products are screened as rigorously as they are in Europe. To avoid the need for any of this be alert, rest often, avoid congested cities and regard other road users as a threat.

Water

In winter it's surprising how little you need to drink in the desert. You may wonder what all the fuss is about. But attempt any work such as digging a car out of the sand and, even in January, you'll soon get a parched mouth in the dry air. If you allow your body to become weakened by dehydration you risk exposure to all sorts of other ailments. Start the day with a full water bottle, keep it handy and use it. Nomads have made an art of water conservation, a habit that takes a lifetime to learn. You may rarely see them drinking and think, if they don't why should I? The fact is your body and your behaviour are far from acclimatised or accustomed to the dry desert, so your water needs are greater than theirs.

Water is as crucial for you as fuel is for your vehicle. At the start of a piste never miss the chance to top up your tanks, hoping that just a jerrican or two will do. Aim to carry **five litres per person per day in winter** and the capacity for double that in spring or autumn, *plus* an emergency reserve. It will in most cases remain half-used by the time the stage is complete but that's as it should be; this reserve could save your life.

WATER AND THE HUMAN BODY

In hot climates (i.e., well into the tropics) you'll be amazed how much water you'll need. Drinking ten litres a day is not uncommon in the Saharan summer and just sitting still in 38°C without shade you're losing a litre an hour. At this rate it takes just five hours for you to become seriously dehydrated and in less than two days you'll be close to death (see the Blenheim story on p.351). In the very end, when everything else has broken down, run out or fallen off, it will be your water that prolongs your life.

Dehydration

The average male, weighing 70kg, is made up of 50 litres (50kg) of water. If even just a small percentage of this volume is lost through sweating, urination or vomiting, the individual will soon begin to experience some of the following symptoms of dehydration:

Water lost	up to	Symptoms
5%	2.5 litres	Thirst, lack of appetite, nausea, headache, irritability, and drowsiness
10%	5 litres	Dizziness, difficulty in breathing, slurring, clumsiness, lack of saliva
20%	10 litres	Delirium, swollen tongue and throat, dim vision and deafness, numb and shrivelled skin

Thirst is of course the first sign of the need for water and this impulse should never be suppressed. Reining in your drinking habits is the last thing you should do. If water is scarce and you can't get more, save on washing and be frugal with your cooking needs; in the desert you should always use water conservatively anyway.

Dehydration is not always immediately obvious in hot, arid climates where sweat evaporates instantly. For this reason (as well as to avoid sunburn) you should imitate the locals by **covering exposed skin** and your head as well as always seeking shade. In autumn or spring in the far south the ambient temperature can exceed body temperature (37°C) so unless you have air-con you should actually *wrap up* to keep the hot air off you – or expect vastly increased water consumption. With engine heat and the sun blazing in through the windows, the inside of a car can reach the mid-40s – it may well be cooler outside! Having the fans full on and windows and vents open may be the only way to cope but is a way to dehydrate very fast. On a **motorbike**, sealing all your clothing apertures creates a mildly humid and cooler sub-climate around your body and greatly limits water loss. You'll feel hot but you'll slow down dehydration.

Extreme and **fast dehydration** can be felt as a progressive drying up of the gullet, something I've read about and encountered myself while riding through hot winds in Algeria. The dryness inches down your moist throat, which becomes parched from breathing very hot air and gradually dries you out from the inside. With ambient temperatures at around 45°C you realise just how quickly you'd die without water and shade, and such temperatures are normal on most summer days, even in Morocco or southern Tunisia.

As a rule you should **urinate** as often as is normal, about four to five times a day. The colour of your urine should also remain the same as normal. A darker shade of yellow means your urine is more concentrated because you're not drinking enough or are losing more through sweating. Drink more water.

Don't forget that having **diarrhoea** is also a fast way of becoming dehydrated (see p.307 for more).

Salt and the body: isotonic drinks

When replenishing water lost from the body, attention must also be paid to **minerals** lost in sweat. The correct combination and concentration of salts is vital to the body's electrolytic balance. This governs the transmission of nervous signals to the brain and explains why your senses become impaired as you become seriously dehydrated. A slight salt deficiency manifests itself in headaches, lethargy and muscle cramps, though it can take a day or two for salt levels to run down enough for these symptoms to become noticeable.

If you feel groggy, taking some **salt in solution** may make you feel better. In fact, after any exertion, such as recovering a car from a deep bogging, a cup of slightly salty water or, better still, a swig of an isotonic drink instantly replenishes the minerals and water you lost during that activity. If you don't want to contaminate your water bottle with salty water and don't have a cup handy, lick the back of your hand, sprinkle on some salt, lick it off and swig it down with some water.

However, **too much salt** in one go (easily done with salt tablets; avoid them) will make you nauseous and may induce vomiting, which means that you lose fluid and so return to Square One. Remember, salt must be ingested with a substantial volume of water. As you become severely dehydrated your body's salt levels actually increase, and taking too much salt at this stage would be catastrophic.

A **rehydration powder** such as Dioralyte, available in sachets from chemists, is designed to replenish lost minerals including salt and sugar and is an essential part of a first-aid kit. Dioralyte is expensive for what it is, so you want to keep it for when you're feeling really rough. So-called **isotonic sports drinks** like Gatorade or Game are a more economical way of doing the same thing but they do lack the precise medicinal range and balance of minerals found in rehydration powders.

Taking regular but moderate doses of salt in hot climates is the best way to prevent feelings of lethargy and possible illness, and it's a good idea to get into the habit of salting your evening meals.

We also found that a lunchtime mug of Japanese instant miso soup was a

If only finding water was always so easy.

good way of keeping our salt levels stable. On one trip, a German we were travelling with proclaimed miso to be the most refreshing drink he'd ever tasted – but we were all pretty thirsty by this stage. Any salty soup will do.

WATER PURIFICATION

The desert is a sterile environment and in the cooler northern Sahara water is usually clean enough to drink without the need for purification, though this doesn't stop some travellers treating their water to be on the safe side. I'm far from immune to stomach upsets but have travelled right across the Sahara drinking water straight from wells and taps without getting ill at all. Anything from a tap is safe to drink in most cases and, as in Europe, bottled water is commonly available in just about all Saharan towns.

Contaminated water is more common around south Saharan settlements where even in winter (better described as the 'dry season') it's always hot. In conjunction with concentrated populations, poor sanitary conditions, unhygienic practices and grazing stock, this all adds up to a health risk to locals as well as yourself. If you're travelling in West Africa, including southern Niger and Mali, you should consider water purification.

Purification and sterilisation

Purification cleans the water physically (i.e. of sediment) as well as bacteriologically. Sterilisation only cleans the water bacteriologically, enough to make it safe but not necessarily palatable.

Water can be treated in one of three ways:
- Boiling for at least two minutes
- Sterilising with a chemical such as chlorine, iodine or silver
- Filtration

Boiling takes time and fuel and, as with the use of chemicals, does not clean impurities from dirty water. It's more of a fall-back should you have no other means of purification.

Sterilising tablets (or liquids) are a more efficient way of getting pure drinking water but can give the water an unpleasant taste (especially chlorine- or iodine-based agents). Some need from ten minutes to two hours to take effect, and they don't clean the impurities from dirty water. Of these, Katadyn's expensive silver-charcoal Micropur tablets do the best job without giving any unpleasant aftertaste. Iodine tablets are expensive compared to iodine tincture (solution) available from chemists, but they do avoid the possibility of a poisonous overdose.

For well water heavy with sediment, **filtration** with a reusable canvas **Millbanks bag** is the traditional solution. This removes cysts in which some bugs like giardia or amoebic dysentery lie dormant. Unfortunately Millbanks bags are so slow you could die of thirst watching one do its job, so they too are best used as an emergency back-up rather than part of a daily ritual. If you're desperate to clean sediment from water, any cloth will do.

The best solution to clean and clear water is a **water filter with a microporous ceramic core**, possibly complemented by other sterilising elements. Any filter with a ceramic core needs to be pumped, either manually or electrically, but it's the quickest way of safely cleaning even the dirtiest of water. Efficient manual units are compact enough for motorcyclists and cyclists. In a car you're much better off setting up an electrically-pumped system. In the UK various overland outfitters sell inexpensive water purification units comprised of a pump with pre-filter and a large ceramic core with a tap and sometimes a shower attachment. The hose can be attached to your water tanks or dropped into a jerrican. The components to make similar units are available from all the main Sahara outlets in Europe. Avoid anything with siphons or hand pumps. Modern electric water pumps which are activated by the drop in pressure as you open a tap take very little power from the battery. All ceramic-core filters need to be brushed clean occasionally with clean water, especially if they've been drawing on heavily-contaminated water. Take care with the brittle cores; if they crack they'll need to be replaced.

A word on **showers**. They sound like a nice idea, especially in the humid Sahel, but they can easily use up to five litres of water just to wet, wash and rinse an individual: all rather a luxury in the desert. Unless you're camped close to a well, save water by not washing till you must, or by taking a standing bath with a flannel. It may feel less refreshing but it can be done with just one litre of water.

WELLS

The surface of the Sahara is almost totally arid but in many places water can be found just a few feet below ground. Over the centuries the desert's inhabitants have dug and maintained wells at these key places, wells which have enabled trade to continue as the process of desertification increased over recent millennia.

Most of the time you can fill up from a tap in town (usually at the fuel station) and carry sufficient reserves to get you to the next. However, in warmer conditions or on longer pistes, you'll find it desirable to replenish your water from wells en route. Wells are a fact of life in all Saharan countries and are marked on

A lone Chaamba well in the Grand Erg. (Route A1)

Fill 'er up please. A Moorish nomad tops up his camel at the Dahr Tichit services on Route R11. © Karim Hussain

all good maps – though this should not be taken as a guarantee that they're still usable. The Michelin 741 map marks many wells in the Sahara with handy tips such as *forage artésien (sulfureuse)* or *eau bonne, trés abondante;* or else warnings like *eau bonne à 8m, puits dangereux* or even *eau mauvaise.*

All frequented pistes will have a well somewhere along the route, which may also support a nomadic encampment. Ancient, hand-dug wells are often found in canyons, along water courses and in depressions. Modern wells can be drilled anywhere. In mixed ground, wells can be hard to find, even with a map location or a GPS waypoint. In this situation it's best to use your instincts. Read the terrain around you, looking for tracks or other signs of visitation. A concentration of trees or even green bushes will identify the presence of underground water. Nomad encampments are usually near wells but rarely right next to them for the sake of privacy, hygiene and over-grazing. For similar reasons you may find it undesirable to camp too close to a well.

Using wells

In the French colonial era many wells were ringed with concrete walls to keep out sand and dying animals. In the Sahel, village wells that are used to irrigate gardens might still have a crude pulley system fashioned from forked tree trunks and a wheeled beam. Some wells even have a rope and bucket, usually based on a sewn-up inner tube, which is more robust than a plastic or metal bucket. However it's best to be prepared with your own rope of up to 30m length and a collapsible bucket. Ten litres is about as much as you can comfortably pull up – anything more soon gets tiring even with a pulley.

Any locals present will often look on pityingly as you struggle to flip and sink the old tin can or inner tube. Or else they'll insist that the incompetent traveller stand to one side as they lean over the well, elbow on one knee, expertly flipping the container and swiftly drawing it up in a few strokes using the full height of their upwardly stretched arm. Water drawn like this is very rarely paid for, although a well-keeper might be tipped for his trouble.

Should you arrive at a well just as a camel herd has taken its fill, you may find the well virtually empty. An overnight wait can see the water rise again.

Frequently-used wells often appear dirty, with litter, animal dung and flies. But this does not mean the water will be unclean; there is no way that crap or flies can harm the water in the well. Tourists are often squeamish about using well water and load it with tablets, but this water is as pure as it gets, so enjoy it.

Nevertheless, as the Michelin map's descriptions suggest, ground water can be **tainted** with the taste of minerals such as salt, magnesium or, at worst, sulphur or poisonous chlorides. Dying animals falling into a well are much more ruinous and will soon render the water undrinkable. The well at the famous Arbre du Ténéré in Niger, on the 700km Agadez–Bilma caravan route, became polluted in this way. The replacement well at 40m is still classed as *très mauvaise* on the Michelin but the water is fine to drink.

Working wells should have ropes and 'inner tube' buckets, but don't depend on it.

If you do find yourself drawing from a well with tainted water, you could save time-consuming filtering by using unpalatable or unpurified water for washing and cooking and keep your better-tasting drinking reserves separate. This is one of the advantages of individual water containers as opposed to having one large tank (see p.140).

Respect this most vital resource of the desert. For you it may be an earthy novelty but for the locals, the lives of their animals and family depend on the well. Avoid larking around on the lip of deep wells or jumping into shallow ones for a bath. Pulling the water out for a wash is much more refreshing and does not contaminate the well with **detergents** which can put off or poison animals desperate for a drink.

Keeping your water cool

The traditional way of carrying water through the desert is to keep it inside a goatskin bag known as a **guerba**. The goaty taste is said to disappear after a few years, and the guerba can be slung over a camel, the outside of a car, or even a shoulder.

The main principle behind the guerba – aside from being a typically innovative use of locally-available materials – is that water evaporates through the skin and thereby keeps the contents cool. The drawback of this method is that water is wasted through the evaporation process.

Modern canvas 'guerbas' hung from the outside of the car reproduce this cooling effect a little more palatably but with the same inefficiency. A less wasteful way of cooling a water container is to wrap it in a damp cloth – as the towel dries out it cools the water, the principle behind those felt-covered ex-army water canteens you still occasionally come across.

In practice these methods are interesting to try out but rarely necessary, even in the Sahara. As long as water containers are kept out of the sun it's rare that the contents get too hot to drink.

Navigation and maps

The Sahara can at first sound a daunting proposition for navigation: an arid wilderness with few landmarks where the consequences of getting lost could be fatal. In fact, route-finding is relatively simple: the few landmarks that exist are usually clear, visibility and weather rarely pose a problem in the cooler months, the entire Sahara is mapped, and in just about all cases you follow a fairly well-defined track – or **piste**, to use the accepted French term.

And this is even before you consider the benefits of GPS. So long as you're equipped with sufficient fuel and water to cover unexpected delays and emergencies and follow the simple guidelines outlined here, you should find Saharan navigation quite straightforward. If you do get lost or disoriented, the best thing you can do is keep a clear head and either stop and work out your error, or try to return to the last point at which you weren't lost. You'll find more detailed advice on not getting lost and what to do when things go wrong below.

NAVIGATION

Successful navigation anywhere requires keeping track of just two things:
- Where you are.
- Which way to go.

To navigate effectively and independently you'll also need most of the following aids:
- Maps to a suitable scale.
- Route descriptions, if available.
- GPS receiver.
- Hand-held compass.
- Distance-recorder or trip meter (incorporated in your vehicle's speedo or in your GPS).

Even with all-singing, all-dancing GPS, maps are vital to desert navigation. © Yves Larboulette

Other useful items include a transparent ruler, pencil and eraser, a roamer (see box p.327) and, even if you don't wear glasses, you might find a magnifying glass useful for reading maps.

For the sake of simplicity, and because it deals specifically with the Sahara, this chapter assumes you're in the northern hemisphere. Some navigational factors will be reversed if you are south of the equator, in which case you're a long way from the Sahara and are already lost; not a good start.

For many this compass may be elementary, but it's worth identifying the **cardinal points**, in particular the intermediate points – ESE, NNW and so on – which are regularly referred to in the itineraries later in this book.

The direction of **north** is the fundamental reference point of navigation. With this immutable point you can reliably calculate your desired orientation. You don't have to know the position of north to a precise degree, usually a general direction to within 20° will do.

This is most easily done using the **sun**. In the northern hemisphere the sun rises in the east and sets in the west. In the cool months it occupies the position of due south at midday, so shadows always point north at this time (but see below). At mid-morning the sun is to the south-east and at mid-afternoon it's in the south-west, more or less.

Try to become familiar with sun angles and so the direction of north. If you happen to have a watch with hands, point the hour hand at the sun: halfway between '12' on the watch and the hour hand will be south. North will be behind you.

North	0°
NNE	22.5°
NE	45°
ENE	67.5°
East	90°
ESE	112°
SE	135°
SSE	157°
South	180°
SSW	202.5°
SW	225°
WSW	247.5°
West	270°
WNW	292.5°
NW	315°
NNW	337.5°

Position of mid-day sun at different times of year.

In the Sahara the sun does not always appear to the south at noon. Because the axis of the earth's spin is not quite perpendicular to the earth-sun direction (the explanation for seasons) the sun's overhead position 'oscillates' over the equator through the course of a year. The **Tropic of Cancer** (N23° 27'; more or less the latitude of Dakhla, Tamanrasset and Kufra) marks the northernmost reach of the midday sun on 21st June. At noon on this day the sun appears directly overhead on the Tropic, with no noontime shadows. Should you find yourself **south** of the Tropic of Cancer during the summer, the midday sun may actually be to the north (depending on the exact time of year) so is not a reliable indicator of north. Rely on a compass at this time of year.

Compass

Anyone travelling through the Sahara should take a **hand-held compass** as well as the more essential GPS unit. Not only is this a sensible and potentially life-saving back-up if your GPS or its batteries fail, it's also more useful than a GPS for taking static bearings. When taking a bearing at a standstill with a hand-held compass, always use it away from the vehicle (say, ten paces) to avoid magnetic interference. Hand-held compasses are also useful for times when you leave the vehicle to explore dunes, scramble around rocks in search of rock paintings, or walk out in an emergency. The best hand-held-compasses are those made by Suunto or Silva. Models with sighting mirrors are not really necessary; the orienteering models with a clear base and a neck cord are ideal.

Assuming there is no magnetic interference, a compass always points to the **Magnetic North Pole**. This is not the same as True North, the geographical point in the Arctic Ocean which, with its southern counterpart, mark the **axis points** on which the earth spins. The position of magnetic north is always somewhere north of Canada, but varies with the earth's oscillating magnetic field, altering its position a bit every year. From Europe and North Africa magnetic north is currently a couple of degrees west of true north; the deviation is not large enough to worry about.

When talking about compasses it's worth mentioning magnetic **inclination** or 'dip' at this point. In different latitudes the earth's magnetic field dips at different angles, being horizontal to the ground only on the 'magnetic equator' while near the magnetic poles this dip is almost 90°, with the lines of magnetism going nearly vertically into the ground. Aware of this problem, quality compass manufacturers balance the needles of their compasses to keep them level in the compass housings, marking the housings with the Declination Zone for which they are balanced. The Sahara falls within the **NME** (North of Magnetic Equator) zone. Europe falls in the adjacent MN (Magnetic North) zone but an MN compass will still be balanced well enough for the Sahara. However, if you happen to have bought your compass in Tierra del Fuego or Tasmania with 'MS' (Magnetic South) stamped on it, the unbalanced needle may drag against the housing in the northern hemisphere and give irregular readings.

A compass for your vehicle

When used in or close to a vehicle, a magnetic compass becomes unreliable because of the massive interference from the vehicle's metal body and electric field. To counteract this interference, special **vehicle compasses** are available, fitted with magnetic compensators which are adjusted to correct the reading. At least that's the theory. As anyone who has tried to align such a compass may know, it can be a frustrating and often unsuccessful job. You get the compensation correct in one position, only for the needle to swing way out of true when you turn the car in another direction – a process that can go on for hours. Dashboard compasses look cool and it would be useful to recommend one, but in my experience only certain models work reliably in certain vehicles.

It's much better to rely on **GPS receivers** which have a built-in compass indicating true north once you're moving (some can now get a bearing at a standstill). The GPS' compass works off satellite readings, not the earth's magnetic field, and this is the compass to use on the move. A hand-held compass used away from the vehicle is a more dependable aid for taking static bearings.

GPS

A GPS (Global Positioning System) receiver is an inexpensive hand-held navigational aid which reads signals from 24 stationary satellites to pinpoint your **position** anywhere on earth with an accuracy of a few metres; pretty

A Thuraya sat phone (with GPS) and a Garmin 72 at the Greenwich meridian (0°W) in London. Neither was right but both were close enough.

impressive. As well as your position, a GPS can also show your **speed** and, once moving, your compass heading or **bearing**. It also has the capability to calculate much else besides, including how far you are from a particular landmark – or '**waypoint**' in GPS terminology – that you've stored in the GPS's memory, in what direction that waypoint lies, and even how long it will take you to get there at your current speed. GPS use has become common in everyday life and not just in the desert or at sea. They are used in construction, surveying and transportation services, and many top-of-the-range cars and some

---

VEHICLE ODOMETERS

Most piste descriptions and distance measurements, including those in this book, begin and end at fuel points, fuel usually being the factor which limits your range. However, your car speedometer's trip meter (odometer) is not an accurate way of measuring true distance.

Fitting **taller than standard tyres**, especially 7.50 or 9.00 Michelin XSs, with their increased circumference, will alter the speedometer reading of your car. Gear ratios will also be raised (higher ground speed per gear at the equivalent engine speed). This may not be immediately apparent but the speedometer's accuracy and fuel consumption calculations – both critical in the Sahara – may read up to 15% **below the true figure**. According to the speedo your car will appear slower and according to the trip meter your fuel consumption will appear worse.

This error translates to having travelled an indicated 500km but having actually covered over 550km, which can result in **navigational errors**, for example when looking for turn-offs on the piste. It's when back-tracking to correct mistakes like this that your fuel reserves can get used up. **Incorrect fuel con-**

sumption gets confusing when you're running low at the end of a long stage. You must know how far you've travelled and how much fuel you're using as exactly as possible.

It's possible to get speedos recalibrated but if you're swapping back to standard tyres when you get home it's simpler to ignore your car speedo and learn to use your infinitely more accurate **GPS** for precise speed, distance and therefore fuel consumption calculations. You can measure your speedo's error (as well as the precision of your GPS) on any European motorway. They all have small white marker posts, set at 100m intervals (even in the UK) and marked with metric distances. Measure a set distance (16 posts almost exactly equal a mile) against your speedo's reading to calculate the error.

UK drivers with **mph speedos** have all the more reason to ignore their odometers as all distances given in this book's routes are in kilometres, as are all road distances in the Sahara (conversion tables appear on p.650).

Motorcyclists, too, would do well to check the accuracy of their speedo which in the pre-GPS era was vital for keeping tabs on fuel and distance. Calculate the error if not using GPS speed-trip readings full time.

motorbikes now feature built-in GPS received and mapping software to provide real-time navigation. In the coming years GPS technology is destined to become even more widespread.

The two dozen satellites which are the space segment of the Global Positioning System are owned and operated by the US military. Russia also has its own version called GLOSSNAS, and the EU and Japan are working on their own. For the moment the US-owned and operated system is the one which all civilian receivers use – and for the moment it's free.

To give an accurate position or **fix**, a GPS unit needs to receive signals from just three but ideally four of these satellites and, so long as you're not in an enclosed space, it should take less than a minute in the ideal circumstances of flat terrain and clear skies that you find in the Sahara. Once your unit has locked onto available satellites, readings are given continuously and nearly instantaneously as you move along, until you turn the unit off. Any information stored up to that point will not be lost. Turning it on again will require a minute or so to get a new fix.

Travel though the Sahara is one of the few terrestrial situations where the potential of GPS is genuinely useful. Since the early 1990s their evolution has transformed desert navigation from a sometimes hit-and-miss affair to one with the ability to pinpoint any location in the desert within a few metres – an incredible feat. There has been the inevitable backlash, with some purists claiming that a GPS makes travelling in the Sahara too easy. But, having done it both ways myself, I feel that a GPS provides a security back-up which greatly extends your potential to explore the desert. You can go deeper into the desert, more safely with a GPS's backup.

Backup is the key word. No matter how clever it is, GPS is only a navigational *aid*. It won't stop you getting lost if you don't pay attention to maps, landmarks, orientation or the cliff face in front of you. More than ever you'll need to **read and understand maps** and *accurately* plot co-ordinates. Even then, knowing exactly where you are is academic if you've run out of fuel or

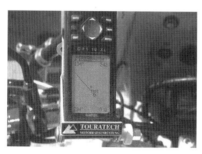

Although by the time you read this the latest models will be able to pick up Euro Sport and dial a pizza, at the time of writing the Garmin 72 was a good basic GPS along the lines of the old Garmin 12. Besides being able to tell you how far you are from Ulaan Bator, its biggest advantages over the 12 are a bigger screen and the need for just two AA batteries.

have broken a leg. At its simplest level a GPS can *quickly stop you amplifying navigational errors* by confirming you're off course.

GPS models and accessories

Recreational GPS units can be of two types: hand-held and fixed, with various levels of gizmology (and even games!) beyond their collective position-fixing ability. In Europe, Garmin and Magellan and to a lesser extent Silva are well-known brands, with the cheapest units now costing under £80/€120. Larger fixed-unit models start at around £200/€300, again going up to three times that price for more bells and buzzers. In recent years the ease of use and range of models has made Garmin the most popular choice, with Magellan, the pioneers of the hand-held GPS, in second place.

Unless you're going to be doing a lot of expeditions, the simplest 12-channel hand-held unit will suffice; its accuracy will be not less than a top-of-the-range unit. However, for use in cars it's best to ensure that the unit you buy has the facility for attaching or extending an **external antenna**. An extension for an external antenna is essential because when fitted in the most convenient position on the dashboard, satellite coverage may be impeded by the car's metal roof. Having an external antenna will enable you to mount your GPS where you like, without having to hold the unit out of the window every time you want to get a reading. This is particularly relevant for Defenders with their steep windscreen angle. On cars with raked windscreens, like Toyotas and Discoverys, the GPS's internal antenna will work on the dashboard.

Get a 12-volt **cigarette lighter adapter** for your vehicle, be it car or motorcycle, so you can keep the unit on all day. Internal batteries would only last a couple of days but obviously are a good backup, enabling you to use the unit away from the vehicle. Especially on a **bike**, this socket can be an unreliable connection with all the shaking around – when the unit turns off you lose your odometer total. Consider fitting better DIN plugs or hard-wiring the GPS cable to the bike's electrics. Keep batteries in the unit even when using the cig socket so that, should it disconnect, the signal will continue on battery power. Without batteries it will switch off when inadvertently disconnected and you'll lose your distance or trip record during that time.

Talking of which, the **time** displayed on a GPS is constantly corrected by the atomic clocks in each satellite, so is accurate to within nanoseconds. 'Daylight Saving' times (usually an hour one way or the other) will not always be registered at the appropriate date, however.

A cut-down juice bottle and two elastic bands is one way of mounting a GPS...

GPS mounts and fixed units The current crop of inexpensive hand-held units have small screens that are difficult to read for a passenger let alone a driver in a bouncing car or motorbike. Most manufacturers produce **swivel mounts** for hand-held units which can be fixed to pretty much any point on the dashboard; for a lone driver it might be a good idea to mount the unit at eye level on the car's windscreen pillar closest to the steering wheel or even the sun visor. Some alternative DIY ideas are suggested on the right.

For a one-off desert holiday hand-held units will do, but if you think you may be doing a lot of GPS-ing in your car, especially without a passenger to help give read-outs, consider buying one of the larger **fixed GPS units**, which typically have screens twice as large as hand-held ones, and keypads to match; they're much easier to read and use on the move. Costing over three times the price of

... but that requires screws so a cable tie and a single elastic band will do. Kits are available on the website (including back-up elastic).

Garmin 152, entry level fixed-mount GPS that is easy to read but not so handy to remove. © Garmin Europe

the cheapest hand-held units (a Garmin 128 goes for around £210/€320, the slightly better 152 model takes mapping and goes for around £250), all fixed units should come with an external antenna. The problem is of course that neither is easily removable when you're away from the vehicle.

Reading anything more than the bearing from a hand-held GPS while riding a **motorbike** is virtually impossible; in fact I like to think my balletic wipe-out at the end of *Desert Riders* was due to an ill-timed glance at the GPS. Rally racers feature a large unit high up in the fairing, but as relating a given GPS reading to a map requires stopping anyway, a plain handlebar mount is best, short of strapping the unit to your left forearm. In my experience the flimsy, quick-release handlebar mounts supplied by Garmin would not last a day riding in the desert. The German company Touratech make strong alloy clamps for many popular models (see picture, p.320), including the large-screen Garmin 126 model which works well externally.

GPS Mapping

Just as symphonic ring-tones and leopard-skin covers are all the rage for mobile phones, so mapping has become the must-have on most popular brands of GPS. **Worldwide map databases**, including city maps, are pre-

Real-time GPS nav set up on Route A14 near the Niger border; demanding conditions for a laptop computer.

loaded into most units and more can be imported from a computer or website. It's a nifty gimmick, giving you the impression that your £200 GPS can guide you along highways and byways like the sophisticated in-car units. However, information databases are usually limited to detailed coverage of America, Europe and Japan. Any built-in GPS map of Africa and the Sahara is likely to show little more than borders and a few major highways and towns. These maps are of no use for desert navigation.

And even if they were, reading a map on a GPS screen that is effectively the size of a cigarette packet at best is extremely frustrating. If you are serious about real-time GPS mapping you'll need to wire in a laptop computer to your GPS and take advantage of its decent-sized screen. You'll also need to import Saharan mapping which means

USING A GPS WITH THE ROUTES IN THIS BOOK

Having used Saharan GPS-guidebooks in German, French, Spanish and Italian, the route information in this book (starting on p.424) has been laid out in what is hoped will be the clearest and most intuitive format for use on the piste.

Nearly all the Saharan itineraries in this book were researched using a Garmin 38, 12XL or 72 set at the 'WGS84' default datum and 'True North'. As mentioned, GPS units are now accurate to within a few metres but even then your distances and GPS positions are unlikely to exactly match those given in this book, especially as even two GPS units of the same brand will not give an identical reading.

Waypoints are given in the **decimal minute** format (DMM) as opposed to the traditional 'degrees, minutes and seconds' (DMS). This means N30° 30' 25" is shown as N30° 30.416', 25" of arc being just under half (0.416) of a minute.

Fractions like .416' have been rounded up or down to a single decimal place (e.g. N30° 30.4'), as fractions beyond one hundredth of a minute represent less than 18 metres on the ground. The decimal method makes plotting these tiny measurements on a map less prone to error, though it's something you're only likely to do with any measure of accuracy on a large-scale 1:200,000 map. (If you can't tell in what form a group of co-ordinates is written in other books, look for a decimal point – in Europe it's a comma – and also for a number over sixty after the minutes. If a 'seconds' figure is over sixty it must be decimal; if it's under sixty it *may* be seconds).

All distances are given in **kilometres and have been taken** from the GPS, not the vehicle speedo. They've also been rounded up or down, as after a couple of hours on any piste you're unlikely to have matched my wheel tracks exactly except on certain mountain pistes. Try to get out of the habit of endlessly re-calculating distance back into miles; learn to think of distance as well as fuel consumption in metric terms (conversion tables appear on p.650) and you are less likely to make miscalculations. Set your GPS to read in metric (as well as decimal fractions of minutes) and learn to rely on the unit as an extremely accurate recorder of distance, time and speed (as well as position).

There are two ways in which you can use the GPS information given in the route descriptions. The simplest is to **use it as a guide** with which to reassure yourself that you're on the right track. In other words the navigator keeps their eye on the GPS, checking to see that its readings match those of the route description in this book.

On the whole, we've given waypoints only for points of significance (landmarks, important changes in direction), except in featureless stretches of piste and in dunes, where we've given them at regular intervals to enable you to plot a course or regain the book's route if you get lost.

Alternatively, you can key **all the waypoints** for a certain piste into your GPS in advance. Done manually this is a laborious process that's prone to keystroke errors but it does give you the reassurance of ticking off each passing waypoint. An infallible way of putting waypoints into your GPS is to use **software** like Ozi Explorer, Waypoint Plus or Touratech QV. These all work with PCs; for Apple Macs I've found GPSPro a bit more usable than GPSy, but I've hardly explored the potential of either program. An **interface accessory cable** is needed to link GPS to a computer.

If you choose these options, you'll find yourself following your route by using the 'Navigation', 'Compass', or 'Highway' page (different descriptions of the same thing) where an arrow points towards the next waypoint on the list.

In my opinion navigating using this method is misleading as it makes you concentrate on the arrow rather than the track ahead. The arrow points directly at the next waypoint but a track on the ground (and the route description of it, where available) is rarely a connection of straight lines between waypoints. Only the bearing and 'distance to' information may prove vaguely useful.

If following this book's routes in this manner, either train yourself to ignore the arrow or keep the GPS on the 'Position' page most of the time where 'trip' and 'bearing' information will be adequate. If you feel you need reassurance as a waypoint approaches, or if you've missed a waypoint, you can move to the 'Navigation' page to find out in which direction and how far away it is.

scanning and calibrating the sheets (or buying them on CD). Touratech QV use Soviet-era base maps with their GPS mapping software (partly because of easy licensing), although the drawbacks of these Soviet maps are addressed below. The better IGN maps don't cover all the Sahara but are also available scanned on CD.

Once you've gone through all this palaver you can enjoy following your position as a moving dot on the map on a laptop screen. All this technology might be handy in military applications, but I've never seen the need for it in the wide open spaces of the Sahara where, if not following a piste, one navigates 'ground to map' rather than 'map to ground'.

2D Nav and other GPS limitations

At times your GPS may come up with a discrete '**2D Nav**' message, a limitation that is played down in the operating manuals. Ideally your GPS wants to read from one satellite overhead and three evenly spaced around the horizon. Sometimes full '3D Nav' may take a couple of minutes to acquire, and until then it is only reading from three satellites: no altitude is given, just lat/long. You may think that's good enough but in fact your GPS has guessed an altitude and used the centre of the Earth as the 'fourth satellite' to estimate your position. This can give readings up to one minute (1800m) in error. Even in the desert that is quite a lot when you're looking for a precise waypoint. Always wait until your GPS is reading in '3D' – it will say so on the 'Satellite' page – for totally reliable fixes.

It won't take you long to discover that even in 3D mode the **altitude** reading is pretty vague, estimated to be half again as inaccurate as the horizontal error. At sea level or known spot heights marked on maps, readings can be up to 200m off. In some cases the mechanical altimeters fitted in some Japanese 4WDs are more accurate. Take GPS altitude readings with a pinch of salt; unless you're flying they're not that important anyway.

On some Garmins I've had problems with the unit **cutting out** repeatedly soon after turning on, doing so even while held quite still in my hand. Eventually it would settle down and remain on. This fault was irritating rather than dangerous as it only lost track of distance covered while turned off. I was told this is a common problem with Garmins (and possibly other brands too), explained by a build-up of carbon on the battery contacts. No dirt was found on the battery contacts but if it happens to you, this could be the cause. Because of this, as mentioned earlier, it is best to run a GPS via a lead off the vehicle battery where possible.

GPS WAYPOINTS FOR ANYTHING, ANYWHERE

The US National Imagery and Mapping Agency (NIMA) lists millions of waypoints for geographical features around the globe. In the Sahara, anything from an erg or mountain range to a hill, well or town can be searched for with just the place's name and country, delivering a waypoint to the nearest minute.

The information was gathered in the 1980s and 1990s from the best maps available, not by any cunning satellite scanning, so is prone to cartographic errors.

The database is available on the Internet at: http://gnswww.nima.mil/geonames/GNS/index.jsp. Click 'GNS Search'. Or try http://wayhoo.com.

Using a GPS in the Sahara

GPS units are user-friendly and easy to learn to use but it's essential to RTFM before you set off. It's not uncommon to see people trying to get the hang of their GPS receivers on the Mediterranean ferries! Once you're familiar with all the elementary **functions** like position, bearing and speed, you can play around with the more complicated facilities if they interest you. These include the ability to store information and do calculations such as upcoming waypoints along your route (if previously entered). There's also a useful backtracking facility, which means that you should be able to find your way back to all previous waypoints along a certain route.

Maps and satellite imagery

The Sahara was originally thoroughly mapped at the demise of the **colonial era** during WWII, principally by France and to a lesser and less detailed extent by Italy (in Libya) and Britain (in Egypt, Libya and Sudan). In the 1970s the evolution of satellites by the Soviet Union and the United States, vying for dominance during the Cold War, brought about global **satellite mapping programmes** that, like the old-fashioned attention to detail found in colonial mapping, is an expensive project never likely to be repeated.

This means that today even the off-piste explorer will find the entire Sahara covered with very detailed, large-scale maps and Landsat images. Some of these maps may be sixty years old but because change in most of the Sahara can be measured in geological rather than historical terms, even these old maps are very useful and, in many cases, are superior in quality and detail to some modern equivalents. In the desert the impression that dunes transform the desert unrecognisably from year to year is exaggerated and, for countries like Libya where the desert actually has developed fast, more modern maps exist.

Get to know your maps

Even if you don't plan to be the navigator, take an interest in your maps. Inspect your route or area closely before you go, study the key and see what everything means and how relief and surfaces are depicted. If you have a route guide, try to relate the description to the map and mark key points with a highlighter or pencil.

The best cartography

There's no shortage of good maps of the Sahara. Many are at least 20 years old but the desert doesn't change much.

offers a combination of **clarity and detail** (not forgetting accuracy!) that enables you to read the terrain like a book. Try and visualise the ground you'll pass over and where confusion or difficulties might lie with junctions, obstructions or surfaces.

Some maps tend to exaggerate surface features to enhance clarity. The dark shading of a cliff may actually turn out to be a long low outcrop, but being a landmark it will still assist in orientation. Once out there you'll soon acquaint yourself with a given map's style in depicting terrain. The desert can be much less dramatic than pre-departure visualisations suggest and you'll probably be brought down to earth, but on the better maps you'll marvel at the incredible detail and wonder how it was so consistently achieved.

Scales

A map's scale is given as a ratio of how much smaller that map is than the actual land surface: a 1:50,000 scale map is 50,000 times smaller than the area it represents. This can cause some confusion as what are called **small-scale maps** have a bigger ratio number and generally cover a larger area with less detail: small scale = small detail; a given feature like a mountain range will be 'smaller'. These maps, with ratios from **two million to five million**, give you a big overall picture of an area which makes them excellent for planning a trip if not necessarily for following a specific route. A good example is the Michelin 741 *North and West Africa* sheet at 1:4 million.

Medium-scale maps with scales between **1:500,000 and 1:2 million** are the optimum scale for driving or riding on desert pistes. On a 1:1 million map, one millimetre represents one kilometre on the ground. If the cartography is of good quality, the terrain's features will be easily read on such a map and the millimetre/kilometre relationship makes distances on the map easy to visualise. A typical one million scale map will cover six degrees of longitude and four degrees of latitude; in the Sahara that's around 600km from east to west and 440km from north to south. The IGN one millions covering

the central and west Sahara are excellent medium-scale maps.

As **large-scale** as you need in the Sahara is a map of 1:200,000. Covering one square degree of the earth's surface (a little over 100 square kilometres), around 800 sheets cover the entire Sahara. At this scale, one millimetre represents 200 metres on the ground, or one centimetre equals two kilometres. These very detailed maps are excellent for precise orientation on hard-to-fol-

A small part of the 1960 'Menzel el Lejmat' (NH-32-XIV) IGN 1:200,000 map covering the Grand Erg Oriental. The entire sheet looks like this, though these days it's full of oil exploration tracks (see photo p.381). © IGN

low pistes or **off-piste** navigation through difficult terrain. With them you can literally pick your way from outcrop to outcrop and along river beds, assuming this details exists of course – some sheets for the Sahara resemble minimalist artworks featuring just a lone outcrop on a featureless 100 square kilometre background.

Amazingly, some major **ergs** can be navigated with a thirty-year-old 200,000 map – all the proof you need to dismiss the theory of 'roaming dunes'. Using a map at this scale it is possible to traverse from one corridor to another and identify individual dune formations. And an erg with rocky outcrops, sand-free clearings or other identifiable features (the western Idehan Ubari in Libya, for example) would be a place where large-scale maps will help.

Latitude and longitude

In pre-GPS days most Saharan travellers rarely knew exactly where they were because the only way to do this required a time-consuming, error-prone process using the stars, a sextant and log tables. In those days, only two decades ago, you travelled with your wits, maps and, if you were lucky, a guidebook with more gaps than Ken Dodd's teeth. Some guidebooks gave consecutive 'waypoints' up to 200km apart, leaving travellers to get through a rather unnervingly long stage without any landmarks or reference points. Now that GPS can give anyone their position within a minute of being turned on, a closer familiarisation with latitude and longitude is necessary.

The difference between latitude and longitude

Latitude and longitude is a method of marking a position on earth using measurements across (horizontally – latitude) and down (vertically – longitude).

WHEN IN ROAM...

Roamers (to give them one name) are pieces of clear acetate printed with a one-square-degree grid. They are useful when trying to read a position on a map which does not have incremental minute scales in the body of the map (only TPCs, see below, have these handy features).

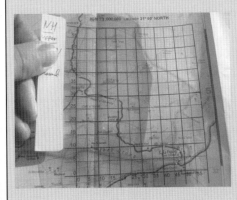

You can work out a position with a ruler and pencil but, especially if your point is in the middle of the sheet, getting an accurate reading from the edge of the map while sitting in a moving car can be awkward. As long as a map has degree lines on it (not all do) roamers can be more convenient.

One roamer does not fit all grid squares because, as mentioned on p.328, a square degree in the northern Sahara is narrower than a square degree in the south. You should use a roamer for a designated latitude.

Across the globe map latitudes are indexed into bands of four degrees: 'NH' (the roamer pictured left) means North of the equator while H corresponds to a latitude band between 28° and 32°N.

Two roamers are available to download and print for the Saharan bands from NE to NH. Visit **www.sahara-overland.com/maps** and take your pick.

The equator is the zero line of reference for latitude, dividing the globe into northern and southern hemispheres. The Greenwich or Prime Meridian is the zero line of reference for longitude, dividing the world into western and eastern hemispheres. The Prime Meridian happens to pass down western Algeria's Tanezrouft, close to Reggane and right through the city of Gao on the Niger River in Mali.

Lines of latitude are parallel, east–west rings that circle the earth. They divide the globe into surface bands at equal distance so that anywhere on the globe **each degree of latitude is about 110km wide** (or 60 nautical miles). One minute of latitude (a 60th of a degree) equals one nautical mile or, more usefully on land, 1.83km. One second of latitude (a 60th of a minute) equals 30.5m.

Lines of longitude all converge at the poles, cutting the earth into vertical segments like a Terry's Chocolate Orange. The width of these segments varies; they are at their widest at the equator, where lines of longitude are (like lines of latitude) around 110km apart. Moving away from the equator lines of longitude converge towards the poles, where they meet.

This can be seen if you look carefully at any map with lat/long grid lines. Putting a **straight edge** along a line of latitude will reveal that the seemingly horizontal line actually curves upwards. Meanwhile measuring the **distance** between vertical lines of longitude will show them a little closer together at the top (see diagram below).

On a map of over one million scale, such as the Michelin 741, lines of longitude will also curve either side of a vertical centre line – on the 741 this centre line happens to be 16°W – though this curvature of longitude is not that important to desert navigation as you'd not expect to navigate with a map of over one million scale.

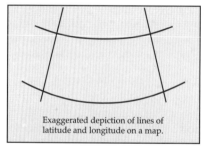

Exaggerated depiction of lines of latitude and longitude on a map.

Degrees, minutes and seconds The latitude and longitude grid divides the globe into **360 degrees** (abbreviated as: °). Each degree is subdivided into **60 minutes** (abbreviated as: ') and each minute divided into **60 seconds** (or: "). Positions are always shown as latitude followed by longitude (longitude in the Sahara may be either west or east of the Prime Meridian).

With this system of co-ordinates it's possible to give a grid reference for anywhere on the planet to an accuracy of 15m using just six digits of latitude and seven digits of longitude. A typical Saharan grid reference looks like this: N20° 27' 23" W12° 21' 39" (Chinguetti in Mauritania). However, these days seconds have been superseded by decimal fractions of minutes, so that the grid reference for Chinguetti would now be written as: N20° 27.38' W12° 21.65'.

MAPS OF THE SAHARA

Most currently available maps covering the Sahara are listed and described below. Only a couple are really useful to desert travellers; others may be more easily available and will offer a good background or modern overlay. For the average Sahara tour choose one large-scale map covering the whole area you plan to visit and then add one- or half-million scale maps for all the areas you plan to cover on pistes. These can be backed up by a selection of 200,000s for areas of special interest, excursions off-piste or places where you expect to have difficulty finding your way. For the latest maps and updated descriptions of new editions go to www.sahara-overland.com/maps.

Michelin 741

Scale 1:4 million.

Date Latest edition: 2003.

Price Around £5/€3.

Availability Any book shop with a good map section.

Description Formerly called the '153' and '953', the 741 covers nearly all the Sahara from the Atlantic to western Egypt (28°E), making this the first choice when considering visiting this region. Supposedly updated every couple of years (though old errors persist) the 700 series (745 covers north-east Africa and Arabia, 746 southern Africa) is renowned for its detail, readability and reasonable accuracy.

The 741 is a good planning map, giving you a clear overview of 90% of the desert, relative distances, borders, major roads and pistes, settlements and surface features, even the depth of wells and quality of water. It's not a map to navigate by, although many novice Saharans have tried! Some pistes are given too much prominence compared to others: many of the thin black lines shown on a 741 are long-obsolete camel trails, yet they are shown to be on a par with much more recognised pistes. This gives a false impression of possibilities – another thing Saharan novices have found to their cost. Nevertheless, the 741 is a must; it's the definitive map of the Sahara and West Africa and offers a quick way of getting to know this huge region.

Michelin also produce maps of **north and west Africa**. Larger scales cover populated areas but the desert is usually 1:4 million, copied from the latest 741. Of interest but not much use in the desert are the 743 *Algeria Tunisia* (actually just northern Algeria) and the 742 *Morocco* (which, lacking grid lines, is not capable of accurately relating to GPS positions).

Institute Geographique Nationale (IGN)

Scales 1:1 million; 1:500,000; 1:200,000.

Date Early 1960s to mid-1970s.

Price 1:1 million: £8 (UK), €8 (France); 1:500,000/1:200,000: €8-13 (France only).

Availability In the UK, 1:1m only, from map specialists. In Europe from specialists or the IGN in Paris (see below). All scales also available on bootleg CD.

Description The **one million** IGNs are to general-purpose desert navigation what the 741 is to planning. They cover the former French African colonies and only extend to the western reaches of Libya (up to 12°E). Readability from 1964 up to the last sheets in 1975 is very good. The few 1961 sheets covering ever-overlooked Mauritania are a little basic by comparison.

The advent of GPS brought up a few errors with the one-millions – mountains misplaced by a few kilometres – but overall the detail and accuracy is excellent as subsequent satellite imagery has proved. Changes in roads are best cross-referenced on a 741 or a modern country map (see below). Don't expect all the marked wells to have been maintained over the last few decades. Particularly in the more populous Sahel, the position of tracks and other man-made features may have altered. Excepting parts of Libya and all of Egypt, these excellent maps are ideal for the basic level of exploration and travel that this book represents. You will find a useful index grid of IGN one-million coverage of the Sahara on the www.sahara-overland.com/maps web page.

Coverage of **half-million** IGNs seems to have been patchy and these days they are very hard to find new, even in Paris. For some odd reason detail is cut off at country boundaries, even adjacent former French ones, which makes them a little less worth searching out, though of course the extra detail makes this perhaps the best scale of all for piste driving. Half-millions are not available at the Espace IGN Cartothèque in Paris.

Just about all the original **200,000s** have been sold or returned to the relevant countries with just the odd sheet turning up in the bookshops of Paris or Geneva. Theoretically still available from the relevant ministries in Algeria, Niger and Mali, their 'strategic' scale makes obtaining them a hit-or-miss affair. Nevertheless, when you can find them, the colour originals are real works of cartographic art, especially in mixed dune and rock terrain. **Black-**

SOME SAHARA MAP SOURCES IN EUROPE

UK
Stanfords
12-14 Long Acre, London WC2E 9LP
☎ 020-7836 1321
www.stanfords.co.uk
For the Sahara it keeps a full selection of ONCs/TPCs but only a patchy selection of one million IGNs. Good selection of modern country maps.

The Map Shop
15 High Street, Upton-upon-Severn, Worcs WR8 0HJ.
☎ 01684 593 146
www.themapshop.co.uk
Fast and efficient mail order service for TPCs and IGN one millions, and cheaper than Stanfords.

Paris
IGN Map Shop
107 rue la Boétie, 75008.
☎ 01 42 56 06 68 (Metro: St Philippe du Roule).
IGN's city-centre outlet, with a full stock of one millions and country maps as well as a couple of Sahara guidebooks.

Espace IGN
2 avenue Pasteur, 75018.
☎ 01 43 98 80 00
www.ign.fr. (Metro: St-Mandé Tourelle).
Mail order service, or head for the Cartothèque department for monochrome 1:200,000 counter sales. Also a small reference library of guidebooks.

Munich
Därrs Travel Shop
Thereisenstrasse 66, D-80333.
☎ 089 20 28 32
www.daerr.de
IGNs including mono 200,000s, Soviet series of Libya or mono copies in all scales, ONCs and TPCs and Quo Vadis Soviet maps on CD.

Amsterdam
Geografische Boekhandel Jacob van Wijngaarden, Overtoom 97, NL 1054 HD
☎ 020-6121901   www.jvw.nl

and-white copies of the full set are available from the IGN Cartothèque at around €6 each and are also widely sold by the major Saharan outfitters in Europe, some avoiding the copyright issue by not crediting the maps as IGNs. In Germany TTQV (www.ttqv.com) sell all the French IGN 200,000s (as well as other scales and the Soviet series) **on CD**, but they are formatted only to work with TTQV 2.5 or later software. Elsewhere, privately-scanned IGNs are available on CD for the desert areas of Mauritania, Niger and Algeria.

The biggest drawback with the 200,000s is that there are **no grid lines** on the face of the map and each degree is only marked in 10-minute increments along the borders. If you look closely there are actually faint crosses in the body of the map at 10-minute intervals, so it's possible to mark your own grid – but draw from cross to cross and not straight across, even though, given their UTM projection, the lines are almost straight. Marking your position accurately without grid lines or a giant roamer is difficult.

Soviet world series

Scales 1:1 million; 1:500,000; 1:200,000.

Date Early 1970s to mid-1980s.

Price Around €12.

Availability Saharan specialists in Germany, Switzerland and maybe in France. Also available on CD (see below).

Description Similar to the American ONC/TPC programme (see below) the Soviet Union produced a range of topographic maps covering the world at the above scales, making them the only ones to cover **Libya**, where they match IGN's earlier efforts to the west but at a lower quality. Difficulties include the **Cyrillic** (Russian) text and what appears to be less than full-colour printing. Their worst feature is representing dunes as a series of still more orange contours rather than with colour and shade as with IGNs. Some are sold as black-

---

USEFUL RUSSIAN

Cyrillic alphabet

А а	a	П п	p		
Б б	b	Р р	r		
В в	v	С с	s		
Г г	g	Т т	t		
Д д	d	У у	u/oo		
Е е	e	Ф ф	f/ph		
Ё ё	yo	Х х	kh		
Ж ж	zh	Ц ц	ts		
З з	z	Ч ч	ch		
И и	ee	Ш ш	sh		
Й й	y	Щ щ	shch		
К к	k	Ы ы	y/i		
Л л	l	Э э	e		
М м	m	Ю ю	yu		
Н н	n	Я я	ya		
О о	o	ь ь	softens preceding letter		

Some towns in Libya

El Gatrun	Эль Гатрун
Germa	Джерма
Ghat	Гат
Idri	Эдри
Kufra	Куфра
Murzuk	Мурзук
Sebha	Себха
Serdeles	Серелес
Ubari	Убари

Features

dunes	Илехан (Пески)
hamada	Хамада
jebel	Джебель
plateau	Плату
wadi	Вади

and-white copies which makes them even harder to read.

Nevertheless, they're the best there are for **Libya**, with the half-million originals noticeably easier to read than the one-millions even if availability of originals seems patchy. In most cases the large scale 200,000s have to be ordered, even from clued-up European outlets.

With workable copyright restrictions organisations like **TTQV** (www.ttqv.com) have scanned the entire Russian series and sell them on **CD**. The fact that the useful 1:500,000 scale is not widely available from IGN makes the Quo Vadis CDs valuable for the entire Sahara and not just Libya, if you can bear them.

When buying these maps on paper, always go for the semi-colour originals if you can and expect to spend an evening familiarising yourself with place names and the Russian alphabet (Cyrillic, see previous page) and writing the translations onto the maps, where necessary. The TTQV CD maps helpfully feature overprinted names of major towns in the Roman alphabet.

US Defence Mapping Agency

Scale Operational Navigation Charts (ONC) 1:1 million. Tactical Pilotage Charts (TPC) 1:500,000.

Date Produced in the 1960s and 1970s, revised in the late 1980s.

Price About £8 or €12 (Or about $7 in the US).

Availability Widely available from map specialists worldwide.

Description While they are of a seemingly useful scale, widely sold as 'Sahara maps' and opening out to the size of a tablecloth, ONCs and TPCs are aeronautical maps and much over-rated for terrestrial use. **Differentiation** of relief and surface is poor and, in the Sahara at least, no attempt is made to distinguish between a mule track and a six-lane motorway. Settlements, where they appear, are rated chiefly by their airport and radio facilities. Well information is also hit-or-miss; some known wells are missing while others which are marked may no longer exist.

ONCs and TPCs also show the UTM grid overprinted in blue, as well as lines of magnetic variation which are also irrelevant with a GPS's built-in true-north-pointing compass. However, as with the Soviet maps, an evening's close scrutiny sorting out which track might be yours is profitable. In some instances the ONC or TPC will give an absolutely accurate orientation of a track (Route L1

Plotting a position on a TPC with ruler and pencil; Route A14.

for example), but most of the time they're confusing and need to be made sense of with another definitive map.

The good thing about ONCs and TPCs is that each grid line across the map has an **incremental scale** in minutes, making accurate position-marking easy without a ruler or roamer (see p.327). The size of the unfolded map can be awkward, but the half-million TPCs are recommended as useful master maps to mark up and plot your own routes over a large area. For actual desert navigation they're more of a backup to use with the IGN or Soviet alternatives.

Moroccan Ministère de l'Agriculture

Scale 1:250,000.

Date From the early 1970s.

Price Unknown.

Availability With difficulty from the Ministry in Rabat (or on bootleg CD).

Description This comprehensive coverage of Morocco is clear to read and a good comparison with the 1GN 200,000s. Grid lines are at half-degree intervals which makes them more useful than the IGNs and the cartographic style is nearly as good. The problem is of course that in the thirty odd years since these maps were printed much infrastructure has changed in Morocco and unless you're planning on doing some exploring in the mountains these maps are rather unnecessary. The one-million IGN Morocco map (or its equivalent) is adequate for all the routes in this book.

Survey of Egypt

Scale 1:500,000.

Date Mid-1930s to mid-1970s.

Price £E10 per sheet.

Availability Egyptian Geodesic Institute, North Giza. *Uweinat* sold out but available on CD off the website ...com/maps.

Description The relevant sheets for the Western and Libyan Deserts are *Siwa*, *Farafra*, *Dakhla* ,*Uweinat*, *Qena* and *Aswan*. The *Uweinat* sheet dates from 1942 and is still a genuinely useful and accurate map for travellers in the area. Other, later sheets have much inferior printing in this region; you're better off with Soviet maps (see above) or the TPCs H4-C and J5-A.

Modern country maps

Various modern map publishers produce country maps for tourists. In most cases these are less useful than 'proper' desert maps like IGN one-millions, but they are of course more up to date. The only Saharan countries where this matters are Morocco and Tunisia. Elsewhere the desert regions are pretty much the same as they were forty-odd years ago.

IGN produces a modern series of country maps which in the Sahara includes Egypt, Mali, Morocco, Mauritania, Chad, Niger (these two unique to

IGN) and Tunisia; some have got newer purple covers. Produced or updated in the 1990s, they have scales ranging from one million to 2.5 million and are easily available in Europe and selectively from the UK map specialists for around £8. With grid lines at one-degree intervals, the 1:1m *Maroc* sheet is superior and in some places more up-to-date than the Michelin 742. The usefulness of other IGN country maps fits somewhere between an up-to-date Michelin 741 and an IGN one-million. *Chad* has no grid lines, for example, and is actually a very old edition (not that that matters much in northern Chad).

Besides the 1:1 million Michelin 742 (no grid) and IGN, other modern maps of **Morocco** which feature grid lines are the German *Reise Know-How* series (1:1m, printed in the UK on plastic paper by Rough Guide.) None of these does a very good job of covering the Western Sahara below 27°N (most get insets at a scale of around 1:2.5 million), but only Route M13 ventures down here and although clear to follow, is not depicted on any map.

Michelin, RK-H and IGN are as good as it gets for **Tunisia**, while there is no modern map of **Egypt** that tells you anything useful about the Libyan Desert in the south-west: it's usually where they slap the key.

For **Libya** the double-sided Lebanese *Malt* 1:3.5 million map may have been produced by Ghadafi himself, so exaggerated are its borders. A better option is the Canadian *ITM* series at 1:1.65m and with grid lines. The second (2003) edition appears better than its predecessor but, as on the 741, there are strings of obsolete or unknown routes going from nowhere to nowhere that give a misleading picture of today's desert tracks in Libya.

ITM also make a 1:2 million sheet of **Mauritania** which gives the latest edition of the ageing 1:2.5 million IGN a run for its money (all IGN have done is change the cover; an old trick).

However, give the ITM *Sahara* map a miss. A rival to the staid Michelin 741 would be nice, and the 1:2.2m scale looks promising, but a quick scan shows countless errors and omissions on the 2000 edition, as well as an inferior design to the Michelin. They had their chance; stick with the 741.

USING SATELLITE IMAGERY

The Space Shuttle passes over the Atlas Mountains. © NASA

Just as the Cold War gave us global mapping, the same arms race launched space missions to record satellite images of the entire planet. The desert makes an ideal canvas on which to record images from space with astounding vividness. Cloud cover is sparse and the combination of rock and sand come up in sharp contrast, even in black and white.

With the whole Sahara mapped down to 1:200,000, the need for satellite imagery is not essential, certainly not when following pistes (though it does help in the east beyond the reach of the large scale IGNs). But now that Space Shuttle and Landsat images from the early 1990s are available free on NASA websites, satellite imagery can provide a new way of looking at the desert, your maps and where you're travelling. At the very least, satellite imagery is an entertaining and educational way of appreciating the desert terrain and in some cases it can help with off-piste exploration.

A good place to start is at http://rove.to, while higher-quality images with distinct navigational uses can be found at the Earth Sciences Applications Directorate at https://zulu.ssc.nasa.gov/mrsid/mrsid.pl, offering incredible high-resolution images. To view them you will need to download software called MrSID (Multi-Resolution Seamless Image Database, from www.lizardtech.com). MrSID enables the viewing of hyper-compressed image data while enabling very fast roaming and zooming. High-resolution means images 25,000 pixels or nearly 10m wide. A typical MrSid ESAD image works out at around 40-45mb and covers around 600 square kilometres.

Zooming in on the Sahara from the zulu web page above you will eventually get to an image classified as N-35-20 for example (Jebel Uweinat in the Libyan Desert) and can download it with MrSID.

These images are not regular photographs; they use false colour, displaying invisible infrared wavelengths as visible colours, so the interpretation of what ground conditions these colours represent takes practice. However, they are not that far off; sand is still lighter than rock which is really most of the information you need.

Two satellite images of the Erg Tifernine and the western Tassili in Algeria. On the image above, the erg is to the right of the central cloud; below, the view is looking over the southern end of the erg in a south-westerly direction. One can clearly make out the delineation of the dunes, suggesting a north–south traversal might be viable. It's nothing that you can't tell from the relevant IGN 200,000 or even one million map, but for the corners of the Sahara which IGN did not reach, sat images can be useful. © NASA

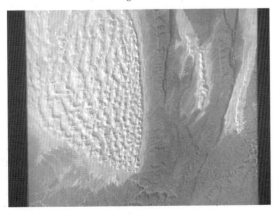

Looking at an actual picture of the desert and relating it to a map will change the way you look at maps. You'll realise why pistes go a certain way but wonder how this was done without the advantage of an overhead view. And seeing a photo from 200km up as a wall of sand moves across the desert floor (see

Jebel Uweinat from N-35-20. On the left the Libyan access oueds of Karkur Ibrahim and Idris are visible. © NASA

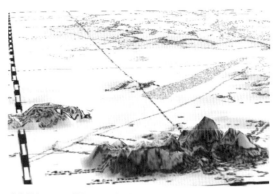

A 3-D image of Uweinat looking north, laid over a map with Jebel Arkenu on the left. Verticality is exaggerated, but gives a vivid impression of the mountain and surrounding relief.

Another 3-D image of Ain Zweia and Dua wells in the south-west (Libyan) corner of Uweinat, using N-35-20. Both images courtesy of Dr K White, The University of Reading.

p.392) will make you truly appreciate the epic nature of Saharan sand storms.

In my experience using high-resolution colour images for short-range off-piste adventuring can come up with exciting possibilities as long as you realise what you're letting yourself in for. The trick comes in *interpreting* images correctly. You may be able to recognise sand from rock but you can't tell the texture of the sand and whether it's drivable. On foot in the mountains, misreading relief from a sat image can also get you into trouble: what might look like a clear wadi leading back to a campsite may be blocked by a 100m-high cliff.

Actual photographs taken at low sun angles are the best, highlighting the relief of the ground which includes the pattern and orientation of dunes.

With foot travel in mind, other more advanced applications of satellite imagery include the ability to use the information in these images to plot a 3-D graphic, which can be useful for climbers (rather than for those in vehicles).

One thing that really helps when printing out or editing a satellite image is adding a Long/Lat grid or even importing it into some GPS software. How to do it with no calibration marks is tricky; the best you can do is re-size the image to the same scale as a map and key on calibration points, or work it out from prominent land marks.

All this may sound very advanced and high-tech, but realistically the best use of satellite imagery is to give a vivid 'photographic' image of the desert floor to compare with a map. Knowing that the image is a true version of the terrain, bereft of any stylistic cartographic vagaries, your maps then take on new meaning.

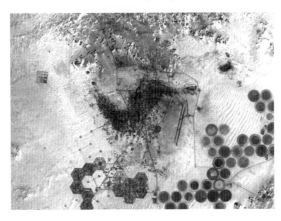

Kufra oasis as seen on a MrSID viewer at maximum magnification, equivalent to a scale of around 1:200,000. The original is in colour and therefore much more readable. Elsewhere in the desert major pistes can just about be recognised, as can the composition of dune belts and possibly passable canyons. © NASA

NAVIGATING A PISTE

In the Sahara, established pistes follow the easiest, clearest and, if possible, most well-watered line between two points (see p.10). Saharan pistes are rarely signposted in a conventional way and may not have any markers along their course. However, once you've travelled your first couple of pistes, you'll find it quite easy to recognise which is a piste and which the tracks of someone driving off behind a rock for a leak.

In the desert the combination of handling your vehicle and navigating is a full-time job, especially if you're alone. If you're ever in doubt, don't hesitate to stop and think – never carry on in the hope that things will work themselves out; a human (and especially male) foible but a sure way to get lost.

Keeping track

To successfully **recognise your piste**, you should first read and digest your route description and try to plot its course on a map. Set your GPS trip function to zero so it matches the distances given on the route descriptions. The beginnings of pistes are often hard to locate, especially near settlements, so keep your eyes peeled for significant signs such as car tracks, cairns, oil drums or other markers (see p.341).

Most recognised desert routes follow a clear and straight course and, because they're established, on frequently used routes you may well find corrugations, which is often a good sign that you're on a main track or one that is converging on a settlement. However, **blindly following tracks** without giving a thought to landmarks, orientation or maps is the most common way of getting lost. It's understandable: there's one track, you assume it must be your track. But if you don't keep an eye on your bearing (orientation), that

338 IN THE DESERT

SAHARA – WEST TO EAST

Although in terms of usefulness it's on a par with ballooning round the world or walking to the North Pole, one of the last motorised challenges remaining in the Sahara is a true lateral crossing of the desert between the Atlantic and the Red Sea.

These types of ambitious expeditions were in vogue for a decade or so from the mid-1960s when at least four attempts were made to traverse the width of the Sahara. What makes a true lateral desert crossing has never been ratified by the United Nations, but it could be said that starting in the desert and keeping three or four degrees latitude either side of the Tropic of Cancer (N23° 27') for the entire crossing has a certain ring of authenticity.

In 1964, with twelve men using three Unimogs, Belgian Richard Petiniot (later involved with the 1968-9 survey of Jebel Uweinat) led a scientific trans-Saharan expedition. Setting out from Tangiers, they headed south and then turned inland at Layoune from where they made things easier for themselves by following established pistes all the way via Reggane, Djanet, Seguedine, Faya and Kufra to Kharga and the Nile (about 10,000km).

One of the few remaining Saviem *balises* east of the Gilf Kebir in Egypt.

A decade later, in January 1975, the British Joint Services Expedition led by Tom Sheppard set out north from Dakar in four Land Rover 101s, two towing powered trailers. Between Ouadane and Tessalit they made the first motorised crossing of the Sahara's 1000km-wide 'Empty Quarter', gathering scientific data along the way. But massive payloads led to problems with trailer suspension, overheating and fuel consumption and, along with politics, saw the expedition drop into the Sahel for the remaining three-quarters of the trip, via Niamey, Kano, Njamena and El Fasher, before coming up the Red Sea coast to Cairo.

Later that year a bunch of young Germans in four Hanomags also set off from the Straits of Gibraltar on an expedition that would take them down to Nouakchott, up to Taoudenni, down again to Bamako, up via Tessalit to Djanet, down to Bilma, up to Tripoli and down again to Kufra, the Gilf and Asyut on the Nile. By this time, nine dizzying months later, three of the overloaded Hanomags had croaked in short succession and the exhausted and demoralised team had suffered all sorts of illnesses, antagonisms and departures along the way. They never intended any grand west–east 'first', but certainly saw a lot of the Sahara and perhaps a bit too much of each other too!

Then in 1977 came probably the last of the big expeditions to cross the width of the Sahara. The French Saviem-sponsored Croisière des Sables objectives included establishing the Piste Saviem across the width of the Sahara, something of dubious value beyond promotion of Saviem (later Renault) lorries. They blew it from the start with a rather Sahelian traversal to Timbuktu, Gao and Agadez before hooking up to Adrar Bous, El Gatrun and on to Kufra and Aswan on the Nile.

(Continued opposite)

track could lead anywhere. In the desert, tracks from yesterday can be blown away by a sandstorm while on some gravel surfaces tracks can survive for decades. Kemal El Din's distinctive *autochenil* tracks can still be recognised in parts of the Western Desert.

On some pistes the tracks can **peter out** altogether. In this case you have to look at the big picture. If your position and bearing are correct it's possible that they may resume on the far side of a wind-smoothed sandy section.

SAHARA – WEST TO EAST

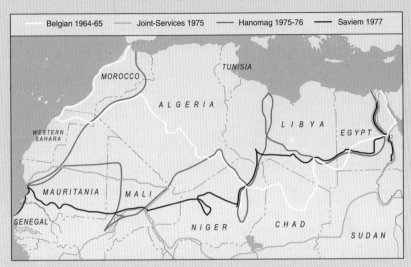

Belgian 1964-65 — Joint-Services 1975 — Hanomag 1975-76 — Saviem 1977

(*Continued from p338*) The Croisière des Sables team used parascenders and trail bikes and even explosives to recce the route, but the heavy TP3s and gnarly-tyred SM8 load carriers saw their fair share of PSP. The Croisière's legacy is a string of Saviem *balises* as marked on the Michelin maps, some still standing today.

Overall then, the true lateral desert crossing of the Sahara within the outlines given above has yet to be done, although from Layounne to Kharga, the 1965 Belgian expedition drew as good a line as possible. These days insecurity in central Sahara can be  added to the perennial difficulty of acquiring local permission to cross uncharted areas.

Once in a while I get enthusiastic enquiries from expeditions set on taking on this challenge, often for charity, but for most it's their first Saharan visit and few have a real idea of what they are taking on. One woman wanted to do it for a cancer charity and I proposed she follow the Tropic and call the expedition 'Operation Cancer'. That was the last I heard of her.

Sources: Werner Lenz; *Sahara Handbook*, (Lascelles); Royal Geographical Society; *Vom Atlantik zum Nil*, Gerd Heussler (Fischer Verlag); *Croisière des Sables*, Christian Gallissian (Arthaud).

Unless you choose to do so, driving on virgin desert without the comfort of existing tracks can be unnerving, so keep a close eye for any markers and tracks and, of course, your bearing.

Tracks can also **braid out** where the terrain allows, such as on flat plains, or where it demands because of awful corrugations (as around KM156 on Route T1 in Tunisia) or patches of soft sand. Though they've been busy sealing it for as long as I've been going to the Sahara, the trans-Sahara route south

The easily-missed 'turn-off' from the Trans-Saharan Highway for In Azaoua on Route A14.

of Tamanrasset spreads out across the plain for several kilometres in either direction. Here it doesn't matter which way you go as long as it's south; eventually all travellers get funnelled between the Laouni dunes and the distant Gara Eker escarpment where parts of the track are sealed. Some inexperienced travellers have picked up a subsidiary track heading south-east to In Azaoua, a case of blindly following tracks and not orientation; for some a fatal mistake.

In some places, tracks also wind **alongside** an old corrugated and undrivable piste, such as the beginning of the Derj–Idri piste in Libya (Route L1) or the northern parts of Route A10. Nervous drivers start off religiously rumbling along the tracks but soon spot locals hurtling along far from the main piste and eventually join them. This situation sometimes offers a choice: the vibrating but consistent ride on the corrugations or the smoother but curving and dipping side tracks. On the first section of the Waw en Namus piste (Route L6) you find yourself trying a bit of one and a bit of the other, an endless search for the smoothest ride. In this situation, you still need to keep within sight of the main track, which is helpful for keeping you in the right general direction if not for driving on. It pays to remember **which side** of the vehicle the track is on. Crisscrossing the track is common but if you lose it somehow, know if it's to your left or right so you can head directly towards it to regain orientation.

It's rare that there's a choice of pistes going to the same place as the easiest and quickest route becomes predominant, and it's usually well marked on the map as well as on the ground, but **junctions** can often be confusing. In the desert they're rarely crystal clear crossroads with 'Give Way' signs. Local drivers who know the way will cut corners to save a few seconds so you may encounter a collection of branches which can be confusing.

This oddly straight piste in Libya is actually an exploration track leading nowhere.

Be suspicious of dead-straight **bulldozed tracks**. In Libya the desert has been extensively explored for minerals and several of these exploration tracks exist, pushed through to take test drillings or seismic readings. They usually criss-cross a certain area and lead from nowhere to nowhere. Anything too straight but with signs of old run-off, and no recent wheel tracks, is not an established piste, which is what most regular routes are in the desert.

Orientation

However clear your piste may seem, and however numerous the car tracks are along it, it's essential to **monitor your bearing** (orientation) throughout the course of any piste. In general this should be quite straightforward: most Saharan pistes on flat terrain follow a consistent heading so the orientation of a piste is usually constant along its whole length, even on pistes several hundred kilometres long. Expect some deviation through rocky hills and around other obstructions though once back on the plain it should resume its former direction.

Always keep half an eye out for the **sun** and get to know the directions of the shadows at various times of the day. After a while, a quick glance at your shadow and your watch will instantly tell you whether you're driving or riding in the right general direction.

For more precise checks on your orientation, the **GPS's compass** has all the answers, giving a continuous bearing reading (though on some models the vehicle must be moving). At times when you're stationary your compass will do the job; get at least five metres from the vehicle and other magnetic influences and be aware of watches, and any keys hanging round your neck. The fine degrees of accuracy a compass can offer are not usually necessary for ordinary navigation and the technique of **triangulation**, taking bearings on two prominent landmarks to pinpoint your position, is redundant now that your GPS can give you that information in seconds.

Markers, cairns or balises

You'll learn to recognise trackside markers, better known by their French name, *balises* (beacons). They take all sorts of forms: colonial-era metal posts at regular distances, painted with cryptic distance markers as in Algeria (pretty irregular these days), small piles of rocks built and rebuilt by passing travellers, oil drums, and ruined tyres dumped by a passing vehicle, which are particularly conspicuous if set upright. The southern section of the Derj piste has beautifully-constructed cairns dating from the Italian occupation, while the plateau section has rather more prosaic half-metre high small pyramids at 5km intervals. The piste to Bordj Moktar has a mixture of metre-high concrete

Left: A line of cairns leads across a clay pan in Morocco (M12).
Right: North to Ounianga, right to Fada (C3). © Reinhart Mazur

From a short distance south of Djanet all the way to the Col des Chandeliers east of Chirfa in Niger, a distance of some 500km, there are nearly 1000 balises, one every half kilometre (not all with oil drums as above; this is Balise 112).
On a good day you can see a few in a row; just as well as there are no other landmarks on Route A15.

pillars after Tim Missao or huge plinths of earth topped with a red-and-white oil drum visible from a couple of kilometres. Even old car wrecks are a sure sign that someone once got at least this far.

Losing track of piste markers which have hitherto been regular is not uncommon. You never know if they've just stopped or you've wandered off onto another piste.

Significant places (usually junctions) have significant markers – more conspicuous than the general trackside markers, but don't count on it. The French used to build huge concrete blocks the size of small huts. You'll find them in Algeria, and on some Moroccan desert pistes.

Natural landmarks

A good map of one million scale or more will offer just enough topographical information to travel by. The most useful natural landmarks are **distinctive hills** and mountains like the outcrop of Grein in the pancake-flat northern Ténéré, a rare chance to pinpoint your position on a map without resorting to plotting a GPS co-ordinate. An escarpment may be less clear if it's low but if it's marked on the map it should be clearly visible as some kind of formation on the desert floor.

'Borne', the junction of the Amguid and Tamanrasset pistes (A6, KM241), used to be hard to find due to the undulating terrain. This new block makes it a bit easier. Mt Tazat, another good landmark, is in the background.

Large **oueds** can provide a vital point of orientation. Any oued marked on a one-million map will be clearly visible as a watercourse on the ground, especially if it has a name. It may be no more than a thin line of grassy tussocks, but in the desert any line of vegetation suggests a watercourse, clearly distinctive as trees such as those at KM200 on the way to Waw en Namus (Route L6). On the direct route from Nouadhibou to Nouamghar, for example, the Oued Chibka north of the fishing village of Tanoudert is a clear marker on your way south – as are the Aguilal hills visible to the SSE.

In the deep Sahara a oued certainly won't appear as a banked watercourse as in Morocco, where you drive down one bank, across the stones and up the other. In the desert a oued may be choked with dunes formed around the vegetation, making a difficult twin-rutted traversal, especially on a bike.

Cairns don't always appear alongside the track, but can be on tops of nearby hills, where they are more prominent.

Driving or riding **off-piste** is, of course, where the natural landmarks become vital, the only means of calculating your orientation or even permitting you to get through. Off-piste driving can be much, much slower than driving on pistes which, as explained elsewhere, follow the easiest and clearest line between two points.

GETTING LOST

Getting completely lost is very rare but even when you're just temporarily disorientated and the landmarks don't match up with the route description or maps, you soon become anxious. The impact of being alone in the desolation sinks in like a spear. At times like this you must use your logic and common sense to work out where you went wrong. The bottom line is that if there's ever the slightest doubt in your mind about whether or not you're on course, you should always stop and consult your map, your GPS and your route description. If you're still not sure, *always* turn back to the last point at which you were certain that you were on the right track.

It is almost always the **navigator's mistake** and not the commonly-blamed map, 'magnetic rocks' affecting the compass (though this can occur) or the Americans messing about with the GPS

Triangular-section steel balises like this are found all over Algeria. This one is at KM168 on Route A5, the old truck route to Djanet before they sealed the Fadnoun.

satellites. Even if reading and trusting the veracity of maps can take some time, good navigators never forget their own fallibility. If you've never used maps before, plotting co-ordinates from your GPS with all those minutes, decimal fractions of minutes or seconds can be confusing. All the more reason then to practise and mark key points beforehand and to draw grids at five-minute intervals on 1:200,000 IGNs (see p.330).

The most common mistake is **jumping to conclusions**, a consequence of wanting to overrule doubt, and allowing the situation to fit the facts. Suddenly you become aware that the piste doesn't quite match the bearing suggested on the map and the tracks become a bit thin. After a few kilometres they fade out and disappear altogether or, worse still, curve away in the wrong direction. You presume they're not marked on an old map so you might veer off towards other tracks crossing the path that look clearer and seem to be heading vaguely your way. The thought of turning back is now frustrating but sooner or later your common sense tells you that things are just not right and you've wandered off-course.

Though illegal in some countries, binoculars are handy when you lose sight of balises. A camera's zoom lens can be as useful. This guy is not as lost as he looks: he's standing on a good sign that he's right on track.
© Jeff Condon

Stop and have a good look around. Get on the roof of the car or onto **high ground** and scan around with a pair of **binoculars** – they can often make the difference in distinguishing between what looks like a burned tree and the next balise. Assess the 'quality' or feel of the piste you're now on: is it the same or does it appear less travelled? Check your position and bearing from the GPS. Have you made a mistake translating the GPS reading onto a map, easily done without a roamer or ruler. Look at all the facts objectively, not just the ones which agree with your expectations and, remember, there must have been a point not too long ago when you weren't lost. If you can't correct your mistake, **go back**.

Taking **short cuts** cross country is a way of trying to deny that getting lost got the better of you. Going back is always psychologically hard, when lost either in the desert or at home. But besides the fact that it may be very slow going, it doesn't take much to get your all-terrain vehicle stuck or damaged off-piste. In such a position, out of sight from the main piste with a burned-out clutch or broken leg, no one is likely to find you. Always play it safe and go back the easy way, however galling it seems.

Confusion near settlements and asking directions

Getting confused near settlements and heading off the wrong way is universal, be it on the Paris Périphérique or out of a desert town. Settlements see a convergence of many tracks and offer a confusing possibility of opportunities. Especially in the more populated Sahel south of the Sahara, routes may leave a village to all sorts of destinations: the river, another nearby village or seemingly in the right direction only to turn away, peter out or end up at a rubbish tip. To-ing and fro-ing across town trying to find the beginning of a piste is more frustrating than unnerving, though

Causing a commotion at Oujeft in Mauritania. Finally we were given the right directions (R5).

it's something that GPS waypoints, where available, now minimise.

At this point you may try asking someone – a hit-or-miss affair in Africa, as one traveller reported. '*I had learned quickly that you never believe what anyone says without getting a few second opinions. Usually you get a variety of contradictory responses and either have to go for the most popular answer or choose the guy who seems most intelligent and trustworthy*'.

A lot depends on *how* you ask. Don't pre-suggest by pointing and asking 'Is this the way to Madame Tussaud's?'. Instead ask 'Which way to Madame Tussaud's?' but don't point. It won't guarantee a correct answer but will avoid the tendency to nod affirmatively to please or to get rid of someone. Although you may be steaming from the ears by this stage, remember to be polite and, as with all exchanges in Africa, start with greetings and handshakes. Avoid showing maps – depending on where you are, only tourists use and understand these – but drawing a mud map in the dirt or in the dust on your bonnet can be useful.

The self-consciousness brought about by your floundering can be hard to handle but it helps if you **ask the right person**. In my own experience I've found policemen, soldiers and older men to be the most reliable, knowledgeable and straight. Women and young girls rarely travel out of the village or are aware of anything beyond a limited radius and are unlikely to speak French, let alone your own language. In some remote places they may also be embarrassed by your attention, elsewhere they'll enjoy teasing you. Some kids will mislead you for a laugh, to get a tip or a free ride to impress their friends. There are a couple of places in Morocco where they practise this evil craft! Sometimes it's less hassle to just try and work it out for yourself, which eventually you always do.

Keeping together

When travelling in large **convoys** the pace is slower and sometimes frustrating, especially for the first few days, but it's as well to remember that you're travelling together for mutual support as much as companionship. **Bikes** in particular will find travelling with cars slow. At times it can be easier to ride for a few kilometres along a clear piste and wait for the cars to catch up. A **rear-view mirror** is useful for bikes in a convoy, and you should always ride with some basic items, most especially maps, GPS, compass and water, even if all your gear is in the car. With a car-only convoy, it's assumed that each vehicle is self-sufficient, as it should be.

Before a group sets out on a new piste **clear rules** should be established and adhered to. Rule One should be to **keep the vehicle behind in sight at all times**. Signals can include flashing lights for a quick photo or toilet stop, and lights kept on for 'Stop now'. Out on the plains, it's sometimes possible to spread out and drive side by side, but when getting back in line establish a pre-determined order.

Losing sight of your companions is unnerving. You end up not knowing if they're behind you or ahead; you race forward or backtrack while they're either doing the opposite or carrying on regardless. It is the responsibility of everyone to look out for each other – this should stop any arguments about whose fault it was. The leader should slow down or stop if he or she gets too far ahead of the rest of the group, who in turn should never stray from the route or stop for long without signalling.

If things look dire, **climb to some high ground**, turn off your engine, look around and listen for the others. In this position you're also more likely to be spotted. Again, binoculars can be very useful. Failing this, an agreed procedure should be strictly adhered to. For example, after a certain time out of contact, you should all return to the point where you last stopped or spoke together. If fuel is critical you should stop ahead at a clear landmark, such as a village or junction.

There is a short episode in *Desert Riders* (see p.208) where I lost the other two guys while we were looking for the track south of Tarat. I had led off one way but they had not followed and within minutes we were separated. The terrain was difficult and it was easier to walk (which may have explained their deviation). I did all the things outlined above, without luck. It's surprising how quickly you can become dejected when you suddenly lose your companions within just half a kilometre!

In this case our situation was far from serious (Tarat was a day's walk away if need be), but had fuel, water or visibility been less than optimal, it could have turned into a survival situation. In this case I was sure they would return as a day or two earlier we'd become separated but all had done the right thing by going back. Sure enough, after a couple of hours I returned close to a spot where we were last together and they soon turned up, having circled me and left me notes on cairns while I searched for them.

Remember, the whole point of keeping together is to give each other much needed support during a risky endeavour. Suppress individualistic tendencies and stay in visual contact when traversing remote tracks, or tell others where you're going. In the above example it was the second and final lesson that we needed to remind ourselves to stay together.

This scenario is not uncommon for groups of people travelling together for the first time; it can take a few days for the team to gel. Expect these sorts of cock-ups in the early weeks when people learn to get a feel for things. Curb any frustration and hope that lessons are learned.

Inter-vehicle communication

Travelling with another vehicle (bike or car) will soon underline the frustration of communication. Turning round to drive back and work out what's going on is not always desirable or even possible. Flashing headlights at one another is OK when rolling along in convoy but it offers a limited range of signals. The sound of vehicle horns tends to get blown away in the wind and may not be audible in a helmet or inside a car with fans roaring. The simple answer is a **hand-held short-range radio** for each vehicle, allied if necessary with a pair of binoculars.

It may sound unnecessarily sophisticated but you'll find radios can save a lot of time and effort, especially in dunes, during recoveries or recce-ing a way through. And even just on a straightforward piste the ability to talk with other drivers can make travelling together smoother and less irritating.

The problem is **reliability**. If it's common to hear of Special Forces in the Middle East getting into trouble because of problems with their state-of-the-art radios, you can be sure that operating cheap consumer units in the Sahara will be no different. Some units work fine, some don't work at all and you never really know why. Another factor is their **legality**. Undoubtedly every country this book covers will want some sort of permit to use radios. If applying for a such a permit officially you can safely add another year to your pre-planning stage. Unless you have good local connections or a healthy, 'decision-enabling' budget your application will sink without trace into the treacle-filled void that is African governmental bureaucracy.

Therefore, take a pair of radios if you think they'll be useful, but make sure you're **discrete** in their storage and use, and be prepared to lose them and face a fine or worse if you get caught. In this situation you want to have your story ready: stress safety and security as your reasons for using them, which is the truth anyway, as well as their innocuous range. It will of course be more believable if you're not wearing a green beret and Desert Storm camo clothing at the time.

CB, VHS or PMR?

To cut a long story short, your choice is between CB (Citizen's Band), VHF and the latest inexpensive PMR (Private Mobile Radio) sets like Motorola Talkabouts. My experience with CB was not so successful and yet this was no surprise. Buying a load of equipment to help film *Desert Driving*, instead of communicating with the crew at little more than shouting distance, I managed to pick up what sounded like minicabbers in Leytonstone, 2000 miles away. Admittedly I did not persevere once I saw it was a lost cause because, to be honest, I was not at all surprised. Others, I've heard, have had more success with CB set-ups in the desert so don't give up on them just because I did.

VHF might be considered a more professional level of comms and VHF retailers will certainly scorn 'nerdy' CB-ers, yet there seems little advantage at short range. Typically a new VHF unit will cost at least three times that of a CB with accessories priced at a similar level, and a licence may be necessary too. I hired a set of Motorola VHFs for a tour once and they all worked well within a couple of kilometres of each other and proved genuinely handy. Hiring was certainly economical as these sorts of radios are often rented out to com-

A PMR446 radio for short range comms: small, handy, cheap and as reliable as anything else. © Mick Baines

mercial users; they worked out around £15 a week. One thing to consider with VHF is that in urban areas of Europe local booster transmitters may enable an outstanding signal but once in the Sahara they may not be so impressive. Supposedly this is not the case with CBs.

In Europe in recent years they've released new frequencies, allowing the growth in inexpensive **PMRs**. A pair of PMRs can easily cost under £100. The units are very compact and light, will easily fit into your pocket and, operating on UHF FM, they have very clear reception. With a licence-free 0.5 watt of power, the range can be up to three kilometres. More powerful one-watt models may receive up to eight kilometres away, but will probably require a licence, depending on where you live.

For recharging on the move you can either use the mains recharger supplied, via an inverter (an inexpensive solution), or try and buy a higher-end model which can take a lead off the car's cigarette lighter socket and doesn't use the radio's battery. Although I have yet to try them in the desert myself, for inexpensive and discrete short-range communications, PMRs are the best bet.

Survival and security

The dangers of travelling in the Sahara are well known (if sometimes misunderstood) and account for part of the adventurous appeal. This frisson of excitement adds an edge that is in fact more often appreciated in anticipation or retrospect. People often overestimate the danger of scorpions and snakes and the risk from theft but underestimate the dangers of poor vehicle preparation, driving and navigation.

Like all desert travellers, I've heard and read various horror stories and also made reckless decisions in my early years. A successful trip is no great story but a fatal trip is no story at all. Few people hear about the people who never come back as their disappearance affects a very small group, but there have been several cases of adventurous but foolhardy bunches of students crossing the Sahara in an old banger during their summer holidays and never returning. Although these unfortunates travelled on fairly straightforward trans-Saharan pistes, it was lack of preparation of an unsuitable car, and driving at the hottest time of year, that made their demise predictable. It may all have been done before, of course, but it does not mean that this trip will not be your last. Broadly speaking in the Sahara a crisis can arise from:
- Serious personal injury.
- Vehicle problems (broken down, destroyed or robbed).
- Being lost or stranded with a combination of the above two.

SURVIVAL DOS AND DON'TS

- Don't travel alone unless you're prepared to face the consequences.
- Know your limitations. In the Sahara there is no rescue service.
- Avoid known danger areas where there are bandits, terrorists, wars or mines unless, again, you are prepared to face the consequences (see box on p.350).
- Don't travel in summer. This is when most desert travellers die. If things go wrong the margins for survival are much slimmer.
- Know where you're going. Keep on the track, avoid dunes and off-piste short-cuts. Carry adequate route information and navigational tools.
- Carry enough fuel and water for your entire planned route, including a reserve. Difficult terrain and physical activity will greatly increase consumption of these fluids.
- Never carry on when lost. Stop before you go too far, accept that you've made a mistake, and if necessary retrace your steps.
- Even before things go wrong don't waste water. Get into the habit of being miserly with your washing and cleaning needs.
- Carry essential spares and tools and know how to use them. You should at least be familiar with tyre removal and repair, and fault diagnosis.
- Keep your companions in sight at all times. Or tell them what you're doing and where you're going, both when driving and when going for an evening stroll.
- Never drive at night. Even on the tarmac roads in Africa there is a danger of unlit vehicles, stray animals and potholes.
- If you check out on departure, check in on arrival. Even if no one seems bothered it's an essential courtesy that may prevent wasted searches.

Injuries are common with motorcyclists. The risks of careless riding and driving, particularly in sand, have hopefully been emphasised in the relevant chapters. Concentration and anticipation are essentials which for motorcyclists, at least, are part of domestic riding anyway. The other danger is around the camp or during car repairs, when injuries from tools, dropping heavy objects, or burns frequently occur. Crashing a car on the highway or having it fall or roll over is one reason why seatbelts should always be worn. The limitations of sand tyres on wet tarmac have already been underlined, especially on heavy, powerful cars, as have the risks of driving a top-heavy car on the piste or in dunes.

Vehicle problems – be it burned out, irreparable or stolen – are more common with travellers in cars. If the vehicle is destroyed or has been stolen the scenario is simple: either recovery is likely (usually the case) or it isn't.

Getting lost need not escalate into a desperate situation if you have a GPS, a map and a compass, and carry sufficient supplies of fuel and water. None of these situations need induce panic if you're on a relatively well-used piste during the cooler seasons. In fact it's hard to see how any traveller who's read this book could become completely unaware of their whereabouts in the Sahara, as navigation dominates so much of your travel. This sort of situation is much more likely to happen to an inexperienced and foolhardy traveller who's ventured into the desert, perhaps in an ill-equipped rental car and without proper equipment.

PREVENTING DISASTER

Some might say that going to the desert in the first place is courting disaster, but this is not true. The very fact that books like this exist proves that adventurous tourism in the Sahara has long been a viable recreational activity and not a lottery with your life. A successful trip depends on thorough preparation

'IF WE'RE DONE FOR WE'RE DONE FOR AND THAT'S ALL THERE IS TO IT'

In February 1959 a team of British oil prospectors came upon an unidentified aircraft in southwestern Libya, about 200km northeast of Kufra. The wreckage had been spotted and its position recorded by a reconnaissance aircraft the previous year. The bomber was soon identified as an American B-24 Liberator, the *Lady Be Good*, so a fifteen year-old aviation mystery began to give up its secrets.

The *Lady be Good* had been part of a squadron of US bombers based near Benghazi, northeastern Libya, which in April 1943 had set off in a sandstorm with two dozen other B-24s on a daylight bombing raid to Naples. On the way the Liberator was blown off course and the crew were forced to abandon their mission and dump their bombs at sea. Around midnight and many hours overdue, the bomber was heard flying over its Libyan base at which time the navigator radioed in to fix a position. Flares were sent up to mark the airfield but were not spotted by the crew and, with no reply to their radio message, the *Lady Be Good* flew on south into the Saharan night.

By 2am on the 5th of April, thinking they were still over the sea, the nine-man crew bailed out as the fuel tanks ran dry. Eight survived the jump and regrouped on the ground, but one crew member was killed when his parachute failed to open.

Still thinking they were just a short distance south of the airfield, the survivors lightened their load and marched north. Their Liberator, laden with emergency supplies and a radio, had landed largely intact 25km to the south.

After five days' marching over nearly 120km, five of the crew collapsed. The remaining trio trudged on, still thinking the base was close, but by April 12th they too were dead.

Following the aircraft's discovery, a search uncovered the remains of all but one of the crew (the ninth man may have been discovered by a British Army convoy in 1953 and hastily buried). Diaries and other artefacts found with the crew helped fill in the tragic details of their doomed mission. In 1995 the wreck was broken up and removed to a police compound in Torbruk.

Not all Saharan air crashes end with such misfortune. In the early 1950s the Hermes airliner was considered the pride of the BOAC fleet, setting new standards in luxury air travel. In May 1952 one such airliner was undertaking an overnight crossing of the Sahara to Nigeria, but when dawn saw the sun rise behind the aircraft the captain knew he was way off course. SOS messages were despatched as the airliner was forced to land in the dunes south of Chinguetti in Mauritania,  some 2000km from its flight path. Amazingly, all eight crew and ten passengers survived.

Nomads from a nearby camp came to help, as did a parachute team of French medics. The survivors set off on foot to a nearby oasis, where sadly one of the crew died of the strain. Two months after the incident an inquiry found gross errors in navigation, and the captain and navigator were dismissed by BOAC.

Forty years later Bob Watt, a London police officer, located the wreck of the Hermes and, following other visits, returned with a TV crew to film the excavation on the crash's 50th anniversary. But in the meantime an enterprising individual from Atar had been alerted to the cache of high-grade aluminium and melted down

Lady Be Good on its rediscovery in 1959 in southeastern Libya.
© U.S. Army Quartermaster Museum

the fuselage for scrap. After much digging only the engines and some other pieces were recovered.

The Sahara's best-known aviator is Antoine de Saint-Exupéry, author of many books including *Wind Sand and Stars* (see p.643). In it he describes undertaking a long-distance record attempt in December 1935 from Paris to Saigon. Disorientated by poor visibility on the Benghazi–Cairo leg, he descended slowly in search of landmarks and hit the ground at full speed. Incredibly both Saint-Exupéry and his co-pilot Prévot survived unscathed. A veteran of previous crash landings which had thus far ended well, Saint-Exupéry was phlegmatic about their fate: 'If we're done for we're done for and that's all there is to it'. Trusting that they had not yet crossed the Nile, they trudged northeast with virtually no water and collected dew from a parachute (an idea later used in *Flight of the Phoenix*). After staggering around for five days and covering 185km they were found, on their last legs, by a nomad, and were safely in Cairo the next day.

WWII Savoia engine cowlings at Karkur Murr, Sudan.

Saint-Exupéry disappeared over the Mediterranean in 1944, but four years earlier an LRDG raid had destroyed an Italian Savoia bomber at Jebel Uweinat (it's still there today). Partially as a result of LRDG activities, by 1942 nearby Kufra was in Allied hands and on Monday May 4th three newly-arrived Bristol Blenheims from the South African Air Force took off on a practice mission towards Rebiana. When one plane's engine began to misfire they all landed, but having lost track of their position, short recces in the operational aircraft failed to locate Kufra or any other landmark.

The twelve men were confident a search party would soon locate them but by

Blenheim IV bomber

Wednesday their water was finished and they were breaking open compasses and gun-sights to drink the alcohol. Very soon half were dying or shooting themselves; hosing themselves down with fire extinguishers during a sandstorm made matters worse as they endured agonising burns and blisters.

On that day the diary of one Major de Wet recorded: '...boys are going mad wholesale – they want to shoot each other – very weak myself – will I be able to stop them and stop them from shooting me – Please give us strength.' The next day he added 'we expect to be all gone today. Death will be welcome – we went through hell'.

Sandstorms delayed the search parties which did not reach the site until the following Monday. Major de Wet was found with a pistol in his hand. Only one of the crew survived. Training and experience apart, Saint-Exupéry's lucky escape and the SAAF's gruelling demise show how the season can radically affect your chances of survival.

In 1920 probably the earliest airborne misadventure in the Sahara led to the death of General Henri Laperine. As a French officer he'd helped pacify the Ahaggar Tuareg who stood in the way of French expansion and a proposed trans-Saharan railway. Setting off from Tamanrasset for Mali, he died of his injuries following a crash near Anesbaraka, well west of In Guezzam. It is said his last words were 'People think they know the desert, people think I know it. Nobody really knows it'.

Unidentified wreck in Libya. © M. Sofiantini

Sources include: www.ladybegood.com; www.tlc-exped.com/LadybeGood.html; www.qmfound.com; www.fjexpeditions.com.

– of your vehicle, your itinerary and your provisions. It's the awareness that this preparation may become crucial to your survival that adds to the challenge of the whole undertaking.

How disasters happen

Disasters in the desert rarely spring up out of the blue. They develop over a period of time, even weeks, and are finally compounded by one more bit of bad luck or one careless decision too many. Paul Stewart's book, *Trek*, describing a mixed group of Brits crossing Africa in the mid-1950s in an old Morris, was a perfect example of how casual carelessness and ill-fortune ended in tragedy near Assamaka. On the web you may still be able to read Karim's 15,000 word epic, *Disaster in the Sahara* (www.desertbiking.co.uk). While anyone with desert experience would recognise that setting off alone on a bike along the 750km Dahr Tichit piste was foolhardy, it's a frank and detailed tale of how a Saharan adventure disintegrates to the point of writing delirious good-bye notes to your parents – as well as a thought-provoking account on the bitter aftermath of rescue.

Most experienced desert travellers don't get anywhere near such desperation because they make the right decisions early on. Wrong decisions can include ignoring any of the guidelines listed on p.349 and not fully appreciating the consequences of your decision. And they don't just happen to tourists. Locals, from young shepherds to experienced desert drivers complacent to the desert's dangers or fatalistic by nature, perish with much greater frequency.

Since the end of the colonial era there has been **no rescue service in the Sahara**, so you are on your own. The local army or police are unlikely to rush off to a set of GPS co-ordinates; better to rely on other travellers who will be much more sympathetic to your plight and flexible in their response. Unless you have impressive diplomatic connections, most local authorities won't lift a finger unless such an endeavour is paid for in advance, in the form of insurance.

We once met a frantic Frenchman in Reggane who'd flown in to try and find his friends, a week overdue from the long but straightforward Tanezrouft piste. (At that time, 1989, it was customary in Algeria to check out and check in between some desert towns.) He was outraged that the local Algerian authorities had not already mobilised a search and had no intention of doing so, and was trying to charter a local plane to search the 1000km of flat reg.

Although to European sensibilities the apathy of **local authorities** can appear callous and even mercenary (as Karim's story vividly describes), to most Africans, getting lost in the Sahara is either seen as Allah's will or tough luck for rich tourists. Mali, Niger, Chad and Mauritania are among the poorest countries in the world and their local authorities haven't got the resources to deal with tourists in trouble. During the 2003 abductions (see p.362) fellow tourists and paid local guides had done much of the initial searching before the local army finally got on the case and used their huge resources.

Satellite phones

You can keep your HF radios, tin-foil kites and SARSAT beacons; the most effective survival aid in an emergency is a satellite telephone. If you can communicate freely your situation is far less perilous. Lately satellite phones have become genuinely portable, cheap enough to buy or rent and much more reliable than long-range radios. A sat phone doesn't have to be stashed for an emergency, of course; you can use it to call or text home every night if you want to. They have become a favourite with many desert travellers, both recreational and clandestine. I've used mine to check on the price of a car part in the UK, send in audio reports for a website, locate a lost companion on Jebel Uweinat (who also had a phone), as a back-up GPS when my main unit was confiscated, and last but not least to call for help when lying injured on the piste.

Thuraya sat phone: low call charges, sends text and comes with a GPS too.

Who you gonna call?

It's comforting to know you can contact someone at home, but in the case of an emergency, do not underestimate the responsibility and strain you may be placing on them to arrange your rescue. They may have little idea of the reality of desert travel and what to do about it when things go wrong. Calling an embassy or your travel insurance company (see box on p.356) in the expectation that they'll get you out of a fix is a tall order.

A much more realistic scenario would be to try and organise it privately by contacting someone locally. If that's not possible, get a message put onto one of the Saharan internet forums to ask for help from other travellers nearby. With today's access to instant communication, it's relatively easy to call upon the network of fellow Saharan travellers, most of whom you'd never meet. They could come from nearby or down from Europe with a spare part or just simply pick you up and take you to safety. Doing it this way, a rescue or assistance can be efficiently organised without a drama.

It can be said that sat phones give you a false sense of security, encouraging you into dangerous situations that you would otherwise have avoided. The same was probably said at the advent of GPS or indeed the wheel. Even in the wilderness mobile personal communications are now an accepted part of modern life as a personal safety device as well as a social one. In the Sahara it may not be essential, but like a GPS it makes sense. Just remember that some countries still regard such items as **illegal** to import by tourists, so pack and use your sat phone discretely.

Thuraya

The most commonly-used satellite phones in the Sahara are Thurayas (www.thuraya.com). Based in Abu Dhabi, they doubtless have plans to cover the world, but currently the network covers India, west and central Asia (not Israel), north and central Africa and Europe (but not Scandinavia) using a sin-

It doesn't have to be an emergency. Ask nicely and you might be allowed to call the kids on Christmas Day.

gle geo-stationary satellite above Somalia. Because of this, costs and therefore call rates are lower than global networks like Iridium.

Made by Hughes or Ascom, Thuraya handsets are the size of a mid-1990s mobile phone and aren't exactly a cutting-edge design either. At present they cost around £500 in the UK, but if you happen to be passing through the Emirates you might get one for less.

The nifty thing about Thurayas is that where there is GSM coverage you can use your regular GSM SIM card inside a Thuraya handset. However, having said this it's not unusual for Thuraya calls to be cheaper than international GSM rates from North Africa, though this too may change. The handset also includes a rudimentary GPS and other features a few years behind the latest mobile gizmographics.

The last price I heard for renting a Thuraya for a month from the UK was US$200 plus usage. For the seasonal Saharan traveller who owns a Thuraya but won't be using it during the year, pay-as-you-go **scratch cards** are best, even if call rates are 25% higher than the monthly subscription service. Should you run out of credit in the desert, it's possible to call a Thuraya agency (or text someone to do it for you at home) and buy a scratch card using a credit card over the phone and receive the code number directly to key in.

With scratch cards I've found calls work out around US$0.90-1.50 a minute. Be warned though that if someone calls your Thuraya on a land line they'll be paying up to US$4.50 a minute! Calls to another Thuraya phone are just US$0.60, making them a viable short-range communications device in the desert, when you think of the added cost of a radio.

One thing to remember is that the smallest 39-unit scratch card (it should cost US$39, but is often more) extends the life of your phone (i.e., your phone number) for only **three months**. If you forget to use the phone for a few months (easily done) you may find it's been disconnected and you'll have to buy a new SIM card and number (about $60). You can ring 151 on your Thuraya free to check your credit and validity and key in more credit if necessary; 151 is also a good way of finding out if the phone is working. In the desert I've found them very reliable, but you must be outdoors and plenty of sky helps. So does keeping the aerial pointing towards Somalia (more or less), if you want to maintain good reception during your calls.

Though the newer units ought to be better, battery life is pretty poor on the original units, so a **car charger lead** that plugs into a cigarette lighter socket is essential. Expect the battery to go flat if stored for a while. Another problem with the early units (as pictured on p.353) is their propensity to turn themselves on inside a pack or pocket. Recessing the red 'on' button would be the answer and may have been done on the current handsets. Besides flattening the battery, the knocking about in your pack might have the unintended effect of keying in random characters. As with any mobile, a password is optional but after three failed attempts you would then need to unlock the phone by keying in a series of PIN numbers that you may have completely forgotten about. Make sure you note these down and take them with you, otherwise you could be stuck.

GSM phones

Though not really an emergency aid, it's worth knowing that the populated areas of just about all the Saharan countries now have GSM coverage. You'll also find towns deep in the Sahara may have coverage and, call costs excepted, having a mobile here is a good back-up to using local services.

WHEN THINGS GO WRONG

Something that few people ever have the opportunity to find out is that in a crisis they do not necessarily fall to pieces. This is especially true of travelling in the Sahara where there's a certain amount of mental preparedness for such an event. In this situation human ingenuity, resourcefulness and determination to survive will enable ordinary, unheroic individuals to do the right thing and perform incredible feats.

But not always. It's been said that the stranded SAAF Blenheim crew (see box on p.350) did all the wrong things which, along with the heat, sped up their ghastly deaths. And I recently heard from a biker who got lost and bogged down in the sand on a desert rally. Instead of turning back he set fire to bits of the bike with little logic and then went off on foot to be eventually found staggering around in his underpants near an oil plant.

Should you break down alone during the tourist season on any of the routes described in this book, unless you're certain help can be found nearby, **stay by your vehicle** and have signals ready. Your vehicle contains many elements you need to prolong survival and it's hard to imagine waiting more than a few hours or maybe a day before someone comes along.

However, if you're stranded on a more remote piste, or if your vehicle is immobilised somewhere **off-piste**, the situation is considerably more serious. In this instance, help is unlikely to pass by unless you've managed to summon it yourself.

Sitting it out in the Idehan Ubari. In the end help came back in hours, rather than days as expected.

MEDICAL EVACUATION (MEDEVAC)

The key to implementing a medical evacuation and repatriation is the **initial telephone call** to the emergency number listed on your travel insurance documents. It is in this situation that a satellite phone can speed things up. It's been said already, but make sure your insurers are clear about the nature of your trip; propose this medical evacuation scenario from the Sahara to them and see how they react. And if you're stuck consider the 'private rescue' scenario outlined on p.353.

To facilitate an evacuation the victim must be transported **back to civilisation** of some sort. A helicopter or air ambulance is unlikely to fly out to you. Be ready to give full and detailed information about the nature of the injuries and the location of the victim. First aid should be applied, including the immobilisation of fractured limbs which, if simple fractures, are rarely life-threatening.

Perhaps the worst medical emergency is not a serious external injury but a stroke, heart attack or even appendicitis where a speedy injection or surgery is necessary to keep the victim alive. In this situation or any critical injury you just have to accept that you're in the desert and can only do so much.

Hospitals may be rare in the Sahara but don't assume that because this is Africa they're unhygienic cesspits. The staff are usually extraordinarily dedicated and working against extreme difficulties and you need not feel at risk there.

There is no prescribed procedure that covers the Sahara as such rescues are extremely rare. Your insurer's loss adjusters will have local agents and details of previous rescues to fall back on and will have to formulate the logistics for a speedy retrieval.

Nevertheless in most serious cases an evacuation back to your home country is guaranteed, as long as you are fit to fly (heart problems can mean that flying is not allowed). You will usually be put on the next commercial flight, with personal assistance along the way including wheelchairs and transportation, etc.

Incoming! After being transported 200km back to Djanet and spending a few days in Djanet hospital, the injured driver flew home on a regular flight. He walked again but the vehicle was dumped © B. Lorsch

Survival priorities

Survival manuals refer to the '**3 Ps**' which need to be addressed in a survival situation: Protection, Position and Provisions. They should be dealt with in that order whether you are on- or off-piste and however soon you expect to be rescued.

Protection (shelter)

Keeping out of the sun and wind is the first priority as this will help reduce water consumption. Erect a tent, awning or whatever you can, even if you think it's just going to be a couple of hours before help turns up, so that you can rest, work or plan in the shade. In a car, shade the sunny windows while allowing the breeze to pass though.

Outside, wear protective clothing and headwear to reduce water loss and the possibility of dehydration. With protection secured you can now turn your attention to either repairing or recovering your vehicle, assisting an injured person, patiently waiting (so conserving energy and water) or as a last resort preparing to walk out.

Position (location)

Easily done with GPS and a good map. Scrutinise the map closely to see exactly where you are and if there may be some place you could get either water or help from other people. Have a look around your immediate area. Climb high ground and scan your surroundings with binoculars. Are there any animal tracks? Is there any vegetation which might attract camels? A camel herder or a nomadic encampment may not be far away. It worked for me once...

Provisions (water and food)

Establish exactly how much food and water you have and how many days it will last, including any emergency rations you may have stashed. Water is by far the more critical and must be conserved and rationed sensibly from the moment you find yourself in trouble. You can last a long time without food (stress will probably reduce your appetite) but not without water. If anything, food should be consumed frugally, as digestion and excretion use up precious supplies of the body's water.

Working it out

If at all possible, getting mobile should be your next priority. Although it might take a day or more, a rolled vehicle can be righted by just two people. Once the chance of repair has been exhausted – something to which everyone should apply every last ounce of their ingenuity and energy – you must face facts and assess the situation.

Try to see if there is a way that you can fix your problem, at least temporarily. It is a well-established fact that people underestimate their ingenuity as well as their strength until faced with a crisis. A car can drive on three wheel rims in two-wheel drive with broken suspension and just one low gear if necessary; a bike can be ridden on its wheel rims if necessary. Make repairs or improvisations calmly, methodically and in the shade or the cool part of the day. Do not be hasty and risk an accident. Conserve your energy.

If you're in a group and have another working car the situation is far less serious. Send some or all of the people to get help or arrange the retrieval of the abandoned vehicle, while being prepared for the vehicle to be stolen or looted in your absence. Don't ration water to the point of thirst. You're better off being lucid for as long as possible rather than slowly dragging yourself down into delirium by not drinking enough. Remember that despite what you see in the movies, in winter your water consumption will be much less than you think, as little as a couple of litres a day.

If there is nothing to be done but wait, keep still and stay in the shade. If your air-conditioning still works, use it in the hot part of the day and shade all the car's windows while enabling good ventilation. It's vital that you minimise water loss.

Stay by the vehicle unless you know it's hopeless. Walking in the desert is tough. If you must walk, walk at night and know exactly where you're heading. See 'Walking out', p.359.

Signalling

Emergency flares should be part of your emergency equipment but are only effective if used at the right time. Never just let off a flare in the hope that

Using a CD as a heliograph made a momentary bright flash across the valley, while the flare's smoke was more visible. But both these stills were shot on full zoom. Thick black smoke is best in day-time: burn plastic or rubber.

someone out there might see it, and don't waste them on anything but the lowest-flying aircraft. **Only make signals when you can see someone who might see it**. Have the flares ready and know how to use them should a vehicle or nomad pass by.

We experimented with signals on *Desert Driving* and found that, while the smoke from a flare was more visible than a CD heliograph (see below), you'd have to be lucky to have it spotted more than a couple of kilometres away. The bright red light it gives off would be much more useful at **night-time**. If you want to attract attention in daylight, the **thick black smoke** from burning rubber or plastic is much more effective, more visible and lasts longer than a flare, and is easily put out with sand. Position a smoke signal on high ground and have it ready to light with a trail of fuel leading to fuel-soaked rags stuffed in the tyre or whatever.

Using a heliograph (signalling mirror) to flash signals using reflected sunlight sounds like a nice idea but in practice is not half as effective as black smoke. Old CDs make useful heliographs as the centre hole enables accurate sighting. Hold the disc with your left hand and rest it on your right shoulder (see the photo on this page). Your right arm should be extended sideways and pointing directly towards the target. Sighting through the hole, angle the disc so the reflection shines on your outstretched hand. If your eye and the hand reflection are in line with the target they will see the very bright flash. Moving the disc's reflection on and off your sighting hand will be seen further off as regular flashes. This sort of sighting is difficult with a car mirror.

At night vehicle lights and their beams can be seen a very long way – 20km is possible on a cool, clear night. If you think there's a chance they'll be spotted, flash your main beam at regular intervals at the same time each night and, if you don't have a powerful torch ready to flash directly at a passing vehicle, remove the battery and a headlight to make a portable torch to shine from a hill should your vehicle be out of sight. Many locals travel at night in the desert, even if they are not necessarily the sort of people you would want to encounter.

There's little chance of an aerial search for tourists in the Sahara but if you think there's a possibility of this or have observed low-flying aircraft, lay out a **regular pattern on the ground**: a cross of stones or any bright colours that contrast with the terrain, the bigger the better. 'Help', 'SOS', '*En panne*' are words you might like to spell out in stones or sand.

Walking out

Many people perish in the deserts of the world because they do not stay by their vehicles. It's already been said that on a piste this is absolutely the right thing to do unless you're certain you can reach help in just a few hours' walk along a clear track. A car contains many things to prolong your life – a motorcycle less so. Off-piste you're on your own. Cyril Ribas, the author of the French Mauritanian GPS guide, spent three weeks by a well on the Tichit piste (Route R11), waiting for a broken suspension arm for his 2CV to be repaired and returned by passing nomads. Walking out would have got him into an early grave, but by scraping along to the piste (he'd come from Chegga, far in the north), he got to the vital well and could wait as long as was necessary.

Walking out should not be considered lightly; in most cases it's a last resort to save yourself when all else has failed. Attempt it only if you're certain your emergency situation cannot be resolved by waiting. **Think carefully about where you are going to walk to**. The strongest person should be chosen to make the march. Aim for a track, road or well that there's a good chance of reaching and once you've decided on your objective, stick to it. Think about the terrain and gradients you must cover; avoid dunes. Remember, this may be the last thing you do, so make it worthwhile. Use the comfort and facilities of your makeshift camp to prepare for the march and leave a dated and timed note, sketch or sand drawing saying in which direction you've gone and with how much water. If retracing your tracks, follow them religiously and avoid short cuts and/or steep ascents unless you're sure they'll save time and energy. Conserve energy and so, water, at all costs.

How far can you expect to get? Who knows? The *Sahara Handbook* suggested a fit person could walk up to 60km through the Bilma Erg in summer. Even

WATER SHORTAGES: LAST RESORTS

As mentioned elsewhere, using antifreeze in your **radiator** makes sense for the vehicle, but it's poisonous to drink. A big-engined car can carry 15 litres of water in its cooling system and another couple of litres in the windscreen washer (probably combined with detergent), which all adds up to a valuable potential water supply.

Antifreeze is blue but if you're not sure or the water is clear, a sweet taste means antifreeze is present so the water must be **distilled**. This can be done by boiling it in a sealed container from which a coiled hose runs into another receptacle – copper brake or fuel lines work best. As the steam escapes through the coiled hose it cools and condenses back into pure water drip by drip. Or try the bottle-to-bottle technique described below. It will take some time to distil useful amounts of water.

Diagrams of solar stills are a popular feature of desert-survival books. The principle is that by making a mini-greenhouse over a pit covered in clear plastic sheeting weighed down in the middle, moisture from plants or urine cast into the pit will heat up and condense on the underside of the sheet and trickle down to the low point to collect in a can. Every time I go to the desert I mean to try this method out because in reality I'm sure a mug of water is all that will be gained.

A better still can be made using two clear **plastic water bottles**. Collect urine (or antifreeze) in one, tape them together at the neck and lay them on level ground in the sun with the empty bottle slightly higher. Pure water will evaporate from one bottle and condense and collect in the other.

Digging down through the sandy bed of a oued is another film favourite. In the Sahara you might soon reach damp, cool sand, but the chances of hitting the water table are pretty slim.

by night I doubt if even a quarter of this figure is possible. As soon as you begin walking your water consumption will shoot up, so your range will be restricted by the amount of water you can carry. On firm ground you're unlikely to average more than 4kph. Aim to rest for ten minutes in every hour.

In **winter**, daytime walking is feasible, but if the daily temperature exceeds 25°C, rest in the hottest part of the day and walk in the early morning and into the late evening. At this time of year 100km over five days would be possible on firm terrain. As you may have read on page 350, Antoine de Saint-Exupéry and his partner managed 185km over five days on a pint of coffee, various medicines, dew from parachutes and an orange, while 500km further south in early May, the SAAF crews were going nowhere and dying in half that time.

The season and therefore temperature makes all the difference: in the **summer** walk at night but don't expect to get far. The stars and/or moon will provide plenty of light. Spare the GPS's batteries and use a hand compass. Stars move through the night but Orion's Belt forms a kite-like arrow which points just west of north until the early hours. Polaris, the North Star, is less bright but is on the axis on which the stars rotate. If you can find the saucepan-like Plough constellation, the edge of the 'pan' opposite the 'handle' points down to Polaris.

Equipment for walking out
Carry as little as possible, wear light and comfortable clothing and, most importantly, cover all exposed skin including your entire head and face for protection against the sun during the day and the cold at night. This equipment should include:
- Lighter or matches – for fire or signalling.
- Rescue flares, heliograph CD and torch.
- Map, compass, GPS, binoculars.
- Compact high-energy food rations – avoid cooking.
- Sleeping bag or emergency space blanket.
- Rope and bucket if expecting to pass wells.
- All the water you can carry.

To **carry water efficiently**, a harness should be made up to support this heavy weight on your back – a rucksack may now be very useful. One 20-litre water container is about the maximum a person could expect to carry. Avoid carrying heavy items in your hands.

SAHARA: HOW SAFE IS IT?
Apart from the pitiless desert and your own bad luck, there are also dangers from other people and their activities, be they fighting each other or terrorising you. Car-jacking and robbery are common in parts of eastern and southern Africa where tourists are an easy target. This has also caught on in the Sahara although, the desert being what it is, to a much lesser degree.

Streetwise strategies
This section could be filled with any number of canny tricks about secret pockets and mouse traps in your money belt, but the only knack you need to devel-

op is common sense along with the option of comprehensive travel insurance. Accept that you may lose something or even everything, through carelessness, theft or robbery. Much has been said about the need to keep your valuables safe, but in the end it's all just stuff that can be replaced, albeit at a price and great inconvenience. This is just a simple fact of travelling. Fear of the unknown is an understandable self-protection mechanism and as long as travellers have travelled, brigands have preyed on them. The perils of travel are probably no greater than they were five hundred or two thousand years ago, and the need for vigilance has always been the same.

On a boat or in a town, carry only things that you can afford to lose – and don't think that Europe is any less risky than Africa. Cities anywhere are the lairs of thieves who prey on ultra-conspicuous tourists – it's one good reason to avoid cities. In these crowded places keep the evidence of your wealth or your confusion under wraps. Wallets should always be zipped into inside pockets and cameras should not dangle temptingly around your neck. Markets and crowded travel termini are favourite haunts for pickpockets. As you wander into these places check that everything is zipped up, and be alert.

Avoid gazing in befuddlement at town plans on street corners in cities like Dakar or Tangiers. Plan your route corner by corner before you walk out of your hotel room and when you do walk, imitate the advice given to women walking alone at night: march with a single-minded purpose that emits the signal loud and clear: 'Kindly leave me alone!'. Beware of pats on the shoulder, newspapers or babies shoved in your face, and other distractions which are well-known set-ups for snatches or pickpocketing.

Petty theft and muggings are of course prevalent in large towns or cities, as they are anywhere in the world. If possible always make use of the secure parking offered by many hotels in towns and cities. Guidebooks advise leaving your valuables in the hotel's safe or at reception, but not all hotels inspire such a feeling of security so some travellers prefer to keep valuables on their person at all times. Never leave valuables in your hotel room.

Smugglers and bandits

As in any wilderness area, **smugglers** – primarily of cigarettes, drugs, arms and people – have certainly taken advantage of the Sahara's unmanned borders. It's a huge industry and all that many locals have to resort to when legitimate tourism work dries up. Many desert travellers have encountered smuggling convoys right across the Sahara and had nothing to fear. In one case in the Gilf the smugglers could not get away from us fast enough and in another, the nocturnal cigarette convoy near Amguid was so large and in such a hurry that, though some vehicles spotted us, they took no interest.

Smugglers may well engage in opportunistic banditry (common in Mali and the Tanezrouft, still a good reason to avoid that area), but as a rule they already have the best of vehicles and a job to do (often with the connivance of local authorities) and don't want the hassle of a robbery.

Banditry also flourishes in any wilderness area beyond the reach of civil law and order, a definition which might be applicable to just about the whole Sahara. All was quiet in the Golden Years from the early 1960s up to the late 1980s when Saharan tourism reached a peak, until the Tuareg rebellions in Niger and Mali and the civil war in Algeria. Today the Toyotas of NGOs, oil

THE TASSILI KIDNAPPINGS OF 2003

The revival of Algerian desert tourism which had begun in 1999 came to a sudden end in early March 2003 when the alarm was raised on the Saharan websites over two missing groups: four motorcyclists and four Swiss travelling alone in a Toyota 4x4 van. They'd not shown up for their pre-booked ferries from Tunis and were last seen on Route A2, west of Illizi.

Soon the Saharan web community was mobilised: bank accounts were opened to help fund the search which friends, relatives and other tourists in the area undertook, and everyone who'd been in the area recently offered their assessments of track and weather conditions, sightings of the missing travellers and their likely movements.

Those familiar with the area and with the disappearance of travellers were certain that they were not simply lost. The Tassili is a rocky plateau where it's hard to stray off the piste, and the bikers were all experienced desert riders who knew Route A2 well.

Records showed a rain storm had passed over the Tassili on February 26th and Imirhou Canyon (east of Illizi and prone to flash flooding) was searched but with no results. Rain on the more open Route A2 would not have immobilised the group; the travellers had disappeared without trace.

Soon more reports came through on the Swiss Sahara forum: another three bikers missing on Route A2; nocturnal movements of cars and motorcycles in the Oued Tikharatine area (KM370 of Route A2); a pick-up driven erratically by armed 'mullahs' near the Oued Samene (KM330); and an aborted satellite phone call from the Toyota's driver from well south of the piste, seemingly on the impenetrable Tamelrik plateau.

By the first week of April no less than seven separate parties, totalling thirty-two people – German, Austrian, Swiss, Swedish and Dutch – in eighteen vehicles, were missing, all within a 200km radius, and all following the clearly defined tracks of the western Tassili.

By this time the media had caught up and began churning out sensational headlines about secret tunnels, flash floods, sandstorms and GPS discrepancies (the invasion of Iraq was underway). The self-interest of groups like UNATA* was even more crass. In a communiqué issued just a fortnight after the first reports, they wasted no time in attacking the missing travellers as *'imprudent and illicit'* engaged in a *'clandestine tourism of defilement'*, deriding their *'sophisticated GPS and sat phones'* and even suggesting they were rock-art thieves sneaking across the border with their treasure! Outdated suspicions directed at Libya were also dredged up and there was a backlash against the 'adventurers' who were foolhardy enough to travel at all in the 'deadly' Sahara.

The fundamentalist connection

It soon became clear that a mass abduction had been orchestrated by Islamic militants from northern Algeria. The fundamentalist GIA had been waging a brutal civil war for over a decade at the cost of 100,000 lives. Now a splinter group, the GSPC (Salafist Group for Preaching and Combat), under the command of former Algerian soldier Amari Saifi (aka Abderrezak Lamari or 'Le Para'), had decided to turn its attentions to Algeria's hitherto peaceful *Grand Sud*. With the aid of a local smuggler the attacks were planned around the popular Routes A2 and A13: easy corridors in which to ambush passing travellers, even though the nature of the terrain there greatly limited escape routes.

Once the disappearances were acknowledged as kidnapping, the search was stepped up. The Algerian military deployed helicopters with heat-seeking sensors (little use in daytime); a hostage's message was found in a oued and missing vehicles, ransacked and half-burnt, were also unearthed. By late April contact had been made and negotiations were in progress.

It emerged the groups had been split into two, one holed up on the Tamelrik plateau southwest of Illizi and the other in the western Tassili near Amguid (see photo, p.372). The authorities eavesdropped on radio messages between the two groups which helped locate them.

Despite pressure from the German government not to go in with guns blazing, the Algerian army launched a raid on May 13th and the western Tassili hostages were freed from their hideout, somewhere southeast of the Mouydir plateau. Most of their abductors were killed.

---

* *Union Nationale des Associations des Agences de Tourisme Alternatif*, a Tamanrasset-based group of tour companies who blame *tourism sauvage* (independent tourism) for ruining the Sahara. See also p.289 and p.399.

The Wintersteller Diaries

Subsequent interviews revealed that their kidnappers described themselves as mudjahedin and, after initial brutality, treated them well. In his newspaper diaries, Gerhard Wintersteller told of their abduction at gunpoint near Gara Khanfoussa (A2, KM190) by a '*Landrover painted in the colours of a tourist company… suddenly, eight masked mudjahedin jump out of the car. They aim their weapons at us, gesture violently and completely overwhelm us.*' A Saharan traveller with many years experience, Wintersteller assumed it was a robbery but the events confused him: "'*Normal' bandits rob tourists and leave them by the side of the road with some food.*" He went on to describe crazed driving, which at one point threw them all out of the vehicle, and of being corralled with other captured tourists and mudjahedin injured in skirmishes.

They walked by night and hid by day, the hostages trying to leave as many signs as possible, strands of toilet paper on bushes and Wintersteller's note '*The Austrians were here!*' which was later discovered. He also described opportunities to grab unguarded weapons while their captors prayed, but thought better of it, and later the emergence of the 'Stockholm Syndrome' as barriers between captor and hostage dissolved under the shared strain.

April brought intense heat, snakes, sandstorms and worsening morale as they pressed into crevices in 50°C heat and drank from putrid *gueltas*. Helicopters regularly passed overhead inspiring both panic and the hope of imminent freedom. But release only came after the captors shot a nomad's camel for food – the nomad tracked them to their hideout and alerted the army.

In the meantime there was talk of the second group – said to be surrounded by Algerian forces on the Tamelrik plateau – being released to avoid another risky raid. Another vehicle was found in Oued Samene, this one booby-trapped.

By mid-June the hostages somehow passed through the armed cordon and off the plateau (there was talk of army collaboration from the start). After travelling through the Mouydir mountains, they turned up a month later in northern Mali, a region long beyond Malian state control following the Tuareg rebellion of the mid-1990s. On the way it emerged that one of the hostages, a German woman, had died of heatstroke.

Negotiations for a ransom continued into August. Libya was involved, or it wasn't; Germany would pay a €5m ransom but denied it. Then on August 17, nearly six months after the first abduction, the surviving fourteen hostages were released, flown to Bamako for a presidential photo call and on home to Europe.

Endgame?

Stories of the hostages' ordeal hit the press and some callously called for them to cover the huge cost of their rescue. There were disputes over the search funds raised via the Saharan websites – a total of €30,000 (including over £1000 via sahara-overland.com) – as it emerged that some involved in the search claimed unusually high expenses. In the end about two-thirds of the money went to African charities like *Medecins Sans Frontières* and a fund for the dead woman's children.

The surviving hostages had come through in remarkably good spirits and health following their ordeal, but the glare of the media soon distorted their accounts of their experiences as some individuals dominated the news while others tried to slip back into normal life. Within months books were produced by members of each group and a film was in the pipeline.

And what of the abductors? Despite denials, there seemed little doubt that they had received a ransom of around €5m. But now that their location was known and with hostages released, many expected them to be shot out. It never happened, many pointing a finger at the indifferent Malian government.

Then in mid-December the US announced the Pan Sahel Initiative (see p.364) and their first task in Mali was to pin down the GSPC who'd been spending their millions on arms and new recruits. An air strike was proposed though not approved, but the GSPC knew their days where numbered in northern Mali. An audacious plan to kidnap leading Dakar Rally racers was foiled by French intelligence and in mid-February 2004 a GSPC group was 'neutralised' trying to bring arms into Algeria. Another group attacked a Nigeran border post and a tourist group in the Aïr. Amari fled across the Ténéré straight into a Chadian ambush near Wour, guided by a US Navy aircraft. Most of the group were killed but Amari and some men were captured by the MDJT Tibesti rebels and in June 2004 handed back to the GSPC or Algerian authorities – no one seemed sure.

companies and sometimes tourists or the tour agencies who guide them are the main prize. Bandits also struck the Dakar Rally in Mauritania in 2001 and threatened to do so again the following year in Niger. Up till late 2002 they have attacked independent and tour groups in the desert regions of Libya, Chad, Mauritania, Mali and especially Niger with one or two attacks a season in the previous four or five years.

A feigned roadside breakdown can be a set-up for a robbery, though this is more common in sub-Saharan Africa. Generally a family group sat by the roadside by a steaming car will be what it seems, but a couple of shifty-looking young men may have other plans. If you are unsure in any situation, keep moving but if the game is up the important thing to remember with banditry is that they have nothing to gain by harming you. A submissive tourist has yet to be killed (though some have been brutalised and shot, see box on previous page). Vehicles and valuables are what they are after. Galling though it may be, let them have it all.

Terrorists and the Pan Sahel Initiative

The Sahara has not escaped the impact of Islamic terrorism that was brought to world attention by the events of September 11. Though thankfully not imitating Al Qaeda's hitherto murderous pattern, the 2003 abductions (see previous page) are the best known, though perhaps an exceptional example, even if some consider the problem may be deeper than that.

Even before the 2003 abductions started, the US had announced the **Pan Sahel Initiative** (PSI), an exercise to help train and equip the local forces of Mauritania, Mali, Niger and Chad to patrol and secure their vast and porous Saharan borders. The PSI kicked off in late 2003, and although one of its first tasks happened to be helping locate the GSPC fugitives, ostensibly the operation was conceived to repel the establishment of Al Qaeda training camps destroyed in Afghanistan following its invasion in 2001.

The setting up of such camps in the Sahara might indeed compromise trade and tourism (they existed in Libya during the 1980s) but the open, arid plains of the central Sahara are not like Afghanistan's mountainous Hindu Kush, and no African government (even the former rogue state, Libya) is likely to give them the support the Taliban had. Training camps in the middle of the Sahara without the assent of a host government or autonomous authority (rebellious or otherwise) could be easily tracked down and picked off.

The PSI may have been a pre-emptive operation against terrorist bases, but it is said that behind that cause lies the need to guar-

In early 2004 US troops moved into several Saharan countries to train local forces in anti-terrorist activities as part of the Pan Sahel Initiative. © USDoD

antee uninterrupted production in West Africa's oil fields on which the US is becoming increasingly dependent.

Terrorists clearly are the type of people one would not want to encounter in the Sahara. Until 2003 they were unknown, and at present it remains to be seen if the GSPC's day is done in the desert or if other groups, emboldened by the GSPC's success in obtaining a ransom, will follow suit.

Dealing with robbery

A bunch of veiled bandits rocking up out of nowhere armed with Kalashnikovs is a sight no owner of a 4WD will be pleased to see. It must be remembered that in just about all cases, it's your car they're after and a Land Cruiser with all the fruit is an especially rich prize. These are basically car thieves and in the current climate of relative calm there is little to be gained by killing you.

Even as early as 1990 a friend of mine lost his Troop Carrier when he popped up from completing an oil-change just outside Tamanrasset to find a machine gun in his face. The two Tuaregs drove him a few kilometres into the desert, from where he walked back to Tamanrasset. Since then he has vowed only to return to the Sahara in the crappiest Series III that no bandit would look at twice. It is certainly a strategy that's worth considering if you insist on exploring certain areas.

In most cases, injuries only occur when the owners try to resist or escape. This happened to one of the Austrians as they tried to evade the *mudjahedin* ambush in the Tassili in 2003. A woman was shot in the back, though amazingly her wound healed quickly when treated with honey by her captors.

Canny items like **hidden fuel-cut-out switches** were also shown to be of little use to other parties involved in this event and merely earned a rifle butt in the face (if you activate this just prior to a robbery, they'll know exactly where they left you when the car staggers to a halt...). A battery-cut-out switch would be better. Fuel-cut-out switches are more useful as additional anti-theft devices. In the end you must remember it's only a car (bikes and bikers are rarely targets except in kidnappings). If you happen to have it insured (as my Land Cruiser friend did, though this is hard to obtain in the UK) there is no financial loss.

Carrying weapons

One of the questions many Africa-bound overlanders consider is whether they should carry **weapons**. Using a knife, tear-gas or even a handgun (as some desert travellers do) might be advisable only if you happen to be in the tiny minority who know how to use them, are prepared to use them and are prepared to face the consequences of doing so and getting it wrong. Guns of course are a huge risk and hugely illegal. Knives and tear-gas can only be used effectively on a single assailant where a punch in the face and a kick in the crotch would suffice. It may be fun to fantasise about, but it's hard to think of a scenario where pulling out a weapon will do anything more than escalate a situation. It all sounds very 'James Bond', but most people appreciate that real-life armed struggles are not smoothly choreographed and endlessly rehearsed, but messy, clumsy and sickeningly brutal. Let the car go and be happy to have got away with your life.

No-go areas

Saharan criminals and insurgents don't relate to national boundaries as we do, but it's still the simplest way of categorising the risk in certain areas.

Lacking the vast natural resources of Libya and Algeria, Morocco, Egypt and Tunisia rely on a flourishing tourist infrastructure and a desire to keep it that way. While the fate of the Saharawi people is far from settled, the conflict in the **Western Sahara** has been dormant for years even if the 'inland' areas of the province remain out of bounds (see map p.459). So, despite the Casablanca bombing in 2003, **Morocco** remains as safe as it gets in the Sahara, as does **Tunisia** despite the underplayed bombing in Djerba in 2002 which killed many German tourists. **Egypt** too suffered a devastating massacre at Luxor as long ago as 1997 but as far as this book is concerned, the area of interest in the Western Desert is about as remote as it gets; the worst one might normally encounter are people-smugglers taking a short cut between Libya and Sudan.

Mauritania has experienced a couple of robberies over the years, and although in the Sahara it's common for authorities to blame criminals from neighbouring countries, it is genuinely thought that Malian Tuareg are the culprits, as the northeast of Mauritania is virtually uninhabited.

Though a few tours do visit the Kidal region, since the rebellion of the 1990s the **north of Mali** has never been really safe for independent travel, and away from the Tanezrouft and Timbuktu, was always a marginal tourist area. Robberies have occurred in the Tessalit region as tourists entered from Algeria and the Tanezrouft is the main route chosen by people-smuggling convoys operating from Gao. **Niger**, as mentioned above, has had its fair share of banditry, mostly in the Aïr or on its eastern fringes, and from which the protection of an organised tour counts for little, but this only temporarily reduces its continued attraction to tour groups.

Algeria, which looked so promising and has so much to offer, is still reacting to the events of 2003 (see box p.362) which at the time of writing have yet to be fully resolved. At Arak in 2002 there was an unrelated robbery of both locals and Swiss tourists in which the culprits were apprehended and quickly released. Most pointed the finger at local authorities and the convoluted municipal politics of the Wilaya of Tamanrasset, rather than at bandits. At the time of writing one needed to hire a guide as soon as one entered the country, but even with the perceived restrictions of a compulsory guide Algeria, like Niger, has much to offer and a long heritage of professional tourism services in the south.

It's not quite what can be said for **Libya** which has lately also insisted on guides at the border. Get-rich-quick *gens du nord* and obstructive tourist police (who also accompany guides) have given it a bad reputation, but as a result of one's limited mobility, security is generally good.

Which leaves **Chad**. Only marginally more accessible than distant Sudan, tours here skirt around the still-untamed Tibesti (where kidnap and/or robbery are almost guaranteed) to the Ounianga lakes and the Ennedi massif. Apart from attempted transit to Sudan via Abéché (itself prone to robbery), letting local tour operators put their vehicles and not yours at risk is your best prospect here, as it is in the other marginal areas of the Sahara mentioned above.

Inevitably this page is already out of date. Check out the latest on each country at www.sahara-overland.com/country as well as 'The S-Files' (travellers' reports) at www.sahara-overland.com/Sfiles.

Landmines

It's well known that certain areas of the Sahara are scattered with minefields, some dating back to WWII, but most laid during more recent conflicts. An anti-personnel mine will blow off your legs and possibly kill you if you step on it, but if you drive over such a mine, you could get away with just a ruined tyre. Larger anti-tank mines will destroy both you and your vehicle. In *In Search of the Sahara* Quentin Crewe described driving his Unimog over a mine near Nouadhibou in the 1970s. The heavy vehicle was destroyed but saved the occupants from injury. Most years a Saharan party sets off a mine somewhere, all known cases being in the areas listed below.

The best way to avoid setting off a mine is to avoid known minefields altogether. However, if you can't or don't want to do that, hire a reliable local guide to steer you through the danger zone. If you decide to go it alone through a minefield using someone else's GPS waypoints, be aware that the slightest deviation could result in a fatal accident. Follow any existing tracks and be wary of any unnatural barriers across a piste.

Known mined areas in the Sahara

Apart from the Atlantic Route (p.464), Route L7 and routes in Egypt's Western Desert, all the pistes in this book avoid mined areas so you should have little to worry about. Nevertheless, it's prudent to list the known locations of Saharan minefields, though this list should not be taken as a guarantee that mines do not exist elsewhere.

Starting from the far west, the horizontal border between **Western Sahara** and Mauritania is mined. Even though by now everyone knows the risks of leaving the piste when crossing the border and a new sealed road is being built, accidents occasionally happen. The danger is in the eight kilometres or so between leaving the tarmac at Fort Guergarat and the first Mauritanian checkpoint on the old 'Spanish Road'. At the time of writing this is a mass of tracks and there are no warning signs till later. In 1998 a Land Rover hit a mine just a couple of metres from existing vehicle tracks, with one fatality. Stay on the clearest tracks and if there is a new road, stay on it.

It's very likely that the entire border to the north with Morocco is also mined from a time when Polisario raiders got as far south as Chinguetti. There are certainly mines alongside the Layounne–Bir Mogrein road; a Paris–Dakar truck caught one here in the late 1990s.

Still in **Mauritania**, areas east and south of Ouadane are also said to be mined although Route R8 to Guelb is safe. There are said to be mines north of Guelb near the El Beyyid well and rock paintings.

There are also mines between Algeria and **Morocco** in the Hamada du Draa and Guir regions between Tindouf and Bechar, though no regular pistes cross this area. Any minefields are well south of the Moroccan routes given in this book.

Mali is thought to be mine-free as is **Algeria**. In **Niger** Tubu rebels laid mines in the Djado region in 1997-8. They were cleared in 2001 after the rebels came to an agreement with the Niger government but in March 2003 three Italian tourists were killed when they hit an anti-tank mine north of Djado. After the accident the military post at Chirfa confirmed there were mines in the area on the route into Enneri Blaka where the former base of the FANS Tubu rebels was located until 2001. There are apparently three routes into the valley of Enneri Blaka: the regular route from the south via Seguidine, one from the north which cuts northeast of Djaba and then goes south down the Enneri Domo, and a new one which cuts directly eastwards from Chirfa. It was this latter route which was reported to be mined.

Besides this, the far eastern reaches of the Seguedine-Zouar piste are mined around Col de Yei Lulu just before the Chad border, and there are reports of wired-off minefields further north.

Libya

Libya has plenty of mines from WWII (mostly in the east) and, along its southern border, following the war with Chad and related to the current Tibesti rebellion. WWII mines still exist east of the line from Ajdabija (south of Benghazi) to Jalu as well as further south. A surveyor working in southeast Libya reported that 'Many areas of country to east of Kufra-Benghazi road are mined' although the run from Al Jakbub close to the border across a passable 'neck' of the Calansho Sand Sea down to Kufra is becoming a popular off-piste excursion with no known reports of mines (see also under Egypt, below). These mines have long been a sore point with Libya, who has insisted that Germany and Britain pay for their clearance. As a result of Libya's continued rehabilitation, in March 2003 the Virgin Group announced a deal under which they would sell an airship-based landmine clearance system using radar to Libya.

Mine warning sign at Ounianga Kebir, Chad. © Ginge Fullen

It's also been reported that the broad plain leading from the tarmac road about 90km north of Sebha, southeast to the Sarir al Qattusah, is mined (in 1989 a traveller was warned by a Libyan police patrol who followed).

In southern Libya, between Serir Tibesti and the Rebiana Erg in the Dohone region, the Passe de Klingue on Route L7 (KM409) has mines from several periods and wrecked vehicles to prove it. Mines located at this point damaged a truck in 1991, nearby in 2001 and again in 2003.

In August 2000 a Swiss party hit a mine on the way back from the well at Gongom on the western side of Dohone. The mine was located in the Oued Oyouroum (N22° 40' E18° 45'), which was not known to be mined. The travellers were returning along their own three-day-old tracks. Later they met a Chadian army patrol near Kilingue looking for Chadian rebels who probably laid the mines, thinking the new tracks belonged to rebels using the well.

It seems the Chadian army has permission from Libya to venture into deep southern Libya to lay mines in their operations against the Tubu rebels so it's simply best to avoid this part of Libya.

Chad

Chad, or to be precise the north as far south as Faya and up to and beyond the Libyan border, is the most mined region in the Sahara, dating from the Libyan war of the 1980s and, as you've just read, is still being mined today. Mines exist alongside tracks; some are well marked, others are not. In August 2002 the leader of the rebel MDJT movement himself was among the dead in a land-mine incident. Near the Libyan border the mines at the Passe de Korizo are well-known with a well developed alternative piste. A truck hit a mine on the track south of the Pass on the Arkiafera Plain north of Wour. Mines also wrecked a Unimog at N22° 19′ E17° 25′ on the way to Aozou and other tracks in this region are well known to be mined, such as the track between Ouri and Aozi, east of the Dohone spur.

There are said to be mines around Ounianga Kebir and the piste northwest to Gouro as well as the piste between Faya and Fada through the Kora dunes (just above N18°). They block the line of least resistance which everyone would follow and you must know the places to avoid by crossing a 50m-high dune belt. South of Ounianga Kebir the ominously-named Wadi Doum (N18° 22′ E20° 23′) – where the Libyans lost the 1980s war and which is now a Chadian military base – is littered with abandoned military hardware, UXO and is heavily mined. Those minefields which are crossed by the clear piste are carefully fenced off with barbed wire. You may be quite safe staying on the piste but walking around to look at the military equipment is dangerous.

In January 2003, in the first reported mine-clearance operation in Chad, the head of an anti-mine unit funded by a UN development programme announced that they had removed some five hundred mines from around Faya Largeau and that the area was mine-free up to 10km from the town.

In this region as well as the western Ennedi it is wise to travel with an experienced guide. Even the sides of the well-used piste about 20km WNW of Fada are mined at a narrow passage. This list is far from exhaustive and stick-ing to previous tracks or travelling with a guide if coming down from El Gatrun all the way to Faya (should it even be safe enough to do so) seems to be the only advice. Guides, however, are not a guarantee that you will avoid mines, which is why northern Chad is, along with its other dangers, the least visited Saharan country.

Egypt

The Western Desert of Egypt saw fierce fighting in WWII and its northern part, between El Alamein and the Libyan border, as well as the Qattara depression, were heavily mined. All mines have been eliminated between the coastal road and the sea, but further inland any number may still remain. The Qattara Depression was never cleared, and both the German and British armies mined the northern parts, below the cliffs, to prevent each other from getting behind

---

CIGARETTE SMUGGLING

The smuggling of cigarettes is big business in the Sahara. Millions of Marlboros and Gauloises, mostly from Mauritania and Nigeria, are brought to Libya and Algeria every year. In North Africa a packet of Marlboros is up to four times more expensive than south of the Sahara. The smugglers are often very rich, driving brand-new four-wheel-drives with petrol engines. In Assamaka, the borderpost between Niger and Algeria, customs officers are well aware of this business but do nothing to stop it. At this border it is not uncommon to see a cigarette smuggler lending his Thuraya satellite phone to a government official so he can call his family in Niamey. Normal phones do not exist at this borderpost. The Algerian authorities are at first sight more serious in fighting the illegal trade. But according to eyewitnesses many government officials are not sincere and are deeply involved in cigarette smuggling themselves.

Gerbert Van der Aa

---

their lines. Given this situation, all parts of the Depression away from travelled roads and tracks are best avoided.

Tensions between Egypt and Libya resulted in some of the border areas being mined. At Jebel Uweinat there is a marked minefield (with large anti-tank mines) blocking the west side of the entrance of Karkur Talh (N22° 02.7′ E25° 07.9′), and also at the low pass where the track skirts the northern spur of the mountain and continues towards the Libyan border at N22° 04.5′ E25° 02.8′. It's also reported that there are mines near tracks passing a series of hills at N22° 04′ E25° 16′, about 20km NE of Uweinat where two red tracks join on the 1942 Uweinat map.

There are unconfirmed reports of mines at the pass between Peter and Paul, and mines may be expected at any easily blockable route close to the border. In February 1999 German tourists ran over a mine in the southern Gilf Kebir at the western entrance of the Wadi Wassa (N23° 00.2′, E25° 51.3′), and it may be expected that the western reaches of the Wadi el Firaq are also mined; a vehicle hit a mine here in 1983 around N22° 53′ E25° 47′, half a kilometre from some iron poles and near a yellow drum.

There have been reports of the Aqaba Pass at the central Gilf Kebir being mined, although this seems extremely unlikely as countless vehicles have gone through this narrow pass over recent years. Old reports suggested that the western entrance of Wadi el Gubba in the northern Gilf Kebir was also mined, but this too is unlikely. A Dakar Rally passed through here in 2000 as have several travellers since, taking the Wadi Gubba route from the western Gilf and heading for the entrance to Silica Glass valley (see p.635).

The minefields recently placed by the Egyptian army are marked with posts and barbed wire, and small stone cairns. If you see any obviously non-natural features (piles of stones, big slabs, steel drums, etc.) placed directly across the track, this is likely to be a warning sign for mines.

Desert landforms

For most visitors it is the dramatic scenery of the Sahara which accounts for the desert's appeal, even if the surrounding landscape is completely devoid of features. Here, where much of the earth is without its usual mantle of vegetation and soil and with little human intervention, the landforms of the Sahara are laid bare in all their magnificence.

The view from Assekrem in the Hoggar (Route A6) is an iconic Saharan vista (© Mike Foster) but most of the Sahara is composed of flat plains of gravel or sand – at times completely featureless apart from surface ripples, as on this vast sand sheet in the Ténéré of Niger (below).

Most of the Sahara is a plateau that lies around 300m above sea level: the desert is a vast flat **plain** creased with low escarpments. As the weathered rock breaks down into sand grains, sand sheets and dunes are formed, some making impenetrable **sand seas**. In places, harder rock has resisted denudation, leaving ancient **plateaux** or hamadas and **mountain ranges**, the most dramatic ones pushed up by volcanic eruptions.

At ground level it appears that wind is the chief **weathering agent** of the desert, most spectacularly apparent in the dune formations and top-heavy outcrops that it sculpts. But, viewed from the air, it becomes clear that **water** has made the deepest mark on the land. Its presence may be brief but the erosive force of a flash flood and all the detritus it carries can achieve in a few hours what might take the wind many centuries to mould.

Desert plains

The typical Saharan landscape is a flat plain dotted with isolated outcrops, inselbergs (isolated mountains) or distant escarpments. A plain of fine sand is known as **serir**, a word commonly used in Libya, as in the Sarir Tibesti or As Sarir in the northeast (spellings of similar words vary). Elsewhere, the northern Ténéré is also a vast serir of flat sand (*ténéré* means 'emptiness' in Tamachek). They can be perfectly smooth to drive over as long as the sand is firm, though unseen soft patches can briefly drag a vehicle down.

Plains of gravel or coarse sand are known as **reg**, the best known being the Tanezrouft (a Tuareg variation on 'emptiness' or 'Empty Quarter') spreading for 1000km across the Algeria–Mali border. Not yet eroded down to grains of sand, a reg has a reliably firm surface though no vegetation apart from the odd grassy tussock clinging to a pocket of sand.

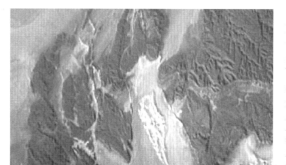

The western end of the Tassili N'Ajjer plateau. In the centre is the Amguid Erg along which pass Routes A7, A9 and A12. On the right can be seen one of the tiers and south-facing escarpment of the Tassili with the drainage flowing north. The narrow pass above the erg is the defile at KM400 on Route A9. © NASA.

Plateaux

In the Sahara it's rare that the land remains totally flat for long. Soon the terrain becomes broken by an escarpment or low cliff, the result of a geological fault and uplifting to form a plateau. In Morocco and Libya these plateaux are known as **hamadas**; examples include the undulating Hamadas du Draa and du Guir south of the Atlas, the flat Tademait and Tassili N'Ajjer plateaux in Algeria and the Gilf Kebir in Egypt. Most plateaux rise gradually to end suddenly in an escarpment: the Tademait, Tassili, Gilf and Hamada el Hamra in Libya all have dramatic south-facing escarpments. The steeper but less broad Adrar massif in Mauritania has a northwest scarp which is descended via the Amogjar Pass.

Some plateaux have several tiers or parallel scarps, most notably the western Tassili. When travelling from Illizi to Djanet you will slowly rise over a barren plateau, drop suddenly, rise again, drop spectacularly at Gara Ihadja Kli, rise and again drop, finally and dramatically, at Tin Taradjeli onto the desert floor.

This tilting gives a pattern of drainage running slowly away from the escarpment, forming **oueds** (see p.378) where vegetation might flourish, with steep gullies cutting down through the plateau's uplifted escarpment. On some escarpments these oueds become dramatic canyons that have cut right back to the escarpment, making a pass; the Oued Samene, Imirhou and Essendilene are three progressively smaller canyons. The former two have cut right through their respective plateau tiers, while Essendilene ends in a dry waterfall and plunge pool.

Outside the canyons and oueds these uplifted plains have had the loose sand blown from them and are covered in larger stones, boulders or hamada-like expanses. Lying at higher altitudes, the surface stones are baked by day and sometimes frozen by night as dew and microbes slowly break down the pebbles into grains of sand to be blown away by the wind or to cre-

The northwest-facing escarpment of the Adrar plateau in Mauritania (R5).

ate the surface varnish known as **patina**. This orangey-brown colour is caused by the oxidisation of iron minerals in the sandstone and is what gives the Tassili and adjacent Akakus their characteristic ochre hue, whereas the volcanic mountain ranges or massifs (see below) do not react in the same way and have a darker hue.

Chad's Ennedi massif and the Djado plateau in Niger are less visited but equally spectacular regions of eroded sandstone plateaux. Such highland areas, with their many rock shelters and waterholes, frequently harbour evidence of prehistoric occupation, be they the paintings of the Tassili, Ennedi and Gilf, the engravings of the Libyan Messaks and the Anti Atlas, or the neolithic tools and artefacts found right across the Sahara.

Plateaux can be very hard to drive across, especially where a sheet of broken basalt boulders lies on the surface as it does in parts of the Akakus, Libyan Messaks and on Route A4 in Algeria. This is the result of an igneous intrusion, a thin bed of lava spreading out from a fissure associated with volcanic activity. You can easily spot this interface between the sandstone plateau and vol-

canic inselbergs on the drive to Djanet. Look closely at the outcrops by the road and you will notice some composed of rounded, potato-like boulders of granite, even though they are the same colour as the distinctive sandstone ramparts forming the edge of the Tassili in the background.

Jebel Uweinat mountain in the Libyan Desert is another location where different types of rock merge

Rough going across a basalt field in the northern Akakus.

PYROCLASTS, STROMATOLITES AND OTHER CURIOSITIES

Even the shortest walk in the Sahara will unearth a range of extraordinary geological curiosities, the discovery of which adds greatly to the desert experience. They're unique to the Sahara only in as much as you can find them so readily, for they exist across the entire planet (and doubtless on other planets too) but across the Sahara's bare expanses of sand they are more visible.

The reinforcing ribbing on these shells just south of Siwa suggests they have a 'high-energy' marine origin.

Some things, like **fossils**, you can find anywhere: on the ground, on a cliffside; plate-sized **ammonites** are sold by the ton at roadside stalls near Erfoud in Morocco. Most common are the shells of marine crustaceans, although it's also possible to find tiny non-fossilised shells the size of a fingernail that would have belonged to freshwater creatures and aren't quite as old as they look.

But elsewhere fossils are truly prehistoric, most notably south-east of Agadez. This is the Sahara's best-known location of **dinosaur** remains, which have been under excavation for several years by American paleontologist Paul Sereno. Vertebrae the size of footballs have been recovered, with new creatures cropping up on each visit.

Sauropod vertebra.
© Michele Soffiantini.

Petrified wood is another type of fossil fragment common in the Sahara. An innocuous shard of rock may in fact reveal a fine wood grain if examined closely. Well-known 'petrified forests' exist west of Hassi bel Guebbour, west of In Salah and south of the Djado plateau.

You can view less dramatic **stromatolite** fossils in the bedrock east of Atar (Route R3). Probably the earth's oldest life-forms, they're still found in the hyper-saline lagoons off Western Australia.

Other geological curiosities of the Sahara include **meteorites**, said to be plentiful along the Hamada du Draa in northwestern Algeria. Aviation pioneer Antoine de Saint-Exupéry once described making a forced landing on a mesa and finding the hitherto unvisited patch of the Western Sahara littered with extra-terrestrial debris.

Strictly earthly in their origins are **sand roses**, the pink, petal-like clusters of gypsum crystal sold by the roadside at Square Bresson junction in Algeria. The added

humidity hereabouts enables the mineralised gypsum to form crystals below the surface. You'll see a gigantic sand-rose sculpture on the entrance to Tozeur in Tunisia.

Found all over the Sahara are hardy fragments of **ostrich eggshells**. In remote locations they may date from the Holocene Wet Phase but were only hunted to extinction on the Saharan fringes in the last century or so.

One of the most extraordinary natural artefacts of the Sahara has to be **fulgarite**, a fused tube of sand (technically a glass), caused by a lightning strike. Often found on dune crests, two types are common, their formation possibly depending on the sand's humidity. 'Finned' fulgarite is a coarse tube 2–10cm in diameter with fins of partially fused sand spiralling round the perfectly glassy hollow core. They can reach several metres into the body of a dune. The fins are thought to be the result of the lightning bolt earthing itself sideways as it drives down into the ground.

Fulgarite

'Plain' fulgarite is a very fragile smooth straw of petrified sand seen in more arid areas like the Great Sand Sea; the electrical energy is dispersed directly down into the arid sands without deviation.

Similar in appearance to fulgarite but possibly of organic origin are what look to be petrified roots protruding from a calceous bedrock in an otherwise totally barren corridor in Egypt's Great Sand Sea. Once dislodged, the rods look as if they have been pressed into the soft bedrock as if it were setting plaster.

Hematite concretions of fossil root casts?

It is possible that this formation is yet another bizarre example of **hematite** concretions. Hematite is an iron-based mineral found in calcareous rock strata across the Sahara. Sometimes forming three-dimensional crosses, or the bud-like formations shown here (from the White Desert in

Strange hematite concretions.

Egypt), with the aid of humidity, hematite can also concentrate and harden on the surface of a piece of sandstone so that after a while only the shell of the stone remains.

On occasion these concretions form tubes which can have the appearance of cooled lava. But if you're in a volcanic area **pyroclasts** are indeed very likely to be present. Pyroclasts are volcanic bombs: globs of lava, spat out from a volcano, which cool and solidify in mid-air into a streamlined lump and land with a thud. The example below was found at Waw en Namus crater.

A corridor in the Great Sand Sea (see p.635) contains a formation unique to the Sahara: **Libyan desert glass**. Although much has been carried away in recent years, look carefully and you will find pieces of a pale green glass-like mineral. Discovered by Clayton in 1932, it's been fashioned into stone tools and a worked piece was recognised in an item of Tuthankamun's jewellery.

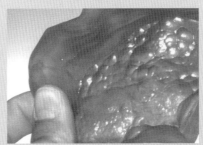

An extraterrestrial impact fusing the sand is one alluring theory (sand metamorphoses similarly into pale green glass following nuclear tests), but the lack of a crater, as well as the presence of partially-fused glass fragments and organic matter in some of the glass, suggests a more mundane terrestrial origin in an ancient shallow lake that became super-saturated with silica.

The Sahara's highest point is the south rim of the volcano Emi Koussi (3415m) in the southeast corner of the Tibesti, one of many volcanoes in that range. Emi Koussi resembles the Martian crater Elysium Mons, suggesting that volcanism once existed on Mars. The white patch in the middle is sodium carbonate collected in a small crater within the main, 10km-wide crater.
© NASA
Below: Fluted columns of basalt in the Atakor.

into one landform (see photos, p.336). The Libyan side of the mountain is again composed of rounded granite boulders, the weathered debris of a massive dome-like structure pushed up from below the earth's crust, not unlike the Guelb er Richat 'crater' in Mauritania. But on the Sudanese and Egyptian side the mountain is composed of the same Nubian sandstone as the Gilf Kebir plateau to the north.

Mountains

The Sahara has four major mountain ranges: the Tibesti, Aïr, Hoggar and Atlas. Other highland areas not considered plateaux include the Adrar des Iforhas, a rarely-visited corner of north-eastern Mali, and the Tefedest, Adrar Ahnet and Mouydir mountains in central Algeria. Some of these mountains, like the **Tefedest** and its inselberg outliers of Tidikmar and Sil Edrar, are as old as any rock in the Sahara, going back to the original formation of the African Plate.

The **Tibesti** of northwestern Chad has the Sahara's highest point, 3415m (11,100ft) **Emi Koussi** in the southeast of the W-shaped massif. The complex Tibesti is actually a mixture of uplifted sandstone plateaux and more recent volcanism such as that which formed Emi Koussi and other volcanoes. Two arms, the massifs of Abo and Dohone, reach northwest and northeast from the cluster of volcanic cones. The Trou au Natron near Bardai is a 700m-deep crater of steaming yellow sulphurous springs.

Pistes ring and even bisect the Tibesti, hinting at possibilities for exploring the wild heart of the Sahara, but rough tracks, landmines, bitterly cold winter winds and ever-warring clans all add up to a hard-won wilderness of isolated oases and gorges which few have ever seen.

THE LAST SAHARAN SUMMIT

Having climbed all the highest peaks in Europe since 2000 ex-Navy diver Ginge Fullen has slowly been ticking off Africa's highest summits.

By early 2004 only two of the fifty-three summits remained. The most remote, dangerous and difficult: Emi Koussi in Chad (3415m) and Bikku Bitti (2267m) just over the border in Libya.

Emi Koussi was the 'easier' of the two, but as Ginge explains, it was still no walk in the park:

The whole area is totally off limits. The last westerners to climb the mountain in 1998 were taken hostage. The entire Tibesti has been mined over the years by the Libyans, Chad Army and different rebel groups. There is no outside influence in the Tibesti. No aid agencies, no missionaries, no UN and the few Government Army troops are only in control of some small towns. Although a recent ceasefire was signed, the new rebel leader did not attend (his predecessor had been killed when his vehicle drove over a landmine).

With the help of a missionary who'd lived in the Tibesti in the 1990s, negotiations were held with Tubu warlords. Eventually, and for a hefty fee, the services of a well-connected guide from the rebel stronghold of Yebbi-Bou were secured.

To the base of Emi Koussi was a hard two-day drive from Faya. Explosive ordinance was evident but landmines are thought to be on the far side of Emi Koussi. As long as I disguised myself as a local when necessary there were no problems. We drove to within 25km of the summit and the peak was climbed in one long day.

Ginge with Tubu friends. Emi Koussi is in the background.

While in the area Ginge hoped to knock off his final and by far the most difficult African summit, Bikku Bitti, part of the Dohone spur of the Tibesti and just a couple of kilometres over the Chad–Libya border depending on whose map you read. A fitting end to his four-year challenge, as far as Ginge could tell there was no record of the peak having ever been climbed – soon he would find out why.

To avoid time-consuming kidnapping, a diversion was taken east of the Tibesti via Ounianga and the mountain approached from the south-east. Even then, minefields had to be negotiated as Ginge and his crew neared the mountain's base. Setting off on foot with three days' water, progress was initially good but soon dropped to just five hard-won kilometres per day. Low on time money and water, Ginge was forced to admit defeat:

The maps do not do justice to the actual terrain which is as broken as anywhere in the world: a maze of ravines, gulleys, pinnacles and gorges. We could not make more than 10km a day due to problems of route finding. Time, food and water were running short. The next week saw several attempts, all ending at deep gorges blocking the way. Finding the way was time-consuming and carrying water for four to five days became quite hard work. I called a halt just 10km from the peak but still maybe two days away.

Nevertheless the recce had been illuminating and, with the difficulties pinned down, Ginge was planning another attempt in late 2004.

Photos: © Ginge Fullen

Hard going on the approach to Bittu Bitti.

The dramatic peaks of the Algerian Atakor massif, part of the **Hoggar**, were formed by a different type of volcanic activity, clearly evident from the profile of the peaks (see photo, p371) as well as from the characteristic polygonal columns formed by cooling basalt. A winter's night in the high passes of the Atakor, rising to an altitude of nearly 3000m, is punctuated by the cracking of rapidly cooling rocks as they tumble to the scree slopes below.

Though only fringing the Sahara, the **Atlas Mountains** running right across Morocco through northern Algeria to Tunisia are the most extensive, forming a rain-catching barrier between the Mediterranean and the northern Sahara. At their highest in Morocco, crossing its southernmost range, the Anti

Atlas drops you directly from lush arable upland pastures onto the desert floor, never more dramatically than when taking the canyon or gorge routes M3, M9, M10 and M11 in a southerly direction. The folded ridges of the Atlas are the result of the African continental plate pushing up against the South European Plate. It is this tectonic movement which caused the earthquake near Al Hoceima in

Acutely folded bedding planes in the Atlas (Route M3).

February 2004 and a far more devastating quake in Agadir on the west coast in 1960 which killed over 12,000 people.

Acute folding is dramatically displayed on many hillsides and cliff faces in the Anti Atlas range, with beds at times folded over on themselves.

Watercourses

All the above landforms are criss-crossed by dry watercourses or creeks known as **oueds** in the former French territories or as **wadis** in the east (as well as many regional variations from 'btâh' to 'enneri' and 'karkur'). As you fly over the plains and plateaux of the Sahara, it is the infinite web of watercourses that is most striking. Rain may be rare but when it comes it carves away powerfully at the land, shifting vast quantities of sediment and rock. In the storms around Tamanrasset in the early 1980s the newly-surfaced Trans-Sahara Highway was swept away or undermined for kilometres at a time. At one point close to Tamanrasset a 3m-deep, 20m-wide channel was carved by floodwaters, as if a bridge over a river had been swept away.

Out in the open desert, the slightest gradient channels the water into the characteristic serpentine watercourses which fill with fine sediment, which in turn retains water and so supports some vegetation. Traversing wider oueds often means driving though the very fine sand which collects in the river bed and can involve negotiating the low dunes which form around the grassy tussocks. Away from highland areas where oueds tend to be more stony and pronounced, the gradient of a plain may not always be evident and you may wonder why a line of vegetation suddenly appears.

Much more conspicuous are the **ancient rivers** which once flowed from adjacent highlands. Mali's Oued Tilemsi, running down from the Adrar des Iforhas, is an example as are the still-active Oued Draa draining the southern Atlas, the Bhar el Ghazal running down to Lake Chad from the north, and Sudan's Wadi Howar, once a western tributary of the Nile. To the west of the Nile beneath the Great Sand Sea, remote sensing using satellites and radar has revealed the presence of a long-extinct river system known as the Gilf River which flowed (and possibly filled its basin with today's sands) many millions of years before the Nile was even formed. During the recent Holocene humid phase the younger of these rivers would have been a focal point for both wildlife and humans and, like the Tassilis, often reveals prolific neolithic artefacts and sightings of wildlife.

Dunes

From the simplest crescent dune to the complex chaos of ergs (sand seas) covering thousands of square kilometres, dunes are as much a Saharan icon as the camel or palm tree. When you see all three at the same time you know you've arrived in the desert.

The origin and formation of dunes is still not fully understood though it's obviously an aeolian phenomenon. But why ergs remain in some places while elsewhere a lone dune marches across a reg, or why a flat sand sheet exists, is unknown and part of the Sahara's wonder. The most popular theory is that, assuming a quantity of sand has been deposited there in the first place, the slightest irregularity of a flat sand sheet will create crests, just as the wind push-

A vivid re-enactment of sand grains blowing over a dune crest.

es up a swell on the ocean. The prevailing winds form a shallow windward slope of compacted grains which get blown over the crest and drop onto the steeper and looser slip face. This is an over-elementary description that does not take into account grain size and character, vegetation which encourages dune formation, latitude, prevailing and alternate winds.

Barchans or crescent dunes are the classic formation but actually quite

THE SOUND OF MOVING DUNES

Few visitors to the desert have been fortunate enough to experience the phenomenon of **singing dunes**, the source of native legends of sinister sirens or *djenouns* (spirits or genies) who lure travellers to their doom.

The sound is actually a deep, loud booming or droning caused by shifting grains sliding down a slip face, and usually occurs in the evening following a very windy day or a sandstorm. The dunes mysteriously resonate as their weight shifts following the wind-borne disturbance.

Ralph Bagnold experienced the sound of dunes in the Libyan Desert and described it as '*a vibrant booming so loud that I had to shout to be heard by my companion*'.

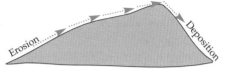

Consistent wind direction

Former position

Erosion

Deposition

Future position

Barchans are less common than you might think in the Sahara. Grains get blown up the left slope and deposited on the steeper leeward side and, in some cases, the dune moves forward.

rare in the Sahara because they form in places where sand is limited, and the Sahara is not one of these places.

A long, shallow windward face drops off to a powder-soft slip face from which extend the two arms of the crescent. A giant barchan was crossing the road south of Dakhla in the Western Sahara the last time I was there but by now passing traffic may have returned to the tarmac. Barchans form along the line of a consistent wind direction with the sands of the windward face being

THE COLOUR OF SAND

Although at first glance the dune sands in the Sahara appear a uniform light brown, in fact they show a remarkable range of colours. Colour is a difficult thing to quantify, as it is as much a psychological perception as a physical characteristic, but dune colour can be identified by comparing a sand sample with a set of colour standards, such as the Munsell colour system. Saharan dune sands mostly fall within a range from yellowish-brown to reddish-brown, but there are exceptions.

Sand colour can be caused by its constituent minerals, as in the case of the white (carbonate or gypsum-rich) sands found downwind of some Tunisian/Algerian chotts. The sorting action of wind transport also concentrates heavier, darker minerals (typically biotite, magnetite or similar 'opaque' minerals), accounting for the dark patches frequently seen on dune slopes. Large quantities of garnet in some dune sands can also impart a pale red colour. The majority of Saharan sands are composed of quartz, whose colour varies depending on chemical impurities, e.g. amethyst and rose quartz.

The transparent nature of quartz means that its colour can also be affected by coatings of clays and iron oxides on the sand grains, imparting a range of red or yellow hues, depending on the type of iron oxide mineral (hematite gives a red colour, goethite a yellow). In some cases, these coatings are the remains of the cement which once held the grains together in a sandstone (e.g. Nubian sandstone, a major source of Saharan sand). Over time, these dune sands become less red as the coating gets worn off as the sand blows around.

Spatial patterns in redness, such as in the Erg Tifernine, which is less red in the north than the south, can arise because the reddish cement is progressively removed as the sand gets transported further from its sandstone source.

However, it is also thought that sand grains can develop coatings similar to the rock varnish that forms on larger rock surfaces, thus becoming redder over time. The perceived colour can further be altered by factors such as grain size (other things being equal, finer grained sands will appear lighter coloured than coarser sands), and the angle of illumination. A particular feature here is the changes in the nature of the illumination as the sun becomes redder as it gets lower in the sky.   Kevin White

constantly blown up over the crest and down the slip face, edging the dune forward. Barchans roaming about are what most people imagine dunes to be doing: a constant if slow-motion swell; it's one of the romantic myths of the Sahara. But **dune mobility** is much exaggerated in the public imagination. The star dunes in the Grand Erg Oriental, pictured here, are much as they were on the IGN map

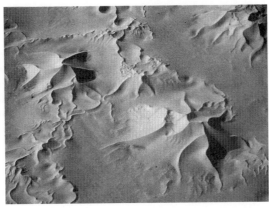

An aerial view of star-dune formations in the Grand Erg Oriental, Algeria (see map p.326). © Andras Zboray

drawn some thirty years ago, so much so that one can still navigate by them.

Other dune formations are more complex to understand, partially the result of seasonal variations in wind direction. Transverse or **seif** (Arabic for sword) dunes are effectively long lines of barchans, curling along with a scalloped edge but, as with all dunes, still having the characteristic shallow gradient of firmer sand and the steep slip face. It is thought that as wind moves along these dune lines a self-perpetuating spiral is set up which helps explain their regular pattern. **Star** or rhourd dunes (see photo above) are unusual isolated dunes with arms reaching out like a starfish in all directions, the result of variable wind directions.

Transverse dunes on the western edge of the Grand Erg.

Ergs

The desert is not blanketed by an ocean of dunes as many people imagine; in fact only around **one-sixth** of the Sahara is covered in sand seas or ergs (also known in Libya as *idehans* or *ramlats*).

Ergs might be considered the ultimate fate of all landforms: the wearing down of rock to its individual grains of silica quartz or sand which are washed away into basins (or

With a wider lens one can see the huge extent and regular pattern of the Grand Erg dunes. © Richard Washington

coastal regions) by rivers or floods and which, as the desert develops, are sculpted by the wind and formed into ergs. But first there must be a large deposit of sand to produce the erg, and this is why one finds them in specific parts of the Sahara, namely in basins where river systems might have once drained (this is also why one finds dunes and beaches on all coasts: the sand has been washed down to this place by rivers from the interior). In the Sahara these huge seas of sand can be the size of a small country, featuring all the dune types already mentioned, and yet they remain uncannily stable, both in their position and extent and in the individual formations within them.

In an erg, lines of seifs or star dunes are separated by **gassis** or corridors aligned to the wind and are usually the easiest way to drive through. The Great Sand Sea is far easier to drive through from north to south – the orientation of the dunes – than from east to west. We tried the latter once and managed just 30km in two days. Similarly the salt caravan route from the Arbre du Ténéré to Fachi and Bilma in Niger is actually quite easy as it goes along the lines of dunes which, coincidentally, also greatly eases navigation.

But smaller ergs can be a chaotic network of dunes with no pattern, technically known as **aklé**. The northern Grand Erg in Algeria and Tunisia (Routes A1 and T1 and T2 near Ksar Ghilane) is much like this, with possibly too small (or too humid) a volume of sand or too weak a wind to break it up into linear or distinct formations. With poor visibility and no pattern this terrain is, not surprisingly, about as difficult as it gets in a car or on a bike.

Oases, gueltas and chotts

Human habitation of the Sahara is dependent on a permanent water supply. Strictly speaking an **oasis** is any village supporting a plantation of date palms. Therefore Djanet is an oasis but Tamanrasset is not. Neither is Ghadames but the entire Vallée du Draa from Zagora south to Tagounite is a string of oases linked by vast palmeries.

The guelta at Toungad (R5).

The Vallée du Draa has a reliable water source in the snow-capped High Atlas of course. Elsewhere in the Sahara any surface water that doesn't evaporate percolates underground through fissures to water-bearing layers of rock capped by impermeable strata. When this upper layer is pierced by a well or a geological fault, water under pressure may rise to the surface (an artesian well), or at least become available by pumping. Much of this water which has collected underground is the result of rainfall thousands of years ago during climatic phases when the desert was less arid. These artesian basins are often centres of population. The unlikely site of the **lake** at Ounianga Kebir amid the arid plateaux of northern Chad is supported by underground aquifers. The lake's vivid blue-green colour is caused by salt-tolerant algae and contrasts strongly with the tawny desert all around. It is estimated that the slender, 3km-long lake loses a depth of 6m of water a year through evaporation, yet miraculously the same subterranean reservoirs that will feed Libya's Great Man-Made River keep Ounianga Serir at roughly the same size.

One of the two lakes at Ounianga in northern Chad, the largest such bodies of water in the Sahara. © Bob Gibbons

Gueltas, rockpools or waterholes sustained by rain, will form in any shady rock crevice where evaporation is minimised. If deep enough they may sustain a permanent population of reeds and grass, or even a village – for example the gueltas near Toungad in Mauritania (see photo on opposite page) and Essendilene (p.538) near Djanet. Being relatively well-watered, the Tassili plateau in Algeria sustains scores of perennial gueltas if you know where to look.

Salt lakes (**chotts** or sebkas) are the result of rain filling a basin from which it cannot drain but only evaporates. A string of chotts runs along the southern base of the Atlas from Morocco to Tunisia. The run-off washes minerals out of the rocks which fill a basin that might elsewhere form a river or a lake like the Dead Sea. Being on the edge of the Sahara, however, seasonal water soon evaporates leaving behind the salts which build up in thick layers over the years.

The best known is Tunisia's huge Chott el Djerid which is actually a hyper-saline lake at times. The Bonneville salt flats of northern Utah in the US are a famously flat venue for speed trials but in the Sahara chotts are best treated with caution. The weak, sun-baked crust may be resting on still-sodden mud. Sink into that and you're in big trouble.

Tunisia's Chott el Djerid salt lake.

Saharan climate and weather

Richard Washington

Imagine planning a Sahara trip for this coming winter with all the gear described in Parts 2, 3 and 4 to hand and a great team on board, except that instead of the current climate, you're setting off 6000 years ago. There would be no need for long-range fuel or water tanks and those sand ladders could definitely stay at home. Instead of a desert trip, you'd be in for a game-viewing safari through the lakes and rivers of the lush Saharan savannah.

Then again, if you were faced with the climate of 18,000 years ago, a Saharan crossing would take you all the way from the Mediterranean coast to the Congo basin – way beyond the range of any vehicle! Today the Sahara lies somewhere in between these extremes but still presents us with the world's largest continuous desert by far, although it clearly has had an amazingly dynamic past.

The prehistoric Saharan climate

Fluctuations in Saharan climate during the last million years (part of the Quaternary Period) can be traced to changes in the distance and alignment of the sun and the earth. This varying distance has been matched by very small differences in sunshine, resulting in ice ages and interglacials, typically set apart by about 100,000 years. These small differences come about because the earth's orbit around the sun is not perfectly circular, but rather varies from being almost circular to slightly elliptical. At the extremes of this oval orbit the amount of sunshine reaching the northern hemisphere during summer is less than usual, allowing winter ice to remain unmelted throughout the year. Taking tens of thousands of years to develop, ice eventually covers much of the northern middle latitudes by the middle of an ice age, the last peaking 18,000 years ago. This ice plays an important role in reflecting sunshine and so maintaining the cold temperatures. Back in the last ice age the world was very dry, windy, dusty and cold, with most of today's deserts double their size.

Superimposed on the 100,000-year ice-age to interglacial cycles are shorter cycles nearer 20,000 years, which result from the tilt of the earth's axis varying from around 21° to 24° (currently it's at 23.5°). This tilt is responsible for the seasons: the larger the angle, the greater the variation between summer and winter.

In the mid-Holocene, some 6000-8000 years ago, summers in the Sahara received significantly more sunshine, resulting in the tropical storms (which these days reach the Sahel in July and August) migrating right over the Sahara, bringing rain and so, vegetation. With this spread of vegetation the usually bright, bare desert surface was replaced by a much darker cover of soil and vegetation which absorbed more sunshine, heated the surface further and so promoted more thunderstorms – which, of course, helped more plants grow and even led to a brief human re-occupation of the desert.

Further back in time the climate over the Sahara changed even more dramatically though it is more difficult to be precise about the causes of these changes because the world was such a different place then. The position and heights of mountains, the location of the continents, the level of carbon dioxide, the amount of solar radiation and so on have all varied, creating wildly different conditions over the Sahara. One thing is certain: dinosaurs stomped about at the end of the Jurassic era; their remains can be found in the western Ténéré and Morocco, and all over the Sahara one can find pieces of petrified wood and other plant fossils (see p.374) from this time.

Why is there a Sahara Desert?

The modern boundaries of the Sahara are the Atlantic coast and the Red Sea, although the more arid and topographically flat Libyan Desert, east of the Libyan Fezzan to the Nile, is sometimes defined as a separate region. Either way this part of North Africa is characterised by extreme aridity in all seasons. But why is this region so dry? Persistent sinking of air on the scale of several hundred (or in this case, several thousand) kilometres is the climatic process necessary to create deserts.

This sinking air (creating a high-pressure zone) comes from the very top of the weather atmosphere (the troposphere), which is as high as moist air can get. By the time air reaches these great heights, any moisture has been rained out in deep storm clouds, often thousands of kilometres from the deserts. And at this altitude air is so cold it can barely retain moisture anyway. From altitudes of 10km the slow sinking process starts. As it is compressed under its own weight, the air's temperature rises, arriving warm and dry at the surface – ideal climatic conditions for desertification.

But what drives this sinking air? Overall there has to be a global balance between the hot, humid rising air in the tropics (picture the towering cumulo-

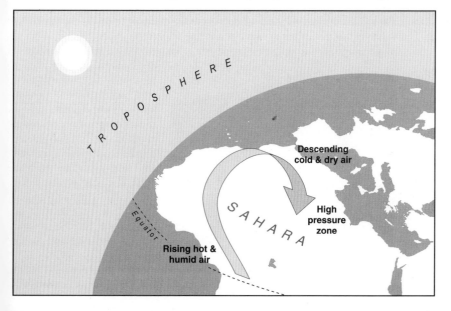

nimbus storm clouds) and sinking air. The air rises over the equator and descends over the subtropics, located between 20° and 30° to the north and the south of the equator, which explains why all the world's deserts, on both sides of the equator, are found within these latitudes.

But something special must happen to make the Sahara a region of such consistently high pressure and therefore such unparalleled aridity. The explanation cannot come from the extent of thunderstorms over central Africa alone; these are comparatively too small. Part of the story, it is thought, is that the Asian Monsoon – the largest region of thunderstorms on earth – forces air to sink on a very large scale over the eastern Sahara, just to keep that balance between rising and sinking air. This part of the Sahara (the Libyan Desert) is by far the driest, a region ten times drier than the central Sahara and so arid that nomadism and trade routes only developed around its fringes.

Another factor is thought to relate to the surface soils and minerals common in the Sahara. Virtually the entire Sahara is simply sand, gravel or bare rock. But minerologically this surface is unusually bright or reflective. Apart from the ice-covered poles, the Sahara is the shiniest part of the earth. This shininess causes a huge amount of sunshine to be reflected back into space. Taken over the year as a whole, the Sahara actually loses more radiation (if you include sunshine and infrared radiation emitted from the earth) than it receives – a highly unusual situation for subtropical latitudes. The upshot of this is that, radiatively, the Sahara is 'seen' as a fairly cool surface and sinking air is drawn to such cool surfaces. So, as in the ice-age example above, the light-coloured surface helps to encourage the high pressure and sustain the desert. And once the air does subside, all the sinking and compression helps to heat the air dynamically.

Saharan rains

For the most part, rain in the Sahara occurs so infrequently and is so sporadic that it's very difficult to measure and even more difficult to map in a meaningful way. Nevertheless, maps of average rainfall from December to February and from June to August (see opposite) really emphasise the vast scale of aridity in the Sahara. Winter rain is confined to the Atlantic and Mediterranean coastal strip, being wetter where the topography is more marked, so that mountainous Morocco, for example, isn't really part of the arid Sahara at all, while along the much flatter coastal strip in Libya or Mauritania, the hyper-arid Sahara reaches right to the coast.

Storm damage to the Trans-Sahara Highway at Arak Gorge.
© Richard Washington

In the summer, mid-latitude storms move pole-

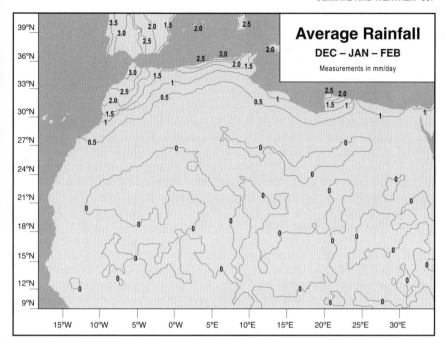

Average rainfall (1961-1990) for December to February in mm per day. One can see that the Atlas and Green Mountains in Cyrenaica catch plenty of rain but in the desert rainfall is negligible.

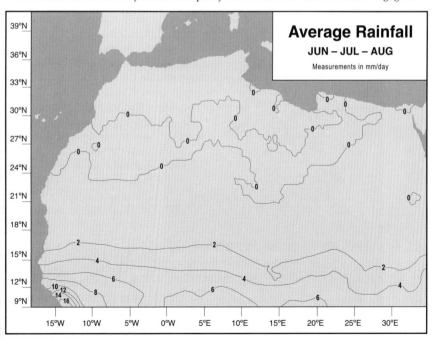

At this time of year some monsoonal cells migrate into the Sahel so that places like Timbuktu or Nouakchott get over 90% of their annual rainfall between July and September.

wards, so that much of the Mediterranean is dry and under the dominant influence of dry, sinking air. Infrequent thunderstorms bring what rain does fall to the coast while, south of the Sahara, the line of tropical storms known as the Intertropical Convergence Zone brings rain to the southern Saharan fringe. This line of storms marks the meeting place between equatorward-blowing winds from both hemispheres.

How often will it rain in the central Sahara? For somewhere like Bilma, Niger, on the eastern edge of the great Ténéré, it only rained in January twice in the thirty years up to 2000. In Timbuktu, no rain fell at all in January between 1961 and 1990. But in August, Timbuktu has experienced rain on just over 200 days in thirty years, this coming from extreme northerly migration of the tropical thunderstorms which bring torrential rain to the Sahel in summer. Meanwhile the ever-arid Bilma has only experienced nineteen rain days in August in 30 years.

Near mountainous regions, like the Hoggar and Tassili N'Ajjer in Algeria and the Tibesti in Chad, topography triggers thunderstorms and rainfall may in places reach over 150mm a year, equivalent to the drier coastal fringes of the Sahara and just enough to support nomadism (London, by comparison, gets 545mm a year). Flash floods are known to occur in these regions so camping in dry river beds needs to be done cautiously if thunderstorms are building in the mountains. The Trans-Sahara Highway passing through the Arak Gorge in Algeria (see photo p.386) regularly gets broken up as floods undermine and wash away the latest layer of tarmac.

Hot days and freezing nights?

Read a travel feature on the Sahara in a Sunday paper and you'll soon get to the lame cliché about 'hot days and freezing nights'. Hot days? Definitely.

Freezing nights? Definitely. But not on the same day nor, for that matter, in the same season. Winter nights in the Sahara are cold but the days are warm, not hot. Summer days are amongst the hottest on the planet (the world record comes from Libya, just south of Tripoli) but the nights are hot too; many days start in the high 20s or low 30s (°C), even in the hours before sunrise.

Yes, some nights *are* freezing and even frosty in the Sahara (though frost requires the humidity of the northern fringes), but the following December day wasn't baking by any means. On another biking trip in September, by 10am it was already 30°C, and I was guzzling 10 litres a day and another couple by night. I opened a tin of spam one evening and a fatty liquid sloshed out over my lap. Even candles melted.

During mid winter you can expect maximum temperatures somewhere in the 20s. Temperatures are mild on the Mediterranean and Atlantic coasts and

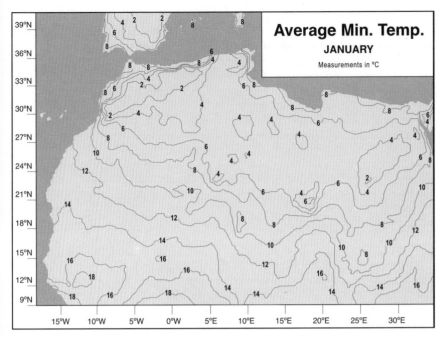

Average minimum temperatures in January. Note the cold spots over mountains, plateaux and the Western Desert of Egypt.

become progressively cooler the deeper into the Sahara you go, as the warming influence of the sea is left behind. South of about 20°N (Atar, Tessalit, Seguedine, Zouar) things start hotting up again (into the 30s) as you travel towards the tropics. Minimum temperatures in winter are in the low teens near the coast (with lots of dew at night if it isn't windy) but soon drop to near freezing in the central Sahara, although the aridity here ensures that dew or frost is very rare indeed.

Following the heat of the day, cooling in the Sahara is very efficient which may explain the impression of 'freezing nights, baking days'. The earth emits infrared heat radiation all day and all night. Unlike most parts of the world, a relatively larger proportion of this Saharan radiation is free to escape to space, owing to the cloud-free skies. When a north wind blows, you'll be particularly cold on winter nights. Many first-time bikers underestimate how cold motorcycling can be in the Sahara in winter, especially at highway speeds on the northern approaches.

It is true that the Sahara does have one of the biggest ranges in daily maximum to minimum temperatures found in the world. But because the maximum temperatures are so high, even a great deal of cooling is not enough to bring cool nights. Summer night-time temperatures are warm to hot: the average minimum July temperature in In Salah, for example, is a little over 29°C. Many nights don't get cooler than 33°C and in July 2002 a heat wave struck the town with night-time temperatures as high as 36.4°C, the highest temperatures for fifty years.

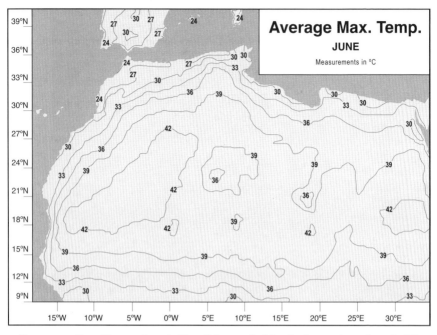

On average, diurnal temperatures in Nouadhibou on the Mauritanian coast vary by only 6°C; in Kufra in the heart of the Libyan Desert and far from the equalising maritime influence the variation is 18 °C.

Summer maximum temperatures are nothing short of dangerous and reliably reach the mid-40s. Bilma in Niger, for example, has an average June maximum of 42.4°C but there have been nearly fifty June days in the last thirty years where temperatures exceeded 45°C; in September 1996, 48.6°C was recorded. Remember that thermometers recording these temperatures are always mounted in nice, white, shady, ventilated boxes well off the ground. On the tar road of the Trans-Sahara Highway near In Salah in summer, the black surface would reach well beyond the 50s and the melting road would feel soft if you could only touch it for long enough (one reason why Saharan roads break up so easily).

It is like this every single summer and it's getting hotter, partly due to global warming brought about by industrialisation. In fact the desert regions are warming faster than any

Summer in the Sahara; hot enough to fry an egg on your car and melt spam. © Toby Savage

other part of the planet. This is an unpleasant and unforgiving part of the year where small mistakes in navigation or minor breakdowns can easily become epics. In May 2001 a truck carrying 120 people on the Marlboro piste into southern Libya suffered a mechanical breakdown. At least ninety-three people died in just a few days and it was only May. Such fatalities, albeit on a lesser scale, occur regularly among locals in the Saharan summer.

The Ceaseless Wind

Coming from Europe, you'll be marvelling at how suddenly the grey and green of home is replaced by the yellow and blue of the Sahara. But before the first day in the desert is out, you'll also be surprised by how restless the wind is and no doubt be spending your first sunset looking for that elusive camping spot where the wind doesn't blow.

The soft chalk of Egypt's White Desert has been carved into strange monoliths by eons of sand-laden wind.

The extremes in heating and the varied surfaces of the Sahara, including the reg, the ergs, and the rocky hamada (see Desert Landforms, p.370) mean that air is always being moved by the constantly changing density, temperature and pressure gradients. Add to that the unusually low friction in the vegetation-free landscape and the wind will become quite a factor in your day.

Wind is simply the movement of air which is driven from regions of higher pressure to regions of relatively lower pressure. Earlier we explained how the Sahara is created by subsidence of air on a huge scale. When that air reaches the surface, it begins to spread out from the centres of high pressure cells. The pressure is relatively lower away from the centre of the high pressures, so air moves steadily away from these cells: the Sahara is a source of wind.

Once this air spreads out it begins to spin slowly clockwise around the centre of the individual high pressure cells. For much of the central Sahara this phenomenon causes the steady north-easterly winds which are pushed equatorward to feed tropical thunderstorms. On the Mediterranean side of these desert highs, the flow is westerly.

Driving down to the Sahara, especially in winter, will invariably take you through these major components of the planet's large-scale climatic circulation. A day or so south of the Mediterranean, the steady westerly winds of the mid-latitudes will be replaced by subtropical north-easterly winds. In winter, this changeover occurs much further south than in any other season (28°N in January as opposed to 35°N in June) since the mid-latitude storm track and all the climatic belts move equatorward following the overhead sun. During the Saharan summer, winds become still more easterly and are typically double

WINDSTORMS

The Sahara is the world's largest source of wind-driven soil dust. Much of this dust is entrained into the atmosphere during dust storms, which occur when the wind is strong enough to lift soil particles from the surface into the prevailing wind. Strong near-surface winds and large expanses of vegetation-free surfaces with fine soil particles ensure that dust storms are a very common phenomenon in North Africa. Rather than simply lifting individual particles of soil, it is now thought that wind tends to bump particles along (a process called saltation, originally described by Ralph Bagnold in *The Physics of Blown Sand*) which leads to disturbances of many other particles, so promoting the entrainment or mobilisation of dust. Once in the atmosphere, the finer particles tend to stay suspended for many days as the natural process of scavenging, where raindrops form around dust nuclei and clean up the air by means of rainfall, is of course very rare in this arid region.

Dust storms are important for a variety of reasons. They disrupt transport (having been associated with Saharan plane crashes – see p.350 – vehicle convoy delays and even the Lost Army of Cambyses), make navigation using landmarks difficult and can even damage vehicles. Climatically they play an important role in either warming the Sahara (by absorbing the earth's radiation which is trying to escape to space) or cooling the atmosphere and surface (by reflecting sunshine back to space). Whether the overall effect is one of warming or cooling depends sensitively on the dust-particle size, shape and colour and the altitude at which it interacts with radiation. Geomorphologically dust storms are evidence of the importance of deflation in moulding the landscape.

Recently released satellite-derived data have helped to pinpoint the major sources of Saharan dust storms. These are rare over the ergs (because the sand particles are usually too coarse there) or the rocky hamada regions. Instead they tend to occur over palaeo (fossil) lakes or oueds where water has previously deposited fine materials. But dustiness or haze (rather than full-blown sandstorms) occurs in all regions of the Sahara as soon as the wind picks up.

In the central Sahara, dust storms are most common in the summer months when intense surface heating drives convection (often dry thunderstorms) and strong surface winds. Dust storms tend to peak near noon, typically occurring between three and six days a month. Dust haze and radically reduced visibility are present on many more days – at least fifteen days a month in mid-summer.

On the Sahel fringe of the Sahara, the wet season (June to September) tends to be the clearest although passing thunderstorms embedded in the easterly waves of the African Easterly Jet tend to throw up the most spectacular dust storms in advance of the storm. The atmosphere is quickly cleaned if the storm brings rain.

The Sahel has experienced the world's longest protracted drought since records began. While the 1940s and 50s were generally wet, the late 60s, 70s, 80s and 90s have all recorded some 30% less rainfall during the summer months. Associated with this increasing aridity has been a trend to greater dustiness and an increased number of dust storms. Timbuktu, for example, experienced fifty-nine dust storms between 1951 and 1975, but between 1976 and 1997, some eighty-nine were recorded. It is not yet clear whether land use or changing circulation patterns are mainly to blame.

Take cover! A sandstorm hurtles towards Djanet. © NASA

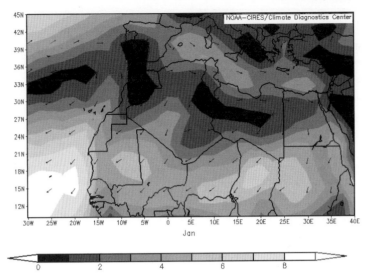

Wind strength and direction in January. In the east, winds are directly from the north, becoming north-easterly as one moves west across the desert, closely matching the orientation of linear dunes in the major ergs. Notice the hyper-windy corridor in north-central Chad; a funnel of sand-laden air is rammed between the Tibesti and Ennedi ranges, strong enough to scar the bedrock.

the speed (see diagram on p.394) owing to the greater heating, closer proximity of the equatorial low pressure region and therefore the higher pressure gradients which ultimately drive the wind.

While all of this is going on at the surface, the mid-latitude westerlies slope over the easterlies with height. So if you took off in a hot air balloon in a steady easterly wind, the balloon would eventually come back overhead in a westerly wind. How long it took for the balloon to find the westerly flow would depend on the season and latitude, but certainly above a few kilometres altitude the flow is always westerly in the Sahara. A very beautiful illustration of this is the sub-tropical jet stream, at its best near 20°N in winter although its position will change by the day. This is a narrow layer of howling winds at an altitude of some 10km which is apparent in the form of a narrow band of cirrus (ice) clouds aligned south-west to north-east across the desert. It provides welcome relief from the relentless sun and does a crucial job in maintaining the angular-momentum balance of the planet*, without which the length of day would change from year to year.

Practically speaking, your experience of wind will mostly be one of finding shelter. This is hard to find behind solid surfaces such as dunes and low rocky outcrops as they tend to create turbulent eddies which can be more annoying than a steady wind. Experienced desert travellers will often carry large wind-breaks of roof-rack height which can be assembled between two or more cars. Low shrubs also offer surprisingly good protection because a reduced wind flows through and minimises the turbulence.

While the winds described here have mostly been associated with large-

* For a full explanation, enrol in an applied planetary geophysics course at your local university.

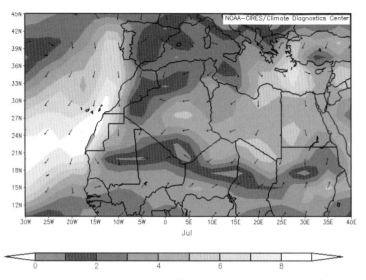

By July the wind strength has increased but its direction is more complex as the developing equatorial monsoon pushes hot, humid air up against the desert's northeasterlies.

scale flow, it's worth recalling the severe heating gradients and varied surface types. It may sound ideal to camp in a valley alongside an erg with an escarpment nearby, but local mountain-to-valley winds are also drawn to these attractive settings. The flow will be up-valley during the day (the anabatic wind) but will reverse soon after sunset (the corresponding katabatic wind) at which time you'll find the wind break or tree is on the wrong side of the camp!

The Dustiest Place on Earth

The Sahara and surrounding dry lands annually throw up about 1.6 billion tons of dust into the atmosphere, making this desert by far the world's largest source. Some of this dust ends up as far away as the Amazon rainforest, pro-

March 27th, 2004, a sandstorm or Sirocco wind moves off the Libyan and Tunisia shore towards southern Italy. ©NASA

viding vital nutrients, while many in Europe as far north as the UK have experienced a dusty rain shower leaving deposits of red Saharan dust on smooth surfaces like cars.

Two regions of the Sahara stand out as pre-eminent dust sources: the Bodelé depression in Chad and the Djouf or Majabat al Koubra region of Mali and Mauritania; the western Sahara's 'Empty Quarter'. This dust is generated

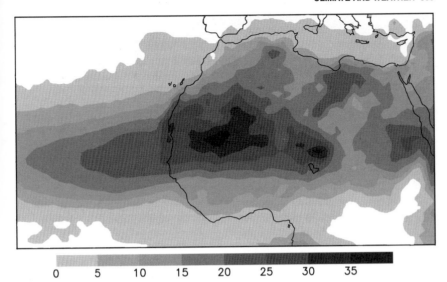

Airborne dust particles in June. Dust is carried far out over the Atlantic at this time and is thought to affect tropical cyclones in the western Atlantic.

from countless 'fossil' or paleolakes which date back to the Holocene Wet Phase. Driven by steady and sometimes gale-force winds, the dust is transported at a height of 3km, blowing east to west across the Sahara in a feature called the African Easterly Jet, easily reaching the Caribbean in ten days or so. In places, sand and dust are transported in a huge conveyor near the surface for many hundreds of kilometres. Examples are the transport system from the Great Sand Sea in Egypt, southwards to the east of the Tibesti and on through the Bodelé where the wind accelerates between the Tibesti and Ennedi massifs.

The Sahara is least dusty from November to January but between May and October, visibility will often be so reduced that scenery beyond a few kilometres is dulled, making navigation by landmarks difficult and greatly reducing visibility (one of the reasons for going to the Sahara in the first place).

When to go

Season is an important factor in the timing of a Saharan visit. For most people the season is from November to February. The heat and dust (and so, reduced visibility) of the summer months are better used for route planning and vehicle preparation at home. One variable does make the winter months less desirable though and this is the short day length. Weighing up temperature, day length and visibility, ideal months tend to be November and January. In the colder parts of the desert like the Gilf, February is ideal.

A March duststorm on Route A12.

Human prehistory in the Sahara

[Expanded from original material by Andras Zboray in previous edition]

One of the enduring fascinations of travel in the Sahara is the opportunity to see evidence of prehistoric human activity, chiefly in the stone tools that were used and in the rock art and tombs left behind. The nature of today's desert environment puts a stone hand-axe on the desert floor beside a burned-out rally racer or the ruins of a Foreign Legion fort. This absence of stratified hierarchy is of course due to the lack of binding vegetation building up soil over the centuries. All there is is sand and rock, and the weathering process of **deflation** continually blows away sand from around loose surface objects, be they gravel or stone tools.

Although desert conditions have existed for millions of years in the Sahara, as the previous section explained, periodic **climatic fluctuations** have occurred with wetter phases creating an environment and ecology very much like today's East African savannah. During these less arid periods our ancestors occupied the valleys around highland areas and followed grazing herds across the plains, as shown by the billions of stone tools or 'lithics', littering the desert floor across the entire Sahara.

The earliest evidence of hominids in Africa was found in the Djourab area of northern Chad, some 2500km west of the Rift Valley, in 2001. The seven-million-year-old skull of a new species, *Sahelanthropus tchadensis*, was nicknamed 'Toumaï'. It is evident that in the much later Lower **Palaeolithic** times (150,000-100,000 years Before Present or BP) the whole of North Africa was populated, as the characteristic pear-shaped Acheulean **hand-axes** (or *bifaces*, see p.398) may be found across the whole region. There were several drier and wetter cycles during the Middle and Upper Palaeolithic, with wet peaks during **Mousterian** (circa. 70,000-50,000 years BP) and **Aterian** (35,000-25,000 years BP) times. This was followed by a long hyper-arid phase coinciding with the last Ice Age, when desert conditions were even more extensive than today.

Neolithic tombs and Stone Age artefacts

The Holocene wet period lasted from about 9000 to 2500 BC, with an arid phase of a few hundred years from around 6000 BC (see diagram p.401). At this time much of the Sahara was habitable for humans. In places, the plains and dunes would have been covered with grassland on which herds of ostrich, giraffe, elephants and various antelopes roamed, just as as they do today in southern Africa.

In the highlands and in shallow basins on the plains several lakes formed, which supported fish, crocodile and hippopotamus. The depleted Lake Chad of today was a much larger body of water fed by run-off from the highlands of northern Chad, Cameroon and Nigeria.

These places were ideal encampments for the early hunters who repopulated the Sahara on the trail of their prey, and later these water sources supported the large cattle herds of the nomadic herders who have left their finely worked stone and bone tools and decorated pottery, as well as heaps of their domestic refuse, at many sites along former lakeshores and highland valleys.

Even in the wetter periods there were regional variations, and true desert conditions have returned several times over the centuries since the Holocene period began. During these times the highlands became refuges for both animals and humans, capturing more precipitation than the lower-lying plains, just as they do today.

Pre-Islamic tombs from finely-built 'keyhole' and 'antenna' tombs (pictured right) to cruder tumuli of piled stones looted long ago, are found alongside many Saharan pistes.

All that can be said about them with certainty is that they predate the spread of Islam into the Sahara (some time after the Arab conquest in the eighth century AD) and probably date from the Archaic Period, whose rock art shows a society developing religious rituals.

Islamic tombs, distinguishable by their small headstones and often aligned on a west–east axis, are sometimes found close to pre-Islamic tombs, showing that, as in the centres of worship of Europe

A pre-Islamic tomb known as a 'keyhole monument'. Inset: Not a pre-Islamic tomb but in fact a 'desert mosque' used by nomads, with the *mihrab* recess pointing to Mecca.

An antenna tomb in the Sequiat El Hamra. © Toby KiteCam.

The famous keyhole tomb near Djanet. © Ian Thompson. Inset: A series of drum tombs on the Tassili (A2); the front tomb's headstones suggest it became a Moslem grave.

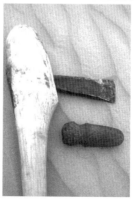

Top: A heavily weathered Paleolithic hand-axe, the original finely crafted Stone Age tool. Note the indentation for the thumb to improve grip. **Middle**: Grinding stones and their 'pestles' at Wadi Bakht, eastern Gilf Kebir. **Bottom left**: A small knife and finely crafted arrowheads, many with tiny barbs. **Right**: modern bush axe and a Neolithic counterpart. One good website describing the manufacture and classification of lithics is the Stone Age Reference Collection: www.hf.uio.no/iakk/roger/lithic/sarc.html.

and the Old World, the sites of pagan worship and the monotheistic religions which follow them are often closely related.

Stone & ceramic artefacts

In the Sahara it is possible to see stone hand tools made by the earliest hominids right up to items still used in the current era, a period spanning millions of years. Distinguishing a piece of rubble from a hand-axe can take practise, but once you've an eye and a feel for likely locations the desert presents a whole new element of fascination and discovery.

The most commonly seen objects are **grinding stones** or their pestles. The actual stones can be the heavy lumps pictured left or more slender and portable oval plates, but all will show a distinctly smoothed and flattened surface (as will pestles) where possibly centuries of grinding took place. They are found across the entire Sahara.

Establishing the age of such objects is an understandable curiosity: the nature of grinding means these tools must post-date the Neolithic revolution when humans advanced from domesticating animals to cultivating crops.

This key moment in the evolution of human society started in the Middle East and Turkey some 12,000 years ago but

COLLECTING ARTEFACTS – THINK TWICE

Our instinct on coming across a Stone Age tool (or anything of interest, come to that) is to pick it up and look at it in amazement and, if we like it, pop it in our pocket as a souvenir of our desert trip. It's a practice that may seem as innocuous as idle beachcombing.

Few of us may be aware of it, but many Saharan countries number their neolithic artefacts as part of their cultural heritage and forbid their removal. In reality few do much about it (Libya has been an exception) but it's worth noting that the more frequently visited regions like the Tassili, Ténéré and lately the Tadrart-Akakus – places where one would expect to see an abundance of these objects – have been cleaned out over the years by early explorers, the colonial occupations which followed, archeological expeditions (some, legitimately) and lately souvenir collectors.

Millions of such objects remain under the Saharan sand seas and in less visited locales, but though numerous and broadly similar, they are a finite cultural and archeological resource, even if they may seem less important (i.e. valuable) than Roman or ancient Egyptian relics.

Picking up a stone knife may sound harmless, but as with so many things (including the geological curiosities described on p.374) they can acquire value. In 2003 a long-established German tour agency, Rolling Rover, was found to be selling Neolithic artefacts, collected during tours in Libya and Algeria, on its website. The fact that they did this so brazenly shows that they saw it like any other commodity. It was the revelation of this systematic looting for commercial gain which contributed to UNATA's overheated accusations during the Algerian kidnappings which occurred almost simultaneously (see.p.362).

The smuggling out of Roman artefacts from Libya has on occasion led to temporary bans on the nationalities involved and these new revelations may have contributed to recent restrictions on independent travel.

Independent tourism and a country's cultural heritage have suffered due to the greed of a few, although in my experience most collecting occurs on organised tours accompanied by a local guide indifferent to or even assisting in the activity.

Legality aside, the collection of these artefacts, cultural and even geological, remains an ethical issue. The search and discovery of such items is an enjoyable recreational and moderately educational pursuit that enhances the Saharan experience. But even if a stone tool or piece of pottery is like countless others spread across the Sahara, think twice before you decide to keep it.

---

would have reached the Sahara a couple of thousand years later. It's also worth remembering that such implements are still used today in parts of Africa; their origin may be ancient but the last time they were used may not have been so long ago. The same could be said for many stone tools up until colonial times. The most remote desert communities may still have had a use for them in recent centuries and items like the tiny **arrowheads** pictured opposite which required great skill to fabricate, may have been passed down or re-used through generations. The crudest choppers, scrapers, blades and hand-axes could be extremely old: 50,000 years or more. All such tools were made by knapping: striking the right sort of rock with a hammer stone to chip off flakes and create a sharp-edged tool.

It's not unusual in sandy areas to come across a **knapping site** where the chips (known as *debitage*) lie scattered where they broke off the cores which became tools as the prehistoric craftsman did his work. A more direct connection with Stone Age activity is hard to find.

Crude stone tools at Wadi Mathendous.

You may also come across **trapping stones** in areas of denser Neolithic habitation. Any hefty stone with a circumferential groove or vaguely 'hourglass' profile would have had a cord looped round it with the other end attached to a snare. Not all animals were hunted to death, some had their mobility reduced by snaring or breaking legs. This way they became a 'live larder' staggering about nearby or easily traced by tracking when the need for them arose. (A 'pre-refrigeration' practice which continues today among surviving hunter-gathering societies). The next stage in controlling these and other 'wild' resources was of course domestication and cultivation: the Neolithic Revolution and the advent of human civilisation.

Ceramics, chiefly in the form of pottery but also sections of bracelets and other items, are as widespread across the desert as stone tools. The oldest examples have been found in Egypt and are thought to be around 9000 years old. As with grinding stones, they imply a post-nomadic, pastoral social order that still exists on the fringes of the region today.

Fragments of decorated pottery, probably from the Archaic period or later.

Rock art

Rock art or petroglyphs (*gravures rupestres* on French maps), be they engravings or paintings, provide the most vivid reminder that the Sahara was not always as arid and desolate as it appears today.

The representation of humans and the animals they at first hunted, later domesticated and even deified demonstrates nothing less than early man taking the epochal step from two and a half million years of nomadic hunter-gathering to gradually controlling and eventually mastering his environment.

The age of Saharan rock engravings and paintings continues to be a matter of heated debate among archeologists but as a rule they're thought not to predate the Holocene wet period, which began about 9000 years ago, and are probably younger than that. Before that time, spanning back past the oldest currently known

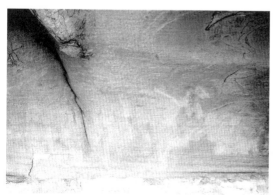

Even the remotest corners of the Sahara yet to be visited by European tourists, such as this location near Tifraiti in Western Sahara, have been damaged in recent years. The thorough scrubbing (as well as attempts at chipping off another fresco nearby) suggests a mixture of bored soldiers, local vandals and maybe even opportunist thieves or strict Muslims who found such images profane.
© Toby Savage

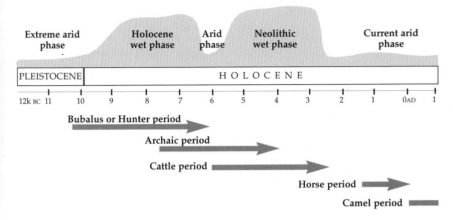

The chronology of Saharan rock art in relation to climate. Not all sources agree on exact dates of either, as most studies have been regional rather than pan-Saharan. Some compress the entire era of petroglyphs into the last 6000 years, although the cattle period is datable with more precision and is uniform across the Sahara. The climate model has also been simplified: the northern Sahara with its Mediterranean influences cannot always be compared to the equatorial factors which affect the southern Sahara.

examples of rock art in the world (France; 30,000 years BP), the Sahara was just too arid to support human life. In the case of **engravings**, relative ages in a single locality can be inferred from differing degrees of **patina** (a varnish-like mineral coating formed during wetter periods) while the **superimposition** of different styles of paintings clearly suggests that those on top are younger. While it is frustrating for us to try and unravel what may be many millennia of images painted or even engraved over one another, it's clear that even then, the makers did not regard the work of their predecessors with any veneration.

Although conveniently classified as a single area, the Sahara is huge, and attempting to apply a relative chronology over widely dispersed regions is very speculative when based on similarities in style and subject matter. However, it has generally been agreed that rock art from the pastoral Cattle period occurred more or less at the same time right across the present-day Sahara.

For visitors looking for answers, that chronological information is adequate; most are satisfied to marvel at the fine artistry of the best examples, to identify individual creatures or decipher scenes, or to visualise the big picture in the context of human evolution and the desert environment today. So, while dating within the Holocene period remains a matter of debate, the various periods and styles are reasonably well defined.

The Hunter or Bubalus period

The earliest examples of Saharan rock art are thought to be **engravings** representing ancient and now partially extinct wildlife such as elephant, giraffe and rhinoceros, as well as various species of antelope and gazelle which were either the main objective of the hunters or had an impact on their imagination. At times these are impressively depicted at almost true scale.

Before the Cattle period big wild fauna dominated rock art; giraffes were one of the most represented motifs (Karkur Talh, Jebel Uweinat, Sudan and Tanakom in the Aïr).

That they were made by hunters can be inferred from the absence of any representations of domesticated animals. Interestingly, human figures, where featured, are small and insignificant.

One of the most prominent and common subjects is **Bubalus Antiquus**, the ancestor of modern domesticated cattle, resembling the East African buffalo but with much larger horns. It became extinct around 5000 BC, so this period is assumed to predate that time.

However, it has been argued convincingly that images of this large horned bovine in fact show an early breed of domesticated cattle, which would imply that the earliest Saharan rock art sites are no older than 5000 BC; an unfashionable suggestion among some archeologists who equate significance with great age.

The best examples of this period are the engravings in Oued Djerat southeast of Illizi in the Tassili N'Ajjer; the many engravings in the eastern Aïr facing the Ténéré; the Tadrart-Akakus; Karkur Talh at Jebel Uweinat; and the thousands of engravings on the **Messaks** in the Libyan Fezzan (probably a richer and more diverse trove than the much vaunted Tassili N'Ajjer). Wadi Mathendous (see Route L5) is the best known and most accessible locality

Hunting an antelope with dogs (Akakus, Libya).

PHOTOGRAPHING ROCK ART

Getting good pictures of rock art can be a rather frustrating activity. With **engravings**, a low sun angle at either end of the day highlights the relief naturally and can make a dramatic picture.

At other times of day, direct overhead sunlight flattens the image. Here a remotely positioned high-power flash can help, as it can for photographing engravings permanently in shade.

A problem of **perspective** also arises from not being able to get sufficiently far away from large engravings, especially if they're flat on the ground, or high on a cliff. The first problem can be solved by having a ultra-wide-angle lens (24mm). The second is best overcome by taking the photo from the valley with a long telephoto lens (200-300mm usually suffices).

Though contiguous friezes can be huge, individual **paintings** are usually much smaller than engravings so the perspective problem does not arise. However, paintings are invariably found in rock shelters that rarely if ever get direct sunlight (one of the factors ensuring their preservation), and their weathered natural pigments are often much less vivid than engravings. Here the best idea is to use a tripod to enable long exposures. **Flash should not be used** as the UV component may damage the paintings.

On no account should you wet a painting to temporarily enhance its relief. This technique was used by many early explorers and archaeologists (including the Lhote team in the Tassili). They knew no better, but it has been found to fade the painting, and the moisture may loosen the rock itself. In this way many of the most beautiful Tassili paintings have been lost. The ones at Ain Doua at Jebel Uweinat await the same fate (see also the photo on the previous page).

Having one good picture is not worth becoming an accomplice to the destruction of this rock art.

Andras Zboray

---

here, where the presence of crocodiles and hippopotami (still found along the Niger River) suggest the significant presence of water.

Examples of the deeply-grooved (rather then pecked) **Tazina style**, often on flat slabs of rock, are found along the Hamada du Draa in Morocco, near Ain Sefra in Algeria and on the Sequiat el Hamra (northern Western Sahara).

The Archaic or Pre-pastoralist period

This period was named **Roundhead** by Henri Lhote after the characteristic round-headed figures of the earliest rock paintings in the Tassili, and the term stuck. This peculiar style is limited to paintings in the **Tassili** (see p.530), but there are similarities with some of the paintings in the Ennedi of Chad (p.613), and possibly also the large cave at Wadi Sora in the Gilf Kebir in southwestern Egypt (p.633). There is some overlap with later Bubalus engravings; the animals depicted are still mainly wild, and the human and human-like figures express a very high degree of symbolism (e.g. the 'Great God' at Sefar, p.535), which seems to imply a more developed society, with well-established **religious beliefs and rituals**.

The exact dating of this period is also a matter of debate, with up to 5000-year discrepancies between different experts. Assuming the average of estimates lies closest to the truth, this period lasted roughly from 6000 to 4000 BC.

The 'swimmers' at Wadi Sora made famous by the *English Patient* film.

War and peace. On the left a battle scene in the Akakus; on the right a tranquil pastoral scene in the Tassili, with the enclosure or homestead depicted in a bird's-eye view. © Andras Zboray

The Cattle period

This period produced the most numerous rock-art sites, both engravings and paintings. Wild-animal representations become scarce, their place taken by innumerable representations of **cattle**, both alone and in herds of sometimes over a hundred. So prolific are they that 'bovine overload' is not an uncommon complaint when you come across yet another cow-studded cave shelter. Today, cows may for us be prosaic milk and burger machines, but these unprepossessing ruminants have endured as key providers to human society as evidenced by the significance of cows and bulls in civilisations from ancient Egypt (mummified bulls encased in gold) and the cult of the minotaur in Knossos, to the India of today.

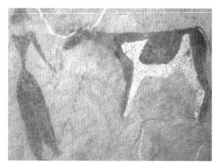

Cattle-period painting from Jebel Uweinat.

Other scenes show people engaged in their daily activities, all depicted in a very artistic and refined manner. Clearly this society was one of nomadic herders, much like the present-day Nuba and Fulani tribes in Sudan and Niger, with their lives revolving around their animals. Many of the most beautiful paintings in the **Tassili** (full details on p.530) and Libyan **Tadrart-Akakus** as well as the lesser known ones at **Jebel Uweinat** in Egypt date from this period. It lasted from about 4500 to 2500 BC, when the increasingly dry climate forced herders to move south.

The characteristic Saharan pottery, which is remarkably similar in form and style across the whole region, can probably be associated with this period. The vessels were typically round, with wavy, combed or dotted decorations (see p.400).

Horse and (Historic) Camel periods

The horse was introduced briefly to the Sahara about 1200 BC, enabling **horse-drawn chariots** to use the Saharan trade routes until classical times, helped by a brief wetter period (which also enabled cultivation in many oases on a much larger scale than today). This period is characterised by small 'double triangle' shaped human figures, often clothed in long robes and described as **Garamantean** after the like-named empire which was based around present-day Germa in Libya during Roman times and whose ruins and tombs survive today along the Wadi Adjal.

Two-horse chariot with 'Garamantean' figures – far cruder than previous artistic styles.

Compared to the much-admired naturalistic styles which preceded it, paintings from this era appear crude, although examples near Germa (possibly by Garamanteans themselves rather than being depictions of them by others) are more sophisticated.

With the **onset of aridity** at the beginning of the Christian era, the **camel** replaced the horse as the beast of burden. Camels are depicted in many places in an even cruder style that has little going for it other than as an aid to dating artefacts with some precision. These are sometimes accompanied by the Tifinar script, formerly used by the Tuareg and thought to have originated in Libya.

... and war again. Be it the horns of a bull or the size of your cannon, exaggeration is as old as human imagination.
Seguiat el Hamra © Toby Savage

Once you begin to appreciate its range, diversity and occasional beauty, Saharan rock art and its associated human prehistory can become quite a fascination. For some recommended reading on the subject, see the relevant section under Books, starting on p.640.

Peoples of the Sahara

Historically, the Sahara has acted like a sea or a mountain range, inhibiting migration and isolating peoples across the breadth of Africa along the Tropic of Cancer. To the north are light-skinned Caucasian peoples who originated in Asia and Europe and spread along the Mediterranean coast from Iberia and the Middle East. To the south are the indigenous black-skinned inhabitants of Africa, where humans originally evolved millions of years ago. In essence all the peoples of the Sahara have their roots in one of the region's three main groups: indigenous **Berbers**; **Arabs**, whose seventh-century conquest trans-

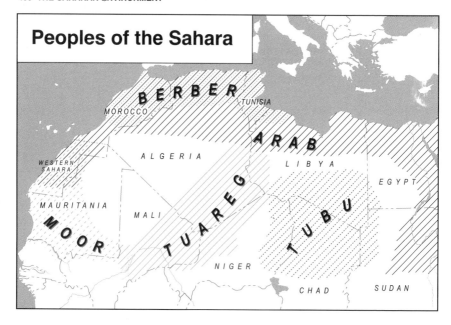

Peoples of the Sahara

formed the face of North Africa and brought Islam to the desert; and **black Africans**, though this is rather a vague definition (some consider the unclassifiable **Tubu** nomads of Chad a race unto themselves). From these ethnic origins, myriad tribes have developed, and centuries of intermarriage, abduction, invasion and economic migration have blurred the lines of ethnicity as they have all over the world. But the desert's remoteness makes the sort of mixing experienced in Europe over the last 500 years much less pronounced and, as the map above suggests, some regions are still clearly associated with certain groups. You can, for example, still be pretty sure you won't find a Tuareg in Egypt or a Tubu in Morocco.

Nomadism

Despite their ethnic and cultural differences, just about all the main groups who live in the Sahara are nomads or nomadic in origin, as indeed are all humans. In the West the term **nomad** is a romantic one, conjuring up images of 'bedouin' tents and a carefree, peripatetic existence. In reality nomads do not wander about aimlessly but move systematically with their camels (or goats, sheep and cattle in the less arid Sahel). Movement is seasonal rather than daily and in winter they may move the herds to higher ground where pasture may develop with rains. It is the availability of **pasture** (the word 'nomad' comes from the Greek term for pasture) with which to feed and fatten their beasts that drives their nomadism. Sometimes they might stay in one spot for months until the area's resources are close to depleted.

A typical nomad's tent or *raïma* (in Hassaniya), houses a family of six. Measuring about 5m square, it can be made of a heavy brown wool of camel hair, supposedly a good insulator and commonly seen in Morocco. Modern *raï-*

mas are made of white heavy-duty cotton, and in Mauritania are lined with colourful, patterned cotton from Senegal. Short sticks raise each corner, creating metre-high walls, and a central pole allows standing room; the front entrance is effectively a raised wall that can be lowered at night or during sandstorms, while on hot days the side walls can be rolled up to let in the breeze.

Small nomad caravan near the Erg Tifernine (A12).

The floor is covered in matting woven by the women from strips of rag, dried grass or palm leaves; bedrolls are tucked away in the corners and during the day cushions are used for lounging. The women spend most of the day in and around the tents, milking camels and goats, preparing meals, looking after the kids and keeping house. Menfolk spend the daylight hours tending to the herds. One spring morning in Mauritania we spent an hour watching an entire nomad clan head off for new grazing grounds. The procession began with about fifty camels under the watchful eyes of outriders. Then came the goats, shepherded along by two boys. They were followed on foot by the other members of the household, some of them leading camels and donkeys loaded with the family tents and the rest of their belongings. Mothers with very young children brought up the rear, perched on howdah-style saddles and wrapped in indigo veils.

Just as in medieval times inhabitants of the greater Sahara were classified as 'Berbers' (or 'Ethiopians' in the pre-Christian era), it's still common for the term **'bedouin'** to be used synonymously and interchangeably with the word 'nomad', especially among the French. This is in fact misleading: the Bedu are a nomadic tribe from Arabia, Syria and Jordan (made famous in the books of T. E. Lawrence and Wilfrid Thesiger) whose ancestors ventured west of the Sinai across North Africa. Used correctly, the adjective Bedouin describes these Arabian nomads.

A Berber encampment in the Anti Atlas (M10).

Rural Berber women at Zagora market.

BERBERS

The indigenous peoples of the Mediterranean coast and the Atlas mountains – or the *Maghreb* as North Africa is known in Arabic – are the **Berbers**. Thought to be the descendants of Neolithic peoples who left their rock art across the Sahara over the last 9000 years, they probably migrated to the north as the Sahara moved into its current arid phase. Following the Arab conquest of North Africa in the seventh century the Berbers were literally forced into the hills where many traditional tribes who have not assimilated into the Arabic culture remain today. Isolated from the Arab cities, they are proud of their non-Arabic origins and traditions. Powerful Berber clans controlled the key passes across the Atlas and resisted colonial control well into the twentieth century. Even today the Rif mountains remain a faintly lawless stronghold of Berbers, who discourage excessive scrutiny of their cannabis plantations.

Nowadays Berber culture is strongest in Morocco, rural Tunisia and northern Algeria and to a lesser degree in Libya. Berbers can be hard to distinguish from Arabs, although rural Berber women are easily recognisable in their brightly-coloured clothes and headscarves, which give them the appearance of

Teatime in outback Mauritania.

Eastern European gypsies (and with a not dissimilar status as social outsiders). They sustain themselves by farming and herding, often living in villages rather than as nomads. However, a few Berbers are nomadic: the strip of desert along the Oued Draa, south of the Moroccan Atlas, is peppered with the tents of Berber families who tend goats, sheep and even camels in pastures that are lush enough to make their lives a little less harsh than those of central desert nomads. Berbers have their own language (similar to the Tamachek of the Tuaregs) with varying dialects from Morocco to Libya, but they'll also speak Arabic and French.

MOORS

The Moors of Mauritania are of Arabic origin and speak Hassaniya, an archaic form of Arabic, as well as French.

Moorish society is strictly hierarchical: the black-skinned slaves or *harratin* from the south occupy the bottom strata, with the fair-skinned *bidan* the highest caste and the *Hassane* nobles who claim direct descent from Mohammed (a common claim to exalted status among Arabs) at the top of the tree. Like many of the Arabic peoples in North Africa, 'white' Moors are proud, haughty people, with a culturally-ingrained superiority complex. Nevertheless, intermarriage and long associations with the higher castes does not mean a black-skinned Moor is considered socially inferior.

Nomadism runs deep in the Moorish psyche as, until the droughts of the early 1970s, the population of Mauritania was almost entirely nomadic. Even though many migrated towards Nouakchott and a life in shantytowns or *bidonvilles*, the desert is still very much lived-in and, in the Adrar region at least, you rarely drive for more than a few hours without passing a nomad encampment. Most town dwellers are only first-generation urbanites and many still go to visit relatives in the desert.

For three months every year many families up sticks for the huge *getna* date harvest around Atar, moving into temporary huts around Azougui, which is transformed into something of a holiday camp, where they tend to their palms and socialise.

Camels and trade

As with all Saharan nomads, the Moors' wealth has traditionally lain in their **camels**. Five hundred years ago this would have amounted to a franchise in road haulage for transporting commodities across the Sahara – or long-range mobility to raid those caravans which did not pay tribute. Today's trading diversity as well as crippling droughts have forced many Moors and other pure Saharan nomads to adopt a modern, sedentary

A family and its camel herd pass by, south of Azogui in the Adrar.

way of life. These days camels are of little practical use, although camel meat is eaten as the staple meat.

Lately camels have become 'back to my roots' status symbols for the well-to-do across North Africa. A few years ago a high-spec Range Rover would have fitted the bill but now owning a herd of camels is *à la mode* and a minor economy has grown up in breeding, transporting and selling camels from Mauritania. Although little more than exotic pets – rather as thoroughbred horses might be in Europe – a fit camel in the right place can be an investment.

Contemporary Moors are comparable with the Jews of medieval Europe, considered to be shrewd **merchants**, shop owners and wheeler-dealers devoted to the acquisition of money. The diversion of the main trans-Sahara route through their territory over the last decade has brought new-found wealth and opportunities from tourists and car sellers. Even in northern Senegal and parts of Mali it will be a blue-robed Moor running the local boutique (general store), and making a few pennies running a roadside stall is a way of supplementing the income of enterprising families.

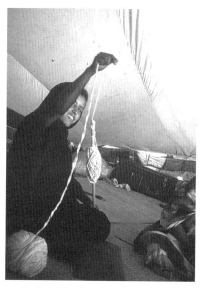

Spinning twine near Oudane.

Moorish dress

All Moorish men wear the billowing, sky-blue or sometimes white *boubou* – basically a folded sheet with a slit for the head and the corners sewn together. This baggy tunic is usually worn over modern Western dress and is embroidered at the neckline and cuffs – the more elaborate the design, the classier the wearer. Boubou are sometimes worn with a white or blue turban (*houli*). The boubou is a very versatile garment: its billowing sides encourage ventilation, and it works well as a wrap against wind and sand, and for sleeping – and with the shoulders bunched up high it gives the wearer a real presence.

The equivalent ubiquitous wrap-around for Moorish women is the *mehlafa*, a length of light, brightly-coloured loose-weave fabric which, wrapped around the head and body, looks not unlike an Indian sari; like the boubou, the mehlafa is always worn over a skirt or dress. Mehlafa come in a wide range of colours and patterns; with the brightly-patterned cottons of Senegal they, too, give the wearer great elegance. As with the boubou, a mehlafa can be used against the elements and as a bed-cloak, and can be pulled right over the face for modesty.

Both sexes spend much of their day endlessly readjusting these loose-fitting garments, which are constantly unravelled by the desert winds. In the bush, women's attire is more conservative and consistent: **indigo-coloured** mehlafa are the norm. When new and lustrous, these garments transfer some of their dye onto their wearers' skins, as they famously do with the Tuareg 'Blue Men'. Active cameleers wear a functional short tunic and baggy *saroual* trousers rather than the impractical, wind-catching boubou.

TUAREG

The Tuareg are the best-known nomads of the Sahara, as their haughty presence and mysterious veils have been immortalised – and romanticised – in countless films and books. They live in the central Sahara, in the desert regions of Algeria, Mali and Niger, and belong to regional clans: the Kel Ajjer occupy the Tassili N'Ajjer and Ghat, the Kel Ahaggar occupy the Hoggar, the Kel Air occupy Agadez and the Aïr, and there are five other groups stretching out as far west as Timbuktu. Kel means 'the people of'. Each clan speaks a different dialect of Tamachek, the Tuareg language, and each has mildly differing social customs and styles of dress, although in Tamachek they call themselves collectively **Kel Taguelmous** in Tamachek: 'the People of the Veil' ('Tuareg' being a less gen-

Kel Ajjer Targui (singular of Tuareg) in Oued Djerat.

erous Arabic label meaning 'the abandoned of God'). In addition to Tamachek, most Tuareg also speak Arabic and French. Tuareg society is matrilineal, and some people like to think it evolved from a utopian prehistoric social system based on the Mother figure. Women inherit wealth and are free to do what they like with it; they also have a strong voice in social affairs.

THE TEA CEREMONY

As a tourist in the Sahara you may be invited into nomads' tents for tea. Traditional nomad hospitality is extended to any stranger, a custom that's essential in the desert where food, water, shelter and news are scarce. The sharing of tea has become something of a ceremonial ritual (although the custom itself is less than two centuries old).

The preferred tea in the Sahara is strong Chinese green tea, which is brewed in a tiny enamel or pewter teapot with chunks of sugar

Tea from a Tuareg: a desert custom.

and sometimes some sprigs of mint. Before serving, the host pours the tea repeatedly back and forth between tiny shot glasses and the teapot, until each glass is lined with foam and the tea is fully brewed. Guests knock the tea back in a couple of gulps – it's strong and very sweet – sling the glasses, and the whole stewing, foaming and pouring ritual is then repeated.

This happens three times and takes at least half an hour; to leave after only one or

two rounds can be considered rude and in some circles is something that's done only if you want to offend your host. Tradition has it that you should only make a move when your host has finished washing the tea tray after the drinking is over.

In Mauritania you may also be offered a swig from a communal bowl of *zrig* while the tea is brewing. This is watered-down camel or goats' milk with plenty of sugar, and is said to be good energy food (young Moorish girls are often brought up on it to make them a plump and marriable 'smina'). But *zrig* can also turn unaccustomed digestive systems inside out, as Yves Larboulette discovered while cycling around the Adrar (see p.253).

Although you're unlikely to be asked to pay for your tea, a small gift is always appreciated, or you may like to buy something from your hosts who'll often unroll a selection of prehistoric artefacts while the tea brews.

The Tuareg are of **Berber descent**, having migrated to the central Sahara from the north-west only a thousand years ago, possibly as an escape from the Arabs. Legend has it that the settlement of Timbuktu was established around this time by a Tuareg matriarch. The excavated tomb of the Tuareg queen Tin Hinan in Abalessa near Tamanrasset, supporting an old Tuareg legend, also upholds this theory. Less prosaic theories claim links with the Knights Templar or the Crusaders (hence the cross emblems on their pendants and camel saddles, and certain 'chivalric' customs), or even that they are the descendants of the 'lost' Garamantean Empire of the Fezzan (see p.572), a thousand-year-old civilisation routed by the Arabs in 668AD. As James Wellard purported in his *Lost Worlds of Africa* (Hutchinson, 1967), there is little physical resemblance with the Berbers though they do share the archaic Tamachek language of the pre-Arabian Sahara. The Tuaregs' written script, Tifinar, is also commonly referred to as 'Libyan script' and has been connected with the Garamanteans. Environmental factors aside, the sudden change from a sophisticated sedentary civilisation to nomadism and piracy is less easy to explain, but for nearly a thousand years they controlled central Saharan trade, guiding or robbing the caravans, depending on allegiances.

Kel Aïr Tuareg in Niger.

Clothes and society

A Tuareg's hallmark is the way he wears his cheche so that, in the company of strangers or superiors, it can be pulled across his face like a **veil**. On ceremonial occasions the men wear indigo turbans, known as a *taguelmous*, whose dye permanently stains the skin of their faces and hands – hence their nickname, the Blue Men. The veil's origin is also debated but it's clearly practical in windy and sandy conditions as well as masking the identity, like a cowboy's neck scarf, when engaged in a raid.

Tuareg women don't wear veils, although a head-covering is common. On special occasions the men don the full regalia including shield and sword. Tuaregness is such a hit with tourists that you'll meet *faux Tuareg* everywhere in the Sahara, especially in the desert areas of Morocco and Tunisia, where wrapping a blue cheche high over your nose and alluding mysteriously to the ways of the desert is enough Tuareg for most camel day-trippers with a camera. In Morocco a dead giveaway is that they are in fact wearing a Moorish *boubou*, easy to obtain and blue enough for most people.

The ubiquitous **Tuareg cross** is the definitive souvenir of the Sahara: a small, silver, cross-shaped pendant that comes in any number of designs and is hawked by genuine and *faux* Tuareg all over the desert, and as an 'ethnic' souvenir as far afield as Indonesia.

As with the Moors and the Tubu (see below), Tuareg society is strictly stratified into **castes** with the nobles at the top, then either warriors or camel owners, and *harratin* vassals at the bottom. 'Slave' is perhaps too emotive a word, bringing to mind chains and degradation. Respected servants or maids might be a better comparison, well treated by the family for whom they work, though without the material ability to leave

A selection of Tuareg jewellery.

and make their own lives; a comparison that might be made with Asian domestic staff in many European countries today.

During the last decade the Tuareg have made headlines (though not in the UK) for their attempts to establish autonomy, something promised by the departing French administration but now difficult to accomplish as their territories lie across three countries that are preoccupied with other civic crises.

Part of the reason for this rebellion was the persecution Tuaregs had suffered at the hands of the governments, particularly in Niger and Mali, from which they'd been excluded and for whose authority they had little respect. This prejudice is partly based on the long-standing acrimony between desert nomads and the sedentary black villagers of the Sahel on whom they had preyed for centuries. At independence the tables had been turned, and age-old scores were being settled. Nowadays, treaties in Mali and Niger as well as prominent government posts have brought a tentative peace, though renegade bands of Tuareg who've developed a liking for their former piratical ways continue to prey on travellers in certain regions, notably northern Mali.

TUBU

Perhaps the true desert dwellers of the Sahara, acclimatised to its hardships over millennia rather than centuries, are the Tubu of northern Chad. Some consider them to be the original inhabitants of the Sahara, preceding even the Berbers of the north. A black-skinned group but with Caucasian features, they are divided into two main tribes: the **Teda** of the Tibesti, southern Libya and north-eastern Niger, and the **Daza** occupying the plains in the centre of Chad as far south as the Lake. Lesser language groups exist in the south-eastern Ennedi and Zagawa regions. The Teda and the Daza each speak their own mutually incomprehensible languages (after

Tubu men. © Ginge Fullen

which each is named) and sport enough clans to keep life interesting.

The Tubu claim indifference to exhaustion, hunger and thirst. It's said that it takes three days for a Tubu to eat a date: one for the skin, another for the flesh and the last for the pith. Compared to the Tuareg and Arab nomadic groups, the Tubu are materially primitive, but stories abound of their toughness and ability to cross deserts on a piece of mutton and a guerba of water. Tubu women often have a ring through one nostril and wear brightly-patterned shawls pulled over their heads. They are used to their husbands being away from home for months at a time, either buying or selling supplies, raid-

Long wait for the AA in Tubu country. © Ginge Fullen

ing or engaged in a vendetta. The men are suspicious and wary of strangers, like some Arabian tribes and mountain dwellers, and rarely parted from their AK-47s which have come to replace the daggers once tied to each limb with a leather thong (all the more easily drawn against an enemy).

Until the 19th century this group, which numbers around 200,000 (compared to 250,000 Tuaregs and 350,000 Moors – these figures can be taken as estimates only), was unknown to the West. Even in the early 20th century, few Teda had come into contact with foreigners until the French got to grips with the Tibesti in 1929.

These days you're most likely to encounter Tubu in southern Libya or the eastern Ténéré while their homelands of the Tibesti in Chad still remain out of reach to tourists. Literature in English is hard to find; Heseltine's *From Libyan Sands to Chad* (1960, see p.640) is recommended. Jean Chapelle's *Nomades Noirs du Sahara* (L'Harmattan, 1982) is by far the most comprehensive modern work and is easily found in Paris.

Reguibat owner of the hotel in Mhamid, Morocco.

OTHER GROUPS

The above constitute the main groups of Saharan nomads but small pockets of other ethnic groups exist that do not quite fit into these categories.

In the far west, the **Reguibat** live in the Western Sahara and are today the dominant tribe of the **Saharawi** confederation. The arid plains of the Western Sahara have moulded an opportunistic and hostile temperament as evidenced by the bitter David-and-Goliath independence struggle of the Polisario (see p.458). Like many strongly traditional nomadic tribes, the Reguibat see themselves as 'The People' and all others as inferior. According to one Reguibat we met, Tuaregs are lightweights, occupying a well-watered part of the Sahara with only short distances between pastures, compared to full-blooded Reguibat nomads in the arid north-west. Tracing their line back five hundred years to the Yemeni, Sidi Ahmad al Rgibi, they are proud of their Arabic ancestry and warlike ways. The French aviator Saint-Exupéry described many encounters with the fearsome Reguibat, who liked nothing more than to ransom back a downed pilot (as Yemeni outlaws still do today). Earlier

mariners shipwrecked or lured onto the western Saharan shore were less lucky.

Chamba nomads in the Grand Erg.

The **Chamba** (pronounced 'shambi') are also of Arabic origin, now occupying the Ouargla–El Golea region of Algeria. They are long-time enemies of the Tuareg to the south (as it seems are all neighbouring groups the world over!) but, like the Tuareg, they used to prey on the trans-Saharan caravans and the hard-working Mozabites of Ghardaia in particular. During the French occupation they were persuaded to give up their raids (*rezu*), and distinguished themselves as trackers and cameleers. In 1902 they were instrumental in the final defeat of the maverick Ahaggar Tuareg, which finally allowed the establishment of a trans-Sahara trade route through French-controlled territory to rival the Turkish dominance of Saharan commerce to the east.

Until recently the **Daouda** lived around the lakes in Libya's Ubari erg (see p.564), leading a rudimentary existence on a diet of date and crustacean mush; the 'Worm Eaters' as British explorer Clapperton described them in 1829. They are thought to be of either Berber or Arab descent and for centuries remained so isolated in the dunes that they did not even know how to weave cloth or make baskets. Due largely to Ghadafi's policy of encouraging desert dwellers to relocate into towns, the Daouda are now dispersed in the new towns along the roads through the wadis Adjal and er Shati.

The **Imarguen** fishermen of the Mauritanian Atlantic coast are famous for using wild dolphins to help herd shoals of mullet into their nets, the dolphins getting a free feed along the way; a practice adopted by other coastal tribes around the world. These days the Imarguen use motorised boats but are still notable for surviving in the extremely arid region along the Mauritanian shore where water is so scarce it's now trucked up from Nouakchott.

BLACK AFRICANS HEADING NORTH ACROSS THE SAHARA

Every year over 100,000 black Africans cross the Sahara trying to get to Europe. From Libya or Morocco they hope to catch a boat to smuggle them across the Mediterranean to Spain or Italy. In Libya, Niger, Sudan and Chad you'll often encounter six-wheel-drive Mercedes *gros porteur* trucks with often over a hundred passengers perched on top, mostly young guys from Nigeria, the country with Africa's biggest population.

Travelling 'roof class' is gruelling. Most of the trucks are old and often have to drive at night to keep the engine cool. It can get very cold at this time and some passengers fall from tiredness or because the trucks are so crowded. The lucky land in the sand, but falling on rocks or being left behind can be fatal.

Only Libya does not require visas for sub-Saharan Africans but this doesn't mean it's easy to get in. Customs officers can make problems and will try to extort money so many truck drivers (who are often carrying contraband anyway) will cross borders illegally along smuggler routes. This makes the trip a lot more dangerous – when vehicles break down (as they commonly do) there may be no passing help. Every year broken trucks are found with many dead bodies lying around; in May 2002 over 100 died when a gros porteur broke down near Tumu.

In the western media these Africans heading for Europe are often described as desperate people, but if you talk to the Nigerians the reality can be different. Heading north through places like Agadez or Tamanrasset you'll be surprised by their good spirits. Many of them see the trip as a kind of adventure, like young Europeans inter-railing or hitching to India. If we don't make it to Europe, they say, at least we'll have a good story to tell.

Gerbert van der Aa

The **Nemadi** were alluringly described in Bruce Chatwin's *The Songlines* as an outcast group of hunters who inhabited the area north of Nema in southeast Mauritania and, unusually, used dogs to catch the gazelles that survived along the Dahr Tichit escarpment. My own enquiry in Tidjikja in 1989 gave the expected 'what do you want to know about them for?' answer but then I was a guest of high-born Hassanes who were probably equally contemptuous of all minor nomadic tribes. Chatwin and Jeremy Swift (*The Sahara*, Time-Life, 1975) described a dwindling troupe of Nemadi thirty years ago so it's unlikely their way of life still exists today.

Colour section (following pages)
- **C8** Rocky spires near Taghrera, Tassili du Hoggar, Algeria.
- **C9 Top left**: Inside the fortified granary, Nalut, Libya. **Top right**: Door knocker, Ghadames, Libya. **Bottom**: Outside the madrasa (Islamic school) in Ghadames, Libya.
- **C10 Top**: New Year's Eve near KM404, A9, Algeria (p.513). **Bottom**: The recently discovered Foginni Cave, Gilf Kebir, Egypt (p.633). **Inset** ©Toby Savage.
- **C11 Top**: Medieval scrolls, Chinguetti, Mauritania (p.476). **Bottom**: Approaching the Sudanese border in Karkur Talh, Egypt (p.627).
- **C12 Top**: Twilight at Assekrem, Algeria (p.508). **Bottom**: Moonlight in the Ubari Sand Sea, Libya (p.553).
- **C13** Afara after a storm, Algeria (p.501) © Yves Larboulette.
- **C14 Top:** The ruins of Djado, Niger (p.596) © Klaus Weltzer. **Bottom**: Kanuri women in Fachi, Niger.

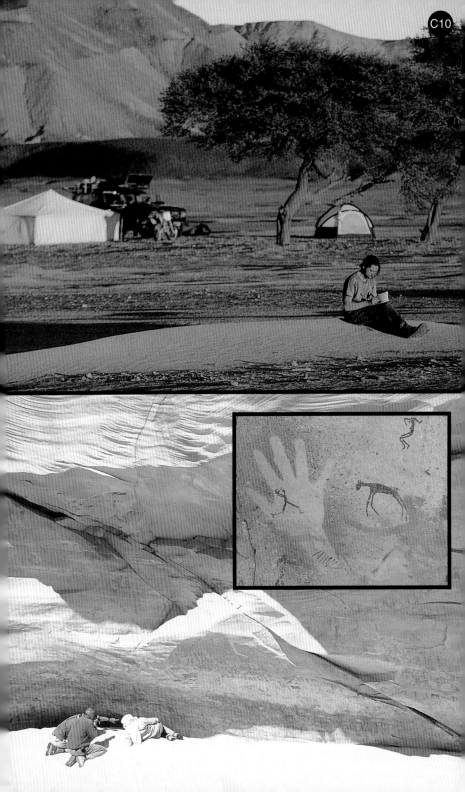

Crossing the Mediterranean

Even though a test run should have ironed out or at least revealed any teething problems with your system, it's good to be aware that the nervousness and distraction of the first few days puts you at risk. Many trips come to a premature end in their early days. Be aware of this. There is a tendency to drive hard as a way of calming yourself down. Instead, aim for easy days, maybe even with visits on the way down; there are plenty of lovely spots in Spain, France and Italy as well as the Sahara. Give yourself time to do some last-minute shopping or even some last-minute repairs.

This initial tension comes to a peak with your first encounter with an African frontier, in most cases the ferry port. By this time you will be gratified to see that there are other 4WDs and bikes also heading overland, which makes the whole escapade a little less daunting.

Once on the African shore it's common to relax a little and even feel elated that at least you've made it this far. Again, give yourself an easy schedule. Big cities in a strange new country are best avoided, especially in northern Morocco, but try to stop off at a few roadhouses or smaller towns to see what's on offer. This is all part of the wonder of travel and you'll have plenty to occupy your senses, not least driving.

MEDITERRANEAN FERRIES

These days there are two principal sea crossings from Europe used by Sahara-bound travellers: across the **Straits of Gibraltar** to Morocco and Mauritania, and from **Marseille or Genoa** to Tunis, Libya, Algeria and the Central Sahara.

Even during the revival of Algerian Saharan tourism from 2000, most people chose to enter the country via Tunis to El Oued, and the formerly popular SNCM sailings to all the Algerian ports have not been used by Europeans for years. There is talk of a new ferry service to **Tripoli** but, because of the distance, it would probably be from southern Italy rather than Genoa or

Ferry Services

EUROPE TO NORTH AFRICA

Marseille which are more useful to Sahara-bound travellers. If you're going to have to drive halfway down Italy to catch a ferry to Tripoli, it's the same distance from Genoa to Libya via Tunisia where costs are less. It will all depend on which European port is used and if it's a RoRo (roll-on-roll-off) ferry.

Spain to Morocco
From southern Spain there are effectively four routes to North Africa:

Algeciras to Ceuta (a Spanish enclave)	**from 30 mins**
Algeciras to Tangier	**2.5 hours**
Malaga to Melilla (a Spanish enclave) or Nador (nearby)	**7 hours**
Almeria to Melilla or Nador	**7 hours**

Clearly the fastest and cheapest is the run to **Ceuta** on the Moroccan coast which has frequent sailings and gives you a chance to take advantage of **duty free-prices** in the enclave, not least of which for fuel (see table on p.421). Long before you get to Algeciras you'll pass countless agencies selling tickets, and there are more in town; wherever you buy from, they all charge the same price. The Moroccan frontier is hassle-free compared to Tangier port, and the road south is straightforward and traffic-free.

    Tangier is a better option only for foot passengers, offering much better transport connections into the country. From Fnideq (the Moroccan town adjacent to Ceuta) you must get a taxi to Tetouan, a reputedly druggy place that is easily bypassed with a vehicle.

Note there is a **height limit** of around 1.85m on routes from Algeciras, above which the tariff is considerably higher. It's a way of charging Moroccans who load two metres of fridges, grand pianos and mopeds onto their hatchback roofs. Most 4WD cars will exceed this height but as long as you're not in a Unimog, ask for the low tariff anyway. During quiet periods away from August,

Hydrofoil leaving Algeciras for Ceuta.

Christmas and Easter no one will bother about your vehicle's height.

Ceuta to Fnideq

During the crossing try and find the white Moroccan immigration cards. Ask at the information desk. Once you've done your business in Ceuta, follow the clear signs leading to the corniche down to Fnideq, 5km from the port. Even on the Spanish side a few hustlers will be waiting, waving you down in an official manner to 'give' you immigration cards. Even if you haven't got your card ignore them and proceed to Spanish Customs who'll likely as not let you through with a wave.

Now you're on the Moroccan side with a line of windows on the left. Here you might want to enlist the aid of a helper, but the procedure is not that complicated. You can always latch on to someone who knows the ropes. Depending on queues it can take from 45 minutes to two hours.

1. Hand in your **passport** and the filled-out **white card** at the first window (ask around for a white form if you didn't get one). Retrieve your stamped passport from the next window about ten minutes later. The white form is retained.

One person can hand in all the passports for a group. Each passport gets stamped with a registration number, something like: '183357QM', as well as a date-of-entry stamp – often not on the same page.

2. **Change money** if necessary. The BMCE counter a few windows along offers normal rates and a receipt.

3. **Vehicle insurance** If you haven't got your domestic insurance (Green Card) extended to cover Morocco you can buy motor insurance (*assurance frontière*) from the office just past the bank. A yellow and white form is laboriously typed out with your details. As a guide, one month for a Mercedes in 2004 cost 815 dirhams, almost the same as it was five years earlier for a Toyota. Ten days is the only other increment: 490 dirhams.

4. **Temporary Importation Document** Get the green *Declaration d'Importation Temporaire de Moyens de Transport* form from one of the booths alongside the

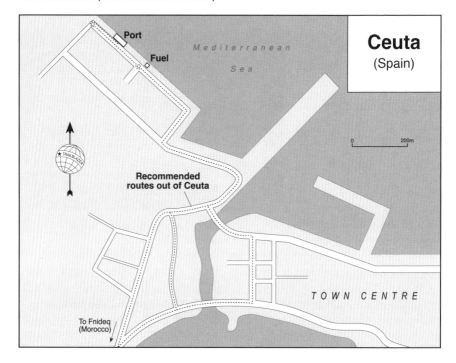

lanes up the steps to the right. Once you've filled it out with your passport registration number and other details, hand over your vehicle ownership papers, Green Card or local insurance, and passport. The green part will be kept while the white copy is stamped and returned to you with the rest of your documents. (If you bought insurance locally you may have to return to that office so they can photocopy your *Declaration d'Importation*.)

5. Drive forward a bit to **Customs** – just a table in the road – where they'll check your papers and do a half-hearted search.

With all this done you then continue to the barrier where they'll check that all your papers are in order and let you loose into Morocco. Tetouan is straight on. There may be a checkpoint or two in the next few kilometres but they usually let tourists through. Note there can be up to a two-hour time difference between Spanish Ceuta and Morocco.

Other options to Morocco

East of Algeciras, there are daily sailings from both Malaga and Almeria to **Melilla**, another Spanish enclave on the east Moroccan coast. The cost is around three times that of Ceuta and in 2004 the fuel at Melilla was about 20% cheaper than in Ceuta. Procedures at Beni Enzar match those for Fnideq, but there is no insurance booth. You can buy some at the first town (Nador).

The weekly SNCM ferry from **Sète**, near Montpellier, to Tangier is expensive but might suit central Europeans who don't mind facing Tangier. The 26-hour crossing saves a two-day drive across Spain to Algeciras.

COMPARATIVE FUEL PRICES

Prices may be higher in remote areas and will of course go out of date. Exchange rates are on p.30 and on the website, as are the latest fuel prices.

	Diesel per litre	Petrol per litre
UK	83p	82p
France	€0.90	€1.15
Spain	€0.70	€0.95
Italy	€0.91	€0.94
Ceuta/Melilla	€0.41/0.49	€0.58–0.68
Algeria	12 dinars	21 dinars
Egypt	£E0.4	£E1.1–1.6
Libya	LD 0.11	LD 0.14
Mali	400 CFA	400 CFA
Mauritania	97UM	134UM
Morocco	5.8 dirham	9.2 dirham
Niger	495 CFA	600 CFA
Chad	500 CFA	600 CFA
Tunisia	0.41 dinar	0.68–0.70 dinar
Western Sahara	2.8 dirham	4.6 dirham

Marseille or Genoa to Tunis

The port of La Goulette near Tunis has become the gateway to the central Sahara from Marseille or Genoa. At either port you have plenty of time to engage in some vehicle spotting as you realise that other people also appear to be heading for the Sahara in ruggedly equipped 4WDs and bikes. Chances are you'll be running into, or even driving with, some of them on the pistes in a few days' time.

The ferries are of a high standard. For Brits the distances to Marseille and Genoa from the Channel ports are almost identical, but the Marseille crossing works out around 15% more expensive than Genoa. A **cabin** is recommended and a self-contained exterior cabin is best (designated 'A**E', meaning A class, cabin code: Exterior). Once on board, go to the information desk to get the door code for your cabin (if you've booked one). There are plenty of lounges, bars, and three standards of restaurant; even the à la carte resto on the *Carthage* is pretty good value, or there's a cafeteria next door. Both sailings take around 22 hours in good weather.

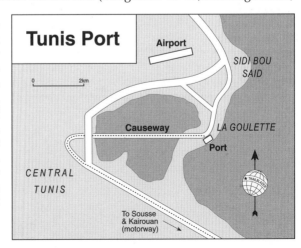

Tunis Port

Airport

SIDI BOU SAID

0   2km

Causeway

LA GOULETTE

Port

CENTRAL TUNIS

To Sousse & Kairouan (motorway)

Tunisian immigration

Doing immigration formalities **on board the ferries** may sound like an efficient use of time while at sea but at busy times can amount to many hours of mind-numbing queuing along the ship's corridors for one form after another. Even though there may be hundreds of you, they employ at most a couple of guys for each task – they have plenty of time after all. With two of you, one can at least take shifts while the other eats, rests or wanders around the decks.

The recently rebuilt port at La Joliette, Marseille.

Form-filling

1. From the information desk get a *Carte de Séjour* which you must fill out and hand in with your passport at one of the temporarily set up desks (on the *Carthage*). The bottom section is stamped and returned with your passport. Staple it in as it's easy to lose.

2. *Fiche d'Entrée ou de Sortie pour Vehicule* is the next form. Fill it out and get it stamped. You hand it in as you leave through the port gate.

3. *Permit de Conduire* is a temporary driving permit for your vehicle. Hand over your vehicle ownership papers and they do it on a computer. You'll get two copies; hand one in as you leave the port.

Leaving the ship, drive through the port as indicated by stewards – tourists go to separate lanes from locals. Here you will be asked to declare any goods (either on board or at the border post get a white A4 list of goods, most of which you will not have) and have a cursory search. The guy will sign one of your documents, keep the A4 sheet and with a final check of papers you are out of the port area. At least **leaving La Goulette** is easy. There is fuel within half a kilometre – continue over the causeway to the traffic lights right at the end by the flyover. Central Tunis is straight on but if you're heading south turn left at the flyover. This leads straight to the (toll) motorway with services, which ends just after Sousse. For Algeria, turn off before the end of the motorway for Kairouan, Gafsa and Touzeur; for Libya hug the coast.

Routes in the Sahara

The following itineraries are divided into three types: those I've done myself in the last few years (by car, 4WD, motorbike or as a passenger on a tour), a few submitted by contributors, and one or two I did before the GPS era and have not been able to update since, but have reasonable route descriptions of without waypoints.

The majority of itineraries were specifically written for this book, with the aid of other guidebooks, local guides or in most cases just following the piste or terrain and working it out. You'll probably find most of the descriptions over-detailed, and on some of the easier routes you may not even need to consult this book at all once you're under way. But it is in conditions of **poor visibility** or if you've somehow lost the track that the detail and especially the waypoints can help you maintain or regain the right course. And if nothing else, it's reassuring to be able to tick off landmarks as you pass them, especially if this is your first visit to the Sahara.

Using the itineraries

Only the countries that are accessible and explorable (or worth exploring) are fully covered here. It's uncertain how Algeria and Libya are going to turn out, but for places like Niger, Chad and Egypt's Gilf Kebir, where various factors limit independent travel by novices, there are written descriptions of recommended routes with highlights and including waypoints but not necessarily accurate distances. Some of these may be of limited use for actual navigation but at least give you an idea what to expect.

The fully logged routes begin and end at key points, usually **fuel stations** at the point of departure and arrival. These are the places to zero your GPS **trip counter** if you want to match your distance readings with those in the book. As a guide to the route's use, the frequency of **traffic** is estimated. This will vary with the time of year of course: busy around Christmas in the central Sahara, and possibly devoid of all traffic at the height of summer.

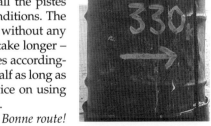

With a long background of riding **motorbikes** in the Sahara, though not necessarily on all the pistes described, I've also estimated riding conditions. The **suggested duration** refers to a traversal without any significant stops. In all cases you could take longer – and you should plan your water supplies accordingly – although motorcyclists might take half as long as a four-wheeler over rough terrain. Advice on using GPS with these routes appears on p.323.

Bonne route!

INDEX OF ITINERARIES AND TRIP REPORTS
(see map pp.12-13)

Morocco

For purists Morocco is not the Sahara, but Africa it certainly is. The country's well-known attractions and easy access from Spain put it firmly on the adventurous side of mainstream tourism. Because the commitment in time, money and distance to explore the Moroccan desert is smaller than elsewhere in the Sahara, stress is also reduced, allowing you to enjoy the wilderness without nagging worries. It's something you won't appreciate until you visit those other places.

All but one of the routes are south of the High Atlas, the barrier between the wild and amicable south and the domesticated north. Some routes venture dramatically into the ranges of the Anti Atlas which makes them more impressive than the pure desert pistes of the plain. Done in a string from east to west they would make an outstanding 2000-kilometre **Grand Traverse of the Moroccan Sahara** from the Rekkam plateau to the Atlantic shore at Tan Tan.

Note that these pistes are much stonier than anything else in the Sahara. Fragile sand tyres and sand ladders will not be necessary, good suspension and underbody protection for low cars and bikes will be. Distances are mostly short; easily within range of a standard 4WD's or desert bike's fuel tank which means no messing about with jerricans.

M1 GUERCIF → AIN BENIMATHAR [270KM]
March 2004; Mercedes 190D

Description
An easy piste across the width of the bleak and often windy Rekkam plateau occupied by Berber nomads in their tents. Not a true desert piste but can be a good shakedown on the way south.

**M1 – RECOMMENDED MAPS
GUERCIF → BENIMATHAR 270KM**

The modern IGN 'Maroc', Michelin 742 or Rough Guide Morocco maps (all 1:1m) all show the major pistes across the Rekkam plateau.

Route-finding and markers
There are no markers but the track is clear all the way.

Fuel Guercif and Aïn Benimathar.

Water
Wells and cisterns along the route.

Traffic
Local traffic serving the Berber encampments is common.

Driving
Easy and rarely corrugated. No need for 4WD.

Suggested duration
Half a day.

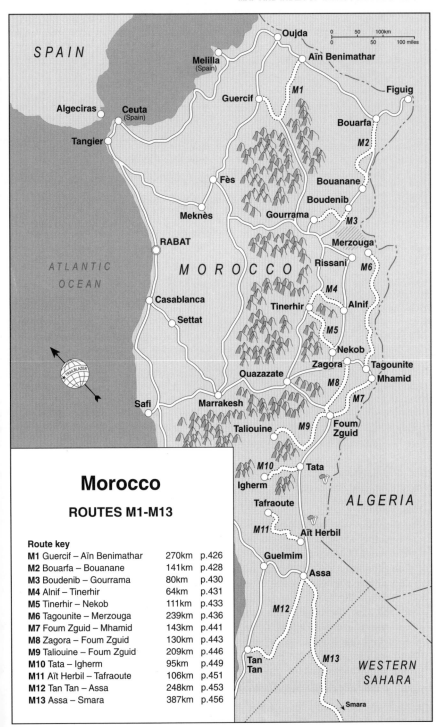

Morocco

ROUTES M1–M13

Route key

0km (270)
Fuel station at the centre of Guercif. Head east out of town on the road to Taourirt and Oujda. After a few kilometres turn south on the single-width road to Missour and Er-Rachidia.

93 (177)   N33° 30.0'   W03° 36.2'
Sign. Turn east on a wide gravel track with the snowy slopes of Jebel Bou Necaur, the eastern limit of the High Atlas, behind you to the south-west.

105 (165)
Well on the north side of the track. Shortly after, you cross a oued alongside a broken bridge.

120 (150)
Piste joins from the north.

127 (143)   N33° 34.2'   W03° 17.6'
A piste turns off to the south-east, an interesting route to Beni Tajite.

140 (130)
Heading NE now on a wide stony piste with two small buildings to the SE.

146 (124)
Tank and cistern with a nearby encampment. In a kilometre you pass a hill with a tripod on top. The old piste is paralleled by a smoother newer piste.

164 (106)   N33° 43.2'   W03° 01.6'
Having passed another water tank a kilometre earlier, you come to a four-way junction with a newer, broader piste heading from Debdou to the south. (Work was in progress on this piste in 2004, as if it was about to be sealed to Tendrara or Bouarfa, but following it south-east, the wide new track soon expired).

170 (100)
Water tank by the piste.

195 (75)   N33° 48.1'   W02° 42.1'
Wide gravel piste. Empty building to the south of the piste.

217 (53)
Small cone hill to the north of the piste with a building on top.

222 (48)
Buildings to the right of the piste.

233 (37)   N33° 58.9'   W02° 21.4'
Track joins a sealed road coming from Debdou and heading east. When you get to a junction, turn left (north) which will lead you to the crossroads south of Aïn Benimathar and the fuel station, below.

270 (0)   N34° 00.4'   W02° 01.4'
Four-way junction and the *Afrique* fuel station south of Aïn Benimathar.

M2 BOUARFA → BOUANANE   [141KM]
March 2004; Mercedes 190D

Description
This should have been a new route to Beni Tajite in the west; many maps show a reasonably clear track between the two via Jebel Korima, but just before Korima well (KM88) the hitherto clear track petered out alongside a oued full of shingle with no clear or recent tracks crossing the oued.

So, either press on and see what happens (the topography appeared correct, it's just the track was not clear or good enough for our 2WD) or turn south towards the border highway running below Jebel Zelmou. We continued across country after KM101 but got trapped by the Oued Zelmou. We then backtracked north-east to what is estimated as KM103 and a nearby mine from where we got back to the highway. A 4WD or trail bike may have more luck finding the way through from KM88 west to Beni Tajite.

Route-finding and markers
No markers but tracks are clear with little chance of straying into the jebels.

Fuel
Bouarfa and Bouanane.

Water
Well at KM70 plus a few nomad encampments and villages along the tracks and pooled water in the bigger oueds.

Traffic
None, but it's not that remote.

Driving
Stony with many washed-out oueds. On a bike there will be a fair amount of bouncing around.

Suggested duration
More than half a day.

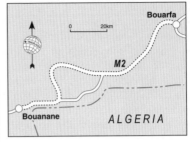

**M2 – RECOMMENDED MAPS
BOUARFA → BOUANANE 141км**

Most of the 1:1m country maps won't show this route beyond KM88 and the old Moroccan 250,000 sheet is only marginally useful here too. But the tracks are easy enough to follow.

0km (141)   N32° 31.8'   W01° 57.9'
Bouarfa fuel. Take the highway west.

56 (85)   N32° 15.6'   W02° 26.2'
Turn off road onto side tarmac.

58 (83)
Tarmac ends, stony piste begins.

70 (71)   N32° 16.4'   W02° 34.6'
Well on south side of piste, which now gets a little smoother.

72 (69)
Wide oued with big stones.

81 (60)   N32° 16.9'   W02° 42.2'
Piste forks, take right track.

85 (56)
Another oued crossing with big stones.

88 (53)   N32° 19.7'   W02° 48.3'
A big oued with a concrete ford. On the other side a piste runs from left to right (N–S) and another carries on ahead (W) into the valley towards Jebel Korima (the aborted direction). Turn south-west at the junction after the oued, passing a few buildings until the track heads south.

91 (50)   N32° 18.1'   W02° 48.5'
Cross the oued with a broken concrete bridge. Half a kilometre later (N32° 17.6'

W2° 48.5') the track splits. Take the right fork, an easy track across a flat valley of gravel with jebels on either side.

93 (48)
A distinctive cone hill to the west as you continue along the valley, soon diverting to the left around a washed-out oued.

99 (42)
On the horizon you can see a radio mast on top of Jebel Zelmou. This ridge marks the border with Algeria. Soon after, a track leads off to the right; you continue south.

101 (40)
Cross another oued and carry on south until you come across a track heading to the south-east. Follow this track via way-point N32° 11.8'   W02° 49.7' (KM103) towards a mine.

104 (37)   N32° 11.7'   W02° 48.2'
Mine buildings. Be careful of trucks and other machinery. Drive out south along the mine access road, to the highway.

110 (31)   N32° 08.7'   W02° 46.6'
Rejoin the highway. A sign here points back to 'Ksar Anbag', possibly the name of the mine.

141 (0)   N32° 02.2'   W03° 03.1'
Bouanane fuel station.

M3 BOUDENIB → GOURRAMA [80KM]

March 2004; Mercedes 190D

Description

A pleasant and easy excursion from the desert town of Boudenib. It passes through the gorge of the Oued Guir to the palmerie and evocative ruins of old Tazouguerte and the Legionnaire's fort of Atchana, to rejoin the tarmac near Gourrama.

After Gourrama the road leads west through the impressive Ziz Gorge and the road south to Erfoud.

Route-finding and markers

A clear piste all the way.

Fuel

Boudenib and Gourrama.

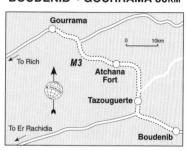

M3 – RECOMMENDED MAPS
BOUDENIB → GOURRAMA 80KM

The whole route is easy to follow without a map, but the 1:1m country maps show the track.

Water

As you're passing several villages as well as following the Oued Guir most of the way, water should not be a problem.

Traffic

Local traffic.

Driving

Straightforward. Possible with care in an ordinary road car or bike with only the oued crossing at KM46 making demands on ground clearance.

Suggested duration

Three hours.

0km (80)　　　N31° 57.0'　W03° 36.5'
Boudenib fuel station (not always open) on the west side of Boudenib. Drive west out of town towards Er-Rachidia.

18 (62)　　　N32° 00.8'　W03° 46.3'
Turn off right onto the piste where the road curves left over the Oued Guir by a shack café. Follow the track up the side of the gorge, with good views of the oued below.

27 (62)
Pass below the crumbling ruins of old Tazouguerte facing the palmerie and gardens alongside the oued. Nice views up the valley from the ruins.

Less than a kilometre later you reach the new town. Take the left fork and fol-

low the signs for Gourrama. Soon you pass by an old water tower – continue along a wide gravelly piste heading NW with the oued still on your left.

35 (45)
Piste drops down and over a oued and follows it through a gap carved in the cliffs. There are ruins on the other side of the oued.

After two kilometres the track runs along the oued bottom, heading east, with gardens on the banks of the oued.

39 (41)　　　N32° 09.4'　W03° 47.0'
Kadoussa village. In just over a kilometre you pass a dam and after another kilometre or so reach the village of El Gorane

(N32° 10.6' W03° 47.1'), surrounded by gardens. Continue following the track along the oued, generally NW.

46 (34)
Cross a wide, stony oued. With the ford churned up, the route snakes about to find a smooth passage, depending on recent flooding.

48 (32)　　　N32° 13.2' W03° 49.2'
Ruins of the Foreign Legion fort of Atchana built just before WWI. This valley saw several battles with renegade tribes in the early decades of the last century right up till 1931. Not that much of interest at the fort but notice the stone pentagram emblem of the *goumiers* (Moroccan troops engaged by the French) set with stones.

55 (25)
Village of Irara.

62 (18)　　　N32° 14.8' W03° 57.5'
Long walled ksar on the left as you enter the village of Méhalla.

66 (14)
Cross the Oued Guir on a concrete bridge.

69 (11)
Village of Toulal, with an old ksar but also satellite dishes.

74 (6)　　　N32° 19.3' W04° 00.6'
Reach the tarmac road a few kilometres before Gourrama.

80 (0)　　　N32° 20.2' W04° 04.1'
Gourrama fuel station. If not carrying on to the Ziz gorges you can make a loop back to Tazouguerte by turning back north and west on sealed roads to Beni Tajite from where a piste leads across the Plain de Snab and over the Belkassem pass to Tazouguerte.

M4 ALNIF → TINERHIR　　　　　　[64KM]
February 1999; Toyota HJ61

Description
This is a satisfying short hop across the Jebel Ougnat from the pre-Saharan plateau to the southern edge of the High Atlas, with its excursions into the gorges of Todra and Dades. North of Alnif you follow a string of villages along the Oued Reg and then climb a clear stony track up to the col at Tizi-n Boujou. From here you'll see the snowcapped peaks of the High Atlas to the north.

Route-finding and markers
The villages at either end are the usual places to get a little confused but the inverted red 'V's sprayed on walls, cairns and other key points should keep you out of people's back yards.

Apart from a few old mining tracks, the lack of major turn-offs on this route makes it pretty hard to get lost. You'll find the description below more useful for judging the state and suitability of the track than for route-finding.

Fuel
Alnif, Tinerhir.

M4 – RECOMMENDED MAPS
ALNIF → TINERHIR 64KM

The IGN, Michelin or Rough Guide Morocco maps (all 1:1m) show a straightish line over the Jebel. With nowhere to go wrong they're all you'll need.

Water

In Alnif and Tinerhir and at villages and wells along the route. There's even a well just before the high point at KM30. There was also an unusually nice roadside café a couple of kilometres after you rejoin the tarmac heading west to Tinerhir.

Traffic

The usual range of Moroccan transporters.

Driving

Nothing worth noting for cars or motorbikes. There are a couple of wide, rubbly oued crossings in the first few kilometres but other than that it's relatively smooth. This, plus the short distance and regular water points, would make this route a fun day out for a **mountain bike**. It's a steady but not agonising slog up to the pass followed by a brief chance to cook the brake blocks.

Suggested duration

Two hours with an engine; an easy day with pedals.

0km (64)　　　　**N31° 07.0'　W05° 10.1'**
Alnif. Turn off north at the western side of the town centre between the mosque and army establishment, passing a 'No Entry' sign shortly after a hotel. After 600m you pass a large school on your left and a radio mast on your right. Take the left fork.

0.9 (63.1)
Football field on right.

1.7 (62.3)
Well on the left of the piste and soon a small palmerie on the right.

2.2 (61.8)
Track passes below some houses on the left and a palmerie on the right. Continue through the village alongside the palmerie.

4 (60)
With more houses on a hill to the left, the track winds around its base. Continue heading north-west.

6 (58)
Track runs between two small stony hills. Half a kilometre later there's another palmerie on the right and more stony hills.

7 (57)
Track crosses a broad stony oued and fol-

lows it north for just over one kilometre.

8 (56)
Leave the oued and pass through another palmerie. After a kilometre you pass some houses in the palmerie and at KM10 you pass a mosque where the track curves left and winds through the small village.

11 (53)　　　　**N31° 11.2'　W05°13.4'**
Having left the village the track forks. Take the right fork, heading N.

13 (51)
Track crosses the kilometre-wide Oued Reg again. Bearing NNE.

15 (49)
A track joins from the right. Two hundred metres later you'll see some ruins on the left of the track and here the piste begins winding NNW up a stony valley along a gravelly track.

19 (45)
Track joins from the left. Five hundred metres later you may see 'Maha Resstera' painted on the side of a concrete building on the left of the track (possibly open in the tourist season).

20 (44)
Having just passed a village and palmerie some distance to the left, the track follows and then crosses a small oued, running

along its western bank as you enter a narrow valley bounded by rocky hills.

22 (42)
Pass through a small oasis (with fossil shop) and cross to the east bank of the oued. Half a kilometre later is another small palmerie.

24 (40)
Elevation 1175m. Begin a gentle climb with the oued now below you on your right. You'll see distinctive grey-green gravel in the bed of the oued and on the hillsides, plus a radio mast on the hilltop ahead.

27 (37)   N31° 18.8'   W05° 16.3'
Pass the radio mast. The landscape is bouldery, with green-tinged cliffsides and soil. Half a kilometre later is a well on the right of the piste.

30 (34)
Having continued climbing you reach the high point of the route, Tizi-n Boujou (1260m). From here you might see the snow-capped peaks of the High Atlas on the northern horizon. Begin smooth descent.

32 (32)
The track flattens out as you continue NNE towards the yellow buildings of Aït el Farsi a kilometre and a half away.

Once in the town drive through the palmerie, passing water towers and follow a line of pylons NNW out of the village towards a red and white radio mast.

36 (28)   N31° 22.4'   W05° 17.6'
Radio mast. Cross a gravelly plain with small grass tussocks. After 1.7km the track forks; take the left fork following the pylons.

42 (22)
Pass a few buildings. The Jebel Tisdaline is visible straight ahead, behind the village.

46 (18)
Having passed some fields just over a kilometre earlier, go through a small village. From the village the track winds NNE across a oued towards the Tinerhir road.

47 (17)   N31° 26.9'   W05° 20.4'
Tinerhir–Goulmima road. Turn west for Tinerhir. If you're doing the piste from the other direction the turn-off is marked with an Arabic sign on the ground and the figures '63'. A white sign opposite also indicates 'Tinghir 25, Ouazazate 190'.

64 (0)
Fuel station on the eastern outskirts of Tinerhir.

M5 TINERHIR → NEKOB   [111KM]
February 1999; Toyota HJ61

Description
Crossing the basalt massif of the Jebel Sarhro, this piste makes a direct and spectacular link between the Todra Gorge north of Tinerhir and Zagora in the south. It rises gradually to the high plains north of Iknioun and then turns west and south crawling up to the 2200m Tizi-n Tazazert pass.

From here the scenery takes a dramatic turn as before you unrolls a series of basalt ridges, flat-topped mesas and ravines of twisted black rock. It's a fabulous descent and you'll want to stop again and again to marvel at your surroundings. For this reason it's preferable to do this piste in the direction described, rather than south–north.

The slightly shorter approach to the pass from Boumaine Dades misses none of the spectacle.

Route-finding and markers
Before Iknioun some mining tracks can cause a little confusion but the notes

M5 – RECOMMENDED MAPS
TINERHIR → NEKOB 111KM

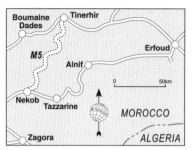

The IGN 'Maroc', NH-30 'Bechar' sheet and Michelin 742 (all 1:1m) are all adequate for this route.

below and the clear mountain track should keep you on the right path. You may spot a few painted red arrow markers as on route M4.

Fuel
Tinerhir and Nekob.

Water
At villages and wells along the route.

Traffic
There was none on our traverse in February and we even gave a few lifts to local villagers. In the warmer season 4WD tourists will be common on this route.

Driving
The tracks get pretty rough near the crest but that's about it. As with all the more northerly Moroccan pistes, rain might cause problems, but otherwise four-wheel drive was not necessary. As with route M4, this too would make a fabulous, if more demanding, ride on a mountain bike.

Suggested duration
One day with a car or motorbike; two full days with a bicycle. If you're planning to spend the night out, the high plains north of Iknioun would be your best bet. Between Iknioun and the Tizi-n Tazazert is either quite populated or rough (as well as cold), and after that there are few sheltered spots until you get to the populated villages in the valley below.

0km (111)   N31° 31.2'   W05° 32.0'
Fuel station at the west end of Tinerhir next to the Banque Populaire. Driving west through the town, after 200m turn left at the sign for the Hotel Timbuktu. Continue down this road for 2.6km until the tarmac ends at a T-junction on the southern outskirts of Tinerhir. Carry straight on (south) onto a rubbly piste that passes through a rubbish dump and a sewage outlet towards a gravel plain and the hills beyond.

4.5 (106.5)
Heading SSW across the gravel plain.

8 (103)
Cross a oued and enter a village with a palmerie. Continue SSW through the village passing a pink mosque on the right after 700m as you leave.

10 (101)
An access track to the radio mast on the right. Keep left. Track becomes stony.

12 (99)
Cross a oued after which the track turns towards 216°, aiming for the hills.

14 (97)
Track drives up a river bed for 500m and soon you start climbing into the hills. After a kilometre or so the track flattens out and snakes along a valley at an average bearing of 135°.

18 (93)
Pass scattered buildings and a cultivated area over the next kilometre or two.

22 (89)
Cross a oued and continue along its west-

ern bank. The heading is generally SW as you sometimes drive along the creek bed.

24 (87)
Leave the oued and start climbing sharply into the hills above. Within a kilometre you get to a distinctive extruded fin of black rock after which the track twists upwards again for the next few kilometres.

28 (83)　　　　**N31° 19.6'　W05° 35.4'**
A track joins from the right, with buildings visible below. Six hundred metres later a circular stone enclosure is visible in the valley below.

30 (81)
Elevation 1850m. The track flattens out to give a view of the (sometimes) snow-topped mountains to the east. Half a kilometre later you begin descending with a village visible in the valley below.

32 (79)
Near some cultivated land on the left a track goes off to the right. Take the left track. In a few hundred metres you pass some houses on the left. Then the track curves upwards again through a landscape of boulders and grassy tussocks.

34 (77)　　　　**N31° 17.8'　W05° 35.6'**
Having flattened out, the track forks. Take the right fork, bearing SSW. A kilometre later you pass a well on the left of the piste and nearly two kilometres later (KM37.6) a thin flat sandy oued, resembling a track, crosses the piste.

40 (71)
After you've passed a few concrete buildings on the left and stone ruins on the right, a couple of tracks join from the right.

43 (68)
Pass a few more buildings up to this point where a track joins from the left.

44 (67)　　　　**N31° 13.1'　W05° 37.3'**
The major junction with the Agoultine mine track (marked on the Michelin map). Soon you begin veering SW and pass a small village at KM45.5.

47 (64)
Irrigation dam on the left and just over a kilometre later another village, with a white mosque.

49 (62)
A large well on the right. In 1km you cross a oued with houses on the right.

54 (57)
Iknioun. Drive through the town and when the road forks (N31° 10.2'　W05° 40.4'), take the right fork, before the colonnade. Head west out of town along the valley with a high ridge to your left.

60 (51)　　　　**N31° 10.2'　W05° 43.6'**
Junction with the '6907' Boumaine Dades piste (sign). Keep left, bearing 252° along the bumpy track to Nekob. In just over 1km you pass through a village where the piste starts climbing and gets rough.

64 (47)　　　　**N31° 09.6'　W05° 45.8'**
Three-way junction with Tiouit mine track. Turn left, descending for a few hundred metres, at which point the track veers left and begins to climb again. Over the next couple of kilometres there are a number of false passes, followed by further ascents.

70 (41)
Tizi-n Tazazert Pass (2200m). Fabulous views all around, especially to the south. Begin the long, spectacular descent.

81 (30)
Concrete block with a faint 'restaurant' sign near a lone palm.

84 (27)　　　　**N31° 03.5'　W05° 46.9'**
Piste junction. Take right fork. Sign for 'bivouac' in a kilometre.

86 (25)
Cultivation and habitation resume as the piste passes between two dry stone walls. In a kilometre you cross a oued of purple stones and then continue along its western bank with fields to your left.

95 (16)　　　　**N30° 58.5'　W05° 49.0'**
Track forks, keep right and climb around the village and palmerie below.

97 (14)   N30° 58.3'   W05° 48.9'
Track forks again. Keep right and drive along the ridge. In just over a kilometre you pass some workings (a mine?) on the right. Continue SW across basalt rubble.

100 (11)
Pass another small mine (?) on the left.

101 (10)
Track forks. Follow the main piste to the right.

109 (2)
A track joins from the left. Cross a oued and approach Nekob which lies directly ahead across a gravel plain.

110 (1)   N30° 53.0'   W05° 52.2'
Tracks join from left and right. Go straight on and pass under electricity pylons.

111 (0)
Outskirts of Nekob. Pass a football field on your left and carry on along a track that emerges from behind a fuel station at the west end of town (N30° 52.1' W05° 52.0').

If you arrive at Nekob as the day ends, there's no obvious accommodation in town and this stretch of the Alnif–Agdz road is pretty exposed for a quiet camp. Tazzarine, 35km east of Nekob, has a big hotel/campsite and the making of a new road to Zagora.

M6 TAGOUNITE → MERZOUGA   [239KM]
Updated: October 2003; mountain bikes (Raf Verbeelen)

Description
Along with Route M13, this route, which runs close to the Algerian border, gives a real taste of the true Sahara a thousand kilometres further south. It's also remarkably smooth to drive compared to other Moroccan pistes. These facts along with an absorbing selection of landscapes make this one of the best desert itineraries in Morocco.

Starting from the Draa Valley you drive north around the Jebel Bou Debgane and then cross Tafenna, a large basin-like formation with Hassi Taffeta well in its centre. Descending the eastern rim you cross the Oued Mird to the fort at Hassi Zguilma and begin the long NNE run up to the town of Tafraoute. From here the track follows a lovely valley to the dune-filled Oued Rheris near Hassi Remlia and then continues over bumpy chotts to Hassi Ouzina and Taouz. After Taouz it's a straight run up to Merzouga and the amazing dunes of Erg Chebbi.

Route-finding and markers
Between Tagounite and KM18 you might find yourself blundering around the villages and irrigation canals of the many villages, but from this point it's a clear run over Tafenna to Oued Mird where the lower loop that goes south of Jebel Bou Debgane joins our piste.

The long smooth run from Hassi Zguilma fort (KM56) up to the eastward turn of the piste has a few turn-offs, so keep an eye on your bearing. 'Agoult' on the Michelin map does not appear to exist, but near here twin tyre markers lead you east over a featureless gravel plain, a few low dunes and a chott (the 'Lac') to Tafraoute. This is the only section that may require concentration.

From the new town to Hassi Remlia and Hassi Ouzina is straightforward. From Ouzina make sure you get south of the Oued Ziz and then follow the tracks (sometimes splitting and rejoining) which all lead to Taouz. At Taouz well-used tracks lead to the mass of Erg Chebbi's dunes visible on the horizon and Merzouga on its western flank.

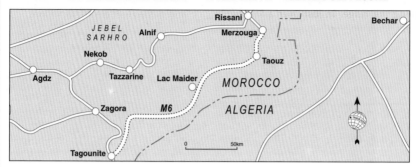

M6 – RECOMMENDED MAPS   TAGOUNITE → MERGOUZA 239KM

The best is the old IGN NH-30 1:1 m which represents the route most clearly. After that the IGN 'Maroc' and Rough Guide country maps are best. The 1:250,000 Moroccan NH-30-5 'Zagora' and NH-30-6 'Taouz' sheets cover the route, but readers have managed without them.

Fuel
Tagounite; Tafraoute and Remlia (from drums); Rissani (50km from Merzouga).

Water
Plenty, from villages and wells along the route. Longest stretch is from the fort at KM56 to Tamassint, KM109.

Traffic
This is a popular route with local tours and tourists alike.

Driving
Rough hairpin tracks lead steeply down into the basin of Tafenna, after which it's remarkably smooth (by Moroccan standards) until you get to the dunes before Tafraoute (mostly avoidable) and another sandy section before Hassi Remlia. From here rough chotts lead to Taouz, though if ground water has seeped up, they could get sticky. The cycle updaters did this route in eight days but think it could be done in five.

Suggested duration
Because it's so smooth, this route could be done in a long day, but it would be a shame not to spend at least one night out in the desert. Any number of spots between Tafenna and Hassi Ouzina would make great overnight stops. Merzouga itself has a number of *auberges* set right by the dunes, stretching in a 20km line north of the town. See Moroccan guidebooks for details.

0km (239)   N29° 59.0' W05° 35.0'
North gate of Tagounite. Drive south into the town centre for 1300m and turn left (N29° 58.6' W05° 35.0') opposite the military barracks. You'll see a very faint sign for 'Blida' (a village marked on the Michelin map) on the east side of the main street. This track leads along canals to a palmerie.

3.2 (235.8)
Walled village on both sides of the track. Heading ESE. When you emerge from the village you'll soon pass a sign for 'central Tagounite' (KM3.9) as you continue through the palmerie.

7 (232)
You reach a scrubby plain and half a kilometre later the track turns almost north

with the mass of Jebel Bou Debgane to the east. The track soon passes two concrete blocks and runs alongside a palmerie to the right (KM8.3).

9 (230)   **N29° 59.0'   W05° 30.8'**
Blida. Having crossed a canal with sluice gates where the track turns ENE and then a major ditch, you arrive at a junction with a small sign on a lamp-post indicating 'Blida'. Turn left towards the red and white mast. Pass the mast on the left and a school on the right and continue through town towards the Jebel.

10 (229)
Pass a health centre and come to a junction. Turn left and continue north with the Jebel to your right. White cairns.

12 (227)
Fork; go right. After a kilometre and a half you pass the village of Aissfou on the left with its long palmerie. Continue NNE.

16 (223)
Ruins on the left and another village 1500m later. Drive straight through it.

19 (220)   **N30° 03.4'   W05° 29.0'**
Junction. Turn right and continue NE. Track sandy and bumpy, veering ENE.

23 (216)   **N30° 04.5'   W05° 26.7'**
Track joins from the WNW coming from Zagora – our track now turns ESE, 110°. The track is slow and bumpy but up ahead you see it rising up the west rim of Tafenna.

28 (211)
The wide, smooth track starts to rise up the hamada and onto the ridge.

31 (208)
Crest of the ridge at 856m (GPS). The descent is very rough and stony. Soon you see the track cutting across the smooth flat centre of the 'basin' to the opposite ridge. At KM34 pass Hassi Tafenna well (N30° 04.5' W05° 20.2').

38 (201)
Begin to climb the track up the eastern rim, which has been improved.

41 (198)
Hut on the right near the crest of the ridge which appears after 300m (951m, GPS). From here a view stretches east over distant plateaux. Begin a very gradual descent over the next 3km.

45 (194)   **N30° 06.6'   W05° 15.1'**
Junction with a cairn on the hamada between the ridge and Oued Mird. Right loop leads south of Jebel Bou Debgane back to the Vallée du Draa.
      Take the left fork NE across the hamada with a line of acacias running parallel to your left.

48 (191)
Cross a small oued and line of acacias.

50 (189)   **N30° 07.7'   W05° 12.4'**
Cross a thicker band of trees as a track joins from the right. In less than a kilometre you get to some buildings and a small palmerie on the left of the track, with a pole marker on the right. The track becomes very sandy for a few hundred metres.

53 (186)
Veer NE towards a reddish escarpment.

56 (183)   **N30° 09.4'   W05° 09.9'**
Hassi Zguilma. Pink fort on a hill. Military checkpoint. The track leaves to the NNE.

60 (179)
Track joins from the left. Smooth going.

66 (173)   **N30° 13.9'   W05° 06.8'**
Tracks diverge. Take the left fork going NE with cone-shaped hill to your right.

70 (169)   **N30° 15.7'W05° 05.4'**
Track splits to the right. Keep left, heading towards big red Ayers Rock-like monolith. After a kilometre more monoliths become visible ahead and to the right. Some corrugations. Bearing 30°.

75 (164)
Track joins from the right (ESE); having passed the red plateaux to the east, another track joins from the right 4km later (N30° 18.6' W05° 03.3').

81 (158)
Distinctive slab cairn with a hole, on the right of the piste. Track still smooth, red sandy gravel.

82 (157)
Track cuts across the piste with two white-painted cairns on the left.

84 (155) N30° 21.8' W05° 00.9'
Signs of an encampment on the right. Possibly a well but does not match any map. Track becomes stonier with scrub and trees to the right.

87 (152)
Stretch of hamada. The bearing in this section varies between 8° and 30°.

90 (149) N30° 25.5' W04° 59.5'
After you've started climbing a bit, a track joins from the right.

92 (147) N30° 25.9' W04° 59.6'
Track heads WNW briefly. In 1999 we were waved down by the 'regional guardian' and various readers report he still crops up. Apparently he's a game-keeper for a group of Saudi falcon hunters who visit the area each February.

95 (144) N30° 27.4' W04° 59.2'
Having passed some soft sand, a cairn on the left and tussocks you reach a pair of tyres on either side of the now corrugated track.

You see more tyre markers as the track heads NNE across a featureless gravel plain.

98 (141) N30° 29.1' W04° 58.4'
Two more tyre markers, another single tyre at KM100 and another pair on a slight rise to the left at KM102. Continue NE across the gravel plain.

109 (130) N30° 33.3' W04° 54.3'
After you've passed another tyre at KM108, the village of Tamassint becomes visible a few hundred metres to the NW (left). The terrain softens a bit and tracks become faint. Keep heading just E of NE aiming for two more tyre markers ahead.

112 (127) N30° 34.7' W04° 53.0'
Two tyre markers on the right. Still on a fast flat gravel piste. There is a single tyre at KM113, another pair at KM116 (N30° 36.2' W04° 51.6'), a single tyre at KM117 and another pair with a cairn at KM118, bearing 56°. After this there are a few cairns.

121 (239) N30° 38.2' W04° 49.3'
Track forks (west fork leads to Zagora). Keep right, heading east towards dunes. Going now gets slow and soft as you cross a low dune (plenty of tracks) and continue over the soft undulating sand.

124 (115)
Ground becomes firmer with dunes and sand-swept cliffs to the right.

127 (112) N30° 38.6' W04° 45.4'
Small mosque, another building and a cemetery on the left of the piste. White buildings visible in the hills to the north. Pink fort visible ahead. Go east towards the fort but do not go to it. Follow the cairns and corrugations around the base of a rubble hill.

129 (110)
Pass pink fort to the right, between two hills, and head ENE across a chott (Lac Maider) towards the palmerie with buildings.

135 (104) N30° 40.0' W04° 41.4'
The pink buildings of Tafraoute, a small town with a radio mast, are 200m to the north of our piste as it heads ENE passing several signs for cafés and auberges. Cairns mark the piste leading east into a pretty valley bounded by a crenellated ridge to the south and dunes to the north.

140 (99)
Valley widens with sand-swept cliffs on both sides. Nice place for a camp. Head E.

154 (85)
Track crosses section of dark rubble.

156 (83)
Small dunes appear as you approach the Oued Rheris. Engage four-wheel drive but probably no need to deflate tyres. The piste winds among the grassy dunes for the next 6km in deep sandy ruts. Follow the tracks at a general bearing of 110-115°.

162 (77)   **N30° 41.0'   W04° 25.5'**
Emerge from Oued Daoura with a palmerie on the right. Drive through Hassi Remlia village over a rough road. Ignore kids' warning of a detour.

165 (74)   **N30° 42.0'   W04° 23.7'**
Stony corrugated main piste joins from the left. It's possible this bypasses Hassi Remlia to the north. Bearing NNE.

168 (71)
Cross a smooth chott marked with cairns.

173 (66)
Pass dunes to the north of the piste while crossing an occasionally bumpy chott over the next 6km.

180 (59)   **N30° 44.5'   W04° 15.0'**
Sign for 'Café Restaurant Ahoir' as you leave the chott and enter a small gravelly valley to the ENE.

184 (55)
Having crossed the rubbly hills over a rise you now reach the Café Ahoir building on the left with dunes behind. Half a kilometre later is the *Hassi Ouzina Auberge*, after which you cross a smooth chott.
    In 2003 a new auberge was being built east of here. Continue ENE with orange dunes on the left and the chott on the right.

189 (50)
Sign on the right for *Ouzina* with a track leading to it.

191 (48)   **N30° 46.7'   W04° 09.6'**
Track forks; go right. (We went left but corrected this by crossing the Oued Ziz.) We rejoined the main cairned track on the right (east) side of the oued at N30° 47.9' W04° 08.5, KM194.) You're heading north now.

200 (39)
A track joins the gravelly piste from the left, followed by some bumpy chotts. You can see the *Auberge Gravure* on a small hill nearby.
    Over the next few kilometres this continues: small gravelly hills, occasional chotts and then stony sections as the track moves back to the ENE.

211 (28)
Having passed through a sunken section of track like a viaduct, you cross a black hamada. In a kilometre the red and white radio mast of Taouz becomes visible.

215 (24)   **N30° 54.0'   W03° 59.9'**
Taouz. There's a well on the right, a water tower and radio mast to the left and possibly the beginnings of hassle from all directions. In 1km you pass a pink fort on the left. Take the track heading NNE to the left of the pink sand hills ahead.

218 (21)   **N30° 55.7'   W03° 58.7'**
Cross a oued on concrete slabs lined with white bollards. The track becomes very corrugated after this with the dark sandy hills to the right. In two kilometres follow tracks across a chott and after another 2km follow the tracks towards a line of pylons on a slight rise.

223 (16)
Track begins to run alongside pylons, bearing NNE. In a kilometre the track turns to the NW and descends into a wide sandy oued.

225 (14)
A couple of balises and 500m later a concrete building on the right and a small brick tower on the left. Heading NW and NNW after a couple of kilometres where the track becomes marked with poles and sticks. Village visible ahead with telegraph poles running parallel to the piste, a few hundred metres to the left.

230 (9)   **N31° 01 .7'   W04° 00.3'**
Pass through small village heading north towards the dunes of Erg Chebbi.

232 (7)
Pass a tower on the left and 2km later a palmerie with a village. The dunes are now close to your right. From here you pass through a couple of small villages with the growing tourist presence of Merzouga beginning to be evident.

239 (0)   **N31° 05.7'   W04° 00.7'**
Southern archway of Merzouga. A new road leads to Rissani. To get to the numerous duneside auberges continue north alongside the Erg and take your pick.

M7 FOUM ZGUID → MHAMID   [143KM]
February 1999; Toyota HJ61

Description
This is as south as you can get in this part of Morocco but there's not a lot going for this route scenically. For the first half the piste follows the Jebel Bani to the north passing the usually dry chott of Lake Iriqui. It's predominantly a rough, rocky trail that can give you a good shaking. After KM100 you then curve ESE down towards the sands of the Oued Draa which soon rise into small dunes as you near Mhamid.

One highlight is that you'll encounter plenty of pastoral desert Berbers herding camels and goats along the piste, though the same can be said for the other pistes around here.

Route-finding and markers
The Michelin map shows a piste following the curve of the Jebel Bani all the way to Tagounite, as do the new and old IGN one millions. This may be possible, the fork might be at KM100 just after the fort. However, the clearer piste continues ESE to Mhamid, the 'last town' in the string of oases down the Vallée du Draa.

Side tracks come and go but route-finding is pretty clear all the way with the Jebel always to the north and either stone cairns or a rubbly track that you can't miss.

Note that all maps show an incorrect alignment out of Foum Zguid. The actual track curves much further south passing just north of the 610m hill (marked on the Michelin and old IGN maps) before curving north towards the pink fort (KM46.4).

M7 – RECOMMENDED MAPS
FOUM ZGUID → MHAMID 143KM

Any of the three main 1:1m Moroccan maps will do.

Fuel
3km north of KM0; Tagounite.

Water
At each end plus the villages, wells and encampments along the route.

Traffic
Reasonable levels of tourists and local traffic. This is not a desolate piste.

Driving
The rough, rubbly tracks are the only thing to watch. Take it easy on your car's springs or your motorbike's wheels. In a car you sometimes just have to crawl along at walking pace. Using the hand throttle can help make progress smoother. Coming through the dunes lining the Oued Draa you'll probably need four-wheel drive.

Suggested duration
Easily done in a day with two good hotels at Mhamid. Most overnight camps will attract a camel herder or two which can be fun.

0km (143) **N30° 04.0' W06° 52.0'**
Southern gate of Foum Zguid. Drive south out of town towards Tata along the tarmac and after one kilometre turn left, SSE onto the piste heading directly for a pink fort.

2 (141)
Fort. Passport check. Continue SSE on corrugations across a rocky basalt plain. Saw-tooth ranges are visible on the southern horizon.

13 (130) **N29° 57.9' W06° 49.8'**
Track forks. Go left, heading SE, to drop into a wide oued. In 700m rise out of the oued with a piste joining from the right (possibly an alternative route across the creek). Continue SE.

19 (124)
As you drop into a dip a track joins from the left.

21 (122)
Fork. Main corrugated track curves right heading towards a large mesa (Jebel Hamsailikh).

29 (114)
Pass to the north of the mesa on your right and in half a kilometre cross a sandy oued with grassy tussocks.

30 (113)
Now you're back on a stony hamada and heading SSE towards Mdaouer Srhir: 'Hill 610m'.

33 (110)
Piste curves around the north-east edge of Mdaouer Srhir.

35 (108) **N29° 50.7' W06° 40.3'**
The piste forks as you're heading east with the mesa behind you. Take the left fork heading ENE. Sand dunes visible ahead.

37 (106)
Fast smooth going for a couple of kilometres. Make the most of it! Then you cross a bumpy claypan and drive through a hummocky oued (KM39.6). Cairns now mark the piste at 100m intervals. This is the far western edge of the Iriqui chott.

41 (102)
Another sandy oued crossing. Continue NE with cairn markers.

45 (98)
As you cross a stony hamada a pink fort becomes visible ahead.

47 (96) **N29° 52.8' W06° 34.6'**
Pink fort. Passport control and probably a tea and chat with the soldiers.

50 (93)
Fast going across Iriqui chott heading ENE. Cairns mark the route.

57 (86)
Still in the chott with cairn markers, the track turns north towards a village at the base of Jebel Bani. You can avoid the track going to the village by veering NE, keeping an eye on the cairns to your left. Dunes visible to the south.

62 (81)
Track turns north through scrubby flats towards a village.

63 (80)
Rejoin cairns as you approach the village at the base of a hill.

65 (78) **N29° 58.0' W06° 26.3'**
Zaouia Sidi Abt en Nebt. Many buildings have solar panels and there's an unusually archetypal mosque: a squat tower with a dome, possibly the mausoleum of Sidi Abt?

In one kilometre you leave the village to the ESE continuing over a stony track with occasional buildings on the left.

72 (71)
Pass tiny palmerie and houses. Heading ESE.

76 (67)
Climb onto a stony hamada from where dunes are visible not far to the south.

83 (60)
Cross a basalt stone field onto an undulating hamada.

89 (54)
Narrow track joins from the left.

93 (50)
The pace slows as the track becomes stony for the next few kilometres. At KM96 you cross a bouldery oued after which the track smooths out a little.

100 (43)   **N29° 53.2' W06° 07.4'**
Pink fort to the right of piste (no check when we passed) after which you pass a small palmerie with a few buildings, one signed 'Bivouac Permanent Iriki'. Tracks diverge here, possibly the fork for the route to Tagounite as marked on the maps, though it seems a bit early. For Mhamid take the right fork which runs east across a hamada.

104 (39)
Track joins from the left then, when another splits off to the right, keep left.

106 (37)
Tracks fan out over a hamada. Continue east. The piste is corrugated but fast. You then cross a small oued with rounded cliffs. From here you begin to head in a more south-easterly direction.

112 (31)
The piste crosses a very sandy oued and forks once on the other side. Keep right and continue SE across the hamada. In a kilometre you should cross 6°W. Here there are lots of tracks (the fork for Tagounite); stick to the most prominent, heading ESE. The going remains relatively fast for the next few kilometres with occasional dips.

124 (19)   **N29° 50.3' W05° 53.1'**
You are now entering the dunes in the bed of the Oued Draa and will need four-wheel drive. The sandy track winds between the bushes and over small dunes after which you cross a bumpy claypan.

127 (16)
Scattered trees and sand hillocks are more numerous now with lots of possible shade. Still on a firm claypan surface.

133 (10)
Track leads east along sandy corridors among small dunes. Continue for a few kilometres until around KM137 the track begins to run ESE along the clearly defined left (north) bank of the Oued Draa.

138 (5)
The tracks emerge from the dunes. Head for the trees, buildings and radio mast ahead. At Km140 you pass a sign for the *Auberge du Soleil*.

143 (0)   **N29° 49.5' W05° 43.2'**
Central square of Mhamid. The *Hotel Sahara* and *Hotel Iriqui* are good places to spend the night or have a meal. Mbarek at the *Hotel Sahara* can also organise a camel trip into the dunes.

M8 ZAGORA → FOUM ZGUID   [130KM]
March 2004; Mercedes 190D

Description
An alternative to Route M7, this route follows the north slopes of Jebel Bani between the two desert towns but is quite stony and scenically no better. Initially it passes through pastoral allotments and gardens, and then becomes more remote, with only a few nomadic encampments.

Route-finding and markers
Many tracks can make make leaving Zagora confusing (if in doubt head for KM11 and work it out from there), but

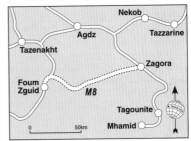

**M8 – RECOMMENDED MAPS
ZAGORA → FOUM ZGUID 130KM**

It's hard to lose the track and any of the three main 1:1m Moroccan maps will do.

as you move further west you follow one clear stony track across the hamada, with an occasional branch. And of course looking at the big picture, you have the Jebel to the south as a guide almost all the way.

From the Foum Zguid end it appears that they may be preparing to seal this track, or part of it. It seems a likely candidate for sealing, greatly improving access between Zagora and the border towns west of Foum Zguid.

Fuel
Zagora and Foum Zguid.

Water
One well at KM31 and several gardens in the western half.

Traffic
None on our traverse.

Driving
Mostly stony, at its worst from KM56 as the route squeezes between two parallel ranges until KM88 after which the piste improves.

Suggested duration
Just over half a day.

0km (130)   N30° 19.7' W05° 50.3'
Zagora fuel station. Head south down the main road towards the famous Timbuktu sign. Immediately as you pass the *Hotel de la Palmerie* on the right (N30° 19.4' W05° 50.4'), turn right (there is a small sign for Foum Zguid). Almost immediately leave this sealed road to the right, right behind the hotel and opposite a *Sahara Aventure* office – head downhill on a track.

1.6 (128.4)   N30° 19.2' W05° 51.3'
Track diverges. Head SW passing an ONEP concrete pump block on your left (they continue for a while) and then a small airstrip to the north.

3.1 (126.9)   N30° 18.7' W05° 52.0'
White concrete bollard on your right.

4.5 (125.5)   N30° 18.1' W05° 52.6'
Track diverges, take right-hand track towards pink building. Pass to the south of this building, heading towards a compound with trees and telegraph poles a short distance further on, and pass it on the north side.

6 (124)
Join a track heading west.

11 (119)   N30° 16.7' W05° 56.3'
Pass some gardens to your north, just

after crossing a oued. Track runs through a spaced-out settlement (Tagourt).

15 (115)   N30° 16.0' W05° 58.2'
Lone acacia to the right with gardens behind it. Piste heads SW for a while.

20 (110)
Piste heads south directly towards Jebel Bani.

23 (107)
Piste now swings SW with buildings visible among the trees at the base of the Jebel. Soon it heads directly west.

25 (105)   N30° 12.2' W06° 01.2'
Pass small oasis garden to the south with a few buildings. There is another oasis 5km further on with rammed earth ruins (N30° 11.7' W06° 03.8').

31 (99)   N30° 11.4' W06° 04.8'
More rammed earth ruins and gardens and a well with water at less than eight metres. Leave the abandoned village with a well on your left.

35 (95)   N30° 10.8' W06° 06.8'
Cross oued, a mixture of sand and stones.

37 (93)
Large pink house to the north of the track

by a fenced-off field, with a walled palmerie and orchards a kilometre later.

42 (88)   N30° 08.8'   W06° 10.7'
Cross a big oued – again rocky and sandy. Within half a kilometre you cross the oued again and pass partially-walled fields and buildings to the south.

50 (80)   N30° 07.0'   W06° 14.2'
Another collection of buildings with fields. Track now heads NW, away from the Jebel.

56 (74)
Piste becomes stony as it heads towards a oued line and the pink town of Bou Rbia at the base of distant cliffs to the NW.

60 (70)   N30° 08.4'   W06° 20.5'
Stony piste splits. Take left (more southern) fork to the west towards Bou Rbia.

61 (69)   N30° 08.4'   W06° 21.4'
White concrete bollard by the track. Cross a stony oued. Bou Rbia is now to the north. A few hundred metres later the track splits again; continue just south of west. In another kilometre there is another white bollard by the piste (N30° 08.1' W06° 22.0').

64 (66)   N30° 07.9'   W06° 22.7'
The track splits. Going straight ahead is more direct but stony. Taking the southern branch SW towards the Jebel is sandier with a sandy oued crossing at KM66 (on the far side of the oued take the track to the right) and is a relief from the stones.

73 (57)   N30° 05.4'   W06° 26.9'
The direct stonier route rejoins the piste from the north and the now stony track continues SW towards the Jebel.

75 (55)
Cross a narrow stony oued, and again 300 metres later. Heading SW.

79 (51)   N30° 03.7'   W06° 30.0'
Cross the 6° 30' line right buy a 'stranded' concrete ford to the north of the track, possibly waiting for a new road to reach it. There are another couple of concrete fords in the next two kilometres.

85 (45)   N30° 02.3'   W06° 33.1'
Track splits; take the left (southern) fork. This is another divergence as at KM64, so you can take the right fork if you like but you may find it stonier. They converge after a concrete ford in around a kilometre. A kilometre later (KM87) there is a stony oued crossing.
Soon after you find yourself heading for a village alongside a long lone dune and the track becomes less stony.

90 (40)   N30° 01.5'   W06° 35.9'
The valley opens out again to the NW as you pass south of the village with the lone dune to the NW. Within a kilometre or two the track starts swinging to the NW passing a white bollard at KM92 (N30° 01.4' W06° 37.3').

104 (26   N30° 05.5'   W06° 42.3'
Route ahead barred with stones. Track now turns N through a big oued and again a kilometre later.

106 (24)   N30° 06.8'   W06° 41.9'
Join a wide, smooth track heading NW. A couple of times it reverts to the old stony piste as it crosses unfinished bridges.

116 (14)   N30° 08.9'   W06° 47.7'
Back on the new surface, you arrive at Smira village. From here we drove alongside pylons through a oued alongside an unfinished road.

124 (6)   N30° 07.5'   W06° 52.4'
Arrive at the outskirts of El Mhamid. Cross the oued and drive through the dense palmerie.

127 (3)   N30° 07.5'   W06° 52.8'
Reach the tarmac road in El Mhamid. If reversing this route, the piste begins opposite a pink building with a white sign on the oued side in three languages asking you to keep the desert clean.

130 (0)   N30° 05.4'   W06° 52.7'
Foum Zguid fuel. Quiet desert town with a few cafés, shops, a hotel and a campsite.
Ask around and someone will take you to see the prehistoric rock engravings south of town.

M9 TALIOUINE → FOUM ZGUID   [209KM]

February 1999; Toyota HJ61

Description

As with Route M10 or M11 in reverse, this is a great (and satisfyingly longer) way of traversing the fabulous Anti Atlas to end up on the fringes of the desert, even if they are busy sealing it.

A few minutes east of Taliouine you turn south across uninspiring high grasslands, passing small villages to either side. Things begin to get interesting as you drop off the plateau at the narrow pass of Tizi-n Ounzour (KM51) to wind your way down to the desert villages along the valley. Once you reach the junction at KM81 you're among the barren Nevada-like ridges north of the Jebel Bani.

Turning east, you pass the Akka Irhen and then make your way north-east along the broad valley, tracing the southern rim of the Anti Atlas before joining the tarmac just north of Foum Zguid.

Route-finding and markers

Reports say that this route has been sealed up to KM81, with a 20-kilometre patch of piste until the sealed road continues to Akka Ihern. There's a lot more going on along the eastern leg of this piste than the 1:1 million maps would have you believe and it's all piste until you reach the road at KM201. Plenty of unmarked villages and associated turn-offs vie for your attention, even though the general orientation is clearly north-eastwards between the ranges. On the remaining piste section markers are few but the track is always well defined.

M9 – RECOMMENDED MAPS
TALIOUINE → FOUM ZGUID 209KM

All the recommended 1:1m maps show the correct orientation of the route.

Fuel

Taliouine and Foum Zguid, or ask around at Akka Irhen.

Water

Plenty of wells, villages and encampments along the route.

Traffic

Not much between the Tizi-n Ounzour pass and Akka Irhen. Otherwise plenty of local taxi vans and mopeds east of Akka.

Driving

Latest news is that this route is sealed up to KM81 and they are pressing on from KM101. The lack of soft sand would make this an especially fine day's run on a motorbike and as it passes plentiful water points, mountain bikers have managed this route over three to four days.

Suggested duration

Plan for one night somewhere off the piste, although a motorbike might do this route in a day.

0km (209)   **N30° 31.5' W07° 53.2'**
Ziz fuel station past the east gate of Taliouine. Go east into the hills.

11.5 (197.5)   **N30° 28.3' W07° 50.6'**
Turn right onto a sealed road signed 'Agadir Melloul 36km'. You will pass several other villages on the way.

32 (181)
Last reports suggested the tarmac ended around here. You cross a low pass and descend towards a small village visible in the distance.

34 (175)
Fork. Keep right, passing a small enclosed field on your left. Small tracks come and go from the left but the main track is clear.

39 (170)
The peaks of the High Atlas are visible on the western horizon. The track heads directly towards the mountains.

41 (168)   **N30° 16.1' W07° 49.0'**
Significant fork down to a village. Keep left. This village, with its brown and white striped mosque, becomes visible to the right in a kilometre.

43 (166)
Track forks near some purplish rock. Stay right, following a small oued.

46 (163)
Colonnaded main street of Agadir Melloul with a radio mast. Drive past the mosque, heading south. In two kilometres pass some pink buildings on the right.

49 (160)
Another radio mast is visible on a hill immediately to the east, with rubbly hills all around.

51 (158)
Tizi-n Ounzour pass, 1950m. Keep right and descend a series of steep, stony bends through the narrow gorge. From here on the scenery becomes more interesting.

54 (155)
Track climbs up above the oued on the east flank of the gorge and then drops down to emerge into a broad valley. The track continues along the right bank of the oued and sometimes gets quite stony.

58 (151)
Large cairn on the left of the track.

63 (146)
The track crosses to the left side of the oued and winds generally SSW.

64 (145)
Track crosses back to the west bank of the oued, still winding about.

68 (141)
Track joins from the left – in 200m cross the oued to the east bank again.

69 (140)   **N30° 03.6' W07° 49.3'**
Tisfrioudine with a palmerie and mosque. Drive past the old ksar and the palmerie heading E. As you leave the town there's a rubbly hill to the right and irrigated fields on the left.

Soon the track turns SE. Between Tisfrioudine and Timassinine the track crosses the oued a few more times.

75 (134)
Timassinine appears on the left of the track. In a couple of kilometres you should cross 30°N.

81 (128)   **N29° 58.5' W07° 48.0'**
Small building and stone block mark the junction with the east–west Akka–Afouzar piste ('6838'). Turn left for Akka.

86 (123)
Rise above the oued to your right. Follow the valley heading NE.

94 (115)
Cross a oued and then another couple of small oueds four kilometres later.

101 (108)
Descend into valley dotted with acacias.

103 (106)   **N30° 03.1' W07° 37.2'**
Track joins from the north. Continue ENE. In one kilometre the piste turns east then continues winding in a general SE direction through a stony oued that runs between low cliffs.

107 (102)   N30° 02.1' W07° 35.5'
Track forks. Carry straight on (the left track leads to a village). Keep right after one kilometre, where another track from the village joins your track from the left.

110 (99)
Ksar visible a couple of kilometres to the right among palms (possibly the fort marked on the maps near Akka Irhen). A track soon leads right, towards the fort. Carry straight on.

115 (94)   N29° 59.7' W07° 31.7'
Having passed a palmerie and a water tower and gone under a gateway you arrive at the roundabout in the centre of Akka Irhen near a pink mosque.

The sealed road right off the round-about leads to Akka Irhem and Tata. You go left, heading NE out of town, past the barracks. The stony track winds out of town over a flat rubble plain of scattered acacia trees with Jebel Bani to the south.

125 (84)
Cross a oued with low banks. One kilometre later a track joins at right angles from the left and in another 500m there's a major junction with red arrows on cairns and trees pointing left (north), possibly to Assarakh. Take the right-hand fork which goes ENE and then meanders a bit.

128 (81)
Two unusually shaped cairns on the hill to the left: one arch-like, the other a small tower of stones. Soon you come to a junction – take the left track marked with cairns. Over the next kilometre other pistes converge as the piste descends past straggly acacias towards a small palmerie.

130 (79)
Village and palmerie to the left. In a kilometre the track runs right past the ruins of an old ksar and then the village itself, leaving to the south-east along a oued.

132 (77)   N30° 04.2' W07° 24.1'
Having crossed the oued after the village you're now heading ESE along the left bank of the oued. Over the next two kilometres you cross and re-cross the oued.

136 (73)
Track forks; go right close to the cliff towards a small palmerie which you pass.

139 (70)   N30° 02.0' W07° 21.8'
Fork; go left. In a kilometre a track joins from the right as you cross a oued that is first sandy and then stony.

At N30° 01.8' W07° 21.6' there's a cairn on the left edge of the piste and you leave the oued and head ESE. When you get to a junction at KM141 continue straight, ESE.

143 (66)
The track is now going NE across a stony hamada. Broad vistas of mountain ranges to left and right.

147 (62)
Track bears close to north for a kilometre then resumes NE bearing.

149 (60)
Curve across a small oued with a few trees then turn NE and soon ENE.

151 (58)   N30° 04.4' W07° 16.3'
Fork. Take the right branch (NE) across a baked muddy stretch to emerge on the right edge of a low banked oued. Then continue heading NE.

154 (55)
Cross a large oued. In two kilometres a track joins from the right by a cairn.

159 (50)
Driving on a hamada, you pass a small palmerie and stone hut on the right.

161 (48)   N30° 07.1' W07° 11.3'
Track passes through a small village with a mosque and well, mostly to the right of the piste. Leave village to the NE. Another village is visible some way ahead at the base of the mountains.

162 (47)
Fork; keep right and keep right again in a kilometre. Tracks to left lead to the village.

166 (43)
Track joins from the left. Now heading generally east.

173 (36)
For the next few kilometres the track bears 10°–15°, occasionally turning NE.

181 (28)
Junction. Turn right along a major piste which curves around a green hill.

183 (26)   **N30° 13.4' W07° 01.8'**
Major three-way junction marked by a large block. North leads to the village of Taourirt n Tilés. Keep right (east). In a kilometre you pass a small palmerie with a small stone building on the left of the piste which then starts to follow the right bank of a broad stony oued.

186 (23)
Cross to the left bank of the oued and head for the village with palms. In a kilometre pass the village (Nisala?) on the left.

187 (22)   **N30° 13.4' W06° 59.2'**
On the other side of the village carry on SE. Keep right despite several left forks which lead to Alougoum on the road north of Foum Zguid.

189 (20)   **30° 13.2' W06° 58.5'**
Fork; keep right. You pass a couple of palmeries on the left in the next kilometre or two: keep right.

195 (14)
Pass a few huts. The track is now heading SE along the Oued Tlite and becomes corrugated on a mauve surface.
   The gap in the ranges marking Foum Zguid (foum means mouth) becomes evident to the SE.

198 (11)
There are a few buildings and palms on the right as the track crosses a claypan.

200 (9)
Pass a large water tank and continue towards a long palmerie. When you get to a junction (N30° 09.6' W06° 53.5') go right. Pylons are visible among the palms.

201 (8)   **N30° 09.5' W06° 52.6'**
Cross a oued and reach the tarmac road. Sign says 'Nisala 17, Tlite 27'. Turn right for Foum Zguid.

205 (4)   **N30° 07.5' W06° 52.8'**
Sign for the Zagora piste which goes north of the Jebel Bani (Route M8).

209 (0)
Foum Zguid fuel station on the northern edge of the town.

M10 TATA → IGHERM   [95KM]
December 2002; Land Rover Defender V8 (Tim Stead)

Description
Even if they've sealed it up to Souk Tleta Tagmout and beyond, this short piste is still well worth doing. Up to the long palmerie of Tleta you pass between the distinctive brown and cream whorled hillsides that line the valley of the Oued Tata. The oued then widens and leads west to the lovely village of Souk Tleta Tagmout. You drive through, passing eye-strainingly green gardens alive with chattering birds. As you drive along the stony oued into the narrow gorge the cultivation continues with water just a foot below the surface and idyllic scenes all around.
   After a few kilometres the 500m ascent out of the valley begins: a rough slow track of tight hairpins and fabulous vistas looking back down over the valley. Once on top you continue across the grassy uplands dotted with herders' enclosures until you get to the mountain town of Igherm straddling the Anti Atlas.
   Like Route M11, this route is probably even better in reverse. If you're coming down the coast from Casablanca and don't want to go all the way to

Tan Tan, turn inland at Agadir, passing south of Taroudant and head up to Igherm. It will be a stunning transition from the drab northern plains, across the Anti Atlas and down into the wild desert, with the dramatic descent unfolding before you rather than behind. And Tata itself is no eyesore, a charming quiet desert town on the edge of the Sahara.

M10 – RECOMMENDED MAPS
TATA → IGHERM 95KM

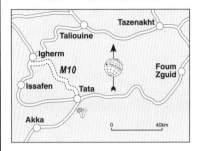

Only some country maps from Michelin and IGN show the full route from Tleta Tagmout up the gorge and over the high plain to Igherm. This route brings you back to the tarmac ten kilometres south of Igherm. It's possible the fork at KM75 would have led directly to Igherm.

Route-finding and markers
After the sealed road ends at Tleta, driving through the gorge you can't go wrong and on the plain the principal track is marked with cairns.

Fuel
Tata and Igherm.

Water
The towns at each end plus wells and villages along the route.

Traffic
All-terrain tours use this route regularly and even light trucks and minibuses rattle up and down the gorge between Tleta Tagmout and Igherm.

Driving
The ascent out of Tleta isn't especially difficult or dangerous, but it can look hard. The track is one car wide through the palmerie as well as on the climb so watch out for oncoming traffic. This section is rough on tyres: keep pressures high and speeds down.

Suggested duration
About five hours. Camping on the high plains south of Igherm would be exposed, away from the odd stone enclosure. A better spot might be the 'busy' oued north of Tleta, the town itself (*auberge*) or anywhere in the desert.

0km (95)
Fuel station at the south end of Tata. Drive along the main street north out of town and into a narrow gorge of whorled rock formations.

27 (68)
A distinctive acacia tree left of the piste.

46 (49)   N29° 57.8' W08° 14.0'
Gate of Souk Tleta Tagmout. Drive through the town, bearing right, past the

square with a water tower on the right, and then head NW towards a hill with the town's name inscribed on it (a regional custom).

A kilometre after the gate the track passes the old town of adobe houses and leads through gardens lined with palms and almond trees.

50 (45)
Turquoise mosque on the right as you head into the hills, passing abandoned

houses. In a kilometre the piste crosses a stony oued with pylons on the left, and then drives alongside it up the gorge.

53 (42)
Picture-perfect oasis spread across the oued. It's a beautiful spot for lunch that even the eventual pestering can't spoil.

55 (40)
Fork just after oued crossing. Go left, getting to a village in a kilometre. The track winds through the oasis for another kilometre where it emerges from the trees and descends into a broad stony oued and follows its course NW.

58 (37)
Pass a small village set in the cliff on the right of the oued.

60 (35)
Pass another palmerie and village. In one kilometre you leave the village and take a sharp hairpin bend to the left (N30° 01.9' W08° 19.0'). Soon the six-kilometre climb begins.

67 (28)   **N30° 02.0' W08° 20.3'**
Cairn with red graffiti at the high point (1735m). Descent begins over grassy plains with plenty of cairn markers.

72 (23)
Pass a walled enclosure on the right.

74 (21)
Tracks join from the left (possible split of the same track?).

75 (20)
Major fork. Go left. It's possible the right fork, which passes an enclosure about 1km ahead, could go directly to Igherm. Continue generally WSW passing many walled enclosures.

80 (15)   **N30° 00.8' W08° 25.3'**
Well near some buildings by the right of the piste.

83 (12)
A group of stone buildings on the right, after which a track joins from the left.

85 (10)   **N30° 01.0' W08° 27.0'**
Join the Igherm–Tata tarmac road. Turn right (north) for Igherm.

95 (0)   **N30° 05.0' W08° 27.8'**
Igherm town sign. Fuel in the town centre.

M11 AÏT HERBIL → TAFRAOUTE   [109KM]
March 2004; Mercedes 190D

Description
This is a great alternative to the now partially-sealed preceding route up to Igherm, a wonderful winding traverse from the desert floor along the gorge of the Oued Smouguene and up onto the eastern ranges of the Anti Atlas. Like M10, reversed from north to south it's a great way to arrive in the desert. On the way you pass cliffside Berber villages as far as Igmir, where the route suddenly climbs steeply out of the gorge onto the highlands leading to the tarmac and Tafraoute.

At the very start of the route there's an opportunity to inspect rock engravings at Aït Herbil, though if you've seen the examples in Algeria and Libya you may not be so impressed.

Route-finding and markers
Road improvements are in progress to the villages north of Aït Herbil, but sealing of the entire gorge route is unlikely. Here the route is clear, though flooding may wash away sections and lead to stony detours. Note that this route is not fully depicted on any of the current country maps of Morocco.

M11 – RECOMMENDED MAPS
AÏT HERBIL → TAFRAOUTE 109km

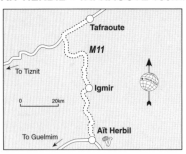

No map, not even the old Moroccan 250,000s, show the gorge section of this route correctly, though many identify a NNE scenic route to Souk El Had d'Afella Irhir. Whatever, even with no map, we worked it out.

Fuel
Aït Herbil and Tafraoute.

Water
From villages along the route.

Traffic
Local traffic serves the villages at either end of the gorge section.

Driving
Stony ruts and oued crossings through the gorge which are fine in a car but may make riding a bike while enjoying the scenery a bit tricky.

Suggested duration
Half a day, but camping around KM29 or spending the night at the guest house at Igmir just before the big ascent (KM35) is more fun and gives you a chance to appreciate the evening/dawn light on the red gorge walls.

0km (106)   N29° 07.9'   W08° 57.9'
Aït Herbil fuel station on the Guelmin–Akka road. To visit the **rock carvings**, drive on the track to the east of the new route (rejoined at KM3.2, see below) which leads into the village of Aït Herbil. Continue north along the narrow main street and when you get to a road turning off to the right with a bougainvillaea-draped wall on the corner at the top end of town (N29° 08.7' W08° 57.1'), turn right and follow the track down to the oued.

Park by the oued at the base of the hill on which stands the old fort. Now walk west across the oued – it may take some scrambling up and over flood-carved banks. To the SW of you on the far side of the oued is a small palmerie and just north of that is a pile of grey tailings where well shafts have been excavated. Behind the grey tailings is a gully, and halfway up the hillside to the right (south) of this gully you will find engravings on the slabs (N29° 08.9' W08° 56.4').

Back at the vehicle, retrace your route to the bougainvillaea corner and here turn right (north) out of the village to rejoin the new bypass road at KM3.2 (N29° 08.8' W08° 57.4').

4.6 (104.4)
Village of Aguerd with houses built into the cliffs. At this point we were led onto a deviation which sent us down a hairpin descent and along the bottom of the oued while the new, high route was being improved. Both tracks converge again (see below), but there may be a small discrepancy in distances.

11 (98)   N29° 11.6'   W08° 59.1'
The high route comes down to the oued and crosses it via a concrete ford. You'll now be driving in or alongside the stony oued and will pass through some dramatically folded strata in the cliffs.

19 (90)
Junction of tracks. Continue west. The other way seems the lesser route but may lead to Souk-el-Had-d'Afella-Irhir which is shown as a scenic drive on some Moroccan maps.

21 (88)
Walled gardens by the piste, a very scenic section leading to the village of Tamesoult (N29° 16.2' W08° 59.5'). There is another village just before KM25, Irhir n'Bell.

25 (84)   **N29° 17.2' W08° 59.6'**
Leave the narrowing oued up the bank to the right and drive through the palmerie. Out the other side turn left uphill into the village where you'll see a couple of hand-painted signs at a junction (N29° 17.2' W08° 59.6') showing distances to Igmir, Tafraoute etc. Follow the signs left out of the village below the cliffs. You're back in the stony oued bottom or alongside it.

29 (80)   **N29° 17.8' W09° 00.7'**
Anywhere around here is a great place to camp among the gnarly argan trees. The pressing of argan nuts makes a highly-prized and nutty-flavoured oil, available at Igmir and widely sold in and around Tafraoute.

32 (77)
Leave the oued as you encounter walled enclosures and pylons on the outskirts of Igmir. Drive through the avenue of palms and trees.

35 (74)   **N29° 20.0' W09° 00.1'**
Igmir guest house on the other side of the oued at the base of a deep, narrow canyon. A nice place to eat, spend the night and meet the locals if there's not a big tour group passing through.

You now leave the Smougeune valley taking a very steep and impressive ascent up into the hills. Great views back down the valley, only spoiled by pylons. Should you stop halfway up the ascent you may find the orange scree full of delicate seaweed fossil prints.

37 (72)
The steep ascent is over at around 1200m. Some nice views just off the track.

40 (69)   **N29° 20.8' W09° 02.4'**
Piste forks with detailed sign. Go right (north) for Tafraoute ('53km').

44 (65)   **N29° 21.5' W09° 04.2'**
Impressive views all around as the piste begins to descend, heading north overall.

49 (60)   **N29° 23.8' W09° 04.3'**
Fork; keep right.

52 (57)   **N29° 25.0' W09° 03.6'**
Having crossed a oued a kilometre earlier, you get to a junction with a sign. Head straight on for 'Agadir', along the pylons.

55 (54)   **N29° 26.4' W09° 03.4'**
Another junction. Left for Tiznit and Agadir, right for Izebi and Tafraoute, passing a windmill water pump.

56 (53)   **N29° 27.1' W09° 03.7'**
Piste meets the sealed road at a T-junction by the village of Tahwawat. We turned left here, then right at the next junction, then left, but a quicker way to Tafraoute may have been turning right here at this point. Either way, it's all tarmac and a nice run through the hills to Tafraoute.

109 (0)   **N29° 43.2' W08° 58.3'**
Tafraoute fuel station. A large town popular with tourists.

M12 TAN TAN → ASSA   [248KM]
February 1999; Toyota HJ61

Route description
The Tan Tan–Assa piste is not an especially interesting route and the bumpy terrain soon gets tiresome, but the piste passes through typical south Moroccan scenery, crossing stony hamadas and oueds as it runs east–west between parallel mountain ranges.

For the record, in 1999 we tried to find the beginning of piste '7092' that passes through the hills north of the Oued Draa (via Aïoun Draa and Tiglite). It starts on the coastal highway about 40km north of Tan Tan. There were a few promising tracks heading east but no clear sign. The Moroccans seem to be opening up the region south of M'said to help reinforce their claim on Western Sahara, and readers report that a sealed road now leads to this town.

Route-finding and markers

The tarmac has reached M'said by now. From this point, the strings of cairns built up on mounds of bulldozed earth (up to KM199) and a single track lead you clearly north-east to Aouinet Torkoz and Assa. This piste was apparently used by one of the Dakar rallies in the early 1990s but does not appear on any map until you reach 10°W near Aouinet Torkoz. Yet it is one of the best-marked pistes in the Sahara. There are so many cairns on this route that you could almost stumble from one to the other blindfolded. We followed it without knowing where we were going and got through without any confusion. From Assa the road is sealed to Foum el Hassan.

Fuel

Tan Tan, Assa.

Water

At settlements plus many wells along the route. You'll pass many nomads and their encampments along the 'unmapped' stretch.

M12 – RECOMMENDED MAPS
TAN TAN → ASSA 248KM

Both the IGN country and 1:1m maps represent the relief much better than the Michelin or Rough Guide country map.

Traffic

Light on the 'unmapped' stretch.

Driving

The roadworks might push you onto some rough driving and you want to hope the many chotts along this route remain dry. Other than that it's the rubble, especially as you cross the course of the Oued Draa at KM133, that will wear you out, either on a bike or in a car.

Suggested duration

A day and a bit in a car; possible in a day on a motorbike.

0km (248)   N28° 26.0'   W11° 04.8'
Fuel station on the north edge of Tan Tan, just after the new camel monuments. The fuel here is priced at standard rates; you have to get to Tan Tan Plage to buy heavily subsidised fuel.

From the fuel station drive south for 400m and turn left onto the road signed for M'said. Follow the tarmac through the low hills to Tilemzoun (KM29) and up over a ridge of the Jebel Rich until it ends.

59 (189)
Cross a broad plain dotted with trees SE towards the long, fluted ridge of Jebel Tassout. M'said sits in a break of the Jebel.

You may want to cut eastwards at this point towards the waypoint at KM77 to follow the valley northeast to Gall Foum Yeraifia.

67 (181)
M'said; not exactly Las Vegas. The alternative piste east to Tisqui Remz was not clear but must cross the range somewhere.

From the village head north back across the valley until you pick up the numerous cairns, many of them painted white. The track soon begins to curve to the NNE and moves towards the north-western edge of the valley below the Jebel Rich escarpment.

77 (171) **N28° 05.5' W10° 48.3'**
Piste crosses at right angles, the left track possibly coming from KM59. Continue NNE up the valley.

90 (158) **N28° 10.7' W10° 43.3'**
Waypoint. Having just come through a bumpy section you head across smooth claypans. The balises continue to be frequent and regularly spaced on either side of the track. After a few kilometres you draw close to the ridge on your left.

100 (148) **N28° 14.2' W10° 38.8'**
Waypoint. In one kilometre you enter some churned up chotts with lots of scrubby bush vegetation.

103 (145) **N28° 15.2' W10° 37.6'**
Piste becomes very stony and starts to rise over low hills. In a few kilometres you come N through a pass and soon see white buildings to the left and right. Stay on the right-hand track, following the cairns. The track runs ENE.

107 (141)
Concrete building to the right at the foot of the escarpment.

109 (139)
Track crosses a broad vegetated oued. On the other side the track forks: go right, following the cairns into the hills, ESE, seemingly crossing back into the valley you've just come over from (but in fact not).

110 (138) **N28° 17.3' W10° 34.8'**
Waypoint. Emerge into a parallel valley.

115 (133) **N28° 18.2' W10° 32.2'**
Pass a double-lidded well on the right of the track just before a oued (on our visit one well was dry, the other locked). Over the next few kilometres there are several very stony oued crossings.

120 (128) **N28° 18.6' W10° 29.6'**
Waypoint. You are heading east across a wide gravel valley with several nomad tents along the foot of the escarpment to the south.

In three kilometres you're heading into another valley and soon pass a concrete building with a green door on the left of the piste. Very stony going for a few hundred metres.

130 (118) **N28° 19.7' W10° 24.2'**
Waypoint. In one kilometre you see a distinctive strip of red rock on an outcrop to the left. You are now entering the course of the Oued Draa as it takes a northern turn through the hills. The track becomes even stonier, making progress very slow for a couple of kilometres.

135 (113)
Climb up onto a stony plateau as the track smoothes out.

140 (108) **N28° 22.1' W10° 20.4'**
In two kilometres you cross a oued with a small palmerie enclosed by a circular stone wall.

143 (105) **N28° 21.5' W10° 19.5'**
Fork. Go right, following cairns. Heading is E with occasional stony patches and minor diverging tracks.

150 (98) **N28° 20.4' W10° 16.1'**
Still on a stony plain with occasional rough oued crossings. Continue E.

154 (94)
Concrete building with two red doors to the left. The terrain is becoming sandy here with a few trees. The pace speeds up. Anywhere in the next few kilometres would make a good spot to camp.

160 (88) **N28° 21.1' W10° 10.2'**
Waypoint. Still fast smooth surface.

170 (78)
Still in the oued heading east along its smooth course with some stony patches. At KM173 a bunch of acacias would make a nice camp.

174 (74) **N28° 22.7' W10° 02.4'**
Concrete building to the right as the terrain gets bumpier.

180 (68) **N28° 22.9' W09° 59.3'**
Waypoint. Fast going along a very smooth claypan. Around this point (10°W) you

have joined the track marked on maps as coming down from the north and curving east to Aouinet Torkoz, although there is no significant cairn or other sign.

187 (61)

Smooth claypan ends but good surface continues over hard sand dotted with small bushes; by KM189 you're back on tennis-ball-sized stones which continue more or less to Aouinet Torkoz.

199 (49)   N28° 28.0'   W9° 51.2'

Aouinet Torkoz. Drive along the town's southern edge and leave eastwards along a track marked with piles of white stones. A radio mast is visible ahead, which you pass to your right at KM202.

206 (42)

Fork to the right. Continue straight ahead (left) along a clear gravel track following cairns, which are now just piles of stones.

208 (40)   N28° 27.9' W09° 46.3'

Another fork. Keep left. In 300m there's a big well and watering trough by the piste. The track is clear from here, heading ENE.

230 (18)   N28° 30.9'   W09° 33.6'

Cross a concrete ford with a small hut on the left. Row of concrete bollards at KM233.

235 (13)

Fork; keep right, following white-painted cairns with another row of bollards marking a water course in a kilometre.

242 (6)

Assa visible ahead. At KM244 you cross a concrete bridge lined with red and white painted bollards.

245 (3)   N28° 36.4'   W09° 26.8'

Piste joins tarmac west of town. Continue east along the tarmac to Assa.

247 (1)   N28° 36.7'   W09° 25.9'

Driving through town ENE you get to a junction with the main road opposite the café El Massina. This is Assa town centre.

To get to Foum El Hassan turn right down the main street, passing a mosque (KM248) on the left. Soon you see a sign to the left for Foum El Hassan. The road is sealed.

M13 ASSA → SMARA   [387KM]

July 2003; Lada Niva (Franck Simonnet)

Description

Running down to the Sequiat el Hamra in the Western Sahara, Route M13 has all the ingredients of a classic Sahara route with a diversity of landscape and terrain: mountains, reg, fast sections, numerous oued crossings, rocky piste and even your old friend, corrugations, all in a remote setting you rarely find in 'mainland' Morocco. The region was the scene of Polisario battles in the 1980s, and today you may spot the *raïmas* (tents) of Reguibat nomads in the mountains between KM200 and KM240.

Route-finding and markers

Easy to follow; most of the piste was used in a Dakar Rally so is well marked. A sign indicates the start of the piste at KM28. After the junction with the Dakar piste at KM52, follow the cairns on earth mounds every 500 metres on both sides of the track.

Crossing the Ga'at Lewar, markers are only cairns and from here on (from KM262 to KM368) you sometimes follow the old corrugated Spanish tarmac as marked on Moroccan maps, but Rally cairns on earth mounds are always present. The track can be done with only three waypoints: Lebouirat (KM114), Hawza (KM277) and Smara (KM387).

Fuel
Assa and Smara.

Water
Water at the start and the end of the route and at the two main towns of Lebouirat and Hawza. In between there are some wells, one at KM187. Other wells near the track are indicated on maps.

Traffic
Light local traffic (but it was summer): one Santana pick-up, two locals at the KM187 well. Hawza is now an important military post (but no checkpoint).

Driving
Varied. Corrugations at junction with the Dakar piste, then fast after which the track follows the vegetated oued. The terrain is rockier between KM190 and KM245 with some sand near the end.

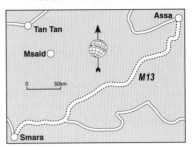

**M13 – RECOMMENDED MAPS
ASSA → SMARA 387km**

This is another ex-Rally route not marked on any map, but as the route description says, it's very well marked with cairns.

If you can get them then Morocco 1:250,000 'Goulimine' NH-29-14, 'Al Mahbas' NG-29-2, 'Hawza' NG-29-1 and 'Smara' NG-29-5 will be interesting.

Suggested duration
Two days.

0km (387)   N28° 36.7'   W09° 25.9'
Assa centre. Take the tarmac road leading south.

28 (359)   N28° 26.1'   W09° 24.5'
Leave the road before the Jebel Ouarkziz at the sign 'Lebouirat 68km' on your right. The track parallels the mountain range, you drive in the oued. Two kilometres before the next point, you leave the oued.

38 (349)   N28° 23.4'   W09° 29.5'
Pass through the range. You will see the first of three walls built during the Polisario war to keep them out. There is a deserted water station two kilometres later.

41 (346)   N28° 22.0'   W09° 29.1'
Leave the Jebel past the third wall. The track becomes corrugated before the junction with the Dakar route.

52 (335)   N28° 17.1'   W09° 32.4'
Junction with Dakar track. Bearing WSW. Fast piste.

63 (324)
Cross oued with vegetation. Bearing WSW.

78 (309)   N28° 12.4'   W09° 47.1'
Cross the multiple courses of the Oued Oum Doul. Bearing SW.

99 (286)   N28° 04.3'   W09° 54.4'
Vehicle wreck. Bearing S.

114 (273)   N27° 57.2'   W09° 57.4'
Lebouirat. Leave it on your left. Bearing W. You are between hills, fast reg.

145 (242)   N27° 53.0'   W10° 14.6'
Tarf An-Nous on your left. Bearing SW, sandy. Oued Gnifida with vegetation.

168 (219)   N27° 45.1'   W10° 24.5'
Two buildings on your left: Sidi Ahmed al Kenti. Sandy.

187 (200)   N27° 37.0'   W10° 31.3'
Cross the Oued Afra with a well on the other side. Bearing SW. In July 2003 I had

to wait eight hours before crossing the floodwaters!

197 (190)   **N27° 32.8' W10° 33.6'**
Climb onto a plateau. Rocky track. Around here you can see Reguibat *raïmas*.

210 (177)   **N27° 29.0' W10° 38.9'**
Crossing with other pistes. Bearing S.

221 (166)   **N27° 23.5' W10° 39.8'**
Junction on your right with another Paris-Dakar track from Msied.

233 (154)   **N27° 17.2' W10° 39.0'**
Change of bearing. Follow the oued W. Five kilometres later there is a well (N27° 16.9' W10° 43.8'). You climb up onto a plateau before a descent with panoramic views.

247 (140)   **N27° 15.8' W10° 45.0'**
Leave the Jebel. Fast section on the Ga'at Mezwar.

262 (125)   **N27° 09.3' W10° 50.2'**
End of fast section. You can now see the old Spanish tarmac ahead (as marked on normal maps). After the plateau, bear W.

277 (110)   **N27° 06.7' W10° 57.9'**
Military checkpoint. By-pass it on the right with a sign for Smara. Nearby is Hawza, destroyed during the war. Bearing W.

297 (90)   **N27° 05.5' W11° 08.9'**
Rocky track.

322 (65)   **N27° 08.0' W11° 22.1'**
Wide track, reg.

339 (48)   **N27° 03.9' W11° 31.0'**
Fortified wall with some sandy sections. You sometimes see the remains of the old Spanish tarmac.

372 (15)   **N26° 51.4' W11° 45.1'**
Junction with the tarmac, near a campsite under restoration in July 2003.

387 (0)   **N26° 44.6' W11° 41.7'**
Enter Smara after a police control; fuel station.

Western Sahara

The province of Western Sahara was once the colony of Spanish Sahara. When Franco died in the mid-1970s Morocco's King Hassan ordered 350,000 volunteers to cross into the territory, based on rather tenuous historic claims to the region. Despite the fact that the UN had been calling for independence and self-determination since the mid-1960s, Spain handed over the colony to Morocco and Mauritania. Up to 160,000 people fled the region.

In 1973 the Front for the Liberation of Saguia-el-Hamra and Rio de Oro (the two provinces which make up the Western Sahara) was formed, better known by its Spanish acronym: **Polisario**. Three years later the **Saharawi**, as the people of Western Sahara call themselves, established the Saharawi Arab Democratic Republic (SADR) as their nation, and were recognised internationally. Saharawi is the collective name for the Western Saharan tribes which include the Reguibat, Oulad Delim, Tekna and Chnagla, a mixture of Arab-Berbers similar to the Moors.

A war ensued with the Algerian-backed Polisario fighting Morocco and Mauritania until 1979 when Mauritania withdrew after a series of Polisario raids as far south as Nouakchott. Mauritania became an ally of the Saharawi while Morocco annexed the part previously occupied by Mauritania.

The Moroccans built a huge wall of sand known as 'the berm' which runs for 2000 kilometres from Tata all the way to Guergarrat on the Atlantic, with mine fields along its base. Morocco now controls three-quarters of the territory west of the berm. On the eastern side, along the Mauritanian border, is what is known as the Free Zone, occupied by the Saharawi. Smara, inland from Laayoune (or El Ayoun), is the unofficial Saharawi capital but on the Moroccan side of the berm. Tindouf, over the border in Algeria, has for many years been the location of refugee towns for the displaced Saharawi tribes.

The UN has not approved the occupation and to this end they have insisted on a referendum which has been postponed year after year. To help legitimise its claim, Morocco has lured settlers into the Western Sahara with various incentives (such as cheap fuel and a road-building programme), aiming to outnumber the Saharawi and so 'win' any referendum.

These days most of the territory remains under Moroccan control and, away from the Sequiat el Hamra in the north, is off-limits to tourists, while the Free Zone is only really accessible via Algeria and therefore difficult to get to. Welfare organisations, archaeologists and journalists can get invitations to Polisario territories via Tindouf, and Michael Palin managed to travel down the Saharawi side of the berm to Zouerat for his *Sahara* TV series.

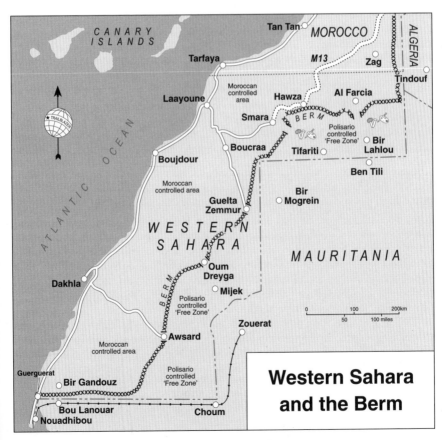

Mauritania

The once little-known country of Mauritania came into prominence in the early 1990s when the collapse of Algerian tourism re-established the trans-Sahara route along the Atlantic shore. Even then the country was only seen as a transit route south to West Africa and rarely appreciated in its own right. As restrictions on independent tourism grow across the Sahara, this is likely to change as the vast and barely-populated Mauritanian Sahara attracts travellers wanting to explore the Sahara for themselves.

The entire northern and eastern half of Mauritania forms part of the Sahara's largest empty quarter: El Djouf or Majabat al Koubra, a million and a half square kilometres (also straddling the Mali and Algerian borders) which contain not one regular piste or town. Alaska would fit in with room to spare.

Primarily this is a flat area of dunes, low escarpments and few wells. But it is the **Adrar region** of plateaux, escarpments and sand-filled canyons that is the focal point of the country's desert life, both contemporary and historic. Its combination of Neolithic remains, historic towns and impressive scenery offer an intimate rather than expansive travel experience.

Atar is the country's date capital and during the mid-summer date harvest or *getna* you'll be lucky to find a spare bed as the whole country moves into the region to celebrate its living nomadic traditions. From Atar to the ghost towns of **Chinguetti** and **Ouadane** and the crater of **Guelb er Richat** are on the tourist trail, and are better enjoyed via the alternative routes. Immediately south of Atar is a less well known but visually more impressive region of little-visited canyon-bound palmeries separated by rocky plateaux and in the Tagant is the 800km route from Tidjikja to Nema, one of the longest in this book but still alive with nomadic activity.

The only disappointment is the lack of substantial rock art sites (although they are said to exist) in the Adrar if not the country itself, even though Neolithic artefacts cover the claypans near some dunes. But as in southern Morocco, you'll regularly encounter the **nomadic lifestyle** which is still closer to this country's roots than anywhere else in the Sahara. It helps support a thriving camel economy (the country's staple meat) and you'll see more, and better fed, camels here than anywhere else in the Sahara except perhaps in Sudan. To see a 500-strong train of camels heading up the Amogjar Pass is an impressive but not at all rare sight.

Ironically, although Algeria has been trying for the last 25 years or more, it looks like sometime in 2005 Mauritania will succeed in building a sealed **road across the Sahara** from north to south. When this happens it will be technically possible to rollerblade while towing a shopping trolley from Dortmund across the Sahara to Dakar. Whether such a road will survive the expected pounding of heavy commercial traffic or Saharan summers remains to be seen, but for the first few months at least, crossing the Saharan overland will never have been easier.

SELLING CARS IN WEST AFRICA

Since the 1990s the Atlantic Route has been a trade route for Europeans and Mauritanians selling used cars in West Africa. If you're lucky and shrewd you can make enough profit to pay for your trip with some money left over. Apart from stony pistes, driving a 2WD in the desert is not that difficult (see p.43), and anyway the Atlantic Route is soon to be sealed – something which may affect the prices listed below. Note that all prices refer to left-hand drive cars; RHDs are worth very little or are locally unregisterable.

In Mauritania and Niger selling used cars is legal. In Mali it's illegal, but in practice does not cause problems. In Senegal it was legal, but not any more; cars more than five years old are no longer allowed into the country without a Carnet which is why most car traders now sell in Mauritania or Mali. Note that the road between Mauritania and Mali is impassable during the rainy season from June to September. Selling used cars in Tunisia, Algeria, Libya or Egypt is either illegal or not viable.

What to sell depends on your destination. In Senegal, Mali and Mauritania diesels are the most popular. In Niger, Nigeria, Chad and Benin people prefer petrol. Everywhere Mercedes is the most popular 2WD, followed by Toyota and Peugeot (the old favourite). If you want to make as much profit as possible bring a model with five doors; two-door models are more difficult to sell. Minibuses of the above brands are also popular. If you bring a 4WD, Toyota is best: (station wagon or pick-up). Old 60 series Land Cruisers are available in Germany or the Netherlands from €4000, returning up to 50% profit in Africa. Other 4WDs including Land Rover are not popular, and only in Nigeria, Niger and Benin are automatic gearboxes appreciated.

Mercedes 190s are seen in almost every African country and cost around €1000 in Europe; in Africa you can get up to €3000. Toyota Corollas and Carinas get the same prices.

A Peugeot 505 or 405 will cost you a little less in Europe but you won't get more than €2000 in Africa. Minibuses of these brands fetch about the same prices.

Don't count on getting the prices mentioned above; selling cars in Africa is a profession in itself. Local dealers are very good at paying a lot less than the market price and can easily sense when sellers are in a hurry. They're also very good at winding you up by coming back many times (especially when you're relaxing in a restaurant at night), or sending friends to offer even lower prices. Many tourists finally sell their cars for a low price just to be free of all these harassments.

In Nouakchott you can sell your car at the campsite. In other countries you're better off visiting car traders. The commissioner system is well established. Basically, some hustler guys will hang around offering their services. They'll find buyers for your car, sort out the formalities and are often a guarantee for a straight deal on both sides. For this, in theory you pay the commissioner 5% of the money you get; in practice the rate is negotiable. Be sure you agree beforehand on who pays the tax at customs and to the police.

For a prestige car like a Mercedes, respraying it in Morocco (about €150) is a good investment if the car is shabby. For a normal workhorse, this is not so important. Failing brakes and leaking exhaust pipes are no problem, as long as the engine is sound. If you expect major problems, going to a garage in Morocco is inexpensive and also a good investment. Just like here, give the car a thorough clean inside and out at a filling station before you try and sell it.

Gerbert van der Aa and Jan Sundstrom

'One owner, FSH, never seen rain' © Sven Torfinn

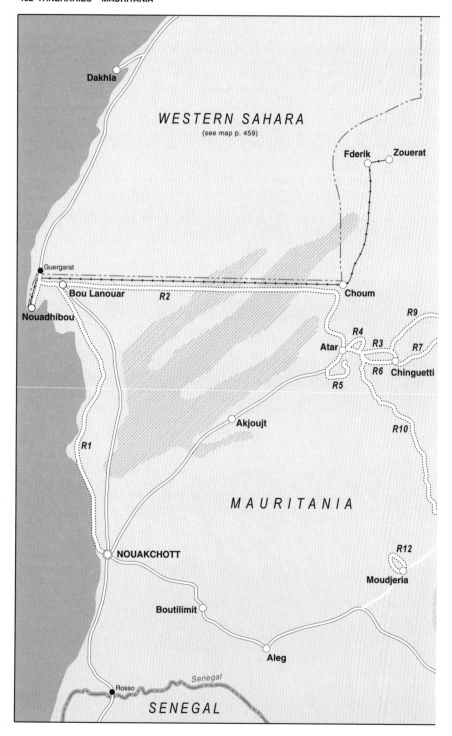

Mauritania

GUELB
ER RICHAT

R8

Ouadane

MAURITANIA

0		100		200km
0	50		100 miles	

Tidjikja

R11

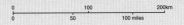

Tichit

DHAR TICHIT

A O U K A R   B A S I N

Oualata

Ayoun al
Atrous

Kifa

Nema

Maps

Because the piste descriptions cover a compact area the small-scale **IGN 1:200,000 maps** are best, available on twin CDs in colour or as mono photocopies sold by the IGN in Paris. Four sheets, 'Atar', 'Chinguetti', 'Ouadane' and 'Guelb er Richat', cover Routes R3–R9. Note that since the last editions of the maps (1963–1975), some of the piste alignments have altered and not all villages and oases are marked. There's more life going on in the Adrar than these maps show. The 1:1 million IGNs are either not good enough to correlate detailed GPS routes or not necessary on the easier routes. Take note of the landmine information on p.466.

THE ATLANTIC ROUTE TO WEST AFRICA

Compared to the central Saharan routes, the Atlantic Route is not particularly scenic, but it does what it's supposed to: get you over the Sahara. As mentioned above this route is soon to be sealed so does not really add up to Sahara Overlanding.

Through the Western Sahara

In recent years Morocco has been building up the infrastructure and improving the desert highway south of Tan Tan in readiness for the Mauritanian connection. This means that since the first edition of this book travel through the Western Sahara down to Mauritania has become straightforward, as has returning north to Morocco, opening up this part of Africa. Fuel stations are frequent, *campements* are on the increase and getting the once-tricky Mauritanian visa has become about as simple as African visas get. Get them either in Europe, in Casablanca, or at the border: see the website for the latest details.

Don't get any ideas about relaxed beachside camps on the way down. Although it's a favourite spot for adventurous European motorhomers, the windswept coast is almost all low rocky cliffs and not especially inviting. South of the Gulf of Cintra the cliffs recede in places and, though occupied by basic fishing settlements, it's easy to get to the beach here.

The border

The end of the road in Morocco is at **Fort Guergarat**. In the days of the convoy, processing of documents would take hours here, but now travellers pass through without delay.

If the new tarmac has not reached here yet you'll face a mass of tracks winding through soft sand and over bare limestone, requiring a mixture of speed and caution in low-slung 2WDs. Remember, **keep to the most used tracks, even if it means getting stuck, as there are mines in the area**. Tourists have been killed here just a couple of metres away from existing tracks.

R1 GUERGARAT → NOUAKCHOTT (via the beach) [483KM]

July 2003; Mercedes 200D (Gerbert van der Aa)

Description

Mauritania is working on a tarred road, but at the time this route was logged work had only just begun and in the first year or so after this edition comes out the following description may still be useful.

The first 300 kilometres to the fishing village of Nouamghar are the most difficult. If you drive too far west the sand gets very soft, if you drive too far east you have to cope with deep truck tracks. (Note that trucks take a different route from cars and 4WDs.) About seventy kilometres before Nouamghar (KM 238) you have to cross four dunes. The first one is especially difficult. Two-wheel drives can only pass with very low tyre pressures.

From Nouamghar you have to drive on the beach, which is only possible at low tide. If the tide is really low you can drive all the way to Nouakchott. If the tide is too high you have to take the improving inland piste that starts at the fishing village of el-Mhaïjrat, about 50 kilometres south of Nouamghar. If you have problems on the beach you'd better fix them fast, otherwise you'll lose your vehicle to the tide. Even with a 4WD it is not always possible to get onto the dunes beyond the high-tide mark.

One nasty thing about this piste is the landmines in the border area between Mauritania and Western Sahara. Two tourists were killed in 1996 when their car exploded. Take care, and always stick to the tracks. Nobody really seems to know where exactly the landmines are. Once you've crossed the railway at Le Bouchon (KM24) you're supposed to be in safe territory, but there are old records of cars setting off mines in the Bay de Levrier.

Route-finding and markers

The piste is far from clear. Lately the Mauritanians have placed some balises (yellow-blue plates on red-white poles). Unfortunately you find them only every ten kilometres, which is not so useful. **Guides** wait for you shortly beyond the border and can be hired for about €35 a car (up to Nouamghar or Nouakchott).

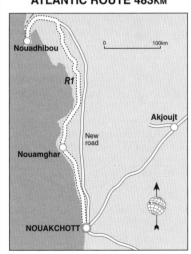

**R1 – RECOMMENDED MAPS
ATLANTIC ROUTE 483KM**

By the time the road's finished you won't need a map but for the moment the old 1:1m NF-28 'Port-Étienne' and NE-28 'St Louis' cover this route as well as anything.

Most guides like to drive to Nouamghar in one day (ten hours), and then directly on to Nouakchott if the tide is low (another four hours). If you don't want to go this fast it's better to spell it out beforehand.

Many guides have a hidden agenda; when cars break down they offer you a derisory price and recover the car themselves. If you have enough time you can easily arrange spare parts or a mechanic in Nouadhibou or Nouakchott. Then again some guides are really nice guys. If you speak French they can tell you a lot about the desert and the life of a nomad.

Fuel

Eighty kilometres north of Fort Guergarat, Nouadhibou and Nouakchott. Also expensive diesel and petrol at Nouamghar.

Water

Eighty kilometres north of Fort Guergarat, Nouadhibou, Tin Alloul, Nouamghar, Nouakchott.

Traffic

Frequent local traffic with tourist cars passing almost every day. Nevertheless, a convoy is a good idea, especially if you travel without a guide. At some stages the piste is so spread out that there's no guarantee other traffic will see you if you get stuck.

Driving

Straightforward. Four-wheel drive only needed occasionally. If you have the water and fuel range it's fun on a bike too. This entire route is currently being sealed and may be completed by 2005. However, if experiences elsewhere in the Sahara are anything to go by, maintenance and repairs will have begun long before the road is completed.

Suggested duration

Two to three days.

0km (483) N21° 25.4' W16° 57.4'
Fort Guergarat. Moroccan frontier in Western Sahara. All formalities are done here. Eighty kilometres to the north (280 km from Dakhla) is the last place to buy fuel and water (unless you deviate to Nouadhibou). You also find a moderately priced hotel near the fuel station.

7 (476) N21° 21.6' W16° 57.6'
End of tarmac, last Moroccan checkpoint. Here the minefield begins, so stay on the tracks. Good piste, with some soft sand. Two-wheel drives should lower tyre pressures.

9 (474) N21° 21.0' W16° 57.4'
Piste splits. Sometimes Mauritanian guides are waiting here. Take the track that turns to the right. The one to the left is a smugglers' piste. It leads directly to Nouakchott without passing Mauritanian customs.

13 (470 N21° 19.1' W16° 57.4'
Old Spanish road. Turn to the south and follow this road to the Mauritanian border post.

16 (467) N21° 17.1' W16° 57.9'
Mauritanian frontier. Formalities straightforward. Both police and customs charge money (around 1000UM or €3.50 plus tax for a car, 2000UM for a 4WD, 3000UM for

a truck). After some haggling they sometimes let you go without paying, but don't count on it. Import of alcohol is not allowed. If they find it you have to empty the bottles.

18 (465) N21° 16.5' W16° 57.7'
Shortly after the border the piste splits again. Here again guides are normally waiting. Take the track to the left and follow it all the way to the railway line, which is about eight kilometres from the previous border post (KM16).

20 (463) N21° 15.8' W16° 57.7'
Turn to the left. If you arrive in an abandoned village you know you're on the wrong track.

24 (459) N21° 13.2' W16° 57.4'
You converge on the railway at the PK46 kilometre marker (46km from the end of the railway). You'll find an old man living in a hut. If you want to visit Nouadhibou you drive for about 25km on the piste on the west side of the railway. If you want to go direct to Nouakchott, cross the railway and head north alongside the rails. There are many different tracks here, because of the soft sand. Watch out for big rocks.

37 (446) N21° 14.8' W16° 53.7'
Rocky terrain, a bit elevated above the rest of the landscape. Around this point you

slowly start turning to the south-east, and leave the railway. Sometimes this area (Sebkha Aoueital) is flooded by the sea. More and more dunes appear. Occasionally you see a small tree.

47 (436)　　　　**N21° 11.0'　W16° 50.5'**
Passage between two dunes.

68 (415)　　　　**N21° 06.1'　W16° 42.9'**
Sandy plain. Don't drive too far west; the sand is very soft there.

83 (400)　　　　**N21° 01.5'　W16° 36.8'**
Wreck of Citroën bus. Shortly after the wreck you have to pass a difficult area with soft sand and rocks.

104 (379)　　　　**N20° 56.9'　W16° 26.9'**
Some huts and tents plus a café and restaurant. There's also a small shop where you can buy spare parts, such as belts and bearings, mostly for Toyota and Mercedes.

137 (346)　　　　**N20° 34.0'　W16° 09.6'**
Sandy plain where you can drive fast. You pass between a balise to your right and a tree to your left.

157 (326)　　　　**N20° 30.9'　W16° 11.6'**
Oued with soft sand. Orange wreck.

181 (302)　　　　**N20° 18.3'　W16° 10.9'**
Plain with occasional dunes.

203 (280)　　　　**N20° 06.8'　W16° 12.8'**
Sign board. You are nearing the coast. The piste to the right goes to Ras Tafarist, about 5km away, where you'll find a nice, but rather expensive, campement. The track to the left leads to the fishing village of Tin Alloul.

220 (273)　　　　**N19° 58.3'　W16° 13.8'**
Tin Alloul. At the checkpoint you have to show your ticket for Banc d'Arguin National Parc. If you don't have a ticket, you can buy it here for 1200 ouguiya (less than €4) a person.

You can buy fish and camp on the beach. The area is famous for sharks, mostly small, which are caught for their fins. The Chinese use them to make shark's fin soup.

238 (245)　　　　**N19° 49.5'　W16° 12.7'**
Some abandoned houses to your left. About one kilometre further a 'steeple-chase' of dune crossings begins. This is the most difficult part of the route and even 4WDs can get stuck.

244 (239)　　　　**N19° 46.8'　W16° 12.6'**
End of first, most difficult, dune crossing. If your engine is hot you can stop here to cool down.

251 (232)　　　　**N19° 43.4'　W16° 14.6'**
End of second dune crossing.

258 (225)　　　　**N19° 40.4'　W16° 15.3'**
End of third dune crossing.

265 (218)　　　　**N19° 36.4'　W16° 14.9'**
End of fourth dune crossing.

292 (191)　　　　**N19° 24.9'　W16° 22.6'**
Deviation. The main piste runs close to the waterfront. To avoid deep tracks take the piste through soft sand over the dunes.

309 (174)　　　　**N19° 21.2'　W16° 30.8'**
Nouamghar fishing village with restaurants, cafés and shops. From here you drive at least 50 kilometres on the beach. Wait for low tide, if necessary.

360 (123)　　　　**N19° 01.6'　W16° 13.9'**
Fishing village of el-Mhaïjarat. Leave the beach if the tide is too high, or if the rocks further on bar continuation. A good inland piste begins here and leads all the way to Nouakchott. Mauritanians are busy working on a tarred road.

368 (115)　　　　**N19° 02.2'　W16° 11.9'**
Police checkpoint.

483 (0)　　　　**N18° 05.9'　W15° 58.4'**
Centre of Nouakchott. The capital has plenty of cheap hostels, where you can sleep in a room or pitch a tent in the courtyard. Cars can also be parked in these guarded courtyards.

The most popular places are *Nomad* and *Menata*, both in the centre of town. They charge around 1500 ougiya per person. *Menata* has an English-speaking owner.

R2 NOUADHIBOU → ATAR [540KM]

November 2003; Nissan Patrol 2.8D and Opel Monterey 3.1D (José Brito)

Description

From Nouadhibou to Choum the piste crosses an endless reg alternating with sandy sections, notably the Azeffal dunes at KM283. Running along the SNIM railway line, it heads north for the first 40km out of Nouadhibou and east for the next 390km. 'Le Train du Désert', as it is locally known, is a 2.5km composition of more than 200 wagons pulled by two or three locomotives.

Near Choum the piste turns to the south and for the last 110km runs along a scenic escarpment, crossing several rock formations and the Azougui oasis in the vicinity of Atar.

Route-finding and markers

The piste is well defined although there are few markers. There are masses of tracks on the way out of Nouadhibou due to the construction of the new road to Nouakchott, and in the sandier sections along the piste. However, as far as Choum the piste runs along the railway, so there are no navigation difficulties (alongside the railway are 'PK' kilometre-posts).

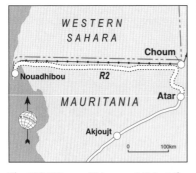

**R2 – RECOMMENDED MAPS
NOUADHIBOU → ATAR 540KM**

The 200,000s would be overkill but the IGN 1m 'Port-Étienne' is rather inaccurate and does not show the railway. Anyway, orientation up to Choum is easy and the 100km from Choum to Atar are easy enough. A TPC may be handy.

Fuel

Nouadhibou and Atar. Probably also in Choum although it is not guaranteed.

Water

Nouadhibou, Atar, Choum and in small villages along the railway line

Traffic

Plenty of local and tourist traffic.

Driving

Overall, it is a very easy piste. There are some sandy sections, but deflating tyres should make the task easier. There are also several dayas (ephemeral ponds), which may be flooded after rainfall. If you are in a 2WD or experiencing difficulties in the sandy sections, you may drive on the railway, but be very careful about trains. Alternatively, you may put your car on a wagon-lit at Nouadhibou but this is a hit-and-miss game with the timetable, and the voyage is said to be a slow, dusty and bumpy ride. Most people don't bother.

Always drive south of the railway due to **mine risk** along the Moroccan border. And avoid driving too close to the railway due to the debris (puncture-making iron stakes) and the sandier terrain.

Suggested duration

Three days, but if you are in a rush it can be done in two.

0km (540)   **N20° 57.8' W17° 02.4'**
Nouadhibou. End of paved road. Head north.

6 (534)   **N21° 01.8' W17° 01.8'**
Le Bouchon checkpoint.

9 (531)   **N21° 03.6' W1°7 01.3'**
Army checkpoint. Piste runs along the new road to Nouakchott.

38 (502)   **N21° 17.2' W16° 54.5'**
PK55. Mass of tracks due to road construction in 2003. Piste turns east.

69 (471)   **N21° 17.2' W16° 37.9'**
End of sandy section.

99 (441)   **N21° 18.4' W16° 21.7'**
Daya (temporary pond).

195 (345)   **N21° 17.0' W15° 28.2'**
Sandy section. Piste turns progressively sandier towards next waypoint.

283 (257)   **N21° 16.1' W14° 39.0'**
Entering Azeffal dunes. Deflate tyres. Mass of tracks and deviations. Avoid deep sand routes near the railway line.

340 (200)   **N21° 11.6' W14° 06.5'**

End of dunes, several dayas to the north. Other smaller sandy sections will follow towards next waypoint.

429 (111)   **N21° 16.8' W13° 18.7'**
End of dunes. Re-inflate tyres. At this point you can head towards Choum (N21° 17.8' W13° 03.9') or turn SE directly for Atar.

442 (98)   **N21° 11.5' W13° 14.1'**
A point on the piste; reg.

480 (60)   **N20° 55.1' W13° 11.6'**
Join the Choum–Atar piste. Head south.

494 (46)   **N20° 47.8' W13° 11.7'**
Piste turns east towards pass in the escarpment on the left.

508 (32)   **N20° 44.3' W13° 06.5'**
Small *auberge*. After a short while leave the main piste and head directly south, through a sandy area.

529 (11)   **N20° 33.6' W13° 06.2'**
Beginning of paved road.

540 (0)   **N20° 31.0' W13° 03.3'**
Atar roundabout. Fuel station on the right.

R3 ATAR → CHINGUETTI (via Ebnou Pass)   [81km]
March 1999; Toyota HJ60

Description
The direct route to Chinguetti takes the Ebnou Pass. When it was opened in 1995 it cut the distance via the *ancienne* or Amogjar Pass by a third and the driving time from a day to two hours!

    The ascent of the pass is the only highlight and nothing compared to descending the Amogjar (which would form part of an 87km loop from Atar). Once you're on the plateau it's the bumps that grab you more than the scenery, but Chinguetti is well worth the excursion.

Route-finding and markers
None, and none needed.

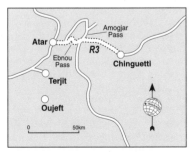

**R3 – RECOMMENDED MAPS
ATAR → CHINGUETTI 81km**

No map yet identifies the Ebnou Pass, but if you need a map to do this route consult your lifestyle guru urgently.

Fuel
Atar and Chinguetti (expensive).

Water
Each end, the Ebnou Pass café and the well near KM32.

Traffic
Regular.

Driving
Five years ago moves were afoot to subdue the corrugations this route is famous for, but only the pass remains sealed.

Suggested duration
You can do it in two hours.

0km (81)   **N20° 31.1' W13° 03.2'**
Atar roundabout. Drive east along the town's main road, going round a couple of bends and keeping right (east) at the *Hotel Dar Salaam* (left goes to Choum). Drive towards the escarpment ahead.

10.6 (70.4)   **N20° 32.0' W12° 56.1'**
Fork. Left goes to Amogjar (Route R4). If you look carefully at the light grey slabs here you'll see they're all rippled with tiny fossil formations. These are stromatolites, sediment-trapping algae that have been dated back three million years and are one of the Earth's earliest life forms. They still survive in a hyper-saline lagoon off Western Australia but even alive sound more interesting than they are.

Go straight on (SE) for the Ebnou Pass. The road begins to climb but the surface is sealed. You steeply ascend a rock-filled canyon on its right-hand face with great views back to the plain.

24 (57)
Ebnou Pass with a shack restaurant. Just after the shack a new track is signed south-west leading 40km to the isolated canyon oasis of Mhaïreth. You are now on top of the stony Dahr Chinguetti escarpment which dips south into the sands of the Ouarane. Continue east.

32 (49)   **N20° 31.9' W12° 46.3'**
Crossroads. North goes to the rock paintings (see Route R4 for description) and the fabulous Amogjar descent, south leads to the windmill well and walled garden of Bir el Greire (4km; the blue dot on the IGN

1:1m) and a stony piste to Chinguetti via the sandy btâh (see Route R6).

This route continues east over stony Dahr with occasional trees. At around KM40 you'll notice dunes to the south: the Ouarane sand sea.

63 (18)   **N20° 34.6' W12° 27.4'**
Junction. Keep right. Left goes NE to Ouadane via the plateau (see Route R9). From here you begin to curve SE and then S down towards Chinguetti. All three IGNs copy one another's incorrect track orientation here, but it doesn't matter, the way on is clear.

As you near Chinguetti, passing the air strip on the right, the track becomes sandier and you'll eventually need to engage four-wheel drive and maybe even deflate the tyres a bit if you don't want to embarrass yourself in the middle of town.

81 (0)
The centre of Chinguetti oasis on the north bank of the broad sandy oued or btâh which divides the old southern quarter from the modern northern part. Fuel is available in jerries from *commerçants* at around double the price in Atar. There was one in the lane directly south of the fort/hotel just to the east of this point.

There are several *auberges* and *campings* in town. We stayed at the *Maison Bien Etre* on the south bank of the oued (keep your foot down!) just to the left (N20° 27.4' W12° 21.7'). Inside are rooms or much more agreeable communal *raïmas*. Its owner can arrange a visit to the famous library.

R4 AMOGJAR PASS → ATAR [55KM]

December 2002; Land Rover Defender V8 (Tim Stead)

Description

Although the best is behind you after 20km, the Amogjar Pass is one of the most spectacular pistes in the Adrar and, as with other routes of this kind, is much better descended with the vista opening up before you. It may no longer be the quickest way to or from the plateau but it's undoubtedly the most impressive.

Route-finding and markers

Once you've found the starting point a few kilometres east of the Ebnou Pass, the route through the canyon is clear.

Fuel

Atar.

Water

Ebnou Pass and the well at the end of the canyon around KM12.

Traffic

With the Ebnou Pass, camel traffic is now restricted to this longer route onto the plateau's pasture. The only other vehicles will be tourists and the decrepit Land Rovers of the nomads.

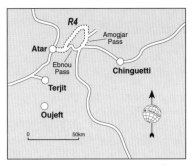

**R4 – RECOMMENDED MAPS
AMOGJAR PASS → ATAR 55KM**

Not essential as you'll have a hard time getting lost. The only map that usefully depicts the curves of the track is the 200,000 IGN 'Chinguetti' sheet.

Driving

Once you come off the dahr the track is rough and corrugated but there are no difficulties.

Suggested duration

Three hours.

0km (55)   N20° 31.9' W12° 46.3'
Crossroads on the Atar–Chinguetti piste (KM32 on Route R3). Turn NE. There is a distinctive stacked outcrop just to the NE at N20° 32.3' W12° 46.6'.

1 (54)   N20° 32.5' W12° 47.7'
The Amogjar rock paintings are no Tassili or Akakus and the 200-oog entry fee makes them even more lacklustre, a few faint figures daubed with little skill.

From the top of the painting outcrop you can just make out Fort Saganne to the west.

3.6 (51.4)
The very stony rim of the Amogjar Pass needs to be driven over slowly in low vehicles. Then the track descends steeply down a few hairpins to the valley below and a branch leading right to the fort (see below).

Turn left to continue down the canyon with more spectacular vistas unfolding ahead.

8 (47)   N20° 32.0' W12° 49.1'
Marmot Junction. Neither a junction nor the lair of marmots, but the domain of

weasel-like *damans* which live in the cliff face hereabouts. Our guide was just telling us about them and there they were, so there's a chance you'll see them too. From here the track heads NE along the canyon. There are some nice camping spots among the occasional trees, but some nomad encampments too. Once past KM20 it's all pretty exposed.

16 (39)   **N20° 36.5' W12° 44.5'**
Fork to the right. This leads to, among other places, El Beyyed well north of Guelb er Richat (a Neolithic site but also with mines reputedly in the area) and after several hundred kilometres the desolate military outpost of Chegga between the Mali and Algerian borders.

From this point the piste passes into more open terrain as it curls round the mountains to continue SW to Atar.

22 (33)
Another track splits right, to the north (marked on the 200,000 map). Keep left, eventually heading SW.

24 (31)   **N20° 37.9' W12° 47.4'**
Abandoned fort by the piste (see box).

45 (10)   **N20° 32.0' W12° 56.1'**
Junction with track to Ebnou Pass. Turn west for Atar.

55 (0)
Atar.

FORT SAGANNE – THE MOVIE

Improbable though it may sound, the fort you see before you was built as a prop for the 1985 French Saharan epic *Fort Saganne*, starring Gerard Depardieu, Catherine Deneuve and a young Sophie Marceau. Set in early 20th-century Algeria, this oddly inert romantic adventure follows the eponymous colonel during his subjugation of the Tuaregs and intervening seductions.

The film is based on the novel by Louis Gardel, itself based on the service of his grandfather, Lt Gabriel Gardel. In April 1913 Gardel was on patrol with the Compagnie Saharienne and came upon a much larger band of Fezzani Tuareg at Esseyen (near

Ghat). Despite the odds Gardel and his men claimed victory; a similar story to Laperine's decisive 1902 battle with the Ahaggar Tuareg.

Gardel died three years later in the Somme and Fort Gardel (near Djanet in Algeria, now the village of Bordj el Haouas, Route A7) was named after him. The publication of his notes about the Kel Ajjer in the early 1960s proved Gardel had been deeply interested in the Tuareg.

In the film you'll recognise several Mauritanian locations, including the real fort in Chinguetti (now a hotel) and the low dunes south of town.

R5 ATAR → TERJIT (via Oujeft)   [96KM]
December 2002; Land Rover Defender V8 (Tim Stead)

Description
Driving south out of Atar along the highway this route leaves the road at the Terjit turn-off but instead of heading for the popular oasis (14km) it takes the next valley south. This is the Oued el Abiod which looks as promising as the map suggests; a black-walled canyon with apricot-coloured dunes resting in huge ramps against the cliffs. The sand gets softer as you pass a few villages and gardens, and just after Toungad palmerie you climb out of the canyon, now blocked by dunes. Having parked the car, it's a kilometre's walk to the lovely guelta, a plunge pool of a transitory waterfall and a rare chance for a swim in the Sahara.

From the village the piste crosses the plateau towards Oujeft, before which it turns back north (KM66) to wind across the stony El Kfeïfir plateau and down the impressive Tourvine Pass into the beautiful canyon that leads to Terjit, itself a jewel when not too crowded.

Route-finding and markers
None needed as far as Toungad. Out of Toungad over the plateau we followed tracks towards Oujeft and eventually almost doubled back. It seems probable that turning left (north-east) at KM66 bypasses Oujeft, a lot of confusion and 4km. These tracks, from Toungad to around KM85, are not marked on the 1:200,000 map.

On the Kfeïfir plateau there are several other unmarked tracks coming and going, mostly to the right, presumably for Mhaïreth, but the main track to the Tourvine Pass is the most prominent. From Tourvine you descend into the valley and turn right for Terjit or left back to KM33 and Atar.

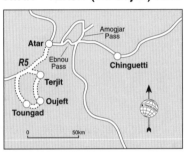

**R5 – RECOMMENDED MAPS
ATAR → TERJIT (via Oujeft) 96KM**

The old IGN 200,000 'Atar' sheet covers the whole route in detail, but does not show all the recent tracks so is best marked up beforehand and scrutinised carefully.

Fuel
Atar.

Water
At villages and several wells in the Oued el Abiod.

Traffic
Regular down the oued, less so over the plateau, plenty around Terjit.

Driving
A combination of very soft sand along the Abiod and a stony plateau. You'd need to ride a bike assertively along the sandy canyon.

Suggested duration
With an early start you could have lunch at Toungad guelta and spend the night at Terjit or even back in Atar – but why rush?

0km (96)   N20° 31.1' W13° 03.2'
Atar roundabout. Head south out of town on the Nouakchott road which should be all sealed by now.

14.4 (81.6)
Canyon and possible guelta on the west side of the road.

23 (73)
Steep descent. The lorry wrecks show that not everyone brakes hard enough.

33 (67)   N20° 16.5' W13° 11.0'
Checkpoint and turn-off for Terjit and,

less obviously, Toungad. Directly to the south you can see the sand piled up against the En Ouakane plateau. Follow the piste leading SSW towards this and the entrance into the El Abiod canyon. (This distance from Atar was measured following the deviations before the sealing of the highway.)

35 (61)
Oued of grey powdery sand.

41 (55)
Track joins from right.

43 (53)
Buildings by the track and a village. You are in the canyon now, heading SE.

47 (49)
Reduce tyre pressures and pass around the dunes. Very sandy from now till Toungad. The canyon's dark grey rocks and orange sand are a striking combination.

58 (38)
Large dune leaning against the left-hand cliff and, in a kilometre, a village (abandoned?) on the right.

59 (37)
Palmerie of Toungad. Drive right through it, passing some buildings and continuing up onto the plateau to your left.

60 (36)   N20° 03.5' W13° 07.5'
Once on the top, turn left (waypoint), drive along the very rocky track as far as you can bear (a couple of hundred metres), and park.

The walk to the guelta takes about 15 minutes and will need more than flipflops. Descend into the gorge and follow it right (upstream), passing some smaller pools and clambering over rocks. The peagreen guelta was around 2m deep on our visit, with a shady overhang and even a bit of grass to sit on. The village children didn't bother us in 1999 – now you may be followed by a *cadeau*-demanding procession all the way.

62 (34)   N20° 03.5' W13° 07.1'
Drive through the village and then turn NE sooner rather than later, to cross the wide flat oued filled with sodom apple bushes. Other tracks lead nowhere and can cause confusion. On the other side ascend a rocky track heading NW, passing a walled enclosure on your left.

66 (30)   N20° 03.6' W13° 06.3'
Fork. We kept right (SE) for Oujeft but it seems certain that turning left here leads less than 2km to what we recorded as KM72 but is marked here as KM68.

68 (38)   N20° 03.9' W13° 05.3'
You are now less than 2km ENE of the fork at KM66. Head generally north.

71 (25)
Cross a sandy oued.

75 (21)   N20° 07.4' W13° 06.0'
Some huts and tents.

79 (17)   N20° 09.5' W13° 05.0'
Track joins from the right. You are now very close to the track on the 1:200,000 map.

82 (14)   N20° 11.1' W13° 04.5'
You have joined the mapped track now. A track joins from the right. Keep left here, and again in a kilometre.

84 (12)
Cross a rocky outcrop with a small dune. In a kilometre keep left again at a junction. At KM90 another track joins from the left. Continue N or NE.

87 (9)   N20° 12.1' W13° 05.4'
The Tourvine Pass is now visible on the horizon as a big track (probably coming from Mhaïreth) joins from the right.

89 (7)
Corrugations appear now as you're drawn towards the Tourvine Pass whose descent begins in 1km, offering a great view.

92 (4)
Road sign for Tourvine Pass.

94 (2)   N20° 15.7' W13° 06.1'
Junction with Atar–Terjit piste. Turn right for Terjit village and the oasis at the very end of the track (about 2km). Left leads back to Atar via KM33.

96 (0)
Terjit oasis. Every tour comes here, but when you arrive you'll understand why. The narrow palm-filled cleft is about 10° cooler than the open air. Water dribbles off the fern-draped walls and birds chatter in the palms (camping 1500 oogs).

After a few days on the piste, Terjit is a welcome tonic. From the car park it's a 300m walk down to the campsite – don't be put off by other *campements* on the way telling you it's not there: it is.

R6 CHINGUETTI → EBNOU PASS (via oued)   [60KM]

March 1999; Toyota HJ60

Description

We were planning to record this route but the guide knew better and we spent two days stuck in the dunes instead, reaching the Mohammed Lemine well near Zarga's east flank out of necessity before heading back north cross country to the oued (or *btâh* as it's known locally), to join the piste around W12° 37', about halfway along.

Nevertheless this looks like a good piste and it would be a shame not to mention it. It should be easy to follow with a 1:200,000 map. Like Route R4, it's an alternative to the Dahr Chinguetti track (R3) and is easy to follow with the sands to the south and the stony dahr to the north plus the Zarga massif to aid orientation.

Nearer to Chinguetti it gets increasingly sandy as it passes several wells and possible encampments. Driven in the opposite direction it would be fun to roll into Chinguetti along the sandy river bed. This does not claim to be a complete route description. Distances are approximate but the waypoints are, of course, as accurate as can be expected.

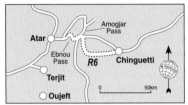

R6 – RECOMMENDED MAPS
CHINGUETTI → EBNOU PASS 60KM

The 200,000 IGN 'Chinguetti' sheet shows the winding course of the piste along the *btâh* as well as the junction at the green hut (KM44) and the well near the end.

0km (60)   N20° 27.4' W12° 21.7'
Chinguetti.

30 (30)
Track passes over a stony surface between dunes to the south and the dahr to the north. Head west with the prominent ridge of Zarga visible to the SW.

37 (23)   N20° 24.3' W12° 40.8'
A barbed-wire fence blocks the piste, marking a large enclosure. Drive around it to the south and carry on west.

The ground in this area has patches of baked mud and there are now plenty of trees and grass. A watercourse is only evident from the trees, and the intermittent track is not always clear among bushes and trees. Some nomadic encampments around. From this point follow tracks tending WNW.

44 (16)   N20° 24.8' W12° 45.2'
Green Hut, the junction of the piste coming down from Amogjar and continuing south 400km to Tidjikja. You are by a sandy oued and among trees directly north of Zarga. Head north up onto the dahr. The piste sometimes becomes very stony at times, winding over the bare rocky plateau.

(South of the Green Hut a piste continues east to the new Mhaïreth piste from where you can turn right up to the Ebnou Pass or down to the lovely long oasis of Mhaïreth.)

59 (1)   N20° 30.9' W12° 45.4'
Bir el Greire. Windmill, well with a generator and a small walled garden. Continuing north for a kilometre you'll soon reach a piste heading west to the Ebnou Pass and Atar, 32km and less than an hour away.

If you carry on 4km north of the well you'll get to the crossroads on the Atar–Chinguetti route: KM32 on Route R3 (N20° 31.9' W12° 46.3'). From here Route R4 leads down the Amogjar to Atar.

HISTORIC CHINGUETTI AND ITS LIBRARIES

One of Islam's Holy Cities, Chinguetti grew to prominence in the medieval era along with places like Ouadane, Oualata and Timbuktu: trading posts on the caravan routes linking the Mali and Ghana empires with the Maghreb and Europe.

In the mid-1990s severe floods uncovered an even older settlement a couple of kilometres down the oued, long ago buried by the sands which press down on the ancient southern quarter of Chinguetti.

The town's famous library near the mosque, itself dating from the 13th century, is actually a repository; one of several in town but the only one open to visitors. In a darkened room you'll be shown centuries-old manuscripts, invoices, letters and grammatical tomes bound in gazelle leather. There are valuable religious texts, too, as Chinguetti was a leading religious school or

Fifteenth-century scrolls.

madrasa. The exquisite calligraphy and geometrical patterns of the grammar textbooks are extraordinary. Bamboo tubes from Asia were used to store rolled-up letters in transit. There are similar but less well-known repositories in Mali and Algeria.

To protect the manuscripts, flash photography is forbidden, so if you plan some photos bring fast film. Expect an impromptu market of souvenir sellers to be waiting for you outside the library as you emerge.

Chinguetti itself is a lovely, relaxed oasis and if you've been travelling a while you might find it more agreeable than Atar. Once the kids get to know you they give up hassling and there are shops in town if you look carefully. There's nothing much to do other than sit around, watch the billowing cloaks of the locals as they cross the btâh, or take a camel trip into the dunes.

R7 CHINGUETTI → OUADANE (via the plain)   [95KM]
March 1999; Toyota HJ60

Description
This is the preferred route for tour groups being led to Ouadane and Guelb, sometimes a little sandy but a great improvement on the bone-shaking plateau piste (Route R9). As there is no recognised piste, route-finding and driving conditions may be demanding although the terrain forms a corridor between the two towns.

Because of the route's increased use by tourists, nomads wait in key locations with a selection of trinkets. Bartering for a souvenir can be an enjoyable pastime, but even here it's money they want, not things to exchange.

Route-finding and markers
Don't expect a clear track all the way to Ouadane. The piste (in fact there are many variations) is unmarked but tracks are fairly frequent. In its first half at least, route-finding requires maintaining your ENE orientation while keeping in the broad corridor of navigable terrain between the dunes to the south and the darker stony dahr to the north. You'll know when you veer too close to these and can adjust your orientation accordingly.

At around KM52 the Herrour ridge becomes a useful landmark; pass over its northern tip and continue ENE until you see the escarpment on which Ouadane lies.

Fuel

Chinguetti and Ouadane. Ask around and expect high prices.

Water

At both towns and at nomadic encampments like Rheouya (KM45.5) along the way. There are other wells marked on the maps.

Traffic

This is the tour operators' route to Ouadane but if you veer from the main route you could be on your own. Better to go with two vehicles.

Driving

There are no dunes to speak of but soft sand is the prevalent theme so deflate tyres accordingly.

Suggested duration

One day. You may find camping before or after Ouadane, although there are *auberges* there.

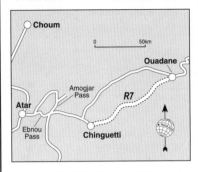

**R7 – RECOMMENDED MAPS
CHINGUETTI → OUADANE 95km**

The two IGN 200,000 maps, 'Chinguetti' and 'Ouadane', are essential for this route and can be improved by drawing lines of longitude at five-minute intervals for the region between the two towns.

0km (95)   N20° 27.4' W12° 21.7'
Maison Bien Etre by the main crossing point of Chinguetti's sandy oued. Drive E down the sandy hummocks of the oued, passing gardens and small palmeries.

3.7 (91.3)
Pass Old Chinguetti, the original 7th-century settlement of Abbeir on the right bank. All you might see are a few palms and sand-covered walls.

7.4 (87.6)   N20° 30.0' W12° 18.5'
Head for a clump of acacias on the north bank where tracks leave the oued and head into low dunes.

8.2 (86.8)   N20° 30.2' W12° 18.2'
Dark tracks lead up into dunes. Continue NE. In half a kilometre you come to a claypan where just about every stone has been worked to some extent.

11 (84)   N20° 31.4' W12° 17.1'
Track passes through trees and over claypans.

12.6 (82.4)   N20° 32.0' W12° 16.5'
Stony patch and in a kilometre some

corrugations after which you pass a line of dunes.

16.8 (78.2)
Heading 70°.

21 (74)   N20° 35.3' W12° 12.9'
Passage through dune corridor.

27 (68)   N20° 37.5' W12° 10.1'
Cross the wide stony Oued Toûchât with trees and grassy tussocks on the far side.

32 (63)
Low rolling dunes and tussocks. Rocks of the dahr visible to the north.

33 (62)   N20° 39.0' W12° 06.8'
Sign on the piste: '*Tingu Maison de Paix*' (in Doueïrât, north of this route). After the sign continue nearly E over soft sand among grassy tussocks. The dunes now are barely visible to the south. Sometimes you cross a patch of stones in the dips.

36 (59)
Broad sandy plain dotted with many tussocks.

38 (57)   N20° 39.7'   W12° 03.7'
Stony patch as the track passes among some acacias (shade and camping possibilities). This is the *steppe arborée* below the 'R' of 'Adrar' on the 1:200,000 map. Heading varies between ENE and E.

41 (54)
Bearing now turns towards ENE. Dunes clearly visible ahead. The 'lightly wooded steppe' continues.

43 (52)
Track veers to NE and becomes more stony and less sandy.

45.5 (49.5)   N20° 41.7'   W12° 00.3'
Encampment on the oued marked on the very edge of the map. A few tents and huts known as Rheouya although the map shows this further south.

47 (48)
Leave the oued and the camp, heading NE. In 500m the track crosses onto stones which continue for a couple of kilometres.

54 (41)   N20° 44.7'   W11° 56.6'
Cross soft sand rises. Heading ENE.

56 (39)   N20° 45.3'   W11° 55.6'
Northernmost point of the Herrour ridge and its dunes. Track now undulates over sandy rises in quite quick succession.

58 (37)
A patch of powdery feche-feche. Heading

now ENE at speeds of up to 55kph .

61 (34)   N20° 46.7'   W11° 53.1'
Lots of big trees with good shadow make a good spot for a rest.

63 (32)
Stony stretch. Bearing 80°-85°.

66 (29)   N20° 47.3'   W11° 50.5'
Sign for 'Enoj' and a fork (just before the 'Oued Enoj' on the map). Go right, heading ENE. In 500m pass half a dozen stone buildings on the left followed by some sharp stones.

68 (27)
Series of rapid undulations over small dunes. Bearing 60°, turning to 70° by KM70.

76 (19)   N20° 50.0'   W11° 45.5'
Sandy undulations continue but are more spaced out. Bearing still 70°.

86 (9)   N20° 52.8'   W11° 40.6'
Still ENE but with smoother, faster terrain with many tussocks.

89 (6)
Heading changes to 60° and within 500m to 45°.

90 (5)
The stone escarpment and buildings of Ouadane become visible. Drive towards the settlement.

The ruins of old Ouadane.

94 (1) N20° 55.6' W11° 37.7'
Entrance to Ouadane at the base of the cliff. Camping. To get to the village cross the rough oued at the base of the cliff and climb up the escarpment past the sign for the Guelb 'hotel'. You may have to pay an arrival tax.

Although easily missed, so well do they blend into the rocks, you can make out the maze of ruined buildings tumbling down the cliff face to the left which made up Ouadane in its trade route heyday.

R8 OUADANE → GUELB ER RICHAT [39KM]

March 1999; Toyota HJ60

Description

Guelb er Richat, a huge crater of concentric rings made by the earth-shaking, dinosaur-annihilating impact of a prehistoric meteor! Alas, no. Impressive looking on a map and doubtless from the air too, the Guelb is in fact an eroded blister of the earth's crust; a dome of rock pushed up from below by a globule of magma. The fractures in the uplifted bending rock hastened erosion so much that now the formation is a worn-down dome, the strata getting older as you near the centre where the heat and pressure has metamorphosed the rock into a colourful conglomerate.

Impressive though this sounds, the view from the centre is unremarkable; nothing more than low hills in the far distance. Without being aware of the Guelb's origins, you'd have no idea you're at the core of a massive geological formation. Like standing on the equator or Ayers Rock, the appeal here rests mostly in getting there and saying you've been, in addition to the peculiarity of driving over the Guelb's rings in order to get to the centre.

Route-finding and markers

From Ouadane you follow the Oued Slit NE towards the key point at KM23.3 from where clear tracks lead in. If you lose the track at any time along the way just head for this point. The rings around the Guelb can only be penetrated in certain places so access into the centre is a bit of a zig-zag. On the 1:200,000 map the heart of the formation is on top of the 'e' in the 'er' of 'er Richat'.

There are said to be mines to the east and south of Ouadane and our guide waved vaguely to the south of Guelb claiming there were mines there. If you're planning to go there it may be wise to ask around at Ouadane.

Fuel

From the *commerçants* in Ouadane at around 100 oogs a litre in 1999.

Water

From Ouadane and the wells near Agouadir, south of the Guelb.

Traffic

Tour groups may still go to the tent hotel at the centre of the crater.

Driving

Sometimes sandy through the oueds and the third ring at KM31.

Suggested duration

The round trip takes half a day but a visit to the ruins at Agouadir and an afternoon bantering or bartering with the nomads encamped here will make the experience complete.

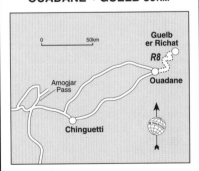

R8 – RECOMMENDED MAPS
OUADANE → GUELB 39KM

If not the 200,000 'Ouadane' sheet, then certainly the 'Guelb er Richat' map is useful in working out your position. Without them you'd have to concentrate heavily on the GPS until KM23.3.

0km (39)
Ouadane, by the pink sign for 'Hotel Guelb er Richat 40km'. Follow the track east out of town with the oued on the right.

2-3 (36-7)
Cross the sandy oued to the southern bank and follow the tracks heading ENE. Good camping spots from here on.

5 (34)   N20° 55.6' W11° 34.8'
Waypoint. From here the tracks lead parallel to the course of the Oued Slit over firm rolling sand. Bearing now NNE.

10.4 (28.6)   N20° 57.4' W11° 32.4'
The low escarpment of the north side of the oued that you've been following (the Torf Tin Terkel) curves away to the north as you cross a chott with some trees.

13 (26)
Trees visible ahead. Still firm rolling sand.

15 (24)   N20° 58.6' W11° 30.3'
Low hills ahead and to the left with trees at their base. Sandy hummocks.

18 (21)
Having passed some dunes on the right (with plenty of Neolithic bits and pieces in the claypans between them), the track continues ENE.

20 (19)   N20° 59.9' W11° 27.8'
You are nearly at the edge of the first map. Cross a oued with grass and trees around. Sandy sections.

22 (17)   N21° 00.1' W11° 27.2'
Waypoint. Continue NE. There may be no distinct track.

24 (15)   N21° 01.4' W11° 27.0'
The key point on the route from where clear tracks lead all the way to the centre of the Guelb. Follow the track NNE through the first ring. Head across the chott crossing over a hard ring of rock like a speed hump (KM25) and continue N. Clear tracks.

28 (11)
Turn sharply E into a narrow and sandy valley between rings two and three.

31 (8)   N21° 03.6' W11° 24.9'
Another key point, where you turn N up a long sandy ramp to cross the third ring. You'll need plenty of speed to get up. The crest is rocky and then the other side is soft sand again. Good view.

(Reversing this pass on the way out is easier, although you'll spot an alternative piste to the W, marked with balises, which ascends over the rocks.)

From here corrugations lead north.

34.5 (4.5)
Drive through a narrow pass, the fourth ring, and over another chott.

37.3 (1.6)
The last pass goes through a sandy oued.

38 (1)   N21° 06.8' W11° 24.2'
Piste forks; go left and follow the tracks through the stony hill to the core.

39 (0)   N21° 07.5' W11° 24.2'
Turn left with the tent hotel ahead (if it's still there), into the small dead-end valley. You are now at the centre. For a view of nothing except the racing wind and distant hills, climb to the 'summit' over black rubble rocks to your west.

R9 OUADANE → CHINGUETTI (via the plateau)   [130KM]
March 1999; Toyota HJ60

Description
To look at, the plateau is not as bad as people say. With a bit of imagination you can visualise the grassy savannah of 5000 years ago, populated with big game. We were surprised at the wildlife too: birds, lizards and even a hare, which you rarely spot elsewhere in the Sahara.

Unfortunately all the birds and the bees can't overcome the hammering you're suffering over the world-class corrugations and stones.

Route-finding and markers
It's a clear if horribly rough track all the way with no turn-offs of any consequence.

Fuel
Ouadane and Chinguetti. Ask around and expect to pay high prices.

Water
Ouadane and Chinguetti.

Traffic
This is the truck supply route to and from Atar.

Driving
Keep tyres pumped up once you're up on the plateau and spare a thought for the suspension or, on a bike, the spokes.

Suggested duration
Half a day.

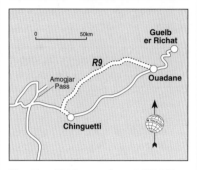

R9 – RECOMMENDED MAPS
OUADANE → CHINGUETTI 130KM

The three IGN maps from 1:200,000 to 1:2,500,000 are all there are.

The location of Ouadane is just off the 1:1,000,000 NF-28 'Port-Étienne' sheet, which doesn't show the last 40-odd kilometres east of 12°N, but it will suffice as the route runs clearly between the two towns.

0km (130)   N20° 55.6'   W11° 37.7'
From the new campsite head WNW to the tracks leading up a light rocky rise with some sand.

9 (121)
Two balises with a track going NE to some villages a few kilometres NW of Ouadane.

30 (100)
The track begins to turn ESE, soon crossing a oued then turning gradually to the SE; it generally keeps that heading until the junction at KM112. Around KM70 you'll pass a sign for the *Maison de la Paix* auberge in Doueïrât, south of the piste.

112 (18)   N20° 34.6'   W12° 27.4'
Junction with Atar piste (KM63 on R3).

130 (0)
Chinguetti oasis. Your car falls apart.

R10 ATAR → TIDJIKJA   [395KM]
November 2003; Nissan Patrol 2.8D and Opel Monterey 3.1D (José Brito)

Description
This route follows the ancient caravan piste between Chinguetti and Ouadane, with the Tagant. You'll see several camel herds, hundreds strong, and plenty of nomadic life. Highlights include the Aoueloûl crater at KM75, Neolithic graves and the remains of ancient Gangara farm settlements (mostly barns) after KM150, and the remains of the ancient village of Rachid after KM335.

The route leaves the Chinguetti piste at KM32 and heads directly south, crossing a bone-shaking hamada alternating with sandy areas (the end of Route R6). After KM80, things get progressively sandier with several dune fields (KM220). The last 100km runs inside the Rachid and Tidjikja oueds.

Route-finding and markers

Easy up to KM32 after which there are few markers. In the dune fields and sandier areas the piste is less well defined, as it circumvents the constantly moving Barkhane fields. In the hamadas, piles of rocks mark the piste in some sections.

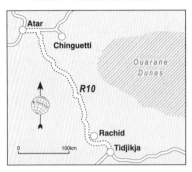

R10 – RECOMMENDED MAPS
ATAR → TIDJIKJA 395KM

This route falls rather awkwardly across three IGN 1:1m sheets – NF-28 'Port-Étienne', NE-28 'St Louis' and NE-29-30 'Tidjikja'. The 1:500,000 TPC J1-C covers the first two IGN maps, with Rachid and Tidjikja just off the map, right of 12°W.

Fuel
Atar and Tidjikja.

Water
Atar, Rachid, Tidjikja and from several wells in the Rachid and Tidjikja oueds.

Traffic
Light, with more traffic between Rachid and Tidjikja.

Driving
Some sandy areas might be difficult to cross. There are some steep sandy ascents, notably the Taoujafet dunes at KM325. If you feel unsure, hiring a guide in Atar is advisable.

Suggested duration
Four days should give you plenty of time to visit the several highlights.

OTHER OPTIONS AROUND ATAR

This whole region south of Atar is a maze of inviting canyons, many with isolated oases, well off the beaten pistes to Chinguetti and Ouadane. If you're feeling adventurous, from Oujeft there are pistes heading south-east to **Faraoun** and **Timnit** and from there north-east up the canyon of the Oued Timnit to the guelta at **Berbera** (about N19° 59' W12° 49'). From here I was told a 'good driver' could continue east cross-country to pick up the Tidjikja piste and turn north towards Zarga and Route R10; not something to try alone and maybe not even possible. As soon as you leave any piste in a car your speed can slow right down to a camel's pace, especially on the plateaus.

Alternatively, crossing the Kfeïfir plateau north of Oujeft, more reliable tracks lead north-east to **Mhaïreth** and across its narrow canyon to the Ebnou Pass (or Chinguetti). It all depends how confident you're feeling about working it out for yourself.

The good thing is that distances are relatively small around here and the canyons make usually navigable passages as well as clear landmarks to relate to a 1:200,000 map. It's also quite a populated area so if you do get stuck, distances are short between the plentiful oases. Cyril Ribas' *Mauritanie au GPS* offers details on some of the above routes, and many more right across Mauritania.

A word about **Azougui**, about 12km north-west of Atar (see Route R1). The regular guidebooks rave about the 'historical ruins of Azougui'. It was from here, after all, that the Almoravid Berber conquest which reached halfway up Spain is said to have begun in 1054. Interesting though this is, what they don't tell you (or have never found out) is that the actual site, by the village of the same name, is nothing more than a walled area of rubble: the Alhambra it isn't.

0km (395) N20° 31.1'W13° 03.2'
Atar roundabout. Leave town heading east towards Chinguetti.

32 (363) N20° 31.8'W11° 46.6'
Leave main piste to Chinguetti and head SE. Rough but well-marked hamada piste.

47 (348) N20° 24.6'W11° 45.3'
Leave Oued El Melga into dune field.

55 (340) N20° 21.2'W11° 46.1'
Exit dune field into sandy hamada.

Rachid and the oued. © José Brito

63 (332) N20° 17.5' W11° 44.9'
Zarga pass.

69 (326) N20° 16.4' W11° 42.2'
Ascent onto plateau.

75 (320) N20° 14.6' W11° 40.7'
Aoueloûl crater. Piste alternates between stony hamada and dune fields.

84 (311) N20° 10.5' W11° 38.2'
Exit of barchan field. Stony piste.

96 (299) N20° 08.6' W11° 32.8'
Exit of barchan field.

101 (294) N20° 07.8' W11° 30.2'
Sandy oued for 5km; N20° 05.7' W11° 27.4'

112 (283) N20° 04.6' W11° 25.7'
Leave daya, head up into a pass.

130 (265) N19° 56.5' W11° 24.7'
Waypoint; reg.

150 (245) N19° 49.4' W11°19.1'
Waypoint. Neolithic graves and remains of Gangara barns south of the piste.

176 (219) N19° 42.4' W11° 09.5'
Waypoint; sandy area.

180 (215) N19° 41.5' W11° 07.8'
Leave sandy area.

202 (193) N19° 32.3' W11° 02.7'
Beginning of reg.

220 (175) N19° 25.7' W11° 58.5'
Contour of hamada. Dune fields ahead

223 (172) N19° 24.4' W11° 58.7'
Dune fields.

228 (167) N19° 22.1' W11° 57.3'
End of dune fields.

265 (130) N19° 06.9' W11° 55.0'
Suzuki wreck.

300 (95) N19° 03.4' W11° 50.8'
Exit of Oued El Khatt into Oued Rachid. Piste now runs inside the oued.

320 (75) N18° 53.2' W11° 49.2'
Leave the Oued Rachid.

325 (50) N18° 52.7' W11° 49.2'
Piste climbs a steep dune to exit the oued. Guelta Taoujafet at the end of the oued.

335 (60) N18° 49.1' W11° 46.7'
Agnânâ wells. Piste runs in Oued Rachid.

365 (30) N18° 41.7' W11° 37.7'
Reg.

372 (23) N18° 39.5' W11° 35.3'
Leave Oued Tidjikja.

395 (0) N18° 32.8' W11° 26.2'
Beginning of paved road. Tidjikja and fuel station on the left 2km down the road.

R11 TIDJIKJA → NEMA [805km]

November 2003; Nissan Patrol 2.8D and Opel Monterey 3.1D (José Brito)

Description

This route follows the ancient caravan piste connecting Tidjikja with the remote villages of Tichit and distant Oualata. To cross this isolated region, the piste uses a west–east orientated escarpment of the Dhar Tichit which separates the Majabat al-Koubra from the Aouker sand sea. Highlights include the rock formations of Le Khcheb (KM142), Makhrougat (KM405), Mhassai (KM407) and Es Sba (KM420, some with Neolithic engravings), the Dreiss gorges (KM193), a Neolithic village near Akrejit (KM322) and of course the UNESCO World Heritage villages of Tichit and Oualata.

The piste heads mostly east until Oualata, where it turns south to reach Nema. Mostly the piste runs close to the escarpment, alternating between the northern and southern faces, to avoid the large sandier areas to the north and south. However, in some places the escarpment is interrupted and the piste crosses large sandy areas. The most extensive is located between KM420 and KM458, where the sands of the Majabat al-Koubra spill into the Aouker basin.

Although it's easy to reach Tichit from Tidjikja, and Oualata from Nema, the bit between Tichit and Oualata is not for beginners as it crosses a remote region with no marked piste. A minimum of two sound vehicles, better still three, navigation instruments and maps, plenty of water and fuel are advisable. If you feel unsure, hiring a guide in Tidjikja or Tichit is advisable. Otherwise you may find your face buried in the GPS much of the time.

Route-finding and markers

Between Tidjikja and Tichit the piste is marked with red/white stakes. After Tichit, the piste becomes less clear and between Es Sba (KM420) and the beginning of the Oualata scarp (KM458) there is no piste. Towards Oualata the piste becomes progressively clearer with cairns on the hamadas. Between Oualata and Nema the piste is clear again and marked with white reflector stakes.

Fuel

Tidjikja and Nema.

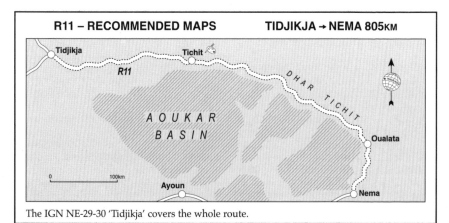

The IGN NE-29-30 'Tidjikja' covers the whole route.

Water
Tidjikja, Tichit, Oualata, Nema and from several wells along the piste (Zig, Touijinet, Aratane).

Traffic
This is a very remote piste so do not count on any traffic between Tichit and Oualata, except for other tourists. Between Tidjikja and Tichit and between Nema and Oualata bush taxis operate regularly.

Driving
This piste is very sandy most of the time so reduce tyre pressures. Nevertheless, some rocky sections, especially after KM480, will force you to re-inflate. There are several steep sandy and rocky ascents and descents, the former requiring a good run up. Between Tidjikja and Tichit there are deep sand ruts and you should beware of sand-covered rocks in the middle of the piste. The sandier areas include the Foum el Boueir (KM223), the approach to Tichit (between KM256 and KM283), between KM582 and KM602, and the approach to Oualata (after KM685). In the larger sandy area between KM420 and KM458 it's necessary to assess the safe passages on foot as there are several giant holes (*aklés*). Recovering the car from such a hole would be very difficult.

Suggested duration
Eight days, with time to visit the several rock formations and the villages of Oualata and Tichit.

NOTE: During the first 40km we were on an older piste following old GPS coordinates. The correct exit from Tidjikja should be a little more to the north.

0km (805)   N18° 32.8' W11° 25.5'
Tidjikja. Beginning of the piste through a sandy oued and agriculture fields.

5 (800)   N18° 30.8' W11° 24.6'
Leave the oued. Piste turns SE.

9 (796)   N18° 28.9' W11° 23.0'
Cross the Oued Tidjikja.

15 (790)   N18° 26.2' W11° 21.9'
Piste diverges. Follow left track uphill.

20 (785)   N18° 24.4' W11° 20.1'
End of hamada. Piste alternates between hamada and sandy areas.

28 (777)   N18° 21.4' W11° 16.9'
Piste turns E.

73 (732)   N18° 21.5' W11° 08.6'
Waypoint.

83 (722)   N18° 20.9' W11° 04.2'
Waypoint.

92 (713)   N18° 23.4' W11° 00.2'
Small house on the left. Piste heads north to avoid the escarpment and becomes less well marked.

114 (691)   N18° 25.4' W10° 51.9'
Waypoint.

121 (684)   N18° 27.4' W10° 48.9'
Nomad encampment. Head E.

142 (663)   N18° 27.7' W10° 37.7'
Rock formations.

156 (649)   N18° 30.8' W10° 30.6'
Le Khcheb wells heading N, but afterwards heading E.

168 (637)   N18° 30.8' W10° 25.6'
Piste heads N and afterwards E across a stony area.

177 (628)   N18° 33.5' W10° 22.0'
Descent into a sandy area.

193 (612)   **N18° 31.8'   W10° 15.5'**
Piste heads SW. You may leave the piste at this point to visit the Dreiss Gorge.

206 (599)   **N18° 32.4'   W10° 09.5'**
Sandy area.

223 (582)   **N18° 36.1'   W10° 01.0'**
Sandy area with some difficult sections.

247 (558)   **N18° 35.2'   W09° 48.9'**
Beginning of the Tichit escarpment. Zig wells on the right in the base of the scarp. Piste heads SE.

256 (549)   **N18° 33.0'   W09° 44.7'**
Very sandy section.

277 (528)   **N18° 29.1'   W09° 34.2'**
Piste very sandy but well marked.

283 (522)   **N18° 28.2'   W09° 31.2'**
End of sandy area.

287 (518)   **N18° 26.7'   W09° 29.9'**
Entering Tichit.

289 (516)   **N18° 26.2'   W09° 29.7'**
Leaving Tichit. Fast piste running along the southern face of the escarpment in a dry salt lake.

302 (503)   **N18° 23.2'   W09° 21.5'**
Enter a small dune area and afterwards an extensive chott.

317 (488)   **N18° 20.0'   W09° 13.7'**
Reg. Head NE to avoid dune fields to the SE.

322 (483)   **N18° 21.0'   W09° 11.3'**
Exit of Akrejit village heading towards a pass in the escarpment.

332 (473)   **N18° 21.4'   W09° 06.9'**
Sandy piste with small sebhka at north.

344 (461)   **N18° 22.7'   W09° 00.5'**
Small pass into plain between scarps.

347 (458)   **N18° 22.9'   W08° 58.7'**
Piste diverges inside dune field. Head SE.

348 (457)   **N18° 22.6'   W08° 58.6'**
Piste heads SSW in a very sandy area.

354 (451)   **N18° 20.3'   W08° 57.1'**
Touijinet wells and diatomite field. Piste heads ESE.

361 (444)   **N18° 20.2'   W08° 54.3'**
Pass between rock formations. Piste heads NE into sandy area along the escarpment.

371 (434)   **N18° 24.9'   W08° 51.3'**
Large sandy area. Piste turns E.

383 (422)   **N18° 23.8'   W08° 45.5'**
Large sandy area with some ascents. Piste heads SE.

395 (410)   **N18° 23.9'   W08° 39.3'**
Dune fields ahead. Piste remains very sandy heading E. Great sandy descent near next waypoint.

399 (401)   **N18° 24.4'   W08° 37.3'**
Piste remains sandy heading E towards Guelb Makhrougat. Several sandy ascents and descents.

405 (400)   **N18° 23.7'   W08° 34.5'**
Leave the Guelb to the south between a small rock outcrop. Piste heads SE.

407 (398)   **N18° 23.4'   W08° 33.2'**
Guelb Mhassai. Piste less well marked, heads ESE.

411 (394)   **N18° 22.9'   W08° 31.2'**
Aratane wells. Piste less well marked. Head N for about 1km and then E to avoid the hamada E of the wells.

415 (390)   **N18° 22.7'   W08° 28.6'**
Waypoint.

420 (385)   **N18° 21.1'   W08° 27.9'**
Es Sba rock formations on the left. From this point forward there is no piste. Until KM458 waypoints are given for guidance only.

422 (383)   **N18° 20.4'   W08° 27.2'**
Waypoint. Head E.

428 (377)   **N18° 20.4'   W08° 26.2'**
Waypoint. Head E.

431 (374)   **N18° 21.0'   W08° 24.6'**
Waypoint. Head NE.

436 (369) N18° 20.9' W08° 21.6'
Leave dune field but more ahead. Head E.

445 (360) N18° 21.8' W08° 17.2'
Sandy area. Head E.

452 (353) N18° 23.4' W08° 13.5'
Exit of sandy area into reg. Head E.

456 (349) N18° 23.3' W08° 11.8'
Exit of reg into small dune field. Head E.

458 (347) N18° 22.7' W08° 10.5'
Piste now clearly visible. Exit of dune field into reg. Small dunes ahead may cover the main piste.

470 (335) N18° 19.4' W08° 06.0'
Piste clearly visible heading S over a sandy hamada.

484 (321) N18° 13.6' W08° 05.6'
Waypoint. Head SW.

487 (318) N18° 12.6' W08° 07.5'
Stony piste over a black hamada.

491 (314) N18° 10.9' W08° 08.8'
Piste remains stony now heading SSE.

497 (308) N18° 09.7' W08° 05.9'
Piste progressively sandier heading E.

498 (307) N18° 09.3' W08° 05.6'
Sandy piste.

500 (305) N18° 08.7'W08° 05.7'
Very sandy ascent up Enji pass.

508 (297) N18° 06.8'W08° 02.0'
Point in piste. Head SE.

513 (292) N18° 06.2'W08° 00.2'
Sandy descent from plateau. Piste heads SW.

526 (279) N17° 59.8'W08° 02.0'
Sandy plain with small rocks.

535 (270) N17° 57.9'W07° 57.5'
Piste diverges to cross a oued.

548 (257) N17° 51.4'W07° 55.2'
Piste visible and marked with stone cairns over hamada. Oujaf

wells to the south with water at 3m.

559 (246) N17° 49.1' W07° 50.7'
Stone cairn. Piste heads SE.

571 (234) N17° 46.5' W07° 44.0'
Exit of hamada into dune field. Contour round the escarpment by the south.

578 (227) N17° 46.8' W07° 41.0'
Exit of dune fields into hamada. Piste well marked heading E.

582 (223) N17° 46.9' W07° 37.8'
Barchan field. Until KM602 the piste is frequently covered by the moving dunes.

583 (222) N17° 46.9' W07° 37.3'
Exit of barchan field into hamada corridor. Piste clearly visible.

588 (217) N17° 44.8' W07° 36.0'
Barchan field ahead. Contour by SSW and then head SE.

595 (210) N17° 42.7' W07° 34.2'
Neolithic vestiges in hamada surrounded by barchan fields.

599 (206) N17° 42.9' W07° 32.5'
Head ENE to contour barchan field.

602 (203) N17° 42.9' W07° 31.3'
Piste now clearly visible heading SE.

610 (195) N17° 39.3' W07° 28.4'
Reg. Heading S.

Sandy going below the Dahr Tichit. © José Brito

624 (181)   N17° 32.7'   W07° 26.9'
Hamada alternating with sandy oueds.

635 (171)   N17° 27.6'   W07° 25.6'
Fast and well-marked piste with some
sandy sections.

650 (155)   N17° 24.4'   W07° 18.7'
Fast and well-marked piste heading ESE
between two escarpments.

660 (145)   N17° 24.4'   W07° 13.2'
Fast and well-marked piste heading SE.

679 (126)   N17° 17.4'   W07° 07.1'
Fast and well-marked piste
heading SE. Nsara wells to the
south.

685 (120) N17°17.4' W07° 3.7'
Pass. Until Oualata the piste is
very sandy.

689 (116) N17°17.6' W07° 01.6'
Oualata. For Nema head SW.

692 (113) N17°16.4' W07° 3.5'
Exit of sandy area. Shortcut
from Tichit joins from right.
Piste well marked.

707 (98) N17°11.9' W07° 7.6'
Fast and well-marked piste
with some sandy sections.

728 (77)   N17° 08.1' W07° 18.0'
Piste well marked, heading SW.

748 (57)   N17° 00.4'   W07° 23.4'
Piste well marked, heading SW.

765 (40)   N16°52.9'   W07° 27.4'
Piste well marked, heading SW.

782 (23)   N16°44.8'   W07° 24.4'
Piste well marked, heading SE.

805 (0)   N16°36.7'   W07° 15.4'
Nema. Beginning of paved road.

Traditional bas-relief doorway decor at Oualata. © José Brito

R12 MOUDJERIA → GUELTA MATMATA (excursion)   [49KM]
November 2003; Nissan Patrol 2.8D and Opel Monterey 3.1D (José Brito)

Description
This piste allows the exploration of the Guelta Matmata and the observation
of relict Nile crocodiles, isolated from their counterparts in sub-Saharan
Africa. Testimony to the time when the Sahara was much less arid, they are
now trapped in several gueltas in the Tagant, Assaba and Affalé massifs.
Extinct in the Algerian Tassili N'Ajjer since 1924 and the Moroccan Oued Draa
since the 1950s, there are also isolated populations of the Ennedi Mountains of
Chad. The isolation of these very small populations threatens their long-term
survival. For this reason, one should approach the guelta in silence, both to
improve your chance of observing these shy animals and to respect their vulnerability.

    The piste leaves the paved road between Moudjeria and Tidjikja and cir-
cumvents the basin of the Tamourt en Na'aj via the north. Rainy season access
may be limited. Apparently there is another piste on the top of the scarp,
allowing the observation of the crocodiles from above. This option should be

used if visiting the guelta during the rainy season.

Route-finding and markers
The piste is clearly visible all the time, although there are few markers.

Fuel
Sangarafa and Tidjikja. Local traders might sell you fuel in Moudjeria.

Water
Moudjeria.

Matmata guelta. © José Brito

Traffic
Bush taxis and tourist operators regularly run this piste.

Driving
Fairly easy. The first and last kilometres are relatively sandy, but deflating the tyres slightly should ease the task. At KM4 you may head directly to the guelta; however, after rainfall this area could be flooded.

Suggested duration
One day, with time to visit the guelta.

0km (49)   **N17° 58.2'** **N12° 14.6'**
N'Beika. End of paved road.

1 (48)   **N17° 58.'0** **N12° 14.0'**
Top of dunes. Tamourt en Na'aj extending to the south.

3 (46)   **N17° 57.9'** **N12° 12.9'**
Point in piste.

4 (45)   **N17° 58.4'** **N12° 12.4'**
Piste splits. Head E directly to Matmata or contour the Tamourt by the NE.

7 (42)   **N17° 58.8'** **N12° 11.2'**
Point in piste.

12 (37)   **N17° 57.5'** **N12° 09.1'**
Point in piste.

16 (33)   **N17° 55.7'** **N12° 08.0'**
Point in piste.

19 (30)   **N17° 54.2'** **N12° 07.6'**
Dar Essala-ma village.

20 (29)   **N17° 53.8'** **N12° 07.6'**
Entering the oued. Head SE to the guelta.

21 (28)   **N17° 53.3'** **N12° 06.8'**
Leave the car at this point to visit the guelta.

25 (24)   **N17° 53.6'** **N12° 08.6'**
Point inside the oued. Head W.

29 (20)   **N17° 53.8'** **N12° 10.8'**
Crossroads in sandy area. From this point you may explore the Oued Bouragga (N17° 51.4' W12° 11.9').

31 (18)   **N17° 54.3'** **N12° 11.4'**
Piste well marked but sandy.

36 (13)   **N17° 55.1'** **N12° 12.9'**
Point in piste.

49 (0)   **N17° 56.5'** **N12° 15.5'**
Reach the road. Moudjeria to the left.

Algeria

Before the troubles of the early 1990s, Algeria was the favourite destination of many desert travellers. Without the complication and expense of actually crossing the Sahara, you could travel far and wide around the world's tenth largest country (the second largest in Africa after Sudan), safely and without compulsory guides or other restrictions. Not only this, but the Algerian Sahara was full of interest: a mixture of big ergs, high mountains, broad plateaux and ancient or colonial history which, with a still-thriving nomadic culture, all provided a rich backdrop without the need to cover vast distances.

Independent desert tourism began to recover in 1999; yearly visitor numbers increased and organised tour operators followed their lead. Then, again, the whole scene crashed overnight following the mass abductions of 2003 (see p.362). Since that time independent travellers have required an accompanying guide from border to border. But even if this rule persists, and provided the abductions prove to have been an aberration with desert security returning to former levels, Algeria still has it all. In no other Saharan country can you see just about everything the desert has to offer.

People still worry about Algeria's bad reputation for civil unrest. But this was always an exclusively northern problem, is less bad than it used to be, and is easily avoidable by entering via Tunisia.

Access and security

The ferries from southern Europe to Algeria are rarely used and the **Moroccan** border posts at Oujda or Figuig have been closed since the mid-1990s. Instead, travellers coming from Europe ferry to **Tunis** and use the road from Nefta in Tunisia to El Oued as the main entry point. The border at Tabel Larbi is

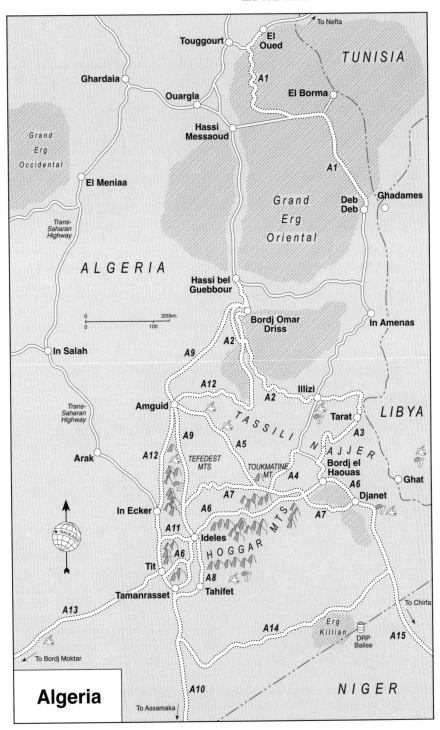

Algeria

Approaching the spur of Erg Tifernine (A12, KM691).

straightforward: the same entry card, customs declaration, driving permit, money change and insurance procedures as Tunis port, with no funny business and forms still in French (as opposed to Arabic-only in Libya). For the latest news on security, access and entry regulations see the 'Algeria' page on the website.

From the south the only viable entry is from **Niger**, either via Assamaka or less conventionally via Chirfa. Entry from **Libya** is only possible from Ghat to Djanet (though not in reverse) while Ghadames to Deb Deb is still not possible (for non-Africans at least.)

Coming up from Mauritania along pistes (rather than cross country through the Erg Chech) has not been done for decades, partly because of the still-sensitive Polisario area in far northern Mauritania and around Tindouf in Algeria. Access from Mali up the Tanezrouft is also rarely used because of the perceived risks in northern Mali.

Although people have managed it recently without incident, venturing too far north of Ghardaia in Algeria may put you at risk, and although things will eventually improve, as things stand it is not recommended.

Also, on the pistes west of the Trans-Sahara Highway (the Tanezrouft), and along the highway itself between El Golea and Tamanrasset there may still be a small risk of banditry or unwanted smuggler encounters. Joining a military convoy may be advisable if not compulsory along the Trans-Sahara Highway (TSH) between El Meniaa and In Ecker (with a time-consuming changeover at In Salah).

The road network in the south

It is possible to drive on tarmac (if not always smooth, unbroken tarmac) all the way from the Tunisian border down to Djanet, Tamanrasset (the TSH) and Reggane from where Algeria's three main trans-Sahara routes lead south into Niger and Mali. These drives in themselves are impressive, particularly the TSH south of Arak and the spectacular drive from Illizi to Djanet – probably the finest in the Sahara. Even then distances between **fuel stops** can be up to 400km, something to consider.

Going down to Djanet, across to Tamanrasset and back up north is the classic tour of Algeria: a great introduction to this country's desert. Inside that triangle – the south-east of the country – is where the best of Algeria's (if not the Sahara's) scenery is to be found and it's no coincidence that most of the following routes are located there. West of the TSH things get a bit flatter, although the Adrar Ahnet west of Arak and Tin Rerhoh escarpment southwest of Tam are also worth exploring if you get through all the routes below.

Despite nearly three decades of work the **TSH** south of Tam still has a couple of hundred kilometres to go before a sealed roads runs all the way from Algiers to In Guezzam on the Niger border. And with no plans for Niger to seal their section, it looks like Mauritania will be first to complete a sealed road across the Sahara. But the Hoggar will always remain the classic desert route through the heart of the Sahara, providing an impression of the desert's magnitude and diversity that the Atlantic Route cannot match.

Maps

To do all the Algeria routes in this book, the readily available IGN 1 millions (chiefly the 'In Salah', 'Djanet', 'In Azaoua' and 'Tamanrasset' sheets) along with the half-million TPC H3-D and a Michelin 741 are all you'll need.

If you want (or are permitted) to get radical, the detailed IGN 200,000s can reveal some interesting, long-forgotten colonial routes on the plateaux.

A1 EL OUED ➜ DEB DEB (via the Grand Erg Oriental) [668km]
March 2002; Toyota HJ61, HDJ80 auto and Defender Tdi

Description

Once you turn off the road and get to KM37.5, well-formed tracks should lead most of the way to the well at KM70, skirting the white patch indicated on the NI-32 map. From this well onwards there were no tracks on the tussock-covered sands and clusters of small dunes.

One highlight is that you'll encounter groups of Chaamba nomads watering their herds around the wells. The northern Grand Erg gets more rain and so vegetation which supports their lifestyle. If you've encountered Tuareg before, you may find these Arab 'bedouins' rather more taciturn and less touristified.

The following highway section gives you a break until you get to the dune-covered section south of Sif Fatimah; they were clearing it in 2002 but they've been doing that for years – it's an ongoing task. You'll also see some huge dunes here, right by the roadside. One often reads that Namibia has the world's biggest dunes at Sossusvlei; they clearly have not seen the Grand Erg.

If you have an appetite for more dune driving when you get to the highway at KM260, it's possible to continue south through the Grand Erg all the way to Hassi bel Guebbour at a bearing of more or less 190° (at least another 300km from KM260). A scan of IGN 1:200,000 maps and even the 1:1 million NH-32 shows regular dune ridges to cross, followed by widening gassis.

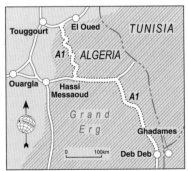

**A1 – RECOMMENDED MAPS
EL OUED ➜ DEB DEB 668km**

Although the 200,000 IGNs can be eye-opening, these maps don't depict the small dunes so the readily available IGN 1:1m 'Sfax NI-32' and 'Hassi Messaoud NH-32' will suffice to establish relative positioning. Once on the road the 741 will do.

Route-finding and markers

Once the tarmac ends there should be tracks up to KM70, but unless plenty of tourists have been through recently, from here on these will fade out after strong winds, and there are no other markers. Through the Erg from KM70 to KM260 this is effectively a cross-country route, although you'll encounter clear tracks on very occasional gravel pans which are as good a landmark as you get out here. Soon after the next well at KM179 the dunes get bigger and become more aligned which makes navigating and driving a bit easier (or maybe you just get used to it).

In between, the problem with route-finding lies with the low, flat terrain; the only time you can get a good look around (and often see where you *should* have gone) is when you're stuck near the summit of a dune cluster. So don't necessar-

The tricky dune pass at KM231.

ily drive directly from one GPS point to another – look at the big picture to work your way through. In general you're trying to keep on the flatter sandy tussock areas and only enter the less vegetated dunes where necessary, even if this means winding around. Up to KM260 this route is hard driving and route-finding, and should not be considered a short cut to In Amenas.

Fuel El Oued, a few villages along the highway before the turn-off, and Deb Deb. Expect maximum fuel consumption up to KM260; typically 5kpl in a diesel. If you're low on fuel at this point, Hassi Messaoud is just 110km west, Deb Deb is over 400km.

Water Fuel stations and villages on the El Oued highway, wells at KM70, KM81 and KM179 in the Erg, roadhouses along the El Borma road and at the checkpoint, and Sif Fatimah, south of the junction.

Traffic Expect none in the dunes, regular traffic on the El Borma road and 4WD taxis south of the KM351 junction.

Driving

Don't assume this is an ideal first piste in Algeria just because it's near the Tunisian border; it's not for beginners. This route has to traverse many small dune formations that are hard on vehicles and the lead driver. Until you're less than 100km from the El Borma road, these dunes are irritating rather than impressive, and in a car you'll be in second gear for two days.

Another problem with small dunes is that if you blow it, there's often not enough space or time to work it out. As a rule try and keep moving on the high ground, even if this means 'wall of deathing' around the rim of a vortex to maintain momentum (see p.190). And of course, **recce on foot if you're not sure**. You may as well keep your tyres deflated all the way to the El Borma road and just drive gently through the non-sandy patches. Just when you think it's all over, south of the junction at KM351 you'll have to work your way around a 30-kilometre stretch of tarmac buried by sand, but at least the surroundings are now impressive.

It's hard to recommend doing this route on a bike unless you feel like a good workout, although the contiguous section through the Erg to Hassi bel Guebbour may be more satisfying as the dune/corridor formations are reportedly more defined.

Suggested duration

Three days. Long enough to get dune driving out of your system.

0km (668)   **N33° 21.0' E06° 49.7'**
El Oued fuel station, west side.

21 (647) Minounsa village (fuel).

26.5 (641.5)   **N33 °10.1' E06° 41.0'**
Turn off S onto tarmac with buildings.

29 (639)
Pass through a village and continue along the tarmac road with pylons on the right.

33 (635)
Sign. Fork left with buildings on right.

37.5 (630.5)   **N33° 05.0' E06° 43.3'**
Junction. End of tarmac. Reduce tyre pressures, turn right to follow southbound tracks over low dunes.

41 (627)   **N33° 03.3' E06° 42.4'**
Tracks turn sharply west out of the low dunes towards a tussock-filled 'valley' about 2.5km away, where it resumes its southern course.

44 (624)   **N33° 03.3' E06°41.0'**
Track passes close to a couple of palm trees on the right. Heading S.

53 (615)   **N32° 58.9' E06° 39.5'**
Track now turns SSE.

63 (605)   **N32° 55.0' E06° 43.8'**
Twin palms in a dip and soon, an old tyre.

70 (598)   **N32° 52.9' E06° 45.6'**
Follow tracks directly east for 500m to reach a sign 'Thelth el Biar' and the well (N32° 53.0' E06°45.7').

Leave the well to the south, crossing an east–west track not shown on maps and head into the dunes and tussocks.

81 (587)   **N32° 47.2' E06° 45.6'**
Another well.

89 (579)   **N32° 43.3' E06° 47.5'**
Cross a track (as on the NI-32 map) marked by a tripod structure nearby.

95 (573)   **N32° 40.2' E06° 47.2'**
Waypoint. Continue south over low dunes, tussocks and the occasional gravel patch with visible tracks.

115 (553)   **N32° 31.7' E06° 49.9'**
Cross a dead-straight track and another, 1km later, before reaching a stony section.

117 (551)   **N32° 30.9' E06° 50.8'**
Tracks head south over gravelly surface.

119 (549)   **N32° 29.7' E06° 50.7'**
Large dunes dead ahead. Go round the east side, crossing a band of dunes around N32° 27.8' E06° 51.2'.

125 (543)   **N32° 27.1' E06° 51.8'**
Dark, gravelly terrain with clear southbound tracks visible 500m ahead and lasting around 500m, then back onto sand with other gravel patches further on.

139 (529)   **N32° 21.1' E06° 53.9'**
Gravelly surface.

143 (525)   **N32° 19.3' E06° 55.2'**
Exit a band of dunes onto a flat gravel surface and then into more dunes.

152 (516)   **N32° 16.0' E06° 57.2'**
Aim for this flat area and not the dunes to the west.

156 (512)   **N32° 14.1' E06° 57.7'**
Corridor between dunes.

161 (507)   **N32° 11.8' E06° 58.4'**
A large area of gravel with clear tracks.

162 (506)   **N32° 11.1' E06° 58.7'**
A point to aim for after a small dune crossing. Flat area ahead.

165 (503)   **N32° 09.5' E06° 59.5'**
Another stretch of gravel with clear straight tracks which end at N32° 08.0' E07° 00.6' just as you cross E07°. Dunes ahead: N32° 06.9' E07° 01.6' is a point in the dunes; at N32° 06.7' E07° 01.8' you exit the dunes onto gravel and at...

174 (494)   **N32° 05.8' E07° 02.5'**
...you enter dunes again and leave them at N32° 05.5' E07° 02.7'.

179 (489)   **N32° 03.6' E07° 02.8'**
A well surrounded by low dunes, followed by occasional gravelly patches, such as at N32° 01.3' E07° 03.7'. From this point the dunes are getting larger and more clearly formed into wide tussocky gassis and ridges.

187 (481)   **N32° 00.0' E07° 04.0'**
Waypoint at N32° among tussocks between patches of gravel. High dunes to the SSW.

193 (475)   **N31° 56.5' E07° 04.2'**
Into high dunes along a tussocky corridor. Aim for N31° 54.4' E07° 05.1' across the dunes. No evidence of the red track as marked on the 741 and NH-32 maps.

202 (466)   **N31° 52.3' E07° 04.6'**
Tussocky waypoint with dunes E and W.

208 (460)   **N31° 49.7' E07° 00.0'**
Tussocks after a 500m patch of dunes.

212 (456)   **N31° 47.6' E07° 07.5'**
Enter dunes again.

216 (452)   **N31° 45.7' E07° 08.6'**
Corridor with big dunes ahead and to SW.

218 (450)   **N31° 44.8' E07° 09.0'**
In the dunes. To exit, wind right, then left and aim for N31° 44.6' E07° 08.9'.

221 (447)   **N31° 43.4' E07° 09.1'**
Guess what: on a tussocky plain with big dunes to either side.

227 (441)   **N31° 40.5' E07° 09.1'**
Out of dunes heading towards a wide bushy corridor with big dunes on all horizons.

231 (437)   **N31 °39.1' E07° 10.8'**
Waypoint in front of an impressive, large star dune. A tricky dune passage begins nearby at N31° 38.5' E07° 11.2'. Wind around their bases.

235 (433)   **N31° 37.2' E07° 11.5'**
Waypoint among sandy hillocks. Head for N31° 35.4' E07° 11.7'.

241 (427)   **N31° 34.6' E07° 12.5'**
Small gravel pan in a corridor among dunes. Wind through for 2km towards N31° 33.7' E07° 12.3' and then N31° 33.1' E07°12.1', a gravel patch with tracks.

247 (421)   **N31° 31.4' E07° 11.1'**
Aim for this point to work your way over a dune ridge.

248 (420)   **N31° 31.3' E07° 11.0'**
Over the dunes. Sheltered camping spots.

252 (416)   **N31° 29.9' E07° 10.0'**
Waypoint as you near the road. Less vegetation around now.

256 (412)   **N31° 28.4' E07° 09.1'**
Cross a new piste which runs NW/SE. There is one more dune ridge to work your way over before the road.

260 (408)   **N31° 26.6' E07° 08.6'**
Hassi Messaoud–El Borma road and pipeline. Turn east. Several low dune banks lie over the road which winds through high dunes.

351 (317)
Junction. Turn south for Deb Deb. After the military checkpoint at Rebba and the Sif Fatimah well, there's a 30km stretch where in places the tarmac is inundated by sand. Afterwards you'll pass monumentally impressive dunes.

668 (0)
Small border town of Deb Deb. Turn right for the fuel station and In Amenas.

A2 HASSI BEL GUEBBOUR → ILLIZI   [470KM]

January 2003; three Honda XR650Ls

Description

This route has all the ingredients of the perfect first Algerian piste: some easy dune driving and navigation, easily-found wells, ruined forts and, on the eastward stage, an almost certain encounter with camel-mounted Tuareg.

There are two main ways of getting to Gara Khanfoussa: turning west at Quatre Chemins as indicated below (the truck route), or continuing down to Bordj Omar Driss and heading west along the foot of the escarpment (the latter stages of Route A12, at times very sandy). They join up anywhere around KM115 or so before heading down to the Gara Khanfoussa dune section.

Once out of the dunes a clear track leads into the valley, passing the wells of Tiskirine, Tabelbalet and Ain el Hadjadj right up to the small cordon of dunes at KM330. As the piste turns eastward, the most scenic part of the route commences with the rosy glow of the Erg Isaouane to the north, vegetated oueds to cruise through and the odd section of hamada and claypan leading to the outskirts of Illizi.

Route-finding and markers

There are virtually no balises on this popular and well-established route, but with a clear track most of the way route-finding is simple. Finding the beginning of the ramp leading into the dunes and Gara Khanfoussa is the only time you may need to use GPS. It's not unusual to get mixed up on this dune section by following misleading tracks (it happens to me every time, in both directions). Take your time, work it out on foot or with the TPC if necessary and don't take chances on steep dune short cuts; backtrack until you rejoin the main tracks which curve around all slip faces. If you're feeling adventurous, it's also possible to get to this point directly from Zaouia Sidi Moussa – a more serious dune route.

The small dune crossing at KM330 is much easier by comparison once you've worked it out on foot. East of here there's a clear track all the way to Illizi. Depending on which track you take you may hit the tarmac either just north-west of town or a few kilometres to the south. Either way, the twin 'RKO' radio towers alongside the fort are just south of the town centre.

Fuel

Hassi bel Guebbour (HbG), Illizi.

Water

As above (limited at HbG, but try the café for bottled water), plus the wells of Tiskirine, Tabelbalet and Ain el Hadjadj.

Traffic

As well as fellow tourists, you may encounter local Tuaregs further south.

**A2 – RECOMMENDED MAPS
HBG → ILLIZI 470KM**

The IGN 1:1m 'Djanet' sheet or the TPC H3-D cover just about all the route.

Driving

This route has it all and there was little hesitation in choosing it as an ideal location for filming *Desert Driving* (the DVD companion to this book, see p.168). The dune crossing around Gara Khanfoussa may sound intimidating, but it passes over rolling dunes, avoiding all crests. As you come out of the dunes heading south, there are a couple of sudden drop-offs right on the old track – drive round to the left or right, recce-ing on foot if necessary to get your speed just right.

Once you're out of the sands the piste through the Ain el Hadjadj valley can be rough when cut up by rains, but there's plenty of room to spread out. The KM330 dune crossing needs a moment's thought before diving in, but from here eastwards the driving is easy, apart from the steep ascent at KM436 which heavy vehicles (if they've got past KM330...) will have trouble ascending. There's an alternative way round a few kilometres to the south.

The only difficulty bike riders might have is keeping it nailed through the churned ruts of the Gara Khanfoussa section – keep an eye on oil and/or water temperatures. The sharp turns in the dunes at KM330 may be a bit tricky too but speeds are low. After that the subsequent 'twin-rut' riding through sandy oueds can be tiring. But, as with cars, this route is one of the best riding pistes in this book. Parts of it, including the infamous Oued Samene Canyon excursion (off this route), appear in the *Desert Riders* DVD.

Suggested duration

Two and a half days.

0km (470)   N28° 41.4' E06° 30.2'
Hassi bel Guebbour fuel station.

2.5 (467.5)
Hot springs behind the reeds just off the road, a popular local washing spot.

62 (408)   N28° 12.0' E06° 48.0'
Quatre Chemins checkpoint. Take the rough W route leading to the waypoint below, or reverse Route A12. Distances work out about the same but this route below is less sandy.

96 (374)   N28° 08.5' E06° 29.3'
Leave the track down a sandy gully heading S alongside the erg's edge, via N27° 53.1' E6° 28.9' to the next waypoint.

171 (299)   N27° 35.3' E06° 37.5'
Having passed a distant metal hut (N27° 39.2' E06° 33.7') and a balise, you see the ramp leading east into the dunes. Reduce tyre pressures, drive up and near the top turn S and follow the track winding SE and NE through the dunes.

190 (280)   N27° 34.5' E06° 46.3'
Gara Khanfoussa visible to the left. Head S along tracks leading through corridors.

197 (273)   N27° 31.7' E06° 47.3'
You're on the southern exit from the dunes. Watch out for the odd drop off, on the old track. Around KM210 you leave the sands (re-inflate) and find yourself on a clear stony track heading ENE and then SE into the valley.

221 (249)   N27° 25.1' E06° 51.8'
Hassi Tiskirine as marked on the Michelin 741. Good water at just a few metres.

234 (236)   N27° 19.4' E06° 54.8'
Hassi Tabelbalet well. Good water at just a few metres. Some old buildings and the ruins of a look-out on the hill behind you. Just before you get to Tabelbalet look out for the pre-Islamic tomb on the hill to the right. Trees offer shade but flies can be a nuisance in daylight. Nearby is a palm tree with a pool of water below it.

Continue along the track southwards between the erg and the jebel.

301 (169)   N26° 50.0'   E07° 15.2'
Ain el Hadjadj well. Good water. An old fort and other ruins and relics from the colonial era. On the ridge to the W you can see a piste which starts just N of here, crosses the Jebel Tahinaouine to A12. Continue S on a clear if rough track initially alongside the jebel.

330 (140)   N26° 36.7'   E07° 22.6'
The track crosses the Oued Samene and ends up facing a narrow band of dunes marked by a high dune to the left. Recce on foot, deflate your tyres and drive over in a series of switchbacks to the east side (N26° 36.3' E07° 23.0').

Now head E towards the tree platforms then turn N, passing more stumps (firewood). Soon you drive through the sandy ruts of a oued. From here on there's a clear track all the way to Illizi with occasional small dune bands and ranges to cross.

436 (34)   N26° 25.0'   E08° 10.1'
Unexpectedly steep ascent up a sand slope with rocks near the top. This point appears to be N of the IGN map's route (in the 'Mennkhour' region) and at other times I've ended up taking the old, more southerly route as the map depicts, avoiding this obstacle. Somewhere there must be a fork which I've yet to recognise but whichever track you end up taking, they all lead to Illizi.

442 (28)
Steep pass and another one 6km later. The terrain becomes more barren and rocky.

467 (3)
Water tower of Illizi visible as you pass through outlying villages. There are various ways of stumbling into Illizi. Once you hit a tarmac road it should guide you in one way or another. South of town is probably easiest: the twin radio towers of the fort on the SW edge of the main town being a good guide. Aim for these, turn a bend to the right with a distance sign on your left and at the T junction turn left for the town centre.

If reversing this route, leave the town towards Djanet to the S, take the tarmac side roads leading W, head south of the cairn hill a couple of kilometres out of town at N26° 26.2' E08° 25.3' and follow tracks W, not some which lead to dead ends SW.

470 (0)   N26° 30.0' E08° 28.3'
Illizi fuel station. The hotel Tabel Larbi is opposite and there's a good basic restaurant just down the road towards the fort.

A3 ILLIZI → BORDJ EL HAOUAS (via Tarat)   [382KM]
January 2003; Three Honda XR650Ls

Description
This is another classic Algerian route through the heart of the Tassili N'Ajjer; a great continuation of Route A2 and alternative to the sealed Fadnoun Highway (itself a spectacular drive). From Illizi it parallels the northern edge of the Tassili up to the Libyan border and then cuts south into the canyon of the Oued Tarat to the town of that name. From here the clear piste contours around the northernmost of the Tassili's south-facing scarps (the plateau is like a series of fallen-over books or dominoes: a gentle rise followed by a sudden drop down the escarpment, then another gentle rise...) until the Oued Imirhou. From here an extremely stony track runs south to the big oued at Dider, rejoining the highway just before Tin Taradjeli for one final drop-off to Bordj el Haouas. It is featured in the *Desert Riders* DVD.

Route-finding and markers
Clear tracks all the way. The only place we lost it was south of Tarat village up to KM172 (see text). At Imirhou junction take the south track to Dider as marked on most maps. It's possible to get mixed up with a newer track which

leads west to the Fadnoun Highway, joining it just below the big Gara Inhaja-n-Kli drop-off. It's not shown on even the 741 map, but it's the main access to Imirhou these days.

Fuel
Illizi and Bordj el Haouas.

Water
Towns at each end, Tarat, Imirhou, some pools around KM324 and Dider.

Driving
Easy, apart from the bone-shaking section from Imirhou south to Dider.

Suggested duration
Two and a half days.

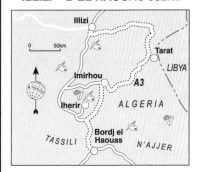

A3 – RECOMMENDED MAPS
ILLIZI → B'EL HAOUAS 382km

The IGN 1:1m 'Djanet' sheet or the TPC H3 -D (with slight misalignment) both cover the whole route.

0km (382)　　　N26° 30.0'　E08° 28.3'
Illizi fuel station. Drive S out of town.

7 (375)
Turn E onto a track. Pass the turn-off for Oued Djerat at KM15 and cross Oued Imirhou around KM38. (It's possible to get to Imirhou at KM261 via this canyon.)

98 (284)　　　N26° 24.0'　E09° 20.2'
Checkpoint close to the Libyan border. Just after turn S onto the rocks, following an old sanded-over track.

112 (270)
Descend into a canyon.

116 (266)
Sandy bottom of the canyon. Tracks lead out into a wide, flat valley.

133 (249)
Follow the valley onto the Tarat plain. Turn E at a crossroads marked with a cairn.

152 (230)　　　N26° 12.5'　E09° 23.3'
Tarat military base. Pass either side towards Tarat village a few kilometres to the S (N26° 08' W09 21').

172 (218)　　　N25° 59.2'　E09.14.3'
We got disorientated here: from the checkpoint we did not keep far enough W of the

oued (not the village/checkpoint side) Whatever, we rejoined the track at a concrete balise just as the track crosses the above waypoint. From here you're on a clear track curving along the base of the escarpment on your right.

253 (129)　　　N25° 43.6'　E08° 44.0'
Nice sheltered spot for a camp just before the descent into Imirhou village where the track gets a bit rougher.

261 (121)　　　N25° 45.5'　E08° 41.2'
Cross Oued Imirhou with a few huts just to the south. This does not feel like the main village which may be further north in the canyon (off this route).

264 (118)　　　N25° 45.8'　E08° 39.2'
Junction. The right turn presumably leads back to the Fadnoun plateau turn-off via Imirhou village. Carry straight on. The track soon becomes very rocky.

284 (98)　　　N25° 37.0'　E08° 35.0'
Twin cairns (see p.208).

316 (66)　　　N25° 22.2'　E08° 33.9'
Sandy descent, then in 2km you cross a oued and enter a narrow valley.

324 (58)　　　N25° 18.2'　E08° 31.1'
Possible pool as you come to the end of

the narrow valley. The track rises up the valley and with one final rocky ascent...

333 (49)   **N25° 14.8'   E08° 28.5'**
... you have the Dider plain before you.

334 (48)   **N25° 14.4'   E08° 28.4'**
Soon you come to a checkpoint. Follow the track erring right and then left to the Fadnoun road.

337 (45)   **N25° 13.3'   E08° 27.3'**
Rejoin Fadnoun road. Turn left for Bordj el Haouas, dropping down the impressive Tin Taradjeli Pass.

382 (0)
Bordj el Haouas fuel station on the Djanet side of the village.

A4 FADNOUN (AFARA) ➔ ROUTE A7   **[99KM]**
November 2002; Toyota HJ61.

Description
If heading south from Illizi, this is a marginally more direct way of getting to Tamanrasset (if that is your next destination), although it's more interesting for its access to the impressive Afara region leading to Tamadjert and the Erg Tihodaine. The first 25km of the route are by far the most impressive, as you descend steeply from the Fadnoun to the Monument Valley-like buttes north of the Afara plain.

A4 – RECOMMENDED MAPS
FADNOUN ➔ ROUTE A7 99KM

The TPC H3-D and IGN 1:1m 'Djanet' cover the route.

From here on, the track passes over a large basalt field and becomes tiresome as you get shaken about for hours, to join Route A7 near KM195. 'Borne' is 14km to the ESE if you want to take the regular Route A6 to Tam.

Route-finding and markers
This bulldozed rocky track is clear throughout its length.

Fuel
None on the route; the nearest fuel is at Illizi (177km north of the start) or Bordj el Haouas (110km east of 'Borne').

Water
No wells were located alongside the piste and the palm huts at Hassi Tirest appear to have fallen into disuse in the thirteen years since this route was first done.

Driving
The descent from the Fadnoun at KM20 is spectacular but is also very washed out and needs to be crawled down slowly to maintain ground clearance. Once at the bottom the piste leads to a boulder-filled defile which also requires care to spare the undercarriage. Although there are some sandy sections around KM11, it's worth keeping your tyres hard until the very stony sections are over at around KM23.

On a bike this first descent is wide enough to pick your own way down, although the boulder-filled defile may be tricky. For all vehicles, after these sections the going is merely rough and corrugated as you cross the basalt field.

Suggested duration
Half a day.

0km (99)   **N25° 22.7'**   **E08° 01.4'**
Large junction and some huts on the sealed Fadnoun road indicating 'Afara'. Turn south.

2.8 (96.2)
Sandy oued and some huts.

11 (88)
Pass through some impressive tassilis (outcrops, good camping) and soon through a low stony pass (N25° 16.5' E07° 57.1') where you wind through low rubbly hills to the west.

20 (79)   **N25° 14.0'**   **E07° 56.3'**
Abandoned cabins and other junk (shelter for camping). Very soon you pass a stone monument and then round a corner for the first steep descent. The first 100m or so are washed out but after that it gets easier as it drops into a valley.

22 (77)
Crawl through a narrow boulder-filled pass and out of a oued which can be trickier than the preceding descent.

25 (74)   **N25° 13.1'**   **E07° 54.4'**
Junction with the piste to Tamadjert to the north-west while the magnificent vista of isolated peaks you've been catching sight of intermittently now reveals itself to the north across the Afara plain. Carry straight on (west).

35 (64)
Junction as you descend to a stony plain. Carry straight on (SW).

46 (53)
A break from the stony going as you pass the abandoned encampment of Hassi Tirest.

57 (42)
A noticeably smooth patch as you head for In Touhoune mountain and then pass it to the west.

78 (21)
As you dog-leg around a hill you see the serrated ridge ending in Tazat mountain to the SE and the conical hills around Serouenout to the south.

87 (12)   **N24° 46.5'**   **E07° 39.4'**
A crossroads (almost correct on the TPC) with the sand of the last few kilometres making for smoother going.

92 (7)   **N24° 44.1'**   **E07° 39.5'**
You have just descended a hill onto the desert floor. This is the key point to aim for if reversing this route.

98 (1)   **N24° 40.2'**   **E07° 39.0'**
A crossing of tracks with a white-quartz topped pile of stones on the east corner of the crossroads. It's easy to get confused with the many tracks here.

99 (0)   **N24° 40.2'**   **E07° 38.3'**
Re-erected balise in a tyre. This is KM195 of Route A7.

From here your options are: A7 west to the Tefedest, A5 taking the same direction north-west towards Amguid. Or you can turn east to Djanet or south-east to intercept Route A6, the main Tam piste via 'Borne' (N24° 35.2' E07° 47.7', see p.342).

A5 TOUKMATINE MOUNTAIN → AMGUID VALLEY [278KM]

November 2002; Toyota HJ61

Description

This route links the first half of Route A7 with the Igharghar valley where it meets Routes A9 and A12. It follows part of the old 1000-kilometre truck route which once supplied Djanet from In Salah or Hassi bel Guebbour until the Fadnoun road was completed in the late 1990s.

Leaving Route A7 at KM235, it follows the mass of still-surviving corrugations past the Toukmatine ridge, across the top of the Amadror plain and south of Erg Tihodaine to follow a valley beneath the edge of the Tassili to the Igharghar valley.

The route through this inselberg-dotted valley becomes rougher and more washed out than what's gone before (you wonder how the supply trucks managed) and overall the route is not a classic unless you take excursions to the north. You emerge at the twin prows of Tazeroukou about 25km south of Amguid.

Route-finding and markers

Apart from the corrugations and wrecked tyres, there are intermittent triangular-section balises – some still standing – along the route. We lost sight of these occasionally, following the braided corrugated tracks which developed over the years.

In the latter section the track is clearer although you should note that the orientation as shown on the NG-31 'In Salah' IGN has 'straightened out' south of the Erg Guidi, heading directly west to Tazeroukou. The TPC shows both routes (and of course every other goat track since the beginning of time). As it stands this route description is probably over detailed.

Fuel

None on route. Nearest sources are at Bordj el Haouas, Arak, Ideles or Hassi bel Guebbour.

Water

There are no wells on the route. In Ebegui is north of KM190 though water here is not confirmed. There is reliable water at Ain Kerma well, just south of Amguid (see Route A12, KM455).

Driving

Initially fast across the Amadror plain after which the route becomes slower over unmaintained sections to the Igharhar Valley. No problems for cars or bikes.

Suggested duration

One and a half days.

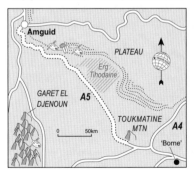

**A5 – RECOMMENDED MAPS
TOUKMATINE → AMGUID 278KM**

The TPC H3-D covers the whole route which is also on the 'Djanet' and 'In Salah' 1:1 million IGNs.

0km (278)   **N24° 45.4'   E07° 16.0'**
KM235 of Route A7. Tracks head directly
for a cone mountain (a slightly misaligned
'Peak 4730' on the TPC H3-D).

12.6 (265.4)   **N24° 46.3'   E07° 09.3'**
Pass a tree on your left with cone mountain to the S and Toukmatine ahead to the
right.

25 (253)
Pass a balise on your left and cross a oued
with Toukmatine right. Heading NW.

28 (250)   **N24° 49.5'   E07° 01.2'**
Balise.

40 (238)
Tyre.

57 (221)   **N25° 04.1'   E06° 52.9'**
Balise. Low dunes of the Erg Tihodaine
directly to the N now.

65 (213)
Sticker-covered balise with another a couple of kilometres later at N25° 06.9' E06°
50.6' near some bits of sheet metal. The
track then becomes rough from the
drainage.

75 (203)   **N25° 11.3'   E06° 49.7'**
Tyre over balise with some blue drums
soon after.

82 (196)
Balises with a track going left of the hills.

99 (179)   **N25° 22.4'   E06° 42.6'**
Fallen balise with a clear track leading to
a cone mountain.

110 (168)
Balise.

117 (161)
Cross Oued Tirhesoutine; cone mountain
ahead to right.

121 (157)   **N25° 30.8'   E06° 35.2'**
Tree in a oued, cone mountain to the right
and an escarpment beyond.

129 (149)
Gara Tindi visible to the NNW.

141 (137)   **N25° 37.4'   E06° 26.7'**
Tracks lead into a oued (cairn on the right;
some nice camping spots) and leave it in
5km (N25° 38.7' E6° 23.5').

165 (113)   **N25° 37.4'   E06° 26.7'**
After recrossing the oued the tracks wind
through low rocky hills. Gara Tindi is
ahead and a ribbon of erg is visible NW of
the mountain. You may encounter the
remains of a stone cobbled track.

174 (104)   **N25° 37.4'   E06° 26.7'**
Erg directly to the N.

179 (99)   **N25° 51.0'   E06° 11.7'**
A corrugated track in a oued between the
erg and Djebel Izzilatene.

186 (92)   **N25° 53.0'   E06° 09.2'**
Balise indicating 'AM 120' on a crest of the
stony track. Another balise 10km later.

210 (68)   **N25° 59.8'   E05° 58.4'**
Road sign and building (coincidentally
near the meeting of N26° and E06°?), still
on the built-up stony track.

231 (47)   **N26° 02.4'   E05° 48.6'**
Ruins, with the Tassili visible to the N.
The route now has clearly diverted from
the NG-32 map (but is in line with the
TPC).

252 (26)   **N26° 07.4'   E05° 35.8'**
Pass. Washed-out track. The edge of
Tazeroukou visible ahead.

255 (23)
Cross the shrubby Oued Tidbar.

268 (10)   **N26° 09.0'   E05° 27.5'**
Pass. White ridge running to the N.
Terrain gets a bit sandier.

278 (0)   **N26° 11.8'   E05° 22.2'**
Gap between two ridges. Tyre over rock.
A track heads W to intercept the Amguid
piste (A9, A12).
     From this point Amguid village (A12,
KM470) is around 20km and Amguid
crossroads (A9, KM350) is 25km. It's also
an easy cross-country drive SSW to the
TSH at Sidi Moulay Lahsene, passing
inselbergs like Sli Edrar on the way.

A6 DJANET → TAMANRASSET (via Assekrem) [676KM]
February 2003; Two Honda XR650L bikes

Description

This has long been the main route between Algeria's two southern towns, linking the Tassili with the Hoggar via the famous viewpoint at Assekrem. If you want to get between one place and the other without fuss or drama, this is the way to go. For a bit more adventure try the first section of A7 which hops over the Erg Admer and saves backtracking along the tarmac and Bordj el Haouas. It meets this route south-east of Tazat mountain.

Leave Djanet along the tarmac road to Bordj el Haouas. From Bordj head south, find the main corrugated track with the right orientation and then curve south-west around the distinctive peak of Tazat, crossing oueds which appear on the NG-32 map. About 100km from Bordj, at 'Borne' (as marked on the 741 map) or spot height '1094' (on the NG-32 map), tracks split at a stone monument. Routes A7 and later A5 head off to the north-west, but this route goes south-west.

On the way to Serouenout are some sandy stretches around the Oued Tafassasset and old car wrecks, with the now re-occupied fort at Serouenout appearing around KM300. West of the fort the piste turns south (as marked on the IGN NG-32 map) for a nice drive along oueds as the mass of Telertheba mountain rises ahead. A less interesting alternative route (not described) heads directly west from the fort.

West of Telertheba it's a fast drive until you near the Hoggar foothills where corrugations reappear as the tracks converge onto a single valley leading into the hills. This track then becomes very rough as it crosses a basalt boulder field close to Ideles. If you don't need fuel (supplies can be irregular

A6 – RECOMMENDED MAPS   DJANET → TAMANRASSET 676KM

Along with the TPC H3-D, the IGN 1:1 million NG-32 'Djanet' shows old alignments of tracks; the slightly newer NF-31 'Tamanrasset' shows the rest of the route.

here) pass the village to your right to KM502 (where Route A8 begins). A turn right sees you pass through the gardens in the oued and out of the south-west corner of Ideles village. A sandy and corrugated track at times follows the pylons to the village of Hirhafok, 30km from Ideles, where you turn left for Assekrem (or straight on to the Tam highway, Route A11).

Route-finding and markers

It's tarmac (and a spectacular drive) to Bordj el Haouas. Leaving Bordj to the south, the ridge to the west ending at Mt Tazat is a good landmark, and a clear cairned track and numerous alternatives continue to the 'Borne' with occasional cairns. At Borne a line of cairns leads SSW into the hills, to Serouenout and Tam. Once in the Hoggar, all routes are clear, if not necessarily easy.

Fuel

Djanet, Bordj el Haouas, Ideles (not guaranteed) and Tamanrasset.

Water

As above, plus Serouenout fort if you're desperate, Oued Tadjeret (deep) and Hoggar mountain villages.

Driving

The tarmac to Bordj may disappoint purists who in most cases will have already taken this route on the way into Djanet – they have the option of cutting through the Erg Admer; see Route A7. Other than that there are no real difficulties until you leave Hirhafok village and turn south for Assekrem. Count on around four hours in a car to cover the next 64km, much of it in low range and pushing your suspension to the limit. The track is deeply washed-out with countless deviations crawling steeply over banks and through the rubble. It's not quite as bad as it looks though.

On a fully-loaded bike this track is also a challenge and there will be difficult sections where you may feel safer walking the bike rather than risk having it fall on you. Harder still is the rarely-used western descent from Assekrem, and even the regular 'tourist' descent will take a few hours to Tam.

Suggested duration

Three days.

0km (676)   N24° 30.8' E09° 29.5'
Djanet south junction fuel station.

78 (598)   N24° 49.2' E08° 55.1'.
Oued Essendilene crosses the road. From here you can take an enjoyable excursion deep into the Tassili up the ever-narrowing canyon – for more details see p.638.

131 (545)
Bordj el Haouas (Tuareg name: Zaouatallaz). Fuel on the east side of town and a shop on the north side of the main street.

There is no sign showing the way to Tam; just leave the village to the south and err SSW with the jagged ridge to the west leading you to Mt Tazat (2165m) at its southern end. You may find the main cairn-lined track or you may not, it doesn't really matter.

222 (444)   N24° 32.1' E07° 58.4'
Waypoint. Flat reg with Tazat behind you to the NE.

241 (425)   N24° 35.2' E07° 47.7'
Stone monument 'Borne' marking the junction of pistes to Amguid and to Tam. A scrawled map shows the routes.

261 (415)   **N24° 29.9' E07° 43.6'**
Key point if you've been stumbling around after 'Borne'. Cairns appear and follow a oued into the hills and on to Serouenout fort.

279 (397)   **N24° 25.2' E07° 38.2'**
2CV wreck, with another couple of wrecks in sandy areas a kilometre further on. Follow the track which now turns more SW through the hills to the fort.

300 (376)   **N24° 18.3' E07° 28.3'**
Serouenout fort with a large cone mountain behind it. Checkpoint.

306 (370)   **N24° 18.5' E07° 24.6'**
Having passed the fort you now head WSW with a flat-topped rubble hill in front of you for the oued route to Mt Telertheba (2455m). Avoid the tracks heading NNW unless you want to take an alternative, slightly more direct (but less interesting) route to the west.

348 (328)   **N24° 10.6' E07° 04.0'**
Track turns northward (bearing 340°) along a oued.

358 (318   **N24° 15.6' E07° 01.0'**
A line of cairns leads north-west.

362 (314)
Track now turns west (260°) as indicated on the IGN and TPC maps.

389 (287)   **N24° 12.6' E06° 46.8'**
Pre-Islamic tomb on the side of the hill on the right. About 15km later you pass the graffiti-covered wreck of a VW bus (N24° 11.5' E06° 39.1').

413 (263) N24° 11.0' E06° 33.5'
Triangular Arabic sign pointing south which matches junctions indicated on the IGN and TPC maps. A few kilometres later you cross the Oued Amadror.

427 (249) N24° 10.6' E06° 25.4'
Having passed a double cairn across the track 3km earlier (N24° 11.1' E06° 27.1'), the

route to Ideles turns SW into the Djebel Tala Mellet.

476 (190)   **N23° 56.6' E06° 04.0'**
Pass a well (water at 15m) and a few palms on the left as you cross the Oued Tadjeret. The distinctive conical peak of Tadêraz (1778m) is visible ahead. Track soon begins to get very rough.

499 (177)
Ideles. Get fuel (N23° 49.0' E05° 56.2') or bypass the town on your right by following the pylons.

502 (174)   **N23° 47.2' E05° 55.9'**
Junction. Turn right and pass through the gardens in the oued and out the other side. When the track forks, keep left and follow the pylons SW out of town. Straight on at the junction leads to Tahifet (Route A8).

530 (146)   **N23° 39.3' E05° 45.7'**
Hirhafok village. For Assekrem turn south (left) at the metal stumps of the missing solar panels, pass a few houses and exit the village. (Straight through Hirhafok leads to near In Amguel and the highway to Tam, Route A11.)

After about 10km the track climbs steeply up off the plain – a taste of what lies ahead. Driving over the plateau, the first half is not so bad, and you pass the palmed guelta of Issakkarassene at around KM560. But up to and beyond the pass at Tin Teratimt (more or less KM580, not marked on most maps but a distinc-

Telertheba, on the way to Tam. © Mike Foster

tive ridge of rock spikes precedes it), you'll be crawling along in low range. A few kilometres after Tin Teratimt there is a mysterious turn-off to the right – ignore this and keep climbing until you get to the signed junction with the Tam–Assekrem piste (KM590) for the final 6km crawl up to the pass.

596 (80)
Assekrem (see box below). The regular route back to Tam returns to the junction and continues straight on, south, with some steep sections.

614 (62)   N23° 09.5'   E05° 43.4'
Big arches indicate the turn-off to the

guelta at Affilal (where you can camp).

647 (29)   N23° 00.9'   E06° 42.4'
Pylons join the main track from the right.

673 (3)
Having passed Iharene volcanic plug a few kilometres earlier, you reach the red and white radio tower on the NE edge of Tamanrasset. Soon the road joins the town's sealed ring road on its north-eastern side.

676 (0)   N22° 47.7'   E05° 31.1'
Tamanrasset central fuel station.

SUNSET AND SUNRISE AT ASSEKREM

No doubt about it, for better or for worse Assekrem is the Ayers Rock of the Sahara – a world-renowned tourist attraction that brings us in in our (relative) hordes. Is it worth it? Yes – you'll probably only be here once and you won't regret the effort.

Most people agree that sunrise is the more impressive event, but sunset over the volcanic plugs is no eyesore either. The steep path behind the lodge up to the plateau takes about 15 minutes of huffing and puffing. Apparently the best viewpoint is not by the chapel (in which you may want to catch your breath and sign the visitors' book) but a bit further west, five minutes past the radio

mast. Follow the crowds. Alternatively, contrary visitors may like to climb the hill on the *opposite* side of the pass up a less well-formed track. But don't tell everyone.

The Assekrem Experience comes at a small price. You have to pay 150D to park in the compound at the Pass, and you can spend the night in the lodge in shared rooms for 12,000D half-board. It's expensive of course and the Tuareg minstrelling may not aid an early night, but if you trek up onto the plateau half an hour before dawn, you and a few similarly bleary companions will be in for a treat.

Western descent from Assekrem

A more challenging but also more spectacular route from Assekrem to Tamanrasset (about four hours in a car, three on a bike) continues off the west side of the pass, passing a left turn (keep going straight, north) and then past the striking volcanic plug of Ilamane, after about 20km.

Right out of Assekrem (if the white gate to the west side of the car park is locked drive around the outside of the compound wall to the south) the rocks are steep and loose with drop-offs and gullies which must be driven over slowly. In fact, even though it is hard-going all the way to Ilmane you lose very little altitude, but from this point the track drops off steeply from the Atakor, passing a ruin on a bend.

The next difficulty is the unusually gravelly oued which leads to the village of Terhenanet (N23° 10.0' E05° 35.5'), 32km from Assekrem, via a couple of other smaller villages. Its consistency makes traction difficult, especially on a bike, and you'll have to air down after the rocks of the Atakor.

Leave Terhenanet to the right (north-east) at which point during our traverse the road had just been regraded following flooding (this deviation was done at the same time as A6), but don't expect it to last. At KM67 from Assekrem is another 'T'-named village with pylons. You then follow or cross more conventional oueds and occasional rock slabs until you near the squat volcanic plug of Ahegher, reaching the highway just south of the airport entrance at KM88 (N22° 49.9' E5° 27.5'). Tam is 8km down the road so the total distance from Djanet to Tam via this descent is 692km, and suspension that needs a holiday.

A7 DJANET → IDELES (via Amadror) [532km]
March 2002; Toyota HJ61, HDJ80 auto and Defender Tdi

Description
This is a satisfying alternative to the regular Route A6 from Djanet to Tam via Serouenout fort. It's not harder and barely longer, but if you've done A6 before, it's a bit more interesting and pleasingly remote. Highlights include the cross-country sections after Erg Admer and across the Amadror plain, and the two lovely passes at KM132 and KM357, followed by the run to Ideles.

Leave the Djanet–Bordj el Haouas road as indicated below, and head into the erg. Once on the south side, head cross-country for Tazat, cross A6 and aim for what I call 'Tazat Pass'. Tazat Pass is a bit of frivolity; if you're not in the mood just follow A6 to Borne. Having got through the pass and reached 'Borne' junction, follow the old truck route NW towards Amguid, leaving it south of Toukmatine to cross over the Amadror plain to 'Tourha Pass' (my name for this unnamed pass). Once you've worked your way through this, head south-west towards Hassi Dehine across the Oued Igharghar, reversing Route A9 back to Ideles.

Route-finding and markers
Only about half of this route is along pistes, but you'll find the cross-country sections easy as there are always bold landmarks to head for (as well as GPS).

Fuel
Djanet and Ideles.

Water
Djanet, Hassi Dehine (unconfirmed), well at KM513, and Ideles.

Traffic
Apart from at each end of the route, you can expect to see no other vehicles.

Driving
Straightforward. Four-wheel drive only needed occasionally. If you have the water and fuel range it would be fun on a bike too.

Suggested duration
Three days.

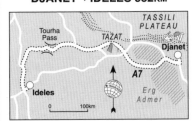

A7 – RECOMMENDED MAPS
DJANET → IDELES 532KM

The TPC H3-D covers the whole route nearly all the way to Ideles.

0km (532)   **N24° 30.8' E09° 29.6'**
Djanet junction fuel station. Head for Bordj el Haouas.

19 (513)   **N24° 30.8' E09° 18.6'**
Leave the tarmac road to the left as it bends right, and follow faint masses of tracks heading 250° across the flat sand towards the dunes. After 7km you begin to curve S, passing over low sand banks that lie across the entrance to the corridor.

30 (502)
You are now in the dune corridor on a bearing of 235°. Eight kilometres later (KM38) you pass along the left side of the corridor, bearing 210°, and in another kilometre (KM39) you turn towards 245°.

42 (490)   **N24° 24.5' E09° 08.7'**
Enter a side valley to the W, bearing 290°, still on firm ground with corrugations.

46 (486)
Curve S, and in a couple of kilometres let your tyres down (if you haven't already).

51 (481)
Gentle ascent of the barrier dune begins. Take a good run up. Once you make it to the crest, turn right and continue down to the desert floor.

56 (481)   **N24° 20.5' E09° 05.0'**
End of the dunes. This is a useful waypoint to know if you're reversing this dune crossing. From this point you can see two conical hills to the W. Head for them or follow a bearing of about 290° – or key in the waypoint for KM127.

71 (461)
Cross a low bank of dunes near the twin hills. This, and a couple of others later on, are easily crossed.

92 (440)
Mt Tazat visible ahead. In 4km (KM96) you cross the first in a series of N–S tracks on around N24° 30'. If you're not already heading for the waypoint below you should do so now.

127 (405)   **N24° 39.4' E08° 10.0'**
Twin cairns on a track heading W across a flat plain towards the mountains.

132 (400)   **N24° 40.0' E08° 07.4'**
The track runs across a oued and enters the hills passing a tree. There's a cairn shortly after and then cairns on hilltops marking the way through the pass. Soft sand with clear, deep tracks.

136 (396)   **N24° 39.2' E08° 05.1'**
Wide sandy amphitheatre surrounded by hills, with Tazat summit directly to the S.

142 (390)   **N24° 37.1' E08° 02.1'**
You're out of the mountains and heading towards a sandy plain with small distant dunes.

148 (384)   **N24° 36.6' E07° 59.3'**
Head S across a gravel plain with dunes ahead and to the right.

154 (378)   **N24° 32.9' E07° 58.7**
Join the main track (A6) and follow it to the W.

176 (356)   **N24° 35.2' E07° 47.7'**
Borne junction. Stone monument. Leave WNW towards Amguid (marked 'AM' on some balises).

186 (346)
Pre-Islamic tomb visible on the hillside to the S.

190 (342)   **N24° 38.4' E07° 40.3'**
Follow tracks heading NW.

195 (337)   **N24° 40.5' E07° 38.3'**
Balise set in a sand-filled tyre. Track heads through a gap in the rocks up past a tree in a sandy pass.

196 (336)   **N24° 41.0' E07° 37.1'**
Top of the sandy pass, with a fallen balise soon after.

203 (329)
Cairn beside the track.

214 (318)   **N24° 43.0' E07° 27.8'**
Upright balise following a fast stretch.

229 (303)   **N24° 44.6' E07° 18.8'**
Two stone cairns atop a rubble hill. Toukmatine mountain visible to the NW.

235 (297)   **N24° 45.4' E07° 16.0'**

Tracks head directly for a cone mountain (a slightly misaligned 'Peak 4730' on the TPC H3-D).

238 (294)   N24° 45.5'   E07° 14.2'
Pass S of the cone mountain and head directly W (or for KM357 waypoint). The going's a bit bouncy over oueds until you pass E06° 50' – then it's a fast gravel plain with the odd oued to catch you out.

321 (211)   N24° 41.7'   E06° 26.7'
The little-known Arbre d'Amadror.

350 (182)   N24° 40.7'   E06° 10.3'
You're now heading for the gap between Tourha and Djebel Amzer Oumfat to the N.

357 (175)   N24° 40.7'   E06° 06.5'
Keep to the N side of the gap and pick up tracks heading NW into the pass. You may spot the turret of Garet el Djenoun 80km to the NW.

365 (167)
In the sandy pass. Firewood.

370 (162)   N24° 44.0'   E05° 59.6'
Tracks turn WSW to get around some dunes. Patches of soft sand.

372 (160)   N24° 44.2'   E05° 59.0'
Junction. Track forks SW towards three cone mountains and continues by winding through low hills.

375 (157)   N24° 43.1'   E05° 57.9'
Small rocky pass and within a kilometre a second pass (N24° 42.9' E05° 57.4') at which you'll get a full view of the Tefedest ahead and with the cone mountains to your left. From here the track goes SSW to ...

379 (153)   N24° 41.5'   E05° 56.4'
... another stony pass where the track turns W and descends into the Igharghar valley. Aheggar outcrop directly ahead.

383 (149)   N24° 41.2'   E05° 54.5'
Leave the hills along a wide oued heading SW.

389 (143)   N24° 39.9'   E05° 51.7'
Mouth of the oued at the approach to the pass behind you. Line of large tussocks.

390 (142)   N24° 39.8'   E05° 51.0'
Tracks leave the oued to head SW across a gravel plain.

394 (138)   N24° 38.4'   E05° 49.8'
Pre-Islamic tomb on the side of a jagged hill to your left. Continue descending in a SW direction. The tracks may disappear, but it doesn't really matter which way you cross the thickly vegetated Oued Igharghar to the Tefedest side (try KM402, N24° 35.8' E05° 46.9'). The first main track you cross running N–S down the oued is not A9, instead keep going until...

412 (120)
... you join the track of Route A9 and turn SW.

437 (95)   N24° 19.7'   E05° 42.0'
Clumps of trees and a cone hill marking the grubby end of Oued Dehine (firewood). This is KM102 of A9.

458 (74)   N24° 10.4'   E05° 38.0'
Junction, take left fork.

459 (73)   N24° 09.8'   E05° 38.1'
Faded green sign marking the Tefedest section of the Hoggar National Park. Scratched on the sign 'Mertoutek 13, Amguid 250'. Continue S along pleasant valleys.

475 (57)   N24° 02.5'   E05° 37.6'
Junction marked with two cairns. A piste runs W for the highway and Tam (this is the red piste marked on the 741 map). Continue S.

490 (42)
Crest a pass. Occasional rough sections of basalt commence with a very rough patch in about 10km.

508 (24)   N23° 50.6'   E05° 48.0'
Ruins of an old colonial compound mark the end of the basalt and a descent into the valley below.
  If you don't need to go via Ideles, follow the tracks south along the valley to N23° 43.2' E05° 50.7' (KM16 on Route A9 and 15km after the ruins) to reach the Ideles–Hirhafok pylon track. Turn W for

Hirhafok and the piste to the highway (Route A11) or the tough ascent to Assekrem (Route A6).

513 (19)   N23° 48.5' E05° 49.1'
However, this route cuts the corner to Ideles by erring E on tracks that lead past a deep well (this waypoint) on the left of the piste. Follow tracks winding SE.

518 (14)
Enter another rough patch of basalt and

then head ESE, about a kilometre later passing Daliesque outcrops with glimpses of the pylons along the piste to the S.

522 (10)   N23° 47.2' E05° 53.1'
Join the Hirhafok–Ideles track and continue NE to Ideles.

532 (0)   N23° 49.0' E05° 56.2'
Ideles fuel station at the N end of town. A6, A8 lead off in various directions.

A8 IDELES → TAMANRASSET (via Tahifet)   [221KM]
December 2001; Toyota HJ61 and six motorbikes

Description
If you're in no hurry to reach Tam from Djanet or fancy leaving Assekrem for later (perhaps to do the full loop from Tam in one go), this makes an enjoyable diversion. The first half of the route up to Tahifet offers the best of the high plateau scenery with rounded granite outcrops or sandy oueds making handy windbreaks, all at around 1800m. This winding piste is especially enjoyable on a bike. The fun is over once you pass Tahifet, with a wide corrugated track leading all the way to the highway south of Tam.

Route-finding and markers
The mountain track is clear all the way, the only tricky point being the fork to the south at KM49 near a Tazrouk turn-off – and later, muddling your way back onto the highway at KM215.

Fuel
Ideles and Tamanrasset.

Water
Ideles, Oued Tazrouk (just off the route), Tahifet and Tam.

Traffic
Local traffic south of Tahifet. Keep right over the many blind crests. If you have a head-on, at least you were on the correct side of the track.

A8 – RECOMMENDED MAPS
IDELES → TAMANRASSET 221KM

The IGN NF-31 'Tamanrasset' sheet covers the route with adequate detail.

Driving
Short of flash floods there's nothing challenging for cars, while on a motorbike the track, as far as the mast at Col Azrou, is as fun as any in Algeria. After Tahifet corrugations set in.

Suggested duration
One day.

0km (221)   N23° 49.0'   E05° 56.2'
Ideles fuel station. Get back on the Djanet–Tam piste which bypasses the town on the east side alongside telegraph poles.

3 (218)   N23° 47.2'   E05° 55.9'
Junction. Continue straight on and begin ascending. Pylons alongside the track.

25 (196)
Enter the Oued Tassakimt which you cross and drive along for 2km.

47 (174)   N23° 29.1'   E6° 06.1'
Tazrouk junction marked with a 2m-high concrete block. Turn right.

49 (172)   N23 °28.4'   E6° 06.5'
Important junction where you should follow easily-missed tracks leading through a gap in the hills to the S (right). If you find yourself driving along a sandy oued, passing wells and cultivated trees, you're heading for Tazrouk village along the Oued Tazrouk and have gone the wrong way
    Having taken the right turn, the track is clear all the way to Tahifet. At KM66 the

conical peak of Assadjene comes into view on the horizon and later you'll see the new radio mast marking Col Azrou at KM82.

82 (139)
Col Azrou. Radio mast, with another older mast 4km later. From here you begin a descent along a oued with some corrugations leading to Tahifet, at times alongside an old collapsed track.

120 (101)
Tahifet village. A good place to get muddled up if you enter the outskirts too far west. Basically drive on the main track through the built-up centre.
    From now on you sit on a corrugated piste for about 95km, passing turn-offs for adjacent villages.

215 (6)   N22° 43.9'   E05° 33.0'
Having passed through a spread-out village, you rejoin the tarmac road which leads north (right) to Tamanrasset.

221 (0)   N22° 46.3'   E05° 31.6'
Tamanrasset south fuel station.

A9 IDELES ➔ HASSI BEL GUEBBOUR   [710KM]
December 2001; Toyota HJ61 and six motorbikes

Description
This route can be a quick and easy way of getting back north or down to the Hoggar from the Gassi Touil, or avoiding slow convoys along the Trans-Sahara Highway. Up to and along the east side of the Tefedest as far as the turreted peak of Garet el Djenoun is a lovely, quiet drive – you won't pass any villages and are more likely to encounter gazelles than people. Make the most of exploring the Tefedest, as north of here things flatten out as you converge with the piste coming up from In Ecker (A12) towards Amguid.
    Moving up the west side of the Erg Amguid (at which point A12 heads east into the Tassili), you pass through a narrow defile at KM404 and continue out across the plain along a clear piste. From here on there's little to distract you until the short ascent up the escarpment leading to the Quatre Chemins checkpoint and the broken tarmac to Hassi bel Guebbour.

Route-finding and markers
Once you get to the green sign at KM81 it's a clear run up the east side of the Tefedest ranges – it's not marked on any maps but a clear track exists all the way and GPS is not essential. Beyond the Erg Amguid, the old truck route that linked Djanet with the north is well marked with oil drums, although you want to keep tabs on your orientation here as other tracks can lead north-west.

Fuel
Ideles and Hassi bel Guebbour.

Water
Ideles, possibly Hassi Dehine, Ain Kerma (off the route at N26°17.8' E05°22.2'– drinkable from the pipe, not the cistern) and Hassi bel Guebbour.

Traffic
Very light once you're past the green sign until Quatre Chemins.

Driving
For both cars and bikes this route poses no technical problems.

Suggested duration
Two and a half days.

A9 – RECOMMENDED MAPS
IDELES → HBG 710KM

Most of the route is on the IGN 'In Salah' sheet; the TPC H3-D covers a bit more.

0km (710)   N23° 49.0'   E05° 56.2'
Ideles fuel station. Get back on the Djanet–Tam piste bypassing the town on the E side alongside telegraph poles.

2 (708)   N23° 47.2'   E05° 55.9'
Junction. Turn left and pass through the gardens in the oued and out the other side. When the track forks, keep left and follow the pylons SW out of town towards Hirhafok. Straight on at this junction leads to Tahifet (Route A8).

16 (694)   N23° 43.2'   E05° 50.7'
Start of the piste to Mertoutek (no obvious sign). Turn right and follow tracks along a oued northwards, turn NE ahead of Ouksem peak. At KM31 the road passes some ruins on the right and enters a very rough patch of basalt rubble and about 16km later crests a pass and descends into a valley with some trees.

65 (645)
The piste crosses another pass and descends into an enclosed sandy valley (nice camping spots).

79 (631)   N24° 09.8'   E05° 38.1'
With the peak '1698' to the E, look out for an old green sign for the 'Hoggar National Park – Tefedest' to your left (scratched on the sign is 'Mertoutek 13, Amguid 250'); keep right of it on the small twin-rut track which leads up the Oued Dehine.

At KM102 you'll see a cone-shaped hill to the W near some trees in the Oued Dehine.

150 (560)   N24° 37.0'   E05° 40.0'
Pass between Aheggar ridge ('2297') and the main Tefedest massif. The distinctive profile of Garet el Djenoun begins to become clear 50km to the N.

200 (510)
Garet el Djenoun; good camping spots. From here to the next waypoint is a fast, flat run along the Oued Igharghar flood plain, passing the low Erg Telachchimt to the E and with prominent peaks to the W including Edjeleh ('1359') halfway between Garet and Amguid.

By this point you may have joined the more frequently used 'Tefedest west' piste from In Ecker (A12). Further north, as the valley narrows the terrain becomes a little more rough, but just head any which way for the next waypoint. Once you see the Amguid Erg ahead, head for its left edge.

350 (360)   N26° 20.8'   E05° 13.9'
Crossroads of the Amguid–In Salah and In Ecker–HbG pistes with a low walled diamond-shaped enclosure nearby and the Erg Amguid before you. Clear tracks lead up the W bank of the erg (corrugations) to the narrow defile at Tebe-n-Teghlamt (KM 404; N26° 44.6' E05° 23.3').

From here the clearly-defined truck piste leads north-east, marked by oil drums, but make sure you keep on the correct orientation as other tracks lead W to In Salah.

453 (257)   N27° 06.5'   E05° 44.2'
Wreck. About 22km later the piste turns directly E and leads through a wide pass and then resumes its NE orientation just as you cross E06°.

486 (224)   N27° 34.4'   E06° 16.9'
Stony crossing, visible as a small kink on the IGN and TPC maps. About 20km later is another oued crossing in the middle of nowhere, just as you leave the NG-31 map or point '402' on the NG-32 map. The track now turns N, then a few kilometres later you cross a major track, but keep going NNE.

608 (102)   N28° 07.0'   E06°24.4'
The piste climbs onto the escarpment and goes E on a rough track to Quatre Chemins checkpoint (KM649). From here head N on the broken tarmac to HbG.

710 (0)   N28° 41.4'   E06° 30.2'
Hassi bel Guebbour. Fuel and cafés.

A10 TAMANRASSET → ARLIT (Niger)   [640KM]
February 2003; Discovery (Gerbert van der Aa)

Description
In the early 1990s this route became dangerous due to the Tuareg rebellion, and several tourists were robbed. Up till then it was the main trans-Sahara route and now the situation seems safe again, at least on the Algerian side (GSPC notwithstanding). In Niger there are still occasional problems with armed robbers, but more in the Aïr, Ténéré and around Agadez.

The Algerians are still working on the tarmac road from Tamanrasset to In Guezzam started in the early 1980s. At the time this route was logged, over 100km had been completed from In Guezzam north past the Laouni dunes, although the original 60km of tarmac south of Tamanrasset are mostly broken up. That leaves about 250km of piste in between. The soft sand south of In Guezzam and around Laouni normally causes problems for two-wheel drives so be prepared for some digging.

Note that Algerian exit formalities are all done at In Guezzam. From there you cross 18km of no-man's land to the Niger frontier at Assamaka. Formalities are straightforward here. Normally you pay 5000 CFA *tax touristique* per person, and 3000 CFA for a *laissez passer* for the car. A carnet is not necessary. You can change all currencies on the black market here: euros are best.

A10 – RECOMMENDED MAPS
TAMANRASSET → ARLIT 640KM

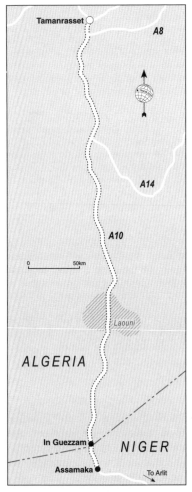

'Tamanrasset' NF-31 and 'Agadez' NE-32 cover ninety per cent of the piste section with the 'Kidal' NE-31 sheet covering an easy 90km section from Gara Eker to In Guezzam and Assamaka.

There's no vehicle insurance at Assamaka (arrange it in Arlit where there are more formalities to be done), but once the police have stamped your passport you're free to move on.

Route-finding and markers

Route-finding is easy. On the Algerian side there are white concrete pillars every kilometre. Local cars sometimes take deviations, but this is not necessary. The main piste is quite good. From Assamaka to Arlit there are metal posts set in oil drums almost every kilometre.

Fuel

Tamanrasset, In Guezzam, Arlit.

Water

Tamanrasset, In Guezzam, Assamaka, Arlit. There are no wells between Tamanrasset and In Guezzam.

Other traffic

Count on seeing around ten vehicles a day in winter. A convoy is a good idea, especially if you don't stick to the main piste. Many ill-prepared tourists have died on this route over the years because they lost the main track.

Suggested duration

Count on three to four days, depending on your vehicle and the speed of border formalities. The border post at In Guezzam is officially open 24 hours a day, but often the head of the police is out, so you have to wait. Assamaka is only open during the day.

0km (640)   **N22° 46.3'   E05° 31.6'**
Tamanrasset south fuel station.

61 (579)   **N 22° 17.7'   E05° 31.1'**
Tarmac ends. Clear piste going south. After about 15km is a sign: 'Military zone. Keep Out'. Ignore this and go on.

95 (545)   **N 22° 02.2'   E05° 38.8'**
Broken sign indicating the turn-off to Taghrera and In Azaoua (see p.340). Continue on southwards.

128 (512)   **N 21° 45.8'   E05° 39.4'**
Remarkable blue stones to your right. Further on you will see them again.

157 (483)   **N 21° 31.5'   E05° 34.4'**
Abandoned buildings to your left. Main

piste passes between two small mountains. Sandy area. Two-wheel drives should take the passage a couple of hundred metres to the west.

216 (424)   N21° 02.5'   E05° 42.7'
Mountain to your right. Shortly afterwards you see two signs in Arabic.

247 (393)   N20° 47.9'   E05° 47.1'
Fast flat sandy area.

284 (356)   N20° 29.5'   E05° 45.3'
Laouni, a sandy area with many rocks. Loads of car wrecks. Take the deviation to the west if the main piste is too sandy.

307 (330)   N20° 20.0'   E05° 45.9'
Beginning of new tarmac to In Guezzam. Most of the time you can drive on it. When the road is blocked with rocks, you have to take the piste running parallel for a while.

400 (240)   N19° 33.9'   E05° 46.3'
In Guezzam fuel station. Just behind the station are a restaurant and some shops.

The piste to the border post is very sandy.

412 (228)   N19° 28.9'   E05° 47.4'
Algerian border post.

430 (210)   N19° 26.0'   E05° 51.2'
Assamaka. Now you are really in Africa. Many people come running, offering to help you. It can be easier to choose one and pay a small gratuity or present later. Leave Assamaka ENE and follow the balises.

470 (170)   N19° 29.9'   E06° 05.9'
Crossroads. Sign with directions to Djanet and Arlit. Head ESE.

523 (117)   N19° 17.7'   E06° 30.5'
Sandy area.

632 (8)   N18° 47.6'   E07° 20.9'
Uranium mine north of Arlit.

640 (0)   N18° 44.2'   E07° 22.9'
Arlit police station, where they stamp your passport and where you probably have to pay again.

A11 TAMANRASSET ➜ IDELES (via Highway)   [224KM]
February 2003; Two Honda XR650Ls

Description
This is the least arduous way of getting on the way to Djanet; or in reverse a way of avoiding the Hoggar if coming from Djanet in an ailing vehicle. Once you leave the highway it's a straightforward run east to Hirhafok and Ideles.

On the way you get a good view of the Atakor massif 40km to the south, with clear views of Ilamane spire (2739m), the bulk of Tahat (2908m, Algeria's highest peak), and the three volcanic plugs facing the plateau of Assekrem.

Route-finding and markers
Easy. At the highway turn-off (KM122), pylons initially follow a corrugated track to Hirhafok and Ideles. There are occasional concrete markers

Fuel
Tamanrasset and Ideles.

Water
Tamanrasset, Hirhafok and Ideles.

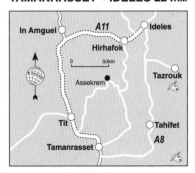

A11 – RECOMMENDED MAPS
TAMANRASSET ➜ IDELES 224KM

The Michelin 741 will get you there.

Traffic
Regular on the highway and light local traffic on the piste.

Driving
Apart from the corrugations and occasional basalt patches, this route poses no problems for bikes or cars.

Suggested duration
Half a day.

0km (224)   N22° 47.7' E05° 31.1'
Tamanrasset central fuel station. Leave the town to the north. Pass the airport, Outoul and Tit villages until you get to the turn-off for Hirhafok.

122 (102)
Turn-off for Hirhafok. Follow the corrugated track east, initially paralleled by pylons.

193 (31)   N23° 39.3' E05° 45.7'
Hirhafok village. Pass through the village and rejoin the pylons for the sandy/corrugated track to Ideles.

220 (4)   N23° 39.3' E05° 45.7'
It's easy to get mixed up when approaching Ideles. Head SE for the avenue of trees which mark the oued crossing on the south end of town. This leads to a junction (N23° 47.2' E05° 55.9') from where you can follow the pylons north to the fuel station.

224 (0)   N23° 49.0' E05° 56.2'
Ideles fuel station. From here it's 499km to Djanet via Bordj el Haouas (Route A6), 221km back to Tam via Tahifet (Route A8, junction above), or 710km to Hassi bel Guebbour (Route A9).

A12 TAMANRASSET → HbG (via Erg Tifernine)   [1040KM]
March 2002; Toyota HJ61, HDJ80 auto and Land Rover Defender Tdi

Description
This is a long route which, instead of being followed to the letter, can be combined with other routes. Combined with the upper half of A10 from KM372 it is a fast way back north to Hassi bel Guebbour (HbG), while once around Erg Tifernine you can leave the route at KM720 to make your way along the (unlogged) old colonial piste to Ain el Hadjadj, KM301 on route A2 (via Jebel Tahinaouine; very rocky and some dunes).

You leave the highway just after In Ecker where it's a smooth run up the west side of the Tefedest and across the plain to Amguid. Uniquely in Algeria Amguid village (as opposed to Amguid military base a little to the south) has long had an odd reputation as a Village From Hell; to avoid getting mobbed you may prefer not to stop here. Just north of Amguid you cross into the valley that leads east below the 'Thala' escarpment, emerging at Hassi Ntsel and the plain west of Erg Tifernine. The highlight of the route is rounding Erg Tifernine and heading north between the erg and Oued Mellene to Gara Khanfoussa. You're bound to encounter Tuareg nomads around here.

Once out of the Gara Khanfoussa dunes this route does not quite reverse the early stages of Route A2 or later stages of A9, but instead turns north-east below the escarpment towards Bordj Omar Driss and the tarmac. Despite some soft sand, feche feche and a couple of dunes, it's worth it for the amazing cliffs at KM946, and to avoid the irritating rubble road leading east to Quatre Chemins.

Route-finding and markers

Right up to the southern spur of Erg Tifernine you are on clear pistes, and up the side of the erg is easy going with tracks. Reversing the maze through the dunes around Gara Khanfoussa can be tricky if recent tracks have been obliterated and confused by oil exploration there (as happened in our case). But by referring to the large TPC to work out your position and heading for KM868 at the right time, you'll find a way out. And even if you don't the dunes and hills to the north-west of Gara Khanfoussa are not that bad and you could work your way through to the west or even directly NNW towards KM922.

Fuel

Tamanrasset, In Amguel, In Ecker and Hassi bel Guebbour (In Ecker to HbG is the longest stage at nearly 900km).

Water

Tam, In Amguel, In Ecker, Abdemezeh village, Ain Kerma, Amguid village, Tin Tadjert well (untested), Hassi Ntsel (untested), KM735, Zaouïa Sidi Moussa gardens (recommended), Bordj Omar Driss, Hassi bel Guebbour.

There are other wells marked on the maps around Erg Tifernine's flanks and in the valley between Amguid and Hassi Ntsel.

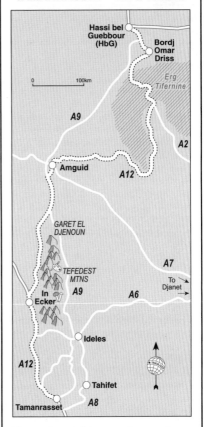

A12 – RECOMMENDED MAPS TAMANRASSET → HBG 1040KM

The section of this route that requires a map is covered on the IGN 'In Salah' sheet or TPC H3-D.

Driving

Mostly fast and easy up to Amguid village where it gets a little sandy. The valley running east to Hassi Ntsel can be both sandy in the oueds and slow going over rocky tracks in between. Ntsel to Tifernine is easy; to turn the spur you follow a very rough colonial track squeezing between the dunes and the jebel. From this point up the side of Erg Tifernine right up to Bordj Omar Driss you're on sand and occasional feche feche.

On a motorbike only the great range required will stop you, but making the effort to explore the Tifernine area would be worthwhile.

Suggested duration

Four days.

0km (1040) **N22° 47.7'** **E5° 31.1'**
Tamanrasset central fuel station.

129 (911)
In Amguel village. Fuel north of town. For café and shops, turn right at the roundabout (water tap in the roundabout).

165 (875)
The rubbish left from the former Base Sonarem leads past the fuel station to In Ecker military base. Checkpoint.

Behind the base, inherited from the French, you can't miss Taourirt Ta-n Afella mountain, surrounded by a long wall and 'Danger Keep Out' signs.

During the 1960s tunnels were drilled into the mountain for nuclear tests, one of which went wrong and blasted fall-out across the plain, poisoning Mertoutek for years. You may have noticed the Greenpeace symbol on an outcrop earlier on.

182 (858) **N24° 08.3'** **E05° 02.4'**
Leave the highway to the north. Sandy piste, sometimes corrugated.

223 (817) **N24° 30.0'** **E05° 07.9'**
Waypoint at N24° 30' just as the tracks divide to go round an outcrop.

247 (793)
Balise 'Amguid 205', after which keep left.

250 (790) **N24° 37.9'** **E05° 09.2'**
Two old signs (in English and Arabic) warning you you're entering the In Ecker Military Zone. A kilometre later you pass a Range Rover wrecked in a Dakar Rally.

261 (779)
Balise 'Amguid 190' with stone cairns alongside the track.

281 (759)
Fork; keep left following the cairns around gravelly hills and continue N or NNE towards Tidikmar mountain.

285 (755)
Another fork, curve left with the cairns as you cross N25°, running between Tidikmar and Garet el Djenoun to the E.

293 (747)
Cross a oued and mudflats.

314 (726) **N25° 11.1'** **E05° 06.8'**
Cross to the W side of the oued.

317 (723) **N25° 12.5'** **E05° 06.2'**
Abdemezeh village (unmarked on maps).

332 (708) **N25° 20.3'** **E05° 05.2'**
Track forks. Keep left following the cairns NNW. 2km later you'll pass a sign: 'Amguid 120, Tamanrasset 330, In Ecker 150'. The track and the cairns now run along the E side of the Oued Taghmert towards the NE.

353 (687)
Isolated peak of Edjeleh visible ahead.

360 (680)
Another Rally wreck by a oued crossing.

372 (668) **N25° 44.6'** **E05° 16.9'**
Edjeleh peak directly to your W.

395 (645)
Balise, 'In Ecker 210, Tam 390'.

408 (632) **N25° 41.7'** **E05° 15.0'**
Pass a small rubble rise on the right – no cairns on this stretch.

425 (615) **N25° 57.2'** **E05° 16.6'**
Cross orange rubble colonial track.

446 (594) **N26° 17.4'** **E05° 16.9'**
Turn off towards Ain Kerma well at the foot of the escarpment. Cross rough ground and soft sand until you connect with a track leading to the well. Or continue N towards Amguid (KM470).

455 (585) **N26° 17.8'** **E05° 22.2'**
Ain Kerma well: some palm trees, rubbish and a building plus a spring filling a concrete cistern via a black pipe. For drinking water separate the pipe, don't take water from the tank.

To leave the well follow the track back NW past Amguid military base (KM465). The sand begins to get soft here.

470 (570) **N26° 25.0'** **E05° 21.5'**
Amguid village.

479 (561) **N26° 30.1'** **E05° 21.2'**
Follow tracks towards the gap in the escarpment to the NE.

482 (558)   **N26° 31.1' E05° 21.8'**
Pass. Turn E into the valley.

485 (555)
The piste crosses a stony embankment with a chott down to the right. You may find smoother going in the oued below to the left.

492 (548)   **N26° 34.6' E05° 26.5'**
Cobbled oued crossing with Tin Tadjert well on the left. The piste now enters a narrow canyon, following a oued as it winds along a stony track.

494 (546)
Re-cross the oued as you exit the canyon and follow a clear piste to the NNE.

496 (544)   **N26° 36.2' E05° 27.5'**
Junction. Take the right fork and turn E towards a cairn on a hill and then ESE along a oued.

503 (537)
Piste winds through a sandy oued. For the next 30km or more the track winds across gravel plains, through oueds and up and over rough rocky sections.

538 (502)   **N26° 28.9' E05° 47.1'**
Lada Niva wreck by the piste.

543 (497)   **N26° 28.7' E05° 49.9'**
Three cairns mark a track heading south. Keep left.

547 (493)   **N26° 29.9' E05° 52.2'**
Stony descent with another in a couple of kilometres, soon followed by a blue Rally wreck.

567 (473)   **N26° 32.1' E06° 01.4'**
Junction. Continue ahead on ENE. The other track to the right is the alternative eastbound route to Hassi Ntsel as seen on the 1 million NG-32 map and which also leads SE down along the Djebel Atafaitafa past Hassi Ta Haft, as on the TPC map.

574 (466)   **N26° 34.3' E06° 04.9'**
The alternative track rejoins our track from the right as it enters the Oued Amassine valley.

594 (446)   **N26° 40.9' E06° 12.7'**
Valley ends at a junction. Take the right fork to the SE.

608 (432)
Hassi Ntsel and a narrow band of dunes. There may be a track around the dunes to the right (SW, a sandstorm was blowing at the time, we could not see), or you can plough through small dunes.

638 (402)   **N26° 25.7' E06° 31.2'**
Waypoint on a gravel plain.

645 (395)   **N26° 23.9' E06° 34.2'**
Cross what must be two smuggling pistes running SW–NE, much more used than the one you're following.

665 (375)   **N26° 20.9' E06° 43.1'**
Pass a large cairn on a mound to the right of the piste as you near the Erg Tifernine.

676 (364)
Cross a sandy oued followed in a couple of kilometres by a chott, in an ESE direction. You'll probably encounter Tuareg nomads for the next 30km.

684 (356)
Start to wind through low sandy hillocks. The ground becomes both sandy and rocky as you get nearer to the erg. The track sometimes splits but is still clear.

690 (350)   **N26° 15.9' E06° 54.5'**
Pass two cairns by the piste as you head NE directly towards the erg in order to work your way through the rubble hills which abut the southern tip of the erg.

691 (399)   **N26° 16.0' E06° 55.1'**
The 4km passage through the rocks begins with a 1km section followed by a descent onto a flat patch by a massive dune and then up onto the rocks again at KM693. Although rough, it's well marked with cairns and fairly clear on the ground when not covered in sand banks.

At times you may have to recce on foot to find the best way.

695 (345)   **N26° 16.0' E06° 57.1'**
Descent from the rocky hills. Join a oued and head N into low dunes at the foot of

the erg. For the next 140km you're driving on, or close to, the eastern banks of the erg. The higher up the smoother the going but the steeper the rises and drops.

720 (320)   N26° 29.0'   E06° 56.5'
Near this point a track winds east through an obscured canyon for around 70km to Ain el Hadjadj on Route A2. Carry on northwards.

735 (305)   N26° 36.3'   E06° 55.4'
Well (not marked on any map) in a region of eroded root-clumps of ancient trees.

778 (262)   N26° 57.8'   E06° 47.6'
Pass between an outlying hill to the right of the erg.

832 (208)   N27° 26.1'   E06° 47.5'
Start of the entry to Gara Khanfoussa dunes, marked by a (possibly fallen) pole and an IGN concrete bollard ('IGN 61'). Head W then NW into the dunes, initially along the remains of an old track.
  If you're lucky there will be recent tracks. The initial section, through to Gara Khanfoussa hill, is relatively easy to navigate. Within a kilometre you'll encounter two or three steep dune faces. Bypass these faces to the right and rejoin the track heading north along a flat section.

838 (202)   N27° 28.8'   E06° 47.3'
Enter steeper dunes with a bit of old road to the right. There are a couple of big dips ahead.

842 (198)   N27° 31.1'   E06° 47.0'
Metal stick set in concrete by the old road. Continue northwards towards Gara Khanfoussa.

849 (191)   N27° 34.7'   E06° 46.1'
Pass west of Gara Khanfoussa with a patch of old road nearby. The later, less straightforward, section of this passage to the W begins here. Tracks may make it clear (the TPC depicts the winding route accurately) but pass the white pole at N27° 36.3' E06° 45.1' and then the balise 2km later at N27°37.0' E06° 44.7'. Soon after you want to be heading W then SW to the waypoint below. If there are clear recent tracks follow these, not waypoints.

868 (172)   N27° 35.3'   E06° 37.4'
Metal pole, exit from the dunes and way out to the plain (KM171 of Route A2). Follow the tracks to the NW and N.

877 (163)   N27° 39.2'   E06° 33.7'
Blue-green metal hut to the west of the many tracks heading N.

922 (118)   N28° 02.2'   E06° 29.3'
Track to Bordj Omar Driss – as opposed to the old truck route to the west (A12).

931 (169)   N28° 06.5'   E06° 31.5'
Around here the flat ground is very soft and you can see a 'lime' track built on it heading NE. Keep up momentum through the flats or take the bumpy white track which turns E towards Bordj Omar Driss below the escarpment. At times you must wind your way around low dunes below the escarpment as you work your way E.

946 (94)   N28° 07.9'   E06° 39.2'
Good place to examine the amazing formations of the cliff: pale green strata mixed with red ochre bands and translucent crystals interlaced with white veins. You may also see tiny shells in the sands.

959 (81)   N28° 07.2'   E06° 46.4'
Having passed the trees and gardens of Zaouia Sidi Moussa to the S, you join the tarmac road and turn left towards Bordj.
  Long neglected Bordj, the former Fort Flatters, seems to be enjoying a rejuvenation, with new homes, roads and even a stadium. At the roundabout turn N up the escarpment – the new road down the cliff may be finished by now.
  A few kilometres after the ascent you pass the checkpoint at Quatre Chemins and after shaking over the patches of broken-up road (may be fixed by now) you pass the warm springs on the right a couple of kilometres before HbG.

1040 (0)
Hassi bel Guebbour. Military base, fuel and a couple of cafés. Fresh water is not so easy to get here or up the gassi to Hassi Messaoud – make the most of the gardens at Zaouia Sidi Moussa.

A13 TAMANRASSET → BORDJ MOKTAR [714KM]

February 1989; Land Rover 101, Toyota BJ75, Honda XL600M

Route-finding and markers

As far as Silet you follow a clear track. From there, earth plinths topped with red and white oil drums lead past Tim Missao directly to Bordj Moktar (the red piste on the 741). At Tim Missao this route follows old grey concrete bollards down to Timiaouine (Timia) where a corrugated track leads back up to Bordj.

Fuel

Tamanrasset and Bordj; possibly at Silet and Timiaouine.

Water

The towns and villages above plus the well at Tim Missao.

Driving

There are corrugations before Silet with sand around the Oued Tamanrasset crossing just before Tim Missao. From Timiaouine to Bordj is also corrugated.

Suggested duration

Three days.

Description

A few people have been in this area in recent years (the waypoint for Tim Missao is from 2003), but its popularity has declined because of continued uncertainties about security in northern Mali, which was most people's desti-

A13 – RECOMMENDED MAPS TAMANRASSET → BORDJ MOKTAR 714KM

The IGN 1:1m NF-31 'Tamanrasset' shows the entire route.

nation after Bordj Moktar. Leave Tam along the highway to the north and at a large concrete block, 42km from Tam, turn west on a corrugated track past the village of Tit and on to Abalessa. Leave this village across a sandy oued and continue along a sometimes corrugated track to Silet, 150km from Tamanrasset, where the surrounding hills begin to sink into the flat reg of the Tanezrouft.

Leave Silet to the north-west, though the route soon curves back to the south-west where the mounds topped with oil drums begin. Forty-three kilometres from Silet you pass through the rocky outcrop of Adrar Isket, from where the piste eventually joins the course of the Oued Tamanrasset; just a faint string of vegetation and small trees. About 140km from Silet you cross the now sandier Oued Tamanrasset with some dunes nearby and head directly south-west to the emerging hills of the Adrar Timekerkaz.

The landmarks for Tim Missao begin 20km from the oued crossing. Look out for a stone hut which, if it's still there, marks the point to head south-east for 5km towards the twin buttresses clearly visible on the horizon. The entrance to the well is through a valley to the right of the two buttresses. Once in the valley keep right, passing over a low dune which leads to the narrow canyon and the well of Tim Missao (N 21° 54.2′ E03° 05.6′). Ancient and modern graffiti cover the canyon walls.

Back at the stone hut, the red and white oil drums continue presumably directly to Bordj Moktar. It's been marked '*interdite*' on the 741 for years, but so are other routes for no apparent reason. The regular piste to Timiaouine can be a little harder to recognise here in poor visibility. Look for the metre-high concrete bollards with 'Timia' stencilled on them. Timia is 260km from Tim Missao across thickening vegetation that gives you the premature impression you've left the Sahara. From Timia it's a corrugated 140km north-west to Bordj.

A14 TAMANRASSET → DJANET (via Erg Killian)   [888KM]
December 2002; Toyota HJ61

Description
This is a long and remote run to Djanet, a 'washing line' hung between the two southbound pistes to Niger (A10 and A15) and mostly cross-country, though there are odd patches of piste at natural bottlenecks. It's not the fastest or shortest way to Djanet but the terrain is mostly open, offering a quiet, scenic and undemanding run across sandy plains and over occasional rocky spurs.

Note that though it's easy driving, this is a long and very remote route, so carry appropriate reserves of fuel, water and back-up. There is no help to be had in the middle part of this route nor any wells you could expect to walk to.

Route-finding and markers
Once you leave the A10 and A15 axes there will be no markers to speak of but you will cross many north–south smuggling pistes, some of them corrugated. We worked it out with just half a dozen 20-year-old waypoints and reading the terrain.

Fuel
Tamanrasset and Djanet.

A14 – RECOMMENDED MAPS   TAMANRASSET → DJANET 888KM

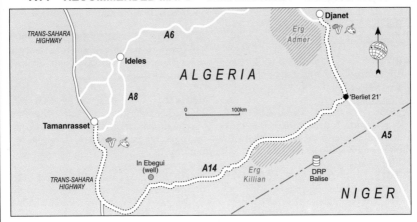

The IGN 'In Azaoua' sheet covers most of A14 with 'Tamanrasset' and 'Djanet' at each end.

Water
Besides the towns at each end, In Ebegui north of KM237 (untested).

Driving
Mostly easy on firm sand planes. Once in a while low N–S rock spurs need either to be picked over slowly or driven through along a line of weakness. Coming into Djanet the sand gets very soft; reversing the less sandy option of Route A15 around Mt Tiska may be an option.

Suggested duration
Three days.

0km (888)   N22° 46.3' E05° 31.6'
Tamanrasset south fuel station.

61 (827) N22° 17.7' E05° 31.1'
Tarmac ends (2003).

95 (793) N22° 02.2' E05° 38.8'
Turn SE at the broken sign for In Azaoua. Over the next 100km you pass signs indicating the distance to In Azaoua.

148 (740)
Double cairn SW of the piste.

170 (718) N21° 32.7' E06° 06.5'
Wrecked desert-racing truck.

201 (687) N21° 25.1'E06° 21.3'
Sandy pass through Tin Tezedjnet. One

In Azaoua junction, KM95.

km later is a green sign indicating 'Tagrera National Park', a region of unusual windcarved outcrops to the north. Head NE.

237 (651)   N21° 39.4'   E06° 33.9'
Leave tracks and turn E.

249 (639)   N21° 37.0'   E06° 38.7'
Old drilling gear. Soft sand, keep ENE.

274 (614)   N21° 43.7'   E06° 51.2'
Head for a gap in the low dunes. In 3km
you cross Tin Tarabine–In Azaoua tracks.

285 (603)   N21° 45.9'   E06° 56.4'
Stony exit from dunes. In 6km you cross
the main channels of the Oued Tin
Tarabine. Tyre visible to the NE.

307 (581)   N21° 46.6'   E07° 04.6'
Pick your way through these low rock
hills. In 1km you pass a rock with a hole.

311 (577)   N21° 47.2'   E07° 06.6'
Crest this rough crossing by a low escarpment and drive SE down the sand banks.
Nice camp spot. It may be possible to
avoid this rocky crossing by going further
S, but it's not that hard. Continue NE
across a sandy plain.

331 (557)   N21° 52.3'   E07° 15.3'
Tracks lead through a low pass; follow the
valley NE.

338 (550)   N21° 54.6'   E07° 18.7'
Exit valley. Open country, distant mountains (Abburak).

360 (528)   N21° 56.8'   E07° 30.5'
Oil drum on N–S track. In 7km split off

right on tracks leaving this piste to the E
(N21° 57.7' E07° 34.0'). In a couple of kilometres there is another low sandy pass.

375 (513)   N21° 58.8'   E07° 38.2'
Oil drum at the N end of the Tissalatine
ridge, south of Abburak. Fast section E
with many tracks.

420 (468)   N22° 05.9'   E08° 02.1'
Having come through a couple more low
sandy passes (Ighellaouane ridge), you
are on a light gravel plain among granite
outcrops.

453 (435)   N22° 11.2'   E08° 18.7'
Follow the mass of tracks going E, uphill
to the pass. In 3km you exit the pass at
N22° 11.7' E08° 20.1'.

496 (392)   N22° 29.8'   E08° 24.7'
Having come through some more passes
you are now approaching the W edge of
Erg Killian. Exit a sandy passage with
dune to the east.

530 (358)   N22° 33.5'   E08° 42.8'
After driving along the N edge of the erg,
a nice camping spot among black rocks.
Continue E, crossing a oued in 14km. The
terrain to the ENE is mostly flat sand
sheet, with some rock slabs and low passes. The crossing of the Oued Tafassasset
around E09° 20' is not as prominent as
you might expect.

From this waypoint it's also possible
to go cross-country directly N, more or
less along E08° 45' to Djanet
(via KM56, Route A7) or on to
Bordj   el   Haouas   via
Amamoukene Oua Mellene.

It is also possible to drive
SE over more complex terrain
to the historic DRP Balise on
the   Algeria–Niger   border
(about 120km) and from there
into the Ténéré, Arbre Perdu
and Chirfa in Niger.

640 (248) N22° 55.6' E09° 37.6'
Another low pass.

663 (225) N22° 57.4' E09° 50.5'
Pass between an impressive
trio of peaks (sheltered camping), part of the Monts Gautier.

The DRP Balise on the Niger border (N22° 13' E09° 44').

669 (219)   **N22° 57.5' E09° 53.3'**
Enter sandy corridor with many tracks
between rocky hills.

676 (212)   **N22° 59.1' E09° 55.4'**
Ascend a tricky sandy pass. Once over
this you can simply head ENE until you
hit the Djanet–Chirfa balise line (A15).

709 (179)   **N23° 10.2' E10° 01.6'**
Berliet Balise 21, erected by a French expedition in 1960. From here simply follow
the balises every 500m N to Djanet.

788 (100)   **N23° 46.4' E09° 43.4'**
Sandy pass, Mt Tiska ahead. Soon the
Tassili is in full view and the sand
becomes very soft. Balises at KM795
(N23° 50.0' E09° 42.5') and KM803 (N23°
54.3' E09° 42.1').

833 (55)   **N24° 08.6' E09° 37.4'**
Sand sheet. Adrar Edehi n-Ergou ahead.
Balise in 3km (N24° 10.1' E09° 36.4').

Balise 112, just south of Berliet 21.

856 (32)   **N24° 18.9' E09° 29.8'**
Intercept built-up dirt road running N-S.
Turn N on this road towards escarpment.

872 (19)   **N24° 25.3' E09° 33.0'**
Join Djanet–Ghat track. Turn left (W).

878 (10)   **N24° 27.1' E09° 30.1'**
Junction with Djanet airport road. Turn
right (N) for Djanet.

888 (0)   **N24° 30.8' E09° 29.6'**
Djanet junction fuel station.

A15 DJANET → CHIRFA (Niger)   [545KM]
December 2000, Land Rover 11A petrol, Patrol 3.3TD (Richard Washington)

Description
This infrequently used piste between Algeria and Niger gives you a great
sense of the immensity of the open desert. Route-finding is made very simple
by balises every 500m (in itself this is quite a sight!) for the entire featureless
section of the crossing.

Only the initial exit from the foothills around Djanet and finding the first
balise on the flat plains east of the Erg d'Admer may be tricky. There are two
ways of starting this route: one heading out over a soft sand sheet south-east
of Djanet's new airport (described in reverse at the end of Route A14), and this
one rounding Mt Tiska to the east. Both routes are depicted reasonably accurately in the TPC H-3D and J-3B maps but this latter route (which leaves the
corrugated piste to Tin Alkoum in Libya around KM29) is recommended for
heavily-laden or under-powered vehicles going to Niger.

From time to time this route is officially closed by either Niger or
Algeria, so check with immigration first. Banditry has occurred on this route
in Niger.

Route-finding and markers

For most of the route balise posts (see p.341) mark the way every 500m, making it impossible to become lost in good visibility. The posts have been removed for a few kilometres around Adrar Mariaou, and end west of the Col de Chandeliers (KM516). The main landmark at the northern end is the distinctive conical peak of Mt Tiska (easily visible from Djanet's new airport which is not on this route) while the west-facing escarpment of the Djado plateau near Chirfa provides a welcome sight at the southern end.

When heading out of Djanet, follow the piste to Tin Alkoum (Libya) before heading south through a gap in the hills towards Mt Tiska. Keep east of Tiska and make your own way through the low hills to the south. The balises appear on the flat plain beyond, at KM101, and run SSE nearly all the way to Chirfa.

Note that the original distances logged on this route were unreliable. As a result they have been estimated from the TPCs and other known points. All the waypoints except KM250 are genuine.

**A15 – RECOMMENDED MAPS
DJANET → CHIRFA 545KM**

The section of this route that requires a map is covered on the IGN 'In Azaoua' sheet or TPC H3-D.

Fuel

Djanet, sometimes expensively at Chirfa, otherwise at Dirkou, another 280km south of Chirfa.

Water

There are no wells along the route.

Other traffic.

Very little.

Driving

Mostly easy, but with soft sections south of Berliet Balise 21, and softer still on the sand sheet south of Djanet airport (if you choose the 'direct' start, reversing Route A14).

Suggested duration

Two days.

0km (545) N24° 30.8' E09° 29.6'
Djanet junction fuel station. Head out of town on a tarmac road to the new airport and after about 10km turn left (east) alongside the old airport onto the well-worn piste to Tin Alkoum (Libya).

29 (516) N24° 19.3' E09° 40.7'
Break in hills (Adrar Tin Amali) on south side of Tin Alkoum road.

33 (512) N24° 17.9' E09 41.8'
Follow tracks through break in hills.

57 (488) N24° 08.0' E09° 46.9'
Sandy sections with the distinctive cone of Mt Tiska in view to the south. Tracks wind to the east of Mt Tiska.

72 (473) N23° 58.7' E09° 50.0'
East of Mt Tiska, nice campsite for early afternoon departure from Djanet.

84 (461) N23° 53.1' E09° 51.7'
Follow a oued SSW through low hills south of Mt Tiska. Adrar Mariaou clearly visible directly to the south.

104 (441) N23° 44.9' E09° 44.9'
Leave the oued.

111 (434) N23° 41.3' E09° 45.6'
Balise 53. The balise line to Niger is now clear to the SSE.

123 (422) N23°36.6' E09° 49.2'
Tree on the piste following a section of missing balises. Possibly due to the military checkpoint visible a few kilometres to the east of the piste on SW slope of Adrar Mariaou. They have been known to intercept traffic on the piste. Follow the balises to the SSE.

Cooling off at KM343 after breaking the sound barrier on the way to Chirfa. © Richard Washington

175 (370) N23° 10.2' E10° 01.7'
Berliet Balise 21 (not one of the regular stick balises – see photo, colour section) erected by a truck-sponsored French expedition in 1960. An uphill sandy section follows for a couple of kilometres with sand soft for at least 10km thereafter.

179 (366)   N23° 08.2'   E10° 02.1'
Balise 112 set by an oil drum with a bottle inside. There's not much to say about the next 60km: at N22° 50.8'   E10° 06.4' (KM211) there is a white concrete marker post inscribed with '133 INCT' then at KM250 (more or less N22° 31' E10° 14') you cross into Niger. About 30km after the border the balise line begins to err to the SE.

343 (202)   N21° 53.2'   E10° 44.9'
Wreck of Nissan Paris–Dakar 1988 press car near Balise 444. A popular camp spot and a bit dirty as a result.

392 (153)   N21° 35.2'   E11° 05.9'
Another burnt-out rally wreck, this time an Aro, near spot height '1790' on the TPC J-3B map.

457 (88)   N21° 10.9'   E11° 34.6'
Toyota Land Cruiser wreck. Surface firms up a little way south and becomes more stony with drainage across piste.

511 (34)   N20° 55.9'   E12° 00.0'
End of regular balises. Piste now turns east towards Chirfa and is marked by stones and the odd balise.

527 (18)   N20° 55.5'   E12° 09.7'
Col de Chandeliers. Tourist piste from Arbre Perdu and Adrar Bous joins in from the WSW. Sandy ascent and nice camp spots in the outcrops to the S of the col.

545 (0)   N20° 55.3'   E12° 19.4'
Chirfa military post. The village with water and possibly fuel is to the north. See Niger, p.593, for more routes from here.

EXPLORING THE TASSILI N'AJJER

The 'Tassili of the Ajjers', a plateau of wind- and water-carved columns or *tassilis* that is not accessible to vehicles, rises 500 or 600 metres above the plain of Djanet. Two very steep passes can only be tackled on foot, though one of them is suitable for pack donkeys. Thirty kilometres to the north, the Akba Assakao pass is accessible by camels, but this is rarely used.

All the plateau in the vicinity of Djanet, encompassing most of the important rock-art sites and among the most fascinating landscapes in the Sahara, lies within the 80,000 square kilometre **Parc National du Tassili** which extends west past Illizi. Do not think that this implies facilities found in national parks elsewhere in the world such as BBQ areas, promotional leaflets, interpretative boards or even rangers or entry signs; in this case the national park designation is more to do with assigning a protected status to the region and probably

The oasis of Djanet, your base for excursions onto the Tassili N'Ajjer plateau.

a condition for it being classified by UNESCO as a World Heritage Site.

There is a **museum** in Djanet at the national parks office, near the old, town-centre fuel station. You may have to pay the entrance fee here if organising a tour yourself. On the last visit this was a rather dusty and uninspiring diorama of stuffed animals and artefacts. The real museum is, of course, out there in the open air on the plateau.

To help protect the area's rock-art heritage, **guides** have long been mandatory for visits onto the plateau above Djanet where the highest concentration of art is to be found. Outside of Djanet, guides and entry fees are also officially required to visit the beautiful Algerian continuation of the Akakus known as the **Tadrart**, south of the plateau, on the road to Tin Alkoum and easily accessible to cars. The highlights here are the engraved rock art in the Oued In Djerane (including a giraffe on a lead, a telling episode in the history of animal domestication), the huge dunes smothering the tassilis at **Merzouga**, and Moul Naga amphitheatre. Many organised tours may, with the obligatory plateau walk, offer a few days in the Tadrart and possibly runs down to the arch at Alidemma, the petrified wood near the Monts Gautier and a return via the Erg Admer – as satisfying as any fortnight's fly-in tour in the Sahara.

A couple of years ago there was a much publicised clean-up operation on the plateau involving local agencies. Over the years the place had taken on the appearance of Everest Base Camp, with litter at the popular camp and rock-art sites. Not unusually, those internationally-acclaimed pariahs, 'tourists',

This section is expanded from original material by Andras Zboray in the previous edition.

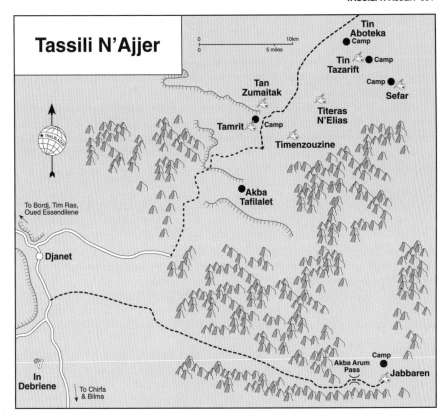

have been cited as culprits despite the fact that for the past two decades all visits here have been accompanied and catered for by official guides presumably approved by the national park and there to protect the environment.

Ensure that you act responsibly on the plateau (or indeed anywhere in the Sahara) when it comes to disposal of rubbish – and if necessary subtly encourage your guide and his crew to do likewise. Remember it is the wilderness in its pristine form that is the great appeal of the Sahara, to you and those who follow. If it cannot be burned, take it back with you.

As far as is known the national park authority does not produce a visitors' **map** of the localities on the plateau. At the moment the best sheet is the 1970 IGN 1:200,000 NG-32-IV 'Djanet', available in mono from IGN in Paris or as a big colour file (see the 'maps' page on the website). The map above is based on part of this map.

There are several **picture books** describing or including the rock art of the Tassili (see Books, p.643). The best known, though probably least admired, is *The Search for the Tassili Frescoes* by Henri Lhote, published (in English) in 1959 and easily available used on the web. He led an expedition to record the art for posterity as the colony of Algeria was slipping out of France's hands. Unfortunately Lhote and those in his service adopted the practice of wetting the rock art to produce more vivid photographs – something which has accelerated their fading in a few decades after surviving millennia on the plateau.

He may not have known any better, though the little-known Neuchatel Museum Swiss expedition recorded many of the Tassili's sites (excepting Jabbaren and Sefar) in the late 1940s, doing a more thorough job than the well-publicised Lhote missions. But Lhote was also accused of turning a blind eye to the inclusion of fakes (painted as a joke) among his recorded discoveries. The slinky quartet known as 'The Bird Headed Goddesses of Jabbaren' (one was embossed on the front cover of early editions of *The Search...*) is known to be one such fake. They were supposedly included (but excised from later editions and indeed the walls of Jabbaren itself) to help attribute the style to ancient Egyptian influences. If anything it was probably the other way round.

Organising tours

Typically a tour on the plateau will last between four days and a week, subject to your appetite for prehistoric paintings and your budget. Be warned that, as mentioned on p.404, it is possible to suffer an overload of bovine images. But the plateau experience is as much a trek through a natural wonderland of tassili ramparts as a dutiful shuffle from one gallery to another; even if you get bored of the rock art, it will still be a great experience.

Depending on the agency as well as the number of people, daily fees for a no-frills tour will range upwards from €30 per person. Double that if food and camping gear are included; costs (including flights) work out at about €150 a day if you book with a European agency.

There are designated camping areas on the plateau; these are no different from any other spot but, as mentioned above, they ensure that litter stays localised. In some places previous travellers have built stone windbreaks which can be handy on windier nights. There are trash areas behind piled-up stone walls, which you should use, as burying opened cans and other litter in the sand can cause nasty surprises for subsequent campers.

POSSIBLE ITINERARIES ON THE PLATEAU

1 day
● Jabbaren via Akba Arum and back plus a visit to the Crying Cows.

4 days
● Akba Tafilalet (antelopes) → Tamrit → Tan Zumaitak → Tamrit.
● Tamrit → Titeras N-Elias → Sefar.
● Sefar → Tamrit.
● Tamrit → Timenzouzine → Akba Tafilalet.

5 days
● Akba Tafilalet (antelopes) → Tamrit → Tan Zumaitak → Tamrit.
● Tamrit → Titeras N-Elias → Tin Aboteka.
● Tin Aboteka → Tin Tazarift → Sefar.
● Sefar → Tamrit.
● Tamrit → Timenzouzine → Akba Tafilalet.

7 days
● Akba Tafilalet → Tan Zumaitak → Tamrit.
● Tamrit → In Itinen → Tin Aboteka.
● Tin Aboteka → Tin Tazarift → Sefar.
● Sefar.
● Jabbaren → Aouenghet → Jabbaren.
● Jabbaren → Akba Arum.

The sites described in this book will give a full coverage of the Tassili rock art. For those wishing to get the full picture, it's also possible to visit several smaller sites lying outside the normal tourist circuit.

Count on walking up to 20–25km a day. If you have particular sites to visit, the guides will show the way, but they're unlikely to make suggestions other than the regularly-visited sites on their 'tramlines'.

The daily routine

At sunrise you break camp and load the animals, which disappear with the herders on the most direct route to the next campsite. The guide sets a more leisurely pace, visiting interesting sites along the route, usually catching up with the animals by early afternoon.

You'll need a small rucksack to carry the daily necessities (water, something to nibble, warm clothes, camera etc). As the plateau is at 1200–1600m, it can be cold in the morning even in the late autumn or in mid-spring, and can remain so all day if there is a thin haze or cloud cover. You're faced with the choice of packing away warm gear in the morning and shivering until the sun makes its presence felt, or having to carry it all until the afternoon. It's a matter of trial and error, but you'll get the feel of it after the first day on the plateau.

For an outline of and background on the recently renamed but still contentiously dated **rock-art periods**, see pp.400–5.

Onto the plateau

Akba Tafilalet, 12km due east of Djanet, is the usual starting point. The travel agencies will drive you out to the bottom of the pass at dawn, where the pack animals will be waiting. By sunrise the animals are loaded and the trek begins. The initial ascent is up a fairly steep slope between two mesas and takes about an hour. It can be quite spectacular as the rising sun strikes the mesa tops high above. At the top the track

On the plateau.

enters a broad valley and turns right into a narrow gorge, following it for a couple of kilometres.

At one point the track splits, with the pack animals taking a zig-zagging path to the right (requiring a long detour on the plateau top), while the footpath turns steeply up the valley slope to the left. A half-hour's climb takes you up to yet another gorge from where a steep path leads up to the edge of the plateau.

Just before reaching the top, you pass a small rock basin which will be full of water if it has rained since the previous summer. The whole climb will take between three and four hours, and even though it looks formidable, can be tackled by anyone in reasonable physical condition; plenty of tourists in their sixties and seventies have made it! The walk through the successive canyons with only the cliff tops illuminated by the rising sun is one of the most spectacular panoramas in the Tassili.

Tamrit

On reaching the top of the rise, the landscape changes dramatically, with eroded humps of sandstone sticking out of the plain, and the fantastic sandstone spires of Tamrit visible on the horizon (the *tassilis* after which the area is named), an hour's walk away. At this point it's possible to take a detour from the main track to the **Antelopes of Tamrit**, a small but refined painting about two kilometres east of the track. The painting is unfortunately much faded, but many of the beautifully-drawn antelopes are clearly visible.

Taking either the main track or the detour, the paths lead to the base of the majestic rock pillars of Tamrit, that are the entrance to the enchanted world of the Tassili. What look like pillars from head-on are in fact wall-like bastions of eroded sandstone separated by narrow canyons. In the last valley to the left there's a small guelta, and the path continues past it to the main valley at Tamrit with its famous cypress trees, a legacy of the last wet period when the vegetation stretched up to the Mediterranean coast. The huge cypresses are thought to be thousands of years old and have survived both the gradual desiccation and the timber-hungry nomads living in the vicinity. After spring and autumn rains the valley floor can bloom with oleanders, giving the impression of a Greek island rather than the centre of the Sahara!

Tan Zumaitak and Timenzouzine

From the northernmost of the two campgrounds at Tamrit, two side excursions can be taken. The shelter of Tan Zumaitak is forty minutes' walk from the campground, via a spectacular natural amphitheatre with perpendicular walls and a perfectly flat sandy bottom. The shelter is on the west side of a shallow and narrow valley that supports some small acacias and plenty of yellow flowers on the oued floor after rain. It's a large rock shelter, with many superimposed human and animal figures from the 'Roundhead' or Archaic period. The quality and preservation of the paintings is excellent. (This shelter was discovered by the Swiss expedition a few years before Lhote; they never used the 'wet sponge' technique and it shows.)

In the opposite direction, about an hour away from the camp, a cluster of sandstone spires rises from the reg. The rock-art sites of **Timenzouzine** are just beyond, in a small oued. Up on the reg, just before the oued, is a large engraved elephant on a flat slab. The paintings here are not as spectacular as the major sites, but there are a few unique ones and they make a pleasant easy afternoon walk. (They are not usually visited because the 'standard' programme calls for Tan Zumaitak for the afternoon of the first day, after the ascent in the morning, and a straight descent on the last day.)

Sefar

The track continues beyond the northern camp to the north-east and soon reaches the edge of the 'stone forest'. This area is probably the most spectacular in the Tassili. Erosion has created narrow streets between the sandstone pillars, as well as a couple of stone arches.

At intervals, avenues cross the streets, and the perpendicular sandstone walls give the impression of walking in a stone Manhattan. On the far side of this area are the rock-art sites of **Titeras N-Elias**. This site offers a compressed

Saharan rock-art course, as in a very compact vicinity there are examples of all the major Tassili art periods (see p.401). The main shelter has an image of a **chariot** drawn by four horses, while on the far bank of the In Itinen oued is a group of paintings from the camel period including an interesting hunting scene. On the nearer side of the oued, there's a large ghostlike figure from the Archaic period, as well as plenty of examples from the Cattle period.

The chariot at Titeras N-Elias. © Andras Zboray

The path continues eastwards along the bed of the oued, and over uninspiring country (by Tassili standards) until abruptly descending into a small oued with a smaller 'town grid' terrain on the other side. This is the **Sefar** oued, and the 'streets' beyond contain the world's largest prehistoric art gallery. The trek from Tamrit to Sefar will take about four hours, covering about 15km and the approved camping area is the first 'street' on the left.

It is impossible to describe all the paintings at Sefar in such a small space. You'd need the best part of a full day to visit all the major paintings, and several days would be needed to see it all. For convenience, the site can be split in half along the line of the 'camp street'. The highlights of the southern part are the costumed dancing figures and the tiny gazelles just beyond the campground, the 'Homestead' scene from the Cattle period, 'the Masked Lady', and the three masks.

The larger northern part contains a very large scene from the Archaic period with a large bovid (bubalus?) and typical roundheaded Archaic figures adoring a 'Great God', and the most famous scene of them all, '**The Great God of Sefar**', which happily is in reasonably good shape, despite some blundered preservation attempts. There are hundreds of others in shelters along the sides of the streets.

Unfortunately many of the paintings are very faint and some have gone altogether due to wetting by Lhote's mission and other visitors, but there is still much left to enjoy.

The Great God of Sefar. © Andras Zboray

Tin Tazarift and Tin Aboteka

Tin Tazarift is about two hours' walk to the north-west in a maze of sandstone streets and pinnacles, or easily visitable as a morning or afternoon side trip from Sefar. The main shelter contains a group of large black figures with horned heads from the Archaic period, plus several others in very good condition. (Again, Tin Tazarift was first explored by the Swiss...). Tin Aboteka lies another hour to the north-west and contains, among others, the famous figure of a large **archer** with characteristic negroid profile.

The two sites can be combined in a single day based in Sefar, though guides may be unwilling to do this as, in their minds, it's two sites so it must be two days (so more money). Alternatively, from Titeras N-Elias it's possible to continue to Tin Aboteka, camp, and go on to Tin Tazarift and Sefar.

Jabbaren

Jabbaren, about 30km south of Sefar, is the second most important rock-art site in the vicinity. This is the one site on the plateau which it is possible to visit in a full single day, including an ascent and descent of Akba Arum pass. It is highly recommended if you don't have the time or inclination to visit the plateau for any longer.

If you're coming over from Sefar the going is good, mainly over gently undulating reg, with some nice rocky sections in the middle. Nearing Jabbaren, there's a small valley with some cypress trees, and the campground is just beyond these in a sheltered cove. Jabbaren itself is about 2km beyond the camp, along the bank of Oued Amazar, one of the main oueds of the Tassili, draining back towards the east. The sandstone here has eroded into conical lumps, with two main streets and many side alleys offering plenty of surface to paint on. Named by Daniken, the 'Great Martian God' from the Archaic

period measures 6m by 3m and is the biggest single painting on the Tassili. There are many scenes from the Archaic and Cattle periods, including a tiny figure of an archer looking over his shoulder with extremely fine detail, like a figure on a Greek vase.

An hour's walk south-east from Jabbaren, across the main oued (and not normally included in a day tour), **Aouenghet** offers some of the most unusual paintings on the Tassili and is a definite highlight. Subjects include the 'Masked God', 'White Lady' and several difficult-to-interpret scenes from the Archaic period.

On to Akba Arum

From Jabbaren you follow the main oued west for a short distance until it reaches a small ridge that is the watershed,

The top of the 600-metre-high Akba Arum.

beyond which the land gradually descends to the western edge of the plateau. A small oued develops and after a few bends ends abruptly in a steep slope littered with car-sized boulders tumbling down between two outlying fingers of the plateau. The path zigzags down the slope which, unlike the Akba Tafilalet, is uninterrupted for the full elevation of the plateau. The descent to the bottom, where a few acacias grow at the foot of the cliff, will take about an hour down a steep path and then another hour or so to where the cars are parked. Coming the other way it takes about three hours to reach Jabbaren.

Djanet environs

While the Tassili above Djanet is known mainly for rock paintings, close to town there is a prehistoric **rock engraving** that is counted among the finest in the Sahara, as well as other sites well worth visiting. It is possible to visit these places without a guide.

Oued In Debriene and the Crying Cows

Take the airport road south from Djanet until you reach the old airport and the crossroads turn-off east (left) to Tin Alkoum (Libya). Turn right here, along a track which leads a couple of kilometres to the Oued In Debriene. At the oued turn right again and a short way to the north on the right side of the track are a couple of boulders with engravings. These are not especially exciting.

To get to the Crying Cows you can either follow tracks south from here to the Crying Cow waypoint below, or head back to the old airport crossroads. From there continue south towards the new airport until you get to N24° 24.4' E09° 29.2'. Turn west here onto very sandy terrain and follow the mass of tracks back to the Oued In Debriene (at one point you may spot an old cobbled roadway). Follow whatever looks likely until you get to a pair of outcrops at N24° 22.5' E09° 25.6' ('Tegherghert' on the 200k map). Look around until you spot the place above. The graceful, naturalistic style is unlike any other engraving in Algeria: three long-horned cows, some with teardrop-like features around their eyes, 'crying' (it is said by local guides) because of the coming of the desert. The scene is in full sun from mid-afternoon, so the relief is better earlier in the day.

The Crying Cows (not to be confused with the cheerful brand of cheese triangles).

Tim Ras and the plateau's edge

Leaving the road to Bordj north towards the plateau edge fifteen kilometres out of Djanet, one enters a wonderful land of pinnacles and mesas rising from sands, a beautiful landscape that makes a great camping spot. Indeed one can drive in and out of the tassilis much of the way from here up to around W09°, with many more secluded camp spots along the way. There is no rock art here, but it's fun to explore all the same.

Essendilene Canyon

Back on the Bordj highway, Oued Essendilene crosses the road 78km from Djanet (see Route A6). Turn north before the oued and follow tracks deep into the ever-narrowing valley for around 18km up to N25° 57.2′ E08° 59.7′. Here you'll probably meet some nomads who, for a small fee, will guide you on the half-hour walk to the end of the canyon and the lovely fern-draped guelta you'll find there.

Tunisia

Being the smallest Saharan country (smaller in fact than some ergs), Tunisia offers limited scope for long-range desert travel. North of the Chott el Djerid, Tunisia is a pleasant Mediterranean country occupying the low hills of the eastern Atlas. Berber life is still very much in evidence away from the coastal tourist enclaves and a scenic drive south during the springtime wildflower season is nice.

Around the Chott, in particular Tozeur, Douz and Matmata, mainstream tourists come to sample the 'Sahara Experience': the nomadobilia zone mentioned earlier in this book. Convoys of white Land Cruisers driven by cheched-up 'Tuaregs' race between these towns and the coastal resorts.

South of the Chott are the true fringes of the Sahara, principally the eastern limits of the Grand Erg Oriental which spills over from Algeria. No piste culture has ever developed in this rarely-visited zone, partly because the dunes here are small and dense (like Route A1 or T2) which makes vehicle travel a struggle. An oil pipeline track reaches down to the southern apex of the country, a stone's throw from Ghadames, and desert rallies have traditionally used the erg to hold small-scale but demanding events. Without having to delve deep into the Sahara these rallies are easy to organise and manage.

A couple of token routes may sound a bit slack. For Brits or even the other non-German and French readers who might use this book, Tunisia is a long way to go via a relatively expensive ferry for not very much. It's hard to imagine anyone going all that way when Algeria and Libya are just down the road and offer so much more.

All in all the best that can be said about Tunisia from a Sahara Overland point of view is that it's a lovely place to visit after Libya. Its green fields, tidy villages and Gaelic ambience are a real tonic for the eye after the half-built squalor and blowing rubbish of northern Libya.

T1 EL HAMMA → TATAOUINE (via Ksar Ghilane)   [221KM]
October 1998; Toyota HJ61

Description
This route makes a good 'shakedown' piste if you're heading for Libya, giving you a chance to become familiar with your GPS, transmission and tyre pressures without putting excessive demands on navigation or driving.

The pipeline piste to Ksar Ghilane is easy, although the short run over the small dunes to the Roman fort will give you something to think about. The scenery improves in the hills towards the end of the piste. If you get a chance the ancient Berber villages around Tataouine are well worth exploring.

Route-finding and markers
Tracks and junctions are all clear using the distances and GPS waypoints below, but as this route may be your first in the desert, references are a little excessive to help give you confidence. Though you'll hardly need them, you'll

T1 – RECOMMENDED MAPS
EL HAMMA → TATAOUINE 221KM

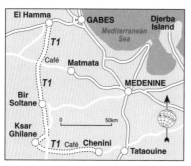

No current map shows the orientation of the piste correctly so use any map with grid lines and a scale of 1:1m or less.

find the odd stretch of orange-topped poles at one-kilometre intervals along the pipeline piste, and stone cairns along the corrugated track east of the pipeline.

Fuel
El Hamma, maybe Ksar, Tataouine.

Water
El Hamma, Ksar Ghilane and Chenini plus a couple of café/souvenir shacks along the piste.

Traffic
Even in the summer you'll encounter a steady stream of local Land Cruisers blasting between Chenini and Douz.

Driving
The pipeline piste is easy for cars and bikes but the 2km dune run to the fort is tricky: a good place to experiment with tyre pressures and dune technique. Note that when we did the piste there was light rain so the soft sand sections, and especially the dune run to the fort, were uncharacteristically firm. East of the pipeline the corrugations are grim right up to the hills. If anything is going to shake loose or break, it will do so here – better now than in Libya.

Suggested duration
You could do it in a day and stay at the plush Ksar Ghilane campements – or the tamarisk groves around KM179 make nice camping spots.

0km (221)　　　**N33° 53.8'　E09° 48.6'**
El Hamma fuel station. Drive west into town, turning left at the roundabout; immediately following a right-hand bend in the middle of town turn left down a narrow street signed 'Matmata'.

Continuing S to the edge of town, the road forks 1km from the turn-off; keep right through the palmerie where the sealed surface ends. Pass under pylons.

6.5 (214.5)
Emerge from the palmerie and after a few hundred metres turn left across a washed-out oued and rejoin the pipeline piste at N33° 50.5' E09° 47.3'. Consider reducing tyres to track pressures and turn right (S) driving S of the broad, shallow valley.

18 (202)
Cross Oued El Hamma.

19 (201)
Pass sign to the east, 'Hjar 10km'. Continue straight ahead. Low dunes to side of track.

22 (199)
Several orange marker poles at 1km intervals from this point.

24 (197)
Cross a oued just after a pipeline valve on the E edge of the track.

28 (193)
Metal sign '690' on the E side of the track.

30 (191)　　　**N33° 38.6'　E09° 44.2'**
Yellow sign for 'Matmata' just N of oued and '240' pipeline sign also visible on the east side. One kilometre later you pass some abandoned buildings on the W.

35 (186)
A side track heads W. Continue S.

39 (182)
Cross over the Douz–Matmata tarmac road (small café). Continue S. About 2.5km later pass an oil camp on the W of the track and after another couple of kilometres a refinery and radio mast.

50 (171)
Douz piste joins from the W. Sign: 'Bir Soltane 25km, Ksar Ghilane 72km, Matmata 60km'. Track becomes mildly corrugated as you are now on the Matmata–Douz tourist route.

66 (155)
Track becomes sandy.

71 (150)   N33° 17.7'   E 09° 44.0'
Bir Soltane army camp visible to the right of the track. Café by the side of the track.

82 (139)
Buildings with radio mast W of the piste. Dunes visible in far distance, the easterly fringes of the Grand Erg Oriental which swamps the borders of Algeria and Tunisia for thousands of square kilometres.

87 (134)
Sandy section for about 3km.

96 (125)
Junction with piste from NE. Continue south. Low hills ahead.

98 (123)   N33° 03.2'   E 09° 46.6'
Turn right for Ksar Ghilane. Track narrows and becomes mildly corrugated.

100 (121)
Track joins laterite road. Turn right continuing SW towards the pink dunes of the Grand Erg Oriental.

113 (108)
Ksar Ghilane village ahead. It doesn't quite match up to the description as 'Tunisia's most beautiful desert oasis' but the dense tamarisk and palm grove on the north side of the settlement is a lovely green interlude and a haven for animals.

116 (105)
Upmarket *Campement Paradis*, popular with excursions from Djerba. Next door is a little tourist enclave with a pond and restaurant, all very pretty.

To get to the fort, 2km away, take the track leading out of the trees NNW from the pond restaurant and over the dunes. If you don't fancy it in your car, you can always hire a camel or even walk. Follow the most recent tracks or head for the GPS point below. The low walls of the fort will become visible after a few hundred metres.

Even though the dunes are only a few metres high the direct route tiptoes along some narrow ridges and along slopes; intimidating if this is your first experience of dune driving. Beware of oncoming traffic: it's a popular route and the 'track' is mostly one car wide. In a car chug along slowly and keep moving; on a bike you may find it easier to blaze your own trail, but take it easy. From the café pool to the fort takes about ten to fifteen minutes.

118 (103)   N33° 01.0' E09° 37.0'
The Roman fort, rebuilt during the French occupation. Some inscriptions are evident in the stonework. This fort would have been an outpost on the *limes*, the frontier or limits of the Roman Empire.

121 (100)
Leave Ksar along the laterite road you arrived on. Depending on where you went while here, the elapsed distance may vary a bit from now on. Drive past the point where you joined this road (KM99) and join the pipeline track...

135 (86)   N33° 02.5'   E 09° 46.7'
... a little further S than where you originally left it. Turn S on the pipeline track.

150 (71)   N32° 54.5'   E 09° 45.0'
Crossroads. Sign on right for Ksar Ghilane. Turn left (E) for Chenini, easily crossing a few bands of dunes as you go downhill. The corrugated track sets in.

152 (69)
Tyre marks piste to SE. Continue E.

On the pipeline piste to Ksar Ghilane.
© Mantec

154 (67)
Tyre marker at fork. Keep right.

158 (63)
Pistes fan out to avoid corrugations. Continue at bearing of around 102°.

165 (56)   **N32° 53.3'   E09° 54.5'**
Hilltop cairns. Mountains visible to left.

168 (53)
'Café Nomade' makes a nice spot for a break.

171 (50)
Sign for 'Café'. Track forks, keep right.

179 (42)
Track rises into hills. After 1km you pass a hilltop cairn S of the track (N32° 53.8' E10° 02.7') with others on ridgetops as you continue E. Scenery improves from here on with distinctive tamarisk groves blocked by a low dam wall evident. Nice campsites if there's no rain about.

182 (39)
Hill with cairn S of the track.

184 (37)
Signs with numbers '1' and '3'. A track turns north. Continue E.

192 (29)
Low pass.

196 (25)
Another pass which you ascend over bare slabs of rock.

197 (24)   **N32° 53.6'   E10° 13.3'**
A third pass immediately after which the track forks. Take the right fork.

198 (23)
Arrive at the tarmac road south of Chenini. Turn left (N) for Chenini along a road through the deep gorge.

203 (18)
Chenini. An impressively-situated Berber hill village incorporating 900-year-old troglodyte dwellings and firmly on the tourist route.

There are other similar villages like Douiret to the S and Ghoumrassen and Guermessa to the N. For accommodation try the famous *Relais du Chenini* (you can't miss it). Otherwise drive through the town on to Tataouine.

221 (0)
Tataouine. If you're heading for Libya, the direct road heading ENE to Ben Guerdane via Kirchaou is not that clearly signposted. Ask around or you'll end up on the road to Medenine.

T2 DOUZ → KSAR GHILANE (direct)   [106KM]

November 2003; Honda XR650R (Karim Hussain, Rally El Chott)

Description

This is a classic route across the dunes to Ksar Ghilane from Douz. Many come to Tunisia just to do this trip. It is accessible, no permits are required and it takes you into dunes without your having to venture to the far south of Tunisia. It starts off on an easy piste, gradually getting harder, with the last 40km on very soft sand and dunes (no piste) ending at the Roman fort of Ksar

Ghilane. You can then recover in the warm spring of Ksar Ghilane and gloat over your accomplishment.

Route-finding and markers
The piste is easy up to the *Sahara Café*, after which a gentle stony piste heads into dunes. The route could be followed GPS point-to-point, but it is preferable to keep your eye on the actual dunes and monitor distances from the route description.

Fuel
Douz, Ksar Ghilane (not guaranteed). Have enough to get you to El Hamma or Tataouine (see T1).

Water
Only from cafés and the well at KM20.4 (unconfirmed).

Traffic
Tourist and tour traffic on the pistes and at the *Sahara Café*.

Driving
In the dunes this route requires a good knowledge of sand driving and recovery if it's not to be impossibly exhausting. You may have to back-track a couple of times to take on less steep routes around some of the high-er crests. Cars should have no great problem; on a bike it is too hard with lug-gage and you should carry at least 3 to 4 litres of water. The trip will take a full day and should be started early. It is not a trip to try alone.

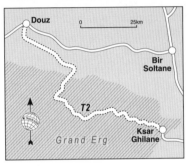

T2 – RECOMMENDED MAPS
DOUZ → KSAR GHILANE 106KM

As with T1 you're on your own. Any map with grid lines and a scale of 1:1m or less will do.

Suggested duration
One day.

0km (106) **N33° 24.0' E09° 0.5'**
Take the road E past the camel racing sta-dium for a couple of kilometres until the piste starts off on the left (this waypoint).
  Turn left onto this piste and after 400m bear right.

1.9 (104.1) **N33° 23.3' E09° 01.2'**
Keep straight.

6.7 (99.3)
A piste joins from right; keep straight.

9.1 (96.9)
Bear right.

20.4 (85.6)
Well.

25.4 (80.6)
A piste joins from left; keep straight.

30 (76) **N33° 15.7' E09° 14.8'**
Sahara Café. Turn right.

47 (59) **N33° 08.9' E09° 09.5'**
A piste joins from right, continue straight ahead.

50 (56)
Bear right.

53 (53) **N33° 06.6' E09° 11.9'**
Waypoint, keep straight.

60 (46) **N33° 03.8' E09° 14.7'**
Crossroads, bear left.

Come in, #72, your time is up.
© Karim Hussain

68 (38)
Crossroads, continue straight across.

72 (34)   **N33° 04.5' E09° 21.9'**
Waypoint, keep straight.

73 (33)
Crossroads, café; turn right.

74 (32)   **N33° 04.6' E09° 23.1'**
'T' junction, turn left.

77 (29)   **N33° 04.3' E09° 24.2'**
Waypoint, keep straight.

80 (26)   **N33° 03.8' E09° 25.7'**
Waypoint, keep straight .

81 (25)   **N33° 04.2' E09° 25.9'**
Dunes end, piste begins.

88 (18)
Bear right.

90 (16)
Crossroads, turn left.

91 (15)
Bad section of road.

96 (10) N33° 02.1' E09° 34.1'
'T' junction, turn right.

99 (7)
Turn left.

100 (6)   **N33° 01.1' E09° 35.8'**
Turn right.

103 (3)   **N33° 00.5' E09° 37.0'**
Fort now visible, head into a basin in the dunes.

106 (0)   **N32° 59.3' E09° 38.4'**
Ksar Ghilane.

Libya

Routes L1 to L5 make up the Classic Tour of the Libyan Sahara, feasible even for a first-timer with a month to spare. They concentrate in the Fezzan region of the south-west which, like the adjacent south-east of Algeria, has just about everything the Sahara has to offer in a relatively compact area. In a clockwise or anticlockwise direction you'll see the very best of the Libyan Sahara – scenically and prehistorically – and still have time to visit the Roman ruins of Leptis or Sabratha on the way back.

L6 is straightforward, but L7 is remote (and not without dangers) and will give you a feel for the remote Sahara that you won't always find in the popular Fezzan. These routes have a lot more distance to cover for not that much more scenic spectacle than you'll find in the Fezzan. And once you've got to Kufra the massif of Jebel Uweinat, only 350km to the south-east on the corners of Egypt and Sudan, is well worth a visit.

Along the southern frontier with Chad there are landmined areas from the 1980s war and more recently laid by Chadian forces trying to limit the mobility of the rebels from the Tibesti (see p.638), especially around the strip north of Aozou and the Kilingue Pass crossing the spur of the Jebel Nuqay or Dohone (Route L7). There are also mines along the Egyptian border, though these are much fewer. In the southern regions you may also encounter smugglers exporting highly subsidised Libyan goods south, as well as the border patrols trying to keep tabs on this trade, but neither is necessarily a threat to travellers.

If you're heading for Egypt, the border formalities at Saloum on the coast are as protracted as any on the planet. For an impression of the drive down from Tazerbu to Chad see page 614, with El Gatrun to Agadez in Niger on page 601.

Access and border formalities
Since the first edition of this book travelling independently in Libya has become restricted: an invitation from a local tour agency is still necessary but since 2002 it is necessary to apply for invitations in groups of three or more (you don't all have to arrive or travel together); you have to travel with a

---

ARABIC NUMERALS

1	١	wahid	11	١١	ihdashr	70	٧٠	saba'i'in
2	٢	ithnayn, tnaan	12	١٢	itnaysh	80	٨٠	tamaani'in
3	٣	tala'ata, tlaat	13	١٣	tala'atash	90	٩٠	tis'i'in
4	٤	arba'a	14	١٤	arba'ata'ash	100	١٠٠	miyya
5	٥	khamsa	20	٢٠	ishri'in	200	٢٠٠	mittayn
6	٦	sita'a	21	٢١	wahid wa ishri'in	1000	١٠٠٠	elf
7	٧	saba'a	30	٣٠	talathi'in	2000	٢٠٠٠	alfayn
8	٨	tamanya	40	٤٠	arba'ati'in	3000	٣٠٠٠	tala'athat aalaaf
9	٩	tissa'a	50	٥٠	khamsi'in			
10	١٠	a'ashra	60	٦٠	sitti'in			

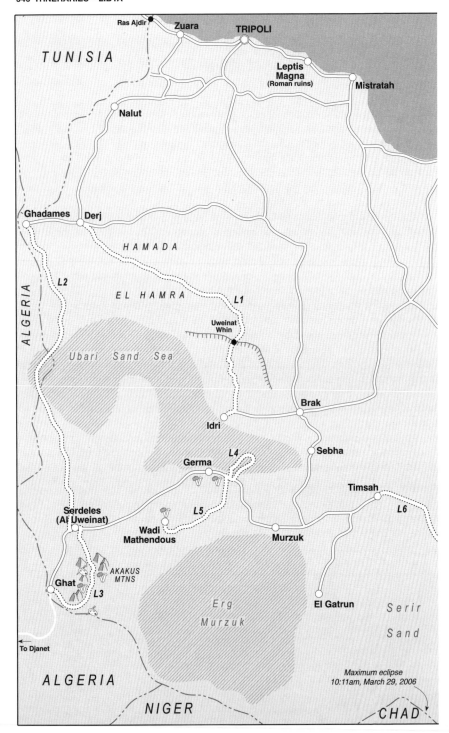

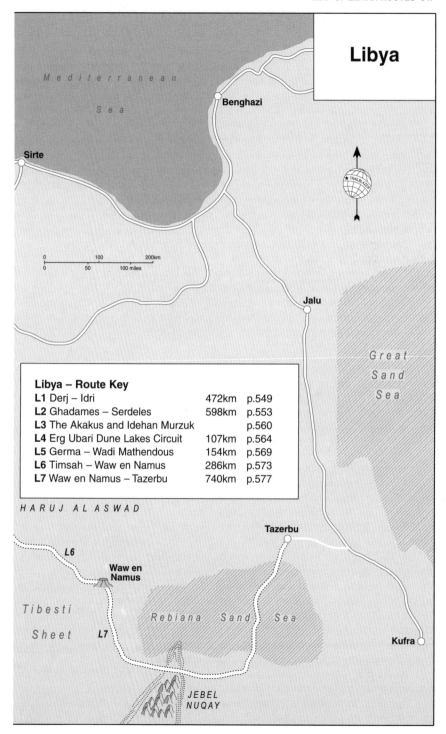

Libya

M e d i t e r r a n e a n

S e a

Benghazi

Sirte

★ TRAILBLAZER

```
0          100        200km
0      50      100 miles
```

Jalu

G r e a t

S a n d

S e a

Libya – Route Key

L1 Derj – Idri	472km	p.549
L2 Ghadames – Serdeles	598km	p.553
L3 The Akakus and Idehan Murzuk		p.560
L4 Erg Ubari Dune Lakes Circuit	107km	p.564
L5 Germa – Wadi Mathendous	154km	p.569
L6 Timsah – Waw en Namus	286km	p.573
L7 Waw en Namus – Tazerbu	740km	p.577

H A R U J   A L   A S W A D

L6

Tazerbu

Waw en Namus

Tibesti

Sheet

L7

R e b i a n a   S a n d   S e a

Kufra

JEBEL NUQAY

guide, and sometimes with a police officer too. This adds up to €100 a day to your costs on top of the typical €200–300 to obtain the visa and services, although the cost does at least include help with documentation at **Ras Ajdir** (the only entry point from Tunisia). As this book was going to press there were rumours that these regulations may be relaxed, allowing tourists again to travel independently without guides, police etc. Find out the latest details on the Libya page of the website. As it is, the above palaver puts many people off.

Your obligatory guide should have all the things listed below ready for you when you arrive, which will speed up your immigration formalities to just half an hour. Without help – worth paying for with your invitation, even if guides become unnecessary – unless you read Arabic you'll just have to hope someone helps you fill in the forms, or latch onto someone who knows what to do. It can take a few hours. The procedure is as follows:

● Get your passport stamped.
● Change money.
● From the hangar on the left, rent number plates – 100LD (have some wire or cable ties ready).
● In the same hangar, buy Libyan carnet – 50LD for a car, 30LD for a bike.
● Buy motor insurance – 80LD for four weeks.

All these documents will be checked as you leave the border post. You get a 50LD refund on your number plates when you leave.

Maps
If you're used to the excellent range of IGN maps available for former francophone West Africa (some of which cover western Libya), you'll find the choice a bit limited. It all adds up to Soviet-era maps, mostly commonly at 1:500,000, and the American TPCs and ONCs. There's more on Libyan country maps and a Russian translation key on p.331.

HEADING SOUTH
If you plan to undertake the classic tour of routes 1–4, the little town of Derj, 520km from the frontier is where you decide whether to head off across the Hamada el Hamra or visit Ghadames first.

From Ras Ajdir the coast road leads 60km to Zuara, a busy northern town the likes of which you won't see further south, so if you need anything, get it here. There's fuel (often queues) about halfway between the border and Zuara and again in Zuara. In all Libyan towns the fuel station is usually located on the edge of town – apparently a safety measure.

Turn right in Zuara centre for Nalut (210km), eventually turning right at an unmanned checkpoint onto the arid coastal plain. A hundred and twenty kilometres south of Zuara turn west along the Jebel Nafusah, passing through nondescript towns. Much more impressive is Nalut, perched on the lip of the Jebel, accessed after a checkpoint and a series of hairpins. Its impressive ksar is well worth a visit, though the *Hotel Nalut* must surely have got better by now.

Turn right at the roundabout at the top of the climb and drive through the modern town, passing the fuel station and the market on your left.

From the far side of town you head into the desert with a runaway dune or two lying over the road before you get to Sinawan. Turn right at the roundabout and drive up through town. There's a fuel station with a café 6km south of town. Beyond Sinawan the grip of the desert tightens with only the marching pylons and vandalised phone boxes for company until you arrive at Derj.

If you're saving the Hamada el Hamra for later, Ghadames is 125km west and its wonderful Old Town of covered thoroughfares is well worth a visit even if you retrace your steps to Derj.

L1 DERJ → IDRI (via Uweinat Whin) [472KM]

November 1998; Toyota HJ61

Description

This is a popular first piste in Libya, drawing you quickly across the bleak Hamada El Hamra plateau rather than the sealed alternative east via Garyat to Sebha. The route can be divided into three parts: an imperceptible ascent along a wadi to Bir Gazell followed by a flat, fast run across the open hamada to its southern escarpment. With little to distract you it's possible (even desirable) to get past the edge of the plateau and the Uweinat Whin checkpoint on the first day. South of here the camping spots are a lot more welcoming. But be warned, the last 120km are slow and rough, winding through spurs of the Jebel Hasawna; it can take a full day to get to Idri, but it's a lot more scenic than the hamada.

Note that unlike every other itinerary in this book, we logged Route L1 in the opposite direction and then reversed the description. Hopefully there are no anomalies, but you may find some descriptions of landmarks conspicuous to southbound travellers missing. Because of this and the fact that this may be your first long Saharan piste, there is probably more information than you'd normally need.

Route-finding and markers

Although many oil exploration tracks cross the Hamada, this route is consistently clear all the way as long as you pay attention to the markers and don't diverge.

Up to Bir Gazell (KM103) you get cairns and the odd concrete pyramid. From here on half-metre high concrete pyramids (see picture, right) lie at almost unbroken 5km intervals alongside the old track all the way to the plateau's edge (KM333) where you drop off the escarpment onto clearer tracks. Smoother tracks run alongside the original track; use these but always keep the pyramids in sight and try to anticipate the next one. And from the point where they all converge there are plenty of clear tracks leading to the edge.

Five-km pyramid markers on the open plateau.

After the checkpoint you'll eventually get the feel for the stony old Italian colonial track lined with its finely-built cairns, some on hilltops and resembling squat bottles or kilns, others square blocks and set right by the track, one on each side. Should you wander onto a smoother piste without these regular cairns, you've made a mistake. Go back to the last cairns and correct your error.

L1 – RECOMMENDED MAPS
DERJ → IDRI 472KM

The cumbersome American ONC H3 shows the entire route with remarkable accuracy, especially the curves around Uweinat Whin and further south. But Idri ('Adri') is misplaced and none of the other villages marked.

The three Russian 1:1 million maps (H-32 'Ghadames', H-33 'Beri Ulid' and G-33 'Sebha') are better in this respect and more pleasing to use, while the French IGN 1:1m NH-32 'Hassi Messaoud' makes a good alternative to the Russian H-32 sheet if you happen to have it already.

Suggested duration
Two days.

0km (472)
Derj fuel station. There's a restaurant opposite but seemingly little else in town apart from a baker about a kilometre back up the Nalut road – an isolated building on the W side of the road. Ask around or use your nose.

For the start of the Idri route drive from the fuel station towards Nalut and turn right along the tarmac road leading east to Garyat.

13 (459)
Leave the tarmac to the S at a blue and white oil drum marked 'IDC 23'. The track leads SE onto the hamada. You'll soon find the actual track very rough and probably choose to drive alongside: a pattern you'll try and maintain for most of this route.

Fuel
Derj and Idri with emergency petrol possibly available at Uweinat Whin.

Water
As above plus the pump house at Bir Rimit (KM72).

Traffic
Popular in winter with southbound tourists. Otherwise sparse. On the plateau don't be distracted or tempted to follow local vehicles which may be using the Hamada's many exploration tracks. Your route is clear all the way.

Driving
Some washed-out cross channels after Bir Rimit then as easy as it gets from Bir Gazell to the escarpment. From here on sometimes agonisingly rough and slow with occasional sandy patches in the valleys. Four-wheel drive is barely necessary though this section can be hard on your tyres and also hard for heavily-loaded bikes.

After less than a kilometre there's a fork; take the right-hand track alongside the old piste.

24 (448)
Buildings visible a few hundred metres south of the track. From here on you'll eventually find yourself driving along the southern bank of a wadi; some bits are washed out, others sanded over. There is also the occasional concrete pyramid, but not at regular 5km intervals as they are later.

57 (415)   N29° 50.7'   E10° 50.9'
Waypoint. You should be driving along the wadi's southern bank with a few shrubs and small trees making a handy spot for a break.

66 (406)
Wide gravel track. Heading is nearly S.

72 (400)
Bir Rimit pumping station. Pass to the north of the buildings, continuing ESE.

The tracks from here lead S to Hassi Ifertas and the difficult route to Idri along the edge of the Idehan Ubari. Should you be tempted to try this route using Göttler's guidebook (1998 edition – Route A9), be warned that the description can be confusing.

73 (399)
Soon after the pumping station the track forks; keep left.

97 (375)
Concrete pyramid.

98 (374)
Bearing 140°.

103 (369)
Bir Gazell approached almost from the N. Cross the wadi to a solitary building with nearby troughs. The Italian-built well is a couple of hundred metres S of the building in the wadi, but it's been dry for years. From here a broad white stony piste leads south from Bir Gazell, later curving to the SE.

105 (367)
Two rusty signs on poles, one fallen over.

130 (342)   N29° 26.8'   E11° 22.0'
A piste cuts across your route with several tyre markers. Continue on a bearing of 134° following the track-side pyramids.

184 (288)
Cross a wadi with some vegetation.

190 (282)
Black oil drum north of the piste. Bearing 125°.

199 (273)
Cross a wide, vegetated wadi.

208 (264)
Diamond-shaped sign on a pole next to a concrete pyramid.

216 (256)
Tyre on pole in an oil drum plus two more tyres lying around. Bearing 104°.

From here on, after you've passed 29°N, the track begins to curve to the S.

250 (222)
Round sign on a pole.

285 (187)   N28° 48.4'   E12° 39.0'
Two rusty signs with graffiti and an oil drum.

289 (183)
Another bulldozed N–S track crosses your piste with a rusty axle as a marker. Continue on bearing 144°.

303 (169)   N28° 40.3'   E12° 44.2'
Concrete pyramid at the crossing of a wide pipeline piste running 20°/200°. Two hundred metres down this pipeline track a red and white sign reads '244' which is probably the distance to Ubari. Cross the pipeline track and continue at bearing 150° to 155°.

313 (159)   N28° 35.2'   E12° 47.5'
Convergence with the wide track from the N. Continue 150°.

323 (149)
Fast going just after crossing a oued. Follow tracks heading just E of N, bearing 167°.

332 (140)
White container with yellow roof to your east. Time to test your brakes and get ready for a complete change of scenery. You are nearing the plateau's edge.

333 (139)
Edge of the plateau and end of concrete pyramid markers. The Uweinat Whin checkpoint can be seen down below to the SW. Steep descent for 1km.

336 (136)   N28° 26.5'   E12° 46.9'
Uweinat Whin checkpoint. From this point your track goes W, curves to the S and then SE. The route follows an old built-up track that for the most part is awful to drive on but very clear to follow. Do not be distracted by other minor or

newer pistes which will feel different and do not have the distinctive stone cairns.

339 (133)
Piste curves to SW.

342 (130)
Driving away from the plateau's edge now at 163°, SSW. Other tracks nearby. Keep on the old track which curves more to the SW.

347 (125)   N28° 22.7'   E12° 49.6'
Small white mosque with green roof. Another track joins from the W, probably from the well at El Hassi, about 30km to the WSW on the edge of the Idehan Ubari.

349 (123)
Beginning of a pretty valley about 8km long with plenty of trees: good camping. Some sandy sections mixed in with rocks can be tricky. But it's best to keep your tyres firm, and use 4WD if necessary.

357 (115)   N28° 20.2'   E12° 54.3'
Carved inscription by the west bank of the track as it crests a pass, indicating (a little inaccurately) 'Idri 120, Uweinat 25'. Route continues SSW along the very stony track which cannot be avoided.

360 (112)
For the next 18km or so the pace speeds up as you pass over flat ground. Either side of the track there is less vibration but more dips. Take your pick, there's no easy way. Head SSW, tending towards SW. You'll pass twin cairns by the track side and others on the hilltops. Make the most of this section. From now on the pace will be rough and slow.

382 (90)
Very stony terrain winding through low hills. After 3km you're going nearly W then you'll curve to the S as you approach 28°N.

392 (80)   N28° 06.7'   E12° 43.5'
Old Peugeot 404 wreck by the track.

399 (73)
You're in the middle of a dead straight bit of track (or more probably driving along-side it) heading 191°. Some stone buildings are visible to the E.

407 (65)
Tree at the beginning of a long cliff wall on the W side of the track. Heading SW, the track follows this distinctive cliff carved by a long-gone river.

413 (59)
After crossing a oued you'll pass some collapsed stone buildings.

427 (45)   N27° 49.4'   E12° 47.2'
Collapsed stone shelter. Track joins from NW. Within 2km you ascend steeply into some hills for more bumpy, sometimes sandy but scenic driving through the Gargaf hills for around 18km. Heading is more or less S and then SE with plenty of Goldsworthyesque cairns to marvel at.

As you near Idri tracks fan out to avoid corrugations and a new parallel track criss-crosses the old colonial track which continues to be marked with twin cairns.

457 (15)   N27° 32.7'   E12° 58.5'
At this point, near a pair of block-shaped cairns the alternative bulldozed track turns S, to the right, away from the old piste. In 6km it joins the smooth, wide El Hassi piste coming out of Idri. Both routes lead to Idri but this way can be a bit less rough.

461 (11)
Continuing along the old track, with a big cairn on a hill to the E, you can see the Idri satellite village of Mansoura ahead. Follow tracks towards its brick water tower.

466 (6)
Mansoura village. Rejoin the tarmac at a S/E bend in the road. S (right) leads 6km to Idri fuel station. Turning E leads to several other fuel stations starting at 28km and eventually to the town of Brak and the turn-off S to Sebha.

472 (0)
Idri fuel station by a roundabout. Restaurant opposite.

OVER THE DUNES TO UBARI

The eastern arm of the Idehan Ubari sand sea separates the string of villages along the Wadi Shati from the Wadi Adjal to the south (the Sebha–Ghat road). Only 120km as the crow flies, you might think that this would make a manageable dune crossing. The 1:500,000 Russian G-33A 'Sebha' map shows various dashed lines joining the two wadis but you can be sure there will be few actual tracks or markers to follow.

I've met travellers who took from four hours (BMW R100GS) to eight days (three 4x4s and a seized bike) to complete the crossing. One to two days is more normal, with a dune camp close to the end near Ubari. Many travellers find the final dunes at the southern edge the hardest to cross.

Like all dune routes, this crossing is hard on your engine and hard on your nerves. There's no set route though the dunes, but as in much of the central Sahara the gassis (corridors) generally run NE/SW. Plan to follow one of these for as long as possible to limit risky dune cresting. GPS waypoints are only moderately useful; you just pick your way along the line of least resistance.

Overall, it's not recommended for first-timers and under no circumstances should you try it alone. But if you hire a reliable guide or meet up with someone who's done the route before, give it a go. Reduce car tyres to 1 bar or less and take only as much fuel as you need to keep weight down while expecting maximum consumption. You may like to see how you get on with Route L3 before taking off across the sands.

Apparently the pipeline piste which you crossed at KM303 on Route L1 from Derj goes through the dunes west of Idri somewhere, but several travellers have reported difficulties in finding it or following it: the otherwise regular red and white km-markers are probably long buried by now.

L2 GHADAMES → SERDELES (Al Uweinat)   [598KM]
February 2000; Toyota, FJ62, Toyota HJ61, Toyota Amazon

Description
Officially this route, a direct link to the fabulous Fezzan of south-western Libya, requires a local guide (you may need one to be in Libya anyway). Nevertheless people do attempt it without a guide, even though the route finding is by no means clear. The description below aims to provide a feel for the route to help you make up your mind. It's this route or L1 if you want to get to the Fezzan, avoiding the highway or long dune routes through the Idehan Ubari. Serdeles is the Tuareg name for the village shown on some maps by its Arabic name of Al Uweinat.

There is no single track, but several variations, with guides taking the way they know. The further west you go the fewer dunes there are to cross and this route describes the westernmost option which includes a continuous dune section of around 24km – most of it a few kilometres inside Algeria. This transgression is tolerated by the Algerians and you won't see anybody, let alone need a visa.

The route takes you right past an army checkpoint at Hassi Tin Hieddan (KM405). If you turned up here without a guide they used to turn you back. It's possible to plead ignorance, talk (or pay) your way out of this daunting prospect – or try and avoid the checkpoint altogether. This is what the more easterly variations of Ghadames–Serdeles do, though the price is up to 100km of dunes – where you may want a guide more than ever.

Scenically, the route, which usually takes two nights and three days with a guide, is not as interesting as you might think, considering the distance. The first eighty kilometres are slow with flat top hills, a few wadis and a lot of

L2 – RECOMMENDED MAPS
GHADAMES → SERDELES 598KM

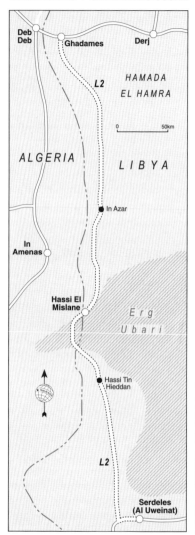

No maps accurately depict this specific route. The ONC H3 covers the whole span and two IGN 1:1 millions also cover the route: NH-32 'Hasa Messaoud' and NG-32 'Djanet'.

NH-32 covers the route accurately as far as In Azar (KM189), but south of here and onto the Djanet NH-32 map none of the few tracks shown corresponds to our route. It's the same story with the Russian 1:1 millions H-32 'Ghadames' and G-32 'Djanet'.

hamada to look at. Expect to cover about 200km by dusk. With the main dune crossing (KM345–369) preceded by a lesser band of sand at KM287, the second day is much more memorable. From the checkpoint south to Serdeles is rocky desert with some speedy sections across salt pans.

You rejoin the Sebha–Ghat road a few kilometres west of Serdeles, at a point 116km north of Ghat. Apart from checkpoints, you can be in Ghat in little more than an hour, with the road paralleled all the way by the long escarpment of the Akakus to your east.

Route-finding and markers
Without a guide, route-finding can be at times difficult and time consuming for first-timers. Even using the GPS waypoints listed below, you're likely to add at least a day to the crossing without the aid of a guide. You'll find the usual mixture of old tyres, oil drums and cairns, and from KM522 the Italian-built square block cairns commonly seen on Route L1.

Fuel
Ghadames and Serdeles. There was no vehicle based at the Hassi Tin Hieddan checkpoint though they may have diesel from the generator. If you're really desperate you could try getting to the Algerian oil towns around Edjeleh (just before Hassi Mislane, KM345), but you could meet trouble.

Water
Despite what the IGNs indicate, we only found water at each end of the route and at Hassi Tin Hieddan (KM405). Water may also be available at the encampment at KM167.

Traffic
Most tourists traverse this route in a southerly direction. In October we came across several groups but only two local bangers heading north.

Driving

Nothing too demanding apart from the dreaded dunes. At KM280, 65km before the main dune crossing, you traverse a band of dunes for about 2km. It's a popular place for beginners to get it all wrong and end up stuck but it's all good practice for the main event down the track.

As with most dune crossings, the 24km section follows gassis and the shallowest inclines. The ascents and most drops are quite easy, but it only takes one short jump or tumble to ruin your day. Take your time and be careful.

At nearly 600km this route is a long stretch for autonomous motorcyclists. With full luggage you'll be gasping through the Algerian section, although at least by then your fuel load should be halved. Other than that you'll find the riding easier than the cars, as long as someone else is taking care of navigation.

Suggested duration

Three days with a guide, with two nights on the piste.

0km (598)
Ghadames fuel station. Head E back out towards Derj.

6 (592) N30° 08.1' E09° 32.8'
Turn off the highway and follow the faint rocky tracks heading ESE (116°). Soon you pass piles of tin cans and other rubbish.

7.3 (593)
Bearing 137°, SE. Soon a cone-shaped hill becomes visible to the WSW.

10.2 (587.8)
Prominent track across stony sand flats. In 1km two pairs of twin-humped hills are visible to the SW.

15 (583)
Cross tracks going N-S. Continue at around 155°.

17 (581) N30° 03.3' E09° 36.5'
At a descent pass a cairn on the right.

26 (572)
Group of flat-topped hills visible to the W.

32 (566) N29° 56.5' E09° 40.1'
Bearing 148°.

33 (565) N29° 56.1' E09° 40.6'
Cross a wadi with some small trees and continue with the wadi on your left.

36.4 (561.6)
Bearing has now altered to around 200°, SSW.

44 (554) N29° 50.5' E09° 40.6'
Broken plateau visible ahead with more flat and pointed hills visible to the SE.

52 (546) N29° 46.5' E09° 41.8'
Bearing 119°. Driving along a broad valley with 'flat-tops' to either side, into a wadi. Some sandy patches and vegetation.

59 (539) N29° 43.7' E09° 43.5'
Cairn visible on hilltop to the W. In 2km you emerge at the far end of the valley.

623 (536) N29° 42.5' E09° 43.4'
Old oil drum marker.

74 (524) N29° 36.2' E09° 46.4'
Drive into a well-vegetated wadi. Within 500m cairns are visible on the ridge tops. Bearing 191°.

81 (517) N29° 32.9' E09° 46.7'
Tyre marker on the right of the track; 1km later you cross a plain with no hills visible on the horizon for about 4km.

95 (503) N29° 27.1' E09° 51.5'
Tyre marker on the left.

104 (494) N29° 22.6' E09° 56.2'
Bearing now 150°.

111 (487)
Long passage through a wadi with bushes and grass.

115 (483)
Wadi now on the left.

126 (472)   **N29° 13.4'**   **E09° 58.4'**
Flat hamada all around.

130 (468)
Tyre marker on the right and oil drums on the left 1km and 2km later.

138 (460)   **N29° 08.1'**   **E10° 01.6'**
La Banat, a former exploration camp, now a collection of abandoned buildings and machinery.

146 (452)   **N29° 03.4'**   **E10° 03.3'**
Waypoint.

152 (446)   **N29° 00.6'**   **E10° 04.9'**
Drive over a thin pipeline which crosses the track.

162 (436)   **N28° 55.4'**   **E10° 06.9'**
Cairn on the right of the piste.

167 (431)   **N28° 53.2'**   **E10° 07.7'**
Abandoned white building and possibly a shepherds' encampment with a vehicle or two. To the S is a grassy wadi. Drive through the wadi in a SE direction, crossing and re-crossing it over the next couple of kilometres, tending towards the SSE.

177 (421)
Low rubble cairn on the right after which the track curves to 146°.

185 (413)   **N28° 44.2'**   **E10° 11.6'**
Track forks; take the one that goes from 140° to 160°. After a few hundred metres there are some bushes on the left and then you turn to a bearing of 180-190°.

187 (411)   **N28° 43.4'**   **E10° 11.5'**
Cross a stony watercourse, descending bumpily, nearing 180°.

188 (410)
Bearing now 240°, SW, soon 202°.

189 (409)   **N28° 42.8'**   **E10° 10.9'**
In Azar. Rejoin a mass of tracks heading S. Low hills to the E. You are now at the series of escarpments 'Etauil' and 'Tigid Accanen' as on the French NH-32 map.

196 (402)   **N28° 38.8'**   **E10° 10.9'**
Oil drum with 'SSL' in white writing.

Broken escarpment edge visible to the SSW. Feels like you're descending (although you're not).

198 (400)
Bearing 169° across a plain. Beginning of a descent.

201 (397)   **N28° 36.6'**   **E10° 10.8'**
Significant drop. Bearing SW.

205 (393)   **N28° 34.6'**   **E10° 09.7'**
Rounded hills on all sides. Track runs at SW around W side of low hills.

209 (389)   **N28° 33.2'**   **E10° 08.4'**
Waypoint, with a small descent towards a sandy wadi 1km later.

215 (383)   **N28° 30.1'**   **E10° 06.1'**
Pass several blue oil drums on the right. Bearing generally SSW.

228 (370)   **N28° 24.1'**   **E10° 03.5'**
Descend into a wadi; hills to the south. About 2km later bearing turns SE.

234 (364)   **N28° 21.0'**   **E10° 03.0'**
Significantly large tree.

244 (354)   **N28° 17.0'**   **E10° 06.6'**
Driving south through a broad valley with flat-tops to left and right.

252 (346)
Noticeably fast stretch across the flat Zerzaitin reg. A chance to see if fourth gear is still working for a few kilometres.

262 (336)   **N28° 08.5'**   **E10° 11.2'**
Cross a sandy ridge onto more flat reg.

265 (333)
Bearing 214°.

274 (324)   **N28° 02.6'**   **E10° 09.5'**
Track goes around large dune.

280 (318)   **N27° 59.8'**   **E10° 07.8'**
The Zerzaitin plain has come to an end and low dune ridges begin.

282 (316)   **N27° 59.1'**   **E10° 06.8'**
Low dune.

287 (311)   **N27° 56.8' E10° 06.5'**
Band of dunes. Before the sand gets soft on the approach ramp it's worth letting your tyres down to dune pressures and then zig-zagging your way through in a southerly direction. They only last for about 1500m after which it's fast and rocky again, but reducing pressures pays off in the long run.

Try to drive round steep ascents, even if snaking in all directions to keep moving. It's not as hard as it sounds.

289 (309)   **N27° 55.9' E10° 06.5'**
End of sandy section. Re-inflate tyres. Continue along a sandy track across a black stone plain. Dunes to the E.

299 (299)   **N27° 51.1' E10° 04.8'**
Rocky bowl with shapely dunes on the left. Drive through the bowl with dunes on three sides. A nice spot.

301 (297)
Bearing WSW.

309 (289)   **N27° 48.0' E10° 00.5'**
Fast driving over rolling dunes with occasional soft patches and some black stone plains. Within 1km or so dark hills appear on the horizon. Bearing SW.

314 (284)
Dunes on left and right close to the track.

319 (279)
Black stone plain after which you'll experience the first corrugations for a while: a sign that the traffic is funnelling through a key passage.

323 (275)   **N27° 42.5' E09° 57.0'**
Algeria is just 2km to the west. Smoke from the oil stacks around Edjeleh may be visible. Continue with dunes on the left.

331 (267)
Dunes still on left. Bearing SSW.

333 (265)   **N27° 37.6' E09° 54.8'**
Waypoint.

339 (259)
Soft sand with patches of sharp stones. Go closely around a huge dune on your left.

340 (258)
Track now turns W.

345 (253)
Approach big dune straight ahead then turn W to arrive at Hassi El Mislane (N27° 34.1' E09° 49.9'), the tip of the west-facing 'nose' on maps marking the Libya–Algeria frontier. Although it is marked as a well, it's more of an occasional water hole.

This is the start of the main dune section, which lasts for 24km. It can make a nice camp or lunch spot. When you're ready, let down your tyres to 1 bar and get ready for digging, pushing, and possibly laying of sand ladders.

348 (250)
An ascent with patches of stones offers an alternative to the soft sand.

351 (247)   **N27° 32.9' E09° 47.3'**
Head into a mass of dunes. The sand is now very soft. You will find the odd tyre and stick marking the way. Note that some crests have short vertical drops or are alarmingly steep, if short descents: you must get the hang of racing up and then easing over the crest. It's a lot easier if someone walks (or rides a motorbike) ahead to guide you through.

From this point it is 18km to the 'Algerian Tree'. Don't pay too much attention to the waypoints below; it's more useful to follow recent tracks and concentrate on the driving and not getting stuck, rather than the GPS.

353 (245)   **N27° 32.2' E09° 47.2'**

356 (242)   **N27° 30.7' E09° 47.8'**

357 (241)   **N27° 30.3' E09° 48.0'**
Oil drum.

358 (240)   **N27° 30.0' E09° 48.3'**

361 (237)   **N27° 28.9' E09° 49.2'**

362 (236)   **N27° 28.4' E09° 48.8'**

363 (235)   **N27° 27.9' E09° 48.5'**

365 (233)   **N27° 27.3' E09° 48.1'**
Oil drums and stick in a white stone.

Cooling off at the Algerian Tree.

367 (231)   **N27° 26.8' E09° 47.2'**

368 (230)   **N27° 26.5' E09° 46.8'**
Tyre marker.

369 (229)   **N27° 26.0' E09° 46.3'**
Tree by a large dune marking the end of the dune section. Popular camping spot.

In his *Sahara* book (see p.642) Michael Palin observed *'This spare, uncluttered, beautiful spot was one of my favourite places in the Sahara.'* (There follows a rather disingenuous implication that they cross the border here into Libya, but over the page he's suddenly in Torbruk!)

You're about 4km inside Algeria. Re-inflate tyres to piste pressures.

374 (224)
Bearing around 150° leading onto hamada with dunes on left. Very stony in 3km.

379 (219)
Fork in the track. Take the left fork: SE.

386 (212)
Cairns alongside the track with dunes still on the left.

392 (206)   **N27° 19.2' E09° 52.0'**
Cairns on top of rocks to the left of the track. Continue over black stone terrain. Hills become crowned with black stone rubble and shale.

400 (198)
Hills subside here as the valley broadens out. Within 1km occasional flat-tops appear to the right.

403 (195)
Grassy patch on the left, head SE.

404 (194)   **N27° 13.6' E09° 55.8'**
Small cairn on a hill to your left. Valley narrows significantly with the track now close to hills on the right.

405 (193)   **N27° 12.7' E09° 56.3'**
Hassi Tin Hieddan well and checkpoint.

412 (186)
Stony plain. Track passes close to flat-topped ridge on the right.

417 (181)   **N27° 07.2' E09° 55.9'**
Waypoint.

422 (176)
Continuing over black stone plains with the continuous flat-top ridge (evident on the NG-32 map) to your right.

424 (174)   **N27° 03.9' E09° 56.3'**
Tyre marker on the left of the piste. A chance to get into top gear.

427 (171)   **N27° 02.4' E09° 57.0'**
Small cairn on the left of the track.

435 (163)
Cross a watercourse. Occasionally fast stretches over black stone plain.

447 (151)   **N26° 53.3' E10° 00.1'**
Cross a wadi.

455 (143)   **N26° 49.6' E10° 00.4'**
Ridge-top cairn on the left of the track.

462 (136)   **N26° 46.0' E10° 01.6'**
Track passes between two trees with another tree on the left.

472 (126)   **N26° 42.8' E10° 06.2'**
Fast going over black stone hamada.

476 (122)   N26° 41.7'   E10° 07.7'
Pass through area of tree stumps perched on car-high mounds of sand.

485 (113)   N26° 38.1'   E10° 11.2'
Mushroom rocks alongside the track.

491 (107)   N26° 35.1'   E10° 11.8'
Small grove of trees.

495 (103)   N26° 32.6'   E10° 11.3'
Cross rocky wadi, then again 500m further on. Then drive along the wadi between its rocky banks.

499 (99)   N26° 30.9'   E10° 11.1'
Wadi widens then you pass a tyre marked with 'R8' and an arrow pointing left on the left side of the track.

501 (97)   N26° 29.6'   E10° 11.3'
Significant descent onto hamada with distant dunes briefly visible to the SE. Track continues winding along escarpments immediately to the right.

504 (94)
Veer away from escarpment, then in 1km track descends through another escarpment with table mountains immediately ahead.

514 (84)   N26° 28.5'   E10° 10.5'
Driving along wadi with a large dune visible ahead. After a few hundred metres leave the wadi and head towards the dunes.

518 (80)
Descend onto a plain in front of the dunes. Curve round to a bearing of 200° to drive through a black stone gap in the dunes, then S again.
    There will be some soft sand later on, but nothing compared with what has passed.

522 (76)   N26° 20.4'   E10° 11.5'
Pair of square-block cairns on either side of the track, then 1km later there is a descent.

530 (68)   N26° 17.2'   E10° 14.0'
Another descent from an escarpment.

535 (63)   N26° 15.0'   E10° 15.7'
Waypoint following some very dusty mud flats.

542 (56)
Very clear track heading SE across black hamada. Fast and easy driving.

550 (48)   N26° 10.0'   E10° 22.2'
Waypoint. Dunes on horizon.

552 (46)   N26° 09.1'   E10° 22.9'
Group of concrete markers on left edge of the track.

561 (37)
Track goes across claypans (sebka) for about 1km then back onto hamada.

566 (32)   N26° 02.1'   E10° 25.7'
Square-block cairn beside track followed by more cairns at about 500m intervals.

570 (28)   N25° 59.8'   E10° 26.6'
Remains of a stone building visible to the left of the track. Stone cairns continue at 500m intervals for another 3km, then become more sporadic.

579 (19)   N25° 56.0'   E10° 28.8'
Oued with bushes on the left, then a short rocky descent followed by a sandy track over a black stony surface.

583 (15)   N25° 53.8'   E10° 29.0'
Another small descent. Trees and radio mast visible ahead.

588 (10)
Palm trees on left.

590 (8)   N25° 50.1'   E10° 30.5'
Tarmac and a small village. Follow the road south to its junction with the Ghat road (N25° 48.4' E10° 31.4'). Turn left (E) for Serdeles.

598 (0)
Serdeles fuel station. There's a good campsite a couple of kilometres to the E, on the other side of town. Otherwise it's a two-hour drive S to Ghat with a couple of checkpoints on the way.

L3 GHAT, THE AKAKUS AND THE IDEHAN MURZUK

The Akakus mountains in south-west Libya form one of the most spectacular regions of the Sahara and are probably the most deservedly popular destination in Libya. The combination of dunes piled against cliffs is both beautiful and impressive and, because the canyons also harbour hundreds of prehistoric rock-art sites as in the adjacent Tassili (they are really one and the same thing), the region has been classified a UNESCO World Heritage Site. This means that tourists can only travel into the Akakus with a guide, a rule that is enforced at numerous checkpoints.

Most independent tourists employ their guides in the small frontier town of Ghat, which stands on the fringes of the Akakus mountains and at the end of the tarmac road, 120km south of Serdeles. It is, however, also possible to enter the Akakus from Serdeles or from the east, though this would be against the general flow, leaving the spectacle till the end. Ghat is also very close to the Algerian border and it is possible to leave the country for Djanet, via Tin Alkoum (though not to come into Libya this way).

At 1:500,000 scale, the best **map** for this region is the Soviet G-32-C 'Djanet' sheet. It shows the 'downslope', eastern edge of the escarpment which you probe as you head northwards on the 'standard tour'. The 1:1m 'Djanet' equivalents from the Soviets and IGN aren't quite so easy to read in the Akakus.

Looking across the Old Town of Ghat. © Lucy Ridout

Ghat

From the abandoned Italian fort that sits on top of a small hill in the centre of town, you get a fine view of the tumbledown mud-brick Old Town below, the new town that now surrounds it and the ring of dunes that encircles the whole lot. As in Ghadames, Ghat's Old Town is worth a leisurely wander and is anyway the only sight on offer. You'll probably be adopted by a guide as you enter the Old Town walls, and he'll ask a few dinars to take you up to the fort. There's a jewellery workshop in one of the houses here, too, and plenty of itinerant trinket vendors along the lanes. There are a few campsites in town, also offering rooms, and the old hotel in the centre.

The main market is at the west end of the main street, with a bakery round the back. You can buy canned and dried groceries in the handful of small stores on the main road between the market and the Old Town.

Ghat's tour agencies are strung along the main road, too, as you come into town, and this is where you should enquire about guides for the Akakus, if you don't already have one.

Into the Jebel Akakus

Hidden behind the escarpment immediately east of Ghat, the Akakus mountains are one of Libya's gems. It's an environment that pretty much has it all: a beautiful approach drive leading to rock arches and other striking geological features; stark canyons with dune-swept cliffs; hidden rock pools and prehistoric paintings.

The only trouble is that you need a guide to visit the region, but that's not as bad as it sounds. Sensitive border areas aside, even if you could go there alone you'd never find half the spots that a guide would lead you to, and even with GPS the maze of pistes through the canyons would require more unravelling than you want to be bothered with.

There is no shortage of agencies in Ghat waiting to help you out. Expect to pay around €30 a day for a guide in your car or €100 for a guide in their own 4WD – the only option if you're on a motorbike but with the big advantage that they can carry your gear. If you can get a few cars together to share the cost, so much the better. They'll organise the permit to enter the national park which ought to be included in your fee, but check this.

Three days covering nearly 400km to Serdeles would give you a good look around, with the first and second days passing through some of the most perfect desertscapes you could point a lens at. Although there's a fairly standard route through, guides have their own variations and personal highlights, so the distances and itinerary outlined below are meant as a rough guide only.

You leave Ghat to the south, towards the Algerian frontier, passing a couple of checkpoints and the villages of El Barkat and Esseyen (see box, p.472). The oasis of Djanet is only 90km across the plateau as the crow flies but nearly 300km on the piste.You'll find more on Djanet and the Tassili on p.530.

Back on the Akakus tour, after around 40km, the canyon of the Wadi Akakus to your right is a popular viewpoint. Then, as you turn south-east and pass along the Erg Takharkhouri the sandy outwash softens at KM66 so you'll need to lower tyre pressures well before the checkpoint at KM83 from Ghat, at the 'entrance' into the Akakus: the **Takharkhouri Pass**. Soon after there are a couple of steep sandy descents that you'd have trouble reversing. At around KM96 you'll reach the huge natural arch (N24° 41.1' E10° 37.9'), an impressive 80-metre-high megalith which is much photographed and, not surprisingly, makes a popular camping spot among the dunes.

After the arch you wind though the canyons and over small dunes, stopping frequently to inspect the many rock-art sites in this vicinity. The rock art might be considered a little disappointing compared to that found in the adjacent Tassili N'Ajjer or the many engravings on the Messaks such as Wadi Mathendous (Route L5).

Nevertheless, some of the naturalistic scenes from the Cattle period are superb (KM101), as were some finely depicted battle scenes. You may also be shown a fine engraving of an elephant at KM124.

Other highlights include a bone-like column carved by the wind from the cliffside (KM141; N24° 51.4' E10° 34.7'), and a couple of rock pools hidden inside a narrow rocky canyon which you walk up to from KM163 (N24° 57.6' E10° 30.2'). At KM197 is an overhang with many things depicted including a Garamantean chariot (N24° 57.4' E10° 32.5') plus other engravings of erotic activity at two sites around KM213-4 (N24° 58.0' E10° 29.0'), and a hippo superimposed on a tiger (N24° 59.0' E10° 28.7').

The further north you go, the firmer the terrain gets. There's a big well pumping into a yellow tank, known as Talouait, at what was for us KM276 (N25° 13.8' E10° 46.7'), and after this we spent the last few hours of the last day travelling across bleaker, stonier ground towards Serdeles, having left the mountains behind us.

At the arch it's possible to branch off to the north-west through the Messak Mellet to Wadi Mathendous and Germa. The news on this route is that once past the dune cordon of Erg Ouan Kasa, it's a long bleak drive over hamada.

Through the Idehan Murzuk
by Ursula Steiner

We set off to cross the Idehan Murzuk from Murzuk town to the ruins of a fort near Tilemsin on the western edge of the sand sea, a distance of around 300km direct. Although it's not expressly forbidden, officially the erg is off-limits. Things will probably stay that way until the first tourists have to be rescued. So if you're heading this way, keep your plans to yourself.

Our group in October 1998 comprised nine people in four cars, a Dodge Ram, a Hilux, a Discovery, a G-Wagen and a quad bike. Having found the tap water salty, no bottled water and little food to buy, we left Murzuk late one afternoon towards Tmissah, but soon turned off south-west across a soft sand plain. Tyre pressures were lowered but we got stuck anyway, so we made camp.

The next day was cold and windy but we made very good progress of about 100km along a broad valley. On the days that followed we managed about a third of that distance between camps, though of course with all the zig-zagging, driving distances are at times double that. We followed fresh car tracks up and over small dunes until the Dodge got stuck on the crest and the others in a dip due to driving too close together.

We passed dry lagoons between beautiful dune chains and from time to time had to cross barrier dunes which blocked the valleys. There were still fresh 4x4 tracks which was comforting, but in the heat of the afternoon one car slid into a hole and it took hours to get it out. We camped, exhausted, on the edge of a dry lake.

Day three dawned hot; by 8am it was already 25°C. Now the dune chains were getting higher but the car tracks were still plentiful. We got stuck several times, which was hard work in this heat, but the colours of the sand, orange, beige and grey, are amazing! We rode up high over sparsely-vegetated dunes and slithered down the slip face into another flat lagoon.

These lakes got smaller as the dunes closed in and there were no more broad valleys to cruise through. From the summits the chaotic dunescape up ahead looked like boiling water. We camped near a small oued with green grass, a little more tired and tense, but happy to be here. Mouse tracks covered the ground and nearby, the brittle white skull of a gazelle lay half buried in the sand.

Up and down, again and again, the next day. If you hesitated you got stuck on the crest but charging over was obviously dangerous. There was no easy way. Often in the depressions there were soft sand fields with white-greyish feche-feche covered with innocuous-looking sand. We were now in the midst of very high dunes with no way to drive around or turn back. Sometimes one car was already on the other side of a dune but we were unable to follow. It was hardest for the last car as the narrow passage over the crest became churned up with every passing vehicle. But once over we floated down the terraces of sand, silently, elevator-like. Golden sand poured away like water. It was absolutely spectacular!

We camped in the dunes near a lagoon filled with white sand. Evidence of Stone Age occupation was everywhere to be seen, from the Acheulian to Aterien and Neolithic eras: 300,000 to 4500 years BC! That evening the G-Wagen crew got a fright when they realised their fuel consumption had shot through the roof.

Our fifth day in the erg was cold but we were only 80km from the fort at Tilemsin as the crow flies. We couldn't go straight on of course, as there were narrow low dunes ahead. Like ants we decided to attack a huge dune and once down the other side found several old lorry tracks. Relieved, we followed this unexpected highway which later disappeared into the side of a dune... So we turned back and climbed a very soft dune, over the crest and down the other side, carefully avoiding a few more craters. Sliding into these 'vortexes' does not bear thinking about. At one point we even had to dig away a small dune to push our way through.

After more effort than anyone could bear, we finally arrived at a dry lake several kilometres long and made camp. We'd travelled only 30km since the morning and the cold evening brought out our sweaters. The atmosphere around the fire was a little edgy. We were close, but not quite there yet.

Day Six. Cold. Loud music for breakfast but then we had to jump-start the speaker-car. We set off but after an hour had to turn back: it was impossible to go on. For an hour we waited while the quad searched the dunes for a way through. And he did a good job too, leading us out of this cul-de-sac like Moses parting the Red Sea. Another lagoon with yellow, red and white sand under the blue sky – colours we had never seen before. Unforgettable landscapes. Some crests, some slopes, some precipices – we were getting used to it now.

But the last pass was the most difficult of the whole expedition. Soft, and after trying again and again softer still. There was no room for 'contour driving' to gain some momentum but somehow, as always, and after a lot of pushing, reversing and flat-out acceleration we got through to enjoy the thrill of cascading down (see p.190) to the next dry lake.

The last day and the dunes got smaller, more muddled. Up and down we went but had to turn back again. Then suddenly a valley and – stones! A wave of relaxation and also a little sadness passed over us as we followed the valley winding through the low dunes. Only at the last minute did we spot, very far away at the edge of a plain, the low dark line of the Messak Mellet on the horizon. We pumped up the tyres and found the so-called fort (just a pile of rubble) at N24° 43.5′ E11° 40.1′. It was nice to be out of the sands at last, but for the evening camp we returned back into the dunes!

L4 THE DUNE LAKES CIRCUIT   107KM
February 2000; Toyota FJ62, Toyota HJ61, Toyota Amazon

Description
The circuit visiting the famous lakes of Gabrun, Um el Ma and Mandara represents a demanding but now very popular dune excursion. Unless you're accustomed to this sort of driving both your nerves and your engine will be in for quite a session. But you'll never know if you don't try.

There are various ways of visiting some or all of these lakes (there are dozens in the area). This itinerary takes you out 45km in a NE direction to Maflu and Gabrun lakes, then retraces itself to cross into the next corridor or valley, close to Um el Ma and Mandara lakes from where it heads south-west back to the Wadi Adjal.

The route generally follows gassis, corridors or valleys which are pretty easy, bar the occasional soft patches. But there are some hollows which require assertive acceleration and quick steering, especially if your vehicle lacks power. The crossing into the Mandara valley at KM65 is also a long slow slog over power-sapping sand, ending in a steep descent. At several other places along this route there are various lesser drops waiting to catch you out.

For peace of mind it is recommend you do this route with a guide (ask at the campsite) or at least one other vehicle.

THE DUNE LAKES

No one knows quite how the lakes manage to exist here in the middle of this elevated erg, but they've been there long enough to support small communities of Daouda, a Berber/Arab tribe (depending on who you ask) characterised by their tightly-bound white cheches which wrap under the chin. These days their villages are all abandoned and they now live in less picturesque but more convenient circumstances in the villages of the Wadis Shati and Adjal.

Each lake is surrounded by a thick band of reeds which help bind its steep banks. Some are warm, others cold, some smell. Small shrimp-like crustaceans are known to thrive on the microbes which inhabit the lakes, and were once the staple diet of the Daouda, mashed with dates. These shrimps were thought to be worms, giving rise to Oudney's description of 'Worm Eaters' when he and Clapperton passed through in 1822.

Lake Maflu.

Route-finding and markers

Usually in pure dunes too many way-points can be misleading or distracting; one must work one's own way through. But this route represents a frequently driven piste and, depending on recent winds, for much of the way you'll find yourself following a mass of tracks. The waypoints listed below should therefore either help confirm your position or lead you back to the main route.

Technically GPS waypoints should greatly help you complete this route without a guide, but there's no getting round the fact that not knowing what's over the next crest makes for slow and tiring driving – an agile motorbike or a quad plus a pair of radios would be of great help here. There are no markers, just tracks.

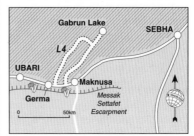

**L4 – RECOMMENDED MAPS
DUNE LAKES CIRCUIT 107KM**

Obviously no map is going to be much good over this short distance. The Russian 1:500,000 G-33-A 'Sebha' covers the route in four square inches, but doesn't tell you much other than marking the three lakes and a route back from Mandara (not L4 which takes a wider corridor to the west).

Fuel

To save weight, fill up with only what you need for the route, plus a reserve. Nevertheless expect consumption to dive to around 5kpl for a diesel, 3kpl for a petrol-engined 4WD and around 13-15kpl for a 600cc single motorbike, depending on traction. There is a fuel station at Gregra, west of the turn-off for the Africa Tours campsite, 15km east of Germa.

Water

Not quite so sweet-smelling at Africa Tours campsite and of similar or worse quality in all the lakes. If you use this water it might be more palatable filtered.

Traffic

Along the main route this can be a real hazard around Christmas time, when unlucky timing can lead to a head-on collision over blind crests. However, the steepest and blindest ascents are only normally possible in one direction, so although people tend to follow tracks, it's usually two-way between dunes.

Driving

Unless you have a super light and powerful car, this can be tense (or exciting!) as you struggle to balance the dune-driving paradox of momentum and prudence. On this route the hardest section can be the first three dunes within sight of the campsite. You could do a lot worse than walking up first to familiarise yourself with the lay of the sand and tracks in the first kilometre. With this foreknowledge you'll then know just how fast to go and which way to turn as you crest the ridges.

We did this route with a guide and even he admitted to being uneasy while among the sands. Dunes represent the most demanding and potentially dangerous desert terrain and the concentration required, even as a passenger, takes some getting used to. Be sure your engine and transmission are up for some full-power driving and travel as lightly as possible, without forsaking essentials like jacks, spare wheels and water. To lighten our vehicles, we left excess baggage at the campsite where we'd spent the previous night.

For bikers the same practice is advisable. Remove those alloy boxes which can get in the way of your legs and enjoy an unencumbered ride. Keep both wheels on the ground and don't take any chances. Accidents here are all too common.

Suggested duration

With a guide the whole circuit can be done in a day, but a night out at Gabrun or wherever you fancy would make a much more memorable experience. And without a guide it'll probably take you that long anyway.

Note: so popular have the dune lakes become in recent years that **rubbish** is now a real problem, especially at Um el Ma lake where many tours overnight and where toilet paper covers the ground like confetti. Even if you don't bother elsewhere, make the effort to burn your toilet paper on the lakes circuit or take it back to the highway along with *all* your rubbish. These lakes are unique to the Sahara – leave them as pristine as you'd want to find them.

0km (107)   N26° 34.0' E13° 15.3'
Africa Tours campsite is signposted at the west end of Terkiba – a blue sign with yellow writing and a tent symbol. Head north between some buildings and along lanes passing fields and palmeries. At the sign for 'Fezzan Tours' (left) go right. Signposting may have improved by now. The campsite is situated next to a fallen pylon broken in half (one of several around here).

Ahead of you is the first ascent, a popular occupation being watching other cars have a go. Even though you have a long approach run it may take a few goes before you get it right and slip over the first crest. Once you've managed this, curve to the right and take a run up anticlockwise round the bowl over the next flattened ridge (see p.87). Drive left along this ridge and then turn right, dive down into the next dip to the right and cross the last dune.

1 (106)
Having got over the tricky initial dunes, ahead of you lies a wide dune corridor full of tracks. There may be some salt flats on the left.

3 (104)
Track does an 'S' to the right and left through dunes.

3.6   N26° 35.6' E13° 15.5'
Another hill to the NE. Sand fairly firm.

4 (103) N26° 35.7' E13° 15.7'
Short rise then flat again. Continue along dune flank.

5 (101) N26° 36.0' E13° 16.0'
The route opens out into a broad, almost flat gassi. Bearing NE.

Looks easy, doesn't it.

6.6 (100.4)　　　**N26° 36.5'　E13° 16.7'**
Small steep dune.

10 (97)　　　**N26° 37.9'　E13° 17.7'**
Steep drop, otherwise as before. NNE.

10.3 (96.7)
Following a big hollow, over the next half kilometre there is a succession of steep rises with short run-ups, so keep your speed up.

10.8 (96.2)　　　**N26° 38.2'　E13° 17.8'**
Within a hundred metres there's another hollow which you drive into and out of, then you're back driving over open, undulating sand ramps. Bearing NNE.

12 (95)　　　**N26° 38.8'　E13° 18.1'**
Start of a long rise up a big sand ramp.

13.3 (93.7)　　　**N26° 39.3'　E13° 18.2'**
Still gradually ascending the ramp which soon flattens out and you're back on an undulating corridor.

14 (93)
Run-up to another dip followed by a soft rise over a small dune.

15 (92) N26° 40.0' E13° 18.4'
After another hairy dip, back onto open terrain.

16 (91) N26° 40.4' E13° 19.1'
Continue NE on firm, undulating surface.

21 (86) N26° 41.9' E13° 21.2'
Still driving along a broad corridor. Within 1km you pass occasional tree stumps, mostly on the right. Bearing ENE.

23 (84) N26° 42.6' E13° 22.4'
Long soft rise. Um el Ma is just 2km NW of here, but in the next gassi.

25 (82) N26° 43.1' E13° 22.8'
Beginning of a mostly flat area dotted with many big tamarisk clumps.

31 (76) N26° 45.0' E13° 25.9'
Still among the tamarisk stumps with a small palm grove on the right. Occasional rounded hillocks with a light covering of stony rubble.

33 (74)
Over the next few hundred metres the undulations tighten giving a rolling ride.

34 (73)
Sizeable palm grove to the right.

35 (72)　　　**N26° 46.1'　E13° 28.0'**
Back on undulating, easy terrain with trees and palms dotted around.

40 (67)　　　**N26° 47.3'　E13° 30.4'**
Maflu, a small lake surrounded by reeds with a dune tumbling into its east bank. Continue NE as before over undulating surface with occasional trees.

43 (64)　　　**N26° 48.1'　E13° 31.6'**
The first buildings of the abandoned village of Gabrun. Drive through the ruins and continue NE to the campsite on the west bank of the long lake.

44 (63)　　　**N26° 48.3'　E13° 32.2'**
Gabrun. Lakeside camping usually occupied during the tourist season. Several lopsided zeribas. The lake itself smells sulphurous – in the salty water you float easily. You can drive circuitously up to the dune overlooking the lake from the east (or trudge up the tracks which ascend it steeply). Once here you'll have a fine view

Looking down on Lake Gabrun. © Yves Larboulette

over a sea of dunes, especially impressive at sunset.

From Gabrun return the way you came for 19km, past Maflu and the trees to the vicinity of KM25. From this point the route takes you over into the next parallel gassi where Um el Ma and the nearly dry Mandara lakes lie. It takes you up long soft dunes' banks and then down a very steep, stepped drop close to Um el Ma.

The waypoints now resume near KM25 which is KM64 as you move W to the next gassi.

64 (43)   N26° 43.1'   E13° 22.8'
Waypoint.

65 (42)   N26° 42.7'   E13° 22.5'
Trees finished now. Start driving into very soft dunes. Consider letting a bit more air out of your tyres if your vehicle finds soft sand difficult.

66 (41)   N26° 42.8'   E13° 21.9'
Begin ascending sandy banks to get into the next valley.

67 (40)   N26° 42.6'   E13° 21.3'
Still rising over the soft sand banks.

68 (39)   N26° 42.9'   E13° 20.9'
The major descent into the Um el Ma valley: two steep and long drops. Down to your left you can see the trees which surround Um el Ma. You can avoid the lower descent by driving to the right once you've reached the flat part of the middle level – then turn left, taking a less steep way down. Bikers might want to walk their bikes down these slip faces but, taken slowly with the correct technique, there is no danger whatever you're driving.

Once you've made it down continue down the valley for 1km to Um el Ma.

70 (37)   N26° 42.7'   E13° 20.2'
Um el Ma, 'Mother of the Waters', considered the prettiest of the popular dune lakes. Ringed by palms and never inhabited (until tourists arrived), it's many people's idealised image of a Saharan 'oasis'.

The water is cold on top but fed by a warm spring from below.

Leave the lake in a generally SW direction, driving up and down over the small humps.

72 (35)
Continue SW with clumps of trees and palms to your left and right.

73 (34)   N26° 41.7'   E13° 18.8'
Mandara lake. A large but nearly dried-out lake with a recently abandoned village on the east bank. Locals guides say it last had water in 1995.

From here you're heading back on a WSW heading along a wide undulating valley with some 'S' traversals through dune bands.

76 (31)   N26° 41.4'   E13° 17.6'

79 (28)   N26° 40.8'   E13° 16.1'

82 (25)   N26° 40.2'   E13° 14.6'
Heading almost due west over rolling undulations.

84 (23)   N26° 40.0'   E13° 12.9'
Descend a steep dune. Over the next 6km there are several undulations and the occasional steep drop so don't relax, it's not all over yet.

91 (16)   N26° 37.2'   E13° 10.3'
Messak Settafet escarpment visible ahead.

93 (14)
Steep drop, head south along wide, undulating corridor.

95 (12)   N26° 35.9'   E13° 10.2'
Easy descent into the Wadi Adjal. Once you're back on terra firma pump up your tyres, turn east and either work your way through the palmerie or head south along any track that will eventually lead to the road. Either way it's around 12km back to the Africa Tours campsite.

107 (0)
Africa Tours campsite.

L5 GERMA → WADI MATHENDOUS   [154KM]
January 2000; Toyota HJ61

Description
No visit to Libya would be complete without an inspection of some of the thousands of rock engravings which cover the Messak Settafet and Messak Mallet plateaux. Wadi Mathendous (pronounced 'Mat-hen-dush') is the best known of these, and easily accessible as an excursion from Germa. Along the northern walls of the wadi you'll find scores of bold depictions of the big game now seen only in East Africa. Most are thought to date from around 8000-6000 BC, and there is no plainer evidence that the Sahara experiences climatic cycles with arid and humid phases.

The road leads up directly through the Settafet's escarpment south of Germa, soon turning rubbly and leading to the agricultural project at Wadi Barjuj. Here you turn WSW, keeping the Idehan Murzuk's dunes to your left and the dark stain of the Messak Settafet far to the north. The drive along the flat serir can be a little disorientating but with these two landmarks, some markers and plenty of tracks, you'll soon reach the checkpoint.

From the checkpoint you rise up onto the sandy plateau immediately to the south and carry on west to the tracks which lead to the many sites here. The last few kilometres to the Wadi cross a grim basalt field where the rocks will have you crawling along at 2kph.

Route-finding and markers
Mostly easy with the only unnerving bit heading into the sandy void after leaving the Barjuj track at KM60, and the many tracks very near the Wadi. There are plenty of markers, tyres and tracks. Keep the dunes to your left and the distant Messak on your right with a bearing averaging around 240°.

On the way back you may find yourself veering north around KM87 cutting off the Barjuj corner and rejoining the track around KM44. It's not a bad idea as the more driving on smooth sand the better.

Fuel
Germa.

Water
Fill up in Germa. Otherwise only available at Barjuj or the checkpoint.

Traffic
In the season you're bound to come across other tourists heading to this popular destination.

Driving
Very easy. You'll only need 4WD to maybe get up to the plateau south of the checkpoint and across the very sandy Wadi itself to the camping spots on the opposite bank.

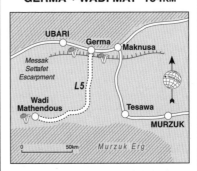

L5 – RECOMMENDED MAPS
GERMA → WADI MAT' 154KM

No map depicts this route or even any of the key landmarks but you'll do all right with this sketch map and maybe the Russian 1:1m G-33 'Sebha' for comfort.

On a bike there's nothing special to worry about except the sandy wadi crossings and not getting carried away and going too fast.

Suggested duration

It takes about three hours to do this route so you could easily do the round-trip in a day. However, it would be a shame not to spend a night at the Wadi, even if you are unlikely to be alone. The shadows at either end of the day make the engravings clearer and more photogenic.

Exploring the Wadi

Once you've parked up here the engravings are in front of your nose. They continue a few hundred metres to the east and over half a kilometre to the west. Seven hundred metres west of the camp you may find an archeological excavation.

You'll see a whole menagerie of beasts depicted along the walls: various bovids and gazelles, crocodiles, ostriches, as well as the semi-enigmatic 'sun wheel', but perhaps most common are giraffes in all styles.

If you're feeling energetic, continuing upstream (SW) for around three hours should bring you after ten kilometres to more engravings at In Habeter (N25° 41.0' E12° 05.0'). On the way you'll pass other sites on the northern wall at around four and six kilometres from the camp. Take the usual precautions when away from your vehicle and wear a stout pair of shoes, as there's no path.

The Secret of the Desert (see Books, p.643) is a great picture book on the petroglyphic riches of the Messaks.

0km (154)   N26° 31.6' E13° 03.9'
Germa fuel station crossroads. There is water round the back. Take the southbound road leading up to the pass. A green sign with white writing indicates '60km' to the Wadi Barjuj project. Rise up to the pass, cutting through the escarpment, and emerge on the southern face of the Messak Settafet.

6 (148)
Road disintegrates into old, broken tarmac. Consider reducing tyre pressures to soften the ride but keep your speed down. The surface improves a bit in 6km.

18 (130)
Road descends from the hamada onto a sandy plain dotted with acacias which would make nice camping spots.

26 (122)
Eroded tarmac becomes a gravel track with corrugations.

42 (112)
Murzuk sand sea may now be visible on the horizon. Surface smooths out a bit

more and is marked with tyres and wire sticks.

52 (102)
The silos of the Wadi Barjuj project are visible ahead, just east of S.

60 (94)   N26° 02.6' E12° 56.5'
Turn W onto the sands before the Barjuj checkpoint at the Lasmo oil exploration sign. The many tracks can be a little confusing. Pass a rubbish dump by the S side of the track after a couple of hundred metres and follow the clearest track heading W, 270°. Firm, easy and, at last, smooth going.

76 (78)   N26° 02.0' E12° 46.8'
Track becomes a little rougher as you cross an arm of the Wadi Barjuj 'east', marked by some large stones and trees. Bearing 260°.

80 (74)
Bearing now 240°, SW.

82 (72)
Track widens and smooths out after wadi

crossing; corrugated but fast. Dunes appear to be a couple of kilometres to the S where some trees are also visible.

87 (67)   **N25° 59.9' E12° 41.5'**
Red and white sign on the right of the track: 'Rig 118'. Then another on the left (S) side of the track. Keep WSW and in 1500m Wadi Barjuj 'west' marked by black stones and vegetation. You'll pass another red and white sign and then leave the wadi over some soft sand.

From here the track speeds up again at a bearing of 235° with tyre markers often visible ahead.

95 (59)
Another red and white Lasmo sign on the left side of the track.

102 (52)
Metal post on left.

108 (46)
Another Lasmo sign.

118 (36)
Dunes peter out to the south. Track gets a bit sandier and bumpier.

121 (33)
Some sandy mounds visible ahead.

123 (31)
Pass sandy mounds. Trees and buildings now visible in the distance: the checkpoint. Leave the main track to the S and drive towards the checkpoint heading WSW.

128 (26) N25° 48.5' E12° 20.5'
Checkpoint. South of the buildings is a rise with a clear track ascending it. Avoid this deeply rutted and sandy track; ascend the slope either side.

Once on top turn SW along clear tracks which become WSW. The dunes are now visible again to the S with the black Messak to the north. The track is fast and smooth. There are occasional tyre markers and small stone cairns.

147 (7)   **N25° 43.1' E12° 11.5'**
Illegible metal sign with yellow border. Here at a small drop the piste turns WNW. Follow the track, bearing 290°.

149 (5)   **N25° 43.4' E12° 10.7'**
Red and white sign and a small cairn marks a fork in the piste. Take the right-hand fork (WNW) through an area of small black boulders.

Within 1km you reach a grey-blue oil drum topped with rocks (N25° 43.8' E12° 10.1'). Continue slowly on the track straight ahead, N, over more basalt boulders. The track slowly descends as you pitch along from side to side.

151 (3)
Bulldozed track crosses your route with a lone acacia tree soon afterwards. After a while the northern cliffs of Wadi Mathendous become visible. Very slow going for cars and bikes.

153 (1)
Another bulldozed track cuts across. Continue straight ahead past a clear sandy patch with low stone walls (shelters?) in it.

154 (0)   **N25° 45.8' E12° 10.1'**
White sign with green and blue writing on the south bank of Wadi Mathendous.

If you plan to cross the Wadi you'll have to let your tyres down – the gravelly sand is very soft. The track continues downstream (E) and carries on out over the northern bank.

Wadi Mathendous.

THE CIVILISATION OF THE GARAMANTES

The Garamantes have often been presented as mysterious, but are now becoming much better understood as a result of recent archaeological work in the Libyan Sahara.

They were depicted by Classical sources in a predominantly negative light, being identified as archetypal 'barbarians' dwelling beyond Rome's southern desert frontiers. Casual reading of this source evidence (spanning the period from the 5th century BC to the 6th century AD) would suggest transient pastoralists and brigands, with no settled roots and an anarchic social organisation.

Ancient Germa excavations from the air. © Toby Savage

Archaeology has revealed a very different picture of sedentary agriculturalists, living in towns and villages, possessing an ordered and hierarchical social structure, and making use of an eclectic, but advanced, material culture. They can be associated with the spread of the horse, camel and wheeled vehicles in the Sahara, with advanced oasis irrigation using underground water channels (*foggaras*), with metallurgy and mining and working of semi-precious stones (including carnelian, known in the sources as 'Garamantian carbuncles'). They are also credited with the development of a written script for the Libyan language which bears a resemblance to the now little-used Tifinar script of the Tuareg.

Roman contacts with the Garamantes were initially antagonistic, with campaigning against their desert heartlands recorded on several occasions between the later 1st century BC and later 1st century AD.

Most famously, Cornelius Balbus led a column against them in *c.* 20 BC, traversing several thousand kilometres of hostile desert terrain and evidently capturing their capital at Garama (present-day Jarma or Germa). By the later 1st century, more stable relations appear to have been established and this heralded a period of trade and peaceful co-existence between the independent kingdom and the Roman empire.

The Garamantes were ruled by kings, evidently controlling a large area of the central Saharan zone and trading with both the Roman empire and sub-Saharan Africa. They can be recognised as the first true civilisation of the central Sahara.

D. Mattingly et al. 2003. *The Archaeology of Fazzan, Vol 1. Synthesis.*

The famous mausoleum at Germa. © Toby Savage

L6 TIMSAH → WAW EN NAMUS [286KM]
November 1998; Toyota HJ61

Description
From the map the crater of Waw en Namus looks a very remote spot, midway between the Rebiana and Murzuk sand seas. Nevertheless, its appeal has led a steady stream of tourists to its reed-fringed lakes and grey ash dunes. The highway drive to Timsah is of little interest and indeed the rough, 300km drive to the crater itself is similarly devoid of much interest: a generally flat, firm and clearly marked piste.

Only once you drive up to the rim of the crater (and even into it) is your perspective altered as you behold the three-kilometre-wide crater, the fluted mound of its cinder cone and the multichrome lakes in between. It's something that sounds impressive in retrospect, but 'a long drive to see a crater' may be your rather drab thought on arrival.

From the crater, Route L7 is a serious proposition – another 740km to Rebiana and Tazerbu on which you'll not see anyone. Or you can continue east round the top of the Rebiana Sand Sea, via Bir Marrouf, about 390km.

Route-finding and markers
Easy most of the way with a very clear built-up track as far as the water project. From here the diversion which avoids Waw el Kebir base itself rejoins tracks from the base at KM200, but is reasonably clear and marked with tyres. From KM200 to the crater, the track is not built up but is frequently travelled, well marked and hard to lose.

All the usual markers line this route: a variety of tyres, oil drums, wire sticks and cairns.

Fuel
Timsah and possibly at the water project if you're desperate. Bikers may find the 600km round-trip quite a stretch and might want to stash a jerrican somewhere well in range to lighten their load.

Water
Timsah and the water project only. The waters at the crater do not look so palatable.

Traffic
This is a popular route and in the season you're bound to encounter other vehicles.

Driving
The only challenging bits are the Timsah sands and the sandy patches between KM260 and KM268. Bikers

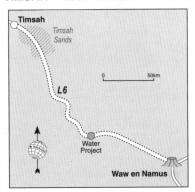

L6 – RECOMMENDED MAPS
TIMSAH → WAW EN NAMUS 286KM

The Russian 1:1m G-33 covers the whole route but only shows the track correctly from the end of the Timsah sands to the Waw el Kebir turn-off checkpoint, and then from the cairn hill at KM223 to the crater.

should take care here as, if you're getting weary after a long day, these nasty sands can catch you out. The rough track for the first 150km is likely to occupy your thoughts more. Most of the time you can drive alongside it.

Suggested duration

You might want to spend a night at the guest house or near the crater. Elsewhere, apart from the acacias at KM200, it's pretty featureless.

0km (286)   **N26° 23.6' E15° 46.6'**
Fuel station at the western end of Timsah.

1.3 (284.7)
Tarmac ends at the eastern end of town. Continue on a light-coloured piste. There may be a bit of confusion here as the reeds from the spring have blocked the piste, so pass just S of the spring, over a soft sand hump and rejoin the track to the N. The white gravel track curves out of town to the NE.

7 (279)
Pass a small lake pit on the left and then a palmerie, and continue out into the desert.

13 (273)
Piste forks here. Take the right fork heading ESE, 115°. But first reduce your tyre pressures as the sand soon gets soft in patches, then soft for good. Tracks run parallel to the main track: it's best if you avoid the sanded-over track altogether. Keep the track in sight to help orientate yourself.

It is best to blast through this sandy outspill without stopping. It gets firmer around KM21 with undulations around KM25.

15 (271)
Sandy rise. A good time to get off the track if you have not already done so.

25 (261)
Low ridge of hills visible in the distance. Sand becomes firmer and soon undulates.

32 (254)
Abandoned trailer by the main track.

34 (252)   **N26° 14.4' E15° 57.6'**
Sandy section ends near a few scattered wrecks on the left of the track. Re-inflate

tyres and continue on or alongside stony and corrugated track, whichever is smoother.

56 (230)
Low plateau on the right of the track.

75 (211)
Plateaux close in on both sides.

80 (206)   **N25° 55.0' E16° 13.5'**
Track rises sharply up an escarpment and descends slowly down the other side.

97 (189)
Slow down for a wadi crossing after which your bearing is 138°. Ahead, the Plateau el Kisa becomes visible. The track becomes very rough.

117 (169)
The track starts climbing into the mountains and smooths off once it levels out.

122 (164)
Watch out for a couple of sharp bends on this stretch.

125 (161)
Lorry wreck followed by a step descent. The old checkpoint will become visible on the horizon.

135 (151)   **N25° 33.3' E16° 34.0'**
Abandoned checkpoint buildings on a hill. Descend down the far side.

150 (136)   **N25° 28.5' E16° 40.8'**
Waw el Kebir checkpoint. Passports checked. Track forks; turn left towards buildings.

151 (135)
Various buildings and cabins. On the right is a workshop with many scrapped

Toyota 75s and other trucks. Continue towards an avenue of trees.

154 (132)

The *Water Project Guest House*. When we came through the wily manager blocked the road so you have to drive around the buildings to get past – and in the confusion you'll be persuaded to eat or spend the night there. Expect to be overcharged in various ways. You can do your own cooking. We thought it was overpriced.

Leave E along wide bands of tracks.

156 (130)

Tyre marker on right. Bearing 65-70°.

158 (128)

White building visible about 2km to the left of the track.

160 (126)   N25° 29.2'   E16° 46.8'

Pass two tyres. Bearing now around 100°. Soon you get to a blue oil drum on a small rise (this waypoint). The track continues on a bearing of around 97° with occasional tyre markers.

164 (122)

Bearing ENE.

166 (120)

Track gets sandy for a few hundred metres.

167 (119)

Oil drum followed by stony surface with sandy dips or patches.

170 (116)

Bearing 122°.

172 (114)   N25° 29.1'   E16° 53.3'

Small stony hill with a cairn. Continue on similar heading.

176 (110)

Stony section ends to become firm. Corrugated sand. Pace speeds up.

178 (108)

Two low hills become visible ahead.

185 (101)

Bearing 155°.

190 (96)

Tyre marker, the first in a while.

197 (89)

Clump of trees visible on horizon.

200 (86)   N25° 19.1'   E17° 03.4'

Line of acacias, about the only trees you'll see on this route. Continue straight ahead, bearing 123°. Junction of the track coming up from the Waw el Kebir army base about 40km to the south-west.

201 (85)

Tyre marker.

202 (84)   N25° 18.4'   E17° 04.4'

White signboard with faint writing and a few tyres.

204 (82)

Rocky hummocks to right of the track.

207 (79)

Two cairns on the right side of the track, which now fans out a bit.

215 (71)

Bearing around 110–125°. Ridge visible ahead.

217 (69)

Small concrete markers appear along the trackside for the next few kilometres.

222 (64)

Large and small cairns by the track.

223 (63)   N25° 12.7'   E17° 14.9'

Track crosses a bumpy stone ridge with a large colony of cairns on top (spot height '484m' on the G-33 map). Descend down the other side over a sandy ramp and then back onto the same sandy gravel corrugated track. Cross-channels slow the pace for a while and the track winds about until KM226 where it resumes 116° and you see another ridge ahead.

227 (59)

Concrete marker.

228 (58)

Tyre marker.

230 (56)
Small cairn on a small hill on the right of the track.

231 (55)
Bearing 100-110°. Pace speeds up.

233 (53)
Tyre marker.

235 (51)
Track passes a hill with white stone graffiti. Patches of white gypsum appear.

240 (46)
Tyre marker.

248 (38)   N25° 06.3'   E17° 26.9'
Climb onto a low ridge of black stones with a stick marker on top.

249 (37)
Oil drum. Bearing 128°.

253 (33)
Stick marker. Bearing 106–115°.

260 (26)
Small gypsum formations on the left, sandy hills ahead.

261 (25)
Cross a wadi and arrive at a sandy ramp leading up to a ridge with a tyre marker and petrol tins. Cross straight over to another sandy rise about 2km later. The sand here is soft and deep, but you should manage it in 4WD rather than having to deflate your tyres.

265 (21)
The track gets very sandy again as you approach the next sandy rise. If you've been having difficulty, now is the time to reduce tyre pressures. Or you can avoid the worst of it by driving over the stony banks to the side. This continues for about 2km where you pass a tin-can stick and within 1km you leave the sandy hills. The total sandy stretch is about 8km in all.

271 (15)
Stony surface, fairly slow.

277 (9)
Tyre marker, bearing now 136°.

278 (8)
Climb up towards first crater. Army checkpoint in 2003.

280 (6)   N24° 57.1'   E17° 43.0'
Either skim through the crater or drive around it. Lots of lava, pumice and unusual rocks around. Were it not for the army the crater would make a nicer camp than mosquito-ridden Namus.

From here you travel over various tracks which lead to the black grit of Waw en Namus. It's not as soft as it looks and appears like a permanent cloud shadow over the land. Bearing about 117°.

286 (0) N24° 55.7' E17° 45.3'
You climb steeply and suddenly you are on the western rim of Waw en Namus. Below you is one of the reed-shrouded lakes which surround the central cone.

Tracks criss-cross the inner surface of the crater. If you decide to drive in, note that the conditions can be dune-like so avoid steep gradients. The 11.6km track which follows the rim is mostly firm, but may need 4WD occasionally.

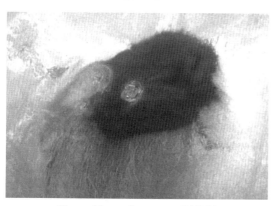

Waw en Namus from space. © NASA

Travelling in the Sahara is unpredictable and can be dangerous.
Every effort has been made by the publisher and the author of Route L7
to ensure that the description below is as accurate as possible. Neither
is able to accept responsibility for any loss or injury sustained by anyone as a result of the information given below.

L7 WAW EN NAMUS ➔ TAZERBU (via Dohone)   [740KM]
December 1999; Toyota HZJ75 (Reinhart Mazur)

Description
Experienced drivers will find no special problem on this route. In contrast to
the shorter and less interesting direct route from Waw to Tazerbu via Bir al
Maruf, L7 offers a variety of magnificent landscapes: the plain of the Serir
Tibesti followed by the volcanoes of the north-west of the Dohone mountains;
the Dohone itself and finally the sands of the Ramlat Rebiana.

It is possible to reach the scenic Rebiana oasis directly from the beginning
of the dune crossing at KM614.

Route-finding and markers
Overall, distinct tracks can be followed, some of which are marked on maps.
Oil drums line parts of the route up to KM278. To the NE of the Kilingue Pass
the dune area of the Ramlat Rebiana has to be crossed at its narrowest point.
Here, the described route leads over comparatively easy going without the
need to traverse steep dune crests, but no tracks are visible in this sandy area.

Fuel
Timsah (on Route L6, 286km from the start of Route L7) and Tazerbu only. In
an emergency you may get fuel at the BUC military post. You may come across
smugglers in Mercedes trucks or Land Cruisers on the eastern side of the
Dohone.

Water
BUC military post (in emergency) and Tazerbu only.

Traffic
There is no traffic on this desolate route. Travel with other vehicles for safety.

Driving
At KM614 a 16km crossing of a narrow neck of Rebiana sand sea commences,
for which you will need to lower tyre pressures. The 1000-plus km range puts
this route tacked onto the end of L6 beyond the range of a motorcycle.

Suggested duration
Three to four days.

WARNING – Kilingue Pass
The Kilingue Pass (N23° 17′ E20° 02′) should be avoided. Instead, follow the
easy track which bypasses the mined Pass a dozen kilometres to the south.
Coming from the eastern side, the Kilingue Pass can only be crossed by
ascending steep, soft sands or, alternatively, by taking a narrow, winding passage through the rocks. This is because the old track approaching the Pass and

L7 – RECOMMENDED MAPS   WAW EN NAMUS → TAZERBU 740KM

Your best bet for this route is a TPC J4-B or whatever Soviet-era mapping you can get hold of.

its broad top are still heavily mined. The wreck of a white mobile home destroyed here in 1991 may be seen, as well as other wrecks from 2001 and 2003 nearby. The ascent from the western side to the pass is much less difficult but dangerous. In order to reach the starting point at the foot of the ramp you have to cross a plain south of the so-called 'Cathedral Mountain' which is still supposed to be mined.

0km (740)   N24° 54'   E17° 44'
Waw en Namus, SW corner. Follow one of several tracks over serir covered with black ash. Huge corrugations must be carefully driven around. Heading 205°.

9 (731)   N24° 52'   E17° 42'
The corrugations end, now fast driving over serir.

59 (681)   N24° 27'   E17° 31'
Join the well-used track, running west–east, between Waw el Kebir and Aozou. Change heading to 120°.

70 (670)   N24° 24'   E17° 37'
Fenced military post 'BUC' (shelters, antennas). Do not approach at night and beware of them using firearms! Do not follow the well-used road which leads to an air strip in the direction of Aozou. Instead, keep to 125° (some faint tracks).

146 (594)   N24° 02'   E18° 13'
Track marked with drums crosses your route in north–south direction. From here some scattered dunes appear but can be easily avoided. Continue to the south-east across fast serir on a well-used piste marked with drums.

206 (534)   N23° 48.5'   E18° 42.2'
Stone inscription on the ground: 'Ozou 200 km, Eghei 140 km, Wau el Chebir 300 km'.

212 (528)   N23° 46'   E18° 43'
Approaching the volcano of Gara Smeraldi. Maintain heading 125°.

278 (462)   N23° 24'   E19° 13'
Gara Desio to the north of the track. Later on you pass through some narrow wadis. The regular marker drums end at this point.

309 (431)   **N23° 19' E19° 25'**
Drum in a narrow, sandy wadi. Another track branches off to the south. Heading is now 80°. Track continues towards a stony plateau.

343 (397)   **N23° 21.9' E19° 43.5'**
Zouma Pass; stone inscription on the ground: 'EGH 60 km, OZU 400 km, W EL KEBIR 450 km'.

347 (393)   **N23° 22' E19° 46'**
End of stony plateau. From here a stony road leads through rough, hilly country to the east.

357 (383)   **N23° 22' E19° 51'**
Wide wadi stretching north–south in front of a mountain range. 'Cathedral Mountain' can be seen to the SE. The track now turns south. Follow this well-used track, passing through wild, stony, hilly country and over narrow wadis, so bypassing the Kilingue Pass.

379 (361)   **N23° 14' E19° 54'**
Emi Kilingue can be seen to the east. Leave the well-defined track which continues to the Dohone mountains in the south. You may find a few tracks leading east which should be followed exactly (there may be a danger of mines on the wide plain).

389 (351)   **N23° 11' E19° 58'**
Scenic region. A wide, easygoing sandy plain with scattered hills. Emi Kilingue is to the north. Heading is now 65° with a few tracks leading in this direction.

409 (331)   **N23° 15' E20° 05'**
Wrecked Magirus mobile home clearly visible on the top of the Kilingue Pass in the distance. Follow tracks across wide plain, heading 65°.

464 (276)   **N23° 30' E20° 40'**
Picnic area used by local truck drivers. Hosenofu may be reached by crossing dune belt to the north-east. Well defined piste heading 35°.

544 (196)   **N24° 02.7' E21° 04.9'**
Junction. Driving north towards N24° 22.4' E21° 08.6', a dune is easily crossed. Alternatively, by driving at 320° this dune may be bypassed after 20km, reaching N24° 12.5' E20° 58.8'. Continuing northwards, you will find yourself driving across a plain of soft sands with no recent tracks.

582 (158)   **N24° 22.4' E21° 08.6'**
Short crossing of a single dune (reducing tyre pressure will help). NE ridges of Jebel Nerastro visible to the west.

592 (148)   **N24° 27' E21° 09'**
Junction: the piste which bypassed that long dune range reappears.

614 (126)   **N24° 37.6' E21° 10.1'**
Starting point of south–north crossing of Ramlat Rebiana: initially keep to a heading of 5°, then change to 20° over relatively firm sand, with isolated dune crests that may be easily bypassed. No recent tracks in your direction.

630 (110)   **N24° 44.6' E21° 14.2'**
End of sandy Ramlat Rebiana. Some scattered tracks. Heading 335°, Tazerbu can be reached without any problem by driving across a fast serir.

665 (75)   **N25° 03.2' E21° 12.3'**
Cross an exploration piste running NE/SW, well-marked with drums.

740 (0)   **N25° 40' E21° 05'**
Tazerbu. Report to the police opposite the radio tower. Water near the police HQ. Diesel available only from the old petrol station near the tower (if you are lucky). If not you can try to get some in drums from private traders, but at a higher price. Petrol is available at the new station when leaving Tazerbu to the east.

Mali

The vast majority of the Malian Sahara has rarely been travelled by tourists. When Algeria was accessible in the 1980s, just about all tourist traffic came down the relatively easy Tanezrouft piste. But since the Tuareg revolt of the 1990s and the growth of smuggling across the area, these days desert travellers are limited to the sandy tracks leading to Timbuktu and the music festivals (see p.582).

The rest of the Malian Sahara is part of a million-square-kilometre void which stretches across to western Algeria and eastern Mauritania with barely a couple of settlements. No recognised tracks cross it bar the dead-end terminating at the salt mines and former prison of Taoudenni, nearly 700km north of Timbuktu (see p.269). Even when the Tanezrouft was open, Kidal and the Adrar des Iforhas region south of Tessalit were still no-go areas for some reason. Since that time it has become a sort of neo-autonomous region for the Iforhas Tuareg, beyond the reach of Malian state control (the sort of province the Tuareg were promised across three countries by the departing French in the early 1960s). The area is not lawless in the way the Tibesti is (Gregg Butensky had no trouble visiting the region in 2004 for the Essouk festival, see p582; but in a car you might be at risk between towns). A few organised tours visit the area with local approval.

In the event of the Tanezrouft ever opening up, an outline of the entire route from Reggane in Algeria to Gao appears below, based on the 1995 edition of *Desert Biking*, but actually traversed in the late 1980s on two different trips and before the GPS era.

B1 REGGANE (Algeria) → GAO   [1370KM]
Algerian sector: March 1988; Land Rover 101, Honda XL600M
Mali sector: January 1989; Toyota BJ75, Yamaha Ténéré

Route-finding and markers
The Algerian section has what remains of the six-metre-high solar beacons at 2km intervals which used to flash by night and be useful marker posts by day. Most have been vandalised and many are missing but their consistent southbound orientation towards Bordj Moktar makes route-finding straightforward.

From Tessalit the track is good past the Adrar des Iforhas while further south, erosion and drifting sand sometimes makes it easier to choose your own route alongside the remains of the main piste.

Maps
IGN 1:1 million: NG-31 'In Salah', NF-31 'Tamanrasset', NE-31 'Kidal', NE-30 'Tombouctou' (the 'In Salah' map is mostly blank and not essential).

Fuel
Reggane, Bordj Moktar, Tessalit and Gao.

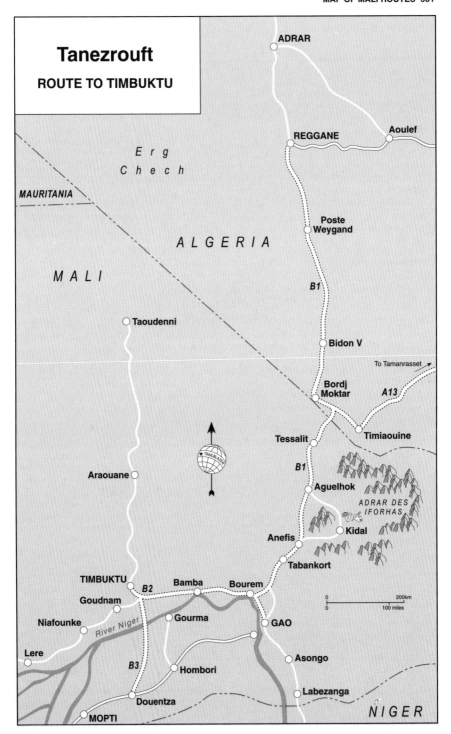

TUAREG FESTIVALS IN MALI

Each January, the desert regions of Mali host at least three Tuareg festivals. Many will have heard of the now somewhat commercialised *Festival au Désert*, held each year at Essakane, near Timbuktu. The other two are held near Kidal and Gao and are at present less well-known and more traditional gatherings.

These festivals emerged as a way of re-establishing tribal contacts following the devastating Tuareg rebellion in the mid-1990s. In 2004 we decided to attend the festivals at Essakane and Essouk using local transport.

Essouk

First up was Essouk, 60km from Kidal in the Adrar des Iforhas. A desert bus runs once or twice a week between Gao and Kidal but not to any kind of schedule. There are also large trucks that take passengers piled atop the cargo. This can be a rough twelve-hour trip but was the way we chose to travel. There were more than fifty of us perched precariously on the truck, high above the desert floor. Keep your essentials handy and note that it gets quite cold at night. Don't count on finding food along the way.

From Kidal to the festival site you can hire a ride or hook up with locals, many of whom will be heading that way. Ask around at the small *Kafe Eteron* near the Radio Tisdas studios (where the group Tinariwen recorded their CD, *The Radio Tisdas Sessions*).

The Essouk festival was a gem. Traditional goatskin tents formed a semicircle around a large sloping expanse. Impromptu music sessions regularly occurred in these tents throughout the three-day festival. Official performances – music and dance, including Tinariwen and the up-and-coming Etran – were held on a small stage after dark. During the day there were colourful camel processions and camel races.

Essakane

With the Essouk over for another year, the toughest part was getting from Kidal to Timbuktu in time for the festival at Essakane. We had just five days in between and the direct route was inadvisable due to banditry and the continued presence of the GSPC (see p.362). It was necessary to head south to Bourem on the Niger River and then west along the river to Timbuktu (Route B2).

No regular transport out of Kidal was to be found but after two days we were able to arrange a ride that would take us via Timbuktu all the way to the festival site. The journey took two-and-a-half days, the last eight hours of which was spent slogging through 70km of sand from Timbuktu to Essakane. The two-wheel drive Toyota Hilux had done OK until that point but 4WD is advisable for the last stretch. We limped into the festival site after dark under the light of one dim headlight, just in time to catch the first of the performances.

The festival at Essakane proved to be the perfect complement to the festival at Essouk. While bigger, less traditional and more commercialised than Essouk, the festival at Essakane included an impressive roster of well-known musicians, mostly from West Africa, but also from Europe and the US, performing with the benefit of state-of-the-art sound and lighting systems.

Other festivals

Making it to the Azawagh festival at the Niger border town of Anderamboukane east of Gao would have been easier as it was not on for about two weeks. But we were bound for Mauritania where we would learn of yet another music festival, this one being held in Nouakchott. Suffice to say, this is a great time to be in the area if you like the local music.

Gregg Butensky

Resources
www.festival-au-desert.org
www.triban-union.com
www.kidal.info

Water
No reliable sources between Reggane and Bordj Moktar. Available at Tessalit and from village wells along the Malian section of the route.

Driving
The Algerian section is smooth and fast reg with occasional soft patches. From Tessalit onwards the route gets bumpier and sandier with increasing vegetation. On a bike it's generally easy riding until you get to the rougher southern sections.

Suggested duration
Five days.

Description
The piste out of Reggane is corrugated and occasionally sandy for the first 50km. After this the reg sets in and driving is easy. Around 200km from Reggane you pass an old emergency water tank (empty) and at KM250 you pass the ruins of Poste Weygand, some dilapidated sheds and, later, a faint piste leading east to the old nuclear test site of Ouallen.

As you cross the Tropic of Cancer at KM360 there is an area of soft sand and small dunes, then at KM400 you pass a second water tank. The historic ruins of Bidon V appear at KM515 (this was originally 'Oil Drum 5', left by the Citroën expedition of the 1920s – the first motorised expedition to cross the Sahara). Around 20km later you drive through the all but fizzled out Oued Tamanrasset with Bordj Moktar appearing at KM640. Check out with the Algerian authorities.

Leave Bordj to the south-west and at the junction 32KM from town, turn south for Mali. Straight on leads to Timiaouine and the piste back to Tamanrasset (see Route A13, p.523). About 100km from Bordj the piste deviates west through a oued to avoid a military area (we became a little disorientated here) and Tessalit is reached after 155km from Bordj, set among rocky hills. In the old days they used to offer to guide you down south along the Oued Tilemsi to the west of the piste, claiming the opportunity to spot some wildlife.

About 100km from Tessalit you pass the village of Aguelhok and the first turn-off to Kidal. Just under 100km south of Aguelhok you enter the tussocks of the so-called 'Markouba Sands' or the Oued Ibdeken on the 'Kidal' map which can be hard work on a bike and has finished many an ageing 2WD which had to blast through to avoid getting stuck.

Seventy kilometres later you pass the main turning east to Kidal. If you've managed to get this far you may as well try and visit Kidal which has fuel smuggled from Algeria, and a hotel. Back at the turn-off after another 15km you reach the village of Anefis. By the time you get to Tabankort, 40km after Anefis, the Oued Tilemsi has converged with the piste and the going gets sandier. Most people avoid the continuation of the sandy oued and head west towards Bourem, 150km from Tabankort, though the going can still be very sandy at times. Bourem is on the River Niger. Here you decide if you continue south to Gao (another 99km), Niamey and the tarmac highway to Bamako, or head 330km west to Timbuktu.

B2 GAO → TIMBUKTU   [430KM]

April 1999; Toyota HDJ80, Nissan Patrol (Tony van Gastel)

Route-finding and markers

Apart from the turn-off north of Bourem and some confusion around villages, it is straightforward.

Maps

NE-30 'Tombouctou' is good enough but the modern course of the piste may not necessarily match these old maps.

Fuel

Gao and Timbuktu (very expensive).

Water

From village wells along the route and even the river.

Driving

In a car the sandy ruts are pretty easy, though tyre pressures will need to be reduced. On a bike the twin ruts winding through the surrounding scrub can be hard work. You have to stay in one rut, stand up and keep the power on – pretty tiring for up to 300km!

Suggested duration

Two to three days.

Laissez-Passer

It's important to note that the Laissez-Passer for Mali is only given for a period of eight days. Thereafter it needs to be extended at customs in any of the larger cities in Mali. We did this in Bamako at the Office du Douane, in the centre of the city. Extension was easy, although I had to write an official *Demande de Prolongation*. The Laissez-Passer was extended for a period of 21 days and the cost was only 100 CFA for a stamp.

Regional security

Concerning the road to Timbuktu, people say that it is safe; bush taxis and so on are going almost every day. However, in the *Sahara Passion* restaurant we were told that only the day before two Toyotas were stolen from the Red Cross, somewhere close to Bourem. [Since this was written Gao has become a centre for people-smuggling, but also a base for the Pan Sahel Initiative – see p.364].

Gao

Gao is a large sandy town, completely built from mud bricks with hardly any stone buildings or tarmac. Fuel is always available. Registering with the police (1000 CFA per passport plus photograph) is friendly and fast. The mosque is not very impressive, but it is interesting to wander around in the city. A visit to the 16th-century tomb of Askia currently costs 1000 CFA per person (it is mud-pile tombs like these that gave rise to the stick-and-adobe 'Sudanese' building style of Mali, the mosque of Djenne being the best-known example). The tomb and its surroundings is basically a mosque, and there are nice views over the town from the top.

Besides the old *Hotel Atlantide*, there are three **campsites** in Gao centre: *Tizimizi* is by far the best.

TIMBUKTU

Today the legendary town long synonymous with the ends of the earth isn't much to look at. Its narrow streets of flat-roofed mud-brick dwellings are filling with sand, and the once-famous Djingguerber mosque is just another mud and stick structure of the sort commonly found in the Sahel. The great mosque was built in the 14th century to celebrate the liberation of Timbuktu from Tuareg control – a problem which beset the town again just a few years ago during the rebellion.

With its golden roof, the Djingguerber mosque helped create the legend of Timbuktu, symbolising the city's reputation for fabulous wealth. These riches were the product of the city's strategic position, a port 'where camel meets canoe' on the shores of the desert and the banks of the Niger. From here salt, gold and slaves were transported across the Sahara to the Maghreb and Europe; business only dwindled after the European empires established their maritime trade routes. Most of medieval Europe's **gold** originated in West Africa, and gold is today still mined in south-west Mali. When the liberating Mali emperor Mansa Musa passed through Cairo on his pilgrimage to Mecca, he gave out so many gold coins (up to a ton and a half) that the price of the precious metal crashed locally for years.

As the wealth and stability of Timbuktu grew, it became established as a seat of learning, accommodating up to 25,000 students. Two years after Columbus sailed for the Americas, the Spanish Moor **Leo Africanus** visited the city and reported 'a great store of learned men, bountifully maintained at the king's expense'. Today many old books from that era still remain in the town's numerous private collections. During this time the Tuareg again began menacing Timbuktu, demanding tribute from the richly-laden caravans converging on the city.

When the Mali kingdom was replaced by the **Songhai dynasty**, Timbuktu was again freed from Tuareg influence and prospered to a degree which is today difficult to imagine. Other strategic cities such as the Songhai capital Gao, 300km to the east, and Oualata (300km to the west, in present-day Mauritania) had similar reputations, thriving as centres of trade, culture and learning.

Gradually word of the Songhai riches spread north to Morocco and Europe so that in 1591 the Sultan of Marrakesh sent an army across the Sahara to sack the Songhai cities, and the overstretched empire collapsed almost overnight. From that date Timbuktu slipped into a dark age of progressive decline.

Over the intervening years the fable born of Africanus' description seeped into the imaginations of Europeans who were themselves discovering the new-found riches of the Orient. By the early 19th century the geographical societies of Britain and France offered huge financial rewards to the first European to return with corroborative reports of the **Saharan El Dorado**.

Marching in full uniform, the stalwart Scottish soldier Gordon Laing was the first of the explorers to actually get there in 1826, travelling across the Sahara from Tripoli. Up till then perhaps forty other adventurers had been less fortunate, most of them falling to disease or the daggers of their guides.

Laing was murdered too, as he left Timbuktu, so never claimed his reward, but two years later the low-born Frenchman **René Caillé** reached the city – without official support and dressed in local garb. Like Laing, Caillé found nothing to match the town's reputation. Dragged across the Sahara by suspicious and cruel traders, he staggered into the oases around Erfoud in Morocco and in December 1828, following initial scepticism, was rewarded with several prizes. But the years of exploration had taken their toll on the 28-year-old baker's son from Poitou; he never fully recovered from his ordeal, and died ten years later.

Today the houses once briefly occupied by Laing, Caillé and the German Saharan scholar, Heinrich Barth, are marked with plaques for the benefit of visiting tourists, where these days fewer than 5000 descendants of the merchants, slaves, conquerors and nomads struggle to survive the ever encroaching desert.

To Timbuktu

The track to Bourem (99km from Gao) is generally firm with some very sandy stretches, particularly the last 20km before Bourem. We had some difficulties finding the track out of Bourem because it initially goes north towards Tessalit and only after some time an illegible signpost points west.

Turn left here and drive through a completely barren area. There were no tracks so we drove cross-country in the direction of our next waypoint. Once you pick up the track, it's generally clear all the way to the Gourma Rharous turn-off, passing through the typical acacia scrub of the northern Sahel. This piste does not always follow the track indicated on the 1:200,000 IGN maps.

West of the Gourma turn-off, the piste mainly follows the river, but the last 15km before Timbuktu is again very sandy, with nice dunes a few kilometres before Timbuktu. We camped in the desert, a few kilometres east of Timbuktu, surrounded by spectacular sand dunes.

B3 DOUENTZA → TIMBUKTU [225KM]
January 2003; KTM640 (Ian Thompson)

There are a few reasonable campsites in Douentza and the track starts next to the fuel station in the centre of town at N15° 00.7' W02° 57.0'. For the first 116km it's easy to follow and in relatively good condition with just a few corrugations. Thereafter it's a different story, with soft sand setting in nearly all the way to the southern bank of the river Niger at KM205. There are many deviations in all directions but none of them offers much relief. I wouldn't like to attempt it on a heavily-loaded bike, in the wet season or in a 2WD (though Dutch contributor Gerbert van der Aa managed this in 2004). The track passes through many creek beds that are dry in the winter months, but which may well make the route impassable during the rains. The scenery is typically Sahelian but quite densely vegetated in places.

Navigation was relatively easy, with the clearly-defined track heading in a northerly direction most of the time. There was one major junction on the route, a track heading off to the east at KM105. Ignore this and continue north.

At KM139 you'll pass through the village of Gare where the sand is at its worse, and shortly afterwards, at KM171, there are a few houses and a campsite (though in January 2003 this looked deserted and closed).

As you near the river the going gets easier (or you've just got used to it) before you arrive at the point where you board the ferry to Korioume at KM205. When I crossed, the small harbour was not in use. Instead everyone boarded at a point on the bank a few hundred metres further east. The **ferry** costs 12,000 CFA, split equally between each vehicle being carried, regardless of size.

From Korioume there's a sealed road all the way to the centre of Timbuktu, but you're back in soft sand when driving around the town. Despite its reputation for hassle, in my experi-

Taking the pinasse. © Ian Thompson

ence Timbuktu was certainly no worse than any other part of West Africa. To make things easy on yourself, it's worth hiring a guide to show you round the sights, some of which can be quite difficult to find. Expect to pay between 3000 and 7000 CFA for half a day. You can also get your passport stamped free of charge at the local tourist information office.

If you're travelling by public transport or on two wheels you might consider leaving by boat from Kourioume to Mopti or Gao. I managed to get myself and my motorcycle on a cargo-carrying pinasse to Mopti for 55,000 CFA, although I'm sure with some negotiation you could get a much better price. The voyage took about fifty hours, and included frequent and long stops at towns and villages on the way, and on the numerous occasions that the boat ran aground.

Basic meals in the form of rice three times a day, twice with fish, were provided by the friendly crew, as were endless glasses of Chinese tea. This is normally included in the price. Accommodation was very basic – I slept on the roof above the engine room. In January there were very few mosquitoes due to the cold wind that forced me to stay fully clothed in my riding suit and in my sleeping bag for most of the trip. Outside of the winter months I guess it would be a different story.

Niger

The Tamachek word 'Ténéré' (the equivalent of the Arabic 'Sah'ra' or 'desert') lights up the eyes of Sahara aficionados. Along with the Aïr mountains, this remote and beautiful region covers the sand sea of the Grand Erg du Bilma in the south (often misunderstood to mean the Ténéré), the serir of the Ténéré du Tafassasset in the north (the genuine Ténéré, a flat void) and the distant plateaux of the far north-east along the Libyan and Chadian borders. The size of France, this mini-Sahara of dunes and plateaux, plains and mountains, iso-lated villages, caravans and prehistoric art sites fulfils the desert expectations of both first-timers on tours and experienced Saharans.

The Ténéré was well traversed by tourists from the 1970s up until the Tuareg rebellion of the early 1990s, which accounts for its firm placement in the Saharan consciousness; it's regularly featured in TV documentaries. For independent

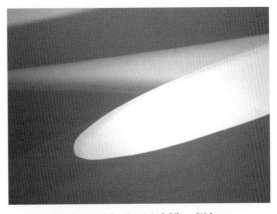

The dunes of the Ténéré. © Klaus Weltzer

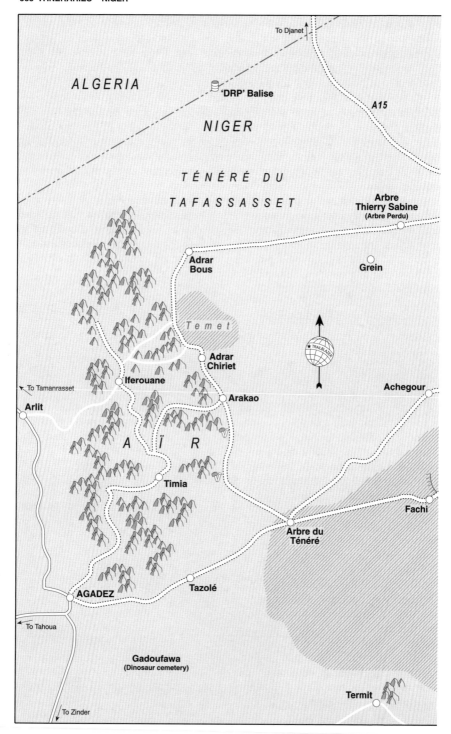

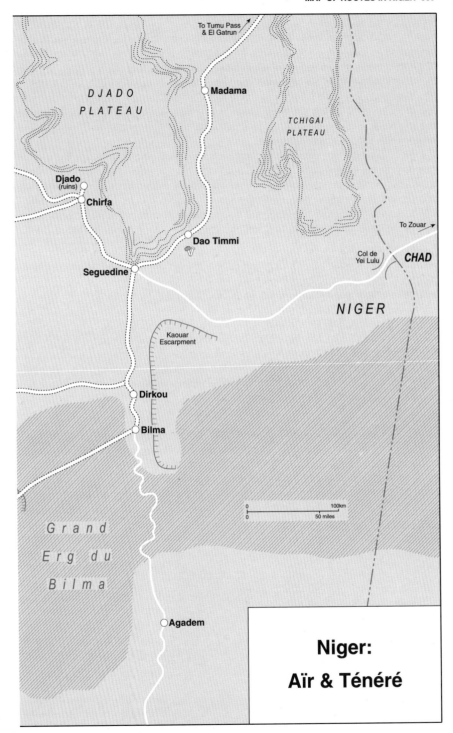

To Tumu Pass
& El Gatrun

Madama

DJADO
PLATEAU

TCHIGAI
PLATEAU

Djado
(ruins)

Chirfa

To Zouar

Dao Timmi

Col de
Yei Lulu

CHAD

Seguedine

NIGER

Kaouar
Escarpment

Dirkou

Bilma

0   100km
0   50 miles

Grand

Erg du

Bilma

Agadem

Niger:
Aïr & Ténéré

travellers accessibility has never really recovered, as problems with renegade Tuareg bandits around the Aïr, and Tubu rebels in the Djado, led to several robberies in the last few years, though both seem to have moved on. Nevertheless Niger has been one of the most robbery-prone countries in the Sahara – not that this stops it being one of the most popular destinations for organised tours.

Either way, a visit here adds up to serious and remote desert travel. Wells are few and far between and, away from the Achegour–Dirkou–Madama route, traffic is sparse. A convoy of two or three sound vehicles is essential rather than merely recommended.

Note that if you are leaving from Agadez, you won't get past the checkpoint without a **guide and permit** (more below). This has long been the rule in the Ténéré and it is not something you should try and get round. The situation is different if you are coming into the Ténéré from Libya or Algeria. At the first town where you stop for fuel and to check in (probably Chirfa, Dirkou or Iferouane) you may be told to take on a guide to your next destination.

Overland access

Security problems notwithstanding, you can get to the Ténéré along pistes from all neighbouring countries:

● Down the trans-Sahara route from Tamanrasset to Iferouane (750km via Arlit) or Agadez (800km); see p.515.
● From Djanet to Chirfa and on to Dirkou (820km); see p.527.
● From El Gatrun in Libya via Madama, Seguedine and Dirkou (810km).
● Along the balised piste from Zouar in Chad (460km, but not done for years and not likely to be soon).

Dirkou is the main fuel point in the Ténéré, although Chirfa, Bilma and Iferouane, in the northern Aïr, may also have supplies.

Guides

Officially it's not possible to bomb around the Ténéré without a guide. Trying to leave Agadez or coming into Dirkou you may have to face awkward questions at control posts which may require paying your way out. It's said that even locals cannot leave Dirkou alone, although again, it's done. There's a checkpoint just out of Agadez and another at the Falaise Tiguidit, both on the

route to the Arbre du Ténéré. They'll want to see your *feuille* or permit issued by an Agadez tourist agency.

But if you head into the Ténéré via the Aïr, for example, there appear to be no checkpoints. The problem comes with the need for fuel: at Dirkou a solo car can buy a *feuille* (3000 CFA for 30 days in early 2001) with no questions asked if they assume you're sticking to the main routes. It's better that you have a *feuille* before you get to the Chirfa control post as the situation is a bit more tense round here.

All this cloak-and-dagger touring can be avoided by **hiring a guide**, useful not so much for finding the way (on the Loop this is fairly easy) but for the local knowledge of people and places. Currently there is a glut of agencies in Agadez so it may well be possible to get a guide for as little as €60 a day in your car or around €130 a day if they drive their own car. Note that local guides' vehicles have not been immune to robberies, and also that the condition of older vehicles (mostly 60-series Land Cruisers) can be rough. Newer 80 and 105-series Land Cruisers are creeping in though, as post-rebellion tourism recovers in fits and starts.

The mosque at Agadez. The protruding sticks help with annual 'replastering'.
© Mike Foster

There are several agencies in Agadez contactable by fax. Rather than listing them here it's best to get an agency, or better still a guide, recommended by other travellers: ask on the website. As everywhere, quality varies where there is money to be made but in general the long history of tourism in Agadez makes it a safe bet you'll get what you pay for.

Having arrived at Dirkou from the north, it may be necessary to get a guide to come out from Agadez unless you're heading directly on to Agadez along the northern truck piste via Achegour (650km) in which case joining a truck convoy may be permitted. Bear in mind that the guide's meter starts running the day he leaves Agadez and ends when he gets back home; either you drop him off, or you pay for his return ride with someone else.

If you don't want to do the full Loop you can still have a very satisfying tour of just the eastern Aïr's flanks with the Ténéré, covering the highlights described below between the Arbre du Ténéré and Adrar Bous. Added to some of the highlights in the Aïr, such as the Timia cascade, the Assodé ruins and rural Tuareg encounters, it will still give you a memorable tour of the region without the long trek east where, realistically, the Djado region is the only highlight. Once you've seen these places the expanse in between is nothing special.

There are many variations on the standard loop outlined below, but these days guides are reluctant to venture away from established routes deep into ergs or remote corners, partly because of banditry but more due to the condition of their vehicles. Most would rather bang out the regular tourist loop and if you've never been there before, it will certainly cover all the highlights the Ténéré has to offer. The following travel reports from Niger may not have the detail of full GPS itineraries but will give you an impression for the area.

THE STANDARD TÉNÉRÉ LOOP [2130KM]

The description of this route dates from 2001 with reference to later information. In an anti-clockwise direction it applies as much to travellers in their own vehicles as it does to organised tours. Travelling in the opposite direction is possible but generally vehicles try to reach the Bilma Erg towards the end of a fuel stage (e.g., Agadez–Bilma) when vehicles are lighter. Either way, the whole route as below can be done in a fortnight.

These long distances make motorcycle travel around the Ténéré barely possible unless a car carries extra fuel.

Agadez to Bilma [610KM]

Leaving Agadez there's a checkpoint just outside town and the piste along the southern edge of the Aïr is corrugated and sometimes rough and stony. Eighty-five kilometres from Agadez you reach the control post at the village of Tourayet (N16° 59.7' E07° 43.3'). At KM138 you cross the dusty Oued Barghot and enter the nominal hunting reserve/Aïr National Park. From here you begin to head north-east, the going gets stony and around KM190 you'll have a good view of Mont Amzeguer. About 25km later (KM215), as indicated on the Aïr Massif map, the sand sets in and you'll want to let your tyres down.

Following the mass of tracks you reach the well at the famous **Arbre du Ténéré** at KM270 (N17° 44.6' E10° 04.9'). Despite what the Michelin map says the water here is perfectly drinkable, but is of course very deep at over forty metres. You'll see the replacement metal Arbre (the original is in Niamey Museum) as well as the Japanese monument: a 15m pylon hung with lenses, plus the usual litter,

Drawing water at the Arbre. It's a big bucket.

other structures and an empty water tank. There are even a couple of 'nouvelle arbres' which you're asked to water when you are there.

Hereabouts the piste splits. Transit traffic heading for Dirkou and Libya takes the easier northern route via Achegour, while tourist groups head into the northern reaches of Erg du Ténéré and the oasis of Fachi (440km). Balises are intermittent on the route to Fachi but the dune corridors line up almost perfectly to lead you there. Soon after the Arbre the grassy tussocks disappear and you're among the low dunes. On our traverse we dropped a few gassis to the south soon after the Arbre and slotted into one around 15km south of the balised route on the IGN maps (via N17° 48.3' E10° 37.8'), which led directly to Fachi.

The dunes are long, low seifs and it's possible to drive without having to regularly negotiate too many crests. Indeed it would be interesting to try and navigate from the Arbre to Fachi without turning on the GPS and just using the orientation of the gassis, as it is hard to miss the Agram falaise with Fachi at its foot. Apart from the soft sands working the engine hard, it's the ripples on the windward side of the sand slopes which can give the car a hammering.

At **Fachi** (KM440), the westernmost Kanure settlement in the Ténéré, you can take a tour of the Old

Old Fachi.

Town after visiting the village chief or sultan, whose house is just east of the big well at the southern end of the main boulevard. Inside the old fort you'll be shown giant storage jars, but overall the tour is nothing special and the hassles from the vendors can be quite a shock after a few days in the desert. Down the road directly east from the main well are the Fachi salines where you'll see the *kantu* pillars (see picture, below) and the smaller **foci** cakes being piled up for the next caravan.

To cross the falaise head north from the village through the palmerie until you get to a broad sandy ramp leading north-east over the ridge (N18° 12.1' E11° 37.6'), more or less the point '579' on the NE-32 one million map. Up the ramp and for a few kilometres after the ridge, the sands get softer and the gassis tighten up a little. Your next landmark might be the lone twin outcrops of Tiguedelane (visible from N18° 30.7' E12° 24. 8'); at this point the gassis spread out and it's around 55km to Bilma with the Kaouar escarpment behind it.

Bilma – Dirkou – Chirfa – Djado [300KM]

The outpost of **Bilma** (KM610) at the southern end of the Kaouar escarpment is famed for its salines, at Kalala just west of the town, and the camel caravans which still carry the salt to the pastoralists of the east and south of Niger. Tuaregs are much associated with this trade but in fact it's a Hausa business; the Tuaregs are hired for their camels and guiding expertise.

Abandoned salt pillars in the erg. Nearby was a dead camel.

An old picture of the fort at Bilma. © Mike Foster

The sandy, tree-lined avenues have a romantic feel but, excepting the seasonal salt and date trade, Bilma is in decline and firmly in the shadow of booming Dirkou. If you need to do any shopping you may as well wait till you get there. You should check in with the police at the fort at the east side of town, among the palms. The palmerie south of here makes a shady place for a lunch break while the two-hour task of pressing a stamp onto your passports is undertaken.

From Bilma a clear truck track leads up to Dirkou, rounding the odd dune and some soft patches. Even if you get off the track the falaise of the Kaouar to the east is always a reliable landmark.

As you near **Dirkou** (KM645) you'll pass the airstrip, with piles of oil drums, to end up at the barbed-wire compound with a shot-up Tubu Toyota maybe still nearby. Here you hand in your passports for more stamps. Still, it gives you a chance to check out Dirkou which over the years has grown into a booming frontier town catering for West Africans drawn by the dubious opportunities for work in Libya or even a way through to Europe. You're bound to see the spectacularly overloaded six-axle Mercedes *gros porteurs* which grind to and fro between Sebha and Agadez, transporting stolen or smuggled goods from Libya. Much of this stuff can be bought in the thriving markets of Dirkou, run by the Nigerians who didn't quite make it to Libya. If you're aching for a beer, there's even a bar here.

Dirkou High Street, a place where you can buy anything.
© Klaus Weltzer

The fuel compound is a couple of kilometres north of the busy centre (N18° 59.8' E12° 53.6'), but in your own car you'll pay up to 300 CFA per litre while locals pay 220. There are stalls with oil drums in town who may siphon you a tank's worth for less.

Having retrieved your passports, you continue northwards on the truck route paralleling the escarpment. Even Dirkou has a *saline*; a rather dank-looking lake at N19° 03.2'

E12° 53.8′ where natron (sodium carbonate) is collected.

This part of the drive up along the Kaouar is not as scenic as you might expect. Few people bother to make the detour to the village of Aney. At Yeguebba (KM745) near the end of the Kaouar (N19° 51.1′ E12° 52.3′) are a few trees offering shade and firewood.

From this point the pale sands of the Kaouar

The saline at Seguedine. © Klaus Weltzer

turn into the orangey-red hues of Djado, the familiar colours of the Akakus and Tassili too. The truck route continues clearly all the way to Pic Zumri and in a dip just beyond is the village of **Seguedine** (KM785).

Trucks head up the escarpment to the north-east of the village on their way to Dao Timmi and Libya, with another, now rarely-used piste leading east to Zouar in Chad. Seguedine has a police post, a small ruined ksar in the style of Djado in its centre and a small saline on the north-east edge of the village. If you're not stopping here, keep to the tracks north-west of the village which lead over stonier terrain. Although you are no longer on the truck route, the regular tours still maintain clear tracks that are easy to follow to the north-east,

though they're further east than those marked on old one million and 'Niger' IGN maps of this area. At N20° 25.3′ E12° 48.8′, about 30km from Seguedine, drivers have kindly erected some chunks of **petrified wood** and 27km later (N20° 33.8′ E12° 37.1′) the landmark of Oleki mountain is visible directly to the northeast. Up ahead, the small oasis of Sara is a shady spot a few kilometres from the edge of the rising Djado escarpment. You reach the control post of Chirfa at KM905 (N20° 55.3′ E12° 19.4′).

To make a visit to **Chirfa** village (KM907), Djado, Enneri Blaka etc, you must deposit your passports here; if you're heading directly across the Ténéré up to Djanet (A15) or across Adrar Bous, the balised piste forks to the west for the Col de Chandeliers (aka Passe de Orida).

There's diesel at Chirfa, costing about 10% more than at Dirkou, or whatev-

Petrified tree trunks.

Tubu women at Djado. © Klaus Weltzer

er they can get away with. Two or three kilometres south of the village are the ruins of Old Chirfa (aka Tebeza, N20° 55.3' E12° 21.8'), part of a series of amazing medieval ksars built on outcrops of rock found right along the western edge of the Djado plateau and dating from the time when a trading route linked Lake Chad with the Fezzan.

Set alongside the escarpment of the Djado plateau, the ruined citadel of **Djado**, 12km north of Chirfa village, is one of the highlights of the Sahara, if not perhaps the single place which most evokes the mystery and romance of the desert. To explore the intricate ruins of this settlement (about the size of old Siwa), now so far from any population centres, is a reminder of the importance of long-vanished cultures and the trans-Sahara trade on which they flourished.

You may want to hire a guide from the village to accompany you there for a few thousand CFA, but it's not essential, more a custom. The ruins are surrounded by a dense palmerie, and standing water in winter. In late summer almost the whole village of Chirfa moves into the *zeribas* beneath the dunes to harvest the dates. Why such a huge settlement was abandoned centuries ago is still unknown, but the decline of the arduous trade route through the eastern Ténéré, as well as the voracious mosquitoes, may have been to blame. Even in the daytime it's possible to get savaged by a swarm of mosquitoes behaving like killer bees, but none of this detracts from the wonder of exploring the mysterious ruins of Djado. The crumbling structure is weakening year by year, something to bear in mind as you explore the alleyways and stairwells inside the main complex.

The fabulous ruins of Djado. © Klaus Weltzer

Ten kilometres north of Djado along a sandy track are the smaller, and some would say more evocative and perfectly-formed, ruins of **Djaba**. To get there requires getting over a distinctive rocky barrier which reaches out southwest from the escarpment – the thin brown line just visible on the NF-33 map

EXCURSION TO ENNERI BLAKA

Enneri means valley, while Blaka, we were told, is the name of a famous Tubu warrior. At the time of our visit in late 2000, *Dunes Voyages* in Agadez had indicated that security in the mountains was no problem; except for a few tribesmen, the Tubu were at peace with the Niger government. Take a local guide and you will be OK. From Chirfa we had to climb up the side of the plateau to get into Enneri Domo, a wide valley with black mountains all around, which leads around the Djebel Kodougihi to Enneri Blaka. The ascent is difficult with sand mixed with rocks*. Once up, we followed the Enneri Domo. The going was very slow and the landscape – although an interesting moonscape – does not change any more and becomes monotonous. The valley is extremely dry; there is hardly any vegetation; just an occasional tree or bush. It had not rained in Chirfa for eleven years and on the plateau it rained only once during that period.

Then we joined the southern end of Enneri Blaka and the scenery changed to white/yellow sand alongside the very black hills, and it was worth the five-hour drive. To get to the famous 'submarine' rock formation (N21° 7.6' E12° 43.8') which holds the rock paintings, we had to drive up a sand dune.

We decided to take a different route back and took the turn-off south towards Seguedine, more or less following the oued line as far as Oleki peak where we were two days before. Just before Oleki we decided to go cross-country to Chirfa. In Chirfa we said farewell to our Tubu guide (CFA 10,000 per day), took fuel (CFA 400 per litre; we were told that there is always fuel in Chirfa) and water. Returning to the military post to retrieve our passports and head west, we were promised we would see *beaucoup de rien du tout*...

Tony Gastel

*There may be landmines here; see p.368.

(although some guides drive around the ridge to the west). Tracks lead to a sandy ramp which requires a good run-up. Once you're on the crest Djaba (KM924, N21° 04.6' E12° 16.0') can just be seen among the palms to the northeast. There is a well near Djaba at N21° 06.4' E12° 15.5' – look for a tyre.

Since Chirfa the monoliths of Orida will have been clearly visible; now they are directly ahead. The biggest, Ouarek, has a well at its base (N21° 07.4' E12° 14.3'), a large cave full of desert melon seeds and, round the back, the **Arch of Orida** (N21° 07.4' E 12° 14.6', KM932).

Across the Ténéré du Tafassasset   [320KM]

Having reclaimed your passports from the Chirfa control post (with the round trip to Orida you are now at more or less KM964 from Agadez), the Loop heads west along a balised track to the **Col de Chandeliers** (KM980) from where the flat serir of the Ténéré rolls away to the horizon. Balises lead up to Djanet (see p.527), but from the Col tour-group tracks also lead WSW, past a wrecked rally truck to the lonely mound of **Arbre Perdu** or Arbre Thierry

Arbre Perdu

Sabine (KM1080, N20° 38.0′ E11°14.9′). The latter, newer name commemorates the Dakar Rally founder whose ashes were scattered here in 1987 after his helicopter crashed near Timbuktu. A slab of Blue Mountain marble (see below) lies engraved with his name.

The tour tracks continue WSW, eventually parallelling the balised Berliet piste (though you'll be unlikely to spot any balises). The next landmark is the north–south string of hills of **Grein** (KM 1117, N20° 29.3′ E10° 13.6′).

From here the sand sheet gets even more featureless, flat and soft – at times even the ripples are absent and there's nothing to focus on apart from a few outlying dunes as you pass the top of the **Erg Capot Rey**. Then, with good visibility, the faint outline of Adrar Bous becomes discernible at around E09° 30′, still some 50km away.

The eastern borders of the Aïr

Adrar Bous (the southern end on E09° is KM1320) is renowned as a site of former Neolithic occupation. From Bous the piste leads west (as marked on the half-million IGN 'Massif de l'Aïr' map) to a garden of mushroom rocks

The oued leading out of Temet (via KM1402). © K. Weltzer

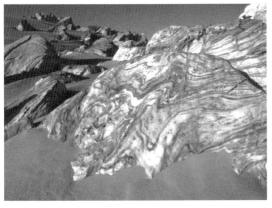

Izouzaouene – The Blue Mountains. © Klaus Weltzer

(KM1355, N20° 13.3′ E08° 41.8′) and then up over a sandy pass (KM1375, N20° 05.7′ E08° 37.6′) to continue along a oued running between the dunes of **Temet** and Mont Greboun. The Temet dunes reach their greatest height at KM1385 (N20° 00.7′ E08° 40.6′), a popular lunch stop or overnight camp. From here tracks lead south along the edge of the Aïr to Tezirzik well (see p.599), but a piste also heads along a oued or gassi back out east into the desert (via N19° 58.8′ E08° 48.2′, KM1402), running southeast (passing a 'blue' outcrop at KM1420, N19° 53.8′ E08° 56.9′) towards the next highlight of the region, Izouzaouene, or the **Blue Mountains** (KM1462, N19° 35.7′ E09° 11.9′). The white marble here (also found elsewhere in the eastern Aïr) is veined with cobalt salts, giving the outcrop its distinctive pale blue hue when seen from a distance.

From the summits of Izouzaouene, the massif of **Adrar Chiriet** is visible directly to the south. The 'Massif de l'Aïr' map suggests a route through the dunes regularly plied by tours; it crosses a pass a couple of kilometres north-east of Chiriet at KM1497 (N19° 21.3' E09° 14.1'), and at Chiriet itself you can drive into a gorge (KM1511, N19° 18.7' E09° 09.7') and out another way. Now the track winds

A foreground of dunes with the ramparts of Adrar Tamgak behind: the definitive east Aïr landscape. © Klaus Weltzer

south-west and crosses a rocky ridge (KM1532, N19° 12.7' E08° 59.3') and soon reaches **Tchou-m-Adegdeg** well (KM1534). This and the nearby well at **Tezirzik** are important sources on the east side of the Aïr and you'll usually meet nomads camped nearby or watering their herds*.

Arakao is another of the eastern Aïr's wonders; a pair of crab's claws ten kilometres in diameter clamped around a tongue of dunes which rolls through the mouth to pile up against the cliffs at the back. To get there you must go out into the dunes and approach the gap between the claws from the east (KM1635, N18° 58.4' E09° 40.3'). It's no surprise that Arakao was occupied for millennia; inside the southern claw

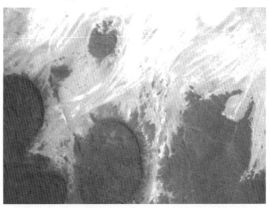

The 'crabs claws' of Arakao and the isolated massif of Adrar Chiriet to the northwest. © NASA

on the slopes of the ridge you'll find pre-Islamic tombs with worked stones and pottery all around. Tours usually visit the southern side of the cirque where access is easier and then camp on the crest of the dune ridge (KM1644). To get to the northern half, cross just as you pass the entrance where the dunes are narrowest.

*From Tezirzik my tour turned into the Aïr and Iferouane, but for the purposes of the Loop, this description continues south from Tchou-m-Adegdeg to Kogo – a sixty-kilometre gap in this account, although the black line on the 'Massif de l'Aïr' map suggests that this section is no less unclear than others in the area. Our group originally came from Timia, up the Zagado valley to Kogo (KM1594) and followed the tour tramlines to a Neolithic site of tombs and artefacts (KM1600, N19° 03.5' E09° 24.9').

The engravings at Anakom. © Klaus Weltzer

Leaving Arakao to the south you pass over low dunes and crest a rise at 'Long Stones Pass' (KM1676, N18° 44.1' E09° 42.7') where the rock has weathered onto long baguettes that have been stood on their end by passing drivers. Looking east you can see 70km to Adrar Madet with the outcrop of Areschima Nord in between. A few kilometres south of here you park up right by the amazingly prolific spread of engravings covering the rocks at **Anakom** (KM1687, N18° 39.6' E09° 43.4'). All the usuals are here – a mini-Mathendous of elephants, bovids, ostriches, and of course giraffes. There's another less well known but no less impressive site of engravings along the boulders of the oued at Tanakom (KM1699, N18° 33.8' E09° 47.3', see p.402).

If you need water the Arbre is now 100km away to the ESE (KM1800). Otherwise you can make your way south and west back to Agadez (KM2070).

In the Aïr

A tour of the Aïr is a complete complement to the exposure of the Ténéré but, like a trip through West Africa, can soon wear you down and have you longing for the desert. The mountains are in reality a Sahelian outlier probing the central Sahara; tracks are clear, villages and gardens are relatively plentiful and the Tuareg still cruise around on their camels with their *takouba* (swords) by their sides. The get-up could well be part of the show, as the price of social

The cascade of Timia. © Klaus Weltzer

activity can be more hassle than you can bear if you stop in one village too many.

Coming up from Agadez the red rocks turn darker as you enter the volcanic part of the massif around the village of **Timia**. Not far from the village with its hilltop fort is the popular waterfall of Timia, a regular on the tourist trail where vendors line up voluntarily behind a line of stones. Their wares are available wherever tourists regularly stop and include the distinctive Tuareg leather 'flap' wallets, pipes, daggers, swords, locks and of course the Tuareg Cross and other jewellery.

North of Timia the ruins of the old Aïr capital of **Assode** have seen better days and are visually less interesting than their history. North of here there is a crossroads with a piste leading east up the lovely Zagado valley to Arakao

The interior of the Aïr, nice for a change but it's not the Ténéré. © Klaus Weltzer

and Chiriet, and another heading west to the highway and Arlit.

Iferouane is the next stop of note, the main town in the northern Aïr with fuel, a police station and maybe still an Italian-run campsite with a pizzeria. Few tours venture north of here except to use the track leading north-east to the Temet dunes and Adrar Bous, and back out into the Ténéré.

EL GATRUN (Libya) → AGADEZ (the Marlboro Piste) [810KM]
November 2001; Toyota HJ60 (Charles Megaw and Jo Butler)

Throughout our time in Libya we had been trying to gather information on the safety of the border areas and routes south. It was difficult to get reliable information and we received a whole range of advice on the security of the so-called 'Marlboro Piste' (a smuggling trade route). We had the option of crossing the border to Djanet in Algeria or, allegedly, even going directly to Agadez across the northern Ténéré from Ghat. However, we resolved to stick to our plan and returned to Sebha before heading south to Murzuk.

Turning off the main Murzuk–Timsah road, we knew we were heading into frontier territory. The tarmac roads in Libya are generally in good condition but this section was appalling and after a few kilometres we took to the sand to save our suspension – the eastern side of the road was easiest to drive on. It took us nearly three hours to cover the 150 kilometres from the junction to **El Gatrun** (see map on p.546).

We arrived to find there was no fuel there or further south in Tajarhi, and no prospect of any arriving in the near future. Although we could have got a few jerries from truck drivers in the town, we decided to do a return trip the following day to Zuweila to get the additional 150 litres we required – another day on the road from hell.

In El Gatrun, we were soon directed to Mohammed Tager who lives in the old Italian fort on top of the hill in the centre of town. Mohammed has done a good job keeping the place in good repair and caters for the few tourists visiting the town. He put us up in the fort and charged us 17 LD per night (5 LD per person and 7 LD for the car).

Mohammed also helped us with the Libyan exit formalities which were as convoluted as the entrance. We managed to negotiate police, customs and immigration in about three hours. The Tourist Police required two photocopies each of our passport and visas (Libyan and Nigerienne) which we were able to do in town. We didn't get our 50 LD deposit for the car number plates back from customs despite our protestations, though we were forced to sign forms to say we'd received the money!

Whilst in El Gatrun we got a formal warning from the Tourist Police that we could have problems as a single vehicle; this news hardened our resolve to find a travelling companion. With very few tourists in Libya as a whole, let alone down here, it quickly became apparent that going with a big Mercedes 6x6 truck was our only option. These huge trucks usually leave in the early evening as it takes them a whole day to unload, have their cargo inspected by customs, and reload. We introduced ourselves to the driver of one and he was very happy for us to join them as if it was the most natural thing in the world for two tourists in a TLC to want to travel with his truck.

Plenty of room on top.

We rolled out of town at 4pm but didn't get more than 10km before stopping. We waited until nightfall and then the lorry was repacked with further cargo loaded on, beyond the view of customs... Packing continued through the night and we eventually headed off the following morning to Tajarhi. The going was painfully slow. We averaged 30kph as the Mercedes groaned under the weight of its load and the seventy-odd returning immigrant workers perched precariously on the roof.

The **sand fields** beyond Tajarhi were a graveyard for trucks. We passed four that had been broken down for days. The occupants of our truck enjoyed throwing cigarettes and dates to the stricken passengers and watching the ensuing scramble. We had to choose between driving in the firm truck tracks with the risk of bottoming out or making our own tracks in the sand and getting stuck. We used both methods and got through needing only two quick recoveries. Once through the sand fields we kept driving along a rockier piste before stopping at midnight for the night.

We continued our slow progress the following day on a much more westerly route than the piste shown on the IGN map. By lunchtime we reached a Libyan military base with a temporary airstrip (N22° 47.8' E14° 01.3'). Customs officers were in evidence and serious negotiations were required to prevent the Mercedes being unloaded for a further inspection.

By early evening we reached the **Libyan border post** (N22° 39.2' E14° 05.4') where we were warned of bandit activity and were advised to stop for the night. We pulled up within sight of the army base and were joined by a further Mercedes, though other trucks continued past us during the night.

By lunchtime the following day we finally reached **Madama**, where a convoy of five empty lorries and two military Toyota pick-ups had just left for Seguedine. We were keen to join this faster group and tried to get through the formalities as quickly as possible. Customs charged us 20,000 CFA for a *laissez passer* (local carnet); with no exchange facilities, they let us pay US$30. The police gave us an arrival stamp and we ended up giving them US$10 in lieu of a random demand for 10,000 CFA so we could get away and catch up with the convoy, which we did after a frantic twelve-kilometre dash.

The terrain here was much easier and the lorries charged south at high speed, quickly losing the army escort after one of the Toyotas got a puncture. We regrouped at the **Mabrous well** [N21° 13.0′ E13° 38.0′] and then it was the turn of the army Toyotas to tear off, leaving us behind when we stopped to make repairs to one of the lorries. We were left wondering whether there was any logic to the escort at all. After a lengthy stop to fix an ailing lorry transmission, we kept going through the night to arrive at the Dao Timmi military base at 2am. The piste between Mabrous and **Dao Timmi** [N20° 33′.5 E13° 32.4′] is rough and heavily rutted with lots of risks of bottoming out. The lorries were pushing on in terrain that was much easier for them. We narrowly escaped being shunted from behind by a brakeless lorry several times.

We descended to the picturesque oasis at **Seguedine**, with a small fort and saline, around lunchtime on the fifth day. Here we were forced to employ a local Tubu guide, Laouel Barka, in line with the current stipulation that all tourists should be accompanied by a guide when travelling in the Ténéré (15,000 CFA or about €23 per day). Although initially exasperated by this demand, given that we already had an escort and only wanted to continue for a further half-day to Dirkou with the same convoy, we decided to use it as an opportunity to explore Djado and we waved goodbye to the trucks.

The local army chief, Lieutenant Ahmoudou Bossi, who had tried to help us reach a compromise with Laouel, invited us to spend the night in his compound and arranged for us to do a day trip to Djado without obtaining the requisite *feuille* (permit) in Dirkou. The following day we set out with Laouel to Chirfa, Djado, Djaba and Orida. The hassle factor seemed high in Chirfa and we were glad of having a local guide. Even though Djado is the most famous site, we thought it definitely worth the extra effort to make it to Djaba and Orida and were disappointed we could not spend more time here. The army say that this area is now free of rebel activity – they wanted to make sure we weren't going up to the plateau though. We bought two jerries of diesel in Chirfa on the way back (US$26 in lieu of 17,000 CFA), continued on to Seguedine for another night with the Lieutenant, and on to Dirkou with Laouel.

In **Dirkou**, we got a *feuille* to cover the rest of the journey to Agadez for 20,000 CFA – the price seems absolutely random. We stayed at Jerome the fuel seller's compound. Jerome died in late 2001 and the place is now run by his son, Sergeant Boubacar Mohamed. We paid 65,000 CFA for a meal, a place to sleep and 200 litres of diesel. We thought this was generous as our friendly Libyan trucks had by now turned up in town and were willing to sell us a drum of diesel for 45,000 CFA. We also took the opportunity to grab a beer, our first for weeks, at *Mariama's Bar*.

Caravan in the southern Aïr. © Klaus Weltzer

Laouel, who had turned out to be somewhat mercurial, decided he did not want to continue to Agadez and we were also happy to be rid of an unstable character.

Sergeant Boubacar arranged a new guide for us and we visited Bilma and then continued to Agadez via Achegour and the Arbre (50,000 CFA for the guide for however long it took). We were taken on a route that followed the balises between Kafra and **Achegour**. The sand was pretty soft and the going was slow with high revs and high fuel consumption needed. Fifty kilometres after the Achegour well we came across a broken-down truck with seventy people who had run out of water. In exchange for some diesel we did a return trip to the well and brought them 250 litres of water.

After spending the night with the truck, we continued on to the surreal **Arbre du Ténéré**. The section between the dunes just south-east of Adrar Madet and the vegetation-covered dunes close to the Arbre was very fast on hard flat sand. We spent the final night at the small Tuareg settlement of **Barghot**. We had bought a gazelle during the day so feasted on gazelle stew, a great change from tuna pasta. Arriving in Agadez, it had taken us ten days to cover the 2200 kilometres from El Gatrun with remarkable travelling companions and fantastic scenery. We were tired but triumphant.

Chad

Along with northeastern Mali, the deserts and mountains of Chad are among the Sahara's least visited regions. Since the last edition the news has got no better in northern Chad; though the MDJT rebels have had some reversals they are still very much in control of the Tibesti, which remains inaccessible.

Following the end of the Libyan war and up to the end of 1998, a few intrepid travellers managed to slip past the Tibesti from Libya, while tour companies still offer Ndjamena-based itineraries in the northeast. Only a handful of independent travellers has managed to explore this area and now that trickle has been reduced to a very occasional drip.

Even in the good years the remoteness of northern Chad placed it squarely on the edge of the Saharan tourist map which, of course, accounted for its appeal. This, plus the fact that much of the north remains **mined** (see p.369), and the scarcity and expense of provisions, put this area beyond the range of first-time desert travellers. Experienced Saharans and even the main local tour agency, *Chad Evasion*, know how to play the game by avoiding towns where local taxes and compulsory guides may be forced on them. But for an independent traveller this sort of 'undercover' tourism is stressful and requires huge autonomy as well as high levels of confidence.

BORKOU, ENNEDI AND TIBESTI

Northern Chad, often described as the 'BET' (the former colonial administrative zones of Borkou, Ennedi and Tibesti), is an untamed land. Civil authority is unknown beyond the few oases, towns and army bases, where life goes on as it did hundreds of years ago, with people tending date palms and herds of camels or goats. Bitter winds blow down either side of the Tibesti massif, scouring the land. With the aid of satellite imagery, geologists have recognised huge parallel scars (marked on IGN maps) several metres deep gouged from the desert floor by the violent winds.

Highlights include the dramatic formations of the Tibesti: buttes and spires rise out of the sandy Arkiafera plain, most notably at the Aiguilles de Sisse, 50km west of Wour. Elsewhere the vertical walls of crumbling mesas line the valleys leading into the massif; a distinctive pattern of striking formations common to all of Chad.

Returning from the Aiguilles de Sisse, close to the Niger border. © Reinhart Mazur

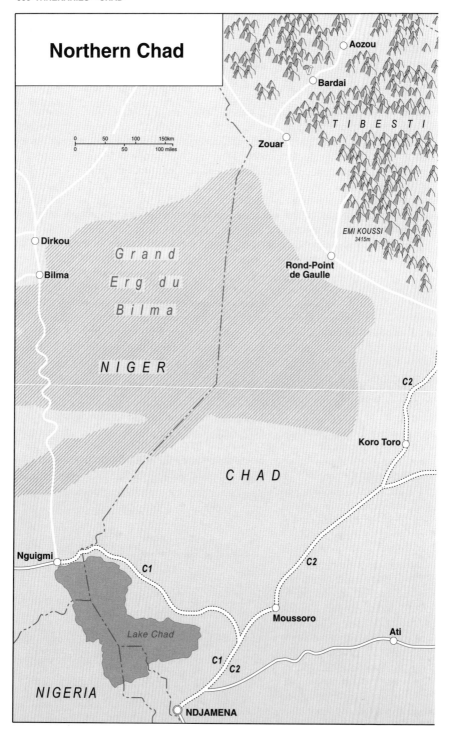

Northern Chad

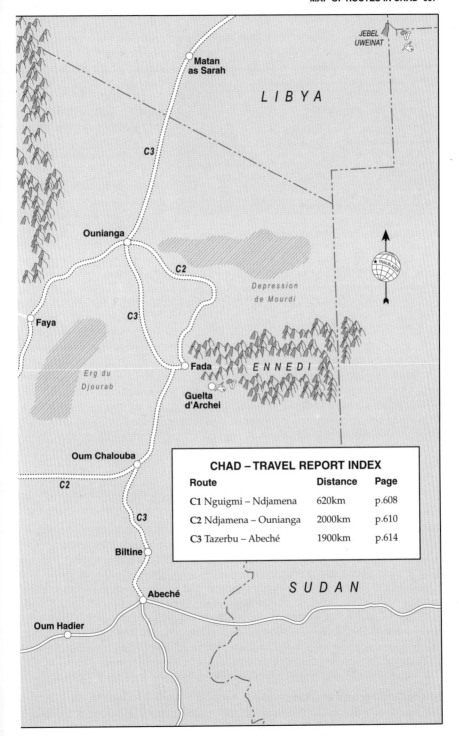

JEBEL UWEINAT

Matan as Sarah

L I B Y A

C3

Ounianga

C2

Depression de Mourdi

Faya

C3

Fada

E N N E D I

Guelta d'Archei

Erg du Djourab

Oum Chalouba

C2

C3

Biltine

S U D A N

Abeché

Oum Hadier

CHAD – TRAVEL REPORT INDEX

The bone-shaking piste from Zouar to Bardai in the heart of the Tibesti passes right by the famous sulphurous crater of Trou au Natron and, when conflicts permit, studies by Italian and German archaeologists are finding the rock art to be no less prolific than in the adjacent Fezzan or Djado plateaux. Without doubt the highlands of the Tibesti have been inhabited for millennia.

The crater of Trou au Natron on the track to Bardai.
© Reinhart Mazur

In the north-east corner of the country, the handful of travellers who are able to appreciate the difference have reported the Ennedi plateau to be even more impressive than the Tibesti. Here, the canyon leading to the Guelta Archai was a firm feature on the itineraries of the few tours which visited the region, both for its rock art and for the reticent population of dwarf crocodiles which, amazingly, have managed to survive here since the last humid epoch. Earlier this century, crocodiles existed as far north as Iherir on Algeria's Fadnoun plateau.

Between the two massifs of Ennedi and Tibesti the unlikely finger lakes near Ounianga Kebir and Ounianga Serir to the east support date plantations which form the core of the Tubu diet. Other than this patchy outline, little is known of this most alluring region of the Sahara, apart from accounts from people who've recently travelled there.

C1 NGUIGMI → NDJAMENA (The Lake Chad Route)   [620km]
March 2003; Discovery Tdi (Gerbert van der Aa).
Additional information: March 2004; Defender Tdi (Graham Jackson).

Description
This route takes an inner course close to the lake with a landscape of savannah with many trees and wadis. You'll see many small villages, and nomads with goats and camels. A carnet for the car is not necessary. At both customs you can buy a *laissez-passer* for a couple of thousand CFA. Passing through Bol is not compulsory, although it's the only place on the route where you can actually see Lake Chad. No one asks for car insurance, like almost everywhere in Chad.

People can be quite nasty, especially in Massakori and Bol. Often kids throw stones at passing cars. Some Germans we met had to pay a lot of money because a small boy asking for a cadeau was hurt when they opened the door of their car. It was not their fault, they said, but the police forced them to pay – 'a lot', they said. We heard many similar stories.

Route-finding and markers
Navigation is the main problem on this route, especially around the many

small towns between Bol and Nguigmi, where many tracks come together. Looking at the Michelin 741 map, it seems that there are two routes; a main one via Mao and this lesser one closer to the lake via Bol. The Mao route may well exist, but all traffic these days seems to go through Bol and we saw no obvious split in the piste that may have gone to Mao.

All border formalities except carnets are completed in Daboua (not on any map). GPS is only helpful to find the towns. On many parts of this itinerary the main route seems to be changing all the time.

Fuel
Petrol and diesel can be bought at many places, but mostly at high prices. Better to fill up in Nguigmi (or better still, Diffa, nearer to Nigeria and so probably cheaper) or Ndjamena.

C1 – RECOMMENDED MAPS
NGUIGMI → NDJAMENA 620KM

Tracks can be confusing on this route and not all maps show all the variations. The IGN 1:1.5 million 'Tchad' country map is the most recent at a useful scale.

Water
Many wells, although the water is not always good. Ask the locals.

Other traffic
This route is not very busy. Count on seeing perhaps two cars a day. Trucks normally take the northern route via Nokou and Mac.

Driving
A big part of this route is a sandy and dusty piste, consisting of tracks in the sand that sometimes are really deep. From Bol to Massaguet the piste is clearer, but most of the time very bad with many deep holes. Only the 80km between Massaguet and Ndjamena are tarred. The first part of this route is especially hard work on a loaded bike, especially because of the long fuel range required; but others have managed, so will you!

Suggested duration
Count on three to four days. Border formalities are straightforward. Driving through deep tracks, winding between the trees is very tiring. Between Nguigmi and Bol you won't make more than 150km a day. It is said that bush camping can be dangerous on this route; if you are going to camp, do so well off the piste, though you will find this more difficult in the less remote stages after Bol.

0km (620) **N14° 14.8' E13° 07.1'**
Police checkpoint on the outskirts of Nguigmi. From here you head to the airport. Should be erring NE. Out of town after this waypoint there are some deep sandy stretches and a lot of tracks. The general direction of the piste is not hard to follow.

43~ (577) **N14° 23.3' E13° 26.1'**
Final Niger military checkpoint. They searched our cars and checked passports, but gave no trouble.

66 (554) **N14° 24.7' E13° 36.8'**
Daboua border post. Have your passport stamped and arrange the formalities for your car. If you have a carnet, the customs will tell you to get it stamped in Bol.

86~ (534) **N14° 17.3' E13° 46.7'**
Good campsite in a oued. Lots of trees and well off the main piste.

118 (502) **N14° 14.4' E14° 05.0'**
Kiskawa. Big village. From here you head directly SSE to Liwa; no need to pass through Rig Rig.

182 (438) **N13° 52.1' E14° 16.0'**
Liwa. Small town, where you can find fuel, restaurants and shops.

235 (385) **N13° 35.2' E14° 38.1'**
Junction. Piste from Liwa to Bol joins another piste from the west. The next 6km are very bad, then the piste becomes better.

The turn-off here to Bol is quite obvious and well travelled though there is no need to go there unless you have to get your carnet stamped. If you do, head all the way through town to the lakeshore where the customs office is. The officer was very nice and indicated that although a bribe wasn't necessary for the stamp, he would really appreciate it. If only all bribe demands were so polite! We gave him an English magazine and a dollar bill and he seemed satisfied. The other people we ran into in Bol were much less friendly and it seemed prudent to get a long way out of town before camping.

241 (379) **N13° 33.7' E14° 41.4'**
Junction. The road to the right goes to Bol, 14km further on. The road straight is the one to Ndjamena.

383 (237) **N13° 37.8' E15° 22.0'**
To your left you see the small town of Ngouri.

471 (149) **N13° 00.4' E15° 44.5'**
Junction near Massakori. The piste to the right goes to the town centre. The one straight on is for Ndjamena.

539 (81) **N12° 28.9' E15° 26.3'**
At Massaguet, take a right onto the tarmac road heading for Ndjamena.

620 (0) **N12° 07.2' E15° 01.4'**
Ndjamena Novotel; about the only place in town where you can camp. Very dirty facilities.

C2 NDJAMENA → OUNIANGA → ENNEDI [2000KM]
March 2002; Tour (Siân Pritchard-Jones, Bob Gibbons)

Perhaps the most difficult thing about trying to visit Chad is finding enough like-minded people to fill the minimum of two cars. We had been contacting a couple of agents in Ndjamena since 1997, and again in 2001, so it was quite a shock when one agent found three other participants and agreed to do the trip for five people. The director, Moussa, then informed us he would be in Mecca on the annual Hajj at the time of our trip, but no problem!

We flew to Chad from Paris. Luckily the agent in Chad had said he would be able to sort out our visas on arrival. At the Paris check-in, nobody questioned our invitation papers hurriedly faxed from Chad, though it was certainly with some trepidation that we landed at Ndjamena, visa-less and clutching only tacky bits of paper for documentation. But a man was there to meet us and the visas were sorted out the next morning.

Our travelling companions were all French. Thierry and Christophe both worked at the French school in Ndjamena. Our third French member, Marie-France, had a daughter and son-in-law working in Chad. They had also only very recently signed up for the trip, which the agent had decided to promote after our repeated requests.

Our first three days followed the well-worn piste through Moussoro, across the dusty Bahr el Ghazal and into the dunes of the Erg du Djourab. Bypassing all the main settlements after Moussoro meant that we avoided unnecessary hassles and demands for money from bored, underpaid officials. However, there were plenty of nomadic herders, camels and goats before Koro Toro, where the short, fine, yellow-coloured grasses of the dry savannah gave way to true desert. Here among the dunes we met one of the heavily-laden trucks loaded with Africans bound for Libya in search of a better life; unfortunately the truck had a very sorry-looking set of battery leads and had been stuck for three days. We took one of the driver's mates on to Faya to get help.

A fiery sunset marked our arrival at the oasis of **Faya Largeau** (N17° 56.1' E19° 06.7'), in a spectacular setting below the rugged escarpments and outlying crags of the Tibesti. At dawn we set off to explore the oasis but the guides suggested we shouldn't wander about on our own. With a fairly reticent population, we supposed the guides needed to be a little cautious, and we ourselves were careful not to offend with our cameras. However, we did encounter some friendly curiosity. We camped in the grounds of the *Emi Koussi Hotel*, with bucket showers and a run-down, decaying atmosphere.

From Faya we were surprised not to be taking the direct route to Ounianga Kebir, close to the Tibesti. We headed generally south-east and made a large loop, later heading north and then north-west to within five kilometres (N18° 22.6' E20° 27.6') of the **Wadi Doum** military camps. We were told that rebel activity in the Tibesti, although curtailed since the latest ceasefire, had resulted in a lot of mines still remaining along that route. In

Ounianga Kebir (N19° 03.3' E20° 29.5') we visited the fantastic lake and heard first-hand accounts of the trouble caused by mines. We met a young man from Cameroon who had recently arrived there. His truck had driven over a mine not far from the oasis, resulting in a few deaths and some bad injuries. In good spirits, he was still hoping to continue his journey northwards when he'd earned enough money to pay his fare.

Depression in the Mourdi.
© Sian Pritchard-Jones/Bob Gibbons

On leaving Ounianga Kebir, we were therefore somewhat concerned when the GPS readings indicated we were heading north-east, rather than east for Ounianga Serir. Somehow in the poor visibility we had missed the ill-defined piste, and were heading towards Libya across some very nasty sand loaded with fractured boulders and very sharp debris. Not much point in worrying by now. Eventually we dropped off the escarpment down a fantastic sandy corridor between dark rugged crags and towers. Back on track, we soon arrived in **Ounianga Serir** (N18° 54.8′ E20° 52.5′), where the various lakes were if anything more spectacular. The most easterly lake (N18° 54.9.8′ E20° 54.6′) was a gem, ringed by orange dunes, bright green reeds and multi-coloured rock outcrops: a truly stunning place. Our camp on the sandy, rocky area high above and just south of the lakes was another spectacular spot to wander at sunset, watching the red and orange shades of the rocky towers become deeper and deeper, before finally fading away into the evening light.

From Ounianga Serir we headed south-east into the **Depression de Mourdi**, hoping to take a track directly from the north into the Ennedi and Fada. En route we visited another superb lake below an escarpment at **Tegguidei** (N18° 51.6′ E21° 23.2′), a place not shown on any of our maps. Here a small transient population mines salt beside the lake, surviving on just one tiny mosquito-infested pool of fresh water. Nobody was here in early March, but we saw the grain stores and evidence of recent visitors.

Just after the lake we became hopelessly bogged in deep orange sand below a jagged black spire of rock (N18° 46.5′ E21° 40.0′). Travelling on south-east we reached **Demi** (N18° 45.9′ E21° 40.3′), another small settlement, again set below spectacular outcrops. Here a very reticent and unfriendly population eke out a poor existence, mining red rock salt. The people claim to be not Tubu but Gorane, and absolutely refused to let anyone even so much as get a camera out.

From Demi there was no piste; we were just heading vaguely south and south-west across the most tortuous terrain. A mixture of sand and broken rocks, low crags and dunes constantly blocked the way forward, necessitating backtracking, diversions and some truly skillful driving. A careless driving mistake in this terrain would have had very serious consequences. Indeed at one point in the middle of nowhere we came across an abandoned, fully-loaded old Toyota, complete with sacks of grain and a guerba on the side. But there was no sign of human life. Had it been recently left there while the driver went for help? We will never know…

Tegguidei salt lake. © Sian Pritchard-Jones/Bob Gibbons

All the next day a raging hot wind blew, with heavy stifling clouds and very poor visibility. Occasionally rain fell as huge droplets of sand-filled water, leaving thick opaque spots on the side windows and windscreen. In the distance we could make out the silhouette of the northern cliffs of the Ennedi, with finger-like towers and broken outcrops where the plateau has eroded. Here we met a solitary overloaded vehicle coming from an oasis deep in the Depression de Mourdi. They advised us not to continue to Fada by this route, as it could take two or three days via a rocky track, so we retreated westerly.

A vague piste eventually led us down an amazing sandy corridor of dunes and rocky towers that marked the western edge of the Ennedi (N17° 46.4' E20° 55.2'). The scene was quite surreal in the yellow hazy light of the storm. We stopped briefly at Wadi Wei (N17° 31.3' E21° 01.4'), an isolated well with acacias and tamarisk trees. From here to Fada the scenery was dominated by rocky towering outcrops and quite hilly areas of sand piled against the rocks. It was dark by the time we approached Fada, and somewhat intimidating to drive through the narrow gorge surrounded by minefields, marked by large signs, barrels, tyres and wire (these mines were being removed.) As we came closer to **Fada**, some military vehicles shot out of the bush to check us out, but we soon arrived in the mud-brick settlement (N17° 11.1' E21° 35.2'). Our camp was in the courtyard of a house belonging to a relative of one of our drivers, at the eastern end of the village.

South and east of Fada lies the spectacular and justifiably famed scenery of the **Ennedi**. Here are the fiery red rock walls and canyons, rock towers, rock art and other amazingly weathered features which are being slowly engulfed by sand and dunes. We camped of course in the **Guelta d'Archei** (N16° 53.9' E21° 46.6') where the canyon walls provided an eerie watch in the moonlight.

Every day the goats and camels of the herders come to water at the black turgid pools of the canyon, in a riot of confusion. During our visit some goats became trapped on the steep vertical cliffs of the canyon and we spent a somewhat sleepless night listening to their tortured cries. Sadly a couple had already fallen to their deaths, but the rest performed amazing feats of mountaineering and communications in their attempts to escape the forbidding cliffs. Alas the famous dwarf crocodiles remained elusive, but tracks and droppings gave some indication of their unseen activities.

In the morning we trekked for a couple of hours each way to the north side of the pools and on to a vantage point overlooking the guelta and the canyon, which is at its most spectacular from this point. It is also far enough away from

Guelta d'Archei in the Ennedi.
© Sian Pritchard-Jones/Bob Gibbons

the herders to take pictures of the camels watering, pictures which were vehemently resisted down at the pools (though when they saw us up on the cliffs, they walked out into the black waters to draw their camels back out of sight!).

The rest of the time in the Ennedi was spent exploring the many canyons and some amazing natural rock arches, as well as visiting some excellent rock-art sites. The paintings here are certainly to be considered the equal of those in the Tassili N'Ajjer in Algeria.

The last three days of the trip took us south to the village of Kalait, shown on some maps as Oum Chalouba or thereabouts. Then we turned west across the scrub to Kouba and back to Ndjamena the same way. We had hoped to return to the capital via Biltine and Abeché, but the route was said to be bad and time-consuming after Abeché on the main road. Most traffic appears to be going further south from Abeché through Mongo to Ndjamena.

C3 TAZERBU (Libya) ➔ ABECHÉ　　　　　　[1900KM]
February 1999; Toyota BJ75 (Reinhart Mazur)

Our short stay in Tazerbu was a complete success. After having been invited at the police station to have tea with the charming head of the local administration, we were allowed to fill up our drinking water containers from a tap off the Great Man-Made River Project water pipe and to replenish our diesel tanks. Supplies had to be sufficient to reach Abeché, two thousand kilometres to the south, near the Sudanese border.

From previous crossings of the Rebiana Sand Sea we knew of some very soft dunes south of Tazerbu so decided to take a direct route across the sands at the narrowest passage through the erg. The gamble proved wise: six months before it had taken us a day to traverse just 30km; this time we got through in one go.

By the afternoon we were within sight of the north-eastern ridges of the Jebel Dohone. Several tracks coming from Kufra and Rebiana converged here, forming a clear piste to the south. Next morning we were up at 6am, confident we'd reach the Chad border the same evening. The piste was fast, allowing us to take in a broad view from the brooding Dohone in the west and distant dunes in the east. We were totally alone until, suddenly, a Toyota trailing a huge cloud of dust drew up on us very fast and waved us down. Our hearts were in our mouths but it turned out to be nothing more than a Libyan customs patrol looking for smugglers. They warned us that the Chad border was a few kilometres ahead but we assured them we were heading for Kufra so were allowed to continue.

This encounter made us wary because now we knew there were patrols who could easily curtail our trip to Abeché. So we decided to leave the piste for a hidden campsite a few kilometres to the east, trying to overlook the fact that anyone could follow our tracks. We were still in Libya.

Across the border
Next morning we crossed the border unobserved. Still nervous, we were relieved when what looked like a group of military trucks up ahead turned out to be a grove of huge acacia trees – completely unexpected in this sandy desert.

Our first destination in Chad was Ounianga Kebir which we intended to reach by a direct route, off-piste. We left the piste leading to Gouro near the border and for the next 500km saw no tracks at all. It seemed as if we were the first people ever to cross this desolate area. **Tekro,** 70km north-east of Ounianga was bypassed to the west and very soon we came across the Kufra-Faya piste along which an unending stream of hopefuls are transported by the truckload to find work in Libya.

As we approached **Ounianga Kebir,** sandstorms were becoming

On the shores of Ounianga Serir. © Reinhart Mazur

stronger and stronger but as we were now following a well-used piste along the foot of the Ounianga plateau, there was no danger of getting lost. This track carried us directly into the marketplace of Ounianga Kebir, passing the incredibly deep-blue Lake Yoa, circled with green palm groves.

We immediately reported to the police, who took our passports, demanding to know where we were heading. When we answered Fada we were told that a guide would be provided by the police. We knew all about this guide business, where a 'guide' might just be a person who needed a lift. However, we did not expect the exorbitant fee demanded from us for a three-day drive. While waiting for our guide we filled up with water from a clear, sweet source by the lake and bought a 200-litre drum of diesel fuel (70,000 CFA) from the market. Luckily a Libyan truck driver was pleased to change our remaining dinars into CFA.

Hali was to be our guide and, being a skinny young man, fitted easily between us on the front seat. However, without our newly acquired roof rack it would have been impossible to transport his masses of luggage, including a 50kg sack of sugar.

To Fada and Abeché

Hali proved to be a reliable and co-operative guide. We first went to the famous lakes of Ounianga Serir and from there crossed a mountainous area to reach the idyllic oasis of Madadi with its old French fort. The sandstorm was getting more and more fierce, and by the evening it was impossible to prepare dinner in the open. Hali contented himself with German brown rye bread and canned fish. So did we.

Next morning we had to cross a 50-metre-high dune belt because the direct passage through the dunes was mined. With the sandstorm blowing stronger than ever, we took refuge behind some huge granite rocks near the well of Mogoro.

Even if he did carry a ton of baggage, we were very impressed with Hali's route-finding skills. We had to trust him as he was sitting on our GPS! Now and then destroyed military trucks and tanks appeared in the clouds of dust and sand and we wondered if the damage had been caused by rockets or mines?

As we approached the Ennedi, the storm eased off and we enjoyed the green oasis of Oum el Adam where we met the first people since Ounianga. The landscape hereabouts opened out into a splendid panorama with magnificent red peaks jutting out of white sandy plains. Joining the well-used piste from Faya, we passed through a mined defile and arrived at the small village of Fada 30km later.

Naturally we had to report to the police at once. 'Where is your permission?' they asked. We had no permission; we had a guide, but this was not enough. So we had to see the Sous-Prefet who was just enjoying his Sunday siesta under a dense tree beside an empty swimming pool. He asked us for our *Autorisation de Circuler*. Without one, he'd have to radio his Prefecture in Faya to ask how to proceed. In any case we'd have to go there to obtain the permission from the Prefet of BET.

The Sous-Prefet turned out to be a kind and educated person who understood the needs of tourists but nevertheless obeyed the orders of his ministry in Ndjamena. He invited us to stay in the garden of his Sous-Prefecture and to join him for dinner. We asked him many questions about Chad, and he warned us of mines in many places in northern Chad, showing us his leg which had been badly scarred by an explosion while driving on the official piste from Gouro to Ounianga. Evidently we would have to go back to Faya (with another expensive guide) in order to apply for the permission. Although we had enough time to do this, we preferred to continue to Abeché, reluctantly accepting that a visit into the Ennedi would have only been possible with official permission and a guide.

But after some days, we were allowed to go directly to **Abeché** with a guide. The 550km is normally covered in a day but we took our time and arrived in Abeché three days later. At Kalait we remonstrated with an unfriendly policeman who let us go only after having received a cadeau. As we neared Abeché, we left the desert behind and the Sahel opened out before us. Said Nemtchi, our young guide, was relieved to be on home turf again. Officials and people in Arada and Biltine proved to be very nice and friendly and we soon grew fond of the lovely region of Abeché with its scenic mountains and splendid herds of cattle. From Abeché we drove across to Mauritania, up through Morocco and home.

Egypt's Sahara: 'The Gilf'

The Sahara fills Egypt from top to bottom but for various reasons the desert here has a different character than elsewhere. It is also known by various confusing names: the 'Western Desert' (west of the Nile), part of the 'Libyan Desert' (another dubious British geographical appellation invented to separate it from the formerly French 'Sahara') or, as I prefer it, abbreviated unambiguously to 'the Gilf', encompassing the Egyptian parts of three distinct formations: the **Great Sand Sea**, **Gilf Kebir** plateau and **Jebel Uweinat** mountain, which between them more than fill the south-western quarter of the country. These are the areas described in this chapter. The areas north of Siwa, from the western oases of Bahariya and Dakhla to the Nile, and east of the Nile, as well as the Sinai, are no less desert but are easily accessible and relatively populated.

The Gilf is in a class of its own, even by Saharan standards: an area rich in history and prehistory, with extraordinary geology and landscapes and an uncompromising remoteness. It was the last part of the Sahara to be explored and discoveries are still being made today. Part of the reason for this is that the eastern Sahara (or Libyan Desert) is much more **arid** than the central Sahara (why? see p.386). There's virtually no vegetation over a huge area, and the number of wells or waterholes can be counted on the fingers of one hand. Because of this, nomadism never gained a foothold after the post-Holocene depopulation of the Sahara. Without wells, no trade routes developed through this region, and with nomads barely visiting the area, little was known and the map remained blank until much later than elsewhere in the Sahara.

Things are changing now as archaeologists and adventure-tour operators take an interest in this little-known area that was for many years difficult to get permits for. This being Egypt, the permit situation for individual travellers is still extremely tedious, but at least the Gilf is now open for organised tours.

Sand Sea, Plateau, Mountain: the three landforms

The depressions of Siwa and Quattara are a geographical barrier. South of Siwa the dunes of the Great Sand Sea unroll for nearly six hundred kilometres to lap the northern reaches of the Gilf Kebir (in fact they spill right through it; see below). Immediately south of Siwa the dune formations are confused and jumbled, making navigation difficult, but as they progress south and get into their stride they form into linear dune barriers on a just-west-of-north orientation. Between these sand barriers the gravel corridors make north–south navigation easy, but in places these passages close up and you need to cross the dune belt into the next corridor. These corridors are generally further apart and lower in the east. Though evidence has yet to be unearthed, it was in these dunes that the '50,000-strong' army of the Persian conqueror, Cambyses,

Some information by Andras Zboray from the first edition is re-used here, though his waypoints (preceded with a '*') were extrapolated from maps. Other waypoints are actual readings following my own visits. His website, www.fjexpeditions.com, is an excellent resource on the Gilf.

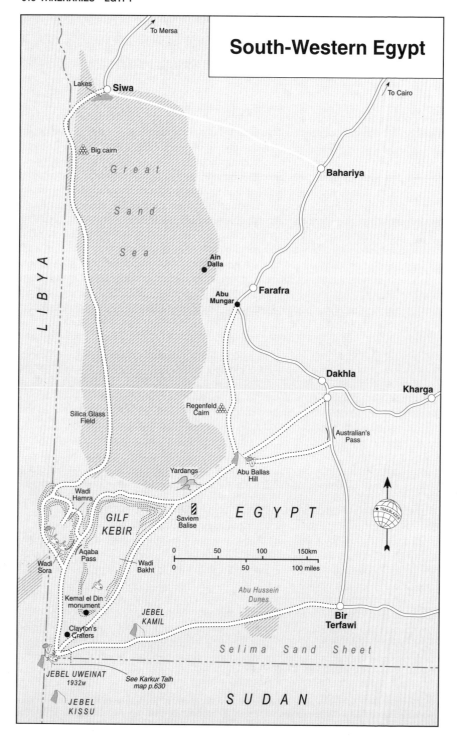

South-Western Egypt

To Mersa

Lakes **Siwa**

To Cairo

Great

⚐ Big cairn

Sand

Bahariya

Sea

● Ain
Dalla

Farafra

Abu ●
Mungar

Dakhla

Kharga

Silica Glass
Field

Regenfeld ⚐
Cairn

Australian's
Pass

Yardangs

Abu Ballas
Hill

EGYPT

GILF
Wadi
Hamra

KEBIR

Saviem
Balise

0   50   100   150km

0   50   100 miles

Aqaba
Pass

Wadi
Bakht

Wadi
Sora

*Abu Hussein
Dunes*

Kemal el Din
monument ●

*JEBEL
KAMIL*

**Bir
Terfawi**

Clayton's ●
Craters

Selima   Sand   Sheet

JEBEL UWEINAT
*1932*м

*See Karkur Talh
map p.630*

SUDAN

*JEBEL
KISSU*

LIBYA

★ TRAILBLAZER

became lost and disappeared during a sandstorm in 522BC while on the march to Siwa. Even today the Sand Sea and the Gilf it runs into remain an effective barrier between Egypt and Libya.

Discovered only in 1926 by Prince Kemal del Din (see p.647), the **Gilf Kebir** or 'Great Wall' rises up to 300m above the desert floor. It is in fact a south-facing escarpment separated by a broad, dune-filled north-south rift through which cuts the Aqaba Pass. The eastern mass of the plateau is the higher and more defined of the two with a west-facing scarp and broad valleys draining to the east such as Wadi Firaq, Wadi Wassa, and Wadi Bakht with its clear evidence of Neolithic occupation. The surface of the plateau is broken up and criss-crossed with drainage channels, making travel by vehicle slow (though Bagnold managed during his 1938 scientific expedition).

The western part of the plateau is less well-defined on sat maps but has a dramatic south-facing escarpment running from the **Aqaba Pass** to almost the Libyan border. Two long, narrow valleys, Wadi Hamra and Wadi Abd El Malik, drain north, the latter thought to be the location of the lost oasis of Zerzura. Both are accessible from the north via the Aqaba Pass or round the west side of the Gilf (although there are a couple of places where you can slither down the escarpment to the south). New rock-art sites are still being uncovered, including the amazing Foggini Mistekawy Cave (see p.634) discovered in May 2002 near Wadi Sora (the real 'Cave of the Swimmers' from the largely fictional *English Patient* movie).

After a short gap immediately south of the Aqaba Pass, a tongue of dunes formed by a 'wind shadow' gets funnelled through the rift in the Gilf, and reaches down between Uweinat and Jebel Arkenu just over the border in Libya. This creates yet another natural border between Libya and Egypt, limiting access from west to east.

And finally, right where the Libyan, Egyptian and Sudanese borders meet at N22° E25° is the ancient granite massif of **Jebel Uweinat** (1932m) and its two outlying cousins: Jebel Arkenu in Libya and Jebel Kissu in Sudan. A bulb of magma pushing up the Nubian sandstone strata gives Uweinat two different appearances: on the Libyan side are the rounded granite boulders and long smooth slab faces so typical of granite formations (like Algeria's Tefedest); the eastern side in Egypt and Sudan is composed of eroded sandstone wadis much like the Gilf, while from the south a band of cliffs rings the summit plateaux.

A couple of waterholes or springs in the perimeter wadis are the only water source for a huge distance – certainly in Egypt northwards until Siwa. The number of rock-art sites is also growing here year by year as exploration continues, with the richest frescoes easily found in the wadi of Karkur Talh on the eastern edge of the massif, mostly in Sudan but only accessible with ease from Egypt.

In between the Gilf and Uweinat are isolated outcrops like Peter and Paul, the Three Castles and Clayton's Craters, while to the east the Selima Sand Sheet runs almost to the Nile, with low escarpments and paleo lakes extending north to the southern edge of the Great Sand Sea.

Like the Tassili–Hoggar of Algeria, Niger's Ténéré and the Libyan Fezzan, the Gilf offers a taste of the diversity of the full Saharan experience in one area. This area is totally uninhabited, virtually waterless and has only a limited num-

A typical two-week tour of the Gilf requires strong vehicles to carry the payload. Most tour operators use tough Toyota Troop Carriers, but their bench seats are not very comfortable. If you're lucky you'll sit in an 80 or 105 station wagon.

ber of axes along which access routes run, although within this area driving cross-country is relatively easy, significantly eased by the lack of surface drainage formations due to the virtual absence of rainfall.

Access

Now the bad news. While it is easy to explore the **Oasis Circuit** that runs in an arc from Cairo through Bahariya, Farafra, Dakhla and Kharga, access to the land to the south and west, considered a border zone, is restricted. This is partly why the area has been so long overlooked by desert tourism. To explore the area you need a permit and an escort which are provided by various ministries via an approved travel agent. You will also have to carry a 'guard', a local soldier, throughout your trip.

These permits and other matters can take months to organise. The permits are given at the discretion of the authorities, sometimes in a straightforward procedure, sometimes after a long hassle, sometimes not at all. Add to this the fact that transporting your vehicle from Europe to Egypt is expensive and lengthy. There is no RoRo ferry from southern Europe to Alexandria, and shipping is asking for delays and expense; the only way is to drive overland through Libya, itself a bureaucratic treadmill. While people have done it, exploring the Gilf with your own vehicle is a serious commitment. Your vehicle must carry a typical fuel load of 400 litres, and enough water and provisions for two weeks. And

Cars are the only way to get around but your days on foot will be the most memorable, for the right reasons.

unsupported travel on a motorbike is of course out of the question (although organised tours do exist).

Unless you have a real no-expense-spared craving to explore the area in your own machine, it is far better to leave the car keys at home and sit this one out on an organised tour. These are more expensive than elsewhere in the Sahara – at least €150 per day plus flights – and the

THE FORTY DAYS' ROAD

From medieval times until its closure by the Mahdi uprising in the Sudan in the 1880s, the eastern Sahara's principal trade route stretched between the Darfur region of Sudan through Kharga oasis to terminate in Assiut, central Egypt. This road, the **Darb el Arbain** or Forty Days' Road, was infamous for its annual slave caravans numbering as many as 80,000 unfortunates on the six-week march. Usually fewer than 20,000 reached Assiut to be sold on to the slave markets of the Middle East. The mortality rate was similarly high among the beasts of burden, and to this day the route of the Darb el Arbain is marked with a trail of white camel bones as well as the occasional human skeleton.

truly professional operators can be numbered on one hand. People have slipped over from the Libyan side but you risk losing your vehicle if caught. One contributor to this book was caught in such a manner and the party spent a few days with the Egyptian Inquisition before being extradited. With the increasing popularity of tours, the chances of getting spotted now are even greater.

On any tour you take in the Gilf you will cherish the days spent on foot, out of the car. Although it's understandable to want to see it all, a typical two-week tour that covers less distance and includes more **walking** (ideally at Uweinat or in the Gilf) will be ultimately more satisfying.

Maps

Even if you are visiting the area as a paying passenger, it's still rewarding to keep tabs on your location. Soviet series maps cover the area but the American **TPCs J5-A and H4-C** cover the area from 2--28°N (which is 130km short of Siwa). Another good map is the **Survey of Egypt's 1:500,000 'Uweinat'** sheet dating from 1942. Originals are now hard to find but it's available on CD from the website. Despite predating GPS by several decades, only a few landmarks are misaligned by a couple of kilometres. In all other respects they depict relief and sandy areas very accurately.

ITINERARIES IN THE GILF

The following route descriptions follow the typical clockwise tour of the Gilf. They start either near Abu Mungar, a roadhouse between Farafra and Dakhla, from Dakhla itself or from Bir Terfawi in the south. All end up in Dakhla, with difficulty at Ain Dalla west of Farafra or, ideally, in Siwa. The starting points of these itineraries are determined by the extreme fuel and water loads vehicles will be carrying in the early days. At this time it is easier to drive on smooth, flat terrain rather than up and over dunes. Some tours do leave fully loaded from Siwa (as indeed did the LRDG), skirting the worst of the northern Great Sand Sea out over the Libyan border.

Abu Mungar – Regenfeld – Abu Ballas

This route contradicts the above advice about starting a Gilf tour in the dunes, but by sticking to a corridor or two we managed to get to Regenfeld without too much pushing and pulling. From there to Abu Ballas was easy.

Leaving the road about 25km south of Abu Mungar around N26° 22' E27° 45', we headed across a sand sheet to the easternmost dunes of the Sand Sea.

ABU BALLAS: THE ZERZURA LEGEND OR SOMETHING MUCH OLDER?

The hill of Abu Ballas lies 140km from the road, at **N24° 26.2′ E27° 38.8′**, about 500m from another similar hill to the south-west, on a plain some distance from the scarp in the north. It would hardly be worth mentioning, except for a large repository of clay urns discovered in 1917 by John Ball who named it Pottery Hill, in Arabic 'Father of Pots', the current name.

The urns were thought to have been placed there by Tubu raiders from Kufra, who regularly attacked Dakhla over the preceding centuries. The legend of the 'black raiders from the west' fuelled speculation about the lost oasis of Zerzura. A couple of hundred years ago the Dakhlans gathered enough courage to mount a pursuit and the water depot was discovered three days' march out of Dakhla – the limit of a camel's range – and was duly destroyed. The raids came to an end though this was only a legend by the time Abu Ballas was actually discovered.

In the meantime, Kufra oasis became known, and the fact that Abu Ballas was one-third of the way to Kufra led to speculation that an unknown oasis, probably the legendary Zerzura, must lie somewhere in the northern Gilf Kebir, another three days' march away.

The main depot of urns, all smashed, lies at the eastern foot of the hill, in a little hollow between the hill and an encroaching dune. In 1932 Almásy photographed intact urns, but today no complete pots survive.

The hill of Abu Ballas.

Remains of pottery possibly dating from the New Kingdom (1500BC).

Abu Ballas is also noted for being the easternmost occurrence of Saharan, and westernmost location of Nilotic, rock art. In recent years the German archaeologist Carlo Bergmann has suggested that this was merely one water cache on a trail of similar depots which led all the way to the Gilf. These depots were in use in the Fourth Dynasty (early Pharaonic era) and dating the Abu Ballas pots has shown them to be much older than previously thought, from the New Kingdom which predates the camel era. At this time donkeys were the main means of transport.

Bergmann's discovery of his so-called 'Djedefre Water Mountain' (Djedefre was the son of Cheops) in the hills south-west of Dakhla proves that Abu Ballas was not the only water cache on this route and, in his opinion, that the western limits of the Old Kingdom may have been much greater, or indeed that the civilisation may even have originated around here, developing from the known Neolithic occupation of the Gilf and moving eastwards to the Nile as desertification took hold. It would certainly tie in with climatological evidence: the end of the Neolithic wet phase occurred about this time.

There is a faint footpath leading halfway up the hill to the foot of the vertical cliff forming the top of the hill. On reaching the rock, take the right-hand path for about five metres and, after a steep scramble, you'll find a carving of a cow and its calf very low on the rock. The engraving is in the typical Saharan style. Taking the left trail, along the west face you'll find a smooth rock face with an engraving of a hunting scene, probably from the early Historic period (see p.405), much like others along the cliffs of the Nile valley. (At the point where the ascending trail forks, there's a small rock shelter with an engraving of an antelope, the work of some playful visitor sometime after 1933.)

Sources: www.carlo-bergmann.de/Discoveries/discovery.htm

At N26° 14.1' E27° 40.4' we picked a SSE-bound corridor and followed it without too much difficulty: the ripples on the sand being harder on the heavy cars' fittings than the occasional patch of soft sand.

After about N25° 55.0' E27° 46.3' we erred to the south via N25° 47.2' E27° 49.7' and N25° 41.1' E27° 49.9', and from N25° 36.2' E27°46.6' headed southwest through an unusual paleo lake with petrified root casts (see p.375). From here it was past N25° 20.4' E27° 36.3' to the cairn at **Regenfeld** (N25° 10.73' E27° 24.8'). From the cairn it's only about 100km and

Regenfeld. This is where the first European to explore this part of the Sahara, Gerhard Rohlfs, on February 5th, 1874, gave up the idea of crossing the Sand Sea to Kufra, and turned north for Siwa. It's named after a shower his party experienced here ('rain field').
The cairn is located on a low ridge facing a long dune line. The cairn used to contain original documents from Rohlfs, Kemal el Din and Almásy. These days passing travellers leave their calling cards.

a very scenic cross-country drive down to Abu Ballas. On the way there's a nice viewpoint looking south from a rise at N25° 05.1' E27° 25.8', after which you start winding in and out of the cone hills of which **Abu Ballas** (N24° 26.5' E27° 38.8') is one of the southernmost examples.

Notwithstanding the theories of German archaeologist Carl Bergmann (see box opposite), there's not much to be said about the drive from **Dakhla** down to Abu Ballas. After a **checkpoint** on the Bir Terfawi road at N25° 28.6' E28° 58.2' (where cars without permits are turned back), you leave the highway 60km from Dakhla, a couple of kilometres after the foot of Australian's Pass, to follow a marked track to Abu Ballas. The total distance from Dakhla is about 180km.

Bir Terfawi to Jebel Uweinat

From Wadi Halfa on the Nile, this was the regular truck supply route to Kufra and is the easiest way of getting directly to Uweinat. From the checkpoint at Bir Terfawi (in the midst of a large agricultural project) a track leads WSW over gently rolling sandy desert. For the first 50km there are small signposts but after a while tracks diverge out into the sand sheet and following the signs is not necessary.

About 35km from the checkpoint you come to the **Abu Hussein dunes**, lying roughly between *E28° 20' and *E28° 25'. The barchans are widely separated at their southern end and are easy to get through. Beyond these dunes you're on the true **Selima Sand Sheet**, a fast, glaring Ténéré-like void with occasional soft patches. There is another more complex dunefield between *E27° 20' and *E27° 30', with a gap at around *N22° 23' along the eastern edge of the dunes.

Alternatively, it's possible to make a detour to the south to **Bir Missaha** well at *N22° 11.3' E27° 57.1'. Straight after leaving the road at the checkpoint one needs to take direct bearings, which will take you onto a flat plain. This bearing will take you close to Bir Sahara, another artificial well in a small depression with some tarfa mounds, at *N22° 52.5' E28° 36.2. At Bir Missaha there may still be a wooden scaffold over the well and a small wooden shed close by – the only visible landmarks. There's nothing much to see apart from the well and the scattered petrol tins of 1930s' expeditions, but it's an historic place, and makes as good a camping place as any other in the desert.

To continue from Bir Missaha to Jebel Kamil, aim for the point *N22° 18' E27° 27' from where the going is good.

The fuel dump at Jebel Kamil. These Shell tins predated the superior German jerrican and are found all over the region.

Jebel Kamil

Jebel Kamil is a conical peak located at N22° 16.7' E26° 38.1', at times visible from as much as 60km away. Coming from the Sand Sheet, about 30km before the hill the landscape changes as outcrops of dark sandstone and patches of reddish drift sand appear. Gradually the terrain becomes rocky, though this is compensated by the dramatic scenery of red sand and low black outcrops with the distinctive Jebel Kamil in the background.

At the southern flanks of the hill there is a depot of Shell petrol tins stacked up on each other, probably from the time when Jebel Kamil was on the track of the convoys supplying Kufra from Wadi Halfa during WWII. Some still retain the original paper label with the yellow Shell emblem of the East India Motor Oil Company on their sheltered sides.

Jebel Kamil to Uweinat

The track towards Uweinat continues almost due west along the southern side of the mountain for about 30km until reaching the edge of a large dunefield occupying the area roughly between *E26° 15' and *E26° 22'. The track is well defined, as the Kufra supply convoys used it regularly, and their trails remain clearly visible even after more than sixty years. At the eastern edge of the dunes the tracks diverge and disappear; there is no easy passage across the dunes, even though the 'Uweinat' map marks a red trail. It saves considerable time to make a detour to the north, around the dunes, rather than to attempt a difficult crossing.

Northwards the dune field extends to *N22° 36', even though the map shows it ending at *N22° 20'. It's easy going north along the dunes once the slope by the granite hill has been tackled. The northern extent of the dunes is abrupt, with good going all around to their western side. The area just to their west is labelled 'broken country', and the area is true to its name. However, by ascending the successive ridges where possible, you'll find the high ground to the west offers easier going. You're aiming for the northern end of a large 40-kilometre-long dune which forms the last barrier to Uweinat, running from *N22° 26' E25° 58' to N22° 02' E25° 40', very close to the Sudanese border.

Once on the west side of the dune, you soon hit the track that comes down to Uweinat from the north-east. At this point Jebel Uweinat is still about 90km away, along reasonably easy terrain.

Abu Ballas to Kemal el Din Monument

From Abu Ballas you can follow the main track south-west, still marked with cairns and steel drums via a low pass at *N23° 44.7' E27° 05.0'. The track continues threading past hills in a broad valley until it reaches an open plain.

On the way it's worth paying a visit to some **yardangs**, also known as mud lions, at N24° 15.3' E27° 29.4', close to the track. The silt from this former lake bed was carved and grooved by the winds coming off the escarpment to the north, and these hardened lumps are the residue, their noses undercut by the prevailing wind. There are more yardang colonies further south.

Following the main south-west track from the yardangs on this plain, several tracks converge at the so-called North-east Gilf Kebir **crossroads**, at around N23° 43' E26° 56' and indicated on maps, an

Yardangs: weathered silt remnants of an old lake bed.

important junction if you're circumnavigating the Gilf and heading back to Dakhla. This used to be the fastest way to Uweinat in the 1930s, but since the road was sealed to Bir Terfawi, it's now mostly used by tour groups. The track towards the northern Gilf Kebir, and eventually Wadis Hamra and Adb El Malik, or down through the Aqaba Pass to Wadi Sora, heads off to the west. The track for Uweinat heads off SSW.

Alternatively, from the yardangs you can cut off cross-country to check out **Saviem Balise 22** at N23° 48.4' E27° 15.5' (see photo p.338 with the full story on the expedition) situated along an obsolete track marked on the TPC which heads off east to Kharga. Just to the north-east, at N23° 48.4' E27° 16.2', is the '**Hill with stone circles on top**' as marked on the 'Uweinat' map. Other hills throughout the Gilf also feature these round enclosures – possibly Tubu hut foundations or much older herders'observation posts.

From here you can head towards the Gilf crossroads through a low point in the relief. On the way you may pass a long straight line of **petrol tins** at

N23° 41.9′ E27° 07.8′, possibly marking a temporary airfield. Once you rejoin the main piste running towards the Gilf, the plateau will slowly rise from the horizon. There's a notable pass around N23° 54.5′ E26° 41.7′ by which time you can see the eastern rim of the Gilf.

The Eastern Gilf

An excursion into **Wadi Bakht**, a dead-end valley reaching into the Gilf, shows the clearest evidence of Neolithic occupation, although the area has been picked clean of artefacts by successive expeditions. For the entrance to the Wadi head for N23° 10.8′ E26° 26.8′ and keep going 'upstream' for about 20km until you reach the dune blocking the narrowed valley at N23° 12.3′ E26° 16.7′. It was here that a lake was thought to have seasonally backed up against this natural dam, making human occupation and maybe even cultivation viable. A line of stones traversing the barrier dune implies that cars should not continue beyond this point (it would be quite hard anyway) and a walk up the valley reveals some curious steps cut into the wall of the narrow cleft where the lake drained. Up above in the lake bed is a selection of grinding stones that have not been picked off by previous visits. Pegs also indicate where this area was studied by the Heinrich Barth Institut in the 1980s – it's certainly as complete a location for investigation as anywhere in the Gilf. Walking up the valley you can wander up some tributary valleys to the south and end up on the top of the Gilf (eg: N23° 12.2′ E26° 14.5′).

Driving back down the valley to the plain you can contour the edge of the Gilf and head into **Wadi Wassa**, the largest wadi to drain the eastern Gilf. About 40km from the entrance, a popular destination here is **Shaw's Cave**, not actually in the valley but almost on the summit of the plateau at N22° 58.9′ E25° 59.1′.

Shaw's Cave.

Unless you're coming from **Wadi Firaq**, the drive up to this height can be quite tricky – at one point you need to get onto the sand banks alongside the valley to gain height (see p.92). Once at the shelter you'll find some well-preserved paintings of red and white cattle, a taster of the many wonders which lie ahead.

This southern spur of the plateau is dissected into many outliers separated by broad 'valleys'. From the Cave you can return to the east side of the Gilf via Wadi Firaq and the group of low hills at its mouth, known as **Eight Bells** (N22° 50.5′ E23° 16.1′). During WWII the place was an airfield and you'll see more of the Shell petrol tins and other rubbish lying around.

An alternative from the Cave is to head west down the back end of Wadi Firaq via a pass at N22° 55.4′ E25° 52.2′. From either Eight Bells or the western edge, you can make your way to the southern point of the Gilf and the **Prince Kemal el Din** monument at N22° 41.7′ E25° 52.3′ (it may take a bit of winding around to find it). The monument was built by Laszlo Almásy in 1933 in honour of Kemal el Din (see p.647) who'd supported Almásy and who'd recently died. The tablet reads: *In memory of His Royal Highness Prince Kemal el Din Hussein, the great explorer of the Libyan Desert. This monument was erected by some who appreciate his great efforts.*

Originally the tablet was set into the cairn but fell off and broke; the pieces are now re-set in concrete. As at Regenfeld, it's the custom for passing travellers to leave notes in one of the tins stashed in the cairn.

Kemal el Din monument.

Gilf to Uweinat

Beyond the monument the next stop is the mountain of Jebel Uweinat, about 120km to the south-west. Immediately to the south of the monument is a churned-up passage of soft sand tracks, the residue of passing rallies. From here on you'll pass various inselbergs, volcanic dykes and craters. One place worth stopping at, either to or from Uweinat is **Clayton's Craters** at N22° 19.3′ E25° 28.3′. The waypoint is among a trio of distinct craters, though there are a few more to the east (and indeed some directly south of the Kemal el Din Monument, at N22° 30.4′ E25° 52.2′).

As the huge ring formation of Guelb er Richat in Mauritania testifies (see p.479), not all craters are the result of dramatic eruptions such as at Waw en Namus in Libya (p.375 and p.573). Here it is likely that a gradual upwelling of magma along subterranean vents and dykes (possibly associated with the uplift of Uweinat itself) forced up 'blisters' in the Nubian sandstone. The resultant dome of fractured, uplifted rock

A dyke leading out from one of Clayton's Craters to the next.

The southern cliffs of Uweinat near the entrance to Karkur Murr.

was more susceptible to weathering and has eroded away, leaving the peripheral rings. Well, that's one explanation. From the craters it's a relatively fast run to Uweinat.

Jebel Uweinat

Jebel Uweinat is the highest point in the Libyan Desert, composed of two very different parts. The western section, lying entirely in Libya, is a circular granite crater not unlike Clayton's, but on a much larger scale. There are several smaller rings inside the largest one, each with granite rims which have eroded into huge boulders resembling, as one traveller pointed out, a pile of giant potatoes. The eastern part, in Egypt and Sudan, is an uplifted sandstone plateau reaching above the peaks of the granite ridges. The bulk of the plateau and indeed the summit lies in Sudan.

The granite part is drained to the west by Karkur Ibrahim and Karkur Idriss. The eastern part is drained almost completely by Karkur Talh to the north and to a lesser extent by Karkur Murr to the south. There are three **permanent springs** collecting the rainwater that drains through the mountain, two in the south-west Libyan quadrant up the mountainside at Ain Zoueia and another at the base at **Ain Doua** (aka Ain Ghazal) where there is a border post (a lot of traffic, legitimate and otherwise, runs between Kufra and Sudan, though it is not possible for a tourist to enter Libya here). There's also another spring at 'Ain el Brins' – as it is known on some maps – in Karkur Murr (see below). In fact the correct name for this formerly-occupied post is **Ain Murr**.

The real Ain el Brins is an as yet unidentified, impermanent spring somewhere on the south side of the mountain between Ain Murr and Ain Doua.

From Egypt access *around* the mountain to the Libyan parts is not permitted (nor unofficially recommended) due to the checkpoint at Ain Doua and passing patrols. However, the Egyptian and Sudanese parts are rarely if ever patrolled

Abandoned border post between Sudan and Libya.

(apart from the guard which each tour must carry). Places like Karkur Murr and even Jebel Kissu are sometimes visited by Egyptian tours as there's been no official Sudanese presence in Karkur Murr for years, if ever, though it is possible the Libyans from Ain Doua set animal traps here.

To get to Karkur Murr there's a pass near an abandoned border post at N22° 00.1′ E25° 17.4′ that leads via N21° 50.0′ E25° 15.3′ to the south side of Uweinat and Karkur Murr. Follow the line of acacias emanating from the valley. You'll pass what looks like some regimental emblem built in stone on the western hillside, some ruins and a plane fuselage (see p.351) but from N21° 53.6′ E25° 07.8′ you'll have to walk a few hundred metres past the odd dead waddan and buzzing flies (a rare experience in the Gilf) to the rather manky, reed-ringed spring of Ain Murr.

Karkur Talh

The entrance into Karkur Talh, the eastern valley of Uweinat, can be difficult to see when coming from the north, although two lone acacias out on the plain serve as landmarks. Aim for the entrance at N22° 02.8′ E22° 07.9′ but note the fenced-off **minefield** on the right as you come in. It's not as dangerous as it sounds and the minefield is easily avoided by driving along the sand drift piling up against the

CCTV on the Sudanese border.

left (east) side of the entrance. There's another way in further east at N22° 01.6′ E25° 12.5′, though this is easier to use when you're leaving the valley and is actually an arbitrary cross-country exit; one of many possibilities to the northeast if you look at a sat photo.

Expect (and hope!) your tour to have scheduled at least two days to explore Karkur Talh. With its winding valleys, trees, reclusive wildlife as well as the prolific **rock art**, it's a highlight of any Gilf tour. About 4km from the entrance the valley broadens into a basin surrounded by hills on all sides. Directly to the south there is a small cove at *N22° 00.6′ E25° 08.2′ with a dry waterfall. The bottom of the cove is littered with huge boulders on one of which you'll find an engraving of a hunting scene with a human figure, a dog and an antelope, while on several rocks at the base of the cliff there are engraved

Giraffe engraving just below the 'cove' as you enter Karkur Talh.

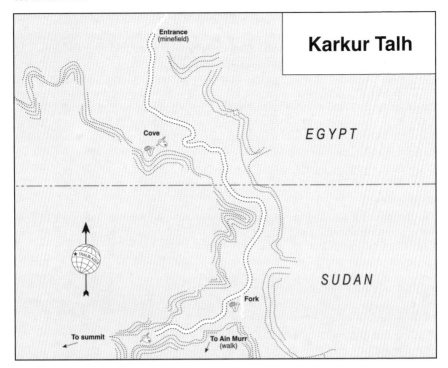

Karkur Talh

EGYPT

SUDAN

Entrance
(minefield)

Cove

Fork

To summit

To Ain Murr
(walk)

giraffes, ostriches and cattle. Coming back out, look out for the giraffe engraved on a slab on your left (pictured p.629). Just above here is an over-hang with some lovely painted figures on its ceiling.

From the cove you can drive west up the wadi, passing an ephemeral lake and soon curving south past an outcrop and dune banks left and right. As you approach N22° you'll notice a black and white border post (literally a post, not a checkpoint!) on the hill on the left (east) – soon you're in **Sudan**.

The *talh* trees which give the valley its name.

Depending on recent rains, vegetation increases significantly here; there are several acacia or *talh* trees after which this valley (or *karkur*) is named. The last significant rain was in 1998 and in 2001 the trees were oozing with sap, bright green bushes were in flower and nets of desert melons spread across the ground. Three years later the valley was as dry as a bone. Part of the reason for this transient herbage is that, even though this is the driest corner of the Sahara, Karkur Talh captures what run-off there is from just about all of the eastern half of the massif. Today's relatively abundant vegetation suggests a river in Neolithic times, making it a good place to live – as the proliferation of rock art seems to confirm.

Less than two kilometres south of the border line the wadi forks at N21° 58.3' E25° 08.3', a point clearly visible as the centre of the blue 'tristar' on the TPC J-5A map. Near the waypoint is a cracked, upturned slab with exposed paintings, while the west side of the outcrop directly ahead, as well as the cove just to the south, are covered with **engravings** depicting mainly giraffe and cattle as

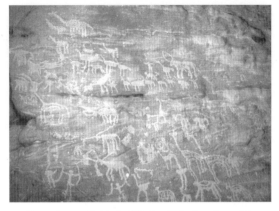

Engravings at the fork of Karkur Talh. See also p.402.

well as battle and hunting scenes. These sites were originally discovered by Hassanein Bey in 1923.

In the valley heading west from the fork several **paintings** were later discovered in 1933 by Almásy-Frobenius and Bagnold's 1938 expeditions. Both sides of this valley display paintings and engravings as well as far younger stone rings demarking former dwellings of Tubus who scraped a living here at the time of the above expeditions but have since moved on to who knows where. On the way into this valley you may spot the mummified *waddan* (mouflon or barbary sheep) which has been leaning against the southern cliff alongside the track for the last few years. **Waddans**, who need never drink fresh water, do survive at Uwienat, though many have been shot out by Libyan hunters. Their horns survive for centuries and we once spotted one on the flanks of the mountain.

A very rare photo of a waddan.
© Yves Larboulette

The best sites are to be found after the valley narrows at N21° 57.6' E25° 06.7'. It's not practical to drive beyond this point but continuing on foot for a couple of kilometres will reward you with the richest density of paintings in Jebel Uweinat: the sites discovered by the 1968-69 Belgian expedition and mostly painted in red ochre. Look out for likely shelters and overhangs to the left and right, some high up on the canyon walls.

Back at the fork, continuing along the southern branch of Karkur Talh, you can't drive beyond N21° 57.1' E25° 06.5'. There are few or no known paintings

CLIMBING JEBEL UWEINAT

For the energetic, the idea of climbing Jebel Uweinat, only 1000m above the desert floor, may be tempting, but because you can't get nearer than 10km as the crow flies from Karkur Talh it's a tough two-day climb. Count on a 30-plus-kilometre round trip and getting through at least **eight litres of water**.

The place to start is the drivable limit of Karkur Talh's west arm. Set off up the valley, curve to the right and turn left where the narrow boulder-filled wadi forks (N21° 58.1' E25° 04.9'). Follow this wadi up onto a series of plateaux, going wherever the terrain allows. With a dawn start you should make it to within a few hundred vertical metres and a couple of kilometres from the top, ready to summit and return the same way the next day.

We tried in 2004 but guessed wrong at the fork using a pixilated sat image and staring at a TPC so hard it caught fire. After 16km of meandering we ended up still 500m below but 3.6km from the summit. Low on water, we turned back the next day.

One thing all this climbing has done in the last couple of years is to prove that **rock art** exists much higher up on Uweinat than previously thought. We found a bovidian scene at 1265m, halfway up a stony valley at N21° 57.2' E25° 01.3', and since then other sites have been found higher still. Stone artefacts were also in evidence, and spotting a waddan on the way down was another bonus.

Ascents from the **Libyan side**, from the head of Karkur Ibrahim, are said to be easier, starting you off half as far from the summit.

Historically the summit has been marked at N21° 54.6' E25° 00.7' (1912m), where there is a cairn with visitors' messages, but the true summit is 1500m away to the south-west, at N21° 54.9' E25° 00.0' and about 20m higher.

Details of both ascents are in the archives of the FJ website. Bagnold's route from the south has not been repeated recently.

here but it is possible to cross over the watershed into Karkur Murr on the southern side of the Jebel; the Karkur Murr waypoint is only 7km to the south-west.

Discoveries in this area are increasing year by year. With a bit of imagination and working outwards from the known locations, it's possible you may find new rock-art sites.

Uweinat to the Western Gilf

It's easy to cover the distance from Uweinat to Wadi Sora in one day even with a stop at Clayton's Craters. The trip passes over firm terrain most of the way

The petroglyph paparazzi in western Karkur Talh.

but if you're thinking of stopping at the conspicuous twin peaks of Peter and Paul, 60km north-east of Uweinat, note that there have been unconfirmed reports of mines at the pass between the twin landmarks and at another hill 3km to the west.

Generally you keep east of N25° 30' to get round the unnamed 'Rough plateau with stone circles' (as marked on the 1942 map). The plateau is a low-level platform of dreary igneous rock and the stone circles at N22° 38.5′ E25° 28.0′, similar to the ones found near Saviem 22, are not really worth the detour along a narrow valley. Although some exploration has gone on here, this plateau is thought to be less interesting than it looks.

Continuing north, if you're heading for Wadi Sora you'll need to work your way round the top of the lee dunes running down to Jebel Arkenu from the Aqaba Pass. At N23° 25.2′ E25° 24.3′ you'll see three conspicuous sand-stone peaks, named the **Three Castles** by Almásy. As you approach the Castles from the south-east, curious tongues of dark orange sand are laid over the lighter base. Almásy used the outcrops as a fuel and water depot during 'Operation Salaam', his daring 1942 traverse from Jalu to Assiut to deliver German spies. Around the foot of the outcrops you'll notice the preponderance of very smooth rounded pebbles, which would normally be found in the bed of an energetic mountain stream.

Wadi Sora – 'Cave of the Swimmers'

Wadi Sora is about 30km beyond the Three Castles, at N23° 35.8′ E25° 13.8′. It's not really a wadi, just an inlet from the main plateau with a couple of detached outliers. Sand spills down the cliff at the back of the inlet, sheltered by a conical rock, all in all making the perfect setting for a sheltered desert camp.

The painted caves discovered by Almásy contain the small swimmer-like figures which inspired the fictitious '**Cave of Swimmers**' in *The English Patient*

movie. The two main caves or hollows at the base of the cliff lie at the right-hand entrance to the inlet. The larger one contains most of the paintings in several groups, including the famous 'swimmers', plus a hoard of other miniature figures. The rock in this cave is in rather poor condition, brittle and flaked, and it has to be said that, quality-wise, the swimmers and associated images are nothing special compared to what you

Wadi Sora.

may have seen at Jebel Uweinat or what lies nearby. In fact at Wadi Sora there are five rock-art sites, two outside and three inside the main valley. At an isolated outlier 3km to the west of the main caves, there's a cave discovered by Clayton with engravings of giraffes; on the other side of the same rock, Almásy discovered more engravings and paintings of giraffes and what look like lions.

From the obligatory visit to Wadi Sora, most tours either head up the Aqaba Pass and back to Dakhla, or round the west side of the Gilf, skirting

The new cave in the western Gilf.

through Libya to get on the way to Siwa via Wadi Gubba and the Silica Glass Field. Either route gives access to either Wadi Abd El Malik or Wadi Hamra, though access to Abd El Malik from the west side is easier, if longer and slower.

In 2002 a **new cave** was found just 10km north-west of Wadi Sora and named the 'Zerzura' or 'Foggini' Cave after the tour company or members of the tour. It contained a concentration, variety and richness of figures unparalleled in the Gilf and was described as the most significant discovery in Saharan rock art for forty years. As with many new archeological discoveries, the exact location of the cave is guarded, although by the time you read this word will have got out and tours will probably include this location on their itineraries.

The shelter is crammed with images, both painted and engraved, most in the well-known 'Wadi Sora' style, others enigmatic or rarely seen elsewhere such as a spread of negative hand prints, or figures 'reflected' along a hori-

Hand prints, achieved by spraying a mouthful of paint over the hand. Also at this site are drawings of a number of headless creatures (inset) whose meaning remains unclear.

zontal crack in the rock. As much as anywhere repetition of a certain image seems to be a theme and it's possible to sit for hours and keep chancing upon yet more detail and new meanings; no danger of 'bovidian overload' here. A curious feature is several 'headless beasts', possibly with a big cat's body. The 'swimming' figures of Wadi Sora are here too, though they are almost certainly not swimming. In and above the shelter there are also carefully engraved figures of antelopes and bovids.

What is interesting is that although it's high off the ground the shelter is not completely in shade and yet the quality of preservation remains high, suggesting that the nature of the rock has much to do with the images' longevity.

Around the west side of the Gilf

From the new cave one curves north past Mushroom Rocks (on the 1942 map, which is better than the TPC around here) and then heads directly north among the western fringes of the plateau. By the time you cross N24° you're about 5km inside the Libyan border, out in the open, trying to avoid the western Gilf's run-off channels. The terrain gets comparatively bleak from here onwards. By N24° 31.8' E25° 00.0' you're back in Egypt and at N24° 37.7' E25° 04.4' you're opposite the **mouth of Wadi Abd El Malik**. To get right into the main, western arm of the wadi takes half a day of slow driving, and although it does not have the petroglyphic riches of Karkur Talh, there is evidence of Neolithic occupation. This wadi was presumed to be the location of the lost oasis of Zerzura by the likes of Almásy and Clayton. No spring is present today although the wadi was used for grazing by Tubu from Kufra within the last century.

From the mouth of the Abd El Malik you get on the Kufra caravan route which, depending on what map you read, once led to Ain Dalla, Abu Mungar or Dakhla. This place, also known as **Wadi Gubba**, is the only ancient trade route that crosses the Gilf and the only place you'll see camel skeletons (around N25° 00.0' E25° 10.6') from long-forgotten caravans. Heading west, within 40km of this point you'll start seeing the low, southernmost dune lines of the Great Sand Sea. Some **cairns** at N25° 09.1' E25° 33.7' mark the entry to the corridor which leads to the **Silica Glass Field** at around N25° 23.3' E25° 30.7' (see p.375). Don't expect to see the ground a-glitter with emerald-coloured glass; successive tours are hoovering the area year by year although the glass is known to exist over a much broader area.

Silica Glass to Siwa – the Great Sand Sea

From Silica Glass it's a two-day, 450-kilometre run north to Siwa, made much easier by keeping to the western limits of the Sand Sea until you need to turn in towards Siwa. In fact no one heads directly north for Siwa unless they have time and fuel to spare, and the drive as described below is not that hard nor that interesting until the very end. Even then, it can have its moments (see pictures pp.176, 191 and 193). It all starts easily enough up the wide Silica Glass corridor; you may spot drums and other rubbish from previous expeditions or even WWII at N26° 11.9' E25° 28.3', N26° 25.6' E25° 24.5' and N26° 41.1' E25° 20.5'. These points are on the trajectory for **Big Cairn** (N26° 57.6' E25° 11.8'), a hill with a few cairns once used as a forward base by LRDG patrols for their

Big Cairn on the western edge of the Great Sand Sea.

raids into Libya. Just before you get there you may notice an old fuel dump. From Big Cairn the going north is fast until around N27° 45'. From here the dunes push you out along the Libyan border. At N28° 15.8' E25° 00.8' you're in a corridor and bushes begin to appear as you head north a couple of minutes inside Egypt until N28° 37' where you'll experience the first corrugations for a while.

Around N28° 51.0' E25° 07.1' you'll come across the first of several old lake beds and yardangs, outliers of the Siwan depression. At N29° 08.7' E25° 13.6' you'll pass some outcrops with embedded sea shells (see p.374) and at N29° 15.0' E25° 20.0' you'll have a view of the westernmost lake of Siwa. From

SIWA TO BAHARIYA VIA AREG, BAHREIN AND SITRA OASES

The road to Bahariya is 380km long, and passes a series of small uninhabited oases and salt lakes. The road itself is in reasonable condition, though covered in places with drifting sand. There is little traffic so the usual desert-driving precautions should be taken and, with checkpoints at both ends, only vehicles and passengers with permits (from the police in Siwa) are allowed.

Leaving Siwa on the Mersa road you turn right after about 6km. The road passes Birket Zeitun, the largest salt lake, followed by the last village to the east, Zeitun. The checkpoint is at the edge of the cultivated area. After the checkpoint the road leads due east for 100km, partially among dunes, then turns to the south-east. About 30km after the turn, a scarp appears on the right (west), and a large depression appears on the left, with white chalk cliffs: this is Areg oasis. There are two tracks making a steep and very difficult descent so you may prefer to explore the oasis on foot. Aside from the impressive scenery, palms and lake, there's a cliff honeycombed with ancient rock tombs.

Soon after Areg the road turns east again, and about 30km later there's a shallow depression a few kilometres to the south of the road, with two salt lakes, and a few rock tombs on a low ridge between the lakes:

Bahrein oasis. It's only accessible with a 4WD (or a fairly long walk, not worth the effort), and the ground around the lakes is very mushy.

At a further 25km there's another shallow depression to the south, with a deep blue salt lake surrounded by hundreds of palms. The descent is easy and it would make an ideal camping spot were it not for the billions of little humming friends that give the oasis its name: Nuwamisa, which means 'Oasis of the Mosquitoes'.

Continuing further along the road a continuous dunefield appears to the south. Thirty kilometres after Nuwamisa the road enters the large depression of Sitra oasis, and crosses it for about 20km. The southern part of the depression, where the road crosses, is not that interesting, but there's a lake and vegetation in the north-western part, only accessible with 4WD.

After Sitra the road enters a region of high barchan dunes, the Ghard el Kebir. It's a spectacular area, and it's possible to drive in among the dunes on firmer ground to secluded camping spots. The dune belt is 80km wide, and is followed by a further 75km of flat featureless reg before you reach the checkpoint at the edge of the descent into Bahariya.

here the dunes can get challenging but it's worth making a visit to the hot spring at **Bir Wahed** (N29° 07.3′ E25° 25.9′ and on the way into the Sand Sea if you are heading south). It may be a popular excursion from Siwa but it's also a great place to soak off a Gilf's worth of grime. The water shortage is over and there's Orangina in the bar!

Though local tour operators take roller-coaster dune routes to thrill their day trippers, you'll have had your share of that; a sanded-over track leads from here past another dry lake the 16km to Siwa. The fuel station in the town centre is at N29° 12.2′ E25° 31.2′, elevation minus 11.4m. Siwa and its environs are well worth a couple of days' visit; any good guidebook for Egypt will have the full story.

Aqaba Pass and the interior of the Gilf

The **Aqaba Pass** divides the Gilf Kebir cleanly in two and is the quickest route back to Dakhla from Wadi Sora – a fact known only to Almásy during his Operation Salaam excursion in 1942. Once up on the plateau you can round the north-east spur and continue over a few dunes before meeting the north-east Gilf crossroads about 250km from Wadi Sora. From the crossroads to Dakhla is another 320km. It is also now possible to get to the very upper reaches of Wadi Abd El Malik via Lama-Monod Pass or to Wadi Hamra over the dune cordon, though neither route is without its difficulties.

Ascending the Aqaba Pass

From Wadi Sora it's roughly 50km to the gap in the cliffs where the plateau is visibly lower for a stretch of about 12km. The western edge of the gap is hidden from the west by a spur with a conspicuous peak at its end, and there are many wadis draining the gap making extremely slow going. Given the numerous watercourses, it's very difficult to find the right one that leads up to the pass. To enter the right wadi aim 5km to the south of the spur, around *N23° 21.7′ E25° 39.6′. From this point follow the creek bed towards the entrance of the pass itself, a narrow valley leading into the cliffs, clearly visible as one rounds the western spur, at *N23° 24.3′ E25° 41.7′. It's worth mentioning that, even though Almásy discovered this pass in 1933 and made several ascents,

during his 1942 traverse he missed the right wadi several times, and spent half a day wandering in the rock field to find the right one. If you take the wrong watercourse, it's better to return to the plain and try the next one in the right direction, rather than attempt to cross the rocks close to the cliff base.

Once in the right watercourse, it's easy going all the way to the pass entrance; at the point

Aqaba Pass. Backing up for another go.

where the valley enters the cliffs, it's about 200m wide. After a large S-turn the valley broadens through an area of sand and rocks which forces you to slow down. On the right an ever-narrowing sand-filled side valley leads to the top of the pass. Churned-up wheel tracks make maintaining momentum difficult, even though the gradient is not that steep. In a heavily-loaded car it's just possible flat-out in Low second (see p.76), though of course reducing tyre pressures helps.

The valley narrows as you reach the crest at N23° 25.1′ E25° 44.1′ and drive up one more steep bank onto the valley's left side. From the plain the height and distance of the total ascent is about 200m over 5km.

The central rift of the Gilf

The gap in the Gilf Kebir is a 10km-wide rift and offers some of the most magnificent scenery in the Gilf, with occasional dunes, sand drifts pressed against the cliffs, and huge outliers and inselbergs dotting the edge of the rift.

For 20km north of the pass it's easy going, skirting outliers. Around here the valley is blocked by several hills. Narrow valleys lead around them, all seemingly passable except the valley leading to the north-west where the TPC map (among others) identifies a track leading towards the western edge of the gap and Wadi Hamra to the north.

In the last couple of years enterprising tours have managed to get through here by crossing a number of dunes and ascending a series of sandy passes onto the plateau top south-west of the head of Wadi Hamra. Once on the plateau the cross-country drive can be easy or excruciatingly slow. It's possible to detour to visit the head of Wadi Hamra, but what is thought to be the only way off the plateau to the north is down the **Lama-Monod Pass**, an irreversable sandy ravine discovered a few years ago by the late Samir Lama (one of the original post-War explorers of the Gilf) while travelling with Theodore Monod (see p.646). It drops into the head of Wadi Adb El Malik and though its exact location is hard to come by, it can be deduced from satellite images, and of course recent tracks. Once in the valley you can drive north to the mouth of the wadi and on to Silica Glass and Siwa (see above).

It's worth noting that despite the rock-art galleries along the southern escarpment of the Gilf, the wadis of Abd El Malik and Hamra are no 'Karkur Talhs'. They are much drier and although stone tools are present, rock art is limited to a few crudely-pecked engravings. Their appeal is more in their extreme remoteness – as hard-won and tranquil as any spot in the Gilf.

Over the cordon to Wadi Hamra

In 2000 we managed to cross the cordon of dunes between N24° 10′ and N24° 15′ (the 'Difficult crossing' indicated by Shaw on the 1942 map) to gain access to Wadi Hamra. Although it took six hours, covering perhaps four times the seven-kilometre width of the dune cordon, the crossing was in fact relatively simple, involving long passes up and down the dune lines to slowly gain height, with two or three places where the precise passage over soft patches or complicated dune crests had to be marked out ahead by passengers and driven through assertively. Since that time it's been crossed in a more reasonable couple of hours, proving that once you know where to go (or that it can be done), it's not so hard.

Once on the west side of the dune cordon it's an easy drive down right into the very top of Wadi Hamra (at the entrance around N25° 58′ E25° 30′ take the western tributary). Once inside, the name 'Red Valley' becomes clear from the sands filling the canyon. From a camp at N25° 37′ E25° 26′, 25km south of the entrance, we walked about 11km across the plateau to the large basin in the otherwise inaccessible eastern arm of Wadi Abd El Malik and back in a day (this sandy basin is only clear on satellite images, not on any map). On the way we found old donkey trails and other evidence of past occupation on the plateau top and plenty more inside the basin itself.

From Wadi Hamra it's an easy run north up to Silica Glass.

Around the northeastern Gilf and back to Abu Ballas

Back to the central rift, 20km north of Aqaba. After 5km you reach a plain at *N23° 40.6′ E25° 40.4′, the centre of which is blocked by a cordon of dunes running north–south, depicted with reasonable clarity on the relevant TPC and very vividly on LandSat images (as opposed to the 1942 map). This is a south-reaching tongue of the Great Sand Sea which goes on to spill through the rift and down towards Jebel Arkenu, west of Uweinat.

At this point the trail to Abu Ballas leads away to the north-east, following the edge of the cliffs for 50km up to a spur on the **northernmost point** of the eastern half of the plateau at *N23° 54.6′ E26° 03.9′. There's a long seif dune extending from the Sand Sea at *N26° 05′, forming a major barrier. Fortunately its end tapers off no more than fifty metres from the northern tip of the spur, offering a convenient pass. And from here it's an easy 40km run across a flat gravel plain to the north-east corner of the Gilf, where another dunefield, composed of dense parallel ranges, blocks the way further east. At *N23° 43.7′ E26° 26.2′ the dunes are low and offer an easy crossing.

From here it's 50km in a straight line due east to the north-east Gilf crossroads. However, the country is very broken and two large north–south seif dunes at *E26° 39′ and *E26° 42′ form seemingly formidable obstacles. Both dunes, however, can be traversed quite easily by searching for a suitable low pass between crests. Beyond the dunes it's easy going to the crossroads at *N23° 43′ E26° 56′ and back to Dakhla via Abu Ballas.

APPENDICES

Sahara book selection

CONQUEST OF THE SAHARA

DOUGLAS PORCH (1986, O/P)

An intriguing and readable account of France's attempts to colonise the Sahara during the 'Scramble for Africa' in the latter half of the nineteenth century. Full of historical detail, it vividly describes the vainglorious expeditions, large and small, which staggered across the desert, often poorly led and suffering greatly for personal prestige and their country's honour. The extraordinary shambles of the doomed Flatters expeditions has to be read to be believed. Out of print but worth the search.

FLYAWAY

DESMOND BAGLEY (1986)

Geographically authentic, fast-paced thriller set in the central Sahara. This is Tintin for grown-ups, where laconic heroes like Burne say 'what the hell…' a lot and casually swap diffs during sand-storms while chased by mysterious assassins. Women are usually other people's sisters and 'strangely attractive'. Compulsively entertaining departure-lounge stuff. In comparison, Clive Cussler's similarly adventuresome *Sahara* is a load of implausible rubbish with a feeble eco-message. It's easily unfinishable and a waste of a good title.

THE FORGOTTEN PATH

DAVID NEWMAN (1965, O/P)

In 1959 Newman decides to drive across the Sahara to visit a friend in Nigeria: 'the sort of adventure that had my nerve endings tingling'. To make matters harder he chooses to do it in a Ford Zephyr, in summer, during the finale of the Algerian war of independence, along a rarely-used piste. Turned back from borders, he decides to literally charge illegally into Algeria: 'To hell with them. It was impos-

sible was it? I'd show them whether it was'. He gets lost near Tindouf and shoots his soup with his '45, the Zephyr begins to break up and, skint, he gets repatriated.

Back in West Africa with new engine bits, his bad reputation precedes him and at one point he threatens to shoot a ferry-man who demands payment to cross the river into Mali. Penniless and with his companion struck down with fever, they lurch from village to lorry, scrounging fuel, push starts and food.

Even allowing for the era, Newman makes even Geoffrey 'Fearful Void' Moorhouse look reasonable. It's this astonishing arrogance and the lively 'what-on-earth-will-the-prat-do-next' pace that drives you through this short book. The guy deserves everything he gets but on another level it's a good warning on what to expect of the Sahara in a 2WD saloon in summer.

FROM LIBYAN SANDS TO CHAD

NIGEL HESELTINE (1960, O/P)

Of the same era but less petulant than Newman, the author sets off on what turns out to be a vexatious journey across the Sahara through Libya to Lake Chad via the Tubu lands of the Tibesti and Ennedi. What makes this book so unusual in the era of unreviewably-lame Travel Book Club adventures is that the author is no fluffy travel writer but a well-read if rather stroppy Theroux-esque character who does not spare those who irritate him.

His Jeep blows its gearbox south of El Gatrun and he is forced to travel on in a lorry with the chirpy M. Gautier in a Land Rover. Having studied his Nachitgal and other material, the author explores the rarely-visited Tibesti Ounianga and the Ennedi and examines the customs of the wily Tubu. It's a credit to the author's detailed research that it was used in the

Full reviews of the above books and many more appear on www.sahara-overland.com/books.
O/P = out of print but available from used-book sellers on the internet.

Saharan turkey *Sahara, The Life of a Great Desert*, see below. *Libyan Sands to Chad* is about the best book available on the little known Sahara of Chad.

IMPOSSIBLE JOURNEY
MICHAEL ASHER (1985)
Asher wants to be a modern-day Thesiger (he wrote Thesiger's biography), with a similar distrust of cars and a love for the desert and its people. In 1986, accompanied by newly-wed wife, Marianetta, they succeeded in completing Geoffrey Moorhouse's ill-prepared attempt to cross the Sahara from Mauritania to the Nile. Unlike Moorhouse, the Ashers had worked in the desert for some years and the author was familiar with nomadic customs, selection of guides and the all-important purchase and care of camels. Once underway they set a gruelling pace that even some of the guides found tough. The mentally-disorientating ego loss and intolerable stress they experienced towards the end of their trek comes close to some of the *Sheltering Sky*'s themes. It's as well to remember that countless pilgrims may have completed the same crossing over the last thousand years. As one perplexed Nigeran border official ruefully observed: 'What will you Westerners think of next?'

LIBYAN SANDS
RALPH BAGNOLD (1987)
Bagnold (see p644) really was quite an exceptional guy and *Libyan Sands* must be the best Saharan yarn written by a Brit. It describes his motor-car adventures and explorations in the Libyan Desert while stationed in Egypt in the 1920s and early 30s. Using Model T Fords loaded down at times with 150 gallons of fuel, Ralph and his chums spent every spare moment of leave exploring the Libyan Desert of Egypt and northern Sudan. His enthusiasm for (often literally) pushing the spindly, steaming Fords across uncharted ergs helped develop today's desert driving techniques such as sand ladders and low tyre pressures. What is striking is that his passionate attraction to the desert is most contemporary, while his energy and curiosity led, among other things, to *The Physics of Blown Sand*, the definitive account of sand formations and features.

Bagnold comes across in the much-admired mould of the self-effacing Brit hero, never complaining or boasting while enacting extraordinary feats of exploration. The book includes his potted history of the exploration of the Libyan Desert up to that time, as well as a prescient spin on the enduring Zerzura legend. An underrated classic.

MAURITANIE AU GPS
CYRIL RIBAS AND SYLVIE BEALLET
(see www.sahara-overland.com)
A route guide to Mauritanian pistes covering 10,000km of pistes, right across the country, up to and beyond the Mali border to places you have never heard of as well as the Beach piste, the rail route to Choum and some interesting excursions in the Adrar south of Atar. The layout of each route is comprehensible even if you're not fully conversant with French. Route maps are laid over old Soviet 1 millions which is a smart idea and there are plenty of boxed asides in the text on Mauritanian culture and history, plus some tasty colour photos. It's pricey but nothing like it exists in any language. A route guide for the truly adventurous – and all researched in a fat-tyred 2CV; stick that in your 4x4 pipe and smoke it!

THE MOST BEAUTIFUL DESERT OF ALL
PHILIPPE DIOLE (1959, O/P)
The same era as Newman (see opposite), but what a different book. Philippe Diolé, a close friend and associate of Cousteau, made a solo camel and lorry journey to the Tassili N'Ajjer and the Fezzan in the early fifties. This was not a journey of science or exploration, it was made for sheer personal enjoyment. The book conveys this beautifully, recalling the impressions, exciting moments and deep moving personal thoughts encountered during the month-long camel trek through the Tassili (including Wadi Djerat), accompanied by a single Turareg guide. In the second part of the book, Diolé recounts one of the earliest visits to the amazing engravings of Wadi Mathendous.

The book's main appeal will be to those already having been to the deep desert. It is a beautiful clear distillation of the emotions experienced by true desert addicts, that many of us are aware of but so few of us have the ability to express in words. It remains one of my all-time favourite desert classics.

ANDRAS ZBORAY

MYSTERIOUS SAHARA

BYRON KHUN DE PROROK (2001)
Mysterious Sahara is clearly written for a market hungry for more ancient treasures following Howard Carter's sensational discovery of Tutankamun's tomb in 1922. It starts off by reminding us how deadly the Sahara is in any number of ways, followed by an over-the-top description of the cave-dwellers of Matmata where the hyperbole starts to froth.

He sets off south for the Hoggar, no mean feat in 1925 but nevertheless embellishing the landscape and events to Victorian literary levels. By chance he learns of the location of the tomb of Queen Tin Hinan (the legendary ancestral 'queen' of the Tuareg) and what follows can only be described as the looting of an ancient and deeply significant burial site for gold, emeralds and Carteresque glory. With Tin Hinan crated up, we're then treated to a fruitless rummage around Siwa to find a legendary 'Temple of Doom' out in the sands. They can't find it but 'we know it's there'.

But what you can't take away is that Prorok was out there and doing it, and in 1926 was indeed the first to ransack Tin Hinan's tomb at Abalessa, even if his partner Maurice Reygasse went on to work with EF Gautier in the 1930s. Strange then that Prorok seems so little known despite his abundant energy for exploration, publicity and self-promotion. While he may have been more toff (in name at least) with a romantic imagination than trained archaeologist, his knowledge of the great European Saharan explorers was more than skin deep. The odd mistake is acceptable and some lurid theories are of their time, while the embellishment of adventurous exploits continues to this day.

SAHARA

MICHAEL PALIN (2002)
Like 'Everest' and 'Yukon', the word 'Sahara' is a good selling tool for Jeeps, hotels, boots, you name it. Palin's book carries the name but, as anyone who saw the BBC series will agree, he spent little time in the desert, failed to get under its skin and instead concentrated on the less arduous and more photogenic aspects of West and North Africa. Fair enough, the product here is MP not where he happens to be or who he's talking to (the book, not much deeper than the TV series, is packed with pics of MP here, there, MP gazing winsomely).

He writes well but for me this sort of heavily-planned faux travel faintly pretending to be continuous, missing key links and with paper-thin spontaneous encounters (like Tom Sheppard) is for undemanding Sunday night armchair travellers; Saharans will be disappointed.

SAHARA, THE LIFE OF THE GREAT DESERT

MARK DE VILLIERS & SHEILA HIRTLE (2003)
The problem here is that the authors have been to the Sahara just a couple of times, more than most it is true but surely not enough to attempt a book such as this. One gets the impression they fell for the enigmatic Tuareg (as you do) and thought 'heck, let's write our new book about Sahara and those shimmering courtly nomads!'. They use the works of 19th century explorers as if they were entirely reliable and relevant today though having done a lot of their groundwork, Porch's *Conquest of the Sahara* gets a good work-out while Heseltine's *From Libyan Sands to Chad* is the veritable horse's mouth for Chad and the Tubu (so never mind about Jean Chapelle's *Nomads Noirs du Sahara* then). So is the online Encyclopaedia Britannica – what a give away!

They certainly do not appear to have visited the desert areas of Morocco, Chad, Sudan, Algeria, Tunisia, Mauritania or even Egypt, or have anything accurate to say about these places. They miss out on contemporary political upheavals too, as if they wrote the book twenty years ago. So it is that comprehending the Tuareg rebellion in Niger, (something which has set them back years and was one of Michael Buckley's better achievements in *Grains of Sand*) isn't allowed to interfere with eulogies on their preternatural guiding abilities, etc; the same, tired old Tuareg schtick. The definitive work on the 'Great Desert' has yet to be written, this turkey is certainly not it.

SHELTERING SKY
Paul Bowles (1983)

A cult novel by the Tangiers literary guru based on his own experiences in North Africa.

Not a thoughtful gift for a visitor to Morocco, but a thrilling read if you like your desert with a bit of sex, madness, infidelity and death. Bertolucci's eponymous film fails to get its teeth into the inscrutable, existential quandaries of the protagonists. The track from the Police's *Synchronicity* album, *Tea in the Sahara*, relates a morbid legend described in this book.

WIND, SAND AND STARS
Antoine de Saint-Exupéry (1987)

An existential adventure classic based on the author's semi-autobiographical escapades in the early days of commercial aviation. This included flying mail across the dreaded *Terres des Hommes* (the Western Sahara) where you saved the last bullet for yourself. It features the almost obligatory near-death experience after crashing in the Libyan Desert. Along with Thesiger and possibly Monod (as yet untranslated into English), Exupéry remains one of the few writers who manages to get close to unravelling the enigma of the desert's appeal.

RECOMMENDED HARDBACKS AND PICTURE BOOKS

Picture or 'coffee-table' books of the Sahara are an enduring genre, though more popular and appreciated in Europe; the best are often in French. The content is inevitably photogenic so for general Sahara books the quality of the printing and the design of the book has much to do with a good impression. Some of these books are out of print but they were all available used on the web.

For an inexpensive start you could do a lot worse than *The Sahara* by Jeremy Swift (1975) from the old Time-Life series of the World's Wild Places. The colour is not brilliant but it gives a good general introduction to the desert.

Despite its misleading title, *Egypt, Civilisation in the Sands* (Koneman, 2000; o/p) is an unusually good photo reportage of the Libyan Desert. Nothing else yet comes close in English for that region though the softback *Desert Libyque* introduced by Theodore Monod (Arthaud, 1994) with its many reproduced engravings and archive photos is a perfect example of this type of book. Monod's biography *Une Vie de Saharien* (Vents de Sable, 1998) is a lovely, large format account of this great Saharan (see p.646).

For cameleers the softback *Azalaï* (Periplo, 1998) comes in three languages and covers the salt caravans to Taoudenni and Bilma.

Hefty, expensive (and this is only Volume 1) *The*

Archaeology of the Fazzan may be most suited to Saharan academics, but the multi-disciplinary approach of the Fezzan Project, covering nearly fifty years of fieldwork brings together a comprehensive study of this rich area.

In the same area but focusing on the engravings of the Messaks is the *Secret of the Desert* (Golf Verlag, 1995) vividly recording the countless images on the plateaux of which the well-known Wadi Mathendous is just a drop in the ocean.

A better than average memoir of exploration for Saharan rock art is Francois Soleilhavoup's *Sahara; Visions d'un Explorateur...* (Transboreal, 1999). There's nothing especially new here but the layout and subject matter make it more than just a log of rock art sites.

Alain Sèbe's series of highly-priced themed Sahara picture books such as *Tagoulmoust, Moula Moula* and *Redjem* are long established but in my opinion the design took a big step forward with books like *Sahara d'Algerie* (2003). Editions Sèbe also produce a mouth-watering range of cards, posters and calendars.

Another book based mostly in Algeria is *Sahara; Les Traces de de l'Homme* (Chabaud, 1989) an account of the French colonial era with much interesting archival material to inspire new travels.

Some Great Saharans

HENRI DUVEYRIER

Henri Duveyrier is remembered as one of the greatest Saharan explorers and the author of the first comprehensive survey of the Tuaregs, *Les Touâreg du Nord* (Paris, 1864).

The young Henri, who lost his English mother in his early years, was expected to pursue a career in business but soon found himself more attracted to travel and exploration. His father, who was deeply influenced by the socialist philosophy of Saint-Simon, accepted his son's vocation with the view of its improving geographical knowledge.

Duveyrier first visited Algeria at the age of 17, after learning German and some Arabic while studying business in Leipzig. In the same year he met Heinrich Barth in London, recently returned from West Africa, whereupon Duveyrier became Barth's favourite disciple. Duveyrier dedicated the subsequent two years to intensive methodological training designed to hone his scientific observation skills, including astronomy, engineering, meteorology, natural history, geology, mineralogy, taxonomy and botany.

He made use of his newly-acquired knowledge during a short exploration of the Algerian 'southern frontier', between Ghardaïa and El-Meniaa. This noted success earned him the commission of surveying the unclear southern boundaries of Algeria and Tunisia. This experience paved the way for his great achievement: the exploration of the eastern Tassili N'Ajjers and the ensuing study of the Kel-Ajjer Tuareg.

Duveyrier's sympathy with the Kel-Ajjer chief Ikhenoukhen proved a valuable asset during his journey of 1859-61 which led him to Ghadames, Ghat, Serdeles, Murzuk and Sabha. Alas, when back in Paris, he suffered from typhoid. The weak and partly amnesic explorer had his magnum opus written on his behalf from his travelogue and notes by an old friend of his father. He slowly recovered, however, and enjoyed public recognition, particularly after he was awarded the Légion d'Honneur in 1862 and in 1863 the gold medal of the Paris Geographical Society.

He was later elected vice-president of this Society. Apart from a study of the chotts south of Constantine, Duveyrier did not carry out any further explorations. Instead, he advised future explorers like Foucauld and Oscar Lenz. After the slaughter of the Flatters mission in 1881 by the Tuaregs, Duveyrier was blamed for his bias in favour of positive relations with them. In an attempt to deflect these criticisms, he demonised the Sennussi Muslim brotherhood in an article published in 1884. Misunderstood, lonely and nearly forgotten, he killed himself on 25 April 1892.

BERNY SÈBE

RALPH BAGNOLD

Ralph Alger Bagnold was the central figure in the exploration of the Libyan Desert in the twentieth century. Born in Devonport in 1896, the son of an army officer, he went to Malvern College (a minor public school of which he was not overly fond) and then on to the Royal Military Academy at Woolwich. In 1915 he joined the Royal Engineers and was sent to France as a member of the British Expeditionary Force. He fought in the bloody, muddy trenches at the Somme, Ypres and Passchendaele and was mentioned in dispatches. After the War he did the Engineering Tripos at Cambridge before returning to the Army in 1921. In 1926 he was posted to Egypt and it was during his leaves that he developed his passion for desert exploration by motor car – Model T Fords and then Model A Fords. Building upon the lessons learnt during WWI by the Light Car Patrols, which also used Model Ts, and by picking the brains of John Ball of the Desert Survey Department, he undertook a series of major expeditions in the Western Desert for which he was awarded the Founder's Medal of the Royal Geographical Society in 1934. After further Army service in the Far East he was discharged as 'a permanent invalid'. The gloomy diagnosis of his condition, 'tropical sprue', proved to be unfounded and he survived and flourished for another five and a half decades. He embarked with gusto on a new career in scientific investigation at Imperial College and became the accepted expert on dune formation and sand movement. In 1941 he wrote his classic *Physics of Blown Sand and Desert Dunes* and was in due course elected a fellow of the Royal Society. He was the first person to use a wind tunnel to study sand movement.

In 1929, using Fords, his expedition proved for the first time, contrary to all accepted wisdom, that the Great Sand Sea could be penetrated by car. It was a journey in which his navigation skills, mechanical ability and the use of sand tracks were honed. In 1930, he and his colleagues were more ambitious and set off for Uweinat and the Selima Sand Sea. In 1932, he went to the disputed Sarra triangle, and this involved a journey of over 6000 miles. In 1938 he went to the Gilf Kebir and carried out a scientific survey of its summit. Some of these expeditions are written up in *Libyan Sands*. These expeditions were quick, cheap, meticulously planned and highly successful. When war broke out in 1939, Major Bagnold was recalled to the Army. He was initially posted to Kenya (a country of which he had no personal knowledge), but en route his ship had to put in to an Egyptian port for repairs, and here he met up with General Wavell, who, recognizing his skills and experience of the desert, immediately arranged for him to remain in Egypt. Exercised by the potential threat that the Italians posed to Egypt and the Suez Canal, he eventually persuaded Wavell, then C-in-C Middle East, that he needed to set up a special force 'to undertake piracy in the high desert'. The Long Range Patrols (later the Long Range Desert Group) were hastily assembled, with Brigadier Bagnold in charge. He managed to recruit some of his colleagues and other explorers from the pre-war expeditions, including Kennedy Shaw, Pat Clayton, and Guy Prendergast. Using Chevrolet two-wheel drive trucks they harried and disconcerted the Italians from the rear.

Bagnold's contributions to desert travel were the refinement of the sun compass, sand tyres, sand tracks, condensors, and wireless fixes for navigation. He developed techniques for driving through dunes, and for identifying suitable terrain. All of this was done with two-wheel drive vehicles, the early versions of which had horribly narrow tyres. He also showed that science and exploration could be combined, most notably on his Gilf Kebir expedition of 1938, when he took along archaeologists, anthropologists and geomorphologists. The LRDG was the precursor of other special forces that played such an important role in World War II, including the SAS, and made a major contribution to the victorious North African campaign.

ANDREW GOUDIE

MANO DAYAK

Mano Dayak, the Western-educated Kel Aïr Tuareg, figured as a contemporary embodiment of the long tradition of 'warlords in the Sahara'. A child of the desert, born around 1950 he learnt to feel at ease in the urban jungle of Paris. Although he reluctantly attended the Ecole Nomade, he gradually adopted Western culture; at the age of 20 he crossed the desert to get to Europe via Algeria. Here Dayak soon established a network of friends among desert-lovers, and resolved to promote interest in his native country, Niger.

He moved on to the US where he hoped to read for a degree in Saharan pastoral practices in order to bring useful new techniques back home. Margaret Mead, the renowned anthropologist, suggested that he would be better educated back in France, where he returned to study under the ethnologist Germaine Tillion at the Ecole Pratique des Hautes Etudes Ethnologiques. In the early 1980s he set up a tour company in Agadez, offering his customers the luxury of V8-powered Range-Rovers. He made a name for himself as a guide and later as a driver for the Paris–Dakar rally, by means of his friendship with its founder Thierry Sabine. When war broke out between the Nigeran government and the Tuaregs in the early 1990s, Mano Dayak launched an association in Paris to heighten European awareness of the problems encountered by the Tuaregs in Niger and Mali. Through TV interviews, extensive press campaigns, several exhibitions and a book, *Touareg, la Tragédie* (Paris, 1996) he soon became an influential icon of the Tuareg rebellion.

He was widely supported in Europe, where he benefited from influential contacts. However, due to his absence from the affected regions, Dayak was unable to put an end to the bloody war which raged in northeastern Niger. In February 1993 he joined the rebel forces but a few months later a disagreement with fellow Tuareg rebel Rhissa ag Boula (now the Nigeran Minister of Tourism) drove him to establish his own faction, the FLT (Front de Libération Temoust).

In 1994, the Ouagadougou peace treaty paved the way for a settlement: the government negotiated with the rebels, represented by a unified Armed Resistance Coordination (CRA) under the presidency of Dayak, and the talks were arbitrated by Algeria, Burkina and France. Alas, Mano Dayak's plane crashed in December 1995 on his way to Niamey, where he was due to revive the peace process. The circumstances of his death are still a matter of controversy today. Agadez international airport is named after him.
BERNY SÈBE

THÉODORE MONOD

Théodore Monod was to West Africa what Wilfred Thesiger was to the Sudan and Arabia. Both were relics of a vanished era, and both recorded threatened ways of life just before they were forever altered. They also shared a preference for the camel's measured pace rather than the motor vehicle.

Théodore Monod was twenty when he first landed on the shores of Mauritania in 1922, at Port-Etienne (Nouadhibou). The young ichthyologist was to experience a decisive encounter with the Sahara when, having studied the area's abundant fishing grounds, he embarked upon a camel ride to Senegal. From then on, Monod's career would be primarily dedicated to deserts. Monod belonged to the last generation of multi-disciplinary scientists; during his innumerable Saharan explorations he studied the desert as a naturalist, a geologist, a botanist, an archaeologist and a writer. His scientific style is sharp, his travel accounts (the most popular being *Méharées*, first published in 1937 and still in print) are instructive and witty. Virtually no region between the Atlantic

Ocean and the Red Sea was unknown to Monod. He thoroughly surveyed the Adrar Ahnet in 1929 and the Tibesti at the beginning of WWII (as a second-class officer), but Mauritania, which he considered 'his diocese', remained his soft spot. In 1954, he and his few camels managed to cross, without resupplying his provisions, the 550 miles of barren reg of the Majabat al-Qubra between Wadan and Arawan, which he dubbed the 'West African Empty Quarter'. An astute investigator when in the field, Monod was also anxious to encourage the scientific study of the French African colonies. In the late 1930s he struggled to found the IFAN (Black African French Institute) in Dakar, designed to be a local replica of Paris' Museum of Natural History. Aged 37, Monod became its first director and quickly established the institute's reputation. His scientific accuracy, his all-embracing knowledge of the Sahara and his wide experience of the wilderness won him the admiration of post-independence Africans and Sahara-lovers. In 1988, he was transformed into a French public figure as a result of a highly-acclaimed TV interview. During the last decade of his life he used his iconic status to campaign for humanitarian causes, including non-violent protests against nuclear testing and support for asylum seekers. Monod's unique combination of ascetism, encyclopedism, commitment and wit appealed greatly to the general public. For that decade he was the French Grand Old Man.

BERNY SÈBE

HASSANEIN BEY

Pasha, Sir Ahmed Mohammed Hassanein Bey was an Oxford-educated, British-Egyptian of Bedouin lineage, and the first Egyptian explorer of modern times, a reputation built on challenging camel journeys across the Libyan Desert in the early 1920s.

In 1920, with Rosita Forbes in disguise; they became the first foreigners to visit the remote oasis of Kurfa since Gerhard Rohlfs, 42 years earlier. At that time Kufra was led by the xenophobic Sanusi fraternity and was out of bounds to all outsiders. Sworn enemies of the British, as WW1 progressed the Sanusi sued for peace in 1917, a process in which Hassanein Bey was involved. It was because of this introduction that he was permitted to pass through Sanusi lands on his two great journeys.

Before departure, Hassanein and Forbes approached the Royal Geographical Society for advice on Rohlfs' account but with anti-German sentiment still running high, they were misadvised that his account was unreliable. Overlooking Rohlfs' detailed description was an error they had plenty of time to regret along the way.

Setting off from Jedabia, eighty miles south of Benghazi, the journey to Kufra took a month; the travellers surreptitiously logging their route. Among the problems they encountered were the inevitable sandstorms, sick camels, long marches, a period of imprisonment as well as fractious guides. They even considered killing one guide, so certain were they that he planned a similar fate for them.

Kufra proved to be as unwelcoming as expected so after ten days' rest they set out for Jaghabub and Siwa, completing their journey two months after they set out from Jedabia. Following their expedition, Rosita Forbes produced *Secret of the Sahara: Kufara*, one of the most enduring books on Saharan exploration. Forbes's account followed a tradition of some pedigree in travel writing and has been the cause of some controversy with its often comical portrayal of her travelling companion, doing little for the natural dignity of the man.

Additionally, questions exist about her claims that she single-handedly planned and financed the trip. Hassanein had been planning the expedition with an old Oxford friend who dropped out at the last moment and it was through this friend that Forbes was introduced to Hassanein. Despite this, *Secret of the Sahara* opens with the following dedication: 'To Ahmed Mohammed Bey Hassanein. In memory of hours grave and gay, battles desperate or humorous, of success and failure in the Libyan deserts.'

The more remarkable of Hassanein's journeys, however, took place in 1923-24. Setting out from the border town of Sollum, Hassanein travelled to Darfur in the Sudan, by way of Kufra. On this trip he discovered Jebel Arkenu and Jebel Uwenait, the latter was of great assistance to Kemal el Din's own efforts the following year. Hassanein Bey was responsible for producing the first charts of large swathes of previously uncharted terrain, including the route from southeastern Egypt into the Sudan. This astonishing 2200-mile trek remains one of the most remarkable desert adventures of any time, for which he was awarded the Royal Geographical Society's Founder's Medal.

He maintained an active interest in desert exploration although his central role in affairs of state prevented further major exploration. He died in 1947 in Cairo following a traffic accident.

EAMONN GEARON

PRINCE KEMAL EL DIN

Considering the circumstances of his birth, it is a surprise that Prince Hussein Kemal el Din became a Saharan explorer at all. In 1914 the British deposed the pro-German Khedive, declared Egypt a British Protectorate and installed Hussein Kamel as sultan. The Sultan, Kemal's father, died in 1917 but Prince Kemal el Din renounced all claims to the throne in favour of his uncle, Fouad. It has been said that Kemal's love of the desert had become so intense that he wanted nothing more.

It was a love of riding and hunting that first drove Kemal el Din into the Egyptian Sahara and as his search for game spread, so did his need to cover greater distances. This led to his development of half-tracked vehicles which allowed him to hunt further afield. Captivated by the thrills of desert exploration, he mounted his first major expedition in 1923 using

HOLLYWOOD ON THE PISTE

The Sahara gives film-makers plenty of opportunities to sensationalise any number of desert phenomena. Ululating tribeswomen and dashing Tuareg warriors are regular staples but *The English Patient* went as far as to have a car buried by an overnight **sandstorm**. In this instance the hapless occupants only realised they'd become completely buried the following morning whereupon by banging from their automotive tomb they managed to alert their rescuers. In the flat desert the sand will just blow through, certainly making a mess of an unprepared camp but not piling up over two metres like drifting snow.

There's a more enduring myth that a sandstorm can strip paint from a car and turn glass opaque. This might be the case with a hand-painted car and a plastic windscreen, but damage to modern car paint and glass is only possible if you're belting flat out into a sandstorm with a combined speed of 300kph. Doing this, you're far more likely to crash catastrophically before the sand has a chance to cause any cosmetic damage to your car. If visibility in either a sand or a dust storm gets too bad, on the highway or a piste, slow down or stop and wait till it clears.

Despite the moving but equally ridiculous scene in *Lawrence of Arabia* where one of Lawrence's companions is sucked down into the depths as they descend a dune (repeated recently in *The Mummy* with an entire biplane!), **quicksands** are a symptom of waterlogged sand and not the soft dry sand of Saharan dunes. You may well sink a few feet into a chott (salt lake), but there is no danger of being sucked into an erg by sinister desert *djenouns*!

This deadly suction was also exaggerated in *Ice Cold in Alex* when John Mills and his crew showed the true mettle of wartime Brits by hauling out a suspected German spy from a bog in the Quattara Depression which somehow still managed to support their 3-tonne ambulance. Later on, at the climax of their run across the Western Desert ahead of the advancing 'Jerries', they resort to ascending a huge dune by reversing the lorry up the slope using the **engine's hand crank**! With the German spy's identity now clear and Mills' alcoholism driving him to distraction, all allegiances are forgotten. There's an utterly implausible battle against the desert as the lorry inches up and over the crest and scrapes home to Alexandria for an ice cold beer and the baddie's dignified confession and arrest.

Mirages are another favourite of the celluloid Sahara. We've all experienced the illusion of a baking hot highway shimmering like a sheet of water, caused by the refraction of light in the hot air. A true mirage is a very rare atmospheric phenomenon where an entire area – at its Hollywood best, a cool oasis but more usually a mountain distant range – is refracted and displaced possibly over hundreds of kilometres in extremely hot conditions. As you approach the mirage it evaporates. In the movies mirages are often confused with plain old hallucinations as our severely dehydrated heroes crawl forth croaking 'water, water...'. A seductive belly dancer turns out to be the swaying rump of a camel and a 20-litre glass of Heineken clutched in both hands becomes a long-dead cigarette butt.

specially adapted Citröen autochenils. The team which included geologists, cartographers, medical men and mechanics, were able to explore large tracts of desert that were previously considered impenetrable. Accompanied by John Ball, director of the Desert Survey Department, the expedition revisited Pottery Hill which Ball had found in 1917 and which the Prince renamed Abu Ballas (see p.622). In addition to the known water jars, the expedition documented three pieces of rock art on Abu Ballas hill and on the same expedition managed to locate the cairn built by the German explorer, Gerhard Rohlfs. In 1873 Rohlfs had been the first foreigner to attempt a crossing of Egypt's Western Desert, an expedition sponsored by Kemal el Din's grandfather, Ismail Pasha. Here they found Rohlfs' message in a bottle which El Din replaced with an Arabic copy.

In December 1924 he left the oasis of Kharga to travel along the ancient Darb el Arbain trade route to Sudan and to explore the mountain of Jebel Uweinat, which had been discovered only the previous year by Hassanein Bey. A detour to the south of Uweinat led to the discovery of Merga oasis, thought by some to be Zerzura itself. While at Uweinat, the team recorded rock art, conducted a great deal of mapping activity and demonstrated that Uweinat was the highest point in the region.

Kemal el Din's third major expedition took place over 1925-26, once again in the company of Ball, and during which his team discovered the plateau he named the Gilf Kebir, or great wall. Not long after this Kemal el Din moved to Paris, where he continued to write about the desert. In 1928 the French Geographical Society awarded him their Gold Medal in recognition of his desert exploration. Despite the end of his own explorations, the Prince maintained an interest in the subject, and the small band of enthusiasts who indulged in it.

In 1932, el Din was pleased to meet with the Hungarian explorer, Laszlo Almásy. The meeting, orchestrated by Hassanein Bey, came after Almásy's expedition to the western Gilf Kebir, and lead to the Prince offering to support future exploration of the area, nominally in search of the legendary oasis of Zerzura. Unfortunately for Almásy, the funding never materialised. Prince Kemal el Din died of blood poisoning in Toulouse in 1932, the result of complications following an operation. In response to his last wish, he was buried in the Moqqatam Hills, overlooking Cairo. In a final, fitting tribute to this lover of the desert, his palace in Cairo, seized by the state following the 1952 revolution, became home to the Desert Institute.

Almásy did return to the Gilf Kebir in 1932, where he erected an engraved marble monument to el Din in recognition of his exploration and discoveries.

EAMONN GEARON

English–French technical glossary

Documents

driving licence	*permit de conduire*
insurance	*assurance*
passport	*passeport*
vehicle ownership	*carte grise*
visa	*visa*

Directions

left	*à gauche*
right	*à droite*
straight on	*tout droite*
over there	*là-bas*
up there	*là-haut*

a long way	*c'est loin*
north	*nord*
south	*sud*
east	*est*
west	*ouest*
south-west, etc	*sud ouest*
back	*retour*
how far to ...?	*quelle distance jusqu'à..?*
which way to...?	*direction...?*
please	*s'il vous plaît*
turn left/right	*tournez à gauche/droite*
pass	*la passe, col*
map	*la carte*

Vehicle – general parts

4WD (4x4)	*le quatre-quatre*	fuel cap	*le bouchon de reservoir*
air filter	*le filtre d'air*	fuel pump	*la pompe à l'essence*
alternator	*le générateur*	fuel tank	*le réservoir*
axle	*l'axe*	fuse	*le fusible*
battery	*la batterie*	garage	*le garage*
bearing	*le palier*	gasket	*le joint*
bolt	*le boulon*	gearbox	*la boîte de vitesse*
brake disc pads	*le jeu de machoires*	glow plug	*la bougie de préchauffage*
brake fluid	*le liquide de frein*	grease	*la graisse*
brake hose	*le flexible de frein*	handlebars	*les guidons*
brake shoes	*les machoires de frein*	hole	*le trou*
brakes	*les freins*	hose	*la durite*
bulb	*l'ampoule*	hose clamp	*le collier*
camshaft	*les cames*	hub	*le moyeu*
carbon brush	*le balai*	ignition	*l'allumage*
carburettor	*le carburateur*	ignition coil	*la bobine d'allumage*
chassis	*le chassis*	inflate	*gonfler*
clutch (plate)	*le (disque d') embrayage*	inner tube	*la chambre d'air*
condenser	*le condensateur*	...is leaking	*...qui fuit*
cylinder head	*la culasse*	jack	*le cric*
diesel	*gasoil*	jerrican	*le bidon*
differential	*le differentiel*	jet	*la buse, le gicleur*
distributor	*l'allumeur*	needle	*l'aiguille*
drain plug	*le boulon*	nut	*l'ecrou*
engine	*le moteur*	oil (filter)	*le (filtre à) l'huile*
engine mount	*le support du moteur*	oil seal	*bague d'étanchéité*
exhaust	*le tuyau d'échappement*	petrol	*l'essence*
fan	*le ventilateur*	2 star/4 star	*normale/super*
fan belt	*la courroie de ventilateur*	unleaded	*sans plomb*
		piston	*le piston*

Fuel consumption conversion table

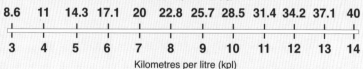

Miles per gallon (mpg)

8.6	11	14.3	17.1	20	22.8	25.7	28.5	31.4	34.2	37.1	40
3	4	5	6	7	8	9	10	11	12	13	14

Kilometres per litre (kpl)

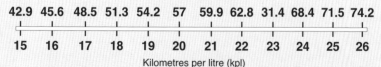

Miles per gallon (mpg)

42.9	45.6	48.5	51.3	54.2	57	59.9	62.8	31.4	68.4	71.5	74.2
15	16	17	18	19	20	21	22	23	24	25	26

Kilometres per litre (kpl)

mpg x 0.35 = kpl   **100 divided by kpl = L/100km**

kpl x 2.85 = mpg   **100 divided by L/100km = kpl**

pump	*la pompe*
puncture patch	*rustine*
pushrod	*tige de culbuteurs*
radiator	*le radiateur*
rim	*la jante*
screw	*la vis*
shock absorber	*l'amortisseur*
spare wheel	*la roue de secours*
spark/spark plug	*l'etincelle/la bougie*
spring	*le ressort*
starter motor	*le démarreur*
sump	*le carter*
suspension	*la suspension*
tie rod	*la barre de connexion*
timing belt	*la courroie dentée*
tyre	*le pneu*
universal joint	*le joint de cardan*
valve	*la soupape*
water pump	*la pompe à eau*
wheel	*la roue*
wheel bearing	*le roulement de roue*

Vehicle – problems

bent/broken	*tordu / cassé*
broken down	*nous sommes en panne*
cracked	*cassé*
...does not work	*...ne marche pas*
leakage	*la fuite*
mechanic	*le mécanicien*
misfire	*avoir des ratés*

overheating	*surchauffer*
puncture	*une crevaison*
recharge	*charger*
repair	*réparer*
spares	*pièce de rechange*
tear, rip	*déchirer*
weld	*souder*

Tools *(les outils)*

hammer	*le marteau*
pliers	*la pince*
ring spanner	*la clé à oeillet*
screwdriver	*le tournevis*
...cross-head	*...cruciforme*
socket	*la douille*
spanner	*la clé*
tyre lever	*le démonte pneu*

Motorcycle specific

drive chain	*la chaîne*
frame	*le chassis*
front fork	*la fourche*
fuel tap	*le robinet d'essence*
gear change lever	*le levier de vitesses*
kickstarter	*le kick*
lever	*le levier*
motorcycle	*la moto*
park the bike (securely)	*garer la moto*
spoke	*le rayon*
swingarm	*le bras oscillant*

DECIMAL DEGREE CONVERTER

Long Lat co-ordinates can be given in different ways; the format given in this book is 'decimal minutes' shown as N00° 00.0' as opposed to the now seemingly obsolete N00° 00' 00'. Sometimes you may receive a waypoint in seconds or even in decimal degrees (N00.0000°, the system preferred by scientists). These formats are sometimes known as DMM, DMS or DDD respectively. GPS units can display waypoints in any of the above formats (and more besides). If you're handy with multiples and divisions of 60 it's not too hard to work out the conversion in your head. Obviously N22.5000° in DDD equals N22° 30.0' in DMM but other fractions can be tricky so use the table below to reduce errors. And if you haven't got a clue what all this is about, don't worry, just keep your eyes on the road and your hands upon the wheel.

1.	0.016	13.	0.216	25.	0.416	37.	0.616	49.	0.816
2.	0.033	14.	0.233	26.	0.433	38.	0.633	50.	0.833
3.	0.050	15.	0.250	27.	0.450	39.	0.650	51.	0.850
4.	0.066	16.	0.266	28.	0.466	40.	0.666	52.	0.866
5.	0.083	17.	0.283	29.	0.483	41.	0.683	53.	0.883
6.	0.10	18.	0.300	30.	0.500	42.	0.700	54.	0.900
7.	0.116	19.	0.316	31.	0.516	43.	0.716	55.	0.916
8.	0.133	20.	0.333	32.	0.533	44.	0.733	56.	0.933
9.	0.150	21.	0.350	33.	0.550	45.	0.750	57.	0.950
10.	0.166	22.	0.366	34.	0.566	46.	0.766	58.	0.966
11.	0.183	23.	0.383	35.	0.583	47.	0.783	59.	0.983
12.	0.200	24.	0.400	36.	0.600	48.	0.800	60.	1.00

Notes on contributors

GERBERT VAN DER AA studied history, specialising in North and West Africa before becoming a freelance journalist. He has contributed to many Dutch newspapers and magazines and visited all the Saharan countries, usually driving an old Mercedes which he sells at the end of each trip.

ALISTAIR BESTOW was born in Kenya in 1960 but has lived in Australia since 1966. In 1996 he travelled from London to Harare on an overland truck and was drawn to return to West Africa in 1999. After travelling overland from Madrid to Timbuktu, he travelled by camel on the first of his journeys to Taoudenni. He is a Senior Patent Examiner (Biotechnology) in the Australian Patent Office.

JOSÉ CARLOS BRITO was born in 1971 in Lisbon, Portugal, and educated at Lisbon University, graduating with a PhD in Biology. Currently works as a post-doc fellow at Porto University. Travelled through Morocco, Mauritania and Senegal; he is currently planning a crossing from Tunisia to Morocco, via Niger, Ghana and Senegal.

GREGG BUTENSKY travels as often as possible and seeks out regional music wherever he goes. Visit him on the web at madnomad.com.

CHARLES FOSTER is a writer, traveller and veterinary surgeon who has extensive experience of desert expeditions, mostly involving camels. Recent expeditions have included the Danakil Depression in Ethiopia (studying water metabolism in mules), the Western Desert of Egypt, Sinai, and the Algerian Sahara. His introduction to deserts was in Saudi Arabia, where he worked on the immobilization of gazelles.

TONY VAN GASTEL left Holland in 1976 to work for 8 years in Kenya and 11 years in Syria. Currently in Ghana. Drove back from Kenya to Holland with his family in a Land Rover and travelled frequently in the Middle East and North Africa. Visited the Sahara several times; Timbuktu and Gao were his most recent trips.

EAMONN GEARON is a writer, photographer and filmmaker who has spent most of the past decade in Saharan Africa. When not exploring by camel, he taught at the American University, Cairo, and wrote and edited various publications. He is currently writing a book about Siwa, where he lived for a year and a half.

ANDREW GOUDIE is a professor of Geography in the University of Oxford and Master of St Cross College. He is the author of *Great warm Deserts of the World* (OUP, 2002) and has worked in many of the world's deserts, undertaking geomorphological research in Egypt, the Middle East, the Namib and the Thar.

KARIM HUSSAIN Born in 1968 in Kuwait of Iraqi-English parents he spent his youth in Kuwait and the UAE. After graduating as a chemical engineer he found a passion for adventuring on an XT600 and has made extensive trips in North Africa. He now concentrates on biking in the Sahara, either on rallies or alone.

GRAHAM JACKSON was born in Lesotho, grew up in South Africa, lives in the USA and is a British national. He is a chemist by trade, but an overlander by passion. He recently completed a trip from the UK to South Africa down the West Coast of Africa.

SIAN PRITCHARD-JONES and **BOB GIBBONS** have been driving across continents for 30 years. They run a small travel company specialising in trips to the Sahara and the Himalayas. During the summer they run trips in the Alps before spending each winter in Nepal, either trekking or working for a local publishing house, researching aspects of the Kathmandu Valley. In 1999 they ran an overland trip for oldies from the UK to Kathmandu, and in 2004 they drove from the UK to southern Africa.

YVES LARBOULETTE (1959) made his first trip to North Africa in 1986. Since then he has travelled in Morocco, Algeria, Libya, Tunisia and Mauritania by motorbike and Land Rover as well as cycling solo once. He started *Redjem Expeditions* in 2001 which was suspended following the Sahara kidnappings in 2003. He works as an IT consultant, runs www.sahara-info.ch and lives in Alosen, Switzerland.

DAVID MATTINGLY is Professor of Roman Archaeology at the University of Leicester, but has over 20 years' experience of Saharan archaeology. He has recently directed work on human adaptation in the desert from prehistory to the present, with a focus on one of the most important ancient peoples of the Sahara, the Garamantes of southern Libya.

Austrian **REINHART MAZUR** is one of those Sahara veterans who started their desert career almost 30 years ago. In many self-organised extended travels by car, he left his tracks in every remote corner of the Sahara. Preferred regions include Chad, Sudan and Egypt. His website www.tlc-exped.net will be available in English soon.

TIM STEAD first crossed the Sahara in 1990 in an aged Peugeot with the idea of making a profit; several disasters later he'd made a loss but discovered a love for the desert. In 2002-3 he returned with a Land Rover for a 20,000-mile round trip – he had disasters but still retains a love of the desert.

TOBY SAVAGE is an advertising photographer but a chance encounter with an archaeologist at a Beaujolais tasting led to an opportunity to travel and write. Since then he's travelled extensively across North Africa in his Land Rover Carawagon describing his adventures in *Land Rover World* magazine. www.tobysavage.co.uk.

BERNY SÈBE (FRGS) has been a Sahara traveller since he was a baby. He has taken part in more than twenty expeditions to Algeria, Morocco, Tunisia, Libya and Egypt. A doctorate student at Oxford University, he is co-author with his father Alain Sèbe of several books on the Sahara, including *Sahara, The Atlantic to the Nile* (London 2003).

IAN THOMPSON Born 1966. Currently lives in England. Has twice combined a passionate interest in both travel and off-road motorcycles by making trans-Saharan trips. Fascinated by deserts and Africa, and hoping to make adventure motorcycling a more regular activity, financed by working as a computer programmer.

MICHELE SOFFIANTINI (1966) has had a passion for the Sahara since his first trip in 1989. On motorcycles and in 4WDs, he has visited Libya, Niger, Algeria, Egypt, Sudan and Ethiopia with his photos featured in many travel and photographic magazines.

RICHARD WASHINGTON is a South African who works at the University of Oxford as a climatologist. His research interests are African rain and Saharan dust. His first Saharan trip was in the late 1990s and he's been every year since then, usually in an old Series 2A Landrover. If it weren't for the proximity of the Sahara to the UK, he'd have given up suffering in England long ago and moved back to Africa.

KEVIN WHITE is Senior Lecturer in Environmental Remote Sensing at the University of Reading. He has been undertaking environmental research in the Sahara since 1985 and has worked extensively in Tunisia, Libya and Egypt. He's a keen overlander, despite several trips with his Camel Trophy Land Rover 110.

RAF VERBEELEN (Belgium, 1974) generated his special interest in the Sahara during his bachelorship in Africa studies. Now trying to combine his passion for bicycle touring and the desert, he forms a trio with soul mates Paul Baccarne and Koen Verheyen to take up the challenge: users.telenet.be/django.

ANDRAS ZBORAY (1964) In his teens he made trips to southern Egypt and northern Sudan where his addiction for the Sahara was fostered. Visits to the Tassili N'Ajjer were followed by the Great Sand Sea, Jebel Uweinat and the Gilf Kebir. In his normal life he runs a software business.

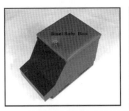

Ferry Tickets
Air Tickets
Shipping

Invitations
Visas
Guides

Travel Advice
Emergency Back-up

Guided Tours & Camel Treks in

ALGERIA – LIBYA – TUNISIA

Support base in Southern Tunisia
with garage and storage facilities

SaharaTravel.co.uk Ltd
Abbey House
15/17 Abbey St Upr
Dublin 1 – Ireland
Tel: 00353-1-4968844
Fax: 00353-1-4968834
E mail: info@saharatravel.com

Licensed and bonded by the Irish Aviation Authority No. TD185

DAVID LAMBETH
RALLY & OVERLAND

0044 (0)1892 853913

N 51 02.476 E 00 13.764
SUSSEX, UK.

Supply, construction and preparation of long distance Rally Raid and Overland expedition motorcycles and 4x4s.

Experienced off road assistance team available for competition events, private expeditions and desert training.

Regular involvement in many international events including:

- **Dakar • Tuareg Morocco**
- **Optic Tunisia • Orpi Morocco**
- **Alto Turia Spain • El Chott Tunisia**

Generously supported by KRIEGA backpacks and MILLERS oils.
Thanks and to the future.

Thanks to Chris and Bryn for producing this and other excellent travel and expedition books that truly keep the spirit of adventure alive.

660 SUPPLIERS' DIRECTORY

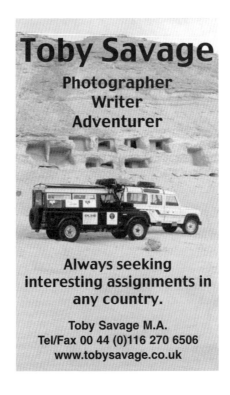

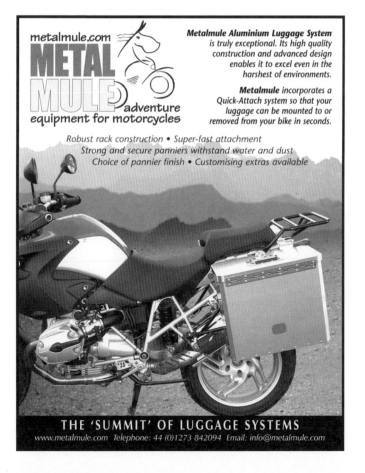

INDEX

BOXED TEXT INDEX

TRAILBLAZER

OTHER GUIDES FROM TRAILBLAZER

Adventure Cycling Handbook	1st edn late 2005
Adventure Motorcycling Handbook	5th edn early 2005
Australia by Rail	5th edn early 2005
Azerbaijan	3rd edn out now
The Blues Highway – New Orleans to Chicago	2nd edn out now
China by Rail	2nd edn out now
Coast to Coast (British Walking Guide)	1st edn out now
Cornwall Coast Path (British Walking Guide)	1st edn out now
Good Honeymoon Guide	2nd edn out now
Inca Trail, Cusco & Machu Picchu	2nd edn out now
Japan by Rail	1st edn out now
Kilimanjaro – a trekking guide to Africa's highest mountain	1st edn out now
Land's End to John O'Groats	1st edn late 2005
Mediterranean Handbook	1st edn out now
Nepal Mountaineering Guide	1st edn early 2005
New Zealand – The Great Walks	1st edn out now
Norway's Arctic Highway	1st edn out now
Offa's Dyke Path (British Walking Guide)	1st edn out now
Pembrokeshire Coast Path (British Walking Guide)	1st edn out now
Pennine Way (British Walking Guide)	1st edn out now
Sahara Abenteuerhandbuch (German edition)	1st edn out now
Siberian BAM Guide – rail, rivers & road	2nd edn out now
The Silk Roads – a route and planning guide	1st end out now
South Downs Way (British Walking Guide)	1st edn out now
South-East Asia – the graphic guide	1st edn out now
Tibet Overland – mountain biking & jeep touring	1st edn out now
Trans-Canada Rail Guide	3rd edn out now
Trans-Siberian Handbook	6th edn out now
Trekking in the Annapurna Region	4th edn out now
Trekking in the Everest Region	4th edn out now
Trekking in Corsica	1st edn out now
Trekking in the Dolomites	1st edn out now
Trekking in Ladakh	3rd edn out now
Trekking in Langtang, Gosainkund & Helambu	1st edn out now
Trekking in the Moroccan Atlas	2nd edn early 2005
Trekking in the Pyrenees	3rd edn early 2005
Tuva and Southern Siberia	1st edn late 2005
West Highland Way (British Walking Guide)	1st edn out now

For more information about Trailblazer and our expanding range of guides,
for where to find your nearest stockist, for guidebook updates
or for credit card mail order sales (post-free worldwide) visit our Web site:

www.trailblazer-guides.com

ROUTE GUIDES FOR THE ADVENTUROUS TRAVELLER